Barron's Review Course Series

Let's Review:

U.S. History and Government

Fifth Edition

John McGeehan
Former American History/Constitutional Law Teacher,
Hampton Bays Secondary School, New York
Writer and Consultant for Curriculum Revision
in United States History and Government for
State of New York

Morris Gall
Former Professor of Education and Assistant Dean,
Yeshiva University Graduate School of Education,
New York

BARRON'S

ACKNOWLEDGMENTS

p. 20   Copyright William H. Sadlier, Inc. with permission of publisher. All rights reserved.

p. 47   Reprinted from *Gavel to Gavel, A Guide To The Televised Proceedings of Congress* with permission from the Benton Foundation, Washington, D.C.

p. 69, 96, 250   Mary Beth Norton, David M. Katzman, Paul D. Escott, Howard P. Chudacoff, Thomas G. Patterson, William M. Tuttle, Jr. *A People And A Nation*, Fourth Edition © 1994 by Houghton Mifflin Company. Reprinted with permission.

p. 90   From The Americans 4E/1-VOL Ed., A Brief History 4th Ed. by Bedford 1985. Reprinted with permission of Wadsworth a division of Thomson Learning. *www.thomsonrights.com*

p. 182   From ETHNIC AMERICANS: A HISTORY OF IMMIGRATION AND ASSIMILATION by Leonard Dinnerstein and David Reimers. Copyright © 1975. Reprinted with permission.

p. 247   "The American Empire" from THE AMERICAN PAST: A SURVEY OF AMERICAN HISTORY by Joseph Conlin, Copyright © 1984 by Harcourt Brace Jovanovich, Inc., reprinted by permission of the publisher.

p. 266   Reprinted from June 1988 New York State Regents Examination.

p. 284   Reprinted from August 1988 New York State Regents Examination.

p. 582   Copyright Daryl Cagle 2001 and CagleCartoons.com. All rights reserved.

p. 597   Copyright Brian Fairrington 2001 and CagleCartoons.com. All rights reserved.

p. 624   Copyright Mike Keefe 2003 and CagleCartoons.com. All rights reserved.

p. 626   Copyright Mike Keefe 2005 and CagleCartoons.com. All rights reserved.

All inquiries should be addressed to:
Barron's Educational Series, Inc.
250 Wireless Boulevard
Hauppauge, New York 11788
www.barronseduc.com

ISBN: 978-1-4380-0018-3

ISSN 2165-1132

PRINTED IN THE UNITED STATES OF AMERICA
9 8 7 6 5 4 3 2 1

10%
POST-CONSUMER WASTE
Paper contains a minimum of 10% post-consumer waste (PCW). Paper used in this book was derived from certified, sustainable forestlands.

TABLE OF CONTENTS

PREFACE

This **Fifth Edition** is designed as a review of the New York State Regents Course in United States History and Government. The material follows the last major revision in the syllabus in Regents Social Studies: United States History and Government, which is used throughout New York State as the basis of a course of study in history on the secondary level. The curriculum incorporates the following Thirteen Enduring Constitutional Issues:

- National Power—limits and potential
- Federalism: the balance between nation and state
- The Judiciary: interpreter of the Constitution or shaper of public policy
- Civil Liberties: the balance between government and the individual
- Criminal Penalties—rights of the accused and protection of the community
- Equality: its definition as a Constitutional value
- The Rights of Women under the Constitution
- The Rights of Ethnic and Racial Groups under the Constitution
- Presidential Power in Wartime and in Foreign Affairs
- The Separation of Powers and the Capacity to Govern
- Avenues of Representation
- Property Rights and Economic Policy
- Constitutional Change and Flexibility

The following concepts and themes in United States history are also emphasized in the curriculum:

- Change
- Citizenship
- Civic Values
- Constitutional Principles
- Culture and Intellectual Life
- Diversity
- Economic Systems
- Environment
- Factors of Production
- Foreign Policy
- Government
- Human Systems
- Immigration and Migration
- Individuals, Groups, Institutions
- Interdependence
- Physical Systems
- Places and Regions

- Reform Movements
- Presidential Decisions and Actions
- Science and Technology

Although the material has been prepared to meet the needs of New York State students, this book can help students in any secondary-level U.S. History and Government course.

What Are the Special Features of This Book?

The arrangement of topical information parallels, for the most part, that of the New York State Regents syllabus in United States History and Government. Each of the seven major units begins with a brief explanation of the key ideas in the unit followed by a list of **connections** emphasized by the state syllabus. Each unit is broken down into several chapters that are consistent with the major divisions in the United States History and Government syllabus.

The format of the Regents Examination is as follows:

- **50 Multiple-Choice Questions**   50 Minutes   55% of grade
- **One Thematic Essay***   45 Minutes   15% of grade
- **One Document-Based Question***   60 Minutes   30% of grade

At the end of each chapter are multiple-choice questions and essays that coincide with the style of questions in Parts I, II, and III of the New York State Regents Examination. Each unit ends with **thematic** and **document-based essays**. In some cases, past Regents Examination questions have been included. The questions range from recall-drill to complex thought questions.

Because of the intimidating amount and complexity of the information presented in a course on United States History and Government, you should find the **Chronology of Events in American History** at the end of the book helpful. It shows the cause and effect pattern of our nation's story. The **Fifth Edition** also contains a **Glossary of Terms**, short biographies of **Notable Americans**, a list of **Historical Documents**, and a collection of significant **Quotations**, organized chronologically. These materials are intended both as reference aids and guides for study and review. Key United States Supreme Court decisions appear at the beginning of the book.

Complementing the text are graphs, political cartoons, maps, and charts to help portray necessary information, express points of view, and allow you to apply interpretive skills.

*There will be no choice in the two essay sections.

The Regents Examination

The **Fifth Edition** of **Let's Review: United States History and Government** follows the syllabus of the New York State Regents curriculum in United States History and Government and is designed to prepare students for the Regents exam. Here are some key tips to consider at test time:

- Preparation for the Regents Exam begins the first day of class. Good study habits, effective note-taking, completion of all assignments, and a positive attitude throughout the year will make success on any exam easier at the completion of the course.
- Follow directions closely on the test itself. Many students are not successful because they do not provide requested information, or they leave sections of the question unanswered.
- **Part I: 50 Multiple-Choice Questions, 50 minutes, 55% of score.** Answer all questions. Budget your time. Watch out for the answer that is correct in itself, but does not answer the question. Do easy questions first, then go back to more difficult questions. Use the process of elimination when necessary.
- **Part II: One Thematic Essay, 45 minutes, 15% of score.** Write a well-organized essay that includes an introduction, several paragraphs that address the task, and a conclusion. Be aware of key terms in the question, for example, **show, discuss, compare.** The thematic essay does not ask for only a recollection of facts, but rather asks the student to focus on themes and to demonstrate critical thinking. Those scoring the essay will use the following generic scoring rubric:

Generic Scoring Rubric
Thematic Essay

5

- Shows a thorough understanding of the theme
- Addresses all aspects of the task
- Shows an ability to analyze, evaluate, compare, and/or contrast issues and events
- Richly supports essay with relevant facts, examples, and details
- Writes a well-developed essay, consistently demonstrating a logical and clear plan of organization
- Includes a strong introduction and conclusion
- Is more analytical than descriptive

4

- Shows a good understanding of the theme
- Addresses all aspects of the task
- Shows an ability to analyze, evaluate, compare, and/or contrast issues and events
- Includes relevant facts, examples, and details, but may not support all aspects of the task evenly
- Writes a well-developed essay, demonstrating a logical and clear plan of organization
- Includes a good introduction and conclusion
- Is analytical and descriptive

3

- Presents a satisfactory understanding of the theme
- Addresses most aspects of the task or addresses all aspects in a limited way
- Is able to analyze or evaluate issues and events, but not in any depth
- Writes a satisfactorily developed essay, demonstrating a general plan of organization
- Uses some facts, examples, and details
- Restates the theme in the introduction and concludes with a simple restatement of the theme
- Is more descriptive than analytical

2

- Attempts to address the theme, but uses vague and/or inaccurate information
- Develops a faulty analysis or evaluation of theme
- Writes a poorly organized essay lacking focus and using few facts, examples, and details
- Has vague or is missing introduction and/or conclusion

1

- Shows limited understanding of the theme; omits concrete examples; details are weak or nonexistent
- Lacks an analysis or evaluation of the issues and events beyond stating vague and/or inaccurate facts
- Attempts to complete the task, but essay demonstrates a major weakness in organization
- Uses little or no accurate or relevant facts, details, or examples
- Has no introduction or conclusion

0

- Fails to address the theme
- Is illegible
- Blank paper

- **Part III: One Document-Based Question, 60 minutes, 30% of score.** The Document-Based Question is divided into two parts: Part A short-answer section (15%) and Part B essay (15%). Following the questions, approximately eight short documents are provided. Each Part A question will address a specific document. Answer the question using the document and the author's point of view, and incorporate information about the time period from which the document has been selected. The Part B essay requires that the student state their position (thesis) in an introductory paragraph, then develop their argument in the body of the essay using information from most of the documents to support their position. Using outside information from the student's knowledge of the time period will enhance the essay. The student should include a brief conclusion restating his or her position. As with the multiple-choice section, budget your time. Those scoring the essay will use the following generic scoring rubric:

Generic Scoring Rubric
Document-Based Question

5

- Thoroughly addresses all aspects of the task by accurately analyzing and interpreting most of the documents
- Incorporates relevant outside information
- Richly supports essay with relevant facts, examples, and details
- Writes a well-developed essay, consistently demonstrating a logical and clear plan of organization
- Uses information from the documents in the body of the essay
- Includes a strong introduction and conclusion
- Is more analytical than descriptive

4

- Addresses all aspects of the task by accurately analyzing and interpreting most of the documents
- Incorporates relevant outside information
- Includes relevant facts, examples, and details, but may not support all aspects of the task evenly
- Writes a well-developed essay, demonstrating a logical and clear plan of organization
- Includes a good introduction and conclusion
- Is both analytical and descriptive

3

- Addresses most aspects of the task or addresses all aspects in a limited way; uses some of the documents
- Incorporates limited or no relevant outside information
- Uses some facts, examples, and details, but discussion is more descriptive than analytical
- Writes a satisfactorily developed essay, demonstrating a general plan of organization
- States the theme in the introduction and concludes with a simple restatement of the theme or topic

2

- Attempts to address some aspects of the task, making limited use of the documents
- Presents little or no relevant outside information
- Uses few facts, examples, and details; discussion simply restates contents of the documents
- Writes a poorly organized essay, lacking focus
- Has vague or is missing introduction and/or conclusion

1

- Shows limited understanding of the task with vague, unclear references to the documents
- Presents no relevant outside information
- Attempts to complete the task, but essay demonstrates a major weakness in organization
- Uses little or no accurate or relevant facts, details, or examples
- Has no introduction or conclusion

0

- Fails to address the task
- Is illegible
- Blank paper

SUPREME COURT CASES

Date	Cases	Concepts	Page
1803	Marbury v. Madison	Judicial Review	50
1819	McCulloch v. Maryland	Necessary and Proper Federal Supremacy	44
1824	Gibbons v. Ogden	Interstate Commerce Federal Supremacy	70
1831	Cherokee Nation v. Georgia	Indian rights	88
1832	Worcester v. Georgia	Judicial Supremacy Native Americans	88
1857	Dred Scott	Slavery/Citizenship Property	212
1886	Wabash, St. Louis and Pacific R.R. v. Illinois	Commerce Clause Property and States' Rights	155
1890	Chicago, Milwaukee, St. Paul Railway Co. v. Minnesota, Corporation as Persons	Equal Protection	143
1895	United States v. E. C. Knight Co.	Antitrust Acts Congressional Power Free Enterprise	156
1895	In Re Debs	Unions/Strikes Commerce Clause	160
1896	Plessy v. Ferguson	Separate but Equal Protection	429
1904	Northern Securities Co.	Trade/Federal Antitrust Commerce	224
1905	Swift and Co. v. U.S. Trade Commerce	Antitirust	224
1905	Lochner v. New York	Work Hours/Property Rights Police Powers	225
1908	Muller v. Oregon	Employee-Employer Contract	225
1919	Schenck v. United States	Speech/Clear and Present Danger/War Powers	56
1935	Schechter Poultry Corporation v. United States	Executive versus Legislative Power	324
1936	United States v. Butler	Taxing Powers	324
1937	National Labor Relations Board v. Jones and Laughlin Steel Corp.	Labor Civil Liberties	338
1944	Korematsu v. United States	Executive Powers/Relocation/ Equal Protection	358
1951	Dennis v. United States	Speech & National Security	406
1954	Brown v. Board of Education	School Integration/ Equal Protection	464

SUPREME COURT CASES (continued)

SUPREME COURT CASES (continued)

UNITED STATES HISTORY DOCUMENTS*

UNITED STATES HISTORY DOCUMENTS* (continued)

*Currently cited in the 11th Grade United States History and Government Scope and Sequence as notable documents.

UNIT ONE

Constitutional Foundations of the United States

KEY IDEAS Unit One explores both the formative stage of our Constitution and its implementation through the Civil War period. Chapters 1 and 2 illustrate the origins of the document, the actual structure and functions of its components, and the tests our constitutional system faced in its early development.

UNIT CONNECTIONS: By the end of the unit you should understand the following points.

- Development of American political institutions
- Reasons for the American Revolution
- Strengths and weaknesses of the Articles of Confederation
- Necessity of Constitutional Convention
- Constitution: Structure, federalism, and basic principles
- Bill of Rights: Balance between government and the individual
- Hamilton and Jefferson; rise of political parties
- Maturing of the Supreme Court, the Marshall Court
- Early foreign policy, Monroe Doctrine, Manifest Destiny
- National unity versus developing sectionalism
- Geographic and economic growth of the new nation
- Early immigrant experience
- The Age of Jackson and reform movements
- Constitutional Crisis: the American Civil War

CHAPTER 1

THE CONSTITUTION: THE FOUNDATION OF AMERICAN SOCIETY

FOUNDATIONS, REVOLUTION, AND CONFEDERATION

> Let Americans disdain to be the instruments of European greatness.
> Let the thirteen states, bound together in a strict and indissoluble
> Union, concur in erecting one great American system, superior to the
> control of all transatlantic force or influence, and able to dictate the
> terms of the connection between the old and the new world!
> Alexander Hamilton, *The Federalist* (1787–1788), No. 11

Before the founding of the American republic, there were few examples in history of a successful republic that included more than a single city or a small confederation of a few cities and territories. The ancient city-state of Athens and the republic of Rome contributed many important concepts to the Western tradition of government, including direct and representative democracy, jury systems, and the development of legal systems. However, when Athens and Rome began to expand and took over new territories, their democratic governments eventually came to an end. They first became tyrannical empires and then either collapsed into anarchy or fell under the rule of military or oligarchic despotism.

Although the U.S. Constitution was not the first one in history, it is the oldest written constitution still in effect. The word **constitution** means the entire legal framework of a nation, or the nation's plan of government. A written constitution that specifically set forth a plan of government, established its institutions, and outlined the rights of citizens as the American Constitution does, is a relatively new development in history.

Foundations

Democratic Roots in the English Experience

During the colonial period (1607–1763) many of the political institutions of England were transmitted to the English colonies in America. Four major landmarks in English history provided a foundation for American constitutional government:

- *Magna Carta (1215).* Although this document was originally designed to protect the feudal nobles from the absolute rule of the king, it later came to apply to all English subjects and provided that (1) the king was subject to the rule of law; (2) Parliament was responsible for the levying of taxes; and (3) all accused persons were guaranteed a trial by jury of peers, or equals.

- *English Bill of Rights (1689).* This document was truly revolutionary because, at a time when absolute monarchs ruled, it established the idea that there were limits on the powers of kings and queens. The English Bill of Rights, much of which was later incorporated into our own, provided that (1) the king could not interfere with parliamentary elections and debates; (2) the king could not suspend laws, levy taxes, or maintain an army without the consent of Parliament; and (3) the people were guaranteed basic rights to **petition the government**, to an **impartial and speedy trial**, to protection against **excessive fines and bails**, and to protection from **cruel and unusual punishment**.

- *Common Law.* In England, the verdicts of judges were written down, collected, and became the basis for future legal decisions. These common practices and legal decisions formed a body of law known as **common law**. Certain **fundamental rights** that developed from the English common law and later became part of statute law were designed to protect the citizen from tyrannical government.

- *A Bicameral Legislature.* By the 14th century, Parliament, the legislative body of English government, had divided into two houses or chambers: (1) the **House of Lords**, consisting of higher clergy and nobility; and (2) the **House of Commons**, representing the wealthy middle class.

Constitutional Development in Colonial America

Many of the democratic characteristics of American constitutional government can be traced back to the colonial experience. Two important precedents that influenced the development of government in the colonies concerned (1) the structure of government (primarily the distribution of power among its parts); and (2) the relationship of the individual to government. By the time the colonies were being settled, English subjects had already developed a theory of **limited government**, or the idea that government did not have absolute power, but was restricted by certain laws and procedures.

- *Colonial Charters.* During the early period of English settlement, the colonies in America were largely self-governing. This was due to the privileges granted by the colonial charters and because geographical distance and other conditions made it difficult for the Crown to tightly control the colonies during the 17th century. Each colony had a charter, or grant, of privileges from the king. There were three basic types of colonial government, the major difference being in the way the governor was chosen. In the **self governing** colonies, such as Connecticut and Rhode Island, the governor was chosen by the colonists. In the **proprietary** colonies, such as Pennsylvania, Maryland, and Delaware, the governor was selected by the proprietor. In the **royal** colonies, such as New York, Virginia, and Georgia, the governor and other high officials were selected by the king. Later in the colonial period, most of the colonies were made royal colonies in order to bring them under direct control of the Crown.

• *Colonial Governing Instruments.* England did not send a governor and a council to each settlement in North America (as was the practice of the Spanish and the French). As a result, other methods of government were used in some of the English settlements in the early colonial period. Among these were the joint-stock corporation, the concept of government by compact, and the proprietorship.

Joint-Stock Principle. Some colonies were settled by a joint-stock company, a form of business organization. The company received a charter from the English Crown granting it a monopoly over trade and colonization for a period of years within a specific area. In return, the company was to give the Crown a share of profits earned and precious metals such as gold or silver that it acquired.

Virginia, the earliest successful English colony, was founded in 1607 by the Virginia Company of London under a grant from the Crown. In 1619 the governor allowed the eligible voters in the colony to elect a local representative assembly. This lawmaking body, called the **Virginia House of Burgesses**, was the first elected legislature in the colonies and marked the first step toward representative government in the colonies.

The Massachusetts Bay Colony, which was also established by a joint-stock company, was founded by middle-class Puritans who wanted to establish a refuge for their religious beliefs in North America.

Government by Compact. Although the settlements of Plymouth, Rhode Island, Connecticut, and New Haven were never as politically important as Virginia and Massachusetts Bay, they were significant in that their governments were based on a **social contract**. In 1620, before they landed at Plymouth, the settlers on board the *Mayflower* realized that they had no recognized authoritative body and made plans for self-government. The adult males drew up and signed an agreement that later became known as the **Mayflower Compact**, in which they agreed to obey the laws that they would adopt. They agreed to consult each other about matters affecting the community and to abide by majority rule.

In 1636, after his banishment from Massachusetts Bay for advocating **separation of church and state**, **Roger Williams** and his followers founded the town of Providence in Rhode Island. They entered into a compact agreement very similar to that of the Plymouth settlers. In 1644 Williams obtained a charter for the colony of Rhode Island that did not require voters to be church members.

The settlements of New Haven and those along the Connecticut River were also settled by Puritan dissenters moving southward. Perhaps the most significant of all the early covenants was the **Fundamental Orders of Connecticut**, adopted in 1639, the first written constitution in America. The Fundamental Orders implied that government rested upon the **consent of the governed** and that it should express the will of the majority.

Proprietorship. The proprietary colonies were established by a feudal patent or a royal grant of land in the New World given by the Crown, usually to friends or relatives. Under this grant, the proprietor, or owner, was given the right to establish a colony and to rule it.

Such a royal grant was used in the founding of Maryland by George Calvert, the first Lord Baltimore, in 1632. James, the Duke of York, the younger brother of King Charles II, became the proprietor of New York after the Dutch surrendered what had been their colony of New Netherland to a British fleet stationed in the Hudson River in 1664.

Signs of Colonial Unity

Colonial unity, within the colonies and among them, evolved slowly. Although each colony maintained independent ties with England and in many ways acted independently, early attempts at achieving colonial union were made both by the colonies themselves and by England in order to gain greater control over its colonies.

- *The New England Confederation (1643–1684).* Massachusetts Bay, Plymouth, Connecticut, and New Haven made up the membership of this Puritan confederacy.

- *Dominion of New England (1684–1688).* In 1686 King James II created the Dominion of New England, which joined the colonies of New York, New Jersey, and the New England colonies of Massachusetts Bay, Plymouth, New Hampshire, Maine, Rhode Island, and Connecticut under one government. **Town meetings**, the basic form of local government in New England, were restricted. James took these actions because the colonists refused to comply with the Navigation Acts, which were designed to regulate the trade of the colonies. As a storm of opposition rose from the colonists, the **Glorious Revolution** of 1688 in England brought about the overthrow of James II and confirmed the supremacy of Parliament over the king. As a result, the Dominion of New England collapsed.

- *The Albany Congress (1754).* In 1754 England called the Albany Congress to establish intercolonial cooperation in dealing with the growing French influence in the Ohio Valley and in lower Canada and to attempt to keep the Iroquois Indians loyal to the British. The **Albany Plan of Union**, drafted by **Benjamin Franklin**, who proposed that the colonies unite in a permanent union for defense. Although the Albany Plan failed, it introduced the concept of a **federal** plan of representative government, with specific powers given to a central authority, which later served as a model for the United States Constitution.

• *The Iroquois Confederation.* The **Iroquois Confederation** included the Six Nations—the Mohawk, Tuscarora, Cayuga, Seneca, Onondaga, and Oneida nations. Its purpose was to keep peace among the tribes and to provide for mutual defense. Based on a federal system, the individual nations maintained their independence while granting some powers to the Confederation. It is likely that the union served as a model for colonial union and influenced the Albany Plan of Union and, later, the Articles of Confederation.

Benjamin Franklin drafted a plan for a colonial union in 1754.

Problems of Control

By the middle of the 18th century, there were thirteen British colonies in North America. By 1750 most of the colonies had been made royal colonies, with governing structures reflecting those of the British government. A governor's council, made up mainly of conservative, wealthy colonists, sat as an upper house of the legislature. It could amend or reject legislation passed by the popularly elected assembly. This lower house of the legislature was chosen by the colonists who met the property qualifications for voting. The assembly could initiate tax bills, exercise administrative oversight concerning the expenditure of funds, and fix qualifications for their own membership. The governor, appointed by the Crown, had the power to veto legislation passed by the colonial assembly and to call or dissolve the assembly.

Frequent conflicts between the popularly elected assemblies and the royally appointed governors symbolized the struggle for colonial self-rule during the 18th century. An early example of this conflict was **Bacon's Rebellion** in Virginia. **Nathaniel Bacon**, a member of the Virginia House of Burgesses, led an uprising against the royal governor Berkeley that resulted in the burning of Jamestown in 1676. The governors gradually lost power to the colonial assemblies largely because the assemblies' control of finances allowed them to deny appropriations of money to governors who defied the popular will. The bulleted factors on page 9 allowed the colonial legislatures to expand their powers and control over colonial government.

Figure 1.1 The English Colonies in North America

- *Expansion of Colonial Suffrage.* Although property ownership was a requirement for voting in the colonies, the abundance of inexpensive land made it possible for many colonists to own property and therefore to vote. By the time of the Revolution, about 75 percent of the adult white males in the colonies were able to vote.

- *Actual Representation v. Virtual Representation.* **Virtual representation** was the belief that all English subjects were represented in Parliament simply by virtue of their status as citizens. However, the colonists came to believe in the concept of **actual representation**, the idea that to be properly represented in a legislature, citizens had to vote directly for delegates who represented their interests. By the time of the American Revolution, the American colonists formally rejected the British argument that they were "virtually represented" in Parliament.

- *Separation of Powers.* Rather than the overlapping of many powers between the executive and the legislature, such as existed between the British Crown and Parliament, the colonists believed that the powers of their legislatures ought to be free from executive (governor) control.

- *England's "Salutary Neglect."* Because of England's own problems—such as the Glorious Revolution of 1688 and wars with Holland, France, and Spain during the 17th century—the local governing bodies of the colonies were allowed to expand their powers and activities. During this period of so-called salutary neglect, the British allowed the colonies a great amount of self-government and economic freedom.

Revolution and Independence

Importance of Locke's Ideas

> The natural liberty of man is to be free from any superior power on earth, and not to be under the will or legislative authority of man, but to have only the law of nature as his rule. The liberty of man in society is to be under no other legislative power but that established in the commonwealth; nor under the dominion of any will or restraint of any law but what that legislative shall enact according to the trust put in it.
>
> John Locke, *The Second Treatise of Government* (1690)

In this quote the English philosopher and political thinker **John Locke** (1632–1704) refers to the law of nature. **Thomas Jefferson** later stated this idea in the Declaration of Independence:

> We hold these truths to be self-evident, that all men are created equal, that they are endowed by their Creator with certain inalienable rights, that among these are **life, liberty, and the pursuit of happiness**.
>
> Declaration of Independence (1776)

9

The second half of Locke's quote stresses the importance of self-rule and the responsibility of a government to those whom it governs. Again, Jefferson's reliance upon the thoughts of Locke becomes apparent when one examines the Declaration of Independence:

> That to secure these rights, governments are instituted among men, deriving their just powers from the consent of the governed. That whenever any form of government becomes destructive to these ends, it is the right of the people to alter or to abolish it, and to institute a new government . . .
>
> Declaration of Independence (1776)

Natural law, as referred to in Locke's *The Second Treatise of Government,* includes those rights essential to the natural existence of humankind. Among these are the rights to life, liberty, and property and the belief that all people are equal in the possession of these rights.

The Fifth Amendment to the United States Constitution was prepared by **James Madison** as a necessary addition to the Constitution (along with the rest of the **Bill of Rights**) to place restrictions upon both the federal and state governments. The Fifth Amendment reads in part:

> No person shall . . . be deprived of life, liberty, or property, without due process of law.
>
> Fifth Amendment to the United States Constitution (1791)

Theory of Limited Government (Locke, Montesquieu, and Rousseau)

The period of English colonization came at a time when European political thinkers were setting forth the idea that governments should be structured on a foundation of law and that a contract existed between the government and the governed. It was not too great a step from that idea to the belief that revolution against those who abused the existing contract was justified. The makers of our own revolution and later the founders of our constitutional system of government were guided in their actions and beliefs by the theory of natural rights and the idea of representative government, as advocated by Locke, the idea of separation of the powers of government by dividing it into **executive**, **legislative**, and **judicial** branches, as outlined by **Montesquieu**, and finally, by the idea of **popular sovereignty**, as championed by **Rousseau**.

Although the common sentiment among the colonists on the eve of the Revolution was that the law of England prevailed, a transformation was taking place. The strong tendency toward political involvement among the colonists, combined with the evolution of a uniquely American form of representative government, made it difficult for the American colonists to find their place in the English parliamentary system.

British Mercantilism and American Capitalism

By the end of the French and Indian War in 1763, the American colonies had grown to be a strong and thriving part of the British Empire. This was a result of lax British regulation under the policy of salutary neglect, which allowed a considerable amount of manufacturing to develop within the colonies. It was also due to the "triangular trade" that involved Africa, the West Indies, and the colonies.

• *Mercantilism.* During the 17th and 18th centuries, England, as did most European countries, believed that power depended upon monetary wealth and that the colonies were a source of wealth in that they would (1) provide raw materials for the mother country; (2) import manufactured products of higher values from England; and (3) not compete with the mother country in economic activities.

After 1763 Britain decided to tighten its control over both the political and economic affairs of the colonies. To carry this out, Britain ended the policy of salutary neglect and began to enforce the mercantilist system, a policy that aroused strong colonial opposition.

Because of the debts incurred from fighting the French and Indian War (1754–1763) and the need to protect the new territory acquired from France after the war, Britain found it necessary to create new sources of revenue. Since the British felt that the colonists should help pay for their defense, Britain decided to raise money by taxing the colonists. In addition, it tried to place restrictions on westward expansion. After the French and Indian War, many colonists began to migrate westward. This invasion of Indian land by white settlers resulted in Pontiac's Rebellion (May 1763), an uprising in which several Indian tribes joined together and attacked settlements and forts on the frontier. The British, who could not protect the frontier, and who wished to avoid further conflicts, issued the **Proclamation of 1763**. This forbade settlement west of the Appalachian Mountains. Encouraged by an adventurous and growing population, which had grown from a quarter of a million in 1700 to over two million in 1770, the colonists continued to settle in western Pennsylvania, Tennessee, and Kentucky.

The New Colonial System and the Formation of the American Resistance Movement

In its attempt to more closely supervise the colonies, Britain's "new" colonial policy had four main objectives: (1) to regulate western expansion and Indian affairs; (2) to keep a standing army in America; (3) to enforce the Navigation Acts; and (4) to raise money in the colonies through taxes including, for the first time, direct taxation of the colonists for the purpose of raising revenue rather than obtaining revenue through the regulation of trade.

• *The Grenville Ministry (1763–1765).* At the urging of George Grenville, the British Prime Minister from 1763 to 1765, Parliament set out to raise money to balance Britain's budget by strictly enforcing the existing mercantile laws and by passing new taxes for the colonies.

The Sugar Act (1764). Designed to replace the Molasses Act of 1733, the Sugar Act lowered the duty on imported molasses in an attempt to stop colonial smuggling.

Currency Reform (1764). The Currency Act of 1764 forbade the colonies from issuing paper money.

The Stamp Act (1765). Passed in February 1765, the Stamp Act was the second measure in Grenville's program that attempted to raise revenue to pay for Britain's costs in defending the colonies. It required that certain documents be written or printed on paper carrying a stamp from the British treasury office.

The tax, a constant reminder of Parliament's authority, affected nearly every aspect of commercial and industrial life in the colonies. Especially hard hit by the new tax were lawyers, merchants, and editors—those with the greatest ability to voice their objections to the revenue-raising measure. Those accused of violating its provisions could be tried in an admiralty court—without a jury.

When news of the passage of the Stamp Act reached the colonies in March 1765, opposition exploded. Following a fiery speech by **Patrick Henry**, the Virginia House of Burgesses adopted the Virginia Resolves, which denied that Parliament had the right to tax the colonies without their consent, claiming that only the House of Burgesses could tax the Virginia colonists.

With Massachusetts in the lead, delegates from nine colonies met in New York in October 1765 to voice their opposition to the Stamp Act. The resolutions drafted by the **Stamp Act Congress** rejected the concept of "virtual representation" in the House of Commons and they agreed to resist all taxes not consented to by the colonial legislatures.

Colonial opposition to the Stamp Act resulted in numerous nonimportation agreements, in which the colonists promised not to buy British goods. Early in 1766 Parliament repealed the Stamp Act, causing much celebration in the colonies.

The Declaratory Act. Early in 1766 Parliament also passed the Declaratory Act, which stated that Parliament had absolute authority over the colonies "in all cases whatsoever." This meant that Parliament had the authority to tax the colonies, in spite of colonial protests over the Stamp Act.

The Stamp Act crisis was significant in several ways. The Stamp Act Congress and the effectiveness of the widespread nonimportation agreements showed that the colonies could unite and work together. Resistance groups, such as the **Sons of Liberty**, coordinated opposition throughout the colonies. Secondly, the crisis helped bring into focus the primary issues that existed between Britain and the American colonies: the status of the colonists in the British Empire, and the taxation powers of Parliament over the American colonies.

- *The Townshend Acts (1767–1770).* Following the repeal of the Stamp Act, King George III appointed William Pitt as Prime Minister and **Charles Townshend** as Chancellor of the Exchequer. The Townshend Acts included new taxes and stricter enforcement of the existing mercantile laws.

Import Duties on Glass, Lead, Paint, Paper, and Tea. These were passed to regulate trade and therefore were within the right of Parliament to create and enforce. However, their stated purpose was for "the support of civil government, in such provinces as it shall be found necessary." That is, they were to raise money to defend the colonies. Therefore, the colonists objected to the import duties because they were a tax measure to raise revenue, not a commercial regulation.

Board of Commissioners and Writs of Assistance. Under the Townshend Acts, Parliament established a special Board of Commissioners within the colonies to enforce the Navigation Acts and to make sure the duties were collected. The use of writs of assistance, or search warrants, by British customs officials to search colonists' businesses, homes, and ships for smuggled goods was approved. Opposition to the writs of assistance was best expressed by **James Otis**, a Boston attorney. Using the principles of natural law, which included the freedom of one's "house" from unauthorized searches and seizures without **probable cause**, Otis argued that an act of Parliament against natural rights was void.

Opposition to the Townshend Acts. Opposition to the Townshend Acts in the colonies was strong. As colonial discontent and resistance grew, the difficulty of maintaining order increased. As a result, more British troops were sent to America. A period of greater disorder followed as customs agents were mobbed and tarred and feathered, and troops were harassed.

- *The Boston Massacre.* On March 5, 1770, ironically the same day the Townshend duties (except the tax on tea) were repealed, a few British soldiers in Boston fired upon a hostile Boston crowd,

The Boston Massacre, in an engraving by Paul Revere.

killing five persons. The event was publicized in newspapers throughout the colonies as a "massacre" against the defenseless colonists. With the help of engravings created by **Paul Revere** and pamphlets of anti-British propaganda written by **Samuel Adams**, the leader of the Sons of Liberty, the American colonists became further inflamed in their resentment of British rule.

• *The Tea Act (1773).* To help the struggling **British East India Company**, Parliament decided to allow the direct shipment of tea from India to the colonies without having the tea go through London, thereby reducing the price of tea sold in the colonies. The Tea Act meant that British tea could now be purchased in the colonies for about half the price of smuggled tea.

The colonists who smuggled and sold the tea took the lead in opposing the Tea Act. On the evening of December 16, 1773, approximately 60 men, thinly disguised as Mohawk Indians, boarded three ships in Boston harbor and threw 342 chests of tea worth approximately £10,000 ($15,000) into the sea.

• *The Coercive, or "Intolerable" Acts (1774).* In March 1774, in response to the Boston Tea Party, Britain retaliated with five acts that the colonies called the "Intolerable" Acts.

The Boston Port Act closed the port of Boston until the colonists paid the British East India Company for the destroyed tea.

The Massachusetts Government Act altered the Massachusetts charter of 1691, giving Britain greater control over the colony and severely limiting self-government.

The Administration of Justice Act provided that, in the cases of crimes committed by officials of the Crown while enforcing British laws, the trial could be moved to Great Britain.

The Quartering Act, passed June 2, 1774, gave British officials within the colonies broad authority to quarter, or house, troops wherever they chose in a town, rather than in barracks provided by the colonies.

The Quebec Act was passed in an effort to maintain the allegiance of the French. It allowed Catholicism and French civil law in Canada and established the boundaries of Quebec as the Ohio River on the south, the Mississippi River on the west, and the Proclamation Line of 1763 on the east. The Quebec Act, though not passed to punish the colonists, outraged them for several reasons. First, it appeared to violate several colonial charters by destroying the claims of three colonies to lands west of the Appalachians. Secondly, it allowed religious freedom to the Roman Catholics, a religion strongly disliked by Protestant colonists.

Declaration and Revolution (1774–1783)

Most colonists strongly opposed the Intolerable Acts, and some came close to outright rebellion. On a call from Virginia, all the colonies except Georgia sent delegates to a **Continental Congress**.

• *The First Continental Congress (1774).* It met at Carpenters Hall in Philadelphia on September 5, 1774. The delegates at the Congress were narrowly divided between those who favored resistance and those who advocated conciliation. Although illness kept **Thomas Jefferson** of Virginia away from the meeting, his *Summary View of the Rights of British America,* claiming Parliament to be only the "legislature of one part of the empire," was used as supportive argument by the more radical members at the Congress.

Declaration of Rights and Grievances. Adopted by Congress on October 14, 1774, the Declaration of Rights and Grievances held that: (1) obedience would be paid only to the king; (2) Parliament did not have the right to tax the colonies; and (3) the following rights were guaranteed to the colonists by the laws of nature, principles of the English constitution, and the several charters or compacts: "life, liberty, and property"; "all rights, liberties, and immunities of free and natural-born subjects within the realm of England"; the right to assemble peacefully, petition the king, list their grievances, and to be free from a "standing army" in the colonies at a time of peace; and the right to popularly selected colonial councils.

The Continental Association. This measure called for an intercolonial effort to prohibit the importation of British goods after December 1774, and exportation of colonial goods to England after September 1775, unless the Coercive Acts were repealed by Parliament.

War in Massachusetts (1775). Nonimportation was enforced so effectively that trade between Britain and the colonies was almost at a standstill. As a result, colonial manufacturing was encouraged and "homespun" garments became symbols of patriotism. Patrick Henry urged that the colonies prepare for war in a famous speech before the Virginia legislature that ended with the words, "Give me liberty or give me death."

Resistance to British measures spread through the colonies in 1775.

15

- *Lexington and Concord.* **General Thomas Gage**, the British commander in Boston, took the offensive against the rebellious colonists and sent British troops to Concord to seize colonial military supplies. Warned by Paul Revere, William Dawes, and Samuel Prescott, an undermanned and underarmed group of colonial minutemen were waiting for the British at Lexington on the morning of April 19th. Shots were fired, and the American Revolution began. After leaving eight Americans dead, the British troops moved to Concord, five miles away. The British were then driven out of Concord and retreated to Boston under heavy colonial fire.

- *The Second Continental Congress (1775).* The Congress met on May 10, 1775, shortly after the outbreak of war in Massachusetts.

Declaration of the Causes and Necessity of Taking Up Arms (1775). On July 6, 1775, deciding on continued resistance, the Congress issued the Declaration of the Causes and Necessity of Taking Up Arms. Prepared by Thomas Jefferson and John Dickinson, it promised armed resistance until the end of unconstitutional imperial control by England and the acknowledgement of the colonials' rights as British subjects.

- **Common Sense** *(January 1776).* **Thomas Paine**, a 39-year-old political agitator and writer who had only one year earlier moved to the colonies from England, wrote a pamphlet entitled *Common Sense* that had tremendous influence. His 47-page document advocated the establishment of an independent American republic. Written in an emotional style in the language of the common people, it sold 120,000 copies in just three months and caused many colonists to favor independence.

Paine attacked the balance of monarchy, aristocracy, and democracy in the English system. Suggesting the abolition of the Crown and nobility, Thomas Paine advocated a republic that would derive its powers exclusively from the governed. Paine's advice would be remembered in one of the restrictions on Congress included in Article II, Section 9, Paragraph 8 of the United States Constitution, which prohibits the granting of titles of nobility.

- *The Declaration of Independence (July 4, 1776).* By the late spring of 1776, independence had clearly become inevitable. The Second Continental Congress formally recommended to the colonies that they individually form governments of their own.

The Drafting. On June 7, 1776, **Richard Henry Lee**, representing the colony of Virginia, introduced into the Continental Congress the following resolution: "That these United Colonies are, and of right ought to be, free and independent states."

On June 11 the Congress referred the resolutions to an appointed committee consisting of Benjamin Franklin, John Adams, Robert R. Livingston, Roger Sherman, and Thomas Jefferson, and asked that they draft a "declaration of independence." The committee delegated the actual writing of the document to Jefferson, who submitted the draft to the Congress on June 28.

The resolution offered by Lee was adopted by the Congress on July 2 with the approval of twelve of the colonies (New York abstained). On July 4, 1776, the **Declaration of Independence** was formally adopted by all the colonies except New York, which finally granted approval on July 15. Congress ordered it printed and distributed to colonial officials, military units, and the press.

The Content. The Declaration of Independence had a profound effect on the political life of the United States. Following are explanations of the four sections and why they were included.

The **Preamble**, an opening statement or introduction, explains that separation has become necessary to preserve natural law and natural rights.

The paragraph following the Preamble contains a theory of democratic government and sets forth four fundamental political ideas: (1) the doctrine of "certain **unalienable Rights**," among them "Life, Liberty, and the pursuit of Happiness"; (2) the compact theory of government; (3) the doctrine of popular sovereignty in the form of governments "instituted among Men deriving their just powers from the consent of the governed"; and (4) the right of revolution to "throw off such Government" that is guilty of "a long train of abuses and usurpations."

The longest section of the Declaration is the list of complaints against King George III that are the reasons for separation. It should be noted that the entire Declaration of Independence is directed toward the king and not Parliament, because Americans claimed that Parliament had no authority over them and they did not want to alienate those members of Parliament who supported them.

The final section of the document is the actual declaration of independence and separation from England, resulting in "Free and Independent States." It is also a formal declaration of war.

The Effects. The Declaration of Independence's immediate effect was a revolution and the establishment of a new nation. However, its longer-lasting effect was to commit the new American nation to carry out the highest political ideals of the age. In Jefferson's own words, the document was "an expression of the American mind."

• *War and Peace (1776–1783).* About one third of the colonists who were called **Tories**, **Loyalists**, or sometimes Friends of the King remained loyal to Britain.

Those Americans who supported the Revolution were called **Patriots**, **Yanks**, or even **Whigs**, a term used in the colonies since the early 1700s to refer to those who opposed various measures of the royal governors. Poorly trained and inadequately equipped, the Patriot army never numbered more than 18,000 soldiers at any one time.

British Advantages and Disadvantages. Among the advantages of the British were a unified effort, greater financial resources, better trained and disciplined troops, and, for most of the war, control of the seas. Disadvantages included the problems of supplying an army fighting 3,000 miles away from home, subduing an enemy that was thinly scattered over a vast area, adjusting to the "guerilla-type" warfare used by the colonists, fighting several enemies, including France, Holland, and Spain after 1778, and cutting off the flow of aid to the colonists from their European allies.

Colonial Advantages and Disadvantages. Colonial advantages included patriotic spirit spurred by defending their towns, homes, and families; superior officers, both native and foreign, including Lafayette of France, von Steuben of Prussia, and Kosciusko and Pulaski of Poland; and the extensive aid in money, supplies, troops, and naval support they received through a treaty of alliance with France in 1778. Major disadvantages of the colonists were problems associated with the lack of central governmental authority as the Continental Congress had little real authority, had not established a sound financial system, and did not have the power to tax; the Tories, who were hostile to independence and aided the British through subversive acts; and the constant struggle to raise and maintain the **Continental Army**.

- *Turning Point and the French Alliance.* The **Battle of Saratoga** (October 1777) was the turning point of the American Revolution. France, eager to avenge its defeat in the French and Indian War, saw an opportunity to split the British Empire apart by allying itself with the American colonies. The alliance provided that if war broke out between France and Great Britain, the two allies (France and the United States) would fight the war together and neither would make peace with the enemy without the consent of the other.

- *British Surrender at Yorktown.* In 1781 the Americans began to win battles against the British in the South. General Cornwallis withdrew his troops to Virginia, near the coast, where the British navy could support him. The British now held only New York City and a few Southern ports. Trapped by the French fleet behind him and a superior combined force of American and French troops before him, Cornwallis was forced to surrender on October 19, 1781. Peace negotiations soon began in Paris.

- *Treaty of Paris (September 3, 1783).* Problems developed between the United States and France because of the Treaty of Alliance signed by the two nations in 1778. According to the terms of the treaty, the United States was obligated to continue fighting Britain until France stopped. France was obligated to Spain to continue fighting until Gibraltar was retrieved from the British.

Although the American diplomats **John Jay**, **John Adams**, and **Benjamin Franklin** were instructed by Congress not to enter into any separate peace agreements with Britain, and to be guided by France in the negotiations, they ignored these instructions. Negotiations were held with the British and a preliminary treaty with very favorable terms was signed in September 1782.

On January 30, 1783, France and Spain signed their own provisional treaties of peace with Britain. The final treaties were signed on September 3, 1783, and the United States Congress proclaimed the treaty of peace and independence, January 14, 1784.

The Revolution in Retrospect

Many historians have offered different interpretations about the American Revolution and its causes. Among them are

- a struggle between the tyrannical control of England and the liberty-loving Americans who saw an opportunity to carry out the beliefs of the Enlightenment thinkers;
- the impossibility of England's maintaining colonies 3,000 miles away as part of its empire;
- a struggle between the growing American free enterprise system and the English mercantile system;
- a conflict of religions—between the dissenting sects that settled America and the Church of England, the dominant religion of English officials and aristocrats;
- the development of a new class structure in the colonies primarily due to the ending of heredity, birthright status, and primogeniture, and the availability of land and the expansion of the franchise (vote) as leveling factors;
- the internal problems of English politics and the inconsistencies of English policy toward the colonies; and
- the fact that the revolution was actually no revolution at all, but a struggle to preserve a social and economic order rather than to change it.

When America freed itself from British control, it also eliminated a system of law and order that had to be replaced if the new republic was to have any chance of survival. The **Articles of Confederation**, the nation's first constitution, was a natural outcome of the revolutionary movement within the American colonies—a constitutional expression of the philosophy of the Declaration of Independence.

This map shows the United States in 1783 after the Treaty of Paris. As indicated, the young country had several territorial disputes. These were soon to involve the new government in serious foreign problems.

Figure 1.2 The United States in 1783

Problems of Confederation

> It has long been a grave question whether any government, not too strong for the liberties of its people, can be strong enough to maintain its existence in great emergencies.
>
> Abraham Lincoln, November 10, 1864

The winning of independence made necessary the establishment of a new government to replace British rule. How would the Americans meet the unprecedented task of establishing a government that was strong enough to govern and protect the nation, but restrained enough to preserve individual liberties?

The British surrender at Yorktown on October 19, 1781, and the Treaty of Paris in 1783 resulted in the establishment of the sovereign state known as the United States. The first years of the new nation under the Articles of Confederation from 1781 to 1789 are called the "critical period." Eventually, this first constitution was replaced by the one written at the **Constitutional Convention of 1787**.

State Constitutions

Between May 1776—when the Continental Congress instructed the colonies to form local governments—and 1780, most of the colonies, which were now states, had written new state constitutions and established governments.

• *Characteristics.* A common characteristic of all these state governments was constitutional republicanism; that is, the source of political authority rested with the people. Another similarity was concern to control the abuses of political power; all of the states developed written constitutions that placed restraints upon the powers of government. All these documents provided for regular and frequent elections to keep the government close and accountable to its constituency. Some of the early constitutions included a list of principles that the government could not violate. Specific guarantees of civil liberties, including freedom of speech and press, protection from arbitrary arrest, the right to jury trial, liberty of conscience, and due process rights were also included in many of them.

Perhaps the most significant feature of these state constitutions was their treatment of the executive and legislative branches of government. The most feared branch, the **executive**, was kept comparatively weak. Most governors were elected for one-year terms by the legislature, stripped of veto power, and usually had only ceremonial functions. The legislature, the branch closest to the people, retained most of the governing power.

• *Separation of Powers.* During the colonial period the belief had developed that good government required the separation of powers between the three branches of government. The 1776 Virginia state constitution specified:

> The *legislative, executive,* and *judiciary* departments shall be separate and distinct, so that neither exercises the powers properly belonging to the other; nor shall any person exercise the powers of more than one of them at the same time.

The constitutions adopted by the American states used the idea of separation of powers as an organizing principle of government.

Figure 1.3 shows how the state constitutions established systems of government that used the concept of separation of powers.

Movement Toward Confederation

The need for a central government was recognized early in the Revolutionary War. The **Articles of Confederation** were accepted by the Continental Congress in 1777, but disputes over western land claims postponed their ratification by the thirteen states until March 1781. At this time, the new league of states came into being.

• *A "League of Friendship."* The most perplexing issue facing Americans during the Confederation Period may have been trying to define the term "United States."

The wording of the Articles of Confederation, especially Article 2, made it clear that state sovereignty was to be maintained. If the states reserved for themselves such a high degree of independence from the central government, what then was the function of the national Congress?

• *Form of Government under the Articles.* The central government, consisting of a **unicameral** (one-house) Congress, acted as an administrative agency for the states. Although Congress was expressly granted the powers to control war and foreign affairs, regulate trade with the Indians, regulate the value of its coinage, maintain a post office, and standardize weights and measures, it could not infringe upon the right of a state to legislate upon matters within its own limits.

Powers of Congress. In the Congress established under the Confederation, each state had one vote. The votes of two-thirds of the states were required to pass legislation, and an amendment to the Articles required a unanimous vote by the states.

Powers of the States. Consistent with Article 2, the states retained all the powers (reserved powers) that were not expressly delegated to the central government. This left the states with such critical powers as (1) authority over commerce with other states and, in part, with other nations; and (2) the power to tax.

Contributions of the Articles of Confederation

The ratification of the Articles of Confederation in 1781 legalized the measures carried out by the Continental Congress since 1775. Despite the severe limitations on its power, the Congress under the Articles of Confederation did make lasting contributions to the nation's well-being.

• *War and Diplomacy.* Under the leadership of the Continental Congress, and the Confederation Congress, the American Revolution was fought and won and a peace treaty concluded.

EXECUTIVE

Powers: Limited administrative appointments, enforcement of laws, limited veto power (New York and Massachusetts) usually reversible by simple majority of legislature.

LEGISLATIVE

Powers: Supreme lawmaker, election of governor in most states, impeachment powers, powers to establish own rules such as meeting frequency, procedures, and membership requirements.

JUDICIAL

Powers: Interpretation of laws (including bills of rights limiting government's authority over the people), life tenure during good behavior, beginning of judicial review (the right to declare acts of the legislature unconstitutional).

THE PEOPLE

Powers: Actual representation through the vote. Although restrictions on suffrage rights still existed (property qualifications, religious exclusions, lack of voting power among women, slaves, Indians), there were movements toward universal manhood suffrage. For example, limited substitution of a taxpayer qualification for property holding took place in Pennsylvania, New Hampshire, New Jersey, Georgia, and Maryland.

Figure 1.3 State Constitutions: Separation of Powers

- *Establishment of a Federal System.* Federalism is the doctrine that advocates the division of powers between the national and state governments. Although the division of powers between the national government—the Congress—and the state governments under the Articles lacked the proper balance, the Articles did outline a federal system that provided a basis for establishment of a government at the Constitutional Convention of 1787.

- *Western Lands.* Perhaps the greatest contribution of the Articles of Confederation was the establishment of a policy for the settlement of western lands and the establishment of government in these new lands. These principles of settlement were used as Americans expanded across the continent throughout the 1800s.

Cessation of Western Land Claims. The United States had acquired the **Northwest Territory**, the land north of the Ohio River and west of the Appalachians, as a result of the Treaty of Paris of 1783 with Great Britain. Maryland refused to ratify the Articles of Confederation until Virginia turned over its claims to much of this territory to Congress, which it finally did, with conditions, in 1781. Formal adoption of the Articles of Confederation came in March 1781 with Maryland's ratification.

Ordinance of 1785. With the passage of the Land Ordinance of 1785, the Congress established a pattern for the orderly division and settlement of the land north of the Ohio River. The Ordinance provided that (1) townships of six miles square would be divided into 36 subdivisions of 640 acres each (the minimal amount to be sold); (2) each section would be sold at auction for at least one dollar an acre with the revenue to be used to pay off the national debt; and (3) the revenue from the sale of one section from each township would be used to support public education—this provided a precedent for federal aid to education. Although some changes in the policy were made in later years, the Ordinance of 1785 remained the basis of public land policy until the **Homestead Act of 1862**.

The Northwest Ordinance of 1787. The Northwest Ordinance combined the concepts of **federalism**, **republicanism**, and **regard for civil liberties** in a plan of national development that ranks in significance with the Declaration of Independence and the Constitution. The Ordinance of 1787, passed by the Confederation Congress and later reaffirmed as federal law by the new United States Congress under the Constitution in 1789, provided for the government of the Northwest Territory, an area of more than 265,000 square miles.

Between 1803 and 1848, Ohio (1803), Indiana (1816), Illinois (1818), Michigan (1837), and Wisconsin (1848) were admitted as states from the Northwest Territory.

Weaknesses of the Articles of Confederation—Foreign Affairs

- *Foreign Occupation of the West.* Great Britain continued to occupy posts in the Northwest Territory, even though the Treaty of Paris of 1783 had provided that the British would leave this area "with all convenient speed."

American problems with Spain included disputes over the boundaries established by the Treaty of Paris of 1783 and the navigation of the lower Mississippi River. Spain's decision to close the Mississippi to American shipping in 1784 led to negotiations between Secretary of Foreign Affairs John Jay and the Spanish minister.

- *Foreign Debts.* Between 1778 and 1783 the United States borrowed several million dollars from the French and the Dutch governments. Because of its failure to meet even the interest payments on these loans, the United States lost the respect of its former allies.

- *Barbary Pirates.* Commerce in the Mediterranean Sea had long been subject to attacks by coastal pirates unless financial tributes, or bribes, were paid. Since the United States was no longer protected by the British navy, and had no navy of its own, it could do little to prevent violations of its commercial rights by the Barbary pirates.

Weakness of Articles—Domestic Affairs

- *Problems of Commerce.* Under the Confederation, Congress lacked the power to control and regulate both domestic and foreign trade. As jealousies over trade developed between the states, they started to levy tariffs on each other's goods. This brought domestic trade almost to a standstill.

- *Need of Revenue.* Most of Congress's difficulties between 1776 and 1787 were related to its inability to raise money. Congressional income was dependent on the whims of the states, since Congress had no power to raise money on its own.

- *Currency Problems.* A postwar depression led to a wide demand for the issuance of paper money by the state legislatures.

During the fall of 1786, an incident in western Massachusetts helped to convince many Americans that changes in the national government were necessary. In Massachusetts, farmers who were crushed by demands for payment of debts and taxes joined together. They took matters into their own hands after the courts ordered that their homes and land be sold to pay their debts. Led by **Daniel Shays**, a captain during the Revolutionary War, some 1,200 armed fol-

Specie, or hard money, was scarce in the new nation.

lowers gathered to attack the federal arsenal at Springfield. This attack was unsuccessful. A militia was raised and sent by the governor to put down the rebellion. It was completely suppressed by February 1787.

Shays' rebellion caused much fear among Americans and was used by conservative forces to bolster their demand for a stronger central government.

• *Political Structure.* It was with Shays' Rebellion and the weaknesses of the Confederation government in mind that the framers of the Constitution included Section 4 of Article IV:

> The United States shall guarantee to every State in this Union a Republican Form of Government, and shall protect each of them against Invasion; and on Application of the Legislature, or of the Executive (when the Legislature cannot be convened) against domestic violence.
>
> Article IV, Sec 4, United States Constitution

Movement Toward a Constitutional Convention

The weaknesses of the Articles of Confederation, combined with the political, social, and economic difficulties faced by the nation at this time, led the states to consider revisions in the Confederation government.

• *The Annapolis Conference (1786).* Although eight states named representatives to the September meeting, delegates from only five states arrived in time for the Annapolis Conference. At the suggestion of **James Madison** and **Alexander Hamilton**, a convention was called to meet in Philadelphia in May of the following year to discuss revising the Articles of Confederation.

From Radicalism to Conservatism

There is evidence to support the idea that the American Revolution, although a concerted effort for independence, was fought by a population with distinct class lines. A conservative group, composed primarily of Northern lawyers, merchants, bankers,

Alexander Hamilton encouraged the rewriting of the Articles of Confederation.

speculators, and wealthy Southern planters and merchants, sought independence from Britain's trade regulations and restrictions on capitalist growth. They had no desire to see the Revolution upset their positions in society, and were firm believers in a government that was controlled by the wellborn who were capable of maintaining the class structure. On the other hand, the small business owners, artisans, and farmers fought the Revolution in order to break America's political ties with England and to destroy the economic and social privileges of the colonial aristocracy. They regarded the principles of the Declaration of Independence as the guidelines for a new social order, as well as the political transformation of power to local representative bodies. The central issue between the conservative and the radical groups in America in the period of the 1780s was still the question of where supreme authority was to be located.

The Articles of Confederation represented the attempt to deny authority to any government superior to the legislative bodies of the states. A change in the balance of political power took place between 1776 and 1787. The movement to centralize power, which was assisted by the problems of the Confederation period, engineered a conservative counterrevolution and created a nationalistic government. Although this protected the interests of the conservative, propertied classes, it also preserved the system of republican government, the primary concern of all groups in the United States.

Exercise Set 1.1

1. "In framing a government which is to be administered by men over men, the great difficulty lies in this; you must first enable the government to control the governed, and next, oblige it to control itself."

    James Madison, *The Federalist,* No. 51

    Which concept of government is being referred to in the quotation?
    A. unicameral legislature
    B. cabinet system
    C. popularly elected assemblies
    D. system of checks and balances

2. In most of the thirteen original colonies, the settlers gained experience in self-government by
    A. choosing governors to administer colonial affairs
    B. electing members of colonial assemblies
    C. regulating trade with England
    D. sending representatives to vote in Parliament

3. Which of the following democratic practices of the American heritage cannot be found in English history?
    A. a written constitution
    B. common law
    C. representative government
    D. the concept of limited government

4. As a result of the Albany Congress of 1754
   A. the Dominion of New England was eliminated
   B. an experiment in intercolonial union was proposed
   C. the colonies were granted limited tax power
   D. an intercolonial legislature was established

5. The most significant step toward intercolonial union was
   A. the New England Confederation
   B. the use of the town meeting in the New England colonies
   C. the drafting of the Mayflower Compact
   D. the formation of the Virginia Company of London

6. Colonial legislatures were often able to control royal governors by
   A. threatening impeachment
   B. controlling finances, including the governor's salary
   C. overruling the governor with authority granted by Parliament
   D. using the colonial militia

Base your answers to questions 7 and 8 on the following excerpt from the Declaration of Independence and your knowledge of social studies:

> "We hold these truths to be self-evident, that all men are created equal, that they are endowed by their creator with certain unalienable rights, that among these are life, liberty, and the pursuit of happiness. That to secure these rights, governments are instituted among men, deriving their just powers from the consent of the governed."

7. According to Jefferson's Declaration of Independence, governments receive their authority and power from
   A. only men
   B. military strength
   C. the people
   D. God

8. The ideas expressed in the preceding excerpt from the Declaration of Independence are consistent with the writings of which pair of Enlightenment thinkers?
   A. John Locke and Baron de Montesquieu
   B. Jean-Jacques Rousseau and John Locke
   C. Sir William Blackstone and Jean-Jacques Rousseau
   D. John Locke and Sir Henry Clinton

9. A review of the events that came before the American Revolution indicates that
   A. the Boston Massacre marked a point of no return toward independence
   B. after 1763 most Americans wanted nothing less than complete independence from England
   C. as late as February 1775, reconciliation was probably possible
   D. Parliament clearly welcomed the armed conflict in hopes of bringing the colonies back under control

10. According to the Declaration of Independence, the purpose of government is to
    A. equalize opportunities for all citizens
    B. provide for the common defense
    C. secure the people in their natural rights
    D. suppress the dangers of "raw democracy"

11. The original reason for adding bills of rights to early state constitutions was to
    A. prohibit state governments from depriving individuals of certain basic rights
    B. deprive the national government of any regulation of natural rights
    C. ensure the supremacy of the legislature over the executive in state governments
    D. provide an example for the eventual Bill of Rights added to the Constitution in 1791

12. The colonial branch of government that Americans had grown to suspect most during the period before the Revolution was the
    A. judicial branch
    B. executive branch
    C. legislative branch
    D. Continental Congress

13. Among the weaknesses of the Articles of Confederation was
    A. the need for a unanimous vote to amend the Articles
    B. the failure to establish a peace treaty at the conclusion of the American Revolution
    C. the abandonment of the principle of federalism
    D. the inability to deal with the western land problem

14. Which of the following best describes the "United States" under the Articles of Confederation?
    A. a confederation of colonies existing within an empire
    B. one nation, consisting of thirteen subordinate components
    C. free and independent states loosely held together by a Confederation Congress
    D. sovereign states with no cohesive element whatsoever

15. The Declaration of Independence
    A. contained a list of grievances against Parliament
    B. was written by Jefferson and adopted without change
    C. contained Jefferson's objections to slavery
    D. directed the grievances of the colonists against George III

CONSTITUTIONAL CONVENTION, RATIFICATION, AND A BILL OF RIGHTS

> The whole people declared the colonies in their united condition, of right, free and independent States .... But there still remained the last and Crowning act, by which the People of the Union alone were competent to perform the institution of civil government, for that compound nation, the United States of America.
>
> John Quincy Adams, *The Jubilee of the Constitution* (1839).

In 1786 James Madison described the Articles of Confederation as "nothing more than a treaty of amity and of alliance between independent and sovereign states." As attempts to amend the Articles failed, and the nation's problems, which stemmed from the lack of a central authority, increased, steps toward forming a new government began.

Constitutional Convention

The Delegates

The Convention met in Philadelphia on May 25, 1787 with 55 delegates from seven states in attendance. By July, twelve states were represented, Rhode Island choosing not to participate.

The delegates at the Constitutional Convention were as brilliant an assembly of statesmen as ever had met in America. The group included **George Washington**, who was selected as presiding officer of the Convention, **James Madison**, who kept a journal of the debates, **Benjamin Franklin**, George Mason, Gouverneur Morris, James Wilson, Roger Sherman, and Elbridge Gerry. Notable absences included the more radical leaders of the Confederation period: **Samuel Adams**, **Patrick Henry**, and **Thomas Paine**. Also absent were **Thomas Jefferson** and **John Adams**, who were serving as ambassadors in Europe.

James Madison (1751–1836) 4th President of the United States. Madison was a key participant in the Constitutional Convention.

Most of the delgates to the Constitutional Convention were men of property, representing primarily the upper classes of American society. Their class status was reflected in their interest in a strong central government. Their goal was to form a government that would avoid the polar extremes of despotism and uncontrolled popular rule. Congress had authorized the Convention only for "the sole and express purpose of revising the Articles of Confederation." Few of them realized at the outset that their efforts would result in a new "constitution," rather than changes in the Articles of Confederation. In order to allow the delegates to debate freely without public pressure, sessions were secret and very little news leaked.

The Virginia, or Large States, Plan

Primarily the work of James Madison and Virginia Governor Edmund Randolph, the plan called for drafting a new document to organize a new form of government rather than for amending the Articles of Confederation. Introduced on May 29 by Edmund Randolph, the Virginia Plan proposed (1) **a bicameral legislature** representing the states proportionately (based on population), with the lower house elected by the people and the upper house to be chosen by the lower house.

The New Jersey, or "Small States," Plan

Presented to the Convention on June 15 by William Paterson of New Jersey, it called for changes in the Articles of Confederation rather than the drafting of a new document. The smaller states claimed that representation in Congress based upon population would allow the larger states to constantly outvote the smaller states. The New Jersey Plan proposed: (1) **a unicameral legislature** similar to that under the Articles with each state having one vote.

The Great, or Connecticut, Compromise

On June 19 the convention decided to scrap the Articles of Confederation and write a new plan of government. The major area of debate concerned the method by which the states would be represented in the national Congress. On July 12, Roger Sherman of Connecticut offered a compromise plan, which provided for a Congress with two houses—a **Senate** and a **House of Representatives**. The lower house of Congress, the House, would be filled according to **proportional representation** (by population) with one member for every 40,000 residents. The upper house, the Senate, would be filled by **equal representation** of the states, each state having two members elected by the legislature of the individual states.

The Three-Fifths Compromise

Three suggestions were made concerning how the population should be counted in order to determine the number of representatives each state was to have in the lower house. Each plan showed strong sectional biases. The first, supported primarily by the slave states, wanted all people (free and slave) counted for purposes of representation, but not for taxation. In the second, the nonslave-holding states of the North wanted only the free population counted. The third proposal, the method which was adopted by the members of the Convention, was to count three-fifths of the slave population for both representation and taxation. (Article I, Section 2, Clause 3. Overruled by Amendments 13 [1865] and 14 [1868].) It was also decided that the method for counting the population would be a census taken every ten years. (Article I, Section 2, Clause 3, Amendment 17.)

Prohibition on Banning of Slave Trade

Linked to the Three-Fifths Compromise, this provided that Congress would pass no law prohibiting the importation of slaves for twenty years. The importation of slaves became illegal after 1808. (Article I, Section 9, Clause 1.)

Fugitive Slave Clause

To placate the Southern states, this clause declared that slaves ("persons held to service or labor under the laws of a state") who escaped to a free state would be returned to their rightful owners. (Article IV, Section 2, Clause 3. Overruled in 1865 by Amendment 13.)

Tariffs

Again, geographic differences surfaced over the question of duties on trade. Southerners who exported agricultural products disapproved of granting power to the national government to impose taxes on exports. Northern business groups, however, wanted tariffs on imports to protect their interests from foreign competition. A compromise was reached and the delegates to the Convention granted Congress the authority to tax imports, but not exports. (Article I, Section 8, Clause 1 and Article I, Section 9, Clause 5.)

The Presidency

The small states desired a weak executive, chosen by and responsible to the legislature. The larger states supported a strong executive selected through direct election by the people. James Wilson's compromise proposal, that the people of the states should choose presidential electors through their own methods who then should meet and choose the executive, was accepted as the method of election. (Article II, Sections 2 and 3, Amendment 12.)

Principles of the Document

Separation of Powers

The arrangement of Articles I, II, and III—the first devoted to the Congress, the second to the President, and the third to the federal judiciary—made it clear that Montesquieu's thoughts, and the experiences of the state governments, were well studied by the members of the Convention. The delegates established a government based on the idea of the separation of powers.

Checks and Balances

The framers of the Constitution were concerned that the government should not act in a hasty or arbitrary manner. The system of checks and balances within our system requires an interaction between the three branches that prevents the abuse of power by any one of them. Figure 1.4 helps demonstrate some of the checks and balances among the three branches of government.

Federalism

This concept of distributing powers of government between one central or national government (usually called the "federal government") and the governments of the several states into which a country is divided was adopted by those at the Constitutional Convention.

Structure of the Document

The final document consisted of a preamble setting forth the reasons the Constitution was adopted and a main body of seven articles divided into sections and clauses. Shortly after ratification, an appendix of amendments to the Constitution was added.

Preamble

This opening paragraph of the Constitution establishes the people as the source of authority for the Constitution and sets forth six goals: (1) to set up a stronger government than had existed under the Articles of Confederation; (2) to improve the judicial system; (3) to guarantee peace within and among the states; (4) to provide protection for the country; (5) to provide for the general welfare; and (6) to maintain liberty for citizens, present and future.

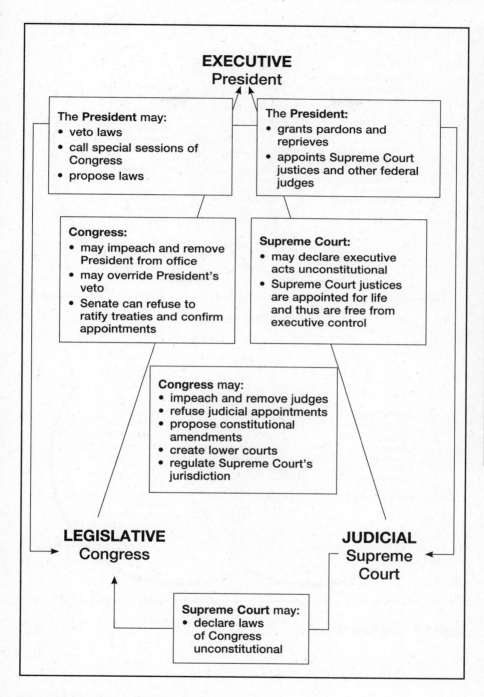

EXECUTIVE
President

The **President** may:
• veto laws
• call special sessions of Congress
• propose laws

The **President**:
• grants pardons and reprieves
• appoints Supreme Court justices and other federal judges

Congress:
• may impeach and remove President from office
• may override President's veto
• Senate can refuse to ratify treaties and confirm appointments

Supreme Court:
• may declare executive acts unconstitutional
• Supreme Court justices are appointed for life and thus are free from executive control

Congress may:
• impeach and remove judges
• refuse judicial appointments
• propose constitutional amendments
• create lower courts
• regulate Supreme Court's jurisdiction

LEGISLATIVE
Congress

JUDICIAL
Supreme Court

Supreme Court may:
• declare laws of Congress unconstitutional

Figure 1.4   Checks and Balances

Federal Government

Enumerated Powers:

- Regulate interstate and foreign trade
- Establish laws for citizens
- Coin money
- Regulate patents and copyrights
- Establish post offices
- Establish federal courts
- Declare war
- Raise and support armed forces
- Pass laws necessary and proper for carrying out preceding powers

Federal and State Governments

Concurrent (Shared) Powers:

- Lay and collect taxes
- Charter banks
- Take property for public use
- Borrow money
- Enforce laws
- Establish courts
- Provide for the general welfare

State Governments

Reserved Powers:

- Determine voter qualifications
- Provide for education
- Establish marriage and divorce laws
- Regulate intrastate commerce
- Conduct elections
- Establish local governments
- Incorporate businesses
- Provide for public safety and morals

Prohibited Powers

Powers Denied

Federal Government:

- Suspend the writ of habeas corpus
- Tax exports
- Show preference to one state over another
- Take money from treasury without right by law

Powers Denied

Federal and State Governments:

- Pass bills of attainder
- Pass ex post facto laws
- Grant titles of nobility
- Deprive persons of life, liberty, or property without due process of the law

Powers Denied

State Government:

- Make treaties with other nations or states without consent of Congress
- Coin money
- Impair the obligations of contracts
- Tax imports or exports
- Keep troops or ships during peace without consent of Congress

Figure 1.5   The Federal System

Articles I through VII

The first three articles of the Constitution describe the organization and functions of the three branches of the federal government: the **legislative**, **executive**, and **judicial**. Articles IV through VII set forth how the powers of the government are to be shared by the federal government, the states, and the people.

Article I:	Legislative Branch
Article II:	Executive Branch
Article III:	Judicial Branch
Article IV:	Relations among the states
Article V:	Amending the Constitution
Article VI:	Supremacy Clause
Article VII:	Ratification Procedures

Amendments

Article V of the Constitution provides that the document may be changed when the need arises. Although there have been many attempts at amending the Constitution, there have been only 27 amendments added to the Constitution since 1789.

Ratification

Article VII provided that state conventions would be called and that, upon the approval of only nine states, the Constitution would go into effect. On September 28, 1787, Congress directed the state legislatures to call ratification conventions in each state.

The ratification of the Constitution led to the formation of **political factions** and the nation's first organized political battle between the **Federalists** and the **antifederalists**.

Federalists

Those who supported the ratification of the Constitution called themselves **Federalists**. In favor of a stronger Union, the Federalists felt that anarchy could result without a stronger national government. Many of the Federalists came from the business and propertied classes and therefore had a personal economic interest in the establishment of a strong stable government. Alexander Hamilton and John Adams were early Federalist leaders.

Antifederalists

The **antifederalists** did not fear strong government as much as they feared a strong centralized government at the expense of local state governments. Another major concern of the antifederalists was the potential danger to individual liberties posed by the lack of a bill of rights.

While the antifederalists wanted the states to maintain a large degree of sovereignty, they also wanted Congress to act for the states in areas where the states could not act for themselves—notably foreign policy, western settlement, commerce, and disputes between the states. Among the early leaders of the antifederalists were Richard Henry Lee of Virginia, and **Thomas Jefferson**.

State Conventions

The debate over ratification took place in conventions within the individual states. By the time New Hampshire ratified in June 1788, the requirement of ratification by nine states had been satisfied. However, New York and Virginia had not yet voted, and most realized that the chances of the Constitution's succeeding without the support of those states were slim.

The Federalist Papers

The most serious criticism of the Constitution by the antifederalists was its lack of a bill of rights. In New York, Governor George Clinton expressed this and other fears in several published newspaper essays, while **Patrick Henry** and **James Monroe** led the opposition in Virginia. Between October 1787 and August 1788, **James Madison** of Virginia, and **Alexander Hamilton** and **John Jay**, both of New York, published 85 essays in New York newspapers above the signature "Publius" to answer the fears of the antifederalists. Madison's leading role in the drafting of the Constitution has made *The Federalist* the most authoritative source for interpreting the Constitution.

A Bill of Rights

The first Congress under the new constitutional government met in April 1789. One of its first tasks was to respond to the calls of the state ratification conventions for amendments to the Constitution in the form of a bill of rights. Of the twelve proposals sent to the states, ten were accepted and officially became part of the Constitution on December 15, 1791, when three-quarters of the states had ratified them. Article V of the Constitution provides for the amending process.

The following cases involving the Bill of Rights will be addressed throughout the text and will demonstrate how the Constitution, in particular the Bill of Rights, has proven to be a "living document" over time:

- *Tinker* v. *Des Moines*, 1969 (First Amendment)—p. 488
- *Engle* v. *Vitale*, 1962 (First Amendment)—p. 506
- *New York Times* v. *United States*, 1971 (First Amendment)—p. 484
- *Mapp* v. *Ohio*, 1961 (Fourth Amendment)—p. 506
- *Vernonia School District* v. *Acton*, 1995 (Fourth Amendment)—p. 523
- *Scott* v. *Sanford*, 1857 (Fifth Amendment)—p. 212
- *Miranda* v. *Arizona*, 1966 (Fifth and Sixth Amendments)—p. 506

Throughout our nation's history, only Congress has proposed amendments for consideration by the states. The procedure allowing for two thirds of the states to petition Congress to call a constitutional convention has never been used. The scope and authority of such a convention are not defined or limited by the Constitution and therefore the method has prompted much debate.

The only amendment to be ratified by popularly elected state constitutional conventions was the Twenty-first Amendment (1933) repealing Prohibition. All other amendments have been ratified by the state legislatures.

By studying the over 80 proposals from the state conventions for ratifying the Constitution, Madison was able to incorporate those he considered most important into his nineteen original proposals.

The **first ten amendments** to the United States Constitution gave formal recognition to certain traditionally accepted natural rights that had been included in the English tradition, colonial charters, and states' bills of rights. The wording of the first ten amendments makes it clear that those powers that are granted or denied to the federal government are powers that come directly from the people. Contrary to our provisions for individual liberties are those systems in which the government grants rights. For example: The First Amendment to the United States Constitution reads in part: *"Congress shall make no law* respecting the establishment of religion . . . or abridging the freedom of speech." Article 125 of the former Soviet Union's Fundamental Rights and Duties of Citizens reads in part: "In conformity with the interests of the working people, and in order to strengthen the socialist system, *the citizens are guaranteed* by law: freedom of speech, freedom of press . . ."

The important distinction is the source of authority in the two different systems of government, the first being the people, the second being the government.

PROPOSAL	RATIFICATION
Amendments to the Constitution may be proposed by a two thirds vote of Congress in both the House of Representatives and the Senate	The amendment must be ratified by at least three fourths of the state legislatures
or	or
when two thirds of the state legislatures request Congress to call a Constitutional Convention, which then proposes an amendment.	be ratified by a majority vote in three fourths of the state conventions called to vote on the amendment.

Figure 1.6 The Amending Process

Amendments	Provisions
I	1. The establishment clause of Amendment I states that Congress shall make no law that establishes religion in any manner. This has been referred to as the "wall of separation between church and state." 2. The second part of Amendment I prevents Congress from restricting the free practice of religion, freedom of speech, press, the right to assemble peacefully, or to petition the government.
II	Amendment II was designed to prevent Congress from denying states the right to have a militia of armed citizens. It is currently argued that the amendment guarantees people the right to own weapons, although states do have the right to restrict such ownership.
III	In peacetime, no citizen may be forced to quarter (house and feed) soldiers. In time of war, Congress may pass legislation allowing for such quartering. The quartering of troops in the colonists' homes by the British government was well remembered by the residents of the states.
IV	Remembering the writs of assistance, supporters of the Fourth Amendment required that search warrants could be issued only under the following conditions: (a) the warrant must be issued by a judge; (b) there must be probable cause (good reason) for its issuance; and (c) the warrant must describe the place to be searched and the items to be seized.
V	1. Grand Juries: A person accused of a serious crime and tried in a federal court must first be indicted (charged) by a grand jury (jury of 12 to 23 persons). 2. Double Jeopardy: A person may not be tried twice for the same crime. 3. Self-Incrimination: A person may not be forced to say anything that would help convict himself or herself. This provision finds its origins in confessions that were obtained through forceful measure, i.e., torture. 4. Due Process: A person may not be deprived of life, liberty, or property (natural rights) except according to law. The Fourteenth Amendment applies this clause to the states as well as the federal government. 5. Eminent Domain: Congress may not (without paying a fair price) take private property for the benefit of the public, e.g., roads, hospitals, and airports.
VI	Amendment VI continues the rights of the accused started in Amendment V. The person accused of a crime must be given a prompt trial in public, and guilt or innocence must be decided by a jury chosen from the state and district where the crime was committed. The accused must be informed of the charges, be present when witnesses testify against him or her, and be provided with a lawyer if he or she cannot provide one. The Fourteenth Amendment has also applied these provisions to state courts.
VII	Amendment VII provides for a jury trial in federal civil cases (trials where one person sues another, usually for damages). The second part of the amendment limits the power of judges to interfere with a jury's decision.

Amendments	Provisions
VIII	If a person is accused of a crime and must await trial, he or she may be released from prison on bail—an amount of money that is put up to guarantee the accused will appear for trial; bail is forfeited if he or she fails to appear. Amendment VIII guarantees that a fine should be calculated according to the wrong done and that "cruel and unusual punishment" may not be inflicted on those convicted. The death penalty continues to be debated on the "cruel and unusual" punishment argument.
IX	Amendment IX was added out of fear that it might be dangerous to make only a partial listing of the basic rights guaranteed in the Constitution. This amendment makes it clear that the federal government may still do only what is authorized by the Constitution.
X	This amendment was added to reserve "all other powers" to the states and the people. The powers of the federal government are listed in Article I, Section 8. The powers denied to the states are listed in Article I, Section 10. All others are reserved to the states.
XIV*	Section 1 of Amendment XIV denied to the states the power to deprive any person of life, liberty, or property without due process of law. This due process clause protects individuals from unfair actions by state government, whereas, Amendment V protected individuals from unfair actions by the federal government.

*Note: The Bill of Rights was added to protect the people from the federal government. The Fourteenth Amendment, ratified in 1868, extended some of the original provisions of the Bill of Rights and applied them to the state governments. It protected individuals from actions by state governments.

Figure 1.7   The Bill of Rights

Exercise Set 1.2

1. Arrested persons claiming they have already been acquitted of the charge for which they are now being tried are claiming the defense of
   A. ex post facto
   B. unreasonable search and seizure
   C. double jeopardy
   D. right to trial by jury

2. The right of government to take private property for public use, providing just compensation is made, is known as
   A. habeas corpus
   B. self-incrimination
   C. Federalism
   D. eminent domain

3. When a judge tells the accused person what he or she is charged with and that he or she may have legal counsel and a jury trial, the accused is being
   A. indicted by a grand jury
   B. denied due process of law
   C. informed of constitutional rights
   D. protected from cruel and unusual punishment

4. The principle of Federalism as established by the United States Constitution provides for the
   A. separation of powers of the three branches of government
   B. placement of ultimate sovereignty in the hands of the state governments
   C. division of power between the state governments and the national government
   D. creation of a republican form of government

5. The Great Compromise of the Constitutional Convention of 1787 concerned the
   A. issue of slavery
   B. representation of the states in Congress
   C. election of the President
   D. allocation of judicial power in the federal government

6. Which of the following compromises made at the Constitutional Convention was later changed by a constitutional amendment?
   A. the establishment of a bicameral legislature
   B. the Three-Fifths Compromise
   C. the tariff-commerce compromise
   D. representation in the House of Representatives

7. The Constitution differed most from the Articles of Confederation in that the Constitution
   A. gave greater power to the federal government
   B. gave greater power to the state governments
   C. made the amending process more difficult
   D. changed the method of admitting new states to the union

8. Which of the following is an illustration of the system of checks and balances?
   A. an individual pays income tax to both the federal government and the state government
   B. New York State requires at least 180 days of school per year
   C. the Senate must approve an appointment by the President to the Supreme Court
   D. Congress may pass no law establishing a state religion

9. The powers of Congress were limited by the Constitution, chiefly because
   A. representatives of the states feared too powerful a central government
   B. the Federalists desired strong, independent state governments
   C. the new government lacked a judiciary to check Congressional power
   D. supporters of a strong central government planned to carry out legislative powers through the executive branch

10. Within the first ten amendments to the United States Constitution is one providing
    A. that under no conditions shall soldiers be housed and fed by citizens at the request of the government
    B. that slavery will be banned
    C. for the right of the people to petition the government
    D. for women's suffrage

CONSTITUTIONAL STRUCTURE, FUNCTION, AND THIRTEEN ENDURING ISSUES

> Our Constitution is in actual operation; everything appears to promise
> that it will last, but in this world nothing is certain but death and taxes.
> Benjamin Franklin, letter to M. Leroy, 1789

Structure and Function

Article I, Congress

- *The Structure.* Congress is organized according to provisions in Article I of the Constitution.

- *Sessions of Congress.* Beginning with the first Congress of 1789–1790, each Congress serves for a two-year term. Each Congress meets in two sessions, each session convening, in accordance with the Twentieth Amendment, on or soon after January 3.

- *Powers of Congress.* The first 17 clauses of Article I, Section 8, detail the power of Congress. Some of the major delegated or enumerated powers of Congress include: the levying and collection of taxes, borrowing money, coining money and regulating its value, regulating interstate and foreign trade, granting patents and copyrights, declaring war, raising and supporting an army and navy, creating courts below the Supreme Court, using state militias to execute the laws of the nation, establishing post offices, controlling naturalization of aliens, and controlling federal property within the states. Powers shared by Congress and the states are referred to as concurrent powers.

- *Necessary and Proper Clause.* Clause 18 of Article I, Section 8 provides that Congress may "Make all laws necessary and proper for carrying into execution the foregoing powers . . ." This is commonly referred to as the **elastic clause**. The Supreme Court case of *McCulloch* v. *Maryland* (1819) provided one of the earliest opportunities to test the use of the powers implied through the "necessary and proper clause." In this case the issue was whether Congress had the right to establish a national bank, even though the Constitution did not specifically grant it that power. Two groups with opposing views on how to interpret the Constitution developed as a result of the dispute:

Strict Constructionists. Those who felt that the Constitution should be read literally and that the elastic clause should be used only for expanding the powers of Congress in cases where the expansion is absolutely necessary.

Loose Constructionists. Those who held the belief that the Constitution, and specifically the elastic clause, should be read broadly and that the fram-

	SENATE	HOUSE
Qualifications	• At least 30 years of age • U.S. citizen for nine years • Resident of state represented (Art. I, Section 3, Clause 3)	• At least 25 years of age • U.S. citizen for seven years • Resident of state represented (Art. I, Section 2, Clause 2)
Term of Office	• Six years • One-third of members elected every two years (Art. I, Section 3, Clauses 1 and 2)	• Two years • Full House is elected every two years (Art. I, Section 2, Clause 1)
Method of Election	• Originally by state legislatures (Art. I, Section 3, Clause 1) • Today, directly by voters of state (Amendment 17, 1913)	• Directly by voters of state and, district (Art. I, Section 2, Clause 1)
Membership	• Two Senators from each state (100) (Art. I, Section 3, Clause 1)	• Now set at 435 by law (1910). Determined by population of a state. Census taken every ten years. As of the 1990 census, each member of the House represented approximately 573,563 persons. (Art. I, Section 2, Clause 3)
Filling Vacancies	• Originally by Governor and state legislature. Today, Governor may appoint until a popular election within the state takes place (Amendment 17, 1913)	• Governor of state calls an election to fill vacancy. (Art. I, Section 2, Clause 4)
Presiding Officer	• Vice-President of the United States; Majority vote in case of tie vote. (Art. I, Section 3, Clause 4) • President Pro Tempore chosen by Senate as presiding officer to preside when Vice-President is absent (Art. I, Section 3, Clause 5)	• Chosen by members, usually represents majority party. (Art. I, Section 2, Clause 5)
Special Powers	• Chooses Vice-President if no majority in electoral vote (Amendment 12, 1913) • Sits as jury in impeachment trial (Art. I, Section 3, Clause 6) • Ratifies treaties with foreign nations by two-thirds vote (Art. II, Section 2, Clause 2) • Approves presidential appointments (Art. II, section 2, Clause 2)	• Chooses President if no majority in electoral vote (Amendment 12, 1913) • Brings impeachment charges (Art. I, Section 2, Clause 5) • All bills for raising revenue originate in the House of Representatives. (Art. I, Section 7, Clause 1)

Figure 1.8 Structure of House and Senate

ers had intended the clause to mean that Congress should have the "proper" powers resulting from its other powers.

Taking a broad view of the elastic clause, the Supreme Court in *McCulloch* v. *Maryland*, in an opinion written by **Chief Justice John Marshall**, held that the national bank was necessary and proper for carrying out Congress's powers of collecting taxes and coining and borrowing money.

The trend throughout our history has been toward loose construction. Examples include Congress's broadened definition of "commerce," increased government control over business practices, labor unions, minimum wages, and the establishment of a Social Security system and Medicare.

John Marshall (1755–1835). As Chief Justice of the Supreme Court, Marshall expanded federal power over the states.

• *How a Bill Becomes a Law.* The primary function of Congress is legislative—to make the laws that govern our nation. Article I, Section 7, provides for the lawmaking procedures of Congress. Except for money bills, which must originate in the House of Representatives, any bill may be introduced by any member of Congress. Of the thousands of bills introduced each year, only a small percentage actually become law.

Article II, The Executive

Perhaps the most powerful political office in the world, the presidency of the United States combines the roles of chief of state, chief diplomat, Commander-in-Chief of the armed forces, chief executive, chief legislator, and head of his or her political party.

• *Structure.* The office of the President and the executive branch are outlined in Article II, Sections 1 through 4, and in Amendments 12, 20, 22, 23, and 25.

• *Election of the President.* The election of the President actually involves two races: the first to be nominated by his or her political party and the second to win the national election for the office of the President.

HOW A BILL BECOMES A LAW

Here's a typical—but greatly simplified—"legislative road map" showing how bills are passed into law. Most proposals, however, never make it through this legislative labyrinth.

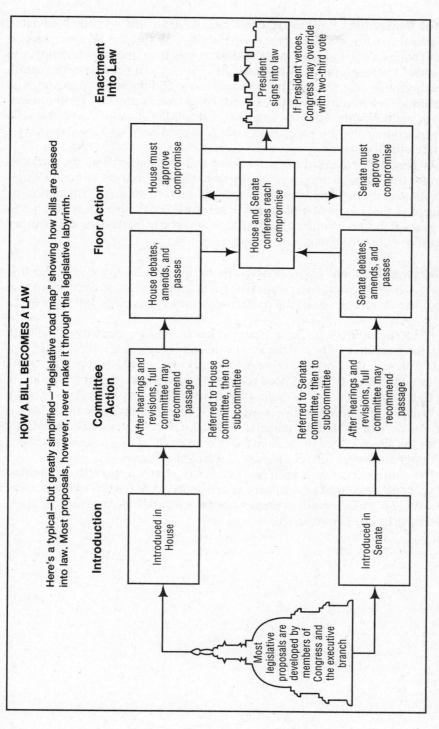

Introduction

Committee Action

Floor Action

Enactment Into Law

Most legislative proposals are developed by members of Congress and the executive branch

Introduced in House

After hearings and revisions, full committee may recommend passage

Referred to House committee, then to subcommittee

House debates, amends, and passes

House must approve compromise

House and Senate conferees reach compromise

President signs into law

If President vetoes, Congress may override with two-third vote

Introduced in Senate

After hearings and revisions, full committee may recommend passage

Referred to Senate committee, then to subcommittee

Senate debates, amends, and passes

Senate must approve compromise

Figure 1.9

The Nomination. Presidential candidates have not always been nominated by political parties. In the first two elections of George Washington, no nominations were necessary as Washington was unanimously chosen by the Electoral College. But as political parties formed and became better established, groups composed of individuals with common political, social, and economic interests competed to have their choice nominated for the presidency. John Adams, Thomas Jefferson, James Madison, and James Monroe were all nominated by party leaders in Congress in what was known as a congressional caucus.

As part of the democratic reforms of the Jacksonian Era, the **national nominating convention**, a gathering of delegates from the different states to nominate a candidate, was developed. It allowed greater participation by citizens in the nomination of a party candidate. Today, delegates are chosen for the national convention either through the caucus method, or the **primary method** within the states.

National Election. Every four years, on the first Tuesday after the first Monday in November, Americans vote for electors pledged to one presidential candidate or another. The road to the presidency is described in Figure 1.11.

• *Executive Branch.* The executive branch consists primarily of the Cabinet, the Executive Office of the President, and independent offices and agencies. Although the Constitution mentions only executive departments (Article II, Section 2, Clause 1) and does not mention a Cabinet (the first mention of the Cabinet came in 1967 with the adoption of the Twenty-Fifth Amendment), the group of presidential advisers was started by President Washington and has become an American governmental tradition. Over the years, the President's office has also assumed the responsibility of overseeing many agencies created by Congress to deal with domestic and world problems.

The entire executive branch has expanded greatly, especially in the past 50 years as the role of government has widened. A President today is aided by some 2.6 million civilian employees working within departments, agencies, boards, and commissions.

Article II, Section 1	Executive power shall be vested in the President, four-year term, electoral system (changed by Amendment 12), date of elections, qualifications for President, succession to the presidency, salary, and oath of office.
Article II, Section 2	Powers of the President: Military, treaties, appointments, powers over executive departments, pardon and reprieve, filling vacancies.
Article II, Section 3	State of the Union Address, calling special sessions of Congress, veto power, receiving ambassadors, execution of the laws.
Article II, Section 4	Impeachment and removal from office for treason, bribery, or other high crimes and misdemeanors.
Amendment 12 (1804)	Amendment 12 alters Article 2, Section 1, Clause 3. Prior to this amendment electors voted for two persons without designating who would become President and who would become Vice-President. Now, electors cast separate ballots for President and Vice-President.
Amendment 20 (1933)	Known as the "lame duck" amendment. Changed office-taking date for the presidency from March 4 to January 20 to shorten length of period a "lame duck" President would stay in office. Also provided that newly-elected members of Congress would take office January 3.
Amendment 22 (1951)	Although Presidents Washington and Jefferson set the two-term tradition, nothing in the Constitution limited a President to only two terms. After President Franklin Delano Roosevelt was elected to a third term in 1940 and then a fourth in 1944, the 22nd Amendment became law limiting a President to two terms or a maximum of ten years.
Amendment 23 (1961)	Gave the District of Columbia three electoral votes and enabled residents to vote for the President and Vice-President.
Amendment 25 (1967)	In an attempt to clarify Article 2, Section 1, Clause 6 dealing with disability and succession of the presidency, Amendment 25 became law.

Figure 1.10 The Presidency

Article III, The Judicial Branch

> Watergate has taught us that our system is not invulnerable to the arrogance of power . . . (and) that our system of law is the most valuable asset in this land.
>
> Judge John J. Sirica, 1974

The Supreme Court is the only federal court specifically mentioned in the Constitution. Article III, Section I provides for a Supreme Court and gives Congress the power to establish inferior (lower) courts. Congress made use of this power with the passage of the **Judiciary Act of 1789**, which established thirteen **district courts** in principal cities, three **circuit courts**, and one **Supreme Court** with a **Chief Justice** and five **Associates**. Because the Constitution does not state the number of Justices to be appointed to the Supreme Court, Congress decides the number by law. Today the Supreme Court has nine Justices.

- *Structure.* The Constitutional provisions for the judicial branch are set out in Article III.

- *Judicial Review.* The Court reviews the constitutionality of legislative acts. Like Federalism and separation of powers, the concept of judicial review is rooted in the principles of **limited government**. Although the framers of the Constitution refrained from specifically spelling out judicial review, they did state in Article III that "the judicial power of the United States, shall be vested in one Supreme Court..." Moreover, Hamilton supported the concept of judicial review in *Federalist No. 78* when he said that when the legislatures are in conflict with the Constitution, "the judges should be governed by the latter rather than the former."

The opinion of Chief Justice John Marshall in the Supreme Court case of **Marbury v. Madison** in 1803 established the precedent for judicial review. In this case, the Court held part of the Judiciary Act of 1789, an act of Congress, to be unconstitutional. The Marbury case marked the first time the Supreme Court ruled an act of Congress to be contrary to the Constitution.

There have been efforts to curb judicial review by those who feel that the Supreme Court has abused its interpretive powers. This occurred after the desegregation decision in *Brown* v. *Board of Education* (1954), when cries for the impeachment of the Chief Justice and other members of the Court were heard. One of the more recent movements for restriction of the Court's jurisdiction has been in the area of religion in schools.

Primary Elections

In states not using caucuses or state conventions, primary elections are held in which voters pick either a candidate by name or delegates to the national convention who will support the particular candidate.

Caucuses and State Conventions

In states not having primaries, party members hold caucuses to pick delegates who then attend state conventions where the state's delegates to the national convention are chosen.

National Conventions

The delegates who have been selected in the state primaries and the state conventions attend the national convention of the party during the summer before the national election. At the convention the delegates vote for their choice for President and Vice-President and adopt a platform on which they run. The individuals selected become the candidates for the national election in November.

Election Day

After intense campaigning by the candidates of the major parties during the late summer and fall, American voters cast their ballots on the first Tuesday after the first Monday in November for electors pledged to one of the candidates. This is the popular vote.

Electoral Vote

In each state the electors of the party that won the greatest popular vote assemble in December and vote for the Presidential and Vice-Presidential candidates, usually of their own parties. Certified copies of these votes are sent to the President of the United States Senate. (Amendment 12)

Counting and Inauguration

The President of the Senate counts the electoral votes (538, the total number of members of Congress, plus 3 for the District of Columbia) in the presence of the House of Representatives and the Senate. The candidates with the majority of the electoral vote are elected and are sworn into office on January 20. (Amendment 20)

Figure 1.11 Election of the President

EXECUTIVE BRANCH

President's Cabinet

(In order of creation)
Department of State (1789)
Department of Treasury (1789)
Department of Justice (1789)
Department of the Interior (1849)
Department of Agriculture (1889)
Department of Commerce (1903)
Department of Labor (1913)
Department of Defense (1947)
Department of Health and
  Human Services (1953)
Department of Housing and
  Urban Development (1965)
Department of Transportation (1966)
Department of Energy (1977)
Department of Education (1979)
Department of Veterans Affairs (1988)

The Executive Office

(Partial Listing)
The White House Staff
Office of Management and Budget
Council of Economic Advisers
Council on Environmental Quality
Domestic Policy Staff
National Security Council
Central Intelligence Agency
Office of Administration

INDEPENDENT FEDERAL AGENCIES

(Partial Listing)

Federal Reserve System
Environmental Protection Agency
Equal Employment Opportunity
  Commission
Farm Credit Administration
Federal Communications
  Commission
Federal Deposit Insurance
  Corporation
Federal Election Commission
Federal Trade Commission

Interstate Commerce Commission
National Academy of Sciences
National Aeronautics and Space
  Administration (NASA)
National Foundation on the Arts
  and Humanities
National Labor Relations Board
Nuclear Regulatory Commission
Securities and Exchange
  Commission
Small Business Administration
Smithsonian Institution
Tennessee Valley Authority
United States Postal Service
Veterans Administration

Figure 1.12 The Executive Branch

Article III, Section 1	Establishment of the Supreme Court and the provision for Congress to establish inferior courts. Judges appointed for life assuming good behavior. Justices are appointed by the President and approved by the Senate (Article II, Section 2).
Article III, Section 2	The power of the federal courts extends to two types of cases: (1) those involving the interpretation of the Constitution, federal laws, treaties, and (2) those involving the United States government itself, foreign diplomatic officials, two or more state governments, citizens of different states, and states or citizens involved in disputes with foreign states. The Supreme Court has *original* jurisdiction in cases affecting ambassadors, public ministers, and in cases in which a state is a party. In all other cases, the jurisdiction of the Supreme Court is *appellate* with such exceptions as Congress shall make.
Article III, Section 3	Treason is the only crime to be defined in the Constitution. Article III, Section 3 provides for the definition and punishment of treason.

Figure 1.13   The Judicial Branch

THE MARSHALL COURT
EARLY SUPREME COURT CASES 1803–1824

CASE	ISSUE	DECISION
1803 *Marbury* v. *Madison*	Can the Supreme Court declare a federal law unconstitutional?	Declared the right of the Supreme Court to annul a law of Congress.
1810 *Fletcher* v. *Peck*	Can a state pass a law breaking a contract? Can the Supreme Court review a state law?	Established the right of the Supreme Court to declare state laws unconstitutional and protected private property.
1816 *Martin* v. *Hunters Lessee*	Can the Supreme Court review and reverse the decisions of the state courts?	Set the appellate jurisdiction of the Supreme Court over the state courts.
1819 *McCulloch* v. *Maryland*	Has Congress power to create a bank? Can the states tax such a structure?	Accepted broad "implied" powers of Congress and sovereign power of the federal government.
1819 *Dartmouth College* v. *Woodward*	Is a charter to a corporation a contract, and is this beyond control of the state?	The Supreme Court limited state powers over individuals and companies and protected contracts.
1824 *Gibbons* v. *Ogden*	What is "commerce" and what is the extent of Congress's power to regulate "commerce"?	Enlarged rights of Congress to control commerce.

Figure 1.14

• *Federal Court System and Routes to the Supreme Court.* The United States is served by 12 regional federal judicial circuits. Each has its own court of appeals and a varying number of district, or trial, courts—94 in all. Each state has its own judicial structure with trial courts, courts of appeals, and a highest court of final state appeal. Cases reach the Supreme Court either through the federal court system or on appeal from the highest court within a state. Of the thousands of cases that seek Supreme Court review each year, only a small percentage are accepted by the Court.

Figure 1.15 Route to the Supreme Court

Comparison to New York State Government

Each of the 50 state governments has political structures similar to the federal government, including republican forms of representative government, division of powers, and a system of federalism between state and local governments. Figure 1.18 shows the similarities between the New York State governmental structure and that of the federal government.

Thirteen Enduring Issues

National Power—limits and potential
Federalism—the balance between nation and state
The Judiciary—interpreter of the Constitution or shaper of public policy
Civil Liberties—the balance between government and the individual
Criminal Penalties—rights of the accused and protection of the community
Equality—its definition as a constitutional value
The Rights of Women under the Constitution
The Rights of Ethnic and Racial Groups under the Constitution
Presidential Power in Wartime and in Foreign Affairs
The Separation of Powers and the Capacity to Govern
Avenues of Representation
Property Rights and Economic Policy
Constitutional Change and Flexibility

National Power—Limits and Potential

The framers of the Constitution carefully limited the power of the federal government by enumerating the delegated powers and, in the Bill of Rights, reserving all other powers to the states and people. Yet, over the years, as our society has become more complex, legislation, executive acts, and decisions by the courts have increased the power of the federal government enormously.

Federalism—the Balance Between Nation and State

Our Constitution balances the powers between the federal government and the states by specifically delegating certain powers to the national government and reserving all others to the states or the people. Throughout the history of our nation, however, the flow of power has gone from the states to the national government.

EXECUTIVE BRANCH
Governor, elected by the people of New York for a four-year term

LEGISLATIVE BRANCH
Bicameral legislature consisting of a 50-member Senate and a 150-member Assembly.

JUDICIAL BRANCH
Court of Appeals: the highest appellate court in the state Appellate Divisions Supreme Courts: the lowest trial courts of the state system

Figure 1.16 New York State Government

The Judiciary—Interpreter of the Constitution or Shaper of Public Policy

Although the Supreme Court has been granted the judicial power of the United States by Article III of the Constitution, has it also become a second legislative body, establishing policy when Congress fails to do so?

Civil Liberties—the Balance Between Government and the Individual

In the famous Supreme Court case of *Schenck* v. *United States* (1919) involving civil liberties during wartime, Justice Holmes wrote, "Free speech would not protect a man in falsely shouting fire in a theatre, and causing a panic." On a larger scale, when does national security require the restriction of civil liberties? How should the Court go about balancing the two forces?

Criminal Penalties—Rights of the Accused and Protection of the Community

How can our government protect the citizens of this country and yet uphold the rights of those who have been accused of committing crimes? If Amendments 4, 5, 6, and 8 protect the accused, what protects the victim of a crime?

Equality—Its Definition as a Constitutional Value

Are all men and women created equal as the Declation of Independence suggests? If our Constitution guarantees equality before the law, does it guarantee equality of opportunities for people, or equality of results?

The Rights of Women Under the Constitution

Although the Constitution does not mention "women," it does make reference to "persons." Yet, the document prohibits only one form of sex-based discrimination, that no state may deny women the right to vote (Amendment 19). The proposed **Equal Rights Amendment**, which has not been approved, would prohibit discrimination on account of sex.

The Rights of Ethnic and Racial Groups Under the Constitution

The trend during the 20th century has been toward much stronger guarantees of minority rights. However, can this go too far and begin to discriminate against the majority? Is it the obligation of society today to make up for the wrongs done to minorities in the past, as affirmative action suggests?

Presidential Power in Wartime

History shows that the President has exercised extraordinary powers during wartime both in restricting civil liberties at home and in sending troops into hostile environments without a declaration of war from Congress. Does the existence of the power of Congress to declare war and the President's power as Commander-in-Chief present an irreconcilable conflict that will be a continuing struggle between the executive and legislative branches?

The Separation of Powers and the Capacity to Govern

Through the system of checks and balances, combined with separation of powers, the framers of the Constitution tried to assure that no one branch would gain oppressive power over either of the other two. As a result, the federal government is often accused of being ineffective, too slow, or pitted against itself to the point of getting nothing done.

Avenues of Representation

Is our system truly a republic, government by the people representing the majority will, or have political parties, special interest groups, and political action committees helped create a government that may be for sale?

Property Rights and Economic Policy

Congress is delegated the power to provide for the general welfare of the United States. Through the enumerated powers and the "necessary and proper" clause, the federal government has assumed economic responsibilities in the areas of trade, taxation, and contracts, and has helped perpetuate a system of free enterprise. However, as Congress uses its powers to promote

American business, it is also responsible for protecting Americans from abuses by businesses.

Constitutional Change and Flexibility

Although the Constitution has been amended only sixteen times since the addition of the Bill of Rights in 1791, in the last decade there have been numerous proposals for amending the document. How many times may the original document be amended without diluting its effectiveness? What are the assurances against insignificant changes to the document? Although the states have never made use of their constitutional power to call a constitutional convention, what would be the limits of such an exercise of power?

Exercise Set 1.3

1. Much of the authority of the United States Supreme Court is based on its power to
   A. propose legislation to Congress
   B. change the distribution of powers as outlined in the federal Constitution
   C. amend state and federal constitutions
   D. interpret the federal Constitution

2. The most serious threat to democracy resulting from high election campaign costs is that, once elected, candidates frequently
   A. owe money to friends and relatives
   B. plan to use public funds to pay their debts
   C. owe loyalty to a few major contributors
   D. have little of their own savings left

3. Base your answer to question 3 on the following headline and your knowledge of social studies.

THOMAS CONFIRMATION FIGHT
CONTINUES FOR HIGH COURT

The confirmation fight referred to in the headline is one that would take place among
A. Supreme Court Justices
B. Senators
C. Cabinet members
D. members of the House Judiciary Committee

4. When Congress makes laws "necessary and proper for carrying into execution the foregoing powers," it is using
   A. enumerated powers
   B. implied powers
   C. concurrent powers
   D. general welfare powers

5. Which headline would be an example of judicial review?
   A. "Impeachment Charges Brought Against President"
   B. "Attorney General Advises Presidential Veto"
   C. "Judiciary Rules Law Unconstitutional"
   D. "Senate Rejects Nomination of Federal Judge"

6. "The Supreme Court is not so much a court of justice as America's ultimate lawmaking body."
   This statement is most concerned with the power of the U.S. Supreme Court to
   A. exercise judicial review
   B. propose Constitutional amendments
   C. exercise original jurisdiction
   D. sit as a jury in impeachment proceedings

7. Which headline is the best example of the application of the system of checks and balances?
   A. "President Truman Fires General MacArthur"
   B. "Senate To Debate Abortion Funding Bill"
   C. "Supreme Court Nominee Rejected by Senate"
   D. "House of Representatives Votes To Discipline Its Own Member"

8. Base your answer to question 8 on the following headline and your knowledge of social studies.

President Bush Refuses to Finish Term as a 'Lame Duck'

An assumption that may be drawn from the headline is that the President has
   A. had numerous bills defeated by Congress
   B. approached the end of his term of office
   C. appointed ineffective staff members to the executive office
   D. dismissed some of his Cabinet directors

LAUNCHING A NEW GOVERNMENT

> All communities divide themselves into the few and the many. The first are the rich and the wellborn; the other, the mass of the people...Give therefore to the first class a distinct permanent share in the government. They will check the unsteadiness of the second...
>
> Alexander Hamilton, 1787

> Men...are naturally divided into two parties. Those who fear and distrust the people...and...those who identify themselves with the people.
>   I am not among those who fear the people. They, and not the rich, are our dependence for continued freedom.
>
> Thomas Jefferson, 1824, 1816

On March 4, 1789, the first Congress under the new Constitution assembled in New York City. The members of Congress were supporters of the new Constitution and many of them had served as delegates in Philadelphia during the summer of 1787. Their primary intention was to carry out the purposes of the nationalists; to make the federal government a lasting institution and to create respect for the republic among the older nations of the world.

George Washington, who had been unanimously elected President, was inaugurated in New York City on April 30th, 1789. **John Adams** had been chosen Vice-President. Congress created three executive departments to which Washington appointed **Thomas Jefferson** as Secretary of State, **Alexander Hamilton** as Secretary of the Treasury, and Henry Knox as Secretary of War. The office of Attorney General was created by Congress as the government's chief law officer.

The Hamiltonian Program: Steps Toward Domestic Stability

Alexander Hamilton, as the first Secretary of the Treasury, formulated an economic program aimed at building the political support and respect necessary to assure the legitimacy of the new government. Hamilton proposed the following financial plan:

Repayment of the Foreign Debt

The national government should repay approximately $12 million to foreign governments and investors, mostly to France.

Federal Assumption of the State Debts

Amounting to $25 million, this repayment was opposed primarily by Southern states such as Virginia, which had partially paid some of their debts. To win their support, Hamilton made a deal with Jefferson to give Northern support for a bill to locate the future national capital on the Potomac River, i.e., Washington, D.C.

Excise Taxes

To raise revenue to help repay both the foreign and domestic debt that Congress incurred during the Revolution and confederation period, a tax was placed on whiskey. Resentment to the tax on whiskey came to a head during the summer of 1794 with the "**Whiskey Rebellion**." President Washington called out 13,000 militiamen to put down the uprising, demonstrating that the new government possessed the power to enforce its authority—a power that had been absent under the Articles of Confederation.

Establishment of a National Bank

Hamilton asked Congress to establish a Bank of the United States that would be a depository of federal funds and able to issue sound paper money on the basis of the securities it held.

- *Jefferson's arguments against the bank:* Using the "strict constructionist" view, Jefferson declared the proposed United States bank unconstitutional. He claimed that the power to create the bank was not listed in the enumerated powers (Article I, Section 8), nor could the power be implied from any other power through the use of the elastic clause.

- *Hamilton's arguments for the bank:* Using the "loose" or "broad constructionist" view, Hamilton held the bank to be constitutional. He claimed that the power to create the bank could be implied from the enumerated powers to coin money, borrow money, and raise money through taxation.

Passage of Hamilton's Program

After listening to the arguments of Jefferson and Hamilton, Washington was convinced that the Bank of the United States was constitutional and advisable. The bank proved to be a sound financial institution and the funding and assumption of the state's debts helped to put the new nation on a solid economic footing.

The Unwritten Constitution (1789–1808)

The reason the United States Constitution has lasted for such a long time is that the document was written so that it could be changed and adapted to future conditions. The provisions that have allowed for adaptation include the elastic clause, the doctrine of implied powers, judicial interpretation, and the amendment process. The flexibility of our Constitution has also been made possible by the practice of custom and tradition, or what is sometimes referred to as the unwritten Constitution.

During the young nation's first three administrations, growth, experimentation, and necessity led to unwritten developments in our constitutional form of government. These included the development of a Cabinet, the formation of political parties, the establishment of judicial review, and a **two-term tradition** for the President. Later developments were the growth of the committee system within Congress, lobbying, and the practice of presidential electors pledging their votes for specific candidates. These elements were not provided for in the Constitution but developed over time through practice.

The Cabinet System

Article II, Section 2, Clause 1 of the Constitution provides that the President may "require the Opinion in writing, of the principal Officer in each of the executive Departments . . ." Functioning at the pleasure of the President, the purpose of the Cabinet is to advise the President on any matter. The evolution of the Cabinet is shown in Figure 1.17.

Political Parties

American political parties began as early as 1796 and the election of John Adams. The followers of Hamilton came to be known as **Federalists** and the supporters of Jefferson as **Republicans**. By 1796 presidential candidates were assuming political party identification.

ORIGINAL CABINET	ADDED, 1798–1913	ADDED, 1947–2006
State Dept., 1789 Treasury Dept.,1789 War Dept., 1789–1946 Attorney General, 1789 (Not head of Justice Dept. until 1870.)	Navy Dept., 1798–1946 Postmaster General, 1829–1970 Interior Dept., 1849 Agriculture Dept., 1889 Commerce and Labor, 1903 (divided in 1913) Commerce, 1913 Labor, 1913	Defense Dept., 1947 (combined War and Navy) Health, Education and Welfare, 1953 (divided in 1979) Housing and Urban Development Dept., 1965 Transportation Dept., 1966 Energy Dept., 1977 Health and Human Services, 1979 Education Dept., 1979 Veterans Affairs Dept.,1988 Homeland Security, 2003

Figure 1.17 Evolution of the Cabinet

The two major political parties in the United States today are the **Republicans** and the **Democrats**. Although third parties have existed in our political structure many times, they have never won real political power. These parties were usually formed because of a single issue. Some of these third parties have included: the **Free Soil party**, which opposed the extension of slavery; the **Greenback Labor party** of the 1870s, which supported farmers and workers; the **Progressive party** in the early 20th century that worked for political and social reform; the **Socialist party** that advocated government ownership of the means of production in American industry; the States Rights party (Dixiecrats) of the 1940s, composed of Southern Democrats who opposed the more liberal wing of the Democratic party; the **Right to Life party** of the 1970s, 1980s and 1990s that opposed abortion; and Ross Perot's United We Stand party in the election of 1992. Third parties have often had their proposals adopted by the major parties and some have been passed into law.

In the United States, political parties perform the following functions: (1) provide qualified and responsible candidates; (2) establish public policy; (3) educate the electorate; (4) encourage voter participation; (5) finance political campaigns.

Judicial Review

The practice of judicial review by the Supreme Court, a power not specifically delegated in Article III of the Constitution, but implied by the Constitution and assumed by the Supreme Court itself, has broadened the authority of the national government. The primary basis of the judicial power in our system of government has been the practice of judicial review, that is, the practice by which courts can determine whether legislative acts, both federal and state, are constitutional.

Two-Term Tradition

Although Article II, Section 1, Clause 1 states that the President shall "hold his office during the Term of four Years," it does not say how many terms a President may serve. George Washington chose to leave office after two terms, and all Presidents followed that precedent until Franklin Delano Roosevelt was elected to four terms (1932–1945; dying during his fourth term). The two-term (or ten-year limit) custom became part of the written Constitution through the Twenty-second Amendment (1951).

Committee System of Congress

Because of the many complex issues that must be considered by the legislative branch, the Senate and the House of Representatives are divided into small legislative bodies called committees. The committee system, which is part of the unwritten Constitution, grew out of necessity and became custom.

Lobbying

The term describes attempts to influence elected representatives during the passage of legislation through Congress. Lobbyists present to legislators the opinion of various groups. They also provide legislators with information concerning issues and bills before Congress. Recently, much criticism has been directed against lobbyists' efforts to influence members of Congress and to purchase the First Amendment "right to petition" with large funds from special interest groups. Deriving somewhat from the concept of lobbying are **Political Action Committees** (PACS), special interest groups who contribute money to political candidates for their election campaigns. PACS now supply more than a third of funds raised by the House candidates and close to a fifth for the Senate.

Pledging of Electoral Votes

Although the Electoral College was designed because of the founders' distrust of the common citizen's capability to select a President, this undemocratic intent has been overcome. Today, political parties name the electors who are pledged in advance to vote for the party's presidential candidate. However, only some states legally bind electors to honor their pledges and, although it is uncommon, electors sometimes do break their pledges and change their vote.

The Birth of American Foreign Policy (1789–1824)

The Administration of George Washington (1789–1797)

- *The French Revolution (1789–1793).* Most Americans supported the French Revolution, until the executions under the Reign of Terror increased. After this and the entrance of Great Britain and Spain into the war against the Revolutionists, opinion in the United States was mixed. It was divided along political lines, with the Federalists supporting England and the Republicans supporting the French.

- *Proclamation of Neutrality (1793).* The French Revolution proved to be one of the most important events in the diplomatic history of the United States, because it established the principles of American neutrality concerning European affairs. Although President Washington recognized the French Republic, he issued a proclamation of neutrality that never used the word "neutral," but stated that the United States would adopt "a conduct friendly and impartial toward the belligerent powers."

- *Problems with England and Jay's Treaty (1794).* Although the United States tried to remain neutral as British hostilities with France continued, its economic ties and trade with both sides placed the nation in danger. The United States and Britain came close to war because of Britain's refusal to abide by rules of international law (primarily the right of neutral shipping), the impressment of American sailors by the British navy, and the failure of the British to evacuate forts in the American Northwest according to the provisions of the Treaty of Paris (1783). President Washington sent Chief Justice John Jay to England to settle differences between the two nations. Jay negotiated a treaty with the following provisions: (1) the British would evacuate the Northwest forts by June 1, 1796; (2) commissions would be set up to establish the amount due to American shippers for loss of goods and other controversies; (3) England's contention that food was contraband was accepted; and (4) direct commerce between the United States and the British East Indies was provided for.

The treaty was a success because it avoided war with Britain at a time when the United States was weak and not ready to fight its former mother country.

- *Washington's Farewell Address (1796).* Before leaving office to be succeeded by Federalist **John Adams**, President Washington conveyed through the press on September 19 his "Farewell Address." Written mostly by Hamilton, Washington advised in the address that the United States should maintain commercial, but not political, ties to other nations, and not enter into any "**entangling**," or **permanent alliances**. While not advocating isolationism, Washington laid out principles that would be followed in the making of American foreign policy until the 1940s and 1950s.

The Administration of John Adams (1797–1801)

- *Failure of Attempts at Neutrality.* Relations between France and the United States grew steadily worse after 1793. Hostile toward the treaties of the United States with England and Spain (the Jay and Pinckney treaties), and unhappy with the fact that the United States had abandoned the 1778 Franco-American Treaty, France ordered its vessels to start seizing American ships carrying British goods. Attempts by the United States to negotiate its differences with France were frustrated by the **XYZ Affair** of 1797 (request of bribes in exchange for negotiations by France) and by an undeclared naval war from 1798 to 1800. In 1800 **Napoleon**, who now ruled France and wanted to avoid war with the United States, agreed to the **Convention of 1800**, which established peace between the two nations and finally recognized an end to the Treaty of 1778.

The Administrations of Thomas Jefferson (1801–1809)

- *Tripolitan War (1801).* The problems of raids on American shipping by the Barbary pirates continued. In 1801 President Jefferson refused the demand of the Tripoli government for payments of "tribute," a form of extortion. Instead of payment, Jefferson sent a naval squadron to protect American shipping. One of the Barbary states, Tripoli, declared war on the United States in 1801, causing hostilities until 1805 when Tripoli was subdued.

- *Problems with England.* After a brief interlude, Britain and France were at war again in 1803. The neutrality of the American shipping was again threatened, as both England and France issued decrees ordering the seizure of ships carrying goods to the other. The British navy resumed its practice of impressing sailors aboard American vessels, claiming they were deserters from the British fleet.

- *The Louisiana Purchase (1803).* During Jefferson's first term, thousands of American farmers had moved west to the lands between the Appalachian Mountains and the Mississippi River. They used the port of New Orleans at the base of the Mississippi River to export much of their produce.

The Louisiana Territory had been given to Spain by France at the end of the French and Indian War. Americans became alarmed when it was learned that Spain had transferred the area back to France by the Treaty of San Ildefonso (1800) and that Spanish officials left in control of New Orleans had ended the right of American farmers to use the port (suspension of the "**right of deposit**.") Jefferson, fearful of a strong and aggressive France as a neighbor and concerned over conflicts concerning the use of New Orleans, sent **James Monroe** and **Robert Livingston** to France to try to buy New Orleans. Napoleon, burdened with problems in Europe, decided to sell the entire Louisiana Territory to the United States for $15,000,000.

Problems arose when the strict constructionist Jefferson realized that the Constitution did not authorize Congress to purchase territory. Jefferson was forced to modify his constitutional theories because of the importance of the purchase, and in 1803 the treaty was ratified authorizing the purchase, which nearly doubled the size of the United States.

- *The Embargo Act (1807).* Seeking to force England to respect American rights while avoiding war, Jefferson pushed through Congress the Embargo Act, which forbade all exports from the United States to any country. Although it caused some harm to England, the act hurt the American economy by causing a depression.

- *The Non-Intercourse Act (1809).* In his last days of office, President Jefferson replaced the disastrous Embargo Act with the Non-Intercourse Act, which opened trade with all nations except France and England.

The Administrations of James Madison (1809–1817)

- *Macon's Bill No. 2.* Congress allowed the Non-Intercourse Act to expire in 1810 and replaced it with Macon's Bill No. 2. This promised both England and France that the United States would resume trade with the first nation that stopped abusing American shipping rights. Macon's Bill No. 2 allowed Madison to resume trade with France and to forbid all trade with England in March 1811.

- *Sectional Politics.* Sentiment for war against England came from land-hungry Southerners and Westerners (**War Hawks**) led by **Henry Clay** of

Kentucky and **John Calhoun** of South Carolina. The commercial interests of the New England states caused them to oppose war because they feared a complete shutdown of trade and continuing depression. Opposition from the New England states increased in 1814 as the British blockade strangled New England commercial interests. At the **Hartford Convention** (December 1814) Federalist representatives declared that a state had the right to oppose congressional action believed to violate the Constitution, thus supporting the doctrine of **states' rights**.

• *War of 1812.* Unable to resist the pressure by the War Hawks in Congress, President Madison recommended that Congress declare war on June 1, 1812. A close vote representing sectional divisions of the country resulted in the declaration of war on June 18, 1812.

• *Treaty of Ghent (December 1814).* For the most part, the peace settlement simply restored the prewar status. Provisions of the treaty included an end to hostilities and British influence in the Northwest Territory, restoration of conquered territory, and arbitration of boundary disputes. Perhaps the longest lasting result of the War of 1812 was the rise of American **nationalism** and the new impulse to expand the nation.

James Monroe (1758–1831), 5th President of the United States. The Monroe Doctrine discouraged European involvement in the Western Hemisphere.

The Administrations of James Monroe (1817–1825)

James Monroe, Madison's Secretary of State, defeated the last Federalist candidate, Rufus King, to become the fifth President. Much of Monroe's success in foreign affairs can be credited to his Secretary of State, **John Quincy Adams**.

John Quincy Adams (1767–1848), 6th President of the United States. As Secretary of State to President Monroe, Adams was the real author of the Monroe Doctrine.

• *Monroe Doctrine (1823).* As the stability of the Western Hemisphere was threatened by European events, the United States could ally with Great Britain in defending its close-to-home interests, or act independently. Russia was threatening to expand and was establishing trading posts on the West Coast. Moreover, the European alliance of France, Russia, Prussia, and Austria was considering an attempt to reclaim as colonies the Latin American states that had recently gained their independence in their war with Spain. President Monroe addressed Congress on December 2, 1823, with a statement of foreign policy that came to be known as the **Monroe Doctrine**. It declared: (1) the American continent was no longer open to colonization by European nations; (2) the United States would not interfere in European affairs; and (3) an act of intervention by a European power in the affairs of a country in the Western Hemisphere would be considered an act against the United States.

Manifest Destiny (1789–1853)

As nationalism grew, Americans came to believe that westward expansion would spread American freedom and democracy across the continent.

The acquisition of large tracts of territory during the 19th century in creased sectional conflict, primarily over the extension of slavery. As the nation expanded rapidly from coast to coast, the American population with its varying social, political, and especially economic interests was able to find harmony only through compromise. However, in time, sectional differences made compromise impossible, and the final result was the Civil War.

Sectional Specialization and Improvements in Transportation

As the nation's economy developed, differences between the sections grew. In the North, industry advanced, helped by the decreased trade before and during the War of 1812, and because of the supply of adequate water power, a wealthy class with commercial capital to invest, and a plentiful labor supply. The South had an agricultural economy based on slave labor. After the invention of the **cotton gin** in 1793, the South had a one-crop economy based upon the cultivation of cotton. At the same time, the grains of the West were quickly transforming that area into the "breadbasket" of the nation.

The need to transport raw materials and manufactured goods between the sections and to ship products to their market created a demand for a better transportation system. Between 1800 and 1825 hundreds of turnpikes (privately built toll roads) and roads financed by the federal government were built to help transport people and products. In 1808, Secretary of the Treasury Albert Gallatin proposed a system of internal improvements at federal expense, an issue that would eventually raise debate between states' righters and nationalists.

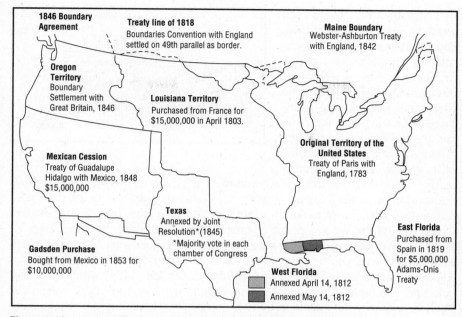

Figure 1.18 Territorial Growth of the United States, 1783–1853

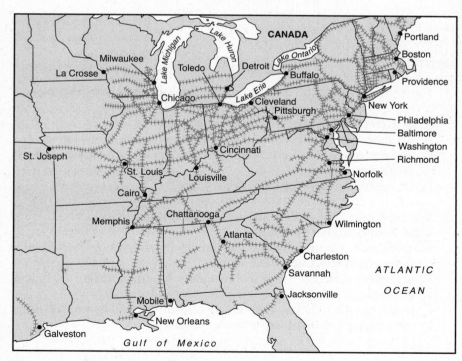

Figure 1.19 Major Railroads in 1860

The years from 1820 to 1850 were the age of the steamboat and canal building to connect interior waterways, which resulted in over 3,300 miles of canals by 1840. In 1828 the first major railroad, the Baltimore and Ohio, was chartered, and by 1840 the nation's total railway mileage equaled that of its canals. At the beginning

of the Civil War, railroads overshadowed all other forms of long-distance transportation in the country. Figure 1.19, showing the routes of the major railroads in 1860, helps to demonstrate the economic interdependency between the North and the West, a factor of great importance during the Civil War.

The growth of transportation brought with it legal questions. One of the earliest questions was who would regulate interstate commerce. The Supreme Court addressed this issue in the case of **Gibbons v. Ogden** (1824), when the Court held that, although Congress did not have the power to control trade within one state, its authority did extend to trade from one state to another and to the navigable rivers on which interstate or foreign commerce could be carried.

Exercise Set 1.4

1. The argument over the creation of the Bank of the United States concerned
   A. its effect on the funds kept in the state banks
   B. whether or not the country needed a central banking institution
   C. whether or not the Constitution provided for congressional authority to create a bank
   D. the creation of the Treasury Department by Congress

2. The Supreme Court under Chief Justice John Marshall influenced United States history in that the Court
   A. stimulated the states' rights movement by supporting the idea that states could reject acts of Congress
   B. helped to create a sense of national unity by strengthening the federal government
   C. weakened the judiciary by refusing to deal with controversial issues
   D. became heavily involved in foreign affairs

3. Which of the following practices has changed from custom and tradition to become part of the written Constitution?
   A. the pledging of electoral votes
   B. the existence of political parties
   C. limiting the number of terms for the presidency
   D. the committee system of Congress

Base your answers to questions 4 and 5 on the following quotation and your knowledge of social studies.

"Now it appears . . . that this general principle is inherent in the very definition of government, and essential to every step of the progress to be made by that United States, namely: that every power vested in a government is in its nature sovereign, and includes, by force of the term, a right to employ all the means requisite and fairly applicable to the attainment of the ends of such power and which are not precluded by restrictions . . . in the Constitution, or not immoral, or not contrary to the essential ends of political society."

4. The quotation expresses the position on the Constitution advocated by
   A. a strict constructionist
   B. one in agreement with Thomas Jefferson
   C. a loose, or broad, constructionist
   D. a states' righter

5. The preceding quotation is most likely from
   A. Washington's Farewell Address
   B. Jefferson's opinions on the constitutionality of the National Bank
   C. Article III of the United States Constitution
   D. Hamilton's opinions on the constitutionality of the National Bank

6. All of the following are characteristic of the Embargo Act of 1807 EXCEPT
   A. it was initially destructive to the American economy
   B. it was generally recognized as a failure
   C. it was America's last attempt at economic pressure on warring European nations
   D. it was beneficial to American industry in the long run

7. The vote in favor of war in 1812 in the House of Representatives indicated that
   A. almost all Americans wanted war
   B. the country was divided over going to war with England
   C. when it came to an issue as serious as the consideration of war, Representatives put aside sectional differences
   D. most Americans desired war with France as opposed to England

8. The original Monroe Doctrine was part of
   A. a joint resolution of Congress
   B. a message to Congress
   C. a Supreme Court ruling
   D. an agreement between the United States and Latin America

9. The significance of the Supreme Court's decision in *Gibbons* v. *Ogden* (1803) was that it affirmed that
   A. intrastate trade fell within the jurisdiction of Congress
   B. tariffs on imported goods were prohibited by the Constitution
   C. the Bank of the United States was found to be permissible by the "necessary and proper" clause of the Constitution
   D. trade involving two or more states on the nation's internal waterways fell under the commerce clause of the Constitution and therefore was subject to congressional control

CHAPTER REVIEW QUESTIONS

1. Which of the reasons listed below was the most important for social and political mobility in the English colonies of North America during the 17th and 18th centuries?
   A. early emphasis on rapid industrialization
   B. existence of a strong cultural heritage
   C. absence of racial prejudice among the colonists
   D. availability of land

2. The best evidence that a nation is a democracy is its provisions for
   A. a system of civil and criminal courts
   B. a limited government responsible to the people
   C. the holding of periodic elections
   D. a two-house legislature

3. Which feature of the current day U.S. government is based upon the principles found in the Magna Carta (1215) and the English Bill of Rights (1689)?
   A. universal suffrage
   B. power of Congress to declare war
   C. power of the House of Representatives to originate all revenue bills
   D. presidential veto power

4. The Mayflower Compact was
  A. an early example of intercolonial unity
  B. a landmark in religious toleration
  C. an agreement to submit to the will of the majority
  D. an example of a successful proprietorship

5. The Dominion of New England was designed to
  A. promote self-government among the New England colonists
  B. enforce the Navigation Acts
  C. encourage fur trading with the French
  D. assist in the development of a Puritan confederation

6. Most English subjects came to America in the colonial period to
  A. enjoy religious freedom
  B. escape political oppression
  C. find economic opportunity
  D. join the forces of slave labor

7. "Direct democracy" is best illustrated by the
  A. New England town meeting
  B. British Parliament
  C. United States Congress
  D. Virginia House of Burgesses

8. The most troubling aspect of the Proclamation of 1763 for the colonists was that it
  A. increased the jurisdiction of the admiralty courts
  B. mandated the quartering of troops in the colonies
  C. discouraged settlement on western lands
  D. was another example of a revenue-raising tax

9. The American victory at Yorktown in 1781
  A. was assisted by French control of the sea
  B. ended fighting in America
  C. marked the end of the French Alliance
  D. convinced the Second Continental Congress to issue the Declaration of Independence

10. The Articles of Confederation
  A. created a supreme national government with subordinate state governments
  B. instituted a system of checks and balances between the executive, legislative, and judicial branches of government
  C. placed control over foreign and domestic trade at the national level
  D. created a national government that did not have adequate taxation powers

11. The convention in 1787 at Philadelphia was called for the purpose of
    A. completing the provisions of the Treaty of Paris (1783)
    B. drafting the Bill of Rights
    C. revising the Articles of Confederation
    D. writing a new Constitution

12. Under the original Constitution, the only government officials elected directly by qualified voters were
    A. Supreme Court Justices
    B. Representatives
    C. Senators
    D. the President and Vice-President

13. The provision that all powers not delegated to the national government are reserved to the states is included within
    A. Article I
    B. the Bill of Rights
    C. Article III
    D. the Preamble

14. In conflicts between the national Constitution and state constitutions, the national Constitution
    A. is silent
    B. states that it is the supreme law of the land and therefore takes precedence over state constitutions
    C. defers to the state constitutions
    D. is restricted by Amendment 10 of the Bill of Rights

15. Political parties were formed early during the country's history and were one of the earliest examples of
    A. the "necessary and proper" clause
    B. the unwritten constitution
    C. the use of the elastic clause
    D. separation of powers

16. Hamilton's arguments in support of a national bank included *all* the following EXCEPT
    A. the bank was among the listed, or enumerated, powers of Congress
    B. the bank would provide a stable currency for the nation
    C. in the use of the "necessary and proper" clause, the ends justified the means
    D. a national bank would benefit the commercial interests of the nation

17. Washington's Farewell Address
    A. favored political parties
    B. condemned all alliances
    C. advocated temporary, nonentangling alliances
    D. promoted economic and military alliance with all major European nations

18. In general, support for war against England in 1812 came from
    A. commercial interests in the East
    B. agrarian interests in the West and the South
    C. the Federalist party
    D. coastal shippers

19. The basis for federal control over interstate commerce was affirmed by the Supreme Court in
    A. *Marbury* v. *Madison*
    B. *Fletcher* v. *Peck*
    C. *Brown* v. *Board of Education*
    D. *Gibbons* v. *Ogden*

20. The Monroe Doctrine was
    A. basically a self-defense measure
    B. an example of an executive check on Congress
    C. soon abandoned for active United States involvement in European affairs
    D. inspired primarily for the defense of European colonies in the Western Hemisphere

ESSAYS

1. The U.S. Constitution has endured for 200 years in part because of its ability to adapt to changing times.
    a. One way in which the Constitution can be changed is through the use of the formal amending process. Following is an excerpt from the Constitution as originally written:

        Article I, Section 3: The Senate of the United States shall be composed of two Senators from each State, chosen by the Legislature thereof, for six Years; and each Senator shall have one vote.

    Discuss how this provision has been changed by amendment. Your discussion must include a clear description of the change and the reasons for the change.

b. The Constitution has also been adapted to meet changing conditions through the use of the following methods:
- Judicial Review
- Custom and Usage
- Loose Interpretation

Choose *two* of these methods. Discuss one way each method has been used to adapt the United States Constitution to meet changing conditions. In your response, describe the specific condition that required constitutional change and describe the specific change that resulted.

2. The concept of democracy has evolved over a long period of time. Throughout history, different societies have contributed to the development of democracy. Some of these societies are:
- Ancient Athens—5th century B.C.
- Roman Republic—509 B.C. to 31 B.C.
- Great Britain—1200 to 1920
- France—1780 to 1820
- United States—1770 to 1800

a. Choose *three* of the preceding societies. For each one chosen, show how a development in that society during the time period indicated contributed to the growth of the concept of democracy.

b. Show how *one* of the democratic developments discussed in the answer to part a. is practiced in a society today.

3. Since the U.S. Constitution was written, many generalizations have been made about it. Some of these generalizations are:
- The Constitution is a "bundle of compromises"
- The strength of the Constitution rests on its flexibility
- The Constitution is what the Supreme Court says it is
- The Constitution is basically an economic document
- The Constitution has both divided and limited the powers of government

Choose *three* of the preceding generalizations. For each one chosen, discuss the extent to which the generalization is accurate and use *two* specific examples to support your position.

4. a. It has been said that the principles of the Declaration of Independence are part of America's debt to European thought. Select *two* principles of the Declaration of Independence, and for each *one* selected, describe how its origin would support the debt to European thought.

b. Select one principle of the Declaration of Independence and describe how that principle challenged previously held political views.

5. Some historians have said that the Monroe Doctrine was America's first statement of foreign policy.

   a. State two provisions of the Monroe Doctrine and explain the reason for President Monroe's inclusion of the provision.

   b. Describe how the Monroe Doctrine was designed to protect and preserve the national interest of the United States.

THEMATIC ESSAY

Directions: Write a well-organized essay that includes an introduction, several paragraphs addressing the task below, and a conclusion.

Theme: Government: Power of the Judiciary

> Shortly after the formation of the new constitutional government, the Supreme Court established itself as an equal to the legislative and executive branches.

Task:

> From your study of the Supreme Court under the leadership of Chief Justice John Marshall, identify two *cases* that strengthened the power of the Supreme Court.
>
> For each case identified:
>
> - Discuss the facts of the case.
> - Describe the court's decision.
> - Explain how the decision strengthened the power of the Supreme Court and the federal government.

You may use cases decided during the Marshall Court era. Some suggestions you might wish to consider are *Marbury* v. *Madison* (1803), *McCulloch* v. *Maryland* (1819), and *Gibbons* v. *Ogden* (1824).

You are *not* limited to these suggestions.

DOCUMENT-BASED QUESTION ESSAY

The following questions (Part A and Part B) are based on the accompanying documents (1–6). Some of these documents have been edited for the purpose of this exercise. The question is designed to test your ability to work with historical documents and to demonstrate your knowledge of the subject matter being presented. As you analyze the documents, take into account both the source of the document and the author's point of view.

Historical Context: American political rights and institutions are derived from English political traditions and 18th century Enlightenment thought.

Task: Using information from the documents and your knowledge of United States history, answer the questions that follow each document in Part A. Your answers to the questions will help you write the Part B essay, in which you will be asked:

> Discuss how American political development was not entirely original in nature, but actually an adaptation of English political traditions and 18th century Enlightenment thought.

Part A
Short Answer

The documents below relate to issues concerning the sources of American political rights and institutions. Examine each document carefully and then answer the questions that follow.

DOCUMENT 1

> They also which do not agree in Christ's religion fear no man from it nor Speak against any man that hath received it,...For this is one of the ancientest laws Among them, that no man shall be blamed for reasoning in the maintenance of His own religion.

—Sir Thomas More, *Utopia* (1516)

1. How were Sir Thomas More's opinions expressed in *Utopia* adopted by the First Amendment to the United States Constitution?

_____

_____

_____

_____

The liberty of man in society is to be under no other legislative power but that established in the commonwealth; nor under the dominion of any will or restraint of any law but what the legislative shall enact according to the trust put in it.

—John Locke, *The Second Treatise of Government* (1690)

2. Which branch of the federal government embodies the thoughts of John Locke expressed above?

_____

_____

_____

_____

3. How have Americans demonstrated their trust in the legislative bodies of both the federal government and the state governments?

_____

_____

_____

_____

DOCUMENT 3

No free man shall be detained or imprisoned, dispossessed, outlawed, exiled,
Or destroyed in any way, except by the lawful judgment of his peers or by the law of the land.

—Magna Carta (1215)

4. Name three rights provided in the Bill of Rights (1791) that were addressed earlier in the Magna Carta.

_____

_____

_____

_____

Unit One **CONSTITUTIONAL FOUNDATIONS OF THE UNITED STATES**

DOCUMENT 4

> The constant will of all the members of the state is the greater will;
> By virtue of it they are citizens and free.

—Jean-Jacques Rousseau, *The Social Contract* (1762)

5. How was Rousseau's comment regarding a consensus adopted by the framers of the United States Constitution?

_____

_____

_____

_____

6. How was Rousseau's comment regarding a consensus *not* adopted by the framers of the United States Constitution?

_____

_____

_____

DOCUMENT 5

> Laws are the necessary relations which derive from the nature of things;
> And in this sense, all beings have their laws; the divinity has its laws,
> The material world its laws……..man has his laws.

—Montesquieu, *The Spirit of the Laws* (1748)

7. Give an example of how the importance of law was adopted in either the American colonial governments or in the constitutional government of the United States.

_____

_____

_____

_____

DOCUMENT 6

> The Crown cannot tax without the consent of the Parliament.

—Bill of English Rights (1689)

8. Explain how the power to tax operated in many of the English colonies and discuss its reference in the Federal Constitution of the United States.

_____

_____

_____

_____

Part B
Essay

Your essay should be well organized with an introductory paragraph that states your position on the question. Develop your position in the next paragraphs and then write a conclusion. In your essay, include specific historical details and refer to the specific documents you analyzed in Part A. You may include additional information from your knowledge of social studies.

Historical Context: American political rights and institutions are derived from English political traditions and 18th century Enlightenment thought.

Task:

> Discuss how American political development was not entirely original in nature, but actually an adaptation of English political traditions and 18th century Enlightenment thought.

Guidelines:

In your essay, be sure to
• Develop all aspects of the task
• Incorporate information from at least *five* documents
• Incorporate relevant outside information
• Support the theme with many relevant facts, examples, and details
• Use a logical and clear plan of organization, including an introduction and a conclusion that are beyond a restatement of the theme

CHAPTER 2

THE CONSTITUTION TESTED: NATIONALISM AND SECTIONALISM

CONSTITUTIONAL STRESS AND CRISIS

> When my eyes shall be turned to behold for the last time the sun in heaven, may I not see him shining on the broken and dishonored fragments of a once glorious Union . . .
>
> Daniel Webster, Speech on Foote's Resolution
> (January 26, 1830)

> I have heard something said about allegiance to the South. I know no South, no North, no East, no West, to which I owe my allegiance. The Union, sir, is my country.
>
> Henry Clay (1848)

Growth of Nationalism

With the end of the War of 1812, the United States experienced a period of nationalism, when westward expansion and internal improvements demanded much of the nation's attention.

Judicial Nationalism

The Supreme Court under Chief Justice John Marshall handed down a number of decisions that increased the power of the national government at the expense of the states, including the doctrine of judicial review.

Economic Nationalism

• *Rechartering of the National Bank (1816).* Under the direction of **John C. Calhoun** of South Carolina, the Second Bank of the United States was established with a twenty-year charter.

Henry Clay (American statesman and orator, 1777–1852). Clay was a lifelong advocate of economic nationalism.

- *Tariff of 1816.* Supported by **Henry Clay** of Kentucky and John Calhoun, a 25 percent tariff was placed on imported goods as a protective measure.

Era of Good Feelings

This term, dubbed by a Boston newspaper to describe the period's absence of political strife, was somewhat deceiving. The election of 1816 gave a victory to the Republicans, with Madison winning the electoral vote 183 to 34, painting a picture of national unity, and the Federalists disappeared as a political party. Yet, by 1819, postwar nationalism and economic stability were eroding, and sectionalism was beginning to become increasingly apparent.

Sectionalism

This term was used to describe the varying interests of the "sections" of the country, which were geographically different and had different economic enterprises suited to their environment. By 1824 three sections were emerging, each with its own concerns and therefore demands on the national government: the industrial Northeast, the cotton-producing South, and the agricultural West. Figure 1.20 lists some of the major issues facing the nation in 1828 and how each section stood on the issue.

Federal-State Relations (1798–1835)

Central to many of the standoffs between the federal government and groups of states' righters was the **nullification doctrine**, which claimed that when the national government assumed rights or powers that had not been delegated to it, the states could nullify the act.

Virginia and Kentucky Resolutions (1798)

In response to the **Alien and Sedition Acts of 1798** (acts passed by Federalists that changed naturalization laws and suppressed criticism of the government to weaken political influence of the Republicans), the Republican-controlled legislatures of Virginia and Kentucky passed resolutions endorsing the doctrine that the Constitution was a compact between states and that the states could legitimately object when Congress exceeded the authority delegated to it by the states. The Kentucky Resolution, authored by Thomas Jefferson, went further and claimed that the states could refuse to obey the law, thereby **nullifying** legislation of Congress.

The Hartford Convention (1814)

Issue	Northeast	South	West
Sale of inexpensive federal land (mostly in the West)	Opposed (early)	Favored	Favored
Internal improvement at federal expense	Favored	Opposed	Favored
Protective tariff	Favored	Opposed	Favored
Territorial expansion (new states)	Opposed (early)	Favored	Favored
Second Bank of the United States	Favored	Opposed	Opposed
Extension of slavery into the territories	Opposed	Favored	Opposed
Attitude toward European immigration	Favored	Opposed	Favored
Attitude toward use of implied powers (elastic clause)	Favored	Opposed	Favored

Figure 1.20   Sectionalism (1828)

Webster-Hayne Debate (1830)

The debate in Congress over the limitation of land sales inspired sharp debate. Senator Robert Y. Hayne of South Carolina defended the right of a state to nullify a federal law that "violated the sovereignty and independence of the states." In response to Hayne, Daniel Webster contended that it was the people, and not the states, who created the Constitution and that if the states could defy the laws of Congress at will, the Union would be a mere "rope of sand." President Jackson, despite his sympathies to states' rights, was against nullification.

The Tariff Controversy (1832)

In 1828 Congress passed the so-called **Tariff of Abominations**, imposing

Daniel Webster (American statesman, lawyer & orator, 1782–1852). Webster believed that the Union took precedence over the states.

high import duties that were opposed by the South. Although the Tariff of 1832 lowered some duties, South Carolina talked of nullification. Calhoun's **Exposition and Protest (1828)** claimed that state conventions had the power to declare laws passed by Congress unconstitutional and to nullify such laws. Calhoun went so far as to suggest secession as a last resort. South Carolina nullified the tariff in December 1832. The Compromise Tariff of 1833, sponsored by Henry Clay, caused South Carolina to withdraw its nullification and prevented a Jackson-Calhoun showdown on the constitutionality of the nullification doctrine. Although the doctrine of nullification is in direct conflict with the Supremacy Clause of the Constitution (Article VI, Section 2), even in recent times it has been threatened in heated debate. After the *Brown* v. *Board of Education* (1954) decision, Southern politicians threatened nullification of the Supreme Court's decree to end segregation "with all deliberate speed."

The Bank War (1832)

When a bill to recharter the Bank of the United States passed in 1832, Jackson vetoed the measure with an interesting constitutional argument. In addition to his dislike for the political power of the bank, Jackson claimed that, although the Supreme Court had affirmed the bank's constitutionality in *McCulloch* **v.** *Maryland* (1819), the separate branches of the federal government were not bound by the judiciary's readings of the Constitution. The bank's charter was allowed to expire, federal deposits were placed in state banks, and control of the nation's banking system returned to the states.

Secessionists

Although actual secession did not take place until shortly after the election of Abraham Lincoln to the presidency in 1860, the theory had been discussed for some time. Those who supported the right of secession claimed that the Union was a league from which member states could withdraw.

The Age of Jackson

A Democratic party emblem from the 1840s.

Historians have long regarded the period that came to be known as that of "**Jacksonian Democracy**" as something unique, and have debated its significance in American history.

The "Revolution of 1828" placed the first westerner in the White House. Although sometimes identified as the representative of the common man, he was truly a frontier aristocrat, owning many slaves and living in the Hermitage, one of the finest mansions in America. Like the antifederalists of the 1790s, he was suspect of the federal government as a body for the privileged.

Although he did not introduce the **spoils system** (rewarding political supporters with public office), he did introduce it into federal government on a larger scale than any of his predecessors. During his eight years in office, he dismissed nearly 2,000 civil servants, replacing them with those loyal to Andrew Jackson.

Extension of the Franchise

Popular participation in politics continued to increase during the first decades of the 19th century, and the right to vote was eventually extended to all white males over 21. Most of the new Western states ended property qualifications for voting, and the older states, concerned about loss of population to the West, followed their example. Whereas less than 4 percent of the population actually voted in 1824, over 14 percent voted by 1840, indicating extension of suffrage rights and participation in politics.

Modern Party Politics

From 1800 through 1820 the congressional **caucus** was the method used to select presidential nominees. However, democratic reforms during the early 1800s led to greater participation by the electorate. By 1824, 18 out of 24 states chose presidential electors by popular vote. The introduction of the convention system of nominating candidates for the presidency by the Anti-Masonic party in 1831 offered a more democratic system that was quickly adopted by the Democrats and the National Republicans. Jackson and his running mate, **Martin Van Buren**, were nominated at the Democratic convention in 1832 and Jackson was reelected easily.

Reform Movements of the 1830s and 1840s

The reform movements of the 1830s–1840s centered around religion, temperance, health, antislavery, women's rights, education, and abolition.

- *Religion.* The **Second Great Awakening**, starting in the late 1790s and continuing through the 1840s, was a prime motivator of reform. Rapid changes, including industrialization, the growth of urban areas, and expansion, helped spark this religious movement to restore traditional community and family values.

- *Temperance.* Because the excessive consumption of alcohol was widespread among all classes of Americans, movements in the 1820s began demanding abstinence from liquor. The formation of the United States Temperance Union in 1833 led to demands for the legal prohibition of alcoholic beverages, and a dozen states passed such laws prior to the Civil War.

- *Health.* The movement to build asylums for the insane rather than housing them in prisons was spurred by the efforts of **Dorothea Dix**. Because of her work, prison reforms were also implemented in some states.

- *Women's Rights.* Among the reform movements of the 1830s was the women's rights movement that sought to overcome the inferior status of women. Chief among the issues were women's lack of rights concerning property, voting, and education. In 1848, **Lucretia Mott** and **Elizabeth Cady Stanton** organized the **Women's Rights Convention** at Seneca Falls, New York. Minimal gains were made, and by the 1850s, women were focusing more and more on the issue of suffrage.

- *Education.* The demand for free public education grew out of the concern that only intelligent voters could support and perpetuate democracy; therefore, the state had the responsibility of financing education. The principal reformer in education was **Horace Mann** of Massachusetts. As Secretary of the State Board of Education, he helped establish public backing for tax-supported schools, lengthened the school year, increased the number of secondary schools, formalized the training of teachers, and broadened educational subjects beyond religious studies.

Elizabeth Cady Stanton (1815–1902), helped organize the first Women's Rights Convention.

- *Abolition.* The Quakers led the earliest antislavery movement in the mid-1700s, preaching that it was a sin for Christians to keep people in bondage. By 1800 most states in the North had abandoned slavery. However, as the South became increasingly dependent on cotton production after the invention of the cotton gin in 1793, slavery was viewed as an absolute necessity.

Frederick Douglass (American abolitionist, 1817–1895) escaped from slavery to become a newspaper publisher and political organizer.

The abolitionist movement of the 1830s differed from earlier movements against slavery by emphasizing that slavery was morally wrong and that blacks were not inferior. This came into direct conflict with the beliefs of "**white supremacy**" in the South. Among the notable abolitionist leaders were **Frederick Douglass**, **Sojourner Truth**, **William Lloyd Garrison**, and **Harriet Tubman**. Garrison, founder of the abolitionist newspaper, *The Liberator* (1831), demanded immediate and complete emancipation, as opposed to the gradual emancipation supported by more moderate abolitionists. Tubman's efforts to assist the escape of Southern slaves to Canada by means of the "**underground railroad**" continued up to the eve of the Civil War.

The slave rebellion led by **Nat Turner** in Virginia in 1831, which resulted in the deaths of sixty whites, and the flow of radical Northern abolitionist literature into the South, turned Southerners from apologists for slavery into aggressive defenders of the institution.

As the Civil War approached, free labor and slave labor were pitted against each other. The North saw free labor as the key to a successful economy and realized that the free labor economic system had to be extended to the territories of the West if future generations were to prosper. Southerners, having built their fortunes and society on the institution of slavery, found it difficult to accept the moral arguments of abolitionists and felt that slavery was necessary to their way of life.

The Indian Removal Act

The reforms of the Jackson Age did not extend to Native Americans. The attempts of Native Americans to remain on their ancestral lands came into conflict with the government's aim to remove them from settled areas in the East and to resettle them in the West. This aim was facilitated by passage of the **Indian Removal Act of 1830**. When the Cherokees were ordered to leave their lands in Georgia, they refused and took the issue to the Supreme Court. In *Cherokee Nation* v. *Georgia* (1831), the Supreme Court ruled that the Cherokees could stay until they voluntarily ceded their lands to the United States. The Court went further in *Worcester* v. *Georgia* (1832) to state that the Cherokee Nation was a distinct political community in which the laws of Georgia had no force. President Jackson, having little sympathy for the Native Americans, refused to enforce the Court's decision.

The rulings of the Supreme Court had little effect on the destiny of the Indian tribes, and many groups, including the Seminole, Choctaw, Creek, Chickasaw, and Cherokee, were moved west. The so-called "**Trail of Tears**," in which thousands of Cherokees died on the forced journey westward, was repeated many times between 1831 and 1840. By 1840, the forced removal of 60,000 Native Americans had been carried out.

Constitutional Debates (1800–1860)

Although most constitutional debate during the first half of the 19th century involved the extension of slavery, the constant battle of state versus federal authority was involved in most issues. It was inevitable that the Supremacy Clause (Article VI) of the Constitution was going to come into conflict with the reserved powers provided for by the Tenth Amendment.

States' Rights v. Federal Supremacy

The early tests of state versus federal authority involved the battles over the **Sedition Act of 1800**, passed by the Federalists to suppress hostile criticism, the **Virginia and Kentucky Resolutions**, and the **Hartford Convention**.

The decisions of the Marshall Court enforced the sovereignty of the federal government and its right to exercise its constitutional powers. The **Louisiana Purchase**, which went against Jefferson's belief in strict construction of the Constitution, required that Congress use its implied powers to purchase the territory. It also demonstrated the need to shift constitutional positions when circumstances such as Napoleon's demands for quick action demanded such flexibility. This "flexibility" in constitutional positions has been used throughout our political history and has become part of our constitutional system.

Slavery and Struggle

The rising dispute over slavery coincided with the territorial expansion of the United States. Although the issue of extending slavery to the territories was solved by the **Missouri Compromise** in 1820, it was only a temporary solution. The controversy arose again after the acquisition of the **Mexican Cession (1848)** and the rapid growth of California's population. At the center of the slavery controversy was the delicate balance in the Senate, where the South was concerned about losing its equal footing with the North. (The larger population of the North had already given them control of the House of Representatives.)

After the Mexican War (1846–1848), Americans held four different views concerning slavery and the new territories: (1) barring slavery forever from the new territories; (2) extending the Missouri Compromise line to the Pacific Coast; (3) no federal interference with the extension of slavery; (4) popular sovereignty (allowing the people of the territory to decide whether or not to permit slavery).

California's application to enter the Union as a free state brought up the slavery problem and marked the last of the great debates among **Daniel Webster**, **Henry Clay**, and **John Calhoun**. The result was the **Compromise of 1850**, which temporarily solved the problem and postponed the Civil War for ten years. The **Kansas-Nebraska Act** (1854), which divided the remainder of the Louisiana Territory into the territories of Kansas and

Nebraska and provided for the admission of the territories as states according to the principle of popular sovereignty, resulted in the repeal of the Missouri Compromise. It also led antislavery elements among the Democrats and the Whigs to join with the antislavery third party Free Soilers to form the **Republican party** in 1854.

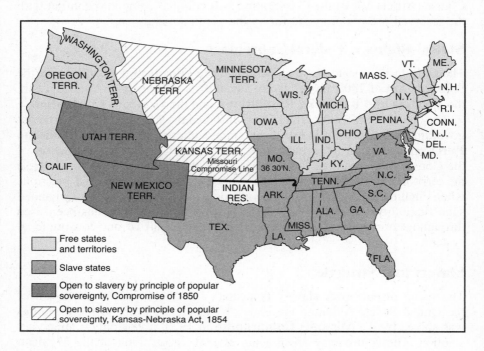

Figure 1.21 Status of Slavery (1854)

Dred Scott Decision (1857)

The Supreme Court decided that the Missouri Compromise was unconstitutional by virtue of the fact that a slave was property and that a slave owner who was protected by the Constitution could bring his or her property into a territory of the United States. It set the stage, in the Illinois senatorial campaign of 1858, for the **Lincoln-Douglas debates**, over the question of popular sovereignty. Although Stephen Douglas offered the Freeport Doctrine, stating that the legislature of a territory could still refuse to pass laws supporting slavery, the stand weakened Douglas in the South and cost him the presidential nomination from a united Democratic party in 1860. Instead, it split the Democrats over the slavery issue and allowed the Republicans to elect Lincoln in 1860.

Event	Issue	Solution
Sedition Act of 1800	Freedom of speech and press	Virginia and Kentucky Resolutions suggesting interposition and nullification; election of 1800 and expiration of act.
Supreme Court decisions of the Marshall Court (1801–1835)	Federal-State relations	Expansion of federal power and jurisdiction.
Louisiana Purchase (1803)	Power of Congress to purchase territory	Jefferson reads Constitution with "loose construction."
Embargo Act (1807)	Does commerce clause imply power to restrict commerce?	Yes; power to regulate includes power to control.
Hartford Convention (1814)	States' rights v. federal supremacy	Matter died down with end of War of 1812.
Slavery	Constitutional or unconstitutional?	*Northern Argument:* Though not claiming that slavery was unconstitutional, provisions had been made in the Constitution for its gradual demise. *Southern Argument:* Slavery was recognized within the Constitution concerning representation (Article I, Section 2), and Fugitive Slave Law (Article IV, Section 2), and therefore legal.
Missouri Compromise (1820)	Power of Congress to prohibit slavery in territories and admit states with conditions	Congress could legislate against slavery in territories but not within states. *Compromise:* 1. Missouri admitted as a slave state. 2. Maine admitted as a free state. 3. No slavery in Louisiana Territory north of 36°30' line.
Wilmot Proviso (1846)	Could Congress ban slavery in territory acquired from Mexico?	*Northern Argument:* Congress could legally bar slavery acquired by virtue of Article IV, Section 3: "make all needful rules and regulations respecting the territory of the United States." *Southern Argument:* People had the right to take their property (slaves) into the territories. Debate over the Wilmot Proviso necessitated the Compromise of 1850.

Figure 1.22 Constitutional Debates (1800–1860)

Event	Issue	Solution
Compromise of 1850	Extension of slavery into California, New Mexico Territory, and Utah Territory	*Compromise:* 1. California admitted as a free state. 2. Utah and New Mexico Territories admitted under popular sovereignty provision. 3. Slave trade in District of Columbia abolished. 4. Stricter Fugitive Slave Law enacted.
Kansas-Nebraska Act (1854)	Status of slavery in remainder of Louisiana Territory	Kansas-Nebraska Act: Popular sovereignty in both territories.
Dred Scott Decision (1857)	Could a slave sue in federal court? If a slave resided in free territory, did that end his or her status as a slave?	1. Slaves were not citizens and, therefore, could not sue in federal court. 2. Congress could not prevent citizens from transporting their property (slaves) into a territory (Fifth Amendment protection of property). The Dred Scott decision declared the Missouri Compromise unconstitutional and the territories open to slavery.
Secession	Constitutional instrument?	*Argument of Calhoun and other secessionist theorists:* Yes. Union is a mere league from which states may withdraw at their pleasure. Constitution is a compact between states and a self-evident right. *Argument of Lincoln and other antisecessionist theorists:* No. Constitution is a compact between the people of the United States, not the states. Constitution is silent on the issue of secession and, finally, the very doing away with the confederation style of government is an argument against the league theory.

Figure 1.22 continued   Constitutional Debates (1800–1860)

Exercise Set 1.5

1. In the *Dred Scott* v. *Sandford* (1857) decision, the Supreme Court held that
   A. slavery could not be prohibited by any state
   B. the Fugitive Slave Law was unconstitutional
   C. Congress could not prohibit slavery in the territories
   D. the Missouri Compromise was valid

2. Chief Justice John Marshall is remembered most accurately for
   A. being a strict constructionist
   B. emphasizing states' rights in his decisions
   C. increasing the power and role of the Supreme Court
   D. frequently deferring to the opinions of state courts

3. The election of Andrew Jackson in 1828 indicated that
   A. political power was shifting to the Western states
   B. the Federalists were making a comeback
   C. Henry Clay was an incompetent opponent
   D. the Bank of the United States was a popular issue

4. All of the following were arguments of Southerners in their defense of slavery EXCEPT
   A. slavery had constitutional support
   B. the Bible justified slavery
   C. blacks were inherently inferior to whites
   D. most European nations still used slave labor

5. The most critical question facing the nation in the 1850s was
   A. what the status of states would be after secession
   B. the political balance between the North and South in the House of Representatives
   C. the extension of slavery into the territories
   D. the significance of a multi-party system in American politics

6. The history of the tariff between 1800 and 1860 shows that
   A. economic issues had little influence over political positions
   B. the North supported low protective tariffs
   C. the tariff issue contributed to the conflict between the North and South over states' rights
   D. higher tariff legislation received uniform support from all sections of the nation

7. The passage of the Wilmot Proviso would have resulted in
   A. the extension of the 36°30′ line of the Missouri Compromise to the Pacific Ocean
   B. popular sovereignty as a means of deciding on slavery in the territory acquired from Mexico
   C. Southern domination of the Senate
   D. the banning of slavery in any territory received from Mexico

THE CONSTITUTION IN JEOPARDY:
THE AMERICAN CIVIL WAR

> My paramount object in this struggle is to save the Union, and is not either to save or to destroy slavery. If I could save the Union without freeing any slave, I would do it; and if I could save it by freeing all the slaves, I would do it; and if I could do it by freeing some and leaving others alone, I would also do that.
>
> Abraham Lincoln, letter to Horace Greeley
> (August 22, 1862)

At the outset, the purpose of the Civil War from the northern point of view was to restore the Union and preserve the Constitution. Lincoln's goal of preserving the Union, even at the cost of tolerating slavery (as expressed in the preceding quote), was paramount. But as Congress became more determined to make emancipation a primary issue of the war, Lincoln drafted his own emancipation proclamation (July 1862) and the South realized that what was at stake was their entire way of life.

Abraham Lincoln opposed slavery, but his first concern was to save the Union.

Just before the outbreak of the Civil War, two issues faced the nation. Slavery in the territories was the first issue. Although the Dred Scott decision had supposedly decided the matter, a new President had been elected (the "Party of the North") and the Supreme Court was in the process of turnover with Chief Justice Taney, the author of the Dred Scott decision, old and ill. Southerners believed that Lincoln's election spelled doom for the property protection reasoning of *Dred Scott* v. *Sandford* (1857).

The second issue was that of secession. As Calhoun had proposed during the 1820s–1830s, supporters of the right of secession held that the United States was merely a league of states, from which member states might withdraw at their pleasure. President Lincoln, among others, argued that secession was not constitutional and that the constitutional system of government was a compact between the people of the United States.

A Nation Divided

Formation of the Confederacy

South Carolina led the way for the formation of the Confederacy when it adopted, through the use of a popularly elected convention, an **"Ordinance of Secession"** in December 1860. Ten additional states eventually followed South Carolina's example and the **Confederate States of America** was formed in February 1861, with **Jefferson Davis** of Mississippi as President.

In seceding from the Union, the Southern states affirmed the **compact theory** of the Constitution and claimed that it was the Northern states that had broken the compact by obstructing the constitutionally mandated return of fugitive slaves.

Lincoln and Constitutional Issues of the War

The Civil War brought an unprecedented clash between the Executive and the Congress in their war power roles. Although minor differences had occurred during the War of 1812 and the Mexican War, the Civil War was about to spell out a new chapter in constitutional history. A reading of the Constitution shows potential

Jefferson Davis was U.S. Secretary of War before becoming President of the Confederacy.

conflict between Article I, Section 8, which grants Congress the power to declare war, raise and support armies, maintain a navy, and to provide for the regulation of the land and naval forces, including militia, and Article II, Section 2, which provides that the President is Commander-in-Chief of the army and navy and Article II, Section 1, which states that the President is vested with full executive power of the government.

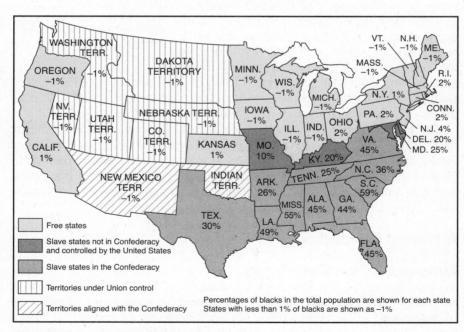

Figure 1.23 A Nation Divided

Lincoln believed that the oath he had taken to "preserve, protect, and defend the Constitution" obligated him to resort to practically any action necessary to maintain the Union.

Emancipation

At the outset of the Civil War, the federal government had been careful to insist that it was fighting to preserve the Union and not to free the slaves. In this way, proslavery forces, primarily in the border states, who were sympathetic to the Union cause were kept with the North. Yet, as the war progressed, Congress moved in the direction of emancipation. The Confiscation Act of 1862 provided that slaves who had escaped from those who were still in rebellion would be "forever free of their servitude." On January 1, 1863, President Lincoln issued the **Emancipation Proclamation** declaring that "all slaves in those regions still in rebellion on that date would be free." Not applying to border states or the regions under Union control, but only to those under Confederate control, the Emancipation Proclamation did not immediately free any slaves. Following the Union victory at Gettysburg, Pennsylvania in July 1863, President Lincoln dedicated the cemetery at the battlefield in his **Gettysburg Address** stating that "government of the people, by the people, and for the people shall not perish from the earth." The actual end of slavery did not come until the passage of the **Thirteenth Amendment** in 1865.

Constitutional Significance of the Civil War

With the surrender by **Robert E. Lee** at Appomattox Court House on April 1, 1865, the Civil War came to an end. Perhaps the most important constitutional result of the Civil War was the repudiation of state sovereignty and the compact theory of union. The concepts of states' rights of secession and the United States as a "league" of states were ended and the nation emerged as a true sovereign entity. The Constitution had survived the war years. The emancipation of the slaves raised numerous issues to be addressed in the following decades, including the rights of states and the role of the federal government in relation to **civil rights**.

Actions by Lincoln	Constitutional Provisions	Justification
Labeled actions by South as "insurrection"	None	South could not legally secede.
Initiation of war by President	Art. I, Sec. 8: "Congress has power to declare war." "Congress has power to suppress insurrections."	President suppressing an insurrection; *Prize Cases* (1863), Art IV, Sec. 4.
Blockade of South	Art. I, Sec. 8: "Congress has power to declare war."	Approved by Congress (1861).
Increased size of army and navy	Art. I, Sec. 8: "Congress shall raise and support armies."	Approved by Congress (1861).
Appropriated funds from Treasury for war effort	Art. I, Sec. 8: "support armies."	Approved by Congress (1861).
Suspension of writ of habeas corpus; disregard for Supreme Court ruling in *Ex Parte Merryman* (1861)	Art. I, Sec. 9: "The privilege of the Writ of Habeas Corpus shall not be suspended, unless in Cases of Rebellion or Invasion the public Safety may require it."	First, none; Supreme Court rules against Lincoln in *Ex Parte Merryman* (1861); Congress later permits with passage of *Habeas Corpus Act.* (1863).
Use of military courts where civil courts still in operation	Amendments V, VI, and VII	Supreme Court in *Ex Parte Vallandigham* (1864) refused to hear case; claimed no jurisdiction; in *Ex Parte Milligan* (1866), Court held Lincoln's actions to be unconstitutional.
Suspension of freedom of speech and press	First Amendment	Permissible to a point during insurrection to prevent prolonged war and additional loss of life

Figure 1.24 Lincoln v. the Constitution

Exercise Set 1.6

1. The Dred Scott decision held that a slave
   A. could bring suit in a federal court
   B. was no longer a slave when he or she entered free territory
   C. was private property even in free territory
   D. could purchase his or her freedom when in a free territory

2. President Lincoln's interpretation and use of the Constitution was
   A. consistently supported by the Supreme Court
   B. influenced by his war aims
   C. never supported by Congress
   D. was typical of Presidents in wartime up to that point

3. The Emancipation Proclamation
   A. ended slavery in the United States
   B. freed slaves only in those areas where the North was not in control
   C. maintained slavery only in those areas that were still in rebellion
   D. was vetoed by Lincoln after passage in Congress

4. Many of Lincoln's actions during the Civil War would have been supported by a
   A. believer in the compact doctrine of the national government
   B. strict constructionist of the Constitution
   C. proponent of the nullification doctrine
   D. loose constructionist of the Constitution

5. The greatest threat to civil liberties during the Civil War was the
   A. suspension of the writ of habeas corpus
   B. blockade of the South
   C. use of Treasury funds by the President without initial congressional approval
   D. identification of the South's actions as an "insurrection"

6. The Emancipation Proclamation was
   A. a law passed by Congress
   B. the result of a Supreme Court decision
   C. a use of the elastic clause
   D. a presidential order

7. The slaves were finally freed by the
   A. surrender of the Confederacy
   B. Emancipation Proclamation
   C. Thirteenth Amendment
   D. capture of Richmond

CHAPTER REVIEW QUESTIONS

1. The most serious problem facing the United States in the first half of the 19th century involved
   A. gaining territory for excess population
   B. the powers of the state governments and the national government
   C. gaining recognition as a sovereign nation
   D. unemployment

2. Sedition can best be described as
   A. preventing aliens from becoming citizens
   B. the illegal criticism of the government
   C. ignoring a law of Congress
   D. obstructing the war effort of a country

3. The Constitution, treaties made by the United States, and laws of Congress are to predominate when conflict arises with state or local laws. This concept, provided for in the Constitution, is called the
   A. reserved powers amendment
   B. elastic clause
   C. supremacy clause
   D. preamble

4. An analysis of the history of the presidency during wartime indicates that executive powers
   A. are usually curtailed severely by the judiciary
   B. operate through a strict construction approach to the Constitution
   C. are expanded and sometimes come into conflict with other branches of the federal government
   D. are unchecked

5. The event that caused the first Southern states to secede from the Union was
   A. the Dred Scott decision
   B. the Compromise of 1850
   C. the election of Lincoln as President
   D. the election of Jefferson Davis as President of the Confederacy

6. The West supported all of the following EXCEPT
   A. internal improvements at national expense
   B. sale of inexpensive government lands
   C. the Second Bank of the United States
   D. squatters' rights

7. In which of the following pairs was the second event a result of the first?
   A. the Mexican War—passage of the Missouri Compromise
   B. Indian land claims in Georgia—*Dred Scott* v. *Sandford*
   C. the application of California for statehood—Compromise of 1850
   D. the Thirteenth Amendment—Emancipation Proclamation

8. The doctrine that indicated that a state could object to a law of Congress if it was felt that Congress had abused its delegated authority was
   A. nullification
   B. sectionalism
   C. interposition
   D. secession

9. The basic cause of sectionalism in the United States during the first half of the 19th century was
   A. economic differences
   B. social differences
   C. political differences
   D. religious differences

10. Regarding the Native Americans, President Jackson favored
    A. upholding Cherokee rights
    B. removal to the trans-Mississippi area
    C. supporting the Supreme Court decision in the Georgia cases
    D. allowing Congressional control of the situation

ESSAYS

1. In the period 1815 to 1860, improvements in transportation and increased interregional trade should have united Americans, but instead produced sectional division and finally disunion.

   Discuss this statement with reference to the sectional impact of transportation and trade developments between the years given.

2. The time period of the late 1820s to the 1840s has been described as the era of Jacksonian Democracy, or sometimes as the "Age of the Common Man." Andrew Jackson played an important role in the controversy concerning Indian removal, the Bank War, the Nullification Crisis of 1832, the spoils system, and the creation of the Democratic party.

   Select *three* of these issues and discuss the following question in relation to the issue. "Was Jackson's role that of a 'man of the people' in the issue, or that of a demagogue?"

3. Throughout United States history, there have been many instances where political, economic, or social difficulties led to demand for reform. In response to those demands, movements or programs have been developed. Referring to the abolitionist crusade (1820–1860) describe:
   • A specific problem that led to the movement or program.
   • A specific reform advocated by the movement or program to deal with the program.
   • Two individuals who were instrumental in the movement.

THEMATIC ESSAYS

Directions: Write a well-organized essay that includes an introduction, several paragraphs addressing the task below, and a conclusion.

Theme: Compromises Necessary for Ratification of the Constitution

> At the Constitutional Convention in 1787 differences between the delegates and the interests they represented made compromise absolutely necessary.

Task:

Identify *two* compromises necessary for the ratification of the Constitution.

- Discuss the two initial positions that led to compromise.
- Describe the resulting compromise.
- From today's perspective, evaluate the compromise reached.

Some suggestions you might wish to consider include: representation, taxation, slave trade, tariffs, and the election of the President.

You are *not* limited to these suggestions.

Directions: Write a well-organized essay that includes an introduction, several paragraphs addressing the task below, and a conclusion.

Theme: Developing Sectionalism and the Need for Compromise

As the United States became politically, socially, and economically sectionalized during the first half of the 19th century, compromise became necessary to avert crisis.

Task:

Identify *two* compromises necessary during the first half of the 19th century.

- Discuss the two initial positions that led to compromise.
- Describe the resulting compromise.
- Evaluate whether the resulting compromise was successful in averting crisis.

Some suggestions you might wish to consider include: The Missouri Compromise of 1820, the Tariff Compromise of 1833, and the Compromise of 1850.

You are *not* limited to these suggestions.

DOCUMENT-BASED QUESTION ESSAY

The following questions (Part A and Part B) are based on the accompanying documents (1–6). Some of these documents have been edited for the purpose of this exercise. The question is designed to test your ability to work with historical documents and to demonstrate your knowledge of the subject matter being presented. As you analyze the documents, take into account both the source of the document and the author's point of view.

Historical Context: The Bill of Rights was added to the Constitution in 1791 to protect individual liberties against government abuse.

Task: Using information from the documents and your knowledge of United States history, answer the questions that follow each document in Part A. Your answers to the questions will help you write the Part B essay, in which you will be asked:

> The Bill of Rights was added to the Constitution in 1791 to protect individual liberties against government abuse. Assess the validity of this statement with particular attention to the areas of search, interrogation, and prosecution.

Part A
Short Answer

The documents below relate to issues concerning the Fourth, Fifth, Sixth, and Eighth Amendments. Examine each document carefully and then answer the questions that follow.

DOCUMENT 1

> I have little patience with people who take the Bill of Rights for granted. The Bill of Rights, contained in the first ten amendments to the Constitution, is every American's guarantee of freedom.

—President Harry Truman, *Memoirs*, Vol. II (1955)

1. What did President Truman mean by the statement "the first ten amendments..........is every American's guarantee of freedom"?

_____

_____

_____

_____

DOCUMENT 2

The right of the people to be secure in their persons, houses, papers and effects, against unreasonable searches and seizures, shall not be violated, and no warrants shall issue but upon probable cause, supported by oath or affirmation, and particularly describing the place to be searched, and the persons or things to be seized.

—Fourth Amendment to the U.S. Constitution

2. The Fourth Amendment mentions "unreasonable searches." Give an example of what has been held to be a "reasonable search."

_____

_____

_____

_____

3. Included in the Fourth Amendment is the provision that a search warrant shall not be issued without "probable cause." Define probable cause. Provide an example if you feel it assists your explanation.

_____

_____

_____

_____

DOCUMENT 3

"....the ultimate measure of the constitutionality of a governmental search is reasonableness...The reasonableness standard is judged by balancing its intrusion on the individual's Fourth Amendment interests against its promotion of legitimate governmental interests..."

—*Vernonia School District* v. *Acton* (1995)

4. What does the Supreme Court mean by "legitimate governmental interests" and what was the government interest in the searches being done in the *Vernonia* case?

_____

_____

_____

_____

DOCUMENT 4

Second, the discovery of the rolling papers then gave rise to *reasonable suspicion* that respondent was carrying marijuana as well as cigarettes in her purse, and this suspicion justified the further exploration....

—*New Jersey* v. *T.L.O.* (1985)

5. In *New Jersey* v. *T.L.O.* the Supreme Court referred to "reasonable suspicion" as justification for further search. How does "reasonable suspicion" compare to the standard of "probable cause" within the Fourth Amendment?

_____

_____

_____

_____

DOCUMENT 5

No person shall...be compelled in any criminal case to be witness against himself...

—Fifth Amendment to the U.S. Constitution

6. In the case of *Miranda* v. *Arizona* (1966), the Supreme Court held that a list of warnings must be read to a person in police custody before questioning could begin. Which two "Miranda" warnings are based on the section of the Fifth Amendment cited above?

_____

_____

_____

_____

DOCUMENT 6

....any person hauled into our court, who is too poor to hire a lawyer cannot be assured a fair trial unless counsel is provided for him.

—*Gideon* v. *Wainwright* (1963)

7. How did the Supreme Court's decision in *Gideon* v. *Wainwright* (1963) affect the interpretation of the Sixth Amendment's provision for an attorney?

_____

_____

_____

Part B
Essay

Your essay should be well organized with an introductory paragraph that states your position on the question. Develop your position in the next paragraphs and then write a conclusion. In your essay, include specific historical details and refer to the specific documents you analyzed in Part A. You may include additional information from your knowledge of social studies.

Historical Context: The Bill of Rights was added to the Constitution in 1791 to protect individual liberties against government abuse.

Task:

> The Bill of Rights was added to the Constitution in 1791 to protect individual liberties against government abuse. Assess the validity of this statement with particular attention to the areas of search, interrogation, and prosecution.

Guidelines:

In your essay, be sure to
- Develop all aspects of the task
- Incorporate information from at least *five* documents
- Incorporate relevant outside information
- Support the theme with many relevant facts, examples, and details
- Use a logical and clear plan of organization, including an introduction and a conclusion that are beyond a restatement of the theme

UNIT TWO ──────────────────────

Industrialization of the United States

> **KEY IDEAS** Unit Two first examines the restructuring of the Union following the Civil War, with emphasis on emancipation and the strengthening of the federal system of government. Chapters 2 and 3 review the growing diversity of the American population, the industrialization of the United States, and the new challenges to American society as a result of growth.

UNIT CONNECTIONS: By the end of the unit you should understand the following points.

- An understanding of American society from 1865 to 1920
- Reconstruction, views on secession, and balance of power between Congress and the Executive
- Impeachment of Andrew Johnson
- Adoption of the Thirteenth, Fourteenth, and Fifteenth Amendments
- Economic changes brought about in the years after the Civil War
- Supreme Court rulings: Civil Rights Cases and *Plessy* v. *Ferguson*
- Political party alignments following the Civil War; the "Solid South"
- Expansion and consolidation of American business; corporations
- Robber barons and the "Captains of Industry"
- Laissez-faire and the eventual need for government regulation
- Antitrust legislation and the formation of labor unions
- Problems faced by farmers; the Populist movement
- The shift from rural living to urbanization
- The "New Immigration" period, nativism, and immigration legislation
- The ending of the frontier and effects on Native Americans

CHAPTER 1

THE RECONSTRUCTED NATION

RECONSTRUCTION AND THE NATIONALIZATION OF CIVIL RIGHTS

During the period of Reconstruction, or the restoring of the South to the Union from 1865 to 1877, the nation had to answer two challenging questions: (1) How should the seceding states be dealt with and on what terms should they be readmitted to the Union? (2) What should be done about the newly freed slaves and what should be their political rights?

The political reconstruction of the South (as opposed to the social and physical rebuilding) can be divided into four stages: (1) the plans of President Lincoln; (2) the years 1865 and 1866 when President Andrew Johnson tried to carry out his policy; (3) Congressional Reconstruction between 1866 and 1868; and (4) the period of Southern reaction in the years after 1868.

Three Plans of Reconstruction

Lincoln's Plan

Lincoln's plan, which became the moderate approach to Reconstruction, was based on the belief that the war was a rebellion of individual citizens and that, since secession was not constitutionally permissible, the South had never legally left the Union. This view was endorsed by the Supreme Court in *Texas* v. *White (1869)* when the Court held that "the Constitution, in all its provisions, looks to an indestructible Union, composed of indestructible states." Lincoln also believed that Reconstruction should be lenient and carried out by the President. In his Proclamation of Amnesty and Reconstruction in December 1863, Lincoln set out his plan of Reconstruction: (1) all Southerners (except high-ranking Confederate political and military officials) would be pardoned and regain citizenship when they took an oath to support the Constitution and the emancipation of slaves; (2) when 10 percent of the voters in a state took this oath they could establish a legal government that would be recognized by the President.

• *Congressional Reaction.* The "Radical" Republicans in Congress did not agree with Lincoln's plan. They looked beyond emancipation to the problem of civil liberties of African Americans and felt that Congress should play a greater role in the assurance of such liberties. In the Wade-Davis bill (July 1864) Congress set its own conditions for readmitting the Southern states. It required that: (1) 50 percent of the voters take the loyalty oath rather than 10 percent; (2) Confederate officials be disenfranchised; (3) Confederate debts be repudiated.

Lincoln killed the Wade-Davis bill with a **pocket veto** because it would have postponed the readmittance of the Southern states. Lincoln and Congress disagreed over Reconstruction, and hopes of compromise and the acceptance of Lincoln's moderate plan ended with his assassination on April 14, 1865.

Johnson's Plan

In May 1865 Johnson issued his plan of Reconstruction, which was similar to Lincoln's: (1) general pardon of all Southerners willing to take an oath upholding the Constitution, except military leaders and those whose wealth exceeded $20,000; (2) recognition of the governments of Virginia, Tennessee, Arkansas, and Louisiana, which had been established under Lincoln's Reconstruction Plan; (3) the remaining Southern states could reenter the Union when they repudiated war debts (bonds sold by the Confederate government to individuals to finance the war), disavowed their ordinances of secession, and ratified the Thirteenth Amendment, thereby abolishing slavery.

By December 1865, when Congress met, all the Southern states except Texas were ready to be readmitted to the Union. The **Thirteenth Amendment**, ending slavery, was ratified in December 1865, giving Congress the power to enforce the amendment with appropriate legislation.

Congressional Plan

The Republicans in Congress believed that the seceding states had reverted to territorial status and therefore required congressional legislation for readmission to the Union. They refused to seat in Congress the representatives and senators who had been elected by the new state governments in the Southern states. Under the influence of Radical Republican Thaddeus Stevens, Congress passed the following laws:

- *The Freedman's Bureau Act (1866).* * This law extended the existence of a wartime bureau that had cared for freed slaves. It helped to provide the freed slaves with food, clothing, and shelter, helped them find jobs, and founded schools. Particularly troubling to Congress were the "**black codes**," laws passed by the Southern legislatures after the abolition of slavery, which were designed to keep freed blacks in a slavelike role. President Johnson vetoed the bill, questioning the constitutionality of its provisions, but it was passed over Johnson's veto in July 1866.

- *The Civil Rights Act of 1866.* This forbade states to discriminate against blacks, guaranteed persons of color equal protection of the laws, and

*Note: The term *freedmen* was used in this period to refer to the freed slaves.

placed jurisdiction of violations of the act in federal courts. President Johnson vetoed the bill, claiming unconstitutional violations of states' rights, but Congress overrode his veto.

- *The Fourteenth Amendment.* This amendment (ratified by Congress and the states) made blacks citizens of the United States. It provided for national citizenship, forbade states from depriving citizens of equal protection of the law, provided penalties for not granting black Americans the vote, excluded Confederates from holding office unless pardoned by Congress, and repudiated the Confederate war debt.

Military Reconstruction Act

The Congressional elections of 1866 gave the Radical Republicans the support necessary to put their Reconstruction plan into effect. On March 2, 1867, Congress took over Reconstruction with its passage of the Military Reconstruction Act, which (1) stated that no lawful governments existed in any of the Southern states except for Tennessee (which had accepted the Fourteenth Amendment); (2) divided the South into five military districts, each under a military governor with federal troops; (3) specified that no state could return to civilian rule and be readmitted to the Union until white and black voters framed a constitution that guaranteed suffrage to African Americans and ratified the Fourteenth Amendment.

Impeachment of Andrew Johnson

The struggle over how to reconstruct the Union provoked a clash between President Johnson and Congress. Johnson, intolerant of opposition and not able to compromise, failed to help his political cause. He wanted to restore the prewar federal system as quickly as possible with one change—that states no longer had the right to legalize slavery. Most Congressional Republicans, on the other hand, believed that sectional conflict would not be resolved until there were guarantees that the old Southern ruling class would not regain power and national influence. After two presidential vetoes and two congressional overrides, the Republicans in Congress took extreme steps to assure that the Military Reconstruction Act was carried out.

Denial of Supreme Court Authority

An act passed on March 7, 1868, denied the Supreme Court jurisdiction over the Reconstruction acts of Congress.

Denial of Presidential Authority

Beginning in March 1867, Congress adopted a series of acts intended to restrict the President's authority.

• *Tenure of Office Act.* Of greatest significance was the Tenure of Office Act (March 1867), which prohibited the President from removing any federal officials without the consent of the Senate. President Johnson, vetoed the act, asserting that the President possessed a separate right of removal without the Senate's consent, a right that had been recognized since the first Congress.

Impeachment

The Constitution provides in Article II, Section 4 that "The President . . . shall be removed from Office on Impeachment for and Conviction of, Treason, Bribery, or other high Crimes and Misdemeanors." During the spring of 1867, the House of Representatives (responsible for bringing the initial charges, Article I, Section 2) searched for a possible charge against Johnson. The opportunity was finally found when Johnson violated the Tenure of Office Act in February 1868 by removing Secretary of War Edwin M. Stanton. Two days later, the House voted 128 to 47 to impeach the President. He was tried before the Senate with Chief Justice Salmon Chase presiding (Article I, Section 3) and was acquitted by only one vote short of the votes of two-thirds of the Senate needed for conviction. The incident appeared to indicate that the impeachment power could be used only for indictable crimes, not offenses resulting from political battles between two branches of government. The Tenure of Office Act was eventually repealed by Congress in 1887.

Reconstruction Comes to an End

Fifteenth Amendment (1870)

Suffrage had been indirectly granted to African Americans in the Fourteenth Amendment. The Fifteenth Amendment authorized the federal government to regulate voting in a limited sense. Although it prevented the denial of the vote based upon race, color, or previous condition of servitude, it did not stop the states from using literacy or property tests to restrict the vote.

End of Reconstruction

By 1872, Americans were tired of Reconstruction. Congress passed the **Amnesty Act**, which restored the franchise to almost all Confederates. As a result, white Democrats gradually regained control of the Southern states. Claiming that the Republican party was the party of corruption, the party of the black man, and responsible for the destruction of the South, the Democratic party became the majority party of the South until well into the 20th century, a phenomenon later referred to as the "Solid South." The withdrawal of the last federal troops took place following the election of 1876.

The Nationalization of Civil Rights

Perhaps with the sole exception of the New Deal era in the 1930s, the period of Reconstruction marked the greatest expansion of federal power in our country's history. The extension of national power over personal liberty and civil rights through the enactment of the Thirteenth, Fourteenth, and Fifteenth Amendments, the Civil Rights Act of 1866, and the Enforcement Acts of the 1870s was carried out at the expense of states' rights and resulted in a new balance of power in the federal Union. Although the states retained the responsibility of regulating civil rights, they did so under the watchful eye of the national government, which now had the right to step in when necessary. Although federal intervention in the South would all but cease by the 1880s, the federal government with greater powers and responsibilities would once again increase its supervisory role over state affairs during the second half of the 20th century.

Exercise Set 2.1

1. Lincoln's plan for Reconstruction was based on the theory that the Confederacy was
   A. to be considered a conquered nation
   B. to be divided into five states which would apply for statehood
   C. to be placed under congressional control
   D. to be considered as never having left the Union

2. By the 1890s Reconstruction had the effect of
   A. bringing complete civil rights to Southern blacks
   B. making the South solidly Democratic
   C. insuring the vote to all freedmen
   D. subduing all racist groups

3. The Reconstruction plan of the Radical Republicans (1867)
   A. established military control in the South
   B. was essentially the plan proposed by President Johnson
   C. was prompted by the South's acceptance of the Fourteenth Amendment
   D. included seating former Confederate military leaders in Congress

4. The most frequent basis for legislation expanding the role of the federal government in the guarantee of civil rights has been
   . A. state court decisions
   B. the war powers of the President
   C. the Fourteenth Amendment
   D. the 18-year-old vote

5. The impeachment of President Johnson by the House of Representatives was based primarily on his
   A. creation of additional Cabinet positions
   B. attempts to exclude the South from the Union
   C. desire to run for a second term
   D. violation of the Tenure in Office Act

6. The "black codes" developed by the Southern states were designed to
   A. keep Southern blacks in the Democratic party
   B. keep freed slaves subordinate to whites
   C. help freed slaves adjust to their freedom through education
   D. divide old plantations and distribute land to former slaves

POST-CIVIL WAR ECONOMICS

In 1860 the United States was still primarily a producer of food and raw materials. However, in the half century that followed the Civil War, the United States became the world's leading industrial power. The statistics in Figure 2.1 demonstrate the extraordinary growth that took place during the 30 years following the Civil War.

Economic and Technological Stimuli

A number of factors were involved in the rapid transformation of American society in the years during and following the Civil War.

Population

Between 1860 and 1890 the country's population soared from 31.5 million to 62.6 million. Besides the high birthrate during this period, millions of immigrants came to the United States. They joined the large number of Americans moving from the farms to the cities. The population boom provided a source of cheap labor necessary during rapid economic growth.

	1860	1890	% of increase
Population	31,450,000	62,600,000	99
Number of factories	140,500	335,400	139
Value of factories	1,000,000,000	6,500,000,000	555
Value of manufactured goods	1,900,000,000	9,400,000,000	394
Industrial workers	1,300,000	4,200,000	223

Figure 2.1 Industrial Growth (1860–1890)

Raw Materials

The new industrial age was based upon steam power and heavy industry that made use of iron and steel. In addition to having about half the world's coal reserves, which were used for fuel, the United States also had abundant raw materials necessary for industrial growth. Iron ore and coal (the two raw materials used in the manufacture of steel with the use of the **Bessemer process** during the 1880s and afterward) were abundant, as were oil, copper, lead, silver, and gold.

Capital

In this period, capital from Americans and from Europe was abundant. As American industry became a lucrative investment opportunity, foreign capital financed many growing industries. By 1900, foreign investors owned approximately $3 billion in American securities. Domestic investment increased in American industry, especially after the decline of American shipping.

Technology

The demand for industrial goods during the Civil War acted as a catalyst to ingenuity and inventions, as American industry had to compete with foreign industry, which could employ labor at lower wages. However, techniques such as interchangeable parts and later the assembly line allowed cheaper production of goods. Inventions of the age included the typewriter (1868), telephone (1876), incandescent light bulb (1880), linotype (1886), and the gasoline engine in the 1890s.

Expanding Markets

Both the domestic and the foreign market for American goods expanded steadily during the second half of the 19th century. This was the result of increased demand by a growing domestic market with greater capability to consume and of increased demand by the foreign market made more accessible through the use of steam-driven iron ships.

Transportation

Before the Civil War, there were only about 30,000 miles of railroad track in the United States, and railroads barely existed west of the Mississippi River. After the war, railroad consolidation united many competing lines into a few giant systems that connected the many fragmented rail systems throughout the nation. By 1900, the New York Central System, created by **Cornelius Vanderbilt**, connected New York to Boston, Cleveland, Detroit, Chicago, St. Louis, Cincinnati, and Indianapolis. The federal government provided land grants to encourage the building of railroads in the sparsely populated West. Initially spurred by the California gold rush of 1849, Western railroad building increased again after the Civil War. The first **transcontinental railroad** was completed with the connection of the Union Pacific and the Central Pacific lines in Promontory, Utah, on May 10, 1869. By 1900, 200,000 miles of track existed in the United States, permitting the rapid transport of people and products.

The shift from wooden sailing vessels to steam-driven steel vessels made the transportation of goods less expensive and helped to expand the world market for American industrial and agricultural goods.

Labor

Before the Civil War, few Americans were wage earners. Most were self-employed in agriculture or small single-owner crafts. By 1900, however, about two-thirds of working adults were wage earners rather than self-employed. As the lives of workers were increasingly controlled by the employers who could hire and fire them at will, the struggle to combine and unionize became important in American labor history.

The Transformation of the South

The Civil War caused both the physical devastation and economic ruin of the South. The financial system based upon Confederate currency and bonds had collapsed, while the emancipation of the slaves stripped the propertied classes of their most valuable and productive assets.

Labor and Agriculture

- *The Freedmen.* Although the Civil War had emancipated the slaves, the adjustment for the freedmen proved to be difficult, since they did not have the means to become self-sufficient. Although Representative **Thaddeus Stevens** advocated the breaking up of large Southern plantations and the allocation of "forty acres and a mule" to each freedman, proposals for an effective program of land distribution failed to get through Congress. In most cases the freed slaves were forced to work for wages set by white landowners under the immediate supervision of a white overseer.

- *Sharecropping.* Black farmers and white landowners turned to a land and labor system known as sharecropping. The farmworker, often a freedman, farmed a tract of land belonging to a plantation owner and, in return for farming the land, was allowed to keep a percentage of the crop. Black sharecroppers lived in freedom, but they often became so indebted to the landowner and other creditors through the crop lien system, where farmers borrowed against their expected harvest, that the system virtually reenslaved the South's black population.

- *Land.* When Southerners returned to producing cotton after the Civil War, they discovered that the world demand for cotton had decreased. During the war, India, Brazil, and Egypt had supplied the cotton needs of the textile industries. The resulting depression in Southern agriculture affected white and black growers alike.

After the war, many large plantations were broken up. Between 1865 and 1880 the number of farms in the Southern states more than doubled, while the size of the average farm decreased. However, because of the sharecropping system, the number of landowners did not increase. As farmers continued to grow cotton and tobacco, overproduction caused prices to plunge, and constant growing exhausted the soil. In time, the necessity of crop diversification and scientific farming methods, including crop rotation, would be recognized.

Industrialization

One of the lessons of the Southern defeat in the Civil War was the realization that industrialization was necessary in the South. While Southern planters, shippers, and manufacturers depended heavily on capital from Northern banks and entrepreneurs, many Southern industries were mere subsidiaries of Northern firms. In the 1870s textile mills were built in the cotton states, and the South eventually replaced New England as the textile manufacturing center. The tobacco industry, aided by the invention of a cigarette-making machine in 1880, added to the industrialization of the South. Lumbering and iron and steel production increased, as did coal mining and railroad production.

Exercise Set 2.2

1. By the beginning of the 20th century, New England was being displaced as the leading textile center of the nation by
   A. the Canadian Provinces
   B. the South
   C. the Northwest
   D. the Southwest

2. Immediately following the Civil War, Southern agriculture
   A. was replaced by industrial output
   B. changed little from the time prior to the Civil War
   C. relied less on tobacco and cotton and became diversified
   D. returned to the plantation-slave labor system

3. The system whereby sharecroppers would borrow against their expected harvest, agreeing to pay a portion of their crops in return for credit, was called
   A. crop rotation
   B. homesteading
   C. nullification
   D. crop-lien

4. To encourage the building of railroads, the federal government
   A. provided land grants
   B. practiced a policy of laissez-faire
   C. increased tariffs on iron and steel products
   D. provided cheap immigrant labor for the railroad companies

Year	Total Value* Millions of Dollars	Cotton Millions of Dollars	Leaf Tobacco Millions of Dollars	Wheat Millions of Dollars
1850	101	72	10	1
1853	124	109	11	4
1855	151	88	15	1
1858	157	131	17	9
1860	270	192	16	4
1863	74	7	20	47
1865	154	7	42	19
1868	206	153	23	30
1870	359	227	21	47

* Selected Exports
SOURCE: U.S. Bureau of the Census, *Historical Statistics of the U.S., Colonial times to 1957*.

Figure 2.2 Value of Selected Exports from the United States

5. According to the information presented in the table on U.S. exports,
   A. the export of leaf tobacco ceased completely during the Civil War
   B. by 1870 the export of wheat had fallen to 1865 levels
   C. the total value of United States exports rapidly recovered from the setback and disruption of the Civil War
   D. the total value of selected exports from the United States increased at a steady rate from 1850 to 1870

EMANCIPATION: AN UNSETTLED ISSUE

> The freedmen were not really free in 1865, nor are most of their descendants really free in 1965. Slavery was but one aspect of a race and color problem that is still far from solution here, or anywhere. In America particularly, the grapes of wrath have not yet yielded all their bitter vintage.
>
> Samuel Eliot Morison,
> *The Oxford History of the American People,* 1965

Political

Although the Civil War and the post-war amendments had changed the legal status of the ex-slaves, in reality their social and economic status had changed very little. With the withdrawal of the last federal troops from the South in 1877, elements of white Southern society looked for methods to prevent blacks from voting.

Since the Fifteenth Amendment prohibited the denial of the vote due to "**race, color, or previous condition of servitude**," Southern state legislatures found other methods of denying the vote. **Poll taxes** and **literacy tests** were two methods used to disenfranchise black Americans. In some states, voters were asked to read and interpret the Constitution. By the late 1800s the **grandfather clause** became a widespread method of keeping blacks from the polls. This was a clause added to state constitutions giving the right to vote to all persons whose grandfathers could vote in 1867, even if the person could not pay the poll tax or pass the literacy test. Since blacks had been slaves and not able to vote in 1867, this clause disenfranchised them while giving the vote to poor illiterate whites. By the early 1900s African Americans had effectively lost their political rights in the South.

Social

The inferior social status of African Americans did not change after the Civil War. Although the Fourteenth Amendment prevented the states from discriminating against individuals, the Supreme Court ruled in 1876, in the case of *United States* v. *Cruikshank,* that the amendment "added nothing to the rights of one citizen against another." In other words, it had to be shown that the state was denying rights for the amendment to apply. The Court went further in the **Civil Rights Cases** (1883) when it invalidated the Civil Rights Act of 1875 that had prohibited **segregation** in public facilities. The Court held that the federal government could not regulate the behavior of private individuals. Later cases, primarily *Plessy* **v.** *Ferguson* (1896), held that blacks could be restricted to "separate but equal" facilities. This opened the door for the **Jim Crow** laws separating white and black Americans in Southern society.

Struggle for Political Control

As the Southern states followed the Reconstruction plan of Congress, they held conventions to draft new constitutions and established new state governments. Black voters exercised their newly acquired right to vote and elected black delegates to participate in these conventions and to the new state legislatures. Although black voters were in the majority in five states, only in South Carolina did they hold a majority in the lower house of the state legislature. Northerners known as **carpetbaggers**, who had recently arrived in the South, dominated the state governments in the early part of the Reconstruction period.

The "Reconstruction governments" passed much admirable legislation and introduced many overdue reforms in the South. The new constitutions were more democratic in that many eliminated property qualifications for voting and officeholding and made some former appointive positions now elective. Provisions for public schools, public works, and general rebuilding of the war-torn South were put through by the new governments.

Unfortunately, the Reconstruction governments under Republican rule were riddled with corruption. White resentment or "backlash" against the Reconstruction governments became widespread, and some secret societies such as the **Ku Klux Klan** were organized and turned to acts of terror. Such groups intimidated the freed slaves to prevent them from exercising their newly gained right to vote. Some relief came with the passage of federal laws, including the Force Act (1870) and the Ku Klux Klan Act (1871), allowing federal supervision of elections and the use of federal troops to control these white supremacy groups. However, the intimidation, including whippings, brandings, lynchings, and murder by these secret societies had already taken its toll.

The "Solid South" developed when white Democrats regained political control in the South. High taxes, corruption, a rising conservative class, and the tradition of white rule combined to end the temporary role of blacks in Southern politics.

The Supreme Court and the Fourteenth Amendment

The Fourteenth Amendment is perhaps the most important amendment ever added to the Constitution, and questions concerning its interpretation began to surface shortly after its ratification in 1868. Did the framers of the amendment intend to bar **discrimination**? If so, did this include private discrimination as well as public discrimination? Perhaps the most perplexing question to face the courts after its ratification: Did the framers intend to make the Bill of Rights applicable to the states as a result of the Fourteenth Amendment?

The wording of Section 1 of the Fourteenth Amendment is critical in understanding the amendment's history and changing interpretations:

> No **State** shall make or enforce any law which shall abridge the privileges or immunities of citizens of the United States; nor shall any State deprive any person of **life**, **liberty**, **or property**, without **due process of law**; nor deny any person within its jurisdiction the **equal protection** of the laws.

The Slaughter-House Cases

During the late 19th century, almost 600 cases involving the Fourteenth Amendment came to the Supreme Court, of which fewer than 30 dealt with ex-slaves. The first detailed discussion by the Supreme Court of the Fourteenth Amendment came in 1873 with the Slaughter-House Cases. When a group of butchers claimed that a monopoly on the slaughtering of livestock deprived them of equal protection of the laws as provided in Section 1 of the Fourteenth Amendment, the Supreme Court answered that the amendment was designed only to protect newly freed slaves. It also stated that the situation the butchers objected to was in the domain of the relationship between the state and its citizens, not the federal government, thus limiting the application of the amendment.

The Civil Rights Cases

In the Civil Rights Cases (1883), the Supreme Court voided the **Civil Rights Act of 1875**, which had forbidden hotels, restaurants, and public accommodations in general to discriminate based on race, color, or previous condition of servitude. The Court held that the Fourteenth Amendment prohibited discrimination only by state governments, not that in which individuals and private citizens engaged. With the *Plessy* case, the power of the Fourteenth Amendment to protect the civil rights of minority Americans reached its lowest point. As of 1896 the amendment was used to sanction "**separate but equal**" facilities and applied only to state actions.

Application of the Fourteenth Amendment to the States

Although the Fourteenth Amendment did not at first apply the Bill of Rights to the states, in time the Supreme Court, explaining the "due process" clause, made certain provisions of the Bill of Rights applicable to the states. The landmark case was *Gitlow* v. *New York* (1925), when the Supreme Court, in incorporating the First Amendment in the due process clause of the Fourteenth Amendment, declared that:

For the present purposes, we may and do assume that freedom of speech and of the press—which are protected by the First Amendment from abridgement by Congress—are among the fundamental personal rights and "liberties" protected by the due process clause of the Fourteenth Amendment from impairment by the states.

Since the *Gitlow* case, the following guarantees of the Bill of Rights have been applied to the states:

- prohibition against unreasonable searches and seizures (Fourth Amendment, *Mapp* v. *Ohio*, 1961)
- privilege against self-incrimination (Fifth Amendment, *Malloy* v. *Hogan*, 1964 and later **Miranda v. Arizona**, 1966)
- guarantee against double jeopardy (Fifth Amendment, *Benton* v. *Maryland*, 1969)
- right to assistance of counsel (Sixth Amendment, **Gideon v. Wainwright**, 1963)
- right to a speedy trial (Sixth Amendment, *Klopfer* v. *North Carolina*, 1967)
- right to a jury trial (Sixth Amendment, *Duncan* v. *Louisiana*, 1968)
- right to confront opposing witnesses (Sixth Amendment, *Pointer* v. *Texas*, 1965)
- right to compulsory process for obtaining witnesses (Sixth Amendment, *Washington* v. *Texas*, 1967)
- right to public trial (Sixth Amendment)
- right to notice as to the nature and cause of the accusation (Sixth Amendment)
- prohibition against cruel and unusual punishment (Eighth Amendment, *Robinson* v. *California*, 1962)

Role of Black Americans in Post-Civil War Society

In the postwar decades of Reconstruction and the rebuilding of the "New South," racial segregation in the form of Jim Crow laws, as well as poll taxes, grandfather clauses, literacy tests, lynchings, beatings, and other forms of violence by white supremacist groups were used to keep blacks in their "proper place." Between 1880 and 1930, three leading figures were instrumental in defining the position of blacks in American society: **Booker T. Washington**, **W.E.B. Du Bois**, and **Marcus Garvey**.

Booker T. Washington

Founder of the Normal and Industrial Institute at Tuskegee, Alabama (1881), and author of the autobiography *Up From Slav*ery, Booker T. Washington stressed the importance of vocational education in preparing African Americans to earn a living and to gain equality. More militant groups and individuals criticized Washington's "willing to wait" methods as "practically accepting the alleged inferiority of the Negro race."

W.E.B. Du Bois

Du Bois's *The Souls of Black Folk* (1903) presented the black American's life to the white public in a series of essays. His **Niagara Movement** (1905), demanded immediate suffrage and civil rights for blacks. Du Bois believed that a small group of educated, talented blacks, referred to as the "Talented Tenth," would save the race by setting an example to whites and other blacks. Du Bois and his associates, black and white, formed the **National Association for the Advancement of Colored People (NAACP)** in 1909 to pursue legal methods to end racial discrimination.

Marcus Garvey

Jamaican-born Marcus Garvey founded the Universal Negro Improvement Association (1916). Preaching racial pride, Garvey insisted that American blacks must return to Africa and create their own civilization in their homeland. Although Garvey's concept of black pride was hailed by many, few chose to leave America and return to Africa.

Exercise Set 2.3

1. Voting rights protection for ex-slaves was provided by the
   A. literacy tests
   B. poll taxes
   C. "grandfather clauses"
   D. Fifteenth Amendment

2. Laws requiring the separation of the races in public facilities were called
   A. equal protection provisions
   B. Amnesty Acts
   C. Jim Crow laws
   D. sharecropper statutes

3. The Supreme Court case of *Plessy* v. *Ferguson* (1896)
   A. mandated integration of public facilities
   B. found the poll tax to be unconstitutional
   C. gave legal support to segregation
   D. affirmed *Gitlow* v. *United States* in applying the Bill of Rights to the states

4. The legislatures established in the Southern states during Reconstruction
   A. excluded blacks
   B. were free from corruption and graft
   C. were primarily dominated by blacks
   D. were instrumental in passing necessary legislation

THE END OF RECONSTRUCTION

The Grant Era

> Let no guilty man escape, if it can be avoided. No personal consider-
> ations should stand in the way of performing a public duty.
>
> President Ulysses S. Grant,
> Endorsement of a letter relating to the **Whiskey Ring**,
> July 29, 1875

The Grant Administration (1869–1877)

Ulysses S. Grant, although a capable military leader, proved a failure at providing strong leadership in the White House. As the nation experienced tremendous economic expansion, incidents of widespread graft and corruption plagued American politics and reflected a low point in public morality.

- *Monetary Policy.* President Grant was not directly involved in the numerous scandals that plagued his administration, but he lacked good judgment concerning those he turned to for advice. During his first term he was influenced by two financial speculators, **Jay Gould** and **James Fisk**. Gould and Fisk helped cause the ruin of many business people, financiers, and workers.

- *Crédit Mobilier.* A scandal involving the construction of the Union Pacific Railroad was revealed during Grant's second administration. The owners of the Union Pacific Railroad created the **Crédit Mobilier**, a construction company, to build the railroad. This company charged the railroad several times the actual amount of construction. To hide the fraud and prevent investigation they gave stock to several members of Congress and the Vice-President.

- *The Whiskey Ring Fraud.* This scandal involved a ring of liquor dealers in St. Louis who, with the assistance of treasury officials, defrauded the government of millions in unpaid taxes.

Urban Politics

Political corruption also existed at the local level. Led by a political "boss," their main goal—to obtain and keep political power—was achieved through graft and bribery. The infamous **Tweed Ring** of New York City's Tammany Hall stole some $100,000 from the tax-

William Marcy "Boss" Tweed (1823–1878) controlled New York City from behind the scenes.

payers before being exposed by *The New York Times* and by the cartoons of **Thomas Nast** in *Harpers Weekly*.

The Solid South

As a result of Reconstruction and political upheaval in the South following the Civil War, the Democrats were able to convince many white voters that the Republican party was the party of corruption that had forced black rule on the South. The Democratic party was dominant in the South from 1876 until the 1970s.

Election of 1876 and the Compromise of 1877

As corruption became more widespread, reform-minded Republicans banded together in 1872 in a new wing of the party known as the "**Liberal Republicans**." They wanted to clean up politics and end military Reconstruction. In 1876, the Republican convention, realizing that the reputation of "Grantism" was hurting the party, nominated a compromise candidate, Governor **Rutherford B. Hayes** of Ohio. The Democratic nominee, Governor **Samuel J. Tilden** of New York, campaigned against Republican scandal and supported reform in the area of federal employment, or "civil service reform."

In the general election to choose the presidential electors who were to cast the Electoral College votes for the President, Tilden won a majority of the popular votes. However, neither candidate had enough undisputed electoral votes to win.

To resolve the unprecedented constitutional crisis, Congress established a fifteen-member electoral commission (Electoral Count Act). After lengthy discussion, the members of the commission agreed to accept the Republican returns, giving Hayes a one-vote electoral victory. In an informal compromise between the parties, the Democrats agreed that Hayes would take office in return for withdrawing troops from the two states where they remained, Louisiana and South Carolina, officially ending military Reconstruction in the South.

The Impact of the Civil War and Reconstruction

Political Alignments

During the Civil War and early Reconstruction era, the political parties exhibited clear-cut differences in ideology, primarily in the areas of race relations and civil rights. After the Civil War, however, sharp policy differences between the two parties faded, although they continued to differ on national issues such as the tariff and currency. The Democrats generally favored low tariffs and the silver standard, while the Republicans favored high tariffs and the gold standard. For the most part, the two major parties failed to develop any clear-cut program to deal with the major social and economic issues that faced the nation.

Nature of Citizenship

The Constitution was silent on the issue of citizenship. The Civil Rights Act of 1866 provided that "all persons born or naturalized in the United States...were citizens of the United States." The Fourteenth Amendment to the Constitution (1868) further defined citizenship on both the national and state level: "All persons born or naturalized in the United States, and subject to the jurisdiction thereof, are citizens of the United States and of the State wherein they reside."

Federal-State Relations

With the nationalization of civil rights by virtue of the Civil Rights Act of 1866, the Thirteenth, Fourteenth, and Fifteenth Amendments, and the Civil Rights Act of 1875, the federal government came to play a far greater role in the preservation of civil rights. The Fourteenth Amendment forbade discriminatory acts by states, not those by private individuals. As white rule returned to the South and attention to the rights of the freed slaves faded, the federal government turned its increased power to national economic issues that were a result of the industrial revolution of the late 19th century.

The North as an Industrial Power

While the Civil War marked a dividing point in American history, with the United States turning from an agrarian nation into an industrial power in a matter of decades, this development was sectional. As industrial development spread over the North, the South remained overwhelmingly rural. The second half of the 19th century saw industrial growth assisted by protective tariffs and corporate development nurtured by favorable Supreme Court decisions. The effect of industry and business would soon find its way into the lives of most Americans.

Exercise Set 2.4

1. In the disputed election of 1876, two different sets of electoral votes were received from
   A. South Carolina
   B. Florida
   C. Louisiana
   D. all of the above

2. By the Compromise of 1877
   A. the Fourteenth Amendment to the Constitution was ratified
   B. Tilden was selected as President of the United States
   C. military occupation of the South ended
   D. the Electoral College system was ended

3. The Crédit Mobilier scandal involved
   A. an increase in the salary of the President and members of Congress
   B. the transcontinental railroad
   C. whiskey and tax fraud
   D. different sets of electoral votes being sent to Congress

4. The section of the Fourteenth Amendment that had the greatest legal significance for the future dealt with
   A. equal protection of the laws guarantee
   B. the apportionment of representatives
   C. the repudiation of the Confederate war debt
   D. the disability clause

1. The Fifteenth Amendment to the U.S. Constitution does not prevent the denial of the vote based upon
   A. literacy
   B. race
   C. color
   D. previous condition of servitude

2. In the decades following the Civil War, the expression "Solid South" was used to refer to the
   A. return of the old plantation system based upon slave labor
   B. dominance by the Democratic party
   C. industrialization of the South
   D. changed attitude on the part of the Southern states toward black Americans

3. Which factor was *least* important in the industrialization of the United States in the 19th century?
   A. abundance of raw materials
   B. inventions
   C. supply of cheap labor
   D. foreign demand for American industrial goods

4. The Fourteenth Amendment is important because, in addition to awarding citizenship to former slaves, it
   A. guarantees women the right to vote
   B. abolishes the poll tax
   C. guarantees equal protection under the law
   D. provides protection against illegal search and seizure

5. The ability to amend the U.S. Constitution lends support to the belief that the document was designed to
   A. preserve the provisions of the original Constitution
   B. adapt to changing times and beliefs
   C. maintain the separation of powers in the national government
   D. accommodate the political party in power

6. Which of the following guarantees would today apply to the states through the "due process" and "equal protection" clauses of the Fourteenth Amendment?
   A. assistance of counsel in criminal prosecutions
   B. ownership of a gun
   C. consumption of alcohol at age eighteen
   D. privilege to drive an automobile at age sixteen

1. Following the Civil War a number of prominent leaders proposed very different programs for the betterment of the black population in the United States.

     Booker T. Washington
     W.E.B. Du Bois
     Marcus Garvey

   For *each* of the leaders listed above, discuss his significance in the drive for civil rights, including each leader's methods used to combat racial discrimination.

2. The nature of the American presidency can be determined by such factors as

     The times in which the President serves
     Relationship with Congress
     Individuals chosen to advise the President

   Referring to the presidential administrations between 1860 and 1877, show how *each* of the factors listed above affected the nature of the presidency. A different President must be used for each factor.

THEMATIC ESSAY

Directions: Write a well-organized essay that includes an introduction, several paragraphs addressing the task below, and a conclusion.

Theme: Separation of Powers

> The balance of the three branches of the federal government has, historically, been in a constant state of flux.

Task:

> From your study of the Reconstruction Period (1863–1876), identify *two* examples of the operation of checks and balances within the federal government.
>
> For each example identified:
>
> - Discuss a specific proposed action by the particular branch of government (executive, legislative, or judicial).
> - Describe the reaction to the action by another branch of government.
> - Finally, explain the settlement or outcome of the debated issue.

You may use any examples from the Reconstruction Period. Some suggestions you might wish to consider are Lincoln's Proclamation of Amnesty and Reconstruction (December 1863) and Congress' Wade-Davis Bill (July 1864), President Johnson's plan of Reconstruction (May 1865) and the reaction of Congress with the passage of the Military Reconstruction Act (March 1867) and the passage by Congress of the Tenure in Office Act (March 1867), President Johnson's veto of the Act (1867), and the subsequent impeachment of President Johnson (1868).

You are *not* limited to these suggestions.

DOCUMENT-BASED QUESTION ESSAY

The following questions (Part A and Part B) are based on the accompanying documents (1–7). Some of these documents have been edited for the purpose of this exercise. The question is designed to test your ability to work with historical documents and to demonstrate your knowledge of the subject matter being presented. As you analyze the documents, take into account both the source of the document and the author's point of view.

Historical Context: The Fourteenth Amendment, ratified in 1868, nationalized civil rights by assuring that no state would deny citizens the equal protection of the laws.

Task: Using information from the documents and your knowledge of United States history, answer the questions that follow each document in Part A. Your answers to the questions will help you write the Part B essay, in which you will be asked:

> Discuss how the Fourteenth Amendment, and its interpretation by the Supreme Court, nationalized civil rights.

Part A
Short Answer

The documents provided relate to issues concerning the concept of equal protection of the laws. Examine each document carefully and then answer the questions that follow.

DOCUMENT 1

Section 1. All persons born or naturalized in the United States and subject to the jurisdiction thereof, are citizens of the United States and of the State wherein they reside. No State shall make or enforce any law which shall abridge the privileges or immunities of citizens of the United States; nor shall any State deprive any person of life, liberty, or property, without due process of law; *nor deny to any person within its jurisdiction the equal protection of the laws.*

Section 5. The Congress shall have the power to enforce, by appropriate legislation, the provisions of this article.

—Fourteenth Amendment, United States Constitution (1868)

1. According the the Fourteenth Amendment, what body was given the power to make sure the amendment was enforced?

_____

2. Keeping in mind the reasons for the addition of the Fourteenth Amendment to the Constitution, why weren't the states given the power of enforcement of the amendment?

_____

_____

_____

_____

DOCUMENT 2

No woman, infant under twenty-one years of age.....convict....nor any free Negro, mulatto, or Indian....shall have a vote.

—Statute, Colony of Virginia (1748)

3. What equal protection of the laws issues are raised by the early colonial Virginia statute?

_____

_____

_____

_____

DOCUMENT 3

4. What rights of citizens does the cartoon show being protected by due process and equal protection?

_____

_____

_____

DOCUMENT 4

......all railway companies carrying passengers in their coaches in this State shall provide equal but separate accommodations for the white and colored races by providing two or more passenger coaches for each passenger train, or by dividing the passenger coaches by a partition so as to secure separate accommodations.

—Louisiana Statute, (1890) issue of *Plessy* v. *Ferguson* (1896)

5. Do you see an "equal protection of the laws" issue with the 1890 Louisiana statute? Why or why not?

_____

_____

_____

DOCUMENT 5

We consider the underlying fallacy of the plaintiff's argument to consist in the assumption that the enforced separation of the two races stamps the colored race with a badge of inferiority. If this be so, it is not by reason of anything found in the act, but solely because the colored race chooses to put that construction upon it.

—Brown, J., Opinion of the Court, *Plessy* v. *Ferguson* (1896)

6. Justice Brown wrote the opinion for the majority in the *Plessy* v. *Ferguson* case. What were his feelings about having races separated in the railway cars?

_____

_____

_____

DOCUMENT 6

In respect of civil rights common to all citizens, the Constitution of the United States does not, I think, permit any public authority to know the race of those entitled to be protected in the enjoyment of such rights. Every true man has pride of race, and, under appropriate circumstances, when the rights of others, his equals before the law, are not to be affected, it is his privilege to express such pride and to take such action based upon it as to him seems proper. But I deny that any legislative body or judicial tribunal may have regard to the race of citizens when the civil rights of those citizens are involved. Indeed, such legislation as that here in question is inconsistent not only with that equality of rights which pertains to citizenship, National and State, but with the personal liberty enjoyed by everyone within the United States.

—Harlan, J., Dissenting Opinion of the Court, *Plessy* v. *Ferguson* (1896)

7. Explain how Justice Harlan's dissenting opinion differs from Justice Brown's majority opinion in the *Plessy* v. *Ferguson* case.

_____

_____

_____

DOCUMENT 7

We come then to the question presented: Does segregation of children in public schools solely on the basis of race, even though the physical facilities and other "tangible" factors may be equal, deprive the children of the minority group of equal educational opportunities? We believe that it does.

—Warren, C.J., Opinion of the Court, *Brown* v. *Board of Education* (1954)

8. Fifty-eight years after the Supreme Court decided *Plessy* v. *Ferguson* (1896), the issue of equal protection of the laws was decided in *Brown* v. *Board of Education* (1954). How did the Supreme Court differ in its view of "equal protection of the laws" in 1954 compared to 1896?

_____

_____

_____

Part B
Essay

Your essay should be well organized with an introductory paragraph that states your position on the question. Develop your position in the next paragraphs and then write a conclusion. In your essay, include specific historical details and refer to the specific documents you analyzed in Part A. You may include additional information from your knowledge of social studies.

Historical Context: The Fourteenth Amendment, ratified in 1868, nationalized civil rights by assuring that no state would deny citizens the equal protection of the laws.

Task:

Discuss how the Fourteenth Amendment, and its interpretation by the Supreme Court, nationalized civil rights.

Guidelines:

In your essay, be sure to
• Develop all aspects of the task
• Incorporate information from at least *five* documents
• Incorporate relevant outside information
• Support the theme with many relevant facts, examples, and details
• Use a logical and clear plan of organization, including an introduction and a conclusion that are beyond a restatement of the theme

CHAPTER 2

THE RISE OF AMERICAN BUSINESS, INDUSTRY, AND LABOR (1865–1920)

TECHNOLOGY AND WORLD INDUSTRIALISM

> The fact is, that civilization requires slaves. The Greeks were quite right there. Unless there are slaves to do the uninteresting work, culture and contemplation become almost impossible. Human slavery is wrong, insecure, and demoralizing. On mechanical slavery, on the slavery of the machine, the future of the world depends.
>
> Oscar Wilde,
> *The Soul of Man Under Socialism* (1895)

The Industrial Revolution

The term "Industrial Revolution" refers to changes in the economic organization of society that include the factory system and machine-made goods. The Industrial Revolution began about 1750 in England with certain inventions in the textile industry and spread to many nations of the Western world, including the United States, during the next century. It involved the replacement on a massive scale of human and animal power with machine power. During the Industrial Revolution there was a shift from manufacturing in the home to the gathering of machines and workers to run them under a single roof (the factory). It also involved improved methods of transportation on land and water, and the growth of modern **capitalism** with the private ownership and control of the means of production.

United States

The Industrial Revolution came to the United States somewhat later than to England. English **mercantilism** had stifled the development of some colonial industry. Moreover, after the Revolution, American capital was used primarily for agricultural development and the shipping industry. The difficulty of importing manufactured goods during the Napoleonic Wars and the War of 1812 provided a stimulus for the development of factories in the United States. The three decades following the Civil War brought economic and social transformation unmatched in the history of the United States. Rich in natural resources, human resources both in labor and scientific development, and capital, the United States approached the coming of the 20th century as a leader in industrial development. Large-scale immigration helped to provide the labor needed in the expanding factory system. By 1894 the United

States was turning out more manufactured goods than any other country in the world. Of course, many problems accompanied the Industrial Revolution. Among them were problems between labor and management, uneven distribution of wealth, and harmful business combinations.

Impact of Industrial Development

On the surface, the Industrial Revolution appeared to benefit most Americans. Statistics suggest that the American standard of living improved in the decades following the Civil War, with prices declining, wage rates remaining consistent, and therefore "real income" increasing. Average working hours decreased and average life expectancy increased. Yet the new industrial age also brought many problems. As wage earners became more dependent on others, times of fluctuation in production resulted in prolonged periods of unemployment in the 1870s and again in the 1890s. The relationship between the factory owner and the workers was no longer personal, and there was little concern for injured or unemployed workers.

Collective bargaining made little progress by 1870 and there was no public welfare program to ease the hardships caused by injury, unemployment, or old age. As industrialism increased and capitalism thrived, the contrast between the rich and the poor increased. As the technology and business organizations of the industrial era generated unmatched powers for creating goods and services, a class of Americans was becoming "enslaved" by the factory system. The words of American social critic Henry Demarest Lloyd in his attack upon monopolies, *Wealth Against Commonwealth* (1894) appeared to be coming true: "Liberty produces wealth, and wealth destroys liberty."

Growth of Capitalism

Capitalism, a form of economic organization characterized by the factory system, private ownership, large-scale production, a free market and wage labor, became the dominant economic system in the industrial societies in the 19th century. Elements of capitalism include (1) **capital**, or the wealth used in producing more wealth; (2) **capitalists**, those who invest money in an enterprise from which a profit is expected; and (3) **labor**, or the working class employed by capitalists.

The leading critic of capitalism and its abuses in the 1800s was the German writer **Karl Marx** (1818–1883). According to Marx, all history involves the struggle between social classes. He saw modern society as divided between the **bourgeoisie** (upper class), which controlled the capital, and the **proletariat** (working class), which sold its labor for wages. Marx supported the organization of workers both as an economic force in **trade unions** and as a political force in a revolutionary movement to overthrow the bourgeoisie.

PRE-CIVIL WAR INDUSTRIAL GROWTH

Although the post-Civil War period has come to be identified with the rapid growth of the Industrial Revolution in the United States, manufacturing and industrial development can be traced back to colonial times. Colonists found that British goods cost nearly twice as much in America as they did in Britain. This situation led the colonists to undertake small-scale manufacturing including the production of textiles (cloth), soap, candles, furniture, and crude tools and utensils. Iron smelteries, some subsidized by colonial legislatures, helped meet the need for farm tools and weapons. Although by 1800 manufacturing was still relatively unimportant to the American economy, soon after the War of 1812 the rise of merchant investors, wholesalers, retailers, and improved transportation marked the early beginnings of industrial transformation.

Textile Industry

Textile manufacturing became an important part of American industry shortly after independence was achieved. The first mill, built in Pawtucket, Rhode Island in 1790, used water-powered spinning machines constructed by Samuel Slater. The **Embargo Act (1807), Non-Intercourse Act (1809)**, and **War of 1812** stimulated manufacturing in the United States, and the number of textile mills increased.

Originally, many industries, including the textile industry, used the "putting-out" or domestic system; workers received supplies at home where they finished the product and then returned it to a merchant who sold it. This system had problems of timing, shipping, and quality control. In 1813 Francis Cabot Lowell and other Boston merchants built the first textile factories in Waltham, Massachusetts, combining all the manufacturing operations at a single location. To satisfy the need for workers, the managers of the textile factories recruited young women from the New England countryside to work in the mills. They offered them appealing wages, boarding houses to live in, and cultural events. This came to be known as the Lowell, or Waltham System and was used in other mills in New England. The textile industry became the most important industry in the country before the Civil War, employing nearly 115,000 workers in 1860.

Iron Production

The iron industry, like the textile industry, was stimulated by the **embargo** on trade before the War of 1812 and by its interruption during the war. A major breakthrough in the iron industry came with the discovery of how to produce **steel** inexpensively and in large quantities. The United States possessed the necessary elements, iron and coal, to produce steel, a mixture of iron, carbon, and other elements. Immense deposits of iron ore lay near the western shores of Lake Superior, and nearly one half of the world's coal reserves lay within our borders. In the 1850s Henry Bessemer of England and William Kelly of the United States independently discovered a revolutionary process for making large quantities of steel inexpensively by burning out the impurities in molten iron. With the use of the **Bessemer process**, steel production soared.

Exercise Set 2.5

1. The introduction of new textile machines in England at the start of the Industrial Revolution increased the employment of textile workers because
   A. the newly developed machinery was less efficient than the hand labor that it replaced
   B. the cost of machine-made textiles fell rapidly, leading to greater demand
   C. the division of labor that developed required more workers to produce the same amount of goods
   D. imported foreign textiles were superior to domestic textiles

2. The primary purpose of the colonies acquired by England during the 19th century was to provide
   A. raw materials and overseas markets
   B. a training ground for military forces
   C. labor for growing industries
   D. settlements for growing populations

3. Which of the following inventions had great influence in the 19th century?
   A. the steam engine
   B. the radio
   C. the automobile
   D. the flying shuttle

4. An important result of the War of 1812 was that it
   A. increased U.S. shipping
   B. encouraged immigration to the United States
   C. encouraged manufacturing in the United States
   D. increased investment in agriculture at the expense of industry

5. America's most important industry before the Civil War was the
   A. rubber industry
   B. machine tool industry
   C. automobile industry
   D. textile industry

BUSINESS ORGANIZATION: SIZE AND STRUCTURE

> They (corporations) cannot commit treason, nor be outlawed nor excommunicated, for they have no souls.
>
> Sir Edward Coke (1552–1634),
> *Case of Sutton's Hospital*

Proprietorships and Partnerships

Before the middle of the 19th century, most American businesses were either **single proprietorships**, with one owner, or **partnerships**, small businesses with two or more owners. However, as American industry and business grew, facilitated by greater amounts of **capital**, improved transportation, greater demand for products, and an available working force, small organizations often proved to be inadequate. If a business wanted to expand, it was difficult for one or two persons to raise the necessary capital. If the organization faced financial difficulties, the owners who were financially responsible often lost their personal assets. Finally, the death of a proprietor or partner often meant the end of the business.

Incorporation

Following the Civil War, the **corporation** became the major form of business organization, gradually replacing proprietorships and partnerships. By selling part ownerships of the business to the public through the sale of **stocks** and **bonds**, the corporation was able to raise the necessary capital for operations and expansion. During the 1880s and 1890s, corporations received important judicial protection when the Supreme Court ruled that corporations, like individuals, were protected by the **Fourteenth Amendment**. This extension of the Fourteenth Amendment meant that corporations could not be denied equal protection of the laws and could not be deprived of rights or property without due process of law. (*Chicago, Milwaukee, St. Paul Railway Co.* v. *Minnesota,* 1890)

Consolidation of Corporations

By 1900 corporations were responsible for nearly two-thirds of all the goods manufactured in the United States. As growth continued, corporate managers searched for ways to expand and increase stability. During the late 1800s, there was a trend toward business combination or consolidation, under new corporate forms such as **trusts** and holding companies that promoted growth and cut down on wasteful competition. Between 1889 and 1903 some 300 business combinations were formed. Perhaps the most spectacular was the **United States Steel Corporation,** the nation's first billion-dollar corporation, which controlled 60 percent of the nation's steel production, created by banker and international financier **J.P. Morgan**.

As investment opportunities increased, greater amounts of capital were necessary. In addition to domestic investments in American industry, foreign investment grew. Between 1870 and 1900 foreign investment in American companies increased from $1.5 billion to $3.5 billion.

TRANSPORTATION, COMMUNICATION, AND RESOURCES

Transportation

Railroads

During the first half of the 19th century, the nation's railroads were anything but a uniform system connecting the different sections of the country. There was little mileage beyond the Mississippi and virtually none beyond the Missouri River. Few tracks were connected; short stretches of lines using different gauges required the unloading and reloading of cargo for transport.

As settlement extended westward, it became apparent that the nation's rail system would have to expand into a uniform system. In 1850 the federal government transferred to promoters several million acres of public land for the purpose of railroad construction. This policy was continued by the government primarily in the construction of Western lines. The nation's first **transcontinental** railroad was completed in 1869 with the joining of the **Central Pacific Railroad** and the **Union Pacific Railroad** at Promontory Point, Utah. Between 1865 and 1890 the total mileage of track in the United

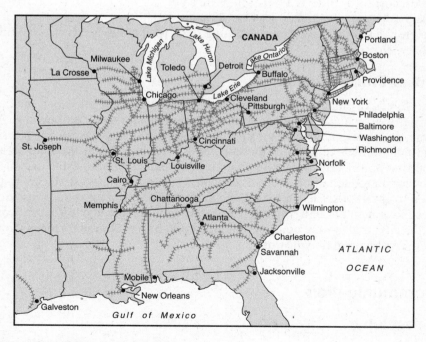

Figure 2.3 Major Railroads in 1860

145

States grew from 35,000 to 200,000, with the greatest growth taking place west of the Mississippi River. Technological advances, including uniform-gauge tracks, the automatic car coupler, the Pullman Sleeping Car, and the Westinghouse air brake, made rail transportation safer and more efficient. By 1910 the United States had a third of all the railroad track in the world. In the half-century following the Civil War, railroads enabled the growing nation to transport its enormous wealth in natural resources to factories, storehouses, marketplaces, and seaports.

Automobiles

Henry Ford, an electrical engineer with Detroit's Edison Company, developed and introduced the **mass production** of automobiles. Copying the meatpacking industry, Ford set up **assembly lines** to produce automobiles, which greatly reduced the time and expense of manufacturing cars. When the **Ford Motor Company** began production of the **Model T** in 1910, 10,000 cars were sold. By 1914, with the help of assembly-line production, 248,000 Fords, costing as little as $490 each, were sold. The production of automobiles also stimulated the growth of other industries, including steel, road building, service stations, rubber, etc.

Automobile manufacturer Henry Ford (1863–1947) developed the assembly-line method of mass production.

Urban Transportation

The forces of industrialization and urbanization accompanied one another during the second half of the 19th century and into the 20th century. As American cities grew, mass transportation became an area of concern. Horse- and mule-drawn vehicles of the late 1800s were inefficient in urban areas. The first power-driven transportation used in the cities were cable cars. The increased production of electricity enabled electric-powered streetcars to be used by the 1890s. Elevated tracks and subways allowed mass transportation free movement through congested areas. As suburbs spread out from the core of the city, tracks were constructed outward to bring commuters to and from their employment downtown.

Communication

Telegraph

The most revolutionary change in communications before the Civil War was the development of the long-distance telegraph by **Samuel F.B. Morse** in 1844. By 1853, 23,000 miles of telegraph wire spread across the United States, freeing the transport of messages from the human messenger. The first transatlantic cable was laid in 1858, making possible instantaneous communication with other continents.

Telephone

In 1876 **Alexander Graham Bell**, a teacher of the deaf in Boston, received a patent on a telephone he had invented. By 1885 the **American Telephone and Telegraph Company** was organized to put the new invention into widespread use.

Sources of Energy

New sources of energy have coincided with industrial development in the United States. During the late 1700s steam energy produced by wood and coal replaced earlier sources of power—humans animal, and water power. By the late 1800s two new sources of energy—oil and electricity—came into use.

Oil

In the early 1850s kerosene refined from petroleum was an efficient and inexpensive fuel used primarily in lamps. Discoveries of oil reserves in Pennsylvania, and later in California and Texas, provided a major source of fuel in the 20th century with the invention of the internal combustion engine. By 1920 the United States was producing about 65 percent of the world's petroleum, much of it controlled by **John D. Rockefeller's Standard Oil**.

Electricity

Harvard President Charles W. Eliot pointed out the enormous change electricity brought to American life, saying, "It is the carrier of light and power; devourer of time and space; bearer of human speech over land and sea; greatest servant of man."

In 1878 **Thomas Edison** formed the Edison Electric Light Company and developed the **incandescent light bulb** which, if not the first, was certainly the most practical light bulb of the time. Another invention of Edison's laboratories, the **dynamo,** solved some of the problems of power production and distribution, enabling the delivery of electrical power. Edison's work was improved upon by **George Westinghouse**. He used alternating current and transformers to reduce high-voltage power to lower voltage levels and was able to make the transmission of electrical power over long distances less expensive. During the 1890s Henry Villard and J.P. Morgan merged various electric companies to form **General Electric**.

Exercise Set 2.6

1. During the period 1860–1890, big business was characterized by
   A. the use of organizational methods to control prices and do away with competition
   B. support for union organization among workers
   C. attempts to curb immigration
   D. lack of adequate leadership in managerial positions

2. Business merger movements of the late 1800s and early 1900s were designed, among other reasons, to
   A. increase hourly wages for workers
   B. control more of the market and reduce wasteful competition
   C. encourage the growth of unions
   D. provide for more equitable distribution of wealth

3. Introduction and improvement of the assembly line and mass production can be largely attributed to
   A. J.P. Morgan
   B. Thomas Edison
   C. George Westinghouse
   D. Henry Ford

4. Railroad building in the period after 1865 resulted in
   A. the end of industrial tariffs
   B. greater population growth west of the Mississippi
   C. a decrease in the growth of towns and cities west of the Mississippi
   D. a decrease in agricultural output

REPRESENTATIVE ENTREPRENEURS

> Upon the sacredness of property civilization itself depends—the right
> of the laborer to his hundred dollars in the savings bank, and equally
> the legal right of the millionaire to his millions.
>
> Andrew Carnegie, *Wealth* (1889)

A new group of business owners appeared during the middle of the 19th
century who later became known as the **robber barons**. Through financial
wizardry, stock manipulation, and fierce competition, these men built corporate dynasties that eventually threatened the free enterprise system in the
United States. Yet their management of business and the nation's resources
also lowered the cost of oil, steel, and other goods for America's consumers
and helped create the modern corporation. Moreover, their willingness to
reinvest profits in further business expansion contributed to the economic
growth of the United States during the last half of the 19th century.

Captains of Industry

John Pierpont Morgan (1837–1913)

Born in Hartford, Connecticut, the son of a prominent international banker,
J.P. Morgan built a reputation after the Civil War as a reorganizer of railroads. By the end of the 19th century, he controlled a vast transportation
network. Morgan founded the J.P. Morgan Company in 1895 and in 1901
organized the first billion-dollar corporation, **United States Steel**.

Andrew Carnegie (1835–1919)

Carnegie became rich investing in oil, ironmaking, and bridge building.
The **Carnegie Steel Company** became America's largest steel concern and
was eventually bought by J.P. Morgan in the formation of United States
Steel. Although he was a shrewd businessman, Carnegie's essay "**Gospel
of Wealth**" (1889) demonstrated his belief in philanthropy, setting forth
the idea that the rich are "trustees" of their wealth and should administer it
unselfishly for the good of the public.

John D. Rockefeller (1839–1937)

Rockefeller's fortune was made in oil, and in 1870 he formed the **Standard
Oil Company** to consolidate his investments. By the 1880s his Standard
Oil Trust controlled almost all the nation's oil refineries, refining 83.7 percent of all the oil produced in the country. A fierce competitor, Rockefeller
explained his ruthlessness in business by comparing it to the American
Beauty rose: "The American Beauty rose can be produced in all its splendor
only by sacrificing the early buds that grow up around it."

The Work Ethic

The American work ethic can be traced back to the Puritan settlements of the 1600s in New England. The Puritans believed that good luck and success during one's life on earth were evidence of the "elect status" necessary to gain entrance into heaven.

Horatio Alger (1834–1899), a 19th-century American writer, dramatized the American dream of success through hard work in over 100 novels based on the idea that virtue is always rewarded. By leading an exemplary life entailing a valiant struggle with poverty and temptation, Alger's heroes all come to wealth and honor.

Public Good v. Private Gain

The principle of **laissez-faire** held that the way to obtain the greatest and cheapest productivity was to leave the individual employer and the individual worker to the free market. Those who favored the laissez-faire doctrine believed that interference by unions or government would upset the market and reduce total production. This would have a negative effect on workers, employers, and consumers. After 1870 the doctrine of laissez-faire received additional support from the principle of **Social Darwinism**, the belief that social progress depended upon competition among human beings resulting in the "survival of the fittest."

The industrial age and the growth of business combinations brought many problems to American life, and concern developed over the abuses of industrialism. As Americans saw the suffering of the poor in city slums, the deteriorating working conditions and failing health of America's workers, the monopolistic practices of major businesses, the lack of consumer protection, the exploitation of the nation's resources, and the widening gap in the distribution of the nation's wealth, many realized that some government regulation was necessary. The **Progressive Movement** in the early 1900s was the culmination of a series of responses to the worst abuses of the new industrial age.

Exercise Set 2.7

1. Major industrial leaders contributed to economic growth during the last half of the 19th century by
   A. promoting further competition among businesses
   B. encouraging government to regulate unfair practices of the nation's businesses
   C. reinvesting profits in the expansion of business
   D. supporting the growth of labor organizations

2. John D. Rockefeller's most significant contribution to the growth of business enterprise in the United States was his
   A. support of labor unions and collective bargaining
   B. elimination of wasteful competitive practices
   C. introduction of assembly line techniques
   D. support of greater government intervention in business and an end to laissez-faire

3. Which of the following groups would have supported greater government intervention in business during the latter part of the 19th century?
   A. the robber barons
   B. supporters of laissez-faire and social Darwinism
   C. owners of the nation's major railroad lines
   D. the working classes

BUSINESS AND GOVERNMENT

> We accept and welcome . . . the concentration of business, industrial and commercial, in the hands of a few, and the law of competition between these as being not only beneficial, but essential for the future progress of the race.
>
> Andrew Carnegie, *The Gospel of Wealth* (1889)

Capitalism and Laissez-Faire

Capitalism

Capitalism can be defined as an economic system in which the means of production are privately owned, production and distribution of goods are determined in a free enterprise system by laws of supply and demand, and there is little government regulation of the economy. A characteristic of pure capitalism is the principle of laissez-faire.

Laissez-Faire

The economic policy known as laissez-faire can be traced to **Adam Smith**, whose *Wealth of Nations,* advocating free international trade, was published in 1776. The concept of laissez-faire was emphasized by Alexander Hamilton in 1791, when he claimed that "it can hardly ever be wise in a government to attempt to give a direction to the industry of its citizens . . . . To leave industry to itself, therefore, is, in almost every case, the soundest as well as the simplest policy."

 • *Principles of Laissez-Faire.* By the middle of the 1800s three characteristics of laissez-faire were obvious in the American economy: (1) Labor should find its price on the market. In other words, an individual's wages were dependent on the price he or she could demand in the market. (2) The value of money should be subject to an automatic mechanism. There should be a uniform standard for currency among trading nations, such as the gold standard, that would stabilize currency among nations and allow greater ease of trade. (3) Goods should be free to flow from country to country without restrictions. Protectionist policies such as tariffs would only hurt trade among nations.

 • *Movement Away From Laissez-Faire.* Beginning in the latter part of the 1800s and continuing through the 1900s, the economic system in the United States moved away from the laissez-faire doctrine. Labor, represented by labor unions and protected by federal and state legislation, could no longer be considered simply a commodity; the country was no longer on a gold standard (ended in 1933), industry was subsidized, and international trade was not free from protective barriers. Today we have a system known as a mixed economy. Under this system, the government exercises some control over the nation's business, monetary system, and labor, while at the same time it allows the economy to regulate itself to a considerable extent.

The Supreme Court, Fourteenth Amendment, and Corporations

During the 1880s the Supreme Court began to change its direction concerning involvement in the economic matters within the states. As the social and political pressures of an emerging industrial nation increased, the Court demonstrated a greater willingness to exercise judicial review against state and federal regulation of industry. More specifically, it gave a new economic interpretation to the due process clause of the Fourteenth Amendment.

In the earlier cases testing the application of the due process clause of the Fourteenth Amendment to economic rights, the Supreme Court, demonstrating judicial restraint, upheld state regulations (*Slaughterhouse Cases,* 1873; *Munn* v. *Illinois* 1877; *Granger Cases,* 1877). The Court had accepted the idea in 1886 that the corporation was a person in the sense of the Fourteenth Amendment (*Santa Clara County* v. *Southern Pacific Railway* 1886). But it was the case of *Chicago, Milwaukee & St. Paul Railway Co.* v. *Minnesota* (1890) that marked the first time the Court declared a state law to be in violation of the due process clause of the Fourteenth Amendment, marking greater judicial protection of corporations.

Competition and Absorption: Mergers and Trusts

As competition among businesses during the second half of the 19th century cut prices and profits, business people sought ways to avoid price wars and increase profits. Combinations in business usually took two forms. Some were organized in a horizontal integration so that an organization under one management controlled different producers of the same product. Others were organized in a vertical integration so that an organization under one management controlled the different steps in the production of one commodity. An example of a vertical combination was the Ford Motor Company, which owned mines, shipping lines, railroads, and other businesses necessary for the production of the automobile. A number of business combinations resulted.

Pools

Agreements among business rivals sometimes managed to fix prices or divide profits and markets. During the 1870s and 1880s railroads made use of pooling agreements to fix prices.

Trusts

A trust was a more formal and permanent agreement than the pooling arrangement. Stockholders of competing companies would turn their stocks and voting rights over to a central board of trustees who controlled the member companies to eliminate competition. The result of the trust agreement was a monopoly, or near total control, of an industry. **John D. Rockefeller**, in an attempt to reduce competition in the oil industry, was the first to employ the trust arrangement with the formation of the **Standard Oil Company**.

Merger

A merger joins two or more companies, resulting in a single corporation. When a merger threatens to monopolize a particular industry, the courts may declare it illegal and a restraint on trade.

During the final decades of the 1800s, mergers and consolidations took place in many industries, including sugar, steel, machinery, tobacco, and copper. As combinations began to have an adverse effect on American society, however, the federal government began to consider intervention, moving away from its former laissez-faire policies.

Railroad Abuses and Government Regulation

Practices of the Railroads

The demand for government regulation of business first came from American farmers. Shortly after the Civil War, agricultural profits fell; some causes were overproduction, greater crop production in other nations, and high prices charged by middlemen. Farmers' grievances were directed against operators of grain elevators, manufacturers of farm machinery, bankers, and primarily, the railroads.

Complaints about the railroads included accusation of monopolistic practices. Railroads were absolutely necessary to the nation's farmers to transport their crops. However, in most farming areas there was only one railroad line. Because of the lack of competition, the railroad was able to charge "all that the traffic would bear" on the "short haul." For example, because of high freight rates, Pittsburgh, a large city served by only one railroad, paid 60 percent more for grain from Chicago than did New York, which was twice as far away. Railroads claimed that this was necessary to make up for the low rates charged on busier routes, or the "long hauls," because of fierce competition among the railroads.

Other unfair railroad practices included granting rebates to large shippers, giving free passes to politicians, bribing members of state legislatures, and entering into pooling agreements to control rates. During the 1870s and

1880s, demands for government regulation of the railroads came from farmers, small shippers, retailers, and reform politicians.

State Regulation

Regulation started at the state level with reform groups winning political control over state legislatures and passing legislation to control abuses. The National Grange of the Patrons of Husbandry, organized by Oliver H. Kelley, numbered 1,500,000 by 1874 and dominated the legislatures of Illinois, Wisconsin, Iowa, and Minnesota. Methods of control initiated by the Granger programs were rate regulation legislation, cooperative buying of farm supplies and machinery, and pressure for federal legislation.

State legislation was dealt a blow when the Supreme Court ruled in *Wabash, St. Louis and Pacific Railway* v. *Illinois* (1886) that states had no power to fix rates on shipments passing beyond their borders. **Interstate commerce** is under congressional control.

Federal Regulation

- *Interstate Commerce Act.* Congress responded in 1887 by passing the Interstate Commerce Act and establishing the Interstate Commerce Commission, which had the power to (1) require that railroads post their rates publicly; (2) require rates to be "reasonable and just"; (3) forbid practices such as pooling, rebates, and rate discrimination; (4) prohibit higher charges for short hauls than for longer hauls over the same line; and (5) investigate complaints against railroads and hand down rulings that could be enforced in courts.

- *Munn* v. *Illinois (1877).* The *Munn* case was one of the several so-called **Granger cases** that dealt with state regulation of railroads and grain warehouses. The Supreme Court, by allowing the Illinois statute fixing maximum charges for the storage of grain (grain that found its way into **interstate commerce** and was therefore under the control of Congress), held that "when one devotes his property to a use in which the public has an interest, he, in effect, grants to the public an interest in that use, and must submit to be controlled by the public for the common good."

- *Sherman Antitrust Act (1890).* In response to increasing pressure to halt the domination of the market by a small number of powerful corporations, Congress passed the Sherman Antitrust Act in 1890. The provisions of the Act included (1) that every contract, combination, or conspiracy in **restraint of trade** among the states or with foreign countries was illegal; and (2) that persons guilty of monopolizing trade or commerce were subject to fines and/or imprisonment.

The weaknesses of the Sherman Act soon became apparent. Although trusts were prohibited, holding companies soon started to replace them and were able to avoid the reaches of the law. The federal courts were hesitant to enforce the Act and continued to define the word "trade" narrowly. The Supreme Court made the law almost meaningless in the *United States* v. *Knight Company* (1895) case when it held that the sugar refining industry did not involve interstate commerce and therefore the Sherman Act did not apply to an almost complete monopoly that the American Sugar Refining Company had over the sugar industry.

Public Opinion

As the end of the century approached, more and more Americans were becoming concerned about the effects of large business combinations. This new social concern led to a mass of progressive social legislation in the 1900s.

Exercise Set 2.8

1. Of the following, the most important cause of agrarian discontent in the United States during the latter part of the 19th century was
   A. the belief that railroads and middlemen were exploiting the farmers
   B. the growth of population in the Eastern states
   C. the rise in prices of agricultural produce
   D. greater government control over public utilities

2. A major problem for businesses entering into a pooling agreement was
   A. falling profits
   B. lawsuits filed against members of pools who went against the agreement
   C. lack of a legal way to enforce the pooling agreement
   D. consumers turning to a company that did not participate in the pooling arrangement

3. Large business combinations of the late 1800s presented a threat to
   A. the currency system
   B. free enterprise
   C. the transportation system
   D. representative democracy

4. A present-day example of laissez-faire economics would be
   A. deregulation of the airline industry
   B. minimum wage laws
   C. farm subsidies
   D. breakup of American Telephone and Telegraph

LABOR ORGANIZATION AND STRUGGLE

> To protect the workers in their inalienable rights to a higher and bet-
> ter life; to protect them, not only as equals before the law, but also
> in their health, their homes, their firesides, their liberties as men, as
> workers, and as citizens . . . to this workers are entitled . . . The attain-
> ment of these is the glorious mission of the trade unions.
>
> Samuel Gompers, Speech (1898)

> Let us not destroy those wonderful machines that produce efficiently
> and cheaply. Let us control them. Let us profit by their efficiency and
> cheapness. Let us run them for ourselves. That, gentlemen, is social-
> isms . . . .
>
> Jack London, *The Iron Heel* (1906)

National Labor Unions

Organized labor in America can trace its roots to 1792 when the journey-
men cordwainers (shoemakers) of Philadelphia organized a local union. Its
successor, the Federal Society of Journeyman Cordwainers, operated until
1806 when, after a strike for better wages, the union was found guilty of
conspiracy in a court of law. Although the strike and subsequent decision
of the courts ended the small union, it marked the beginning of decades of
struggle for the **bargaining power** of workers in the workplace. In the case
of *Commonwealth* v. *Hunt* (1842), the Massachusetts high court held that
labor unions had a right to combine and strike "in such manner as best to
subserve their own interests."

The modern labor movement is essentially a product of the Industrial
Revolution. The development of the factory system made it impossible for
individual workers to bargain on equal terms with a powerful employer.
Only by organizing and presenting their demands as a group were the workers able to secure higher wages, shorter working days, improved working
conditions, and protection against being discharged without just cause.

National Labor Union

Formed in 1866 under the leadership of **William Sylvis**, the National Labor
Union helped to push legislation through Congress for an **8-hour workday**
for laborers and mechanics employed by the federal government.

The Knights of Labor

Founded in 1869 by Uriah S. Stephens, the Knights of Labor started as a
secret organization whose aim was to unite skilled and unskilled workers

into one great national union. They advocated higher wages, 8-hour working days, equal pay for equal work by men and women, abolition of child labor (under 14 years), arbitration of labor disputes, prohibition of foreign contract labor, safety and health laws, workers' cooperative associations, a graduated income tax, and government ownership of railroads and other public utilities. Under the leadership of Terence V. Powderly, the Knights of Labor gained influence, and membership reached 700,000 by 1886. The union declined rapidly after 1886 for several reasons, including the failure of a strike against the Texas and Pacific Railroad and the blame attached to the Knights for the bombing at the **Haymarket Riot** in Chicago.

The American Federation of Labor

Founded in 1881 by **Samuel Gompers**, the AFL was organized as a federation of many separate skilled craft unions rather than a general organization of workers. Each member craft union enjoyed a degree of autonomy in matters affecting its own trade. The goals of the AFL stressed "bread and butter" issues: higher wages, an 8-hour workday, improved working conditions, use of union-made products, and passage of state and federal legislation to benefit labor. The methods used by the AFL to obtain its goals included the **strike** (a work stoppage until goals are met) and the **boycott** (the practice of not purchasing the

Samuel Gompers (1850–1924) founded the AFL in 1881.

product of the employer). By 1900 the AFL claimed 500,000 members and eventually was successful in winning the **closed shop** (plants hiring only union workers) and the abolition of **yellow-dog contracts** (requirement by the employer that a newly hired employee sign an agreement not to join a labor union). Yet, as a union of skilled workers, the AFL excluded 90 percent of the American workers who did not have a craft or the skills to qualify for membership in one of its affiliated unions.

International Ladies Garment Workers Union

Of the 8 million female workers in 1910, only 125,000 were members of unions, primarily because most unions refused to accept women as members. A strike by thousands of women shirtwaist workers in New York in 1909 laid the foundation for the International Ladies Garment Workers Union. The ILGWU was instrumental in bringing relief to the families of the victims of the **Triangle Shirtwaist Factory fire** in New York City in 1911. This tragedy claimed the lives of 146 workers and subsequently brought about a modern factory inspection system and laws to regulate the labor of women and children.

Struggle and Conflict

Between 1881 and 1900 there were over 24,000 strikes in the United States that involved nearly 128,000 establishments. Many tried to blame labor unrest on the infiltration of socialists and anarchists into the work forces. However, the unrest among the American workers who faced great inequities in the late 1800s was typical of the activist undercurrent that flowed throughout American history.

Major Strikes

- *Haymarket Riot (1886).* Following a nationwide strike for an 8-hour day by the **Knights of Labor**, trouble broke out in Chicago as sympathetic **anarchists** addressed a protest meeting held by the strikers. After police entered the crowd to break up the meeting, a bomb was thrown, killing seven police and wounding sixty more. Because of this incident, the Knights of Labor became identified with anarchism and violence, and this led to the union's decline. It also helped to turn American public opinion against labor unions.

- *Homestead Strike (1892).* When the **Carnegie Steel Company** threatened to cut wages and crush the **Amalgamated Association of Iron and Steel Workers** in 1892, workers picketed the plant. Management called in Pinkerton guards to protect the plant, but they were attacked by the strikers and run out of town. An appeal to the governor of Pennsylvania brought in the militia. Although the workers struck for nine months, public opinion eventually turned against them and they went back to work, agreeing to the company's terms. The strike crushed the Amalgamated Union and left the steel industry unorganized for 40 years.

Eugene V. Debs (1855–1926) led the American Railway Union in the strike against the Pullman Company.

- *Pullman Strike (1894).* Workers at the Pullman Palace Car Company struck in protest over policies at the company town near Chicago and cuts in wages. The strike spread, bringing railroad traffic west of Chicago to a standstill when the American Railway Union, under the leadership of **Eugene V. Debs**, aided the strikers by calling a boycott in which union members refused to work on any train with a Pullman car. The railroads appealed to the federal government for protection. President **Cleveland** sent troops to Chicago to "protect the mails," but more probably to crush the strike. The federal government obtained a court **injunction** (order) that forbade the union to strike. Within a month the strike was ended, and Debs was imprisoned for failing to abide by the court injunction to end the strike. The Supreme Court upheld the conviction of Debs in the case of *In Re Debs* (1895) on the grounds that an injunction was valid under the federal government's power to remove obstacles to **interstate commerce** as provided by the Sherman Antitrust Act. The injunction became a powerful weapon of employers to combat strikes.

• *Lawrence Textile Strike (1912).* Unskilled industrial workers ignored by the American Federation of Labor were organized by the **Industrial Workers of the World** (or **Wobblies**) formed in 1905 under the leadership of "**Big Bill**" **Haywood**. They advocated militant agitation, willful obstruction of industry, and damage to businesses. Although the IWW gained few victories, national attention was focused on the union in 1912 when 30,000 textile workers in Lawrence, Massachusetts, struck for better working conditions and higher wages. The American Woolen Company met nearly all of the union's demands. After America's entry into World War I, the federal government prosecuted various IWW leaders for their attempt to obstruct the draft.

Management's Position

Management (owners and managers of means of production) has been at odds with labor throughout modern industrial history. Management's position has usually included (1) conducting production and operations with as little interference from labor unions as possible; (2) increasing productivity and profits through efficiency and laborsaving techniques; (3) being free to increase and decrease work forces according to need; and (4) maintaining an **open shop** (the choice of the employer to hire both union and nonunion labor) as opposed to a **closed shop** (the employment of only union workers).

Tactics Employed in Disputes by Management and Labor

A strike by workers is usually the final means of attempting to gain demands and often hurts both labor and management. Very few disputes end in strikes because of the following techniques:

• *Collective Bargaining.* Representatives of management and labor meet, discuss issues and differences, and settle on a contract acceptable to both sides.

• *Mediation.* The Federal Mediation and Conciliation Service offers the services of mediators, or neutral third parties, who sit in on the negotiations between management and labor, offer suggestions of concessions to both sides, and encourage the two sides to reach an agreeable contract. The mediator's decision is not binding.

• *Arbitration.* Both management and labor agree to a neutral third party. That person hears the dispute and hands down a decision that will be accepted by both sides according to an agreement beforehand. In other words, the arbitrator's decision is binding.

- *Fact-Finding Board.* When a strike affects the welfare of the nation, the President may appoint a board to hear the dispute and hand down a decision.

Weapons Used by Labor and Management

When collective bargaining is not successful in settling labor-management disputes, more drastic means may be used:

- *Labor.* Workers may resort to a **strike**, **picketing** (demonstration by workers usually outside of the workplace), a **boycott**, and **publicity** to convince the public of the legitimacy of their demands and to seek support.

- *Management.* Employers may use **strikebreakers** (sometimes referred to as **scabs**), **lockouts**, in which the employer keeps the workers from their jobs until they accept management's terms, **injunctions** (court orders that say workers must return to work), and **publicity**, or appeal to the public for support.

Attitude and Role of Government

Beginning in the late 1900s government has played a crucial role in affecting the balance between labor and management. Examples of government intervention include:

- *Sherman Antitrust Act (1890).* This was used to restrain activities of unions, finding them to cause "unreasonable restraint of trade."

- *Clayton Antitrust Act (1914).* This act reversed some of the interpretations used under the Sherman Act and declared that legitimate union activities were not subject to antitrust laws. The Clayton Act also restricted the use of injunctions against unions in labor disputes.

- *Norris-LaGuardia Act (1932).* Federal courts were prohibited by this act from granting injunctions against workers who engaged in strikes, boycotts, or peaceful picketing. The Norris-LaGuardia Act also made unenforceable **yellow-dog contracts** (contracts that prevented a worker from joining a union after being employed).

Socialism, Communism, Anarchism

Marxist socialists in America at the end of the 19th century were primarily Germans who brought their political and economic theories with them from Europe. The Marxist Workingmen's party and the Social Democratic party attracted some support during the 1870s. In the early 1880s the socialists split into two groups: those who rejected capitalism and those who rejected both capitalism and organized government. The latter group was known as **anarchists**.

In 1900 the **Socialist party of America**, with **Eugene V. Debs** as its presidential candidate, won about 100,000 votes. In the next decade, after the arrival of many eastern Europeans and continued political interest among American workers, membership in the Socialist party grew. In 1912 its growth peaked and Debs received nearly one million votes as the Socialist presidential candidate. However, unlike labor in many European countries, American labor never established a major political party in the United States. Instead, it used its influence to seek its goals within the "two-party" system.

"Radicalism" was not restricted to politics and labor movements. The Socialist party's commitment to democratic gradualism attracted many members of the clergy, writers, and others who believed reform was not possible under the two major parties. Writers in the early 20th century who spoke for socialism and criticized the capitalist system included some of the most notable American literary figures, such as Upton Sinclair, Jack London, Theodore Dreiser, and Frank Norris.

Middle-Class Labor Support

Not all advocates of better working conditions and higher wages came from the "radical fringe" of politics and the labor movement. The Women's Trade Union League combined the forces of the wealthy elite with reformers, like **Jane Addams**, to aid working women in their efforts to organize. The Consumers' Union was a "watchdog" organization formed to promote the purchase of only those goods produced in factories with approved working conditions.

Exercise Set 2.9

1. While the Knights of Labor included both skilled and unskilled workers, the American Federation of Labor consisted of
   A. only industrial workers
   B. the fringe element of radical labor
   C. craft unions of skilled workers
   D. primarily immigrant labor

2. An important reason for the growth of labor unions in the second half of the 19th century was
   A. the passage of the Clayton Antitrust Act
   B. a decrease in immigration to the United States
   C. the growth of a socialist movement in the United States
   D. the indifference of business to the welfare of employees

3. The primary reason for support of free compulsory public education by labor unions was to
   A. decrease the number of children in the work force
   B. educate youth for eventual union leadership
   C. provide day care for the children of union members
   D. train youth in different industrial skills

4. A powerful weapon used by employers to end strikes was
   A. the closed shop
   B. the injunction
   C. picketing
   D. the use of a mediator

CHAPTER REVIEW QUESTIONS

1. Which is a fundamental idea of laissez-faire capitalism?
   A. workers should own the means of production
   B. employers should provide social benefits for all workers
   C. government should control output and wages
   D. businesses should gain and lose according to their own efforts

2. In the United States, economic opportunities for women expanded during the last quarter of the 19th century primarily because of the growth of
   A. opportunities to buy farms in the West
   B. industry and technology
   C. big-city political machines
   D. organized labor

3. In which way did the joint-stock company help lay the foundation for the modern corporation?
   A. the major reason for forming a company was to produce industrial goods on a large scale
   B. the company made low-risk investments and thus could guarantee a profit
   C. the government sponsored and controlled the company
   D. the company was owned by more than one individual, each of whom received a share of any profits

4. Urbanization
   A. slowed the industrialization of the United States
   B. occurred primarily along the West Coast of the United States
   C. and industrialization stimulated one another
   D. would have progressed faster if industrialization had grown at a slower pace

5. In most of the major labor disputes that took place before 1900, the federal government
   A. supported organized labor
   B. maintained a completely laissez-faire attitude
   C. supported management
   D. claimed that strikes did not affect interstate trade and therefore did not become involved

6. Which was a major obstacle to the formation of labor unions in the United States during the period 1860–1900?
   A. prohibition of labor organizations by the Constitution
   B. general government support of management
   C. excellent working conditions in United States factories of the time
   D. status of factory workers as equal partners with management

7. A major reason for the passage of the Sherman Antitrust Act in 1890 was to
   A. encourage competition in business
   B. protect the rights and safety of workers
   C. promote free trade among nations
   D. raise protective tariffs in the United States

8. Methods used by management to combat the activities of unions included
   A. general strike
   B. blacklisting
   C. antitrust legislation
   D. the injunction

9. An event that hurt unions and caused many Americans to associate labor with anarchism and socialism was the
   A. Triangle Shirtwaist fire
   B. candidacy of Eugene V. Debs for President in 1912
   C. formation of the National Women's Trade Union
   D. Haymarket Square incident

10. During the 20th century, labor unions in the United States were most strengthened by legislation that guaranteed workers
   A. the right to boycott
   B. the right to bargain collectively
   C. adequate retirement pensions
   D. a share of company profits

ESSAYS

1. Many aspects of United States society have been greatly affected by technological changes.

   Choose *three* of the aspects of United States society listed below. Explain how *each* one chosen has been affected by a specific technological development. (Use a different development for each aspect.)

   Aspects of United States Society
   Urbanization
   Industrialization
   Agriculture
   Politics
   Environment
   Rights of the individual

2. The position or status of workers in the United States has been influenced by a wide variety of factors.

   Factors
   Immigration
   Labor Unions
   Government Action
   Technology

   Choose *three* factors from the list above. For *each* one chosen, show how that factor has influenced the economic and/or social and/or political position of workers in the United States. Use specific information to support your discussion of each factor.

3. The concept of due process helps to guarantee that all "persons" receive justice before the law.
   a. Using the Supreme Court cases of *Santa Clara County* v. *Southern Pacific Railway* (1886) and *Chicago, Milwaukee & St. Paul Railway Co.* v. *Minnesota* (1890), show how the Supreme Court furthered the concept of due process in the legal system of the United States.
   b. Discuss the impact of the two cases mentioned in part a. (*Santa Clara* and *Chicago, Milwaukee & St. Paul Railway*) have had on corporations and their development.

THEMATIC ESSAY

Directions: Write a well-organized essay that includes an introduction, several paragraphs addressing the task below, and a conclusion.

Theme: Third Party and Local Political Movements Have Been an Important Factor in the Democratic Process.

> Problems faced by farmers in the expanding industrial economy of the late 1800s led to the formation of local political movements and the development of third parties.

Task:

> From your study of the period of agrarian protest (1870–1890), identify *two* political movements formed to address problems faced by farmers.
>
> For each movement identified:
>
> - State one issue viewed as a problem by the political movement.
> - Discuss what farmers saw as the cause of the problem.
> - Describe legislation or court decisions that resulted in addressing the problem.
> - Discuss the success or failure of the legislation or court decisions.

You may use any political movements and resulting legislation and/or court decisions. Some suggestions you may wish to consider regarding political movements and third parties include the Greenback party, National Grange of the Patrons of Husbandry, Populist party, and Farmer's Alliances. Legislation and/or court decisions may include the Interstate Commerce Act (1887), Sherman Silver Purchase Act (1890), *Munn* v. *Illinois* (1877), and *Wabash, St. Louis and Pacific Railway* v. *Minnesota* (1886).

You are *not* limited to these suggestions.

DOCUMENT-BASED QUESTION ESSAY

The following questions (Part A and Part B) are based on the accompanying documents (1–6). Some of these documents have been edited for the purpose of this exercise. The question is designed to test your ability to work with historical documents and to demonstrate your knowledge of the subject matter being presented. As you analyze the documents, take into account both the source of the document and the author's point of view.

Historical Context: The rise of American business and industry during the second half of the 18th century.

Task: Using information from the documents and your knowledge of United States history, answer the questions that follow each document in Part A. Your answers to the questions will help you write the Part B essay, in which you will be asked:

> The second half of the 19th century was one of economic transformation in the American experience. Using the issues identified in the documents (for example, increased governement involvement in economics, varying economic theories), discuss why this is an accurate statement.

Part A
Short Answer

The documents below relate to the rise of American business and industry during the late 1800s. Examine each document carefully and then answer the questions that follow.

DOCUMENT 1

> Let us inquire for a moment what are the proper functions of government, and how far, if at all, it may interfere with the natural laws governing commerce, manufactures, and agriculture.....When these general functions are exceeded the result is generally injurious to government. It is better always to leave individual enterprise to do most that is to be done in the country.

—Daniel Knowlton, New York City Merchant, September 27, 1883

1. How are the opinions of the New York City merchant consistent with the concept of laissez-faire?

_____

_____

_____

DOCUMENT 2

> The argument is that....in the exercise of the power to regulate commerce, Congress may suppress such monopoly directly and set aside the instruments which have created it......

—Chief Justice M.W. Fuller, *United States* v. *E.C. Knight Company* (sugar refining company) (1895)

2. Chief Justice Fuller found that Congress had the power to regulate monopolies. Under what Constitutional provision did Chief Justice Fuller find Congress' power to regulate monopolies?

_____

_____

_____

DOCUMENT 3

The "Gospel of Wealth" but echoes Christ's words. It calls upon the millionaire to sell all that he hath and give it in the highest and best form to the poor, by administering his estate himself for the good of his fellows, before he is called upon to lie down and rest upon the bosom of Mother Earth. So doing, he will approach his end no longer the ignoble hoarder of useless millions, poor, very poor indeed, in money, but rich, very rich, twenty times the millionaire still, in the affection, gratitude, and admiration of his fellow-men....

—Andrew Carnegie, *The Best Fields of Philanthropy*, December, 1889

3. Andrew Carnegie was one of 4,047 millionaires in the United States in 1892 who had amassed wealth through industry, trade, and the railroads. According to his thoughts expressed above, what was the best use of the millionaire's fortunes?

_____

_____

_____

DOCUMENT 4

	Growth of Manufacturers in the United States (includes all factories, hand, and neighborhood establishments) (in thousands)			
Year	Number of Establishments	Wage Earners	Value of Products	Amount of Capital Invested
1859	140	1,311	$ 1,886,000	$1,009,000
1869	252	2,054	3,386,000	2,118,000
1879	254	2,733	5,370,000	2,790,000
1889	355	4,252	9,372,000	—
1899	512	5,306	13,014,000	9,835,000

4. According to the chart concerning manufacturing growth between 1859 and 1899, the largest amount of capital invested was during what year?

_____

5. The amount of capital invested increased approximately how many times between 1859 and 1899?

_____

DOCUMENT 5

In the late 19th and early 20th centuries, socialists throughout the world were under the spell of Marx's seemingly impregnable analysis....The United States was undeniably a rising industrial colossus with a pronounced tendency toward industrial monopoly. Marx's theory of capitalistic accumulation and concentration surely applied to the American republic. Yet....there had not come into being, for example, a sizable class-conscious proletariat dedicated to the overthrow of capitalism; the economic well-being of American industrial workers was not deteriorating, but improving;...the middle class was expanding, and the Socialist Party....had not made a significant dent in the traditional party loyalties of American voters.

—Professor Howard H. Quint, University of Massachusetts

6. According to Professor Quint, what were the reasons that Marxist socialism did not become deeply rooted in the American political and economic system in the late 1800s?

_____

_____

DOCUMENT 6

Percentage Distribution of Gainfully Occupied Persons 16 Years of Age and Over, 1870–1900				
Occupation Group	1870	1880	1890	1900
Agriculture and allied occupations	52.8	48.1	41.2	35.9
Mining	1.5	1.6	1.8	2.1
Manufacturing and mechanical industries	22.0	24.8	26.3	27.5
Trade and transportation	9.1	10.7	13.6	16.3
Clerical services	1.7	2.0	2.5	2.8
Domestic and personal service	9.6	8.8	9.7	10.0
Public service not elsewhere classifed	.6	.7	.9	1.0
Professional service	2.7	3.3	4.0	4.4
TOTAL	100.0	100.0	100.0	100.0

7. According to the chart, what was the trend of the percentage of persons employed in agricultural positions compared to the number of persons employed in manufacturing and mechanical industries?

_____

_____

Part B
Essay

Your essay should be well organized with an introductory paragraph that states your position on the question. Develop your position in the next paragraphs and then write a conclusion. In your essay, include specific historical details and refer to the specific documents you analyzed in Part A. You may include additional information from your knowledge of social studies.

Historical Context: The rise of American business and industry during the second half of the 18th century.

Task:

> The above-referenced documents address varying aspects of the transformation. Using the issues identified in the documents (for example, increased government involvement in economics, industrial leaders, varying economic theories, statistical information), discuss why this is an accurate statement.
>
> The second half of the 19th century was one of economic transformation in the American experience.

Guidelines:

In your essay, be sure to
• Develop all aspects of the task
• Incorporate information from at least *five* documents
• Incorporate relevant outside information
• Support the theme with many relevant facts, examples, and details
• Use a logical and clear plan of organization, including an introduction and a conclusion that are beyond a restatement of the theme

CHAPTER 3

ADJUSTING SOCIETY TO INDUSTRIALISM: AMERICAN PEOPLE AND PLACES

IMPACT OF INDUSTRIALISM

Urbanization and the Quality of Urban Life

Between the Civil War and 1910, the urban population increased dramatically. In addition to the general increase in the number of people living in cities—from about 6.2 million to 42 million—during the period from 1860–1910, there was also an extraordinary expansion in the size of large cities such as New York, Philadelphia, and Chicago.

Attractions of the City

People moved to the cities because they offered opportunity. In the urban centers there were jobs in offices and factories, employment for both the skilled and the unskilled. American cities became marketplaces for people, resources, and ideas and centers of transportation, communication, and capital.

Cities also became centers of educational and cultural institutions. In some instances, business leaders accepted the responsibility for using their wealth and resources to improve urban communities. During his lifetime, Andrew Carnegie gave $60 million to help cities establish free public libraries. Wealthy leaders of industry, including John D. Rockefeller, Matthew Vassar, and Cornelius Vanderbilt, founded or endowed colleges and universities. Others, including Andrew Mellon and J.P. Morgan, built extensive art collections, which were eventually opened to the public.

Problems of the Cities

As the American city grew, so did its problems, especially widespread poverty among city residents. Fast-spreading **slums** housed masses of low-income workers. In 1893 there were 702 people per acre in New York's Lower East Side. Poor workers lived in tenements and small apartments that lacked adequate space, safety, or sanitation.

Inadequate **sanitation** and the spread of disease became a by-product of rapid urban growth. By the 1870s few American cities had installed underground sewers, relying instead on cesspools.

Crime, though not exclusively an urban affliction, flourished in the slums of urban areas with their poverty and overcrowding. The fifty percent increase in the prison population between 1880 and 1890 reflected the fact that crime had become a way of life in American cities. Police forces were still at an infant stage and in some cases easily corrupted by various interest groups.

City Architecture

Housing was a pressing problem in most rapidly growing urban centers. With the lack of adequate transportation, workers were forced to live near their jobs no matter how poor and congested the buildings were. The growth of tenements and the terrible sanitary conditions that caused outbreaks of disease eventually forced the passage of Tenement House laws.

The growth of structures in the downtown areas of the city was extraordinary. The concentration of business and professional offices along with the inflation of real estate value made tall buildings inevitable. The development of wrought iron, then steel, and finally the discovery that walls themselves could be supported on steel columns embedded in them allowed **skyscrapers** to grow in height. Finally, the development of the **elevator** allowed architects to overcome the problem of access to higher levels of the building.

Social Darwinism

The publication of *The Origin of Species* in 1859 by the Englishman **Charles Darwin** marked a major step in the **theory of evolution**. It proposed that many more individuals of each species are born than can possibly survive. As a consequence, there is a constant struggle for existence, and only the fittest survive. Social Darwinism affected American political thought by delaying legislation that required factory inspection, the limitation of work hours, and other protective measures.

• *Unequal Distribution of Wealth.* Along with industrial expansion and the growth of American cities came a growing gap between the rich and the poor. As the national wealth increased from $16 billion to $65 billion between 1860 and 1890, the distribution of wealth grew more uneven, with fewer Americans controlling more of the nation's wealth. By 1890 only 9 percent of the population owned 71 percent of the nation's money and 88 percent owned only 14 percent. Yet those who advocated Social Darwinism held that the capable would rise to the top and that eventually the wealth would seep down to the masses in the form of greater employment opportunities.

- *Philanthropy.* The philanthropic activities of the wealthy were consistent with Social Darwinism. Adhering to the laissez-faire beliefs that government should not pass welfare legislation, some of the wealthy believed they had a social responsibility to assist those who were less fortunate.

- *Calls for Reform.* With the unequal balance of wealth and power, it seemed that the rich were growing richer and the poor, poorer. As the growing poverty of America's workers became increasingly apparent, many called for public and private relief that was not forthcoming. Movements for reform were spurred by the humanitarian concerns reflected in literature (*How the Other Half Lives,* Jacob Riis, 1890, *The Bitter Cry of Children,* John Spargo, 1906, *Progress and Poverty,* Henry George, 1879). Early efforts to help included the **Society for the Prevention of Cruelty to Children** (1874), settlement houses such as **Hull House** in Chicago, founded in 1889 by Jane Addams to offer social services, and the establishment of religious institutions such as the **Young Men's Christian Association** (1851), the **Salvation Army** (1879), and city missions.

Work and Workers

Peopling the Cities

Prior to 1870 relatively few Americans were wage earners. The United States was still primarily an agricultural nation, with most Americans owning farms. By 1900, as a result of the Industrial Revolution, the transfer of America's population to the cities and the growing employment in factories, about two thirds of the working population were selling their labor to employers for a daily or weekly wage.

The flow of workers to the cities came from two sources; first, the movement of large numbers of native-born Americans from the rural areas and second, the thousands of immigrants from Europe who settled in the cities where they found employment opportunities. The growth of American industry and the absence of restrictions on immigration drew a steady stream of immigrants, which reached its peak in 1907 when 1,285,000 immigrant entries were recorded.

Working Conditions

Gone were the days when workers and employers maintained an intimate and caring relationship. The impersonal relationship between labor and management was a direct result of the urban factory system and led to deteriorating conditions for the average wage earner. Long hours, low wages, child labor, and dangerous working conditions were common during the 19th century when **collective bargaining** was nearly nonexistent and **unions** were looked upon as conspiracies. As the pool of workers increased with the flow of native-born Americans and immigrants to the cities, the plight of workers grew worse. Although the Thirteenth Amendment (1865) had ended "slavery and involuntary servitude except as punishment for a crime," the employees of the factory system were becoming "wage slaves" of industrial America.

A related problem was that of **child labor**. By 1870 many of the nation's industrial workers were children, under the age of twelve. Working in the factories brought problems for children including lack of education, emotional disruption, family breakdown, and physical abuse. Working from "dark to dark," children toiled six days a week earning little for 12- to 13-hour shifts.

The Working-Class Family

Industrialization also brought changes in the American family. The participation of family members in outside institutions, including schools, political organizations, social clubs, and places of employment replaced some of the companionship that had existed in the rural household. As mother and father each became wage earners, usually out of economic necessity, broken families were sometimes the result. At the turn of the century, the majority of American households consisted of the nuclear family—a married couple with or without children, living with no other relatives. About 15 to 20 percent of households were made up of extended families—households with grandparents, grandchildren, aunts, uncles, cousins, or in-laws.

Ethnic and Racial Impact on Workers

American labor was affected by society's feelings concerning race and ethnic differences. Few labor leaders welcomed blacks into labor unions, the **Industrial Workers of the World** being the exception. Immigration, both early (consisting mostly of northern Europeans), and later (made up primarily of eastern and southern Europeans), provided labor competition that kept wages low and hampered unions' attempts to organize.

Women and the Industrial Age

With the new Industrial Age, the Victorian ideal of women as the pampered and weaker sex quickly disappeared in American society. In early colonial America, women worked as hard as their husbands to build families and homesteads on the frontier. Success in colonial life required a partnership between the sexes. Although life was hard and women did not have equal political rights, they had more equality with men during these times because of the common goal of survival. As conditions became more settled and life easier, women lost their equal status. By the early 1800s most women stayed home to tend to household chores and to raise the family, "protected" from the demands of education, politics, and business.

From Home to Factory

With the arrival of new inventions in the early part of the 19th century, some women began to work away from the home. **Textile mills** in New England provided the earliest industrial opportunities for women to enter the work force. Yet, factory work proved to be a mixed blessing, since women were often exploited and usually hired at wages far below those paid to men doing similar work. Throughout the 19th century the supply of women looking for work increased with the arrival of immigrants from Europe. Employers who had little trouble finding replacements for those women dissatisfied with pay and working conditions were able to impose wage cuts and work speedups. In 1870 women who worked in mills earned $5 to $6 for a 60-hour week, while those who did sewing piecework at home received about 6 cents per shirt and earned little more than $3 per week.

Technology and Women

In the late 1800s, business expansion and new inventions, including the type-writer and telephone, brought about an increasing need for office workers with special skills. Since these jobs were usually filled by women, education became more important; by 1890 twice as many young women were finishing high school as young men.

A profession that welcomed women throughout the 1800s was **teaching**. By the 1890s there were twice as many women teaching as men. Women teachers in city schools earned about $13 a week, while men teachers received two to three times that amount.

Religion in a Diversified Society

As poverty, urban overcrowding, and social disorder increased during this age of government laissez-faire, religious groups joined social reformers in attempting to ease society's problems. Emphasizing social responsibility as a means to salvation and service to fellow human beings as a Christian duty, religious reformers built churches in slum neighborhoods, provided community services, and joined drives to make businesses socially responsible.

The Growing Middle Class

Industrialism helped to create a growing middle class consisting of salaried workers, professionals, salespeople, government workers, and the like. A transformation was taking place in the lives of many Americans, in their homes, work, and leisure time.

Standards of Cultural Values

The buying power of the growing middle class fueled further industrial growth. Goods that had once been available only to a few were becoming available to many. American inventiveness, combined with technology, mass production, and mass marketing, provided goods such as ready-made clothes and home appliances—necessities rather than the luxury they had once been.

Middle-Class Materialism and Morality

As luxuries were being transformed into commonplace articles of everyday life, the difference between those who could afford such goods and services and those who could not became accentuated. As the turn of the century approached, incomes continued to rise. For example, the average yearly pay of a clerical worker rose from $848 a year in 1890 to $1,156 a year in 1910. But as wages increased, the cost of living also rose. For most ordinary workers, it was becoming harder to pay for even the necessities. As the concerns of the working class, middle class, and farmers—the group often referred to as the "common man," "taxpayer," or "man on the street"—began to coincide, they joined to support the Progressive Movement that began in the 1900s.

Leisure Activities

Along with industrialism and the development of laborsaving devices in the factory and at home came a greater amount of leisure time for some

Americans. The average work week for manufacturing workers decreased from 66 hours per week in 1860 to 51 hours per week in 1920. The most popular leisure activities were sports. By 1860 there were at least 50 baseball clubs in the country; football became the most popular collegiate sport; and cycling, tennis, golf, and basketball were also enjoyed. Of course it was the wealthy, with more free time and money to spend on sporting activities, who were able to take the greatest advantage of America's leisure-time revolution.

As they worked fewer hours, Americans had more time for leisure activities.

Art and Literature

Although critics have characterized the post-Civil War era as the "Gilded Age," suggesting crassness and lack of taste in a materialistic society, progress in art and literature was noteworthy.

Literature

As the degree of literacy in America increased, book reading by all levels of society increased. The popular press was reflected in the "dime novels" (low-priced, paperbound adventure novels about the wild West), detective stories, and science fiction, which became favorites of America's young people. Leading dime novels included stories of The Lone Ranger, Old Cap Collins, and Tom Swift.

"Local-color" writers produced regional literature, which depicted the people and environment of a particular region of the country. Bret Harte wrote about the West *(The Outcasts of Poker Flat)*, **Mark Twain** wrote of the South *(The Adventures of Tom Sawyer, The Adventures of Huckleberry Finn)*, and **Jack London** wrote of the West and Northwest *(The Call of the Wild)*.

Art

The Society of American Artists was formed in 1877 to organize and popularize a new trend in American art: the breaking away from the romanticized works of the earlier generation. Among the new school of American artists were George Inness, a leading landscapist, Winslow Homer, whose art was best demonstrated in his bold paintings of the sea, and James A. McNeill Whistler, painter of realistic portraits. The development of photography helped to free the early American painters from realism and led to impressionism and abstract art.

Music

American music reached its greatest stage of development later in the 20th century. The later 19th century saw the spread of musical appreciation with the formation of the New York Symphony Orchestra in 1878 and the Boston Symphony Orchestra in 1881. A major discovery in the area of music was the reproduction of music by mechanical means. By 1900 over 150,000 American homes had a **phonograph**, an invention of Thomas Edison.

Role of Philanthropists

Cynically described as those who "stole privately and gave publicly," the **"robber barons,"** including **John Rockefeller** and **Andrew Carnegie**, gave considerable amounts of money for the development of cultural centers promoting art, music, and education.

Exercise Set 2.10

1. The trend toward urbanization involved
   A. the growth of rural America due to the unsafe conditions of the city
   B. the movement of people from rural areas into the cities
   C. decrease in metropolitan population
   D. a decrease in immigration

2. Urban political bosses and machines in the latter part of the 19th century
   A. took advantage of the needs of newly arrived immigrants
   B. contributed nothing to their cities
   C. were closely regulated by civil service organizations
   D. had little influence in urban politics

3. The belief concerning poverty that was consistent with Social Darwinism was that
   A. the poor were weak individuals
   B. the federal government had the responsibility of assuring economic equality
   C. systems of public welfare and relief had to be implemented to ease the hardships of the poor
   D. the problems of the poor were the fault of the wealthy

NATION OF IMMIGRANTS

> All of our people all over the country—except the pure-blooded Indians—are immigrants, including even those who came over here on the Mayflower.
>
> Franklin Delano Roosevelt,
> November 4, 1944

The heterogeneous nature of the American population throughout our history has been due to the continual influx of various immigrant groups. The American pluralistic society consists of many subdivisions known as **ethnic groups**, identified by race, religion, places of origin, culture, and history.

Old Immigration (1609–1860)

Motivations

Early immigration to North America came primarily from northern and western Europe. Settlers from the British Isles included English, Irish, Scots, and Welsh. Among the settlers from continental Europe were the Germans, Dutch, Swiss, Swedes, and French.

During the period of "colonial immigration" (1609–1789) most settlers came to the American colonies for one or more of the following reasons: desire for land, political strife at home, religious persecution, or economic opportunities. In the latter part of the old immigration period (1780–1860), motivations for immigration included the availability of land as the United States expanded westward, jobs provided by the early stages of the Industrial Revolution, and opportunities for social mobility that did not exist in Europe. Problems in Europe also encouraged emigration. Political and religious unrest in Germany, France, Austria, Hungary, Ireland, and Denmark during the middle of the 1600s increased rates of emigration. Between 1789 and 1815 Europe was ravaged by the French Revolution and Napoleonic Wars, while in the 1830s revolutions spread through Poland, France, and Belgium. Between 1845 and 1849 Ireland experienced a devastating famine. The European population doubled between 1750 and 1850 and emigration restrictions were relaxed in a number of nations. Improved transportation facilitated the movement of those who wanted to emigrate. Moreover, portions of our diverse population were acquired through conquest and annexation, including the French population of the lower Louisiana Territory and the Spanish population of the Southwest.

Indentured Servants and Forced African Immigration

In the English colonies labor was scarce and most newcomers were unwilling to work for others, because it was easy to acquire land and become independent farmers.

One answer to the labor shortage problem was the use of **indentured servants**. Europeans who lacked the funds to pay for their transportation to America (poor and landless farmers, unemployed and low-paid workers, debtors) were able to sign indentures, or contracts, in which they agreed to work from 4 to 7 years in exchange for their passage to America. Once they had fulfilled the terms of their indentures, they were free to find independent employment. Indentured servants accounted for nearly 80 percent of the 130,000 settlers in the Virginia and Maryland colonies in the 17th century.

Between 1492 and 1770 more **Africans** than Europeans came to the New World, most of them settling in the Caribbean and in South America. However, they were brought in chains against their will. At first, most slaves were brought to the English colonies from the Caribbean islands, but as time passed, they were imported directly from Africa. By the 1660s most blacks in the colonies were legally held as slaves, numbering approximately 400,000 by 1775. The English settlers justified slavery, a tradition that did not exist in England, with the **ethnocentric** belief that fair-skinned people like themselves were superior to dark-skinned races, and with the economic need for labor in the colonies.

Early Nativism

In the early years of settlement, there was little opposition to immigration because labor was needed in the growing country. Moreover, most immigrants to the United States who came from northern and western Europe **assimilated** easily. One group, formed in the 1850s, that supported nativism, or favored native-born Americans and opposed immigration, was the American party, commonly known as the "**Know-Nothing**" **party**. Much of their opposition was directed at Irish and German immigrants who, they claimed, threatened native labor by taking jobs, were clannish, and failed to quickly assimilate. But the most important source of conflict between Protestant native-born Americans and immigrants was religion, specifically objections to Irish Catholics. Many feared that if the Catholics "took over" America, the Pope in Rome would rule, and religious and political liberty would be destroyed. Goals of the American party were the limitation of political officeholding to native-born Americans, a 21-year residency requirement for naturalization, and greater restrictions on immigration.

Ethnic Distribution (1820–1930)

Between 1820 and 1930 more than 37 million immigrants came to the United States, mostly from Europe. While most came from northern and western Europe prior to 1880, most came later from southern and eastern Europe. Figure 2.4 illustrates the geographic distribution of immigration to the United States during these years.

Decade	Germany	Ireland	England, Scotland, Wales	Scandinavia	Italy	Austro-Hungary	Russia & Baltic States	Totals
1820	968	3,614	2,410	23	30		14	7,059
1821–30	6,761	50,724	25,079	260	409		75	83,308
1831–40	152,454	207,654	75,810	2,264	2,253		277	440,712
1841–50	434,626	780,719	267,044	13,122	1,970		551	1,498,032
1851–60	951,657	914,119	423,929	24,680	9,231		457	2,324,073
1861–70	827,468	435,697	607,076	126,392	11,725	7,800	2,515	2,018,673
1871–80	718,182	436,871	548,043	242,934	55,795	72,969	39,287	2,114,081
1881–90	1,452,970	655,540	807,357	655,494	307,309	362,719	213,282	4,454,671
1891–1900	505,152	388,416	271,538	371,512	651,873	574,069	505,281	3,267,841
1901–10	341,498	339,065	525,950	505,324	2,045,877	2,145,266	1,597,308	7,500,288
1911–20	143,945	146,199	314,408	123,452	1,209,524	901,656	921,957	3,841,141
1921–30	412,202	220,564	330,168	98,210	455,315	214,806	89,423	1,920,688
Totals	5,947,883	4,579,182	4,198,812	2,343,667	4,751,311	4,279,285	3,370,427	

Figure 2.4 Immigration to America (1820–1930)

New Immigration (1870–1930)

New Sources

Emigration from southern and eastern Europe at the end of the 19th century affected cities worldwide. Although cities like Warsaw, Berlin, Vienna, Naples, and London received new immigrants, the United States, with its higher standard of living and reputation for being a land of opportunity, received the bulk of the new immigrants. Between 1880 and 1930 over 27 million immigrants came to the United States, many to Ellis Island in New York Harbor. The new immigration included Italians, Greeks, Jews, Poles, Rumanians, and those emigrating from the Austro-Hungarian Empire and Russia.

Reasons for Immigration

The "new immigrants" sought to escape the same economic problems that had caused many earlier immigrants to leave their homelands in northern and western Europe. Unemployment, high birth rates, overpopulation, and epidemics of malaria and cholera drove many southern Italians abroad, for example. The easing of immigration restrictions and faster, less expensive transportation made immigration into the United States a more viable option for many.

Attractions of the United States

America's greatest attraction was the opportunity for social mobility through economic opportunities not available in Europe and Asia. America's rapidly growing industries continually needed inexpensive labor, and the numerous foreign immigrants provided the necessary hands. As older immigrants were less likely to tolerate the deteriorating working conditions of unregulated industrial expansion, Slavs and Italians replaced British, Irish, and Germans in coal mines, while Portuguese, Greeks, and Italians found employment in New England textile mills. East European Jews took jobs formerly held by the Irish and Germans in New York City's garment factories, and the Japanese on the West Coast replaced many Chinese in agricultural and service tasks.

America's democratic and constitutional form of government, allowing for civil liberties and political freedoms not available in many European countries, was a strong attraction. Those persecuted in other countries, as the Jews were in Russia, were able to combat discrimination in their new home with the formation of constitutionally protected groups such as the **B'nai B'rith Anti-Defamation League**.

Urbanization and the Ghetto

As the decades following the Civil War saw increased immigration, many large cities developed a patchwork of ethnic neighborhoods. The new immigrants settled together in ghettos called "Little Germany," "Little Italy," and so on, where they clung to their own language and customs. Because immigrants felt more comfortable working and living among friends and relatives, ethnic groups concentrated in particular industries and locations.

Americanization Process

Most new Americans experienced stages of change as the "Americanization process" took place. The first stage, especially with the later immigrants from southern and eastern Europe, usually included discrimination by native-born Americans. Many times, these immigrants were excluded from better residential areas, received little protection in employment, and were belittled.

As immigrants began to adopt the ways of American society—the English language, an understanding of the legal system and government and its customs and traditions—they experienced the stage of acculturation, or the adaptation to the American culture.

A later stage of Americanization occurred when the immigrant was finally absorbed into American society. This is known as the stage of assimilation, which usually does not occur until the second or third generation of immigrant families.

Contributions of Immigrants to American Society

Most immigrants came to the United States seeking political, economic, and social freedom. As a result, they have continued to contribute to the American democratic heritage and its preservation. The rich cultural heritage that came to the United States with different groups of immigrants has continued to add to our heterogeneous society.

Notable immigrants:

Business: Andrew Carnegie (Scotland), James J. Hill (Canada), Eleuthère Irenee Du Pont (France)

Science: John Audubon (Haiti), Alexander Graham Bell (Scotland), Albert Einstein (Germany), Enrico Fermi (Italy), Isador Rabi (Austria)

Government and Law: Felix Frankfurter (Austria), Thomas Paine (Great Britain), John Peter Altgeld (Germany), Carl Schurz (Germany), Albert Gallatin (Switzerland)

Music: Igor Stravinsky (Russia), Hans Kindler (Holland), Bruno Walter (Germany), Victor Herbert (Ireland), Arturo Toscanini (Italy), Artur Rodzinski (Yugoslavia)

Literature and Journalism: Jacob Riis (Denmark), Joseph Pulitzer (Hungary), Thomas Nast (Germany), John Peter Zenger (Germany), Peter F. Collier (Ireland), Ole Rolvaag (Norway), Louis Adamic (Yugoslavia)

Reaction to the "New" Immigration

Cultural Pluralism

The long held concept of the "melting pot" suggested that all immigrants absorb the aspects of a uniform American culture and, as a result, become "Americanized." However, in reality, the patterns of acculturation and assimilation have not produced such homogeneous results. Although American society does have a homogeneous core including the English language, a democratic political system, and uniform economic institutions, our society is at the same time quite heterogeneous. Although different ethnic groups become Americanized, they also maintain a degree of their cultural heritage. This idea of "cultural pluralism," rather than a pure melting pot, was first expressed in 1915 by the Jewish-American philosopher Horace Kallen in his articles entitled "Democracy Versus the Melting Pot."

Nativist Reactions

Ironically, although the majority of the original settlers and immigrants to the English colonies and early United States came for economic opportunity, political freedom, and religious freedom, they lacked tolerance for anyone who deviated significantly from themselves. Americans of every generation have feared that newcomers would subvert established customs and undermine the traditions of society. Opposition to immigrants began toward the Scotch-Irish and Germans in the middle of the 19th century, followed by discrimination against Italians, Chinese, Jews, Poles, and Japanese at the turn of the century, and Mexicans, Puerto Ricans, Latin Americans, and Vietnamese in the 20th century. Native-born Americans have demonstrated "nativism" toward immigrants of minority groups who have deviated from the dominant culture. Stereotyping, or a fixed conception of groups, became a common form of discrimination.

Nativist groups discriminated against individuals because of race, religion, political beliefs, and economic fears. In 1887 the **American Protective Association** was founded, based on anti-Catholicism. The **Ku Klux Klan** originated as primarily an anti-black organization during the Civil War era and resurfaced as an anti-Semitic, anti-Catholic, anti-immigrant group in the 20th century. White workers in 1877 organized the **Workingmen's party** in California as an anti-Chinese organization based primarily on economic fears and racism. Pressures from nativists helped lead to legislation early in the 1920s designed to keep those with "radical" political beliefs from entering the country.

Nativist discrimination against minority groups, including black Americans, has had numerous effects, perhaps the greatest being economic. Although **affirmative action** legislation has attempted to remedy this trend, minority groups continue to remain at the lower end of the economic scale in the United States.

Legislation	Provisions	Causes
Chinese Exclusion Act (1882)	Restricted Chinese immigration for a 10-year period	Racism, economic fears
Gentlemen's Agreement (1907)	Japan persuaded to deny passports to those who wanted to emigrate	"Yellow Peril" racism, economic fears
Literacy Test (1917)	Immigrant required to pass literacy test in either English or another language	To keep out immigrants from eastern and southern Europe; most immigrants from northern and western Europe were literate
Immigration Act of 1921	Quota system set at 3% of total of that nationality in U.S. in 1910; general limit of 350,000 immigrants per year	Fear of Bolshevism (quota reduced immigration from eastern and southern Europe)
Immigration Act of 1924	Lowered quota set in 1921 to 2% and set base year at 1890	As nativisim grew, greater cutbacks desired
Immigration Act of 1927	Congress set limit to 150,000 immigrants per year with most from western and northern Europe and virtually no Asians	Continued nativism and desire for racial purity
National Origins System of 1929	No more annually than 150,000 from outside Western Hemisphere; quotas enacted based upon numbers in 1920; no restrictions on immigration from Western Hemisphere; prohibited all immigration from Asian countries	Extreme post World War I nativism
Refugee and Displaced Persons Acts (1940s–50s)	Provisions to admit immigrants (refugees) from Nazi Germany and later from eastern Europe	Exceptions made by Congress consistent with U.S. foreign policy

Figure 2.5 Immigration Restrictions (1882–1929)

Legislation	Provisions	Causes
McCarran-Walter Act of 1952	Annual total of 156,000 immigrants with quota on those from outside of the Western Hemisphere; 2,000 yearly from Far East; and screening for Communists	"McCarthy Era," fear of Communism
Immigration Act of 1965	Ended quota system; set annual number from outside Western Hemisphere at 170,000; 120,000 from within Western Hemisphere; preference for those with "special talents" and relatives	Improvement on earlier acts claimed to be racist and unfair

Figure 2.5 continued   Immigration Restrictions (1882–1929)

Immigration Restrictions

On a number of occasions in our history, Congress has responded to nativist sentiments with the passage of restrictive legislation. Figure 2.5 provides a listing of the major restrictive legislation passed by Congress during the 1800s and 1900s.

The immigration restriction acts of the 1920s, combined with the depression of the 1930s, drastically lowered the numbers of foreigners coming to American shores. Only 23,068 came in 1933, 28,470 in 1934, and 34,956 in 1935.

Exercise Set 2.11

1. Which is the main way that ethnic groups in the United States have helped to shape the national identity?
   A. most of the newer groups have blended in and adopted the ways of earlier immigrants
   B. each group kept cultural characteristics that became part of the general culture
   C. each group attempted to become the dominant force in society
   D. ethnic groups made large financial contributions in support of the arts in the United States

2. The immigration laws of the 1920s were noteworthy because they
   A. satisfied the Chinese and Japanese governments
   B. limited immigrants to 25,000 per year
   C. encouraged immigration from eastern and southern Europe
   D. established systems of quotas designating specific numbers of immigrants from different countries

3. Which of the following immigrant groups assimilated with the greatest ease?
   A. the Irish in the 1850s
   B. the Chinese in the 1880s
   C. the English in the 1920s
   D. the Vietnamese in the 1970s

4. Which of the following statements is true about immigration to the United States during the last two decades of the 19th century?
   A. United States immigration laws sharply reduced the number of eligible immigrants
   B. nativist objection to immigration drastically reduced the numbers of foreigners coming to the United States
   C. quotas were placed on immigrant groups coming from the Western Hemisphere
   D. many immigrants of this period faced problems in assimilating into American society

5. The hostility of the Know-Nothing party was aimed primarily at
   A. slaveholders
   B. Protestants from northern Europe
   C. Irish and German Catholic immigrants
   D. labor unions

6. A major reason that no significant restrictions were placed on immigration to the United States before the end of the 19th century was that
   A. the American economy was in need of additional workers
   B. there were no signs of nativist objections to immigrants before the 20th century
   C. the numbers of immigrants coming to the United States continued to decrease as the 19th century came to a close
   D. European and Asian nations halted all emigration

THE LAST FRONTIER

> The result is that to the frontier the American intellect owes its striking characteristics . . . that restless, nervous energy; that dominant individualism, working for good and evil, and with all that buoyancy and exuberance which comes from freedom—these are the traits of the frontier.
>
> Frederick Jackson Turner,
> *The Significance of the Frontier in American History* (1894)

The Significance of the Frontier in American History, an essay by University of Wisconsin professor **Frederick Jackson Turner**, was read to a conference of historians in connection with the World's Fair in Chicago in 1893 and presented a new theory to the age-old question, "What is the American?" Professor Turner, contemplating the effects of the closing frontier, proposed that one of the major differences between European and American civilization was that the American was in part the product of the distinctive environment of the New World. The "free land" offered by a continuing westward moving frontier offered hopes of economic gain and adventure, changed the social stratification that typified European society, demanded new political institutions, changed traditional economic practices to meet the demands of self-sufficiency, and gradually produced an "Americanization" of the society that was making up the United States. Although the simplicity of Turner's thesis has been criticized over the years, the operation of the frontier process still remains a well-respected explanation of the development of the American character.

Land West of the Mississippi

By the early 1800s the "American West" continued to move as the white frontier advanced beyond the Mississippi River. The nation gained new territory with the purchase of the **Louisiana Territory** (1803), the annexation of Texas (1845), the acquisition of the **Oregon Country** through a treaty with Great Britain (1846), the **Mexican Cession** by treaty with Mexico (1848), and the **Gadsden Purchase** from Mexico (1853), fulfilling the emotional drive for expansion (**manifest destiny**). (See Figure 1.18 on page 69, "Territorial Growth of the United States, 1783–1853.")

Native Americans

As the white population continued to press westward, the original settlers, the American Indians, were ruthlessly forced onto poorer lands or onto **reservations**. The newcomers who desired land for railroads, farms, and speculation could not tolerate the nomadic Indian who recognized no individual ownership of land. By 1873, white settlers, with the assistance of federal troops, had subdued most of the native population.

The Homestead Act (1862)

Passed by Congress during the Civil War, the Homestead Act provided 160 acres of federal land for settlers who would inhabit plots of land for at least five years. Problems with the Homestead Act included the inadequacy of the small plots and abuse by mining and timber companies who gained considerable amounts of free federal land by having employees put in claims for homesteads.

The Impact of Industrialization

Transportation

During the 1820s and 1830s trade routes in the United States began to indicate greater **East-West economic interdependency**. The transportation improvements of the 19th century helped connect the agricultural interests of the West with the markets of the East, and the industrial centers of the East with the growing need for manufactured goods of the West. The building of canals, the steamboat, the railroad, and the telegraph helped to open up the frontier and brought many farmers into the market economy. Self-sufficient farmers who at one time produced many agricultural products began to specialize in one or two crops.

Immigration

Increased immigration during the 19th century increased the market for agricultural goods in the Eastern cities. Immigrants also contributed to the growing population of Western territories and states. Both public and private interests in the West encouraged the migration of immigrants westward to promote their economies.

Investment Opportunities

Public and private investment and a growing population stimulated economic growth during the 19th century. Lucrative investment opportunities in the nation's growth encouraged investment by banks, insurance companies, corporations, and private individuals.

Development of Urban Centers

As the population of the United States increased, the frontier moved steadily westward and rural settlements became towns and cities. Early cities grew along major river routes (Cincinnati, Louisville, Pittsburgh) and along the shores of the Great Lakes (Cleveland, Chicago, Detroit). With the continued growth of the railroad and telegraph, new cities grew along major lines (Omaha, Kansas City, Denver, Salt Lake City, El Paso, Sacramento, Los Angeles).

Native Americans

Advancing White Settlement

White settlement took its toll on the Native American population almost immediately. The greatest destruction of the American Indian population started long before the infamous wars of the 1800s between Western settlers and the Plains Indians. Diseases carried from Europe killed hundreds of thousands of Native Americans who had no natural immunity to these germs. Most deadly of the diseases was smallpox, which drastically reduced the Indian population in the Caribbean, Central America, the English colonies, and Canada.

Legal Status and Treaties

Early on, the British settlers viewed the American Indian as a type of "savage"—an inferior race, much the same as they viewed the black African. During the colonial period, British policy toward the Indians was to slowly push them westward and avoid conflict. The **Proclamation of 1763** (preventing settlement west of the Appalachians) was passed to prevent friction with the native populations, a problem the financially strained British government could ill afford.

Once independence was gained, the United States government found that conflict with the "red man" was "inevitable." The **Northwest Ordinance** of 1787 called for the Indians to be treated in "good faith," and the **Treaty of Greenville** (1795) accepted Indian tribal sovereignty by virtue of their residence in part of the Northwest Territory. However, both provisions were eventually violated.

The Indians, exempted from taxation and not counted in apportionment of representation and taxes, possessed an indefinite status under the Constitution. During the 1820s the federal government urged the removal of the tribes to the West, and several states took independent action to remove the Indians. Congress passed the **Indian Removal Act of 1830**, which appropriated $500,000 for treaties to remove tribes, primarily in the Southeast, west of the Mississippi.

In 1827, following attempts by the state of Georgia to have them removed, the Cherokees of Georgia adopted a written constitution and declared themselves an independent state. In ***Cherokee Nation* v. *Georgia*** (1831) the Supreme Court held that, although the Cherokee Indians could not bring a suit in federal court, they had a right to their own land until the time they chose to voluntarily cede it to the United States. In ***Worcester v. Georgia*** (1832), the Supreme Court went further in stating that citizens of Georgia had no right to enter Cherokee lands without the consent of the Indians. President **Andrew Jackson**, who, as a general, had led the expedition against the Seminoles in Florida in 1818, had little sympathy for the Indians. Jackson refused to implement the Supreme Court's decisions and, with support from Congress (**Removal Act of 1830**), he ordered the removal of Indians to lands west of the Mississippi, starting with the Choctaw in 1831. In 1835 a minority group of Cherokees signed a treaty agreeing to exchange their land in Georgia for Western land. In 1838, when many Cherokees refused to move, President **Martin Van Buren** sent federal troops to force the Indians from their land and march them to Oklahoma. Nearly one quarter died of disease and exhaustion on this forced move, which has come to be known as the **Trail of Tears**.

Indian Wars (1850–1900)

Although early policy toward the Indians called for their resettlement west of the Mississippi River, by the 1840s the movement of whites to the West forced a change in policy. Government policy now called for the establishment of **Indian reservations**. The legal status of the Indian under the reservation system was that of a ward, or one under the care of the federal government. However, this did not bring peace because whites entered reservation land and the Indians found the reservations too confining after their nomadic lifestyle. Battles continued throughout the 19th century with cruelties and brutalities committed by both sides. The last occurred in 1890 when unarmed Teton Sioux of South Dakota were massacred by federal troops armed with Gatling guns at **Wounded Knee**, South Dakota. The final "taming" of the American Indian came with the destruction of the buffalo, or bison. Depended upon by the Plains Indians for survival, the buffalo became the white man's source of food, sport (buffalo hunters such as "Buffalo Bill" Cody), and leather, and 9 million bison were killed between 1872 and 1874.

Legislating Indian Life

Reform movements in the late 1800s urged change in federal policy toward the Indians and organizations such as the Indian Rights Association awakened concern. The aim of most reformers was to **assimilate** the Indians into white society. The **Dawes Severalty Laws** of 1887, providing for the division of Indian lands among individual families and citizenship to those Indians who abandoned tribal allegiances, was passed in hopes of accelerating assimilation. Unfortunately, the Dawes Act failed. Attempts at assimilation violated Indian traditions and under the act nearly one half of the Indian lands was lost to white settlement.

Partially in recognition of those Indians who had served in World War I, Congress passed the **Snyder Indian Citizenship Act** in 1924, granting citizenship to all Indians born in the United States. In 1934 Congress passed **the Indian Reorganization Act**, a reform measure designed to stress tribal unity and autonomy. By returning surplus lands to the Indians, authorizing tribes to form corporations, and providing for elected tribal councils, the act attempted to restore the tribe as the center of Indian culture and life. In 1953 Congress began a policy of "**termination**," or the ending of federal responsibility and social services (education, health, welfare) in an attempt to assimilate the Indian into American society. The policy of termination ended in the 1960s and a new militancy surfaced among groups of American Indians in the 1960s and 1970s. The occupation of **Alcatraz Island** in San Francisco Bay in 1969 and the holding of hostages at Wounded Knee in 1973 by the **American Indian Movement** (AIM) are examples of attempts by the American Indians to regain lands that they felt were rightfully theirs.

The Mining Frontier

The **California Gold Rush** of 1849 brought nearly 100,000 new settlers. After gold was discovered near Denver in 1858, many settlers came to Colorado, and the discovery of the **Comstock Lode** in 1858 increased the population of the **Nevada Territory**, bringing statehood in 1864.

The Cattle Frontier

The grasslands of the Great Plains, east of the Rocky Mountains, were well suited for grazing and quickly became the cattleman's frontier, where large herds of cattle grazed on

Discoveries of gold helped draw settlers to the West.

the "open range." The original market value of the Texas longhorn was for its hide, processed in the tanneries of the Northeast. However, after the Civil War there developed the "**long drive**," or the driving of cattle herds north to the nearest East-running railroad for the Eastern beef market. By the 1880s the long drive became less common as increased numbers of farms closed in the open range and the railroads were located closer to local ranches.

By the 1890s overproduction of cattle caused the prices in the Eastern markets to decline. Prices of steers dropped from $30 apiece to only $8. Over the next few years the "open range" approach to cattle raising ended and, assisted by the invention of **barbed wire** by Joseph Glidden (1874), ranchers turned to smaller herds on fenced land.

The West, sparsely populated and lacking law enforcement officers, lawyers, and judges, developed an unwritten body of customs sometimes known as the Code of the West. Justice on the frontier was carried out by federal district courts and United States marshals, who often employed hired guns to assist them. Some of the more notorious lawmen of the frontier were Wyatt Earp, Bill Tilghman, Texas Ranger Ira Aten, and Judge Isaac C. Parker. At times, when the legal system proved to be incapable of curbing gamblers, gunmen, and desperadoes, groups of self-proclaimed law enforcers formed vigilante committees to cope with lawbreakers.

Much cowboy dress was adopted from the Mexican *vaqueros*.

The Farming Frontier

Farmer versus Nature

The frontier farmer found the turf of the Great Plains hard to manage, for the roots of the grasses extended deep and intermeshed to form sod up to twelve feet thick. Turning this hindrance into an advantage, the ingenious plains farmer used special plows to cut the sod into bricks ("Nebraska Marble"), which was then used to build homes. In an area lacking wood, rock, and brick clay, the **sod house** solved the problem of shelter for the plains farmer.

Perhaps the farmer's greatest foe was nature itself. Drought and wind combined to scorch the crops and lift the dry topsoil, creating swirls of dust that were deposited hundreds of miles away. Prairie fires raced across the plains in the fall when grass became dry. Winter blizzards and subzero weather froze farmers and livestock alike, and plagues of grasshoppers turned millions of acres into a wasteland.

Technology

New farming inventions allowed the plains farmer to cultivate the soil in spite of nature's resistance. **Barbed wire** enabled farmers to enclose the fields, keeping their own livestock in and the rancher's herds out. An improved prairie **plow** made of steel that did not break when it cut through the tough sod was devised in 1868. The **windmill** allowed the farmer to draw spring water from deep underground and cultivate the fields, while improved systems of irrigation made use of limited amounts of water. Laborsaving devices like the horse-drawn **reaper** and later the **combine** helped turn the plains into the "bread basket" of the nation, and later the world.

Government Policy

The railroads held tremendous amounts of land through federal grants and sold many acres to the farmers. The **Homestead Act** (1862) encouraged further settlement and about 600,000 homesteaders benefited. The **Morrill Land Grant Act** (1862) provided for the sale of federal land to finance agricultural colleges, promoting scientific agricultural development.

Life on the Great Plains Farm

Besides the hostile environment, the isolation and loneliness of the plains farm added to the challenge of survival. It was not uncommon for families to walk many miles to the nearest farm for simple conversation. Medical needs were met by self-proclaimed physicians who, with a mixture of folk remedy, medieval methods, and improvisation, served the needs of the prairie population. Frontier schools, usually an early priority in a prairie settlement, were financed by local districts, and the success of plains education was surprisingly high. By 1900, Nebraska, Kansas, and Iowa boasted the highest literacy rate in the nation.

Agrarian Protest

The Grange Movement

The transition of the American farmers from self-sufficiency to the market economy brought hardships that eventually caused them to form political organizations. During the 19th century, farmers found themselves at the mercy of forces—commodity prices, grain storage charges, interest rates, and shipping costs—that were beyond their control.

The **National Grange of the Patrons of Husbandry** was founded in 1867 to organize farmers into local chapters dedicated to education, culture, and socialization. However, in the 1870s its aims became less social and more political, with membership reaching 1.5 million by 1874. The Grange accused the railroads of discriminatory practices (long haul compared to short haul, rebates, monopolizing practices), the grain-elevator operators of monopoly practices, charging "all that the traffic would bear," and manufacturers of raising prices and the cost of credit so that farmers were unable to make a profit.

Legal Efforts; Court Cases

By the middle of the 1870s the Grangers held the political balance in several of the Midwestern states. In four states **Granger laws** were passed to regulate railroad rates and the practices of the owners of grain elevators. The Supreme Court, in a series of landmark decisions, upheld the principle that government could regulate all those industries "affected with a public interest."

- **Munn *v.* Illinois** *(1877).* The Supreme Court upheld state regulation of grain elevators storage rates, declaring that "**the public has a direct and positive interest**" in private businesses "**clothed with a public interest.**" As a consequence, the rates and services of public utilities could be regulated, departing from the tradition of laissez-faire economics.

- **Wabash, St. Louis and Pacific Railway *v.* Minnesota** *(1886).* In this case, based on congressional control over interstate commerce, the Supreme Court restricted state control by holding that the states had no power to fix rates on shipments of goods passing beyond their borders.

- **Chicago, Milwaukee and St. Paul Railroad *v.* Minnesota** *(1889).* The Supreme Court ruled that corporations could not be denied property rights without being afforded equal protection of the laws and due process.

National Government Response: Interstate Commerce Commission

In response to the Supreme Court's decision in the *Wabash* case, Congress passed the **Interstate Commerce Act** (1887) establishing the Interstate Commerce Commission, which had among its powers the right to require that railroads post rates publicly, demand that rates be "reasonable and just," forbid pooling, rebates, and rate discrimination, prohibit "long haul vs. short haul discrimination," and investigate complaints against the railroads.

Populism

- *Farmers' Alliances.* As the agrarian crusade continued into the 1880s, farmers' alliances were formed to demand change concerning a number of issues. In 1887 the Southern Farmers' Alliance had a membership of 3 million. The Northern Farmers' Alliance attracted 2 million members by 1890. In 1889 delegates from both alliances met to discuss a common platform that included demand for free silver; graduated income tax (percent of tax rate increasing with amount earned); government ownership of the railroads; and the direct election of Senators. In the elections of 1890, members of the alliances were elected to many state positions and 53 members of Congress who were sympathetic to the desires of the farmers' alliances were sent to Washington, D.C.

- *Populist Party.* The **People's party**, or **Populist party**, was formed in 1891 through the efforts of the Farmers' Alliances. **James B. Weaver** ran for President on the Populist ticket in 1892 and received a million popular votes. The Populist platform, known as the **Omaha Platform**, included a graduated income tax, postal savings banks, government ownership of railroads and telegraph lines, the direct election of Senators, and the use of initiative (popular introduction of legislation) and referendum (the provision for the popular vote on laws rather than that of the legislatures). The Populist platform also continued to support an increased amount of currency in circulation, an issue endorsed by the **Greenback party** of the 1870s. Since most farmers were debtors, borrowing and buying on credit, the deflationary trends of the later 1800s proved to be devastating. The Populist platform continued to be pushed by Progressives for a generation. As with many third-party movements in the nation's history, much of the Populist platform was later adopted by the major parties.

- *Election of 1896.* In the election of 1896, **William Jennings Bryan** ran on the Democratic ticket advocating increased coinage of silver. Speaking on the free-silver issue at the 1896 Democratic Convention, Bryan spoke his famous words, "You shall not press down upon the brow of labor this crown of thorns, you shall not crucify mankind upon a cross of gold." The platform of the Democrats was progressive and adopted much of the Populist platform, including reduced tariffs, antitrust legislation, and outlawing the injunction in labor disputes. A vigorous Republican campaign, combined with rising farm prices due to overseas crop failures, resulted in a victory for the Republican candidate, **William McKinley**.

Exercise Set 2.12

1. The Dawes Severalty Act (1887) changed previous policy toward Native Americans by
   A. abolishing the reservation system
   B. granting them citizenship
   C. halting attempts at assimilation of the Indian
   D. dividing tribal lands among individual families

2. As the 19th century progressed, farming on the Great Plains became
   A. less threatened by a hostile environment
   B. further dependent upon the railroad
   C. less important to the economy of the United States
   D. primarily a one-crop economy

3. Which of the following was true of the Grange Movement?
   A. it was primarily a southern agrarian movement
   B. it started as a social organization and became increasingly political in the 1880s
   C. it had little effect on future state and federal legislation
   D. it avoided politics

4. Cattle raising in the semi-arid lands of the West greatly increased as a result of the
   A. Homestead Act
   B. invention of the reaper
   C. extension of the nation's railroad network
   D. Morrill Land Grant Act

AMERICAN SOCIETY AT THE TURN OF THE CENTURY

In the late 1800s and early 1900s many changes were taking place that helped the nation become a world power. A once predominantly rural nation was becoming a nation of cities. A country whose economy was once based on agriculture was rapidly becoming an industrial giant. From 1860 to 1910 towns and cities developed and grew at a rate unmatched in modern times. While the rural population almost doubled during these years, the urban population multiplied nearly seven times.

Urbanization and Cultural Development

Urbanization stimulated cultural development by the mixing of many different types of people, the establishment of facilities including libraries, schools, museums, orchestras, and theaters, and the concentration of wealth that contributed to cultural growth. While public school systems and colleges received greater support from both government and private sources, curriculums broadened and specialized. The American Library Association was formed in 1876. Daily newspapers increased in number from 700 in 1870 to 2,500 in 1900, while circulation increased from 2.5 million to 15 million and magazines numbered 1,800 by the turn of the century. Museums began display the works of American painters and sculptors. The rise of the city contributed to cultural progress in the United States.

Growth of American Imperialism

American expansionism turned to **imperialism**, or the imposition of control over other peoples. **Manifest Destiny** was completed by the turn of the century and the United States was continentally complete. Imperialism was beginning to play a role in American foreign policy. By 1900 the "American Empire" included Alaska, the Midway Islands, Samoa, the Philippines, Guam, Puerto Rico, Hawaii, and Wake Island.

Problems Caused by Industrialization

America's rise as an industrial power and its race to greatness brought many problems. With the coming of the new century, these problems started to be addressed. With the conquest of the continent had come reckless **abuse of the environment**—the soil, forest, and water. Rapid industrial growth had brought the **exploitation** of women, children, and workers. The belief in

"Social Darwinism" had led to disregard for the incompetent and the infirm. Wealth and power was concentrated among only a few, and **poverty** was becoming widespread. Although slavery had ended, **racism** plagued American society. Finally, corruption poisoned the political system. To remedy the nation's problems, it was necessary to cleanse politics and to regulate the business interests that controlled government.

The "**Progressive Era**" was an attempt to solve the many problems caused by an industrial society. In 1906 President Theodore Roosevelt labeled those individuals who were working to uncover corruption "**muckrakers**." These philosophers, social scientists, and novelists included **Henry George** *(Progress and Poverty,* 1879), **Lester Ward** *(Dynamic Sociology,* 1883), **Edward Bellamy** *(Looking Backward: 2000–1887,* 1887). **Thorstein Veblen** *(The Theory of the Leisure Class,* 1899). They produced a literature of protest in the late 1800s. The common theme in most of their works was that laissez-faire had not worked and progress was possible only through social planning. The Progressive era was a reaction to laissez-faire and included greater governmental and legal control of big business and greater government accountability.

CHAPTER REVIEW QUESTIONS

1. Between 1890 and 1914 most immigrants to the United States came from
   A. Latin America
   B. northern and western Europe
   C. southern and eastern Europe
   D. Southeast Asia

2. Which of the following accurately describes the Ku Klux Klan of the 1920s?
   A. its activities were limited to the South
   B. it favored immigration restrictions as well as white supremacy
   C. many of its members were elected to Congress
   D. it appeared for the first time during this decade

3. The destructive impact of white settlement on the Native American population was most strongly felt through
   A. the spread of disease unknown to Native Americans
   B. immediate elimination of the native population through warfare
   C. wholesale enslavement of the Indians
   D. immediate relocation of Indians to lands west of the Mississippi

4. All but which of the following major transportation developments affecting United States history took place in the period before the 20th century?
   A. the steamboat
   B. the airplane
   C. the stagecoach
   D. the railroad

5. In the 40 years following the Civil War, which of the following areas was affected by only state and local legislation?
   A. women's suffrage
   B. interstate commerce
   C. immigration
   D. civil rights

6. Which of the following American authors was least concerned with social criticism of America?
   A. Frank Norris
   B. Jacob Riis
   C. Upton Sinclair
   D. Horatio Alger

7. During the second half of the 19th century, an open immigration policy was generally opposed by
   A. factory owners
   B. land speculators
   C. sparsely populated Western territories
   D. labor unions

8. The Populist movement of the 1890s can best be described as a
   A. political coalition of farming interests directed against banking and railroad interests
   B. trade union movement located in major Eastern cities
   C. reform movement seeking to eliminate urban poverty and slums
   D. political interest group desiring war with Spain to protect United States interests in Cuba

ESSAYS

1. Throughout U.S. history, there have been many instances where political, economic, or social difficulties led to demands for reform. In response to those demands, movements such as those listed below developed.

   Agrarian Protest/1870–1900
   Movement for Immigration Restriction/1870–1930

 For the *two* movements listed above:

- Describe a specific problem that led to the movement or program
- Describe a specific reform advocated by the movement or program to deal with this problem
- Discuss the extent to which this reform was successful in solving the problem

2. During the second half of the 19th century, literary figures in the United States produced works critical of society and advocating change.

Select *three* writers. For *each one* chosen, identify an issue that was addressed by the listed work and discuss the author's approach to the issue, including suggested change or reform.

   Lester F. Ward, *Dynamic Sociology* (1883)
   Ida M. Tarbell, *History of the Standard Oil Company* (1902)
   Thorstein Veblen, *The Theory of the Leisure Class* (1899)
   Henry George, *Progress and Poverty* (1879)
   Edward Bellamy, *Looking Backward: 2000–1887* (1887)
   Jacob A. Riis, *How the Other Half Lives* (1890)

THEMATIC ESSAYS

Directions: Write a well-organized essay that includes an introduction, several paragraphs addressing the task below, and a conclusion.

Theme: Government and Economic Systems

> During the time period of 1865–1900 the federal government departed from the principles of laissez-faire.

Task:

Identify *two* examples of the federal government's departure from the principles of laissez-faire.

- Discuss the problem that led to the government's change in economic policy in each example.
- Discuss each specific federal government action.
- Evaluate whether the government actions were successful in addressing each problem.

Some suggestions you might wish to consider include: control of interstate commerce, antitrust activities, and railroad land grants.

You are *not* limited to these suggestions.

Directions: Write a well-organized essay that includes an introduction, several paragraphs addressing the task below, and a conclusion.

Theme: Diversity and Government Action

During the time period between 1875 and 1925 the views of the American people changed with regard to immigration, and the federal government responded with changes in immigration laws.

Task:

Identify *two* pieces of immigration legislation passed by the federal government during the 1875–1925 time period.

- For each immigration law identified, discuss changes in the views of the American people that contributed to the change.
- Discuss each specific immigration law.
- Compare each of the 1875–1925 immigration laws used to current immigration legislation.

Some suggestions you might wish to consider include: Chinese Exclusion Act (1882), Gentlemen's Agreement (1907), Literacy Test (1917), Immigration Act of 1921, and Immigration Act of 1924.

You are *not* limited to these suggestions.

DOCUMENT-BASED QUESTION ESSAY

The following questions (Part A and Part B) are based on the accompanying documents (1–6). Some of these documents have been edited for the purpose of this exercise. The question is designed to test your ability to work with historical documents and to demonstrate your knowledge of the subject matter being presented. As you analyze the documents, take into account both the source of the document and the author's point of view.

Historical Context: The industrialization of the United States following the Civil War had a tremendous impact on labor.

Task: Using information from the documents and your knowledge of United States history, answer the questions that follow each document in Part A. Your answers to the questions will help you write the Part B essay, in which you will be asked:

> The organization of American labor into such early unions as the Knights of Labor and the American Federation of Labor was a natural response to the industrial revolution during the second half of the 19th century. Assess the validity of this statement.

Part A
Short Answer

The documents below relate to issues concerning workers in the period of industrialization following the Civil War. Examine each document carefully and then answer the questions that follow.

DOCUMENT 1

—Bibb Mill No. 1, Macon Georgia

1. Provide two observations of the picture above that were later addressed by labor unions.

_____

_____

_____

DOCUMENT 2

The laboring classes constitute the main part of our population. They should be protected in their efforts peaceably to assert their rights when endangered by aggregated capital, and all statutes on this subject should recognize the care of the State for honest toil, and be framed with a view of improving the condition of the workingman.

—President Grover Cleveland, Albany, N.Y., August 18, 1884

2. How would organized labor use President Cleveland's statement to support their goals?

_____

_____

_____

DOCUMENT 3

1. Accidents and casualties are very numerous, partly owing to the exposed machinery and partly owing to carelessness.....It is really painful to go round among the operatives and find hands and fingers mutilated, in consequences of accidents.
2. Unnatural or monotonous working positions...in some cases make the worker round-shouldered, in other cases producing curvature of the spine and bow-legs.
3. Work by artificial light. It is very injurious to the eyes.

—Dr. John B. Whitaker, Impact of Factory on Worker Health, 1871

3. Describe how labor could use Dr. Whitaker's report in its demands for improved working conditions.

_____

_____

_____

DOCUMENT 4

An 1889 Payroll Ledger			
Names	Total Hours	Price	Amount
Overseer			
J. W. Doran	60	40	24.00
Sec. Hands			
P. Clifford	60	18	10.80
P. Smith	60	18	10.80
P. King	60	20	12.00
Third Oilers and Roving H'ds			
R. Lathrop	60	12	7.20
A. Blanchard	60	10	6.00
Scrubber			
J. Moriarity	60	5	3.00
Picker Men			
M. Grincovitch	60	10	6.00
M. Goetz	60	10	6.00
J. Chazee	60	10	6.00
A. Icyk	60	10	6.00

—An 1889 Payroll Ledger

4. After studying the payroll ledger, discuss two arguments the workers may have against the employer.

_____

_____

1. To secure to the toilers a proper share of the wealth that they create.
2. The adopting of measures providing for the health and safety of those engaged in mining and manufacturing.
3. The substitution of arbitration for strikes.
4. The prohibition of the employment of children in workshops, mines, and factories before attaining their fourteenth year.
5. To secure for both sexes equal pay for equal work.

—The Knights of Labor Charter

5. From a reading of the Knights of Labor Charter, discuss what the early labor union saw as major problems of workers in the post-Civil War period.

_____

_____

_____

DOCUMENT 6

HOURS AND WAGES, 1860–1900

—Hours and wages, 1860–1900

6. Explain how both management and labor could use the information in the graph to support their position.

_____

_____

_____

7. Since it appears that wages and hours improved for the worker between 1860 and 1900, how do you account for the increasing number of strikes during the time period?

_____

_____

_____

Part B
Essay

Your essay should be well organized with an introductory paragraph that states your position on the question. Develop your position in the next paragraphs and then write a conclusion. In your essay, include specific historical details and refer to the specific documents you analyzed in Part A. You may include additional information from your knowledge of social studies.

Historical Context: The industrialization of the United States following the Civil War had a tremendous impact on labor.

Task:

> The organization of American labor into such early unions as the Knights of Labor and the American Federation of Labor was a natural response to the industrial revolution during the second half of the 19th century. Assess the validity of this statement.

Guidelines:

In your essay, be sure to
• Develop all aspects of the task
• Incorporate information from at least *five* documents
• Incorporate relevant outside information
• Support the theme with many relevant facts, examples, and details
• Use a logical and clear plan of organization, including an introduction and a conclusion that are beyond a restatement of the theme

UNIT THREE ⎯⎯⎯⎯⎯⎯⎯⎯⎯⎯⎯⎯⎯⎯⎯⎯⎯

The Progressive Movement

> **KEY IDEAS** The rapid growth of the United States during the second half of the 19th century, and the problems that accompanied this development, resulted in a period of transition and reform. The age of laissez-faire was coming to an end as social conditions/governmental responsibilities for social conditions increased. As the United States entered the 20th century, expansionist desires, including economic imperialism, became a major component of its foreign policies.

UNIT CONNECTIONS: By the end of the unit you should understand the following points.

- Political, economic, and social problems lead to need for reform
- Muckrakers and the exposure of evils in American society
- Progressivism and the role of the federal government
- Progressivism and farmers, women, labor, African-Americans, and Native Americans
- Theodore Roosevelt, Woodrow Wilson, and the power of the presidency
- The spread of Manifest Destiny to Latin America and Asia
- Imperialism versus anti-imperialism
- The failure of Wilsonian attempts at neutrality
- World War I and the restrictions on civil liberties
- The failure of the United States to ratify the Treaty of Versailles
- Isolationism and diplomacy (1920–1933)

REFORM IN AMERICA

THE REFORM TRADITION

The American Republic was founded on the concept of equality. The founders of the nation held it to be a "self-evident truth" that all people are created equal, being endowed with the same basic rights to life, liberty, and the pursuit of happiness. Reform movements were started in various periods as a response to changing social conditions with the belief that the betterment of society was a possibility. Americans believed that in a democracy the people could create a better society through their own efforts.

American Revolution

The American Revolution was the first of a number of conflicts throughout the world that furthered the ideals of the **Enlightenment** thinkers. What distinguished the United States from other 18th century countries was that the American Revolution allowed the political theories of the Enlightenment to be put into practice. The United States based its government upon **Locke's** and **Rousseau's** idea of a "social contract." The purpose of government was to preserve people's natural rights to life, liberty, and property (Locke). The new Constitution, which proved to be an enduring plan of government, included **Montesquieu's** concept of separation of powers and checks and balances.

Abolition Movement

The movement to abolish slavery was a major reform movement during the first half of the 19th century. With the invention of the cotton gin in 1793 cotton exports rose from half a million pounds in that year to 83 million pounds in 1815. Increased demand for cotton intensified the South's dependency on the cotton-slave economy and slavery spread with great speed. The issue of slavery threatened the Union when it became entangled with problems raised by westward expansion.

The earliest reform movements opposing slavery originated with the **Quakers**. Before the American Revolution they freed their slaves, claiming it was a sin for Christians to hold people in bondage. By 1830 there were at least fifty black antislavery societies. However, in the 1840s, the movement became more widespread as many Americans came to believe that slavery was morally wrong. As whites became more involved in the movement, black abolitionists, including Sojourner Truth, Harriet Tubman, and Frederick Douglass, worked with white reformers to end slavery. **William Lloyd Garrison's** newspaper, *The Liberator,* launched a militant abolitionist movement in the North.

By the 1850s the question of slavery was dividing the country. A major setback to the abolitionist movement came with the Supreme Court's decision in ***Dred Scott v. Sandford*** (1857). The Court held that slaves were not protected by the Constitution. The Court said that Congress could not prevent citizens from transporting their slaves into a free territory because slaves were property, protected by the due process clause of the Fifth Amendment to the Constitution. Rather than settling the slavery question, however, the Dred Scott decision increased sectional conflict over the issue of slavery, especially over its expansion to western territory.

The end of slavery and the granting of citizenship and civil rights to black Americans did not come until after the Civil War and the passage of the Thirteenth, Fourteenth, and Fifteenth Amendments. Although the slavery question was finally resolved, reform movements for extension of civil rights to African Americans and other minorities continued through the 20th century.

Women's Rights

Women in the 1800s were expected to keep house and raise children. Politics and work were the domains of men; women were the guardians of the home. The laws reinforced these perceptions. For example, married women in many states had no rights over property they inherited or wages they earned. They did not have legal control over their children, could not sue in their own name, and could not be a party to a contract.

Between 1820 and 1860, as other reforms began to sweep America, the women's movement began to develop. Women were active in all the reform movements in this period. Their involvement in these other reform movements made them realize that they were as oppressed as many of the groups they were attempting to assist.

As economic and social conditions changed with increased industrialization, equality slowly came to women. Early industrialization allowed women

Susan Brownell Anthony (1820–1906) was a leader in the women's suffrage movement.

to develop some financial independence and opened new areas of employment. Women's colleges, including Wellesley, Vassar, and Smith, opened between 1865 and 1875. By 1900 about 70 percent of all colleges admitted women. The efforts to gain political equality by reformers such as **Elizabeth Cady Stanton**, **Lucretia Mott**, and **Susan B. Anthony**, and groups such as the **National American Woman Suffrage Association** started to gain results during the second half of the 19th century. By 1895 sixteen states allowed women to vote, and in 1920 the Nineteenth Amendment was ratified, granting women throughout the nation the right to vote.

Civil Service

The movement to appoint people to government jobs based on merit rather than through the **spoils system** aroused great interest following the Civil War. The scandals of the Grant era and later the assassination of President Garfield in 1881 by a "disappointed office seeker" focused attention on the need for civil service reform. The abuse of the spoils system led to the demand that certain offices be filled only by those who had performed adequately on a "civil service" examination. The **Pendleton Act** (1883), adopted during President Arthur's administration, authorized the President to appoint civil service commissioners to administer examinations for "classified" government positions. Today, most government jobs are filled through civil service exams.

The Mentally Ill

Before the 1840s the mentally ill had been treated either as criminals and placed in jails, or as social misfits placed in poorhouses. A pioneer in the reform movement for the mentally ill was a Massachusetts schoolteacher, **Dorothea Dix**. After reporting to the state legislature the shocking treatment of the mentally ill in Massachusetts—"confined . . . in cages, closets, cellars, stalls, pens! Chained, naked, beaten with rods, and lashed into obedience . . ."—legislation was passed to set up a state hospital for the insane. Dorothea Dix carried her crusade across the country, resulting in improved care for the mentally ill in many states.

PRESSURE FOR REFORM

So long as all the increased wealth which modern progress brings goes but to build great fortunes, to increase luxury and make sharper the contrast between the House of Have and the House of Want, progress is not real and cannot be permanent.

Henry George, *Progress and Poverty* (1879)

In the face of the facts that modern man lives more wretchedly than the caveman, and that his producing power is a thousand times greater than that of the cave-man, no other conclusion is possible than that the capitalist class has mismanaged . . . criminally and selfishly mismanaged.

Jack London, *The Iron Heel* (1906)

Struggle for Fair Standards

As industrialization continued to cause poverty for millions and an unequal distribution of the nation's wealth, movements for change gained momentum. Reformers demanded that government begin to regulate industry, finance, working conditions, and agriculture in the interest of the many rather than the few. A new movement known as the **Progressive Movement** resulted in the reform of the worst abuses in government and business. Although Progressives attacked many of the same grievances as **Populists** did in the 1890s, they received wider support from Americans, especially the growing middle class, and from government leaders.

Increasing Inequities of Wealth and Poverty

By 1900 the unequal distribution of the nation's wealth was beginning to threaten political democracy in America. Only 1 percent of the population owned 50 percent of the nation's wealth, while the top 12 percent controlled 90 percent. With so much wealth concentrated in the hands of such a small group, their influence over legislatures and candidates increased. Such class inequities helped to spread **Marxist** thought in the United States. **Karl Marx** predicted that discontent among the proletariat (working class) would result in the overthrow of capitalism and the subsequent end of class struggle. However, change came in the United States through reform legislation passed under the banner of the Progressive Movement rather than through revolution.

Rising Power and Influence of the Middle Class

An important result of industrialization in the United States was the rise of the middle class, which included professionals, technicians, government workers, salespeople, service employees, teachers, social workers, and clerical workers, among others. As the problems caused by business abuses and consolidation began to affect the middle class, they began to support the Progressive Movement and demand reform.

Communication of Progressive Thought

The Progressive Movement in the United States was assisted by a variety of nationwide organizations. Interest groups including the National Consumers League, **National Association for the Advancement of Colored People**, National Child Labor Committee, and **National Housing Administration**, joined with occupational groups such as the **American Bar Association** and the American Health Association, with nationwide membership. Technological improvements in communication—the telephone and telegraph—improved the availability of information and allowed progressivism to become a national movement.

The "Muckrakers" and Reform

> Men with the muckrake are often indispensable to the well-being of society, but only if they know when to stop raking the muck.
> President Theodore Roosevelt, April 14, 1906

The term "**Muckrakers**" was first used by President Theodore Roosevelt in referring to a character in John Bunyan's *Pilgrim's Progress* who rejected a crown for a muckrake (a rake used to gather dung into a pile). The term was applied to writers who investigated and attacked social, political, and economic wrongs. Books and magazine articles in *McClure's, Collier's,* and *Hampton's* exposed the worst abuses of the period and stirred public outcry against them.

The Authors

Magazine articles by **Ida Tarbell** exposed the abuses of the Standard Oil Company. **Lincoln Steffens** published stories of corruption in major American cities. These sensational accounts stirred popular concern. Novelists of the late 19th and early 20th centuries who spoke for socialism and criticized the capitalist system are among the most famous American literary figures. They include **Upton Sinclair, Jack London, Theodore Dreiser**, and **Frank Norris**. Sinclair's novel ***The Jungle*** (1906) brought the conditions in the meat-packing plants of Chicago to the attention of the nation and stimulated demand for laws regulating the meat industry. Jack London, a member of the Socialist party, wrote *The Iron Heel* (1906), warning of a Fascist America and idealizing a Socialist brotherhood of man. Theodore Dreiser's *The Financier*

(1912) and *The Titan* (1914) exposed the ruthlessness of promoters and profiteers. Frank Norris's ***The Octopus*** (1901) showed the control of the railroads and corrupt politicians over California wheat-ranchers.

Legislation

The power to legislate for the health, safety, and welfare of the community belongs principally to the states, but during the early 20th century, Congress began to use its commerce and taxing powers to legislate for the "general welfare." Usually, such legislation followed revelations of corruption and immorality by muckraking publications. The **Pure Food and Drug Act** of 1906 barred adulterated and misbranded foods from interstate commerce. The **Meat Inspection Act** of the same year, passed shortly after the publication of Upton Sinclair's novel *The Jungle,* provided for local inspection services by the Department of Agriculture and banned from interstate commerce uninspected and rejected meat. The **Mann-Elkins Act** of 1910 extended the jurisdiction of the Interstate Commerce Commission over telephone and telegraph lines. The **Keating-Owen Act** of 1916 barred from interstate commerce any products made in factories, canneries, or similar workshops that employed children under fourteen. In *United States* v. *Darby* (1941), the Supreme Court ruled that goods manufactured in violation of the **Fair Labor Standards Act** of 1938 could be barred from interstate commerce.

Contemporary "Muckraking"

Literature designed to make the public aware of problems and abuses in America did not end with the Progressive Era. Societal problems were the subject of many of **John Steinbeck's** novels during the Depression years. The Supreme Court ruled *(New York Times Co.* v. *United States, 1971)* that *The New York Times* could print the "**Pentagon Papers**," a secret document that revealed behind-the-scenes decision making during the Vietnam War. The case provided a classic national security versus First Amendment confrontation, in which the Court ruled that

> paramount among the responsibilities of a free press is the duty to prevent any part of the government from deceiving the people and sending them off to distant lands to die of foreign fevers and foreign shot and shell.
>
> *New York Times* v. *U.S.* (1971)

Finally, investigative reporting by two writers on the *Washington Post* newspaper helped to uncover the **Watergate** scandal during the early 1970s and eventually led to the resignation of President **Richard Nixon**.

Other Areas of Concern

Problems of Poverty

As the imbalance in the distribution of wealth increased during the second half of the 19th century, poverty among the working class grew. The acute housing problems of the poor were described by reformer **Jacob Riis** in *How the Other Half Lives*. He advocated providing housing for low-income families in model tenements. Help for the urban poor also came from individuals like **Jane Addams**, who wanted to improve the lives of working class people by enabling them to obtain an education, better jobs, and better housing. **Hull House**, a settlement house established in Chicago in 1889 by Addams, served the needs of the city's urban poor.

Women's Rights and Efforts for Peace

The movement for women's suffrage rights, which continued throughout the 19th century, culminated in the adoption of the **Nineteenth Amendment** in 1920. The **Fifteenth Amendment** had given the right to vote to black men, but it had ignored women. Prominent women's leaders, such as **Elizabeth Cady Stanton** and **Susan B. Anthony**, led the movements to gain the vote and organized the **National American Woman Suffrage Association**.

The **birth control** movement was led by **Margaret Sanger**, who distributed information about contraceptives in the hopes of preventing unwanted pregnancies among poor women. Although most states still prohibited the sale of contraceptives in 1921, the formation of the American Birth Control League by Sanger enlisted physicians and social workers in the effort to convince the courts to allow the distribution of birth control information.

As the United States approached entry into World War I, **peace movements** developed in the nation. "Peace is a woman's job," Representative Jeannette Rankin believed, "because men have a natural fear of being classed as cowards if they oppose war." Representative Rankin was the first woman ever to be elected to Congress and she voted against the declaration of war in World War I and World War II.

The Black Movement

The **National Association for the Advancement of Colored People**, originally a predominantly white organization, was formed to battle discrimination by **W.E.B. Du Bois** and his supporters in 1909. The 1920s saw the emergence of a revised version of the **Ku Klux Klan**, determined to reach its goal of "native, white, Protestant supremacy." Using violence and political pressure, the Klan terrorized black Americans as well as Catholics, Jews, and immigrants. One response to discrimination was the formation of movements that advocated black independence, such as the Universal Negro Improvement Association (1914) headed by **Marcus Garvey**. Garvey's movement believed that blacks should separate themselves from the corrupt white society. Advocating the "uniting of all the Negro peoples of the world into one great body to establish a country and government absolutely their own," Garvey led a "**Back to Africa**" movement.

The Temperance Movement

During the Progressive Era the temperance movement made great gains and was supported by several organizations. The **Women's Christian Temperance Union** (1876) with **Frances E. Willard** as its leading spirit, preached that alcohol was the primary factor in crime, poverty, and vice. The Anti-Saloon League carried on a campaign against the evils of alcoholic beverages and saloons. Both organizations worked to outlaw the manufacture and sale of alcoholic beverages. However, they did not approve the methods of **Carrie Nation**, who invaded saloons with her hatchet and smashed bottles and bars. The temperance movement was assisted by the coming of World War I. The **Eighteenth Amendment** was passed in part to conserve grain that was to be used for feeding the armed forces and Europe instead of for alcohol production. It was ratified in 1919; in 1920 **Prohibition** began.

Anti-Defamation League (1913)

Pogroms in Russia brought attention to the plight of **Jews** abroad and encouraged the formation of the American Jewish Committee. The Committee pledged itself to protect the civil rights of all Jews throughout the world. In 1913 Jews organized the **B'nai B'rith Anti-Defamation League**, dedicated to combating prejudice in the United States.

1. The Nineteenth Amendment to the U.S. Constitution provided for
   A. the direct election of senators
   B. voting rights for women
   C. a national income tax
   D. end of slavery

2. The Progressive Movement, on the whole, did not focus attention on
   A. impure food and harmful medicines
   B. poor living conditions in urban areas
   C. the unhealthy results of industrialization
   D. the plight of African Americans

3. Of the following pairs, the one that is not correctly matched is
   A. John Steinbeck—*Grapes of Wrath*
   B. Upton Sinclair—*The Jungle*
   C. Frank Norris—*Uncle Tom's Cabin*
   D. Jack London—*The Iron Heel*

4. Jane Addams worked to help people in city slums by establishing
   A. the American Red Cross
   B. the National Association for the Advancement of Colored People
   C. the Salvation Army
   D. Hull House

5. The National Association for the Advancement of Colored People
   A. subscribed to the beliefs of Marcus Garvey
   B. intended to fight discrimination through legal action
   C. was founded by William Lloyd Garrison
   D. attracted most of its members from the African American working class

6. The reform movement which resulted in having a 19th century amendment added to the Constitution was the
   A. women's suffrage movement
   B. temperance movement
   C. advocates of better housing conditions
   D. abolition movement

PROGRESSIVISM AND GOVERNMENT ACTION

> We demand that big business give the people a square deal; in return we must insist that when anyone engaged in big business honestly endeavors to do right he shall himself be given a square deal.
> President Theodore Roosevelt, *Autobiography* (1913)

Emerging Progressive Movement: Political Reform

The **Progressive Era**, which began about 1900 and came to an end with the outbreak of World War I, was primarily a response to the industrial and urban growth of the 1800s. In the late 1800s, labor unions, churches, Populists, publicists, and utopian novelists called attention to the worst abuses of the industrial age. Yet, by the turn of the century, class division was even more obvious, the abuses of business had increased, and the poverty and squalor of the cities had deepened.

Municipal Reform

A major aim or objective of the Progressive reform movement within the cities was to "clean up" municipal governments. The attack on city "bosses" and "machines" was led by civic-minded mayors and groups determined to abolish corruption. The concepts of the city manager (a specially trained official in city government), civil service reform, supervision of public expenditures, and city commissions (a commission of experts to assist city government) were introduced. As cities rapidly expanded, pressure was put upon city governments to provide and maintain public utilities. In some of the more progressive municipalities, there were movements for public ownership of utilities such as gas, electric, telephone, and transportation systems. Settlement houses, similar to **Jane Addams' Hull House**, were established in a number of cities. They provided education, health care, child care, cultural events, and recreation.

State Reform

Reformers began to look to the state governments and the federal government for progressive legislation to address the nation's problems. Governors became important figures in state reform, including **Woodrow Wilson** of New Jersey (administrative reforms), **Theodore Roosevelt** of New York (improvement of urban tenements and tax revision), and perhaps most outstanding, **Robert M. La Follette** of Wisconsin. La Follette, organizer of the **Progressive American League** in 1911, who was later elected to the Senate and was instrumental in guiding progressive reform at the national level. With the help of other reformers, he supported labor legislation, federal aid to farmers, and the continued government operation of federally owned utilities such as the hydroelectric dam at **Muscle Shoals**, Alabama.

Many cities and states adopted measures that provided for increased popular control of government. Among these were the **referendum**, which provided for a popular vote on laws rather than, or in addition to, that of the legislatures, **recall**, or popular removal of government officials, and **initiative**, the popular introduction of legislation. **Ballot reform** included the use of the secret ballot. The **Seventeenth Amendment** (1913) eventually provided for the direct election of senators, the **Nineteenth Amendment** (1920) gave the franchise to women, and **direct primaries** allowed more widespread participation in the selection of candidates by registered voters.

Theodore Roosevelt and the Square Deal

Progressivism emerged in full force during the presidency of Theodore Roosevelt between 1901 and 1909. In addition to calling for greater government intervention to protect the welfare of the American people from big business and the social evils of rapid industrialization, the Progressive Movement was marked by a change in the perception of executive leadership. Now reformers looked to the President to be both politically powerful and to demonstrate legislative leadership, while resisting the pressures from powerful business interests.

President **William McKinley** was assassinated in 1901 shortly after his inauguration for his second term. McKinley's successor, Vice-President **Theodore Roosevelt**, finished out the term and was reelected in 1904. Roosevelt's program of domestic reform was called the "**Square Deal**," a term developed from his promise to bring a "square deal" and "opportunity" to every citizen.

The Stewardship Theory of Theodore Roosevelt

Roosevelt looked upon the presidency as a "**stewardship**" in whose care the common welfare and destiny of the American people were entrusted. In this way, he revived the **Hamiltonian** doctrine that the President was not limited in authority by the exact functions listed in Article II. In other words, the President was restricted only by what the Constitution or acts of Congress specifically said he could not do. Roosevelt's use of the office of the President has come to be known as the "**bully pulpit**."

PROGRESSIVE REFORMS

Reform Area	Goals	Accomplishments	Key People
Extension of Democracy	Women's Suffrage Representative government	1895—16 States 1920—19th Amendment 1913—Direct Election of Senators Amendment Referendum, Recall, and Initiative	Susan B. Anthony Robert M. La Follette
Honesty and Efficiency in Government	Appoint people to government based on merit	Pendelton Act (1883) Civil Service Commission (1883) City Manager System	Chester Arthur
Regulation of the Economy—Business	End child labor End abuses of monopolies Regulation of business	Pure Food and Drug Act (1906) Meat Inspection Act (1906) Clayton Antitrust Act (1914) Keating-Owen Act (1916) Fair Labor Standards Act (1938)	Theodore Roosevelt Ida Tarbell Upton Sinclair Frank Norris Woodrow Wilson
Regulation of the Economy—Transportation/ Communication	Reduce discriminatory practices of natural monopolies	Mann-Elkins Act (1910) Hepburn Act (1906) *Northern Securities Co. v. United States* (1904)	Theodore Roosevelt
Social Issues	Municipal reform Equitable distribution of wealth Race relations Prohibition Effective national monetary system	Hull House (1889) Graduated Income Tax (1913) NAACP (1909) Women's Christian Temperance Union National Monetary Commission (1908)	Henry George Francis E. Willard Louis Brandeis Jane Addams Jacob Riis
Conservation	Preservation of natural resources	Desert Land Act (1877) Forest Reserve Act (1891) Newlands Reclamation Act (1902)	Theodore Roosevelt John Muir Gifford Pinchot

Theodore Roosevelt called the office of President a "bully pulpit."

Square Deal Legislation

The legislation passed during Roosevelt's administrations reflected his belief that the modern industrial era demanded government that was powerful enough to guide national affairs. Although Roosevelt has been termed a **"trust buster,"** his goal actually was government regulation of uncontrolled competition in order to eliminate unfair practices of bad trusts. Congressional legislation between 1901 and 1909 included (1) establishment of the **Department of Labor and Commerce** (1903) to regulate business and enforce economic regulations; (2) the **Elkins Act** (1903), which added strength to the Interstate Commerce Act by making the granting or acceptance of secret rebates illegal; (3) the **Hepburn Act** (1906), which increased the power of the Interstate Commerce Commission by giving it the power to reduce discriminatory rates of railroads and placing the burden on the railroad to show that the rates were not unreasonable, and forbidding most free passes; and (4) the **Pure Food and Drug Act** and **Meat Inspection Act** (1906), which responded to the efforts of "muckrakers," including Upton Sinclair's *The Jungle,* by giving the government greater power in the protection of the public from inferior and unhealthy foods and drugs.

President **Taft**, who succeeded Roosevelt, was as sympathetic to reform as Roosevelt was. He prosecuted twice as many trust cases in four years as Roosevelt had in eight years.

The Supreme Court and "Trust-Busting"

The regulation of trusts had been inefficient under the administrations of Grover Cleveland and William McKinley. Under Roosevelt and Taft many trusts were broken up. The Roosevelt administration initiated several federal government suits and won notable victories in two cases, *Northern Securities Co.* v. *United States* (1904) and *Swift and Co.* v. *United States* (1905). In *Northern Securities* the United States government brought a suit to break up the Northern Securities Company, a railroad holding company organized by James J. Hill and E. H. Harriman. The Supreme Court held that the company was an "**unlawful combination**" within the meaning of the Sherman Act. In the *Swift* case the Supreme Court affirmed the power of Congress to punish conspiracies in "**restraint of trade**." The Court found that livestock and packing houses were "commerce among the states" and therefore within the Article I, Section 8 powers of Congress.

In *Standard Oil Co.* v. *United States* (1911), the Supreme Court announced its "rule of reason" to be applied to the Sherman Antitrust Act. Ordering the dissolution of the Standard Oil Company of New Jersey, the Court held that the Sherman Act forbade only "**unreasonable combinations**" or "contracts" in restraint of trade. "Reasonable" monopolies, it held, were legal, and size alone was not to be a determinant.

Presidential Mediation

Roosevelt led the way for government's role as an **arbiter** (judge or umpire), in labor disputes affecting the **public interest**. In May 1902 the **United Mine Workers** walked out of the anthracite coal fields of Pennsylvania demanding a shorter work day, better wages, and union recognition. Forcing both sides to accept arbitration, Roosevelt appointed an arbitration board, which decided in favor of a 10 percent increase in wages and a nine-hour work day, but also declared that the owners did not have to recognize the union.

Conservation

President Roosevelt, a lover of the outdoors, was a determined **conservationist**. Roosevelt was effective in pressuring both Congress and the states to pass conservation measures. Roosevelt added nearly 150 million acres to the national forests and was instrumental in protecting natural resources from private exploitation.

The Newlands Reclamation Act (1902) authorized, for irrigation purposes, the use of money obtained from land sales in the arid Western states. In 1908 the President called 44 governors and 500 natural resource experts to a

National Conservation Congress, to plan nationwide resource management. Yet, in spite of his efforts, timber and mining companies continued to destroy the environment.

New York State's concern for its environment began in 1885 with the passage of the New York State Forest Preserve Act providing for the protection of much of the Adirondacks and the Catskills. The 1895 **New York State Constitution** provided that the forest preserves would be kept forever wild and not wastefully developed.

The Supreme Court and Labor

Progressive thought entered the legal field and did battle with traditional laissez-faire views. The Supreme Court interpreted the Fourteenth Amendment as protecting the sanctity and freedom of contract at the expense of reforms for workers. In *Lochner* v. *New York* (1905) the Court ruled that a New York law that limited working hours was an infringement upon the **contract rights** between "the master and his employees" and therefore unconstitutional. The Court continued the *Lochner* reasoning in *Adair* v. *United States* (1908) with the Erdman Act of 1898, which made it a crime for an interstate carrier to dismiss an employee for membership in a labor union, an unconstitutional interference with the employer's and employee's liberty of contract.

However, in *Muller* v. *Oregon* (1908) the Supreme Court modified its *Lochner* v. *New York* decision by upholding an Oregon statute that limited the length of the work day for women to ten hours. The Court's conclusion that women were physically inferior and dependent upon men would later work against the continuing equal rights struggle of women.

Woodrow Wilson and the New Freedom

Progressivism was surging as the presidential election of 1912 approached. The victor, Democrat **Woodrow Wilson**, expressed his philosophy of Progressive government when he declared, "Freedom today is something more than being let alone. Without the watchful, resolute interference of the government, there can be no fair play between individuals and such powerful institutions as the trusts."

Election of 1912

The Republican party found itself split between the conservative followers of incumbent **William Howard Taft** and the Progressives, who themselves were split between **Theodore Roosevelt** and Senator **Robert M. La Follette** of Wisconsin. The Republican convention nominated Taft. Roosevelt and his followers formed the **Progressive party**, which nominated Roosevelt as the "**Bull Moose**" candidate on a platform embodying **New Nationalism**, the balancing of big business and big government through government's supervision of economic enterprise for the general welfare. The Socialist party nominated **Eugene V. Debs** as their candidate.

The Democrats, realizing the advantages of a race against the divided Republicans, nominated the Progressive governor of New Jersey, **Woodrow Wilson**. The Democrats' platform included the enforcement of the Sherman Act, better banking and currency laws, and tariff reform. The electoral outcome of the race was 435 votes for Wilson, 88 for Roosevelt, and 8 for Taft. The Socialist party received its greatest support in the election of 1912 with nearly a million popular votes cast for Debs. The Progressive measures supported by Wilson, Roosevelt, and Debs received the support of three fourths of the voters, demonstrating the strong national support for Progressivism.

The Underwood Tariff and the Graduated Income Tax

Upon entering office, President Wilson prepared for his attack on what he called the "**triple wall of privilege**": the tariff, the trusts, and the system of banking and currency.

Wilson saw the high rates of 40.8 percent established by the Payne-Aldrich Tariff (1909) as protecting the "special interests" of business while preventing consumers from benefiting from lower prices resulting from international competition. After Wilson's personal delivery of his message to Congress, a practice revived from the times of Washington and Adams, and the revelation of the pressures used by business lobbyists in Washington, the Underwood Tariff was finally approved in 1913. It lowered rates to 27 percent, the first significant tariff reduction since the Civil War.

Reformers during the administrations of Roosevelt and Taft introduced **income tax** legislation, which had been held unconstitutional by the Supreme Court in 1895 *(Pollock* v. *Farmer's Loan and Trust Company, 1895)*. As a result, the **Sixteenth Amendment** was proposed and sent to the states for ratification in 1909 and, to the surprise of many, was passed and became part of the Constitution in 1913. Within a short time, the income tax became the principal source of federal revenue. The federal income tax is an example of a **progressive**, or graduated, tax. A person earning a greater income pays taxes at a higher rate. A **regressive** tax, such as a sales tax, is designed so that all people pay the same tax rate, no matter what their income.

Clayton Antitrust Act and the Federal Trade Commission

Wilson's battles against the trusts gained their greatest victories with the passage of the **Federal Trade Commission Act** and the **Clayton Antitrust Act**. Wilson's special message to Congress during January 1914 asking for measures to break up monopolies was answered with the creation of the Federal Trade Commission. It was empowered to issue "**cease and desist**" orders to any business found guilty of unfair methods of competition.

The Clayton Antitrust Act, also passed by Congress in 1914, provided the following: (1) it expanded the definition of "unfair methods of competition" to include interlocking directorates, price discrimination, and purchase of a corporation's stock by a competing corporation; (2) it made officers of corporations liable for illegal acts of the corporation; and (3) it exempted labor unions and agricultural associations from antitrust acts and restricted the use of the labor injunction.

The Federal Reserve System

The third part of the "triple wall of privilege" identified by Wilson was the nation's banking and currency system. A major problem with the existing system, which was a product of the Civil War National Banking Act, was the inability of the amount of currency in circulation to adjust to the needs of the economy. Reform was needed.

The **Federal Reserve Act** was passed in 1913 and it included (1) the division of the country into twelve districts, each having a Federal Reserve bank; (2) the use of the Federal Reserve banks as "bankers' banks" for deposits of cash reserves of national banks and of state banks who wished to join the system; (3) the issuance of Federal Reserve notes (nation's paper currency); (4) the provision for loans from the Federal Reserve banks to member banks in times of need (adding to currency "flexibility"); and (5) the establishment of a Federal Reserve Board.

Direct Election of Senators

The Constitution provided that the state legislatures would elect senators (Article I, Section 3). The Seventeenth Amendment (1913) provided for the direct election of senators by popular vote.

Women's Suffrage Amendment

The women's suffrage movement was part of the reform movement to improve the legal and social status of women in the second half of the 19th century. The franchise was granted to women by the Wyoming Territory in 1869, the state of Wyoming in 1890, and the state of Colorado in 1897. By 1914 twelve states, all of them Western, had granted women the right to vote. The increased role of women in business and industry during World War I finally led Congress to approve the women's suffrage amendment and to send it to the states for ratification. The Nineteenth Amendment was added to the Constitution in 1920.

World War I: Effect on Domestic Reform

The Progressive Era ended when the United States entered World War I. American reform efforts now turned to a "crusading zeal" to make the world "safe for democracy." The war left Americans disillusioned, and after the war they reverted to **conservatism** and **nationalism**, typical of postwar periods.

Exercise Set 3.2

1. Which of the following was not true of the Progressives?
   A. they believed that the age of laissez-faire should come to an end
   B. among their members were representatives of the growing middle class
   C. they did not like the boss-ridden, business-dominated political parties of the day
   D. they did not believe in a strong, responsible government

2. Which of the following reforms was not achieved during the Progressive Era, 1901–1914?
   A. tariff reform
   B. railroad legislation
   C. banking reform
   D. a national minimum wage law

3. The public's response to Upton Sinclair's novel *The Jungle* helped bring about
   A. passage of the Clayton Antitrust Act
   B. the Pure Food and Drug Act
   C. adoption of the Nineteenth Amendment
   D. America's entry into World War I

4. Which of the following functions of the federal government came later than the other three?
   A. guaranteeing the welfare of the poor and unemployed
   B. the regulation of trusts
   C. promoting industrial growth by means of a protective tariff
   D. regulating immigration

CHAPTER REVIEW QUESTIONS

1. The name "Boss" Tweed is most closely associated with
   A. civil service reform
   B. referendum and recall
   C. increase in city "bossism" politics
   D. fair and open elections

2. All of the following were major reforms of President Wilson's "New Freedom" program except
   A. tariff reform
   B. antitrust legislation
   C. social security
   D. banking and currency reforms

3. A Progressive measure used at the state and local level that permits voters to introduce legislation is referred to as
   A. initiative
   B. recall
   C. impeachment
   D. referendum

4. Wilson's first administration (1912–1916) was characterized by
   A. greater protection of trusts
   B. reforms in the country's banking and currency system
   C. increases in most tariff rates
   D. the end of the temperance movement

5. The main objective of the Muckrakers was to
   A. establish communism
   B. cleanse capitalist society
   C. overthrow the existing form of government in the United States
   D. end government censorship of American literature

6. The Federal Trade Commission Act of 1914
   A. made all business combinations that resembled trusts illegal
   B. established the nation's first income tax
   C. established an investigatory board with the power to issue "cease and desist" orders
   D. replaced the Clayton Antitrust Act

ESSAYS

1. In Andrew Jackson's day it seemed to be in the public interest for banking and government to be separated; in Woodrow Wilson's day it seemed to be in the public interest for them to be joined.

   a. Select *two* issues from the list below and explain how they may have contributed to the change in economic philosophies.

   Issues
   Distribution of wealth
   Elasticity of currency
   Growth of industry
   Population increases
   Economic cycles

   b. *Explain* the economic philosophies for *both* Jackson's and Wilson's views concerning banking and government.

2. "The ability of the Constitution to respond to changing conditions of society has been made possible in a large part by the amending provision." Assess the validity of this statement with reference to three of the issues listed below.

   Issues
   Women's suffrage
   Tax revision
   Temperance
   Election of senators

3. Reform has been a continuing process in United States history.

   a. Listed below is a major reform movement with some of the problems it attempted to solve. For the reform movement provided, discuss why reform was needed in the problem areas listed. Show how the reform movement responded to that need.

   Progressive Movement (1890–1920)
   Practices of big business
   Actions to make government more democratic

   b. Listed below are problem areas that many people believe are in need of reform today. Choose one of the areas and identify a specific problem related to it. Describe one proposal that has been made to deal with the problem.

   Areas in Need of Reform
   Quality of education
   Providing adequate housing
   Dealing with crime

· THEMATIC ESSAY

Directions: Write a well-organized essay that includes an introduction, several paragraphs addressing the task below, and a conclusion.

Theme: Diversity, Reform, and the Black Movement

> Techniques advocated by civil rights leaders at the end of the 19th century and beginning of the 20th century ranged from gradual evolution to demands for complete, immediate equality.

Task:

> Identify *two* African American civil rights leaders during the 1875–1925 time period.
>
> - For each leader identified, discuss the method(s) he used to obtain equality for African Americans.
> - Discuss the differences in the techniques used by each of the leaders.
> - Assess the success or failure of the methods used by each leader.

Some suggestions you may wish to consider include: Booker T. Washington, W.E.B. Du Bois, and Marcus Garvey.

You are *not* limited to these suggestions.

DOCUMENT-BASED QUESTION ESSAY

The following questions (Part A and Part B) are based on the accompanying documents (1–7). Some of these documents have been edited for the purpose of this exercise. The question is designed to test your ability to work with historical documents and to demonstrate your knowledge of the subject matter being presented. As you analyze the documents, take into account both the source of the document and the author's point of view.

Historical Context: Although the United States entered the 20th century with the vast material strength that placed it among the great powers of the world, the rich human values of the past were being lost. The Progressive Period was a time for social justice to catch up with industrial capitalism.

Task: Using information from the documents and your knowledge of United States history, answer the questions that follow each document in Part A. Your answers to the questions will help you write the Part B essay, in which you will be asked:

In the view of the Progressives, what was wrong with American society? What solutions did the Progressives support to correct these wrongs?

Part A
Short Answer

The documents below relate to issues concerning the Progressive Period. Examine each document carefully and then answer the questions that follow.

Meat scraps were also found being shoveled into receptacles from dirty floors, where they were left to lie until again shoveled into barrels or into machines for chopping. These floors, it must be noted, were in most cases damp and soggy, in dark, ill-ventilated rooms, and the employees in utter ignorance of cleanliness or danger to health expectorated at will upon them. In a word, we saw meat shoveled from filthy wooden floors, piled on tables rarely washed, pushed from room to room in rotten box carts, in all of which processes it was in the way of gathering dirt, splinters, floor filth, and the expectoration of tuberculosis and other diseased workers. . . . Where comment was made to floor superintendents about these matters, it was always the reply that this meat would afterwards be cooked, and that this sterilization would prevent any danger from its use. . . . In one well-known establishment we came upon fresh meat being shoveled into barrels, and a regular proportion being added of stale scraps that had lain on a dirty floor in the corner of a room for some days previous.

—Upton Sinclair, *The Jungle* (1902)

1. What were the popular reactions to the passage above from Upton Sinclair's book, *The Jungle*? What was the response of the government? (Provide at least one piece of legislation in your answer.)

_____

_____

_____

_____

DOCUMENT 2

> I stand for a square deal. But when I say that I am for the square deal, I mean not merely that I stand for fair play under the present rules of the game, but that I stand for having those rules changed so as to work for a more substantial equality of opportunity and of reward for equally good service...now the great special interests too often control and corrupt the men and methods of government for their own profit.

—Theodore Roosevelt, *New Nationalism* (1910)

2. What are the "special interests" referred to by Presidential candidate Theodore Roosevelt?

_____

_____

_____

_____

DOCUMENT 3

> The Senate of the United States shall be composed of two Senators from each State, elected by the people hereof, for six years; and each Senator shall have one vote. The electors in each State shall have the qualifications requisite for electors of [voters for] the most numerous branch of the State legislatures.

—Seventeenth Amendment (1913)

3. Describe how the Seventeenth Amendment could be considered a "progressive amendment."

_____

_____

_____

Sadie is an intelligent, neat, clean girl, who has worked from the time she got her working papers in embroidery factories. She was a stamper and for several years before she was poisoned, earned $10 a week. In her work she was accustomed to use a white powder (chalk or talcum was usual) which was brushed over the perforated designs and thus transferred to the cloth. The design was easily brushed off when made of chalk or of talcum, if the embroiderers were not careful. Her last employer therefore commenced using white lead powder, mixed with rosin, which cheapened the work as the powder could not be rubbed off and necessitate restamping. . . . None of the girls knew of the change in powder, nor of the danger in its use. The workroom was crowded and hot, the stampers' tables were farthest from the windows and the constant use of the powder caused them to breathe it continually and their hands were always covered with it. . . . Sadie was sick in the hospital for six months (losing $10 per week). She said her employer bought off several of her witnesses, but before the case came to trial two years later several of them also became ill and consequently decided to testify for her. The employer appealed to the girl's feelings and induced her, on the day of the trial, to accept $150. He said that he had had business reverses and consequently would be unable to pay in case she won.

—Preliminary Report of the New York State Factory
Investigating Commission (Albany, N.Y.:
The Argus Company, 1912), vol. 1, pp. 488–489

4. Who would use the account provided in the New York State Factory Investigating Commission to promote their interests—labor or management? Why?

_____

_____

_____

_____

DOCUMENT 5

As to the forest reserves, their creation has damaged just one class, that is, the great lumber barons: the managers and owners of those lumber companies which by illegal, fraudulent, or unfair methods have desired to get possession of the valuable timber of the public domain, to skin the land, and to abandon it when impoverished well-nigh to the point of worthlessness.

There are some small men who have wanted to get hold of this lumber land for improper purposes, but they are not powerful or influential, and though they have sometimes been put forward to cause an agitation, the real beneficiaries of the destruction of the forest reserves would be the great lumber companies, which would speedily monopolize them.

If it had not been for the creation of the present system of forest reserves, practically every acre of timberland in the West would now be controlled or be on the point of being controlled by one huge lumber trust. The object of the beneficiaries of this trust would be to exhaust the resources of the country for their own immediate pecuniary benefit, and then when they had rendered it well-nigh worthless to turn it contemptuously over to settlers, who would find too late that those responsible for such conditions had betrayed them and had been false to the public.

—President Theodore Roosevelt Letter (1907)

5. President Theodore Roosevelt has been credited with having been a great conservationist. How does the 1907 letter support this reputation?

_____

_____

_____

_____

6. According to President Roosevelt, what are the objectives of the lumber trusts?

_____

_____

_____

_____

DOCUMENT 6

> The right of citizens of the United States to vote shall not be denied or abridged by the United States or by any State on account of sex. Congress shall have power to enforce this article by appropriate legislation.

—Nineteenth Amendment (1920)

7. How did the Nineteenth Amendment expand social justice in the early part of the 20th century?

_____

_____

_____

_____

DOCUMENT 7

Triangle Shirtwaist Factory Fire, "Devil Rising."

8. What message is the cartoon conveying regarding the 1911 Triangle Shirtwaist Factory Fire?

_____

_____

_____

_____

Part B
Essay

Your essay should be well organized with an introductory paragraph that states your position on the question. Develop your position in the next paragraphs and then write a conclusion. In your essay, include specific historical details and refer to the specific documents you analyzed in Part A. You may include additional information from your knowledge of social studies.

Historical Context: Although the United States entered the 20th century with the vast material strength that placed it among the great powers of the world, the rich human values of the past were being lost. The Progressive Period was a time for social justice to catch up with industrial capitalism.

Task:

In the view of Progressives, what was wrong with American society? What solutions did they put forth to correct those wrongs?

Guidelines:

In your essay, be sure to
• Develop all aspects of the task
• Incorporate information from at least _five_ documents
• Incorporate relevant outside information
• Support the theme with many relevant facts, examples, and details
• Use a logical and clear plan of organization, including an introduction and a conclusion that are beyond a restatement of the theme

CHAPTER 2

THE RISE OF AMERICAN POWER

THE INDUSTRIAL-COLONIAL CONNECTION

Economic Imperialism

In the 1870s and after, several developments combined to shift America's attention across the oceans. The end of the frontier, announced officially in the census report of 1890, an increase in American agricultural and industrial output, and fluctuations in the American economy fostered the belief that the fixture of the country's growth and prosperity lay outside its own continental borders.

United States Industrial Productivity

By the end of the 19th century, factories and farms in the United States produced more goods than the domestic market could consume. As American industry continued to grow, industrialists looked abroad for new sources of raw materials, additional markets for American goods, and places to invest surplus capital. Both farmers and industrialists were eager to enter new overseas markets, and the growing volume of exports began to change American trade relations. In 1870 United States exports totaled $451 million; in 1880, $853 million; and by 1900, $1.5 billion. In 1898 the United States exported more than it imported, a status known as a favorable balance of trade, beginning a trend that lasted through the 1960s.

Theories of Expansionism

As overseas trade expansion continued to receive more attention, a school of thought developed that held that the only way to save and promote nationalism was through overseas territorial expansion.

President Lincoln's Secretary of State, **William Seward**, had envisioned an American empire that included Canada, Cuba, Central America, Hawaii, Iceland, and Greenland. Although his ambitious designs resulted only in the 1867 purchase from Russia of **Alaska** for $7.2 million, it was an important step toward American territorial expansion. Josiah Strong, a Congregational minister and strong advocate of expansionism, wrote a popular book, *Our Country: Its Possible Future and Its Present Crisis* (1885), that called for overseas missionary work to "civilize the world under the Anglo-Saxon races." A growing popular belief was that Americans, the bearers of civil liberty and Christianity, were members of a God-favored race destined to lead the world. "As America goes, so goes the world," Strong claimed. Others in America who supported expansion drew on **Charles Darwin's** theories of evolution, applying them to human and social development and calling for the triumph of the fit and the elimination or subjugation of the unfit.

Naval Power

The importance of naval power became increasingly obvious toward the end of the 19th century. The American fleet had fallen into disrepair and by 1880 consisted of only 48 ships that were capable of even firing a gun. Big-navy proponents pointed to the growing fleets of Great Britain, France, and Germany, arguing that the United States needed a stronger fleet to protect its growing overseas interests, and Congress began to authorize new naval construction. One of the main forces behind naval expansion was Captain **Alfred T. Mahan**. After graduating from the Naval Academy in 1859, he devoted a lifetime to studying the influence of sea power in history and for over two decades he headed the Newport Naval War College.

Technological Advances

Technology continued to improve machinery, means of transportation, and methods of communication, as the "need" for expansionism grew. Exports to other countries included the inventions of **Thomas Edison** (electronics, communications) and **Alexander Graham Bell** (communications), **George Westinghouse** (air brakes), **Cyrus McCormick** (farm machinery), and **George Eastman** (photographic equipment). Improvements in transportation and communication accelerated America's involvement in world affairs with the speed and safety provided by **steam-powered ships** and the linking of the United States with other parts of the world through **underwater cables** to transmit **telegraph** communication. Finally, technological improvements in industry increased output and hastened the need for additional foreign markets.

European Imperialism

The last third of the 19th century was characterized by a worldwide scramble for empires. Great Britain, France, and Germany had established colonial claims in Africa and now looked to Asia for further gains. As imperialist expansionism grew throughout the world, Americans considered the acquisition of colonies necessary to attain a position of power in the world.

The Tariff Controversy: Free Trade vs. Protectionism

The tariff question, which was an issue throughout American history, continued to be raised during the expansionist period at the turn of the century.

Through the mid-19th century, tariffs were continually raised to protect American manufacturing and agriculture. Those who advocated protectionism believed that a high tariff was necessary to allow continued economic growth at home. Those who claimed that tariffs were benefiting certain groups and were making prices artificially high for most consumers favored lowering the tariff rates to approach a system of free trade among nations.

The tariff question continues to be an issue today in international economics. Those who favor protectionism claim that the higher standard of living in the United States has resulted in a higher cost of production requiring protection from less expensive foreign goods. Advocates of free trade argue that the American consumer deserves a greater choice of goods at lower prices and that foreign competition would force an increase in the efficiency of American production.

Exercise Set 3.3

1. Which of the following was not a reason for United States expansion between 1880 and 1914?
   A. the desire to extend Christianity
   B. the search for overseas markets
   C. the desire to maintain a position in the international race for power
   D. the search for outlets for surplus population

2. U.S. expansion abroad following the Civil War indicated that
   A. the demand for industrial and agricultural goods within the United States exceeded industry's ability to produce
   B. advocates of isolationism influenced national foreign policy
   C. economic expansion, nationalism, and cultural values worked together as reasons for overseas growth
   D. domestic growth and international growth were unrelated

3. Before 1898, possessions of the United States beyond its immediate boundaries
   A. included Alaska
   B. did not exist
   C. consisted of Alaska, Canada, and Mexico
   D. included most of Central America

4. A high protective tariff rate on imports into the United States may reflect
   A. an isolationist view of economic matters
   B. a desire for free trade
   C. the need to become more involved in the international market
   D. the desires of the average American consumer

AN EMERGING GLOBAL INVOLVEMENT

> Recent events—the navigation of the ocean by steam, the acquisition and rapid settlement by this country of a vast territory on the Pacific—have practically brought the countries of the east in closer proximity to our own. The intercourse between them has already greatly increased and no limits can be assigned to its future extension.
>
> Instructions by Secretary of State Conrad
> to Commodore Matthew Perry, 1852

Manifest Destiny and Expansion into the Pacific

The concept of "**Manifest Destiny**" was first expressed when journalist **John O'Sullivan**, responding to the question of the annexation of Texas, stated that "the fulfillment of our manifest destiny is to overspread the continent by Providence for the free development of our yearly multiplying millions." With the additions of the **Mexican Cession** (1848), the **Oregon Country** (1846), the **Gadsden Purchase** (1853), and **Alaska** (1867), the continental boundaries of the United States were established.

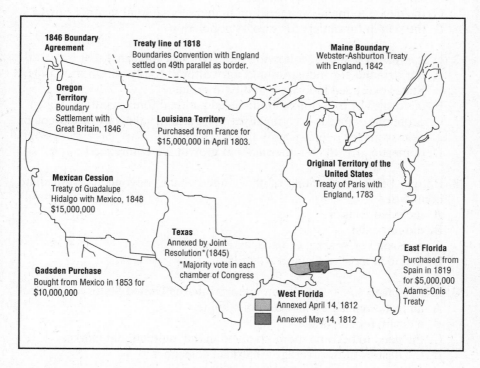

Figure 3.1 Territorial Growth of the United States (1783–1853)

The Opening of Japan

In 1852 President **Millard Fillmore** sent **Commodore Matthew Perry** to end Japan's isolation and to convince the Japanese to open certain ports to American trade. In March 1854 Perry secured a treaty of friendship with Japan that granted some trading concessions. In 1857 Townshend Harris, the first American minister to Japan, negotiated treaties expanding the diplomatic and commercial relations between the two countries.

In the face of American and European imperialism, Japan quickly transformed itself from a medieval feudal state to a modern nation. By establishing a strong central government, creating a powerful army and navy, and encouraging industrialization, Japan soon became a leading trading and manufacturing nation. Japan's need for raw materials and markets for its manufactured goods turned the nation to active imperialism by the end of the 19th century.

Increased Japanese immigration into the United States by the beginning of the 20th century brought about considerable nativist opposition. Newspapers, state and local governments, and labor unions, among others, pressured for immigration restrictions, resulting in the **Gentlemen's Agreement** (1907), which curtailed the flow of Japanese laborers into the United States.

Early Relations with China

The United States had long been involved in trade with China, opening a small, but profitable, exchange of goods in 1784.

During the 1800s many Chinese immigrants came to the United States and settled on the West Coast. Nativists aroused widespread anti-Chinese feelings, claiming that the Chinese worked for low wages and were not able to assimilate into American society. The **Workingmen's party**, formed in 1877, included in its platform an anti-Chinese stance, and was instrumental in the passage of state and local laws discriminating against Chinese workers and shopkeepers. In 1882 Congress, responding to nativist pressures, passed the **Chinese Exclusion Act**, prohibiting Chinese immigration for ten years. A later law passed in 1902 excluded the Chinese completely. The Supreme Court addressed the problem of *Yick Ho* v. *Hopkins* (1886), in which the Court struck down a San Francisco ordinance on the grounds that it arbitrarily classified persons so as to discriminate against the Chinese.

Other Pacific Overtures

The Open-Door Policy

Following the **Spanish-American War** (1898–1899) and the **Philippine-American War** (1898–1902), which was a revolt against American rule, the United States annexed the Philippines and increased its Pacific trade. Anticipating increased trade with China, but realizing that the United States had entered the competition late and trade was threatened by the European spheres of influence, President McKinley's Secretary of State, **John Hay**, suggested an **Open Door Policy** in 1898. He proclaimed that "we do not seek advantages in the Orient which are not common to all. Asking only the open door for ourselves, we are ready to accord the open door to others." In 1899 Hay addressed identical diplomatic notes to Germany, England, and Russia, and later to France, Japan, and Italy, asking them to join the United States in respecting the preservation of China's independence and territory. However, the Open Door Policy failed to slow the pace of imperialism in China. The **Russo-Japanese War** (1904–1905) threatened the open door in China by making Japan the dominant power in the Far East. President Theodore Roosevelt persuaded both Japan and Russia to recognize the neutrality of all Chinese territory outside of Manchuria and brought the warring sides to Portsmouth, New Hampshire (September 1905) to draft a peace treaty.

The Boxer Rebellion

As their nation continued to fall into the hands of European and Asian imperialist nations, the **Boxers**, a Chinese society encouraged by Manchu leaders, vowed to drive the "foreign devils" out of China. In June 1900 members of the Boxers attacked the foreign holdings (concessions) in Peiping and massacred 300 people. A joint expeditionary force of European, Japanese, and American troops suppressed the rebellion. The Manchu Dynasty was overthrown in 1912 by the Nationalists (Kuomintang) under **Sun Yat-sen**, and China was proclaimed a republic.

The Acquisition of Hawaii

During the early 19th century, American traders, missionaries, and whalers visited the Hawaiian Islands. In 1842 the State Department announced that the Hawaiian Islands would not be open to colonization by any other nation. In 1875 the Reciprocity Treaty granted commercial favors to the islands if the Hawaiian king assured the United States that he would not allow other powers to acquire territory. A treaty in 1887 between Hawaii and the United States provided for the leasing of **Pearl Harbor** as a naval station.

As American interests, represented primarily by sugar plantations and missionaries, grew in Hawaii, the white population of the islands became increasingly influential. When **Queen Liliuokalani** attempted to nationalize the sugar plantations and drive foreign investors out, American planters revolted (January 1893). They overthrew the queen, set up a provisional government establishing the **Republic of Hawaii**, and asked for annexation by the United States. President Cleveland withdrew the annexation treaty from the Senate, and arguments concerning the fate of Hawaii continued through the 1890s. After the victory in the Spanish-American War, annexation of the Philippine Islands, and emphasis on naval buildup heightened the expansionist excitement in the country, President McKinley obtained a joint resolution from Congress annexing the Hawaiian Islands on July 7, 1898. Hawaii remained a territory until it was admitted as the fiftieth state in 1959.

Samoa and Naval Bases

The Samoan Islands, some 3,000 miles to the southwest of Hawaii, provided strategic locations in the South Pacific shipping lanes. Like Hawaii, the islands had been visited by American sailors and missionaries since the 1830s. In 1872 a United States naval officer negotiated an agreement granting the United States use of the harbor of Pago Pago, the site of a later naval station. Great Britain and Germany also secured treaty rights in Samoa and tensions between the three powers came to a showdown in 1889 when German threats of annexation brought fleets from the three countries face-to-face in the harbor at Pago Pago. A timely hurricane wrecked the fleets and subsequently the three nations established a **tripartite protectorate** over the islands.

Hesitant Colonialism

Review of the Monroe Doctrine (1823–1898)

On December 2, 1823, in a message to Congress, President James Monroe, influenced by Secretary of State John Quincy Adams, put forward an independent American foreign policy that later became known as the **Monroe Doctrine**. Claiming that the Western Hemisphere was no longer open to European colonization, the Doctrine proved to be of great importance to future foreign policy determinations of the United States. But it was not until

The expansion of American interests led to a need for overseas naval bases.

after the Civil War that the United States was powerful enough to enforce the Monroe Doctrine throughout the Western Hemisphere.

Mexico's sovereignty was threatened in 1863 when the French took advantage of internal instabilities and created a puppet state under **Archduke Maximilian**. Secretary of State **William Seward** objected to French intervention by **Napoleon III**, emperor of France. In 1865, with the end of the Civil War, American troops were sent to the Mexican border. French troops were withdrawn in 1867, and Maximilian was executed by the Mexicans. The United States saw this as a victory for the Monroe Doctrine and a sign of growing American power in the Western Hemisphere. By the end of the 19th century, the United States had become powerful enough to enforce the Monroe Doctrine.

The Spanish-American War (1898–1899)

American interests in Cuba increased with economic investments totaling over $50 million by 1895 and an annual trade worth $100 million, the strategic importance of the island, (especially as plans for a canal across Central America developed), and the growing spirit of manifest destiny. When Cuban Nationalists revolted against Spain in February 1895, American sympathy for an independent Cuba was encouraged by the sensational stories printed in the "**yellow press**"—**Joseph Pulitzer's** *New York World* and **William Randolph Hearst's** *New York Journal*.

Following Cuba's refusal to accept President McKinley's plan for increased self-government under Spanish control, and the sinking of the American battleship *Maine* in Havana Harbor on February 15, 1898, popular support for war resulted in a declaration of war against Spain on April 17. At the same time, Congress adopted the **Teller Amendment**, pledging the United States to acquire no Cuban territory and to turn the island over to the Cuban people as soon as their independence was won.

Spain was defeated in Cuba after the battles of El Caney and San Juan Hill, and the fall of Santiago on July 13, 1898. A bloodless conquest of Spanish Puerto Rico was conducted by General Nelson A. Miles. While the war was being fought in Cuba, American Commodore George Dewey defeated the Spanish fleet in the Philippines and captured Manila on August 13.

Empire Building

The **Treaty of Paris** ending the Spanish-American War was signed December 10, 1898. The treaty provided that American troops would remain in Cuba until 1902 while the Cuban constitution was prepared. Included in the Cuban constitution was the **Platt Amendment**, which required that any treaties involving Cuba would have to be approved first by the United States; Cuba was to grant permission to the United States to intervene, if necessary, to preserve the island's independence, and a naval base at **Guantanamo** was to be

246

leased to the United States. The Platt Amendment governed Cuban-American relations until 1934.

- *Puerto Rico.* As a result of the Treaty of Paris (1898), Puerto Rico was ceded to the United States. The **Foraker Act** of 1900 provided that the President of the United States would appoint Puerto Rico's governor and the executive council of its legislature. The **Jones Act** of 1917 granted Puerto Ricans American citizenship and the right to elect both houses of their legislature. In 1948 Puerto Ricans were granted the right to elect their own governor and in 1952 Puerto Rico voted in favor of **commonwealth** status.

- *Guam.* After it was annexed to the United States by Spain in 1898, the island of Guam, located east of the Philippines, was governed by the United States Navy. In 1950 Guam received limited self-government, American citizenship for its inhabitants, a governor appointed by the President of the United States, a popularly elected legislature, and a bill of rights.

- *The Philippines.* When the Treaty of Paris ending the war between Spain and the United States came before the Senate, the question of the annexation of the Philippines sparked heated debate. Anti-imperialists argued that annexation would violate the sacred concept of self-determination. Imperialists stressed the commercial and strategic advantages of ownership, along with the fact that Germany and Japan would most likely move into the Philippines if the United States were to pull out. The arguments of the imperialists triumphed, and the treaty was ratified on February 6, 1898, by a 57-to-27 vote.

When the Philippines did not receive independence following the Spanish-American War, a rebellion under the leadership of **Emilio Aguinaldo** broke out. This insurrection, known as the **Philippine-American War**, was a war

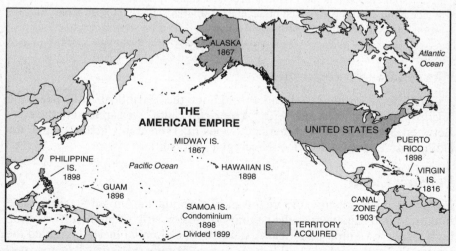

Figure 3.2 The American Empire (1903)

of larger proportions than the Spanish-American War, and resulted in more American casualties. After the rebellion was suppressed, the United States imposed its regime on the Philippines. English was made the official language, public works were introduced, and sedition acts and political imprisonment silenced critics. Beginning in 1907 the Filipinos elected the lower house of their legislature. The **Jones Act** of 1916 granted the citizens of the Philippines the right to elect both houses of their legislature and promised eventual independence. During the administration of Franklin Roosevelt, the **Tydings-McDuffie Act** (1934) was passed, providing for eventual independence and allowing the Filipinos to write a constitution. In 1946 the islands formally received independence and the following year granted the United States military bases within their country.

Constitutional Issues

America's new overseas territories raised a constitutional question concerning the status of alien peoples and whether constitutional protections of the United States were extended to them. In the so-called "**insular cases**," particularly *Downes* v. *Bidwell* (1901), the Supreme Court ruled on the question, "Does the Constitution follow the flag?" It concluded that the Constitution protected the basic civil rights of inhabitants of colonial possessions, but did not confer citizenship or political rights on them.

Latin American Affairs

> There is a homely adage which runs, 'Speak softly and carry a big stick; you will go far.' If the American nation will speak softly and yet build and keep at a pitch of the highest training a thoroughly efficient navy, the Monroe Doctrine will go far.
>
> President Theodore Roosevelt, September 2, 1901

West Indies Protectorates

As American influence spread throughout the Caribbean following the Spanish-American War, the term "**American Lake**" was applied to the area. Between 1900 and 1917, American troops intervened in Cuba, Panama, the Dominican Republic, Mexico, Nicaragua, and Haiti.

Panama Canal

Following the acquisition of Oregon and California, the United States became interested in a canal across the isthmus (a narrow strip of land with water on both sides) in Central America. A treaty with Colombia in 1846 granted the United States the right to build either a canal or railroad across Panama (part of Colombia until 1903), and in 1850 the United States and Great Britain agreed to exercise joint control over a future canal.

• *Acquisition and Construction.* America's new possessions in the Caribbean and Pacific underscored the need for a means of faster transportation across Central America. Remembering the seventy-one days required for the battleship *Oregon* to sail from San Francisco around Cape Horn to its battle station in the Pacific at the outset of the Spanish-American War, President Roosevelt pushed for the construction of a canal. The **Hay-Pauncefote Treaty** (1901) with Great Britain gave the United States sole control over a future canal in return for the guarantee that the canal would be open equally to all nations. Colombia, seeking more money, rejected the **Hay-Herran Treaty** (1903), which was to give the United States a ninety-nine-year lease on a canal zone in the Colombian province of Panama. Frustrated by Colombia's lack of cooperation, President Roosevelt hinted at a Panamanian revolt and shortly thereafter (November 1903), Panamanians rose in revolt against Colombia for independence. Panama's independence was recognized immediately by the United States.

The **Hay-Bunau-Varilla Treaty** (1903) with Panama granted the United States perpetual control of a canal zone ten miles wide across the isthmus of Panama in return for a lump sum payment and an annual fee. On August 15, 1914, the first ocean steamer sailed through the completed canal, which had cost $275 million to build.

• *Current Treaty.* During the 1960s and 1970s Panama demonstrated resentment over the presence of the United States and its sole control over the canal. In January 1964 Panama broke off diplomatic relations with the United States resulting in negotiations over the treaty between the two countries. President Lyndon Johnson announced in December 1964 that he would propose a renegotiation of the 1903 treaty. Although a new treaty granting Panama greater control over the canal was concluded, increased tensions between the countries prevented its ratification. In August 1977 the United States and Panama ended years of negotiations when President Carter and General Torrijos Herrara signed two treaties providing for the return of the Panama Canal Zone to Panama in the year 2000. The treaties were ratified by the Senate in 1978 and the return took place on December 31, 1999.

Interpretations of the Monroe Doctrine

As you read, the implementation of the Monroe Doctrine came years after its introduction in 1823. The Monroe Doctrine was tested in 1895 over a boundary dispute between Venezuela and the British colony of British Guiana. The United States demanded that Great Britain accept arbitration concerning the Venezuelan boundary dispute. President Cleveland's Secretary of State **Richard Olney** claimed that the Monroe Doctrine implied that the United

States was justified in intervening in Western Hemisphere affairs because "the United States is practically sovereign on the continent." After military force was threatened, Great Britain agreed to arbitration, and Olney's stand became known as the **Olney Interpretation of the Monroe Doctrine**.

President Theodore Roosevelt's interventions in the Venezuela debt dispute (1902) and the Dominican debt default (1904–1905) illustrated his belief that the United States had to assume "international police power" in the Western Hemisphere. This policy of United States intervention in Latin American affairs, excluding intervention by European nations, became known as the **Roosevelt Corollary** to the Monroe Doctrine. Latin American countries soon objected to the paternal and dominating role of the United States.

President Taft and Dollar Diplomacy

United States influence continued to expand in Latin America during the administration of President **Taft** (1909–1913). Under a policy referred to as **"dollar diplomacy,"** United States bankers and businesspeople were encouraged to invest in areas of importance to the United States and were guaranteed full military and diplomatic support. In 1899 two of the largest banana importers merged to form the **United Fruit Company** which, by 1913, owned over one million acres and most of the railroad and steamship lines in Central

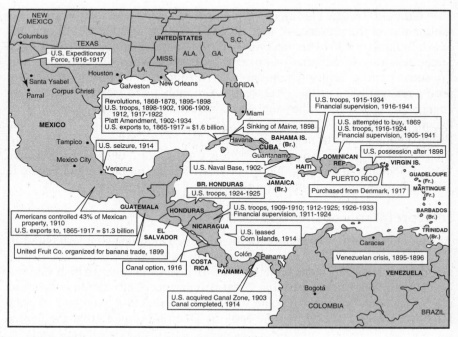

Figure 3.3 The United States and the Caribbean

America. Because of American investments in the countries of Honduras, Nicaragua, and Haiti, the United States felt able to justify military intervention to protect American interests. Intervention came when the United States Marines were ordered into **Nicaragua** in 1912, **Haiti** in 1915, and the **Dominican Republic** in 1916.

President Wilson and Mexico

Porfirio Diaz, the dictator of Mexico for 37 years, was overthrown by a revolution in 1911. After a period of constitutional government, General **Victoriano Huerta** seized power in 1913. President Wilson withheld recognition of his government during a time of "watchful waiting," because he considered Huerta a "butcher" whose regime was oppressing the Mexican people. Wilson stationed United States naval units off Mexico and seized the **Port of Vera Cruz** in 1914 to block a German arms shipment. In July 1914 Huerta resigned and Wilson recognized the new government under Venustiano Carranza.

In 1916 **Pancho Villa**, a rival Mexican leader, revolted and led raids into New Mexico, hoping to bring the United States into an action that would help him seize power. American forces under General **John Pershing** were ordered into Mexico to capture Villa. Objections from Carranza, and an elusive Pancho Villa, caused Wilson to recall Pershing. As Mexican objections to "**Yankee Imperialism**" continued, relations between the two countries worsened. As part of the **Good Neighbor** policy in the 1930s, Mexican control of its own resources was recognized, while compensation came to the United States in return for **nationalized oil properties**.

Good Neighbor Policy

The United States changed its policy toward Latin America in the 1930s. In 1933, under the "Good Neighbor" policy of President Franklin Roosevelt, the United States agreed that "no state had the right to intervene in the external or internal affairs of another," thus abandoning the (Theodore) Roosevelt Corollary. Some people feel that the end of the 20th century saw a resurgence of the Roosevelt Corollary to the Monroe Doctrine in the attempts of the United States to curb Communist influence in Nicaragua, El Salvador, and on the island of Grenada.

Exercise Set 3.4

1. Which is the most valid conclusion that can be drawn concerning the territorial acquisitions of the United States?
   A. the use of a show of military force was always necessary
   B. the "fruits of war" rarely include territorial gains
   C. the addition of territorial gains increases a country's involvement in international affairs
   D. the territorial gains of the United States did not extend beyond the Western Hemisphere

2. The Platt Amendment provided for relations between the United States and
   A. Cuba
   B. Panama
   C. Hawaii
   D. Alaska

3. Which of the following is *not* an example of formal imperialism?
   A. annexation
   B. colonialism
   C. military occupation
   D. humanitarian aid

4. Which of the following did *not* become a United States possession as a result of the Spanish-American War?
   A. Puerto Rico
   B. Panama
   C. the Philippines
   D. Guam

5. The Roosevelt Corollary to the Monroe Doctrine
   A. was widely accepted by Latin America
   B. was reinforced by Franklin Roosevelt in the 1930s
   C. had been used since the introduction of the Monroe Doctrine in 1823
   D. made the United States the peace keeper in the Western Hemisphere

6. The right of American citizens living in China to be tried in American courts was called
   A. "following the flag"
   B. the Open Door Policy
   C. extraterritoriality
   D. dollar diplomacy

RESTRAINT AND INVOLVEMENT (1914–1920)

The United States must be neutral in fact as well as in name.
President Wilson, Message to U.S. Senate, 1914

America cannot be an ostrich with its head in the sand.
President Wilson, Address to U.S. Senate, 1916

The world must be made safe for democracy.
President Wilson, Address to Congress
asking for declaration of war, April 2, 1917

On July 28, 1914, **Austria-Hungary** declared war on **Serbia** following the assassination of **Archduke Franz Ferdinand**, heir to the Austro-Hungarian throne, by a Serbian nationalist. Germany backed its ally Austria, while Russia mobilized to protect Serbia. Germany in turn declared war on Russia and France, Russia's ally. German troops marched through Belgium to crush France; Britain, honoring its pledge to defend Belgian neutrality, declared war on Germany. The Great War had begun with the Allies (Britain, France, Russia, Serbia, and Belgium) opposing the **Central Powers** (Germany and Austria). Later, the war would engulf most of the nations of the world.

*entente → int'l understanding re.
a common course of action*

European Background to World War I

Nationalist Rivalries and Alliance System

Following the French Revolution, the nations of Europe had created a "**balance of power**." However, after the unification of Germany in 1871, **Chancellor Otto Von Bismarck** first made an alliance with Austria-Hungary (**Dual Alliance**, 1879); later Italy joined, forming the **Triple Alliance** in 1882.

Seeing the Triple Alliance as a threat, France and Russia ratified a secret alliance in 1894. Although Great Britain did not immediately join the alliance with France and Russia, early in the 20th century an "understanding," which came to be known as the **Triple Entente**, developed between the three nations. Thus, by 1907 the chief European powers had organized themselves into two opposing camps — the Triple Alliance composed of Germany, Austria-Hungary, and Italy, and the Triple Entente, with France, Russia, and Great Britain.

Colonialism and the Spread of War

Underlying reasons for World War I included conflicting **territorial claims**, **imperialistic rivalries**, and **destructive nationalism**. Although the nations of Western Europe had not come into direct conflict, their armies and navies continued to grow in size and the "peace" that existed was an "armed peace," based upon a **"balance of terror**."

Importance of Control of Sea Routes

Great Britain had long followed a policy of keeping its navy superior in strength to any other nation's naval fleet. Germany, realizing that a naval buildup was necessary to compete with Great Britain, began an effort to create a navy second to none. When war broke out in Europe, the fleets of the Allied Powers were effective in forcing German ships to seek the shelter of their home ports. Throughout the war the Allies maintained a **blockade** of Germany and Austria-Hungary that enabled the Allies to import food and raw materials, transport troops, and effectively destroy the commerce of their enemies.

Germany's power on the seas increased with the use of the submarine, or **U-boat**. Although first used to destroy enemy warships, the submarine was eventually used to destroy merchant ships as well. According to international law, a merchant ship was to be warned before attack. However, Germany began a policy of "**unrestricted submarine warfare**" that was so destructive it appeared to spell defeat for the Allies.

United States Involvement

Efforts at Neutrality

When war broke out in Europe in 1914, Americans reacted with horror and wanted to stay out of the hostilities. President Wilson declared American neutrality on August 4, 1914 and, in a message to the Senate, he proclaimed that the United States "must be neutral in fact as well as in name."

Neutrality proved to be a difficult policy as Americans became either pro-Ally, pro-German, or pro-neutral. Those who sympathized with the Allies felt a bond with England and remembered that France had come to the aid of the Americans during our Revolution. The movement to enter the war on the side of the Allies was helped by propaganda describing Germany's militarism and unprovoked invasion of Belgium. A considerable part of the country was either pro-German, pro-neutral, or pacifist (anti-war). Irish-Americans were traditionally anti-British, and approximately 8 million Americans were of German descent. Among Progressives in the United States, war was seen as violating and interrupting the spirit of Progressive reform. In 1915, Progressives, including Jane Addams, Florence Kelley, and Lillian Wald, formed the American Union Against Militarism to stop the "machinery of war." Shortly thereafter, Addams and Carrie Chapman Catt formed the Women's Peace party to organize women against the war. But on the whole American sympathies went out to Britain, France, and the other Allies, and against Germany, Austria, and the

Central Powers. The memory of their Anglo-Saxon background and cultural heritage, along with the gross violations of Belgian neutrality by Germany, gave the Allied cause in the United States the momentum to quiet the dissenting opinions.

Neutrality became difficult to maintain as the United States continued to trade with both the Allies and the Central Powers. Violations of American neutrality came from both the British and the Germans. The British demanded that ships bound for Germany be first inspected in British ports for contraband (smuggled goods). Germany, to compensate for British naval superiority and to blockade Britain, turned to unrestricted submarine attacks in the war zone around the British Isles. The sinking of the British passenger liner *Lusitania* on May 7, 1915, resulting in the deaths of 128 Americans, outraged the American people. The **Sussex Pledge** (1916) by Germany halted unrestricted submarine warfare temporarily, but torpedo attacks began once again in January 1917. Although Woodrow Wilson had been reelected in 1916 on the slogan, "He kept us out of war," the situation in Europe continued to bring the United States closer to entry. After continued strikes against American ships in 1917, President Wilson asked Congress for a declaration of war against Germany. Congress declared war four days later on April 6, 1917.

Causes of United States Entry into War

Although Germany realized that the resumption of unrestricted submarine warfare might force the United States into the war, they felt that United States aid to the Allies would come too late to prevent a German victory. The publication of a telegram ("**Zimmermann Note**"), intercepted by the British in February 1917, turned American opinion against Germany. In the telegram, written by the German foreign minister to Mexico, Germany promised Texas, Arizona, and New Mexico to Mexico in return for its support in the war.

Economic ties with the Allies, including a profitable trade and numerous loans, was an added incentive for Americans to support the Allies. British propaganda, which represented Germany as a threat to democracy, helped convince many Americans that victory for the Allies meant victory for democracy. Finally, when the **Russian Revolution** (1917) resulted in the overthrow of the czar and the establishment of a temporary republican government, the war became more clearly a struggle between democracies and autocracies.

United States Role in the War

Besides American troops, the Allies desperately needed naval power, munitions, industrial goods, and food. The American fleet was primarily responsible for ending the U-boat threat and transporting troops and supplies. The American Expeditionary Force under the leadership of General **John J. Pershing** arrived in France in 1917, and in July 1918, along with French troops, drove the Germans back close to their border. Following major victories by the Allies, Germany agreed to consider a peace plan as provided for by Wilson's **Fourteen Points** (January 1918) and an **armistice** (cease-fire) was signed on November 11, 1918.

Communist Russia

Although the United States was initially pleased to see the overthrow of the czar in Russia, the seizure of power by the **Bolsheviks** and the establishment of communism caused concern. After the war, Europe was ravaged by poverty and chaos—conditions that made the area vulnerable to Communist propaganda and ideology.

Exercise Set 3.5

1. U.S. entry into both the War of 1812 and World War I was caused in part by
   A. foreign troops on American soil
   B. Presidents who encouraged entry into war
   C. interference with American shipping
   D. a foreign nation's threat to Mexico

2. The factor that was most significant in causing President Wilson to ask Congress for a declaration of War on Germany in April 1917 was
   A. the German invasion of Belgium
   B. the Russian Revolution of 1917
   C. the sinking of the *Sussex*
   D. the resumption of unrestricted submarine warfare by Germany

3. What was the primary focus of United States foreign policy in the decade after World War I?
   A. to defend the price of freedom of the seas
   B. to reduce United States commitments to other nations
   C. to contain the spread of communism in Eastern Europe
   D. to fulfill collective security agreements with Western European nations.

4. Wilson was reelected to the presidency in 1916 because of his claim that
   A. entry into World War I was inevitable
   B. he had kept the United States out of war
   C. he would immediately bring the United States into the war
   D. he would begin submarine attacks against the Germans

THE CONSTITUTION AND WORLD WAR I

> The question in each case is whether the words used are used in such circumstances and are of such nature to create a clear and present danger that they will bring about the substantive evils Congress has the right to prevent.
>
> Majority Opinion, *Schenck* v. *United States* (1919)

> Anarchy stands for the liberation of the human mind from the domin-ion of religion, the liberation of the human body from the dominion of poverty, liberation from the shackles and restraints of government.
>
> Emma Goldman, *Anarchism* (1910)

War Opposition and Patriotism, the Draft Issue

As America approached entry into war, public opinion was by no means uni-fied. Heated debate continued between those who advocated military support for the Allies, supporters of neutrality, and antiwar critics.

Anti-German Feelings

Anti-German feelings were building before 1917, much the result of subma-rine warfare. After American entry into the war, preparation was encouraged by groups such as the **National Security League** and the Navy League, while public opinion was mobilized by George Creel's **Committee on Pub-lic Information (CPI)**. Recruiting the services of thousands of people in the arts, advertising, and film industries, the CPI effectively publicized the war. Films like *The Prussian Cur* and *The Kaiser, the Beast of Berlin* brought the message to the screen while the Division of Industrial Relations rallied labor around the war effort. As the anti-German sentiment increased, many schools stopped offering instruction in the German language, sauerkraut be-came "liberty cabbage," and orchestral works by German composers were not performed by American symphony orchestras. Extreme patriotism reached the point of vigilantism in some cases. Radical antiwar leader Frank Little, a member of the **Industrial Workers of the World**, was captured in Butte, Montana and hanged.

Antiwar Sentiment

Antiwar activists claimed that war was repressive to the progressive spirit, needlessly cost the lives of a nation's youth, violated Christian morality, and was a profit-making endeavor of the industrial-military leaders. Leaders in Congress including Senator Robert La Follette and House Majority Leader

Claude Kitchin fought United States preparation for entry. Pacifist Progressives such as **Jane Addams** and Paul Kellogg contributed to the efforts of the American Union Against Militarism. Addams helped found the **Women's Peace party** and even **Andrew Carnegie** and **Henry Ford** helped to finance the peace movements.

The Draft

In 1917, after entry into the war, Congress passed the **Selective Service Act** establishing a system to **draft**, or **conscript**, men into the armed forces. All males between the ages of 18 and 45 were required to register. By the war's end, 24 million men had been registered by local draft boards, with over 4 million serving in the armed forces. In the *Selective Service Cases,* the Supreme Court decided in January 1918 that the draft was constitutional under Congress's power to "declare war and raise and support armies."

Espionage and Sedition Acts

America's participation in World War I raised again, as it had earlier in the Civil War, the conflict between the Bill of Rights and the needs of war. Two laws passed by Congress in 1918, the **Espionage Act** and the **Sedition Act**, placed certain restrictions and limitations upon the freedoms of the press and speech. The Espionage Act outlawed any obstruction with military registration and enlistment and banned "treasonable and seditious" material from the nation's mails, at the discretion of the postmaster general. Publications seized for violation of the Espionage Act included *The New York Times* and the *Saturday Evening Post*. The Sedition Act, an amendment to the Espionage Act, was passed in reaction to activities of pacifists' groups, certain Labor leaders, and "Bolsheviks and radicals." Extending restrictions on interference with enlistment procedures, the act also made it a felony to "utter, print, or publish disloyal, profane, scurrilous, or abusive language about the form of government, the Constitution, soldiers and sailors, flag or uniform of the armed forces . . . ."

For the most part, the Supreme Court endorsed the repressive measures used against radical political activities during the war years. When Secretary **Schenck** of the **Socialist party** was convicted under the Espionage Act for distributing antidraft leaflets, the case (***Schenck v. United States**, 1919) was appealed to the Supreme Court on the grounds that the act violated the First Amendment and was therefore unconstitutional. **Justice Holmes**, writing for a unanimous court, upheld the constitutionality of the Espionage Act. Explaining that free speech was never an "absolute" right, he held that, during war, civil liberties could be restricted. "Free speech would not protect a man in falsely shouting fire in a theatre, causing a panic," was an example he provided for the court's reasoning that freedom of speech was not absolute. His approach in determining whether speech could be restricted became known as the **"clear and present danger"** rule. According to this, if words presented a "clear and present danger" of causing evils that Congress had the right to prevent, the speech could be curtailed. Holmes, in the later case of *Abrams* v. *United States* (1919), warned in a strong dissent that restriction of speech must be carefully applied so as not to stop the **"free trade in ideas"** so important in a democratic society.

Wartime Convictions

The decision in *Schenck* by the Supreme Court supported the government's prosecution of those who violated wartime security measures. The Espionage Act was upheld again in *Debs* v. *United States* (1919), an appeal from the conviction of Socialist party leader **Eugene V. Debs**. Debs was found guilty of felonious acts after delivering a speech denouncing capitalism and the war. **"Big Bill" Haywood**, leader of the **Industrial Workers of the World**, joined forces with 75-year-old **Mother Jones** and radical **Elizabeth Gurley Flynn** and appealed mostly to unskilled workers to join in destroying capitalism and stopping the war. Federal prosecutions during the war years sent Haywood and many radicals to prison. American anarchist **Emma Goldman**, imprisoned earlier for advocating birth control and pacifism, was deported to Russia in 1919.

The Red Scare 1918–1920

During the war, the **Bolshevik Revolution** in 1917 brought a Communist government to Russia. After the new Russian government under the leadership of **Lenin** withdrew from the war and made a separate peace with Germany, Americans felt betrayed. They were also frightened by the Bolsheviks' calls for workers everywhere to revolt. A **"Red Scare"** in the United States intensified as communism began to spread in Europe.

American Foreign Policy and Russia

American foreign policy also reflected hostile feelings toward Russia. In June 1918 President **Wilson**, without the consent of Congress, ordered American troops into Siberia to guard allied supplies and to observe Japanese influence in northern Russia. Wilson hoped to smash the Bolshevik government whose Communist influences were felt in short-term uprisings in both Germany and Hungary in early 1919.

Violations of Civil Rights

During the "Red Scare," extreme actions were taken against radicals. The civil liberties of "radicals," including many socialists and communists, were violated when Wilson's Attorney General, A. Mitchell Palmer, ordered the deportation of suspected radicals, raided homes of those suspected of being involved in "subversive" activities, and arrested hundreds whose economic and political views were unorthodox. The political implications of the trial and execution of anarchists **Nicola Sacco** and **Bartolomeo Vanzetti** for murder in 1920 brought worldwide attention to the "blind patriotism" of the Red Scare period.

Exercise Set 3.6

1. Where in the Constitution would you find the "freedom of speech" guarantee?
   A. the Preamble
   B. Article I
   C. the "elastic clause"
   D. the First Amendment

2. The leader of the Industrial Workers of the World who was prosecuted for subversive activities during World War I was
   A. Emma Goldman
   B. George Creel
   C. "Big Bill" Haywood
   D. Eugene V. Debs

3. A study of the Supreme Court's decision in the case of *Schenck* v. *United States* (1919) indicates that
   A. during times of war civil liberties may be restricted
   B. the First Amendment is absolute in nature
   C. all political speech is protected by the First Amendment
   D. the activities of subversive groups may be restricted without any review by the courts

4. The case of Sacco and Vanzetti aroused sympathy for them and criticism of government measures because they
   A. were executed immediately
   B. were found innocent of all charges against them
   C. probably did not receive a fair trial as a result of unsubstantiated fears
   D. were imprisoned without a trial

THE SEARCH FOR PEACE AND ARMS CONTROL (1914–1930)

> A general association of nations must be formed . . . for the purpose of affording mutual guarantees of political independence and territorial integrity to great and small states alike.
>
> President Woodrow Wilson
> Address to Congress, January 8, 1918

The Peace Movement

The movement that had objected to America's entry into World War I gained further support when the United States considered the peace settlement following the war that included membership in an international **League of Nations**. Americans were tired of war and were no longer receptive to President Wilson's justification of America's role in the Great War. Groups including Representative Jeannette Rankin's American Women Opposed to the League of Nations and the Women's International League for Peace and Freedom opposed American membership in the League of Nations. They viewed the League as a vehicle for bringing the United States into future international conflicts. Ironically, later in the 1920s and 1930s, some of these same groups, including the Women's International League for Peace and Freedom, advocated cooperation with the League of Nations and membership in the World Court as preventive measures to avoid war as a solution to international problems.

Wilson's Fourteen Points   *perception of* 1½

President Wilson was able to transform the war, which was an ugly grinding struggle, into a noble crusade for liberty, democracy, and permanent peace. Wilson's peace aims were developed in a long series of speeches and public papers from 1914 to 1918. His **Fourteen Points** were listed in an address to Congress on January 8, 1918; a list would be circulated among the populations of Europe in millions of leaflets.

President Wilson's Fourteen Points included the following:

- the replacement of secret treaties with **open diplomacy** among nations
- **freedom of the seas**
- **removal of economic/trade barriers** between nations
- **reductions in armaments**
- **adjustment of colonial claims** with respect for native populations

- redrawing of European boundaries with a respect for nationalities and **"self-determination"**
- the formation of an **association of nations**

By the fall of 1918 the Allied Armies, with the assistance of American forces, were advancing toward the German border. Shortly thereafter, the German government opened negotiations with Wilson for a peace on the basis of the Fourteen Points.

The Versailles Treaty

Although President Wilson sailed for Paris in December 1918 with the intention of writing his Fourteen Points into the peace treaty, problems for his ambitious plans had already started. Worried about legislative support in the approaching peace negotiations, the President appealed to the American people for Democratic victories in the midterm elections of 1918. However, this appeal backfired. The Republicans captured both houses of Congress and they resented Wilson's partisan tactics. Wilson's second blunder was his failure to take any members of the House or the Senate with him to Paris, instead bringing with him a delegation he expected to dominate in the treaty-writing process.

The **Paris Peace Conference** began its work in January 1919 under the direction of Woodrow Wilson and Prime Ministers **Georges Clemenceau** of France, **David Lloyd George** of Great Britain, and **Vittorio Orlando** of Italy. The final **Treaty of Versailles**, signed by delegates from Germany on June 28, 1919 (separate peace treaties were drawn up with Germany's allies), provided for (1) an admission by Germany of its **war guilt**; (2) stripping Germany of its **colonies**; (3) **adjusting German borders**, taking away Alsace-Lorraine, Posen, the Saar Basin, parts of Schleswig and Silesia; and (4) stripping Germany of most of its military and naval forces.

Reluctantly, President Wilson agreed to a treaty that did not mention freedom of the seas, or reduced tariffs. Negotiations had been secretive and the reparations assigned to Germany were impossible to repay. Wilson's last hope was an effective association of nations in which the United States would have a major role.

The League of Nations and United States Rejection

The **Covenant** for the League of Nations was incorporated into the Versailles Treaty. It provided for an **Assembly** to represent all member nations, a **Secretariat**, permanently located in Geneva, Switzerland, a **Council** controlled by the permanent members (United States, England, France, Italy, and Japan) and four other nations elected by the Assembly, and a separate **Permanent**

Court of International Justice (known as the **World Court**). Under the Covenant the members of the League were pledged to seek disarmament, to arbitrate differences, and to act together against outside aggressors or covenant breakers in a system of "**collective security**."

The Struggle over Ratification

The struggle over American ratification of the Treaty of Versailles, including the League of Nations, became a bitter duel between Woodrow Wilson and the Republican Chairman of the Senate Committee on Foreign Relations, **Henry Cabot Lodge**. Much of the objection to the treaty was based on political jealousy, largely due to Wilson's refusal to consult Republican Senators in creating the treaty. However, many feared that participation in the League of Nations might draw the United States into European troubles.

As the Senate carried out its Constitutional role of "Advise and Consent" concerning foreign treaties (Article II, Section 2), three groups developed: Democratic followers of Wilson who favored immediate ratification; hard core "irreconcilables" (including William Borah of Idaho, Robert La Follette of Wisconsin, and Hiram Johnson of California) who opposed American membership in the international organization; and moderates who preferred a watered-down version of the League that would include certain "reservations" to protect American interests. President Wilson decided to appeal directly to the American people, but in the midst of a speaking tour through the Middle West, he suffered a paralytic stroke and remained an invalid during the critical period of debate on the League.

Rejection of the Treaty

On November 19, 1919, Wilson's Democratic supporters and the "irreconcilables" combined to defeat the treaty with the Lodge reservations. The reservationists and the "irreconcilables" then voted down the treaty in its original form. Once again, in March 1920, the treaty failed to receive the necessary two-thirds approval of the Senate, although the vote was 49 to 35 in its favor. Finally, when the Republicans were victorious in the election of 1920, sending **Warren G. Harding** to the White House, they saw their victory as a mandate against the League of Nations. A joint resolution was adopted by Congress on August 25, 1921, declaring the war to be over.

Washington Naval Disarmament Conference

President Harding sponsored the Washington Disarmament Conference of 1921, which led to the limitation of battleship construction among the chief naval powers (Britain, United States, Japan, France, and Italy) and stabilized the balance of power in the Far East. Temporarily, the Conference seemed to be a substantial step toward **arms control** and **economic rehabilitation**.

Kellogg-Briand Pact (1928)

An agreement, eventually signed by 62 nations, and named for United States Secretary of State Frank Kellogg and French Foreign Minister Aristede Briand, was negotiated in 1928 "condemning recourse to war for the solution of international controversies, and renouncing it as an instrument of the national policy." The **Kellogg-Briand Pact** passed the Senate by a vote of 85 to 1, but was looked upon skeptically by many because it provided no means of enforcement.

The World Court

Periodic proposals for U.S. membership in the World Court (the League's judicial agency) were defeated in the Senate during the administrations of Presidents Harding and Coolidge. The Court itself rejected America's admission in 1926 when certain conditions were insisted upon by the United States. Attempts by Presidents Hoover and Franklin Roosevelt to gain America's membership were also frustrated by a Senate that was heavily influenced by isolationist forces and by those who feared that membership in the Court would involve the nation in League affairs and the problems of Europe.

1. The major flaw of the Kellogg-Briand Pact (1928) was that it
   A. was signed by only four nations
   B. was discouraged by the League of Nations
   C. had no provisions for enforcement
   D. violated the provisions of the Washington Naval Disarmament Conference of 1921

2. The primary reason for the United States Senate's rejection of the Treaty of Versailles was
   A. the forced assumption by Germany of war guilt
   B. the fact that the war continued in the Western Hemisphere
   C. the inclusion of the League of Nations Covenant
   D. the refusal of the Allies to repay their war debts to the United States

3. At the Paris Peace Conference, President Wilson pushed for
   A. U.S. occupation of Western Europe
   B. the establishment of a League of Nations
   C. the immediate repayment of all war debts to the United States
   D. military occupation of Germany

4. European nations claimed they were having difficulty paying their war debts to the United States because
   A. the United States failed to join the League of Nations
   B. Germany had defaulted on its reparations to the Allies
   C. the United States lowered its tariffs
   D. American bankers were investing in Germany

CHAPTER REVIEW QUESTIONS

INTERRUPTING THE CEREMONY

McCUTCHEON, CHICAGO TRIBUNE-NEW YORK NEWS SYNDICATE, INC.

Base your answers to questions 1 and 2 on the cartoon and on your knowledge of social studies.

1. The main purpose of the cartoon is to express opposition to which President's action?
   A. Woodrow Wilson's support of the Treaty of Versailles
   B. Franklin Roosevelt's announcement of the Good Neighbor Policy
   C. Harry Truman's decision to send aid to Europe after World War II
   D. Ronald Reagan's 1985 summit meeting with Chairman Gorbachev of the Soviet Union.

2. According to the cartoon, the United States should follow a foreign policy of
   A. collective security
   B. noninvolvement
   C. detente
   D. imperialism

3. Supreme Court decisions in cases involving the First Amendment to the federal Constitution generally reflect the principle that
   A. if an action is based on a religious belief, it must be allowed
   B. only demonstrations that support the beliefs of the majority may be held
   C. freedoms of speech and press are absolute
   D. individual rights must be balanced against the needs of society at the time

4. An advantage of the United Nations that has contributed to its success when compared to the League of Nations is
   A. the provision that no armed forces are used to carry out its goals
   B. the membership of all the world's major powers
   C. the lack of a judicial body
   D. its complete prevention of war in the world

5. The most accurate statement concerning U.S. foreign policy is that the United States has generally
   A. used military confrontation to solve disputes
   B. reacted forcefully to imperialism around the world
   C. acted according to national self-interest
   D. formed entangling alliances with countries in need

6. The major foreign policy issue facing the Wilson administration between the outbreak of the First World War in 1914 and United States entry in 1917 was
   A. freedom of the seas
   B. German aggression in the Caribbean
   C. the future of United States overseas possessions
   D. tariff controversies with Japan

7. After the Spanish-American War Cuba was
   A. left completely independent
   B. restricted by the Platt Amendment
   C. admitted as a state to the United States
   D. reoccupied by the Spanish

ESSAYS

1. Foreign policy actions by the United States, including American involvement in the Spanish-American War and World War I, have been based upon factors such as those listed below.

   Factors
   Ideology
   Pressures from other countries
   National self-interest
   Domestic pressures
   Geography

   Select *three* factors from the list above and discuss their significance concerning the involvement of the United States in the Spanish-American War *or* World War I.

2. Different individuals and governmental bodies have had roles in foreign policy determinations of the United States government. Between the years 1898 and 1920, describe *one* way in which *three* of the following individuals or government body affected the direction of foreign policy of the United States.

   The President
   Political parties
   The Congress
   Special interest groups/Lobbyists

THEMATIC ESSAY

Directions: Write a well-organized essay that includes an introduction, several paragraphs addressing the task below, and a conclusion.

Theme: Changing American Society

> The first quarter of the 20th century experienced the testing of civil liberties in a number of ways.

Task:

> Identify *two* events in the first quarter of the 20th century that tested the civil liberties of Americans.
>
> - For each event identified describe its immediate causes.
> - Discuss the specifics of each event.
> - identify the constitutional issue(s) involved in each event.

Some suggestions you may wish to consider include: the Red Scare of 1919, the Scopes Monkey Trial of 1925, *Schenck* v. *United States* (1919), the Trial of Sacco and Vanzetti, and the Rise of the Second Ku Klux Klan.

You are *not* limited to these suggestions.

DOCUMENT-BASED QUESTION ESSAY

The following questions (Part A and Part B) are based on the accompanying documents (1–6). Some of these documents have been edited for the purpose of this exercise. The question is designed to test your ability to work with historical documents and to demonstrate your knowledge of the subject matter being presented. As you analyze the documents, take into account both the source of the document and the author's point of view.

Historical Context: Late 19th-century and early 20th-century expansionism by the United States was seen by many as a continuation of earlier 19th-century Manifest Destiny.

Task: Using information from the documents and your knowledge of United States history, answer the questions that follow each document in Part A. Your answers to the questions will help you write the Part B essay, in which you will be asked:

> Late 19th-century and early 20th-century expansionism by the United States was seen by many as a continuation of earlier 19th-century Manifest Destiny. Using the issues identified in the documents, discuss why this is or is not an accurate statement.

Part A
Short Answer

The documents below relate to both continental and overseas expansion of the United States during the 1800s and early part of the 1900s. Examine each document carefully and then answer the questions that follow.

DOCUMENT 1

> Our Manifest Destiny is to overspread the continent allotted by Providence for the free development of our yearly multiplying millions.

—John L. Sullivan, *Democratic Review* (1845)

1. Which continent is being referred to by John L. Sullivan?

_____

_____

_____

DOCUMENT 2

Go West, young man, and grow up with the country.

—Horace Greeley, *New York Tribune* (1850)

2. The opinion of John L. Sullivan (see Document 1) and the advice of Horace Greeley in Document 2 both supported westward expansion and settlement by Americans. Which groups of North American inhabitants would have been likely to object to the positions of both of these men?

_____

_____

_____

DOCUMENT 3

We make treaties—that is, we pledge our faith—and then leave swindlers and knaves of all kinds to execute them. We maintain and breed pauper colonies. The savages, who know us, and who will neither be pauperized nor trust our word, we pursue, and slay if we can, at an incredible expense....The fact is that these Indians, with whom we have made a solemn treaty that their territory shall not be invaded, and that they should receive supplies on their reservations, have seen from one thousand to fifteen hundred miners during the present season entering and occupying their territory....

—*Harper's Weekly*, August 5, 1876

3. How does the author of the article in *Harper's Weekly* view the treaties made by the United States government with the various Native American populations?

_____

_____

_____

_____

DOCUMENT 4

The Philippines are ours forever...And just beyond the Philippines are China's....markets. We will not retreat from either....We will not abandon our opportunity in the Orient. We will not renounce our part in the mission of our race....under God, of the civilization of the world....And we will move forward to our *work*.....with gratitude....and thanksgiving to Almighty God that He has marked us his chosen people.

— Senator Albert Beveridge, Speech to 56th Congress,
Congressional Record (1900)

4. What is the "work" that Senator Beveridge believes the United States must move forward with in the Orient?

_____

_____

_____

_____

5. What occurrence had taken place that would lead Senator Beveridge to state in 1900 that "The Philippines are ours forever?"

_____

_____

_____

_____

Our interests and those of our southern neighbors are in reality identical. They have great natural riches, and if within their borders the reign of law and justice obtains, prosperity is sure to come to them.... We would interfere with them only in the last resort, and then only if it became evident that their inability or unwillingness to do justice at home and abroad had violated the rights of the United States or had invited foreign aggression to the detriment of the entire body of American nations.

—President Theodore Roosevelt, Message to Congress, December 6, 1904

6. The segment above is many times referred as the Roosevelt Corollary to the Monroe Doctrine. What geographic area is being referred to by President Roosevelt?

_____

_____

_____

_____

7. What are President Roosevelt's opinions regarding United States intervention in the "southern neighbors?"

_____

_____

_____

_____

DOCUMENT 6

—Swinging the Big Stick (1905)

8. Who is the President portrayed in the cartoon?

_____

_____

_____

_____

9. The big stick in the cartoon is labeled "The New Diplomacy." What were the new diplomatic policies that were proposed by the President portrayed in the cartoon?

_____

_____

_____

_____

DOCUMENT 7

Alaska and Hawaii

10. Give one advantage to the United States for each of the acquisitions (Alaska and Hawaii) in the map.

_____

_____

_____

_____

Part B
Essay

Your essay should be well organized with an introductory paragraph that states your position on the question. Develop your position in the next paragraphs and then write a conclusion. In your essay, include specific historical details and refer to the specific documents you analyzed in Part A. You may include additional information from your knowledge of social studies.

Historical Context: Late 19th-century and early 20th-century expansionism by the United States was seen by many as a continuation of earlier 19th-century Manifest Destiny.

Task:

> Late 19th-century and early 20th-century expansionism by the United States was seen by many as a continuation of earlier 19th-century Manifest Destiny. Using the issues identified in the documents discuss why this is or is not an accurate statement.

Guidelines:

In your essay, be sure to
- Develop all aspects of the task
- Incorporate information from at least *five* documents
- Incorporate relevant outside information
- Support the theme with many relevant facts, examples, and details
- Use a logical and clear plan of organization, including an introduction and a conclusion that are beyond a restatement of the theme

UNIT FOUR

At Home and Abroad: Prosperity and Depression

KEY IDEAS Unit Four details the effect of World War I on the nation and the political, social, and cultural aspects of the decade of the 1920s. The second part of the unit examines the causes and effects of the Great Depression and the changing government role as it dealt with social and economic problems.

UNIT CONNECTIONS: By the end of the unit you should understand the following points.

- Postwar return to peacetime economy
- Fear of Communism and civil liberties at risk
- Warren G. Harding and a scandalous administration
- Henry Ford's automobile and mass production
- Economic problems of the 1920s lead to disaster in the 1930s
- Responses to economic problems by Herbert Hoover and Franklin Delano Roosevelt
- New Deal and Socialism; checks and balances; two-term presidential tradition
- President Roosevelt's "Court Packing"
- Shift of political alliances of African Americans
- The Dust Bowl and Depression Age literature

WAR AND PROSPERITY (1917–1929)

THE FIRST WORLD WAR AT HOME

> We are glad . . . to fight thus for the ultimate peace of the world and for the liberation of its peoples. . . The world must be made safe for democracy.
>
> Woodrow Wilson, Address to Congress, April 2, 1917

> The highest and best form of efficiency is the spontaneous cooperation of a free people.
>
> Bernard M. Baruch, in *American Industry at War: A Report of the War Industries Board, March 1921.*

Selective Service

World War I, like all wars, brought about a dramatic change in people's lives. The **Selective Service Act** of May 28, 1917 required all men 18 to 45 years of age to register for military service. From the nearly 10 million who originally registered, some 700,000 names were drawn by lot for service. By the end of the war, Selective Service had registered 24 million names as a pool from which names could be drawn as needed for the armed services. Of these, close to 5 million were in uniform by the war's end, and more than 2 million were sent overseas. Women served in the Army and Navy Nurses Corps and in the auxiliary forces of the regular Navy.

Mobilizing American Industry

American industry was mobilized for the war. A **War Industries Board** was created, headed by the financier **Bernard M. Baruch**. The Board established priorities for the production of necessary war materiel.

Providing Food and Fuel

Food and fuel were basic to the conduct of the war both for our troops and for our allies. **Herbert Hoover**, a mining engineer with a Quaker background, was put in charge of food distribution. His task was to see that adequate supplies of basic foods were produced and distributed as needed. He instituted "wheatless" Mondays and "meatless" Tuesdays on a voluntary basis as a means of conserving these essential staples. People responded readily to his request that they plant "victory gardens."

Conservation of fuel was achieved under the direction of a fuel administration headed by **Harry A. Garfield**. Daylight savings time was introduced and motorists were urged to observe "gasless" days to aid the war effort.

Financing the War

The war was financed partly by increased taxes but primarily through borrowing from the American people, who bought **government bonds** in four "Liberty Loan" drives and one final "Victory Loan" drive. These drives yielded $22 billion. Another $10 billion, approximately the amount lent to our allies, was raised through income taxes and by special taxes on liquor, tobacco, and theater tickets.

Transportation and Communication

To facilitate the transportation of troops and war supplies by rail, the railroads were placed under the direction of Secretary of the Treasury William G. McAdoo. Government control was later extended to the communication industries—telephone, telegraph, and cable.

Labor and the War

Support of the A.F.L.

Led by Samuel Gompers, the **American Federation of Labor (A.F.L.)**, which had two million members at the outbreak of the war, actively supported the war effort. As millions of men left their jobs to serve in the armed forces, the burgeoning war industries demanded more and more workers and a new labor force had to be formed.

Women in the Labor Force

The labor gap was filled, in part, by women who stepped in to "man" the factories, farms, mills, mines, and railroads in place of their brothers, sons, and husbands. The ranks of labor were filled also by a quarter of a million African Americans who moved from the South into the coal mines, steel mills, and railroads of the North.

Mobilizing the Arts for War

The arts, too, proved to be a mighty force in the war effort. Artists created posters to encourage enlistment and to sell war bonds. The classic "I Want You for the U.S. Army" by Samuel Montgomery Flagg and the Liberty Bonds poster by Walter Whitehead provided stirring visual war messages.

Song writers used their talents to support the war effort in music. The nation sang **George M. Cohan's** "Over There" with gusto. Another popular World War I song was **Irving Berlin's** "Oh How I Hate to Get Up in the Morning." With millions of American boys in France, the nation sang war-inspired songs such as "Hinky Dinky Parlay Voo" and "How 'Ya Gonna Keep 'em Down on the Farm after They've Seen Paree?"

Propaganda

Propaganda was also a war weapon. The Germans were "Huns" who committed terrible atrocities. The Kaiser was "The Beast of Berlin," and many schools discontinued teaching the German language.

Voices of Dissent

Yet, there were voices of dissent in the country despite the prevailing atmosphere of support for the war. Six members of the United States Senate and 57 members of the House of Representatives voted against Wilson's call for a declaration of war against Germany on April 6, 1917. The dissenting members included the first woman member of Congress, Republican Jeanette Rankin of Montana. In the Middle West, where many areas had large German-American settlements, sentiment against the war was strong. Republican Senator Robert M. La Follette of Wisconsin voted against the war resolution, asserting that "Germany has been patient with us," and Republican Senator George W. Norris of Nebraska charged that the United States was being manipulated into the war by financial and commercial interests that stood to profit from the war. Many parents were singing the popular 1915 antiwar song "I Didn't Raise My Boy to Be a Soldier."

The "Return to Normalcy"

Reconversion and "Normalcy" (1918–1921)

A spirited demand for reconversion to a peacetime economy set in almost immediately after the war. Both the administration under President Wilson, and the Republican opposition, agreed that the dominance of government over industry must be reversed. The **Esch-Cummins Act** of 1920 provided for the return of the railroads to private control. The Jones Merchant Marine Act of the same year authorized the sale of government-built ships to private operators. The Republican campaign slogan in the election of 1920 was "back to normalcy," and the presidential candidate Warren G. Harding of Ohio declared, "We want a period in America with less government in business and more business in government."

The Fordney-McCumber Tariff

A month after his inauguration, Harding called Congress into special session and asked it to pass legislation for higher tariffs, reduction in taxes and spending, and a bonus for the veterans. Congress responded by passing the "protectionist" **Fordney-McCumber Tariff**, whose high rates were designed to keep foreign goods out of the United States. International trade was reduced when European nations retaliated with tariff restrictions of their own.

Tax Reduction

Congress approved Harding's tax proposals by reducing income taxes substantially. "Normalcy" had returned, but a rocky road lay ahead.

1. "To protect the workers in their right . . . to be full sharers in the abundance which is the result of their brains and brawn . . . is the glorious mission of the trade unions."

   Samuel Gompers, Speech, 1898

   In pursuit of this goal during World War I, organized labor
   A. resisted efforts to draft union members into the armed services
   B. opposed the entrance of women and blacks into the labor market
   C. engaged in a crippling general strike
   D. essentially cooperated with and supported the U.S. war effort

2. Which of the following was *not* used during World War I as a means of securing an adequate food supply?
   A. planting of "victory gardens" by people who were not farmers
   B. raising the price of wheat to stimulate increased production
   C. government restriction on the shipment of food to Europe
   D. encouragement of voluntary reduction in the consumption of food through "wheatless" and "meatless" days during the week

3. Woodrow Wilson's doctrine of "strict accountability" had specific application to
   A. submarine warfare
   B. loans to belligerents
   C. investment in foreign countries
   D. treatment of prisoners of war

   Base your answers to questions 4 through 6 on the cartoon that follows and on your knowledge of social studies.

4. Which economic concept is illustrated in the cartoon?
   A. depression
   B. protective tariff
   C. supply and demand
   D. government price controls

5. Cotton farmers in the South experienced the situation shown in the cartoon because of the region's reliance on
   A. sharecropping
   B. government subsidies
   C. subsistence farming
   D. a single-crop economy

6. Between 1914 and 1916, which factor helped bring about the change in the financial position of the cotton farmer as shown in the cartoon?
   A. the demand for cotton became high during World War I
   B. climatic changes in other cotton-growing nations greatly reduced their cotton crops
   C. American cotton became more resistant to destructive insect pests
   D. new styles of clothing required large amounts of cotton

7. In World War I public opinion
   A. remained strictly neutral until Wilson asked for war
   B. remained disinterested in the war until the sinking of the *Lusitania*
   C. preponderantly favored the Allied nations
   D. was evenly divided between the two opposing sides

8. During World War I, one method of financing the war effort by the United States was
   A. printing additional greenbacks
   B. selling bonds
   C. decreasing taxes
   D. eliminating all tariffs

9. The Republicans returned to power with the election of Warren G. Harding in 1920. The new President's call for a "return to normalcy" turned out to mean
   A. low tariffs and high taxes
   B. active participation in international affairs
   C. a huge increase in government expenditures
   D. isolationism and protectionism

THE TWENTIES: BUSINESS BOOM OR FALSE PROSPERITY?

> I have no fear for the future of our country. It is bright with hope.
> Herbert Hoover, Inaugural Address, March 4, 1929

> There is little question that in 1929 . . . the economy was fundamentally unsound.
> John Kenneth Galbraith in *The Great Crash,* 1929

The Election of 1920

The country entered a new era with the election of 1920. The Republicans chose Senator **Warren G. Harding** of Ohio as their presidential candidate, and Governor **Calvin Coolidge** of Massachusetts as his running mate. The Democrats nominated Governor **James M. Cox** of Ohio for President and Assistant Secretary of the Navy **Franklin Delano Roosevelt** for Vice President.

Wilson called for a "solemn referendum" on the League of Nations as a key issue in the election. The Republicans accepted the challenge. The war-weary nation supported the Republicans in rejecting the League and the idealism of Woodrow Wilson. The "Red Scare" of 1920, resulting from the Bolshevik revolution in Russia, was another factor contributing to the overwhelming Republican victory—404 to 127 electoral votes and 61 percent of the popular vote—for Warren G. Harding.

The Nineteenth Amendment to the Constitution, granting women the right to vote, was ratified by the required three fourths of the states on August 26, 1920, and, as a result, women were able to vote in a national election for the first time.

Economic Recession (1921–1922)

A severe economic recession, caused in part by the conversion of the industrial war machine to a peace economy, staggered the nation in 1921. The market was glutted with heavy inventories of goods produced during the war. Exports dropped sharply. As 20,000 businesses failed in 1921, unemployment reached 4,750,000 or 11.5 percent of the labor force. As the war demand for food slackened, the American farmers experienced falling prices that resulted in mass bankruptcies and foreclosures. The war's end also brought on serious labor strife. Major strikes occurred in the coal, steel, and railroad industries.

The average work week of steel workers was 68.7 hours. Their demand for an eight-hour day and the right to unions of their own choosing was met

Coal miners struck for better working conditions following World War I.

with outright rejection by powerful corporations. Grievances of the coal miners included extremely dangerous working conditions, a work week often limited to two or three days, and company ownership of the miners' homes and of the markets in which they purchased food, clothing, and other necessities. Railway labor went on strike when wages were reduced by President Harding's Railway Labor Board. The textile industry, which had migrated to the South where labor conditions were more favorable to mill owners, witnessed strikes by employees, many of them young women, whose wages were generally 18 cents an hour for a 56-hour work week.

War Loans and Debts

When the United States entered the war, the Allies had been at war with Germany almost three years. Their financial resources were exhausted. Consequently, loans were extended by the U.S. government to enable them to pay for the food and war materiel supplied by the American farmers and manufacturers. The British war debt, including postwar loans (in money and goods) for rehabilitation, amounted to $4.3 billion; the French $3.5 billion; the Italian $1.6 billion, and smaller amounts were owed by Belgium, Greece, and other Allies. The Allies argued that these debts should be canceled because they had been incurred in a common cause, but the Harding administration insisted they be repaid.

France and Britain presented Germany with a bill for $33 billion in **reparations** for damages caused by the war for which the Versailles Treaty had laid the blame on Germany. To enable Germany to pay, the United States adopted the **Dawes Plan of 1924** proposed by the Illinois financier Charles G. Dawes. Essentially, the plan scaled down reparations payments and provided for American loans to Germany. The entire war debts-reparations issue came to a halt with the **Great Depression** of the 1930s.

Scandal in the Harding Administration

President Harding died suddenly in San Francisco on August 2, 1923, and his Vice-President **Calvin Coolidge** was sworn in as President. Shortly before, Harding's death rumors began to circulate about corruption in his administration.

Teapot Dome

A major scandal, but by no means the only one, centered around government oil resources at Teapot Dome in Wyoming and Elk Hills in California. About two months after Harding's death, a Senate committee under Thomas Walsh of Montana was formed to investigate oil leases made to private companies from these government oil reserves. The reserves had been set aside under Presidents Taft and Wilson for the use of the Navy.

Soon after his inauguration, President Harding transferred the Teapot Dome and Elk Hills oil reserves from the Navy Department (Secretary Edwin C. Denby) to the Interior Department (Secretary Albert B. Fall). Denby approved of this transfer. Fall then entered into a secret, illegal, and corrupt deal with two oil men, Harry Sinclair and Edward Doheny. Without competitive bidding and at a bargain price, Teapot Dome was leased to Sinclair, who had made a large contribution to the Republican campaign in 1920, and the Elk Hills reserve was leased to Doheny, a close friend of Fall. In March 1923, Fall resigned from the Cabinet.

The investigation committee discovered that Fall had received a "loan" of $100,000 from Doheny on which he was charged no interest, put up no security, and made no arrangement for repayment. Fall went to jail for accepting a bribe from Doheny. The Supreme Court declared the leases invalid because they were made by a "conspiracy" involving "fraud" and "corruption."

Coolidge Prosperity Not for Everyone

The Business of America is Business.
Calvin Coolidge

In the election of 1924, the Republicans won an easy victory with President Calvin Coolidge triumphing over the Democratic challenger John W. Davis, a New York corporate lawyer. "Coolidge prosperity" was the keynote of the Republican campaign, which resulted in a popular vote of nearly 2 to 1 and an electoral vote of 382 for Coolidge and 136 for Davis.

Despite the conservative Republican victory, there were disquieting rumblings in their own party, indicating that the Coolidge prosperity was not for everyone. Charging that Coolidge "had literally turned his back on the farmers," Senator **Robert M. La Follette**, Republican of Wisconsin, ran for President on the newly formed **League for Progressive Political Action**. He received support not only from the farm belt but also from labor groups and Socialists. The Progressive program called for federal assistance, including low-interest credit to farmers, social legislation for the benefit of labor, and government ownership of railroads and water power. La Follette received almost 5 million votes, about 16 percent of the total cast.

The election of 1924 was marked by a surge of women candidates in state elections. Two women, Miriam A. "Ma" Ferguson of Texas and Nellie T. Ross of Wyoming, were elected Governor of their states. Both were wives of former Governors. And 123 women were elected to state legislatures.

Slump in Agriculture

Agriculture, like other segments of the economy, had enjoyed economic prosperity during the war, heightened by greatly increased demand for food in the European war zone. As prices of wheat, meat, and other farm products rose rapidly, farmers borrowed money to buy farm machinery and to increase their acreage under cultivation. The **gasoline-engine tractor** could sow and cultivate more in an hour than the horse-driven plow could accomplish in a day. As farm hands returned from the war and European farms again entered the market, an over-abundance of farm produce caused a severe slump in farm prices. The wholesale price index of farm products (1910–1914 = 100) was at 211 in 1920 and dropped to 121 in 1921. Its high during the 1920s was 149 in 1928. In 1932 it was 68, lowest in 33 years. Farm mortgage debt rose from $7.8 billion in 1920 to $10.8 billion in 1923.

Government support of farm prices was repeatedly vetoed by President Coolidge.

288

The "Golden Twenties"

"Golden Twenties" was the name given to the period of economic prosperity for many, but not all, segments of the American economy. As we have seen, farmers generally were experiencing hard times. Coal and textiles remained in a slump after the recession of 1921. But most manufacturing, retail trades, transportation, the growing service industries, and other segments of the labor force were earning good wages and spending freely. Business was booming. Few doubted that good times would ever end.

Speculation in the "Big Bull Market"

The stock market offered an almost irresistible temptation to make easy money. People from all walks of life began to "play the market" and watched the paper values of their investments soar. The accelerating boom of the "Big Bull Market" led more and more people to risk their savings in the "get rich quick" orgy.

Exercise Set 4.2

1. The economic sector that benefited *least* from the Coolidge prosperity was
   A. agriculture
   B. labor
   C. large and small business
   D. banking and finance

2. Loans made by the United States during World War I to Allied nations
   A. remained largely unrepaid by the debtor nations
   B. were payable in full under the Dawes Plan
   C. were repaid in full during the two decades following the war
   D. were voluntarily canceled during the Coolidge administration

3. In the 1920s the farmers demanded a change in the government's farm program in order to obtain
   A. a higher tariff barrier on agricultural goods
   B. a legislative program that would limit farm production and reduce farm indebtedness
   C. a farm program that included direct farm supports
   D. agricultural prices designed to give the farmer an equitable share of national income

4. Which of these was a general characteristic of the period 1920–1930 in the United States?
    A. strong executive leadership
    B. a retreat from a policy of laissez-faire
    C. apathy toward reform
    D. increase in federal tax rates

5. The main cause of the recession of 1921 was
    A. monetary policies
    B. a decline in American exports to Europe
    C. war scares
    D. greater use of machinery in industry

OPTIMISM AND MATERIALISM

> The good old times were not good old times. Neither master nor servant was as well situated then as today.
>
> Andrew Carnegie, June 1889

Mass Consumption

Rapid Rise of the Automobile

A brief recession in the years between 1921 and 1922 was soon followed by seven years of phenomenal growth in the American economy. The automobile, which was driven by a gasoline engine and was invented as a result of experiments in Europe and America in the late 19th century, played a key role in this economic development. Passenger car registration in the United States reached 8,000 by 1900, jumped to 1.3 million by 1913, rose to 8.1 million by 1920, and catapulted to 26.5 million by 1930—one automobile for every five Americans.

Henry Ford

Industrialist Henry Ford was largely responsible for this phenomenon. Ford, of Dearborn, Michigan, built his first automobile in his shop in 1896. The famous **Model T**, first produced in 1909, began to be turned out on the Ford **assembly line** by **mass production** techniques at the rate of one car every 10 seconds by 1925. In 1914 Ford startled the industrial world by introduc-

Ford's assembly line turned out one Model T every ten seconds.

ing the eight-hour day with a minimum daily wage of $5. The rising standard of living of the average American, coupled with an increase in leisure time, created a ready market for the sale of automobiles.

Economic and Social Developments Related to the Automobile

The transformation in the American way of life brought about by the automobile was accompanied by other significant economic and social developments. New road construction, required to accommodate the automobile, was also a spur to automobile production. By 1925 there were more than half a million miles of surfaced highways in the United States. Twenty years later the number had tripled. Other industries associated with the automobile came into being or grew to giant proportions—vulcanized rubber for tires, refined petroleum for fuel, steel, glass, batteries, paint, upholstery and other components of the automobile, as well as gas stations, repair shops, sales agencies, advertising, and insurance. Soon one in every nine American workers was earning a living directly or indirectly from the automobile.

Growth of Suburbia and the Middle Class

In other ways, too, the automobile transformed the character of American life. The movement of the urban middle class from the larger cities to their suburbs was due to automobiles that made it possible to commute to jobs. The growing middle class could afford to move to the suburbs where there was fresh air, space, better homes, and status, and to escape the congestion and the automobile fumes in the cities. This resulted in a real estate boom in suburbia and it accelerated the process of decay in the inner cities.

Decline of the Railroads

The construction of highways and superhighways marked the decline of interurban railroads and trolleys. Railroad mileage, which reached a high of 260,570 miles in 1929, declined to 231,494 thirty years later. Maintenance of the railroads was neglected while expenditures for road building soared.

Impact of Superhighways

Superhighways wrought havoc with planning as they intruded through tree-lined urban neighborhoods and gobbled up parkland. The popular trolley gave way to air-polluting buses. The toll of deaths, injuries, and property damage on the highways mounted steadily.

Life in Suburbia—New Political and Economic Growth

In the suburbs new regional political and economic units developed. Local boards of education, elected town officials, and neighborhood associations assumed added importance with the growth of suburbia. Highways began to be lined with shopping centers, gas stations, and chain restaurants.

Installment (Credit) Buying

Installment buying—buy now and make weekly or monthly payments later—enabled families to purchase durable goods on credit. Sales of automobiles, radios, refrigerators, vacuum cleaners, and other home appliances soared as consumers went deeper and deeper into debt. Chain stores and department stores promoted consumer credit by introducing charge accounts and time payments.

Advertising played a key role in promoting the business boom of the 1920s. **Montgomery Ward** and **Sears Roebuck** issued massive illustrated order catalogs from which buyers nationwide could purchase by mail virtually every consumer item on the market. Ads for soap, cigarettes, and other products in daily use appeared in newspapers, magazines, on outdoor billboards, and over the radio. By 1929, American business was investing $3.5 billion annually to promote its products by advertising.

New Media

Both **radio** and **motion pictures**—destined to have profound influence on American culture—became important media in the 1920s. Regular radio broadcasting began in 1920 with station WWJ in Detroit. The results of the 1920 presidential election were the first to be broadcast over the radio by station KDKA in Pittsburgh. Sales of radio sets and parts which had already reached $60 million in 1922, skyrocketed to $400 million by 1929. In 1933 President Roosevelt was speaking to the entire nation in his radio "fireside chats."

Motion pictures, which first appeared early in the 20th century, became a major influence in American life during the 1920s. Large motion picture theaters were catering to 100 million viewers, to whom Charlie Chaplin, Mary Pickford, Douglas Fairbanks, Gloria Swanson, Greta Garbo, Harold Lloyd, and Rudolph Valentino became as familiar as their own neighbors. These stars of the silent screen faced a new challenge in 1927 when Al Jolson appeared in the first "talking picture," **The Jazz Singer**, released by Warner Brothers. Color films soon followed and Hollywood, California, became the center of the film industry.

With people all over the country listening to the same radio programs and viewing the same movies, a process of **homogenization** of American culture began. Colorful local speech patterns, dress, music, recreation, manners, and morals tended toward standardization as people took their cues from what they watched and heard on the radio and in the movie theater. This trend was greatly accelerated when television emerged two decades later.

Constitutional and Legal Issues

Attacks on Civil Liberties

In the years after World War I, there was a vigorous drive against Communists, anarchists, and Socialists by the federal government and state governments. The Espionage Act passed during the war remained in effect, and suspected revolutionists were arrested and fined under this law. This postwar concern over radicals in the United States was largely due to the Bolshevik Revolution.

- *The "Big Red Scare."* Toward the end of World War I, the revolutionary **Bolsheviks**, led by **Nikolai Lenin**, overthrew the czarist government of Russia and established a **Communist** regime. A wave of hysteria, the "**Big Red Scare**," swept through the United States. The country had experienced similar periods of fear and hate before. The Alien and Sedition Acts of John Adams' administration, the attacks on life and property of abolitionists in pre-Civil War days, and the rampaging violence of the post-Civil War Ku Klux Klan all had threatened civil liberties guaranteed by the Constitution.

- *The Palmer Raids.* Between 1919 and 1920, during the Big Red Scare, Attorney General A. Mitchell Palmer conducted raids, arresting some 6,000 suspects, 500 of whom were deported as undesirable aliens with little regard for their constitutional rights. It was at this time that the **American Civil Liberties Union** was founded by a group of prominent citizens including Roger Baldwin, its director from 1920 to 1950, attorney **Clarence Darrow**, settlement house founder **Jane Addams**, philosopher **John Dewey**, and Harvard law professor, later Supreme Court Justice, **Felix Frankfurter**.

- *Supreme Court Decisions.* Cases involving the constitutionality of these acts came before the Supreme Court. These cases raised the question of freedom versus order—the need to balance the liberty of the individual with the peace and order of society. Justice **Oliver Wendell Holmes** expressed this balance in two classic opinions. Writing for the Court in *Schenck* v. *United States* (1919), he upheld the conviction of the defendant for distributing leaflets advocating refusal to enlist in the armed services and expressed the "**clear and present danger**" doctrine. Holmes said, "The most stringent protection of free speech would not protect a man in falsely shouting fire in a theatre and causing a panic." (The wartime Espionage Act was found not to have violated the First Amendment.)

In the case of *Abrams* v. *United States* (1919), where the defendant appealed his sentence of twenty years imprisonment for violating the 1918 Sedition Act by publishing and distributing leaflets alleged to bring the form of government of the United States into contempt, Holmes wrote, in a classic dissenting opinion, "In this case sentences of twenty years imprisonment have been imposed for the publishing of two leaflets that I believe the defendants have as much right to publish as the government has to publish the Constitution of the United States now vainly invoked by them."

- *The Case of Sacco and Vanzetti (1920–1927).* On May 5, 1920 two Italian aliens, **Bartolomeo Vanzetti**, a fish peddler, and **Nicola Sacco**, a shoe factory employee—both anarchists opposed to all organized government—were arrested and charged with the murder of a payroll official and his guard, at a factory in South Braintree, Massachusetts. The case was tried before Judge Webster Thayer. The defendants were found guilty and sentenced to death, but many believed they were convicted because of their beliefs and their Italian nationality. Harvard law professor **Felix Frankfurter**, in his book *The Case of Sacco and Vanzetti,* wrote of Judge Thayer's opinion, "His twenty-five thousand word document cannot accurately be described otherwise than as a farrago [mixture] of misquotations, misrepresentations, suppressions, and mutilations." Protest meetings were held throughout the world. Appeals to the U.S. Supreme Court were turned down. Protesting their innocence to the end, Sacco and Vanzetti died in the electric chair at Charlestown, Massachusetts, August 23, 1927.

- *The New Ku Klux Klan.* Another attack on civil liberties was mounted by a renewed Ku Klux Klan in the postwar political climate. Targets of the Klan, which was especially strong in the Midwest and the South, were African Americans, Catholics, and Jews. The Klan spread terror by beating and lynching innocent people and by setting fire to homes and houses of worship.

Prohibition—the Eighteenth Amendment

I believe in liberty . . . . But I have never believed that democracy involved the liberty to guzzle when that liberty to guzzle was a menace . . . to the integrity of that society which constitutes the America we love together.

The Reverend John Haynes Holmes, 1924

The **Eighteenth Amendment**, which went into effect on January 16, 1920, outlawed the "manufacture, sale, or transportation of intoxicating liquors." For decades the **Anti-Saloon League** and the **Women's Christian Temperance Union** (WCTU) had been agitating for Prohibition. Several factors combined to make the period between 1917 and 1920 a favorable time for the adoption of this amendment. During the war many people thought it was wrong to use vast quantities of grain in the production of beer and liquor when food was needed for the Allies and armed forces overseas.

- *The Volstead Act.* The Volstead Act, or the Prohibition Enforcement Act, passed by Congress in 1919 over President Wilson's veto, defined "intoxicating" (as used in the Eighteenth Amendment) as any beverage containing over 1/2 of one percent alcohol. This made even beer and wine illegal. From the beginning, opposition to Prohibition was too strong and widespread to permit effective enforcement. Longtime habits, such as the workingman's pint of beer after a hard day's labor, could not easily be wiped out by law. Making "home brew" became a fad throughout the country. "**Speakeasies**," where patrons had to use passwords before the door was opened, flourished.

• *Repeal of the Eighteenth Amendment—the Twenty-first Amendment.* The movement to repeal the Eighteenth Amendment gained adherents when it became apparent that popular resistance can make a law virtually unenforceable. The Twenty-first Amendment to the Constitution, providing for the repeal of the Eighteenth, was proposed by two thirds of both houses of Congress on February 20, 1933, and was quickly approved by the necessary three quarters of the state legislatures, so that it was ratified on December 21, 1933.

Science, Religion, and Education

In the summer of 1925, the nation became absorbed in the **Scopes Trial**, or so-called "monkey trial," taking place in Dayton, Tennessee, where John Scopes' job was in jeopardy for teaching evolution to his high school biology class. Laws prohibiting the teaching of Darwin's theory had been passed in three Southern states, including Tennessee, in support of Fundamentalist theology.

The case attracted added attention because of distinguished counsel on both sides: **William Jennings Bryan** for the prosecution, and **Clarence Darrow** for the defense. Bryan, a gifted orator, had run for President three times as the Democratic party candidate. The law under which Scopes was convicted was ultimately repealed, but Fundamentalists continued to demand that "**creationism**" (the Bible account of creation) be taught in the schools on a par with the theory of evolution.

Native Americans

The legal status of Native Americans throughout our history is viewed by many as a test of our adherence to the Constitutional guarantees of civil liberties. From the earliest colonial times, the Indians were driven off their lands and forced to retreat westward by the guns of white settlers and their army units. Treaties with the Indians were repeatedly broken as valuable minerals—gold, silver, copper—were found on their territory or as white farmers and ranchers sought the western lands promised forever to the Indians by the treaties. The Indians were forced to live on reservations located in areas that were usually arid lands of little use to white settlers. Traditional tribal boundaries conflicted with those drawn by the federal government in the interest of white settlers, miners, hunters, and trappers. Government army units often suppressed Indian opposition with wanton cruelty at times amounting to genocide. The story is told by Helen Hunt Jackson in her book, published in 1881, aptly entitled *A Century of Dishonor*.

• *The Dawes Act (1887).* In an effort to make the Indians adopt white culture, the Dawes Act was passed in 1887. It attempted to substitute the single-family farm of 160 acres for the traditional Indian tribal way of life. After 25 years of "good behavior," the Indian would get title to the land plus American citizenship. The Dawes Act failed to achieve its purpose because most of the Indians preferred to remain on the reservation and retain their tribal ways. In 1924, citizenship was extended to all Native Americans by an act of Congress. But their plight remained desperate as they continued to have the lowest standard of living of all Americans.

• *Indian Reorganization Act (Wheeler-Howard Act) 1934.* Failure of the policy adopted under the Dawes Act was finally recognized in 1934 by the Indian Reorganization Act, also known as the Wheeler-Howard Act. The former policy was reversed. Native Americans were no longer to be urged to adapt to the "individual" American norm. Traditional tribal life was to be preserved and encouraged. Self-government of the Indian tribes on the reservations was to be protected by law. Education was to receive a high priority. The Indian population began to increase. From a low of less than 250,000 in the 1920s, it rose to 800,000 in 1970.

• *Indian Policy from the 1950s to the 1970s.* In the 1950s the federal government adopted a new Indian policy whose goals were termination and relocation. Its intention was to end all federal responsibility to Indians, transferring responsibility to those states that had large Indian populations. A second goal was to assimilate Indians into the American culture by relocating them to cities. Relocation and termination proved to be a failure, and in 1970, termination was ended. It was replaced by a new policy of "**self-determination**," which encouraged Indians to develop their own tribal life on the reservations. In the 1960s and 1970s, under a new spirit of militancy, Native Americans began to assert their rights, sometimes by direct action. They turned to the courts for redress, as far as possible, for injustices of the past.

Immigration

> Give me your tired, your poor,
> Your huddled masses yearning to breathe free,
> The wretched refuse of your teeming shore,
> Send these, the homeless, tempest-tossed to me,
> I lift my lamp beside the golden door!
>
> Inscription on the Statue of Liberty in New York Harbor
> From "The New Colossus" by Emma Lazarus

The Golden Door, which had beckoned millions of underprivileged and oppressed to seek refuge in America, was almost sealed after World War I. Prompted by the economic recession of 1920–1921 and the "Red Scare" with its fear of alien ideas, Congress enacted the **Emergency Quota Act of 1921**. This act limited the number of immigrants from any country annually to 3 percent of the number of persons from that country who were living in the United States according to the census of 1910. This was only the beginning. In a calculated decision to limit the number of immigrants from southern and eastern Europe, the immigration laws of 1924 limited the number of immigrants from any country to 2 percent of those living in the United States from that country as determined by the census of 1890 (instead of 1910). Total immigration was reduced to 164,000. The **National Origins Act of 1929** set the annual limit at 150,000 with quotas for each European nation. The Immigration Act of June 25, 1948, authorized the admission of 205,000 European displaced persons. The number was increased to 341,000 by the act of June 16, 1950. The **McCarran-Walter Act of 1952** included new measures designed to keep out "subversives" and gave the Attorney General the power to deport immigrants (even if they had become citizens) for belonging to "Communist or Communist-front" organizations.

The **Immigration Act of 1965** discontinued quotas based on national origin. Race, religion, and color are no longer factors in admission. Occupation and skills of the applicant are key considerations, as is having relatives already living in the United States. The act thus ended almost half a century of discriminatory immigration policy. The **Immigration and Control Act of 1986** (**Mazzoli-Simpson Act**) provides for legalizing the status of aliens who have been in the United States illegally since before January 1, 1981. Within six months, more than 300,000 aliens sought legal status under this provision. The 1986 law also imposes civil and criminal penalties on employers who knowingly hire, recruit, or refer aliens who are not authorized to work in the United States. The Refugee Act of 1980 provided for granting asylum in the United States to refugees who have good reason to fear persecution in their homeland. Under this act refugees have been admitted from Vietnam, Cambodia, Laos, Afghanistan, Poland, Czechoslovakia, and Central America.

Shifting Cultural Values

A Revolution in Morals and Manners

A revolution in morals and manners that began prior to World War I was greatly accelerated by the war and its aftermath. The psychoanalytic discoveries of **Sigmund Freud**, which opened the hither taboo field of sexual research, was interpreted as a warrant for rejecting the prevailing ethic of premarital chastity for women. The "flapper" of the 1920s "lost generation" took to smoking and drinking, wore short dresses, and found the automobile and movies a way to escape from the scrutiny of a chaperone. Women began to reject the double standard that permitted freedom for men but not for women. The Nineteenth Amendment, adopted in 1920, had finally guaranteed women's suffrage in national elections. By 1923, a **National Women's party** was campaigning for the adoption of an **Equal Rights Amendment** to the Constitution.

Changing Role of Women

World War I had a dramatic effect on the status of women in American society. During the war, women served in the armed forces. They filled the gap in farms, factories, mills, and mines left by the men who were in military service. The new freedom gained during the war manifested itself in new moral and social behavior. Women were now openly drinking and smoking, and their clothing was more revealing.

The role of women in all aspects of life—economic, political, social, and cultural—was changing rapidly. A majority of women now lived in cities and they increasingly entered the work force. In 1920, one of every five employed people was a woman. By 1950, 18 million—nearly 30 percent of the work force—were women. Electric irons, washing machines, refrigerators, vacuum cleaners, canned goods, and ready-made clothing freed women from the relentless pressures traditionally associated with homemaking. Women began playing an active role in politics, civic affairs, the arts, and the pursuit of their individual interests and talents. Women in the work force began playing an equal role with their husbands in supporting the family. In response to these developments, Congress enacted the 1922 Sheppard-Towner Act, extending financial aid to the states for the welfare and health of pregnant women and newborn infants. The act authorized the appropriation of $1 million annually for maternity and infant care.

• *The Nineteenth Amendment (1920).* The Nineteenth Amendment, guaranteeing women the right to vote in state and national elections, was proposed by Congress on June 4, 1919, with little opposition. President Wilson urged its adoption, noting the part played by women during World War I. "The services of women during the supreme crisis have been of the most signal usefulness and distinction." The Amendment became the law of the land when it was ratified by the 36th state on August 26, 1920. It declared: "The right of citizens of the United States to vote shall not be denied or abridged by the United States or by any state on account of sex."

Literature and American Life

> And I wish American novelists would give up trying to make business romantically interesting. Nobody wants to read about it unless it's crooked business.
> F. Scott Fitzgerald, *This Side of Paradise* (1920)

> He serenely believed that the one purpose of the real-estate business
> was to make money for George F. Babbitt. True, it was a good adver-
> tisement at Boosters Club lunches . . . to speak sonorously of unselfish
> public service . . . and a thing called ethics . . . But they didn't imply
> that you were to be impractical and refuse to take twice the value of a
> house if a buyer was . . . an idiot. . . .
>
> Sinclair Lewis, *Babbitt* (1922)

The 1920s became known as "The Roaring Twenties," "The Gilded Age," and "The Jazz Age." Writers of the period, such as **Sinclair Lewis**, **F. Scott Fitzgerald**, **Theodore Dreiser**, **Ernest Hemingway**, and **John Dos Passos**, cast doubt on prevailing values and caused the participants in the giddy whirl to be dubbed "the lost generation."

- *The Search for Heroes.* It is doubtless significant that the period witnessed a frantic search for heroes. As a model, **Charles A. Lindbergh** was almost too good to be true. A tall, handsome, modest young man, Lindbergh startled the world by his solo, nonstop flight in his single-engine propeller-driven plane, "**The Spirit of St. Louis**," across the Atlantic from New York to Paris, May 20–21, 1927. The overnight flight took 33 hours, 39 minutes. On his return to New York, Lindbergh, the "Lone Eagle," was greeted with a triumphant parade up New York's Broadway. A year later, **Amelia Earhart**, a pioneer woman in aviation, made a similar trans-Atlantic nonstop flight.

In sports, the all-time baseball hero, **Babe Ruth**, came to the New York Yankees in 1920 as an outfielder after previously winning 24 games as a pitcher with the Boston Red Sox. He established a lifetime record of 714 home runs and led the great Yankee ball club to seven pennants and four world championships. Other sports heroes of the period included Jack Johnson, world heavyweight boxing champion (1910–1915); Jack Dempsey, who attracted the first million-dollar gate in 1921; Bill Tilden, who was ranked first in the world in tennis, throughout the 1920s; "Red" Grange, who scored 31 touchdowns for the University of Illinois; and Gertrude Ederle, the first woman to swim the English Channel and break the existing men's record on August 6, 1926.

On the screen, the object of fascination was **Rudolph Valentino**. Born in Italy, Valentino came to the United States in 1913 and became a national idol for his performance in two 1921 blockbusters, *The Four Horsemen of the Apocalypse* and *The Sheik*.

- *The Black Renaissance.* The post-World War I period witnessed a great black renaissance in Harlem. Poets Langston Hughes and Countee Cullen, political activist Marcus Garvey, writer Zora Neale Hurston, scholar and nationalist leader W.E.B. Du Bois, as well as gifted painters and musicians, gathered in Harlem and made this part of New York, with its wide streets and classic buildings, an exciting place to live in the 1920s.

1. Which of the following was a prime *cause* of the other three?
   A. imposition of immigration quotas
   B. the Big Red Scare
   C. raids conducted by Attorney General A. Mitchell Palmer
   D. rapid growth of the new Ku Klux Klan

2. Federal government policy toward Native Americans may properly be described as
   A. generally one of hostility to their best interest as fellow Americans
   B. a policy designed to destroy or basically alter their traditional culture patterns
   C. a series of changes in policy including making treaties with them, attempting to exterminate them, and treating them as wards of the government
   D. all of the above

3. Which of the following does *not* apply to the immigration policy of the United States during the 1920s?
   A. it sought to limit the number of immigrants
   B. it restored the traditional American immigration policy of keeping the Golden Door open
   C. it established the principle of selective immigration by favoring immigrants from some areas of the world over those from other areas
   D. it was enacted over the objection of a sizeable minority of public opinion

4. Between 1920 and 1930 passenger car registration in the United States leaped from 8.1 million to 26.5 million. A direct result of this increase was
   A. less movement of people to the suburbs
   B. a stimulation of such related industries as advertising, insurance, and finance
   C. a decrease in road and highway construction
   D. a decline of the importance of the assembly line

5. Which was *not* a characteristic of the economic life of the 1920s?
   A. new methods of production
   B. installment buying and borrowing to finance consumer growth
   C. a government tax policy that retarded accumulation of large personal fortunes
   D. investment by banks in real estate, mortgages, bonds, and stocks

6. A major effect of the new radio and motion picture industries was
   A. a steady decline in the circulation of newspapers and magazines
   B. a tendency toward homogenization of American culture
   C. a shift away from sports as a major source of recreation for both spectators and participants
   D. a decline in the influence of religion due to falling attendance at religious services

7. The rapid growth of the automobile industry was made possible by
   A. the introduction by Henry Ford of an eight-hour day and a minimum wage of $5 a day in 1914
   B. a ready market created by the rising standard of living and the increase of leisure time of the average American
   C. cooperation of labor and management in the trucking industry
   D. failure of trolleys and railroads to maintain a high standard in their facilities and operations

8. Which of the following pairs are associated with the Harlem Renaissance of the 1920s?
   A. Sigmund Freud and Ernest Hemingway
   B. Gertrude Ederle and Rudolph Valentino
   C. Sinclair Lewis and F. Scott Fitzgerald
   D. Langston Hughes and Countee Cullen

9. Which of the following was, at least in part, a cause of the other three?
   A. the changing role of women in economic, social, and cultural affairs
   B. the adoption of the Nineteenth Amendment
   C. the active participation of women in World War I
   D. the emerging emphasis on wife rather than mother

10. The adoption of the Nineteenth Amendment to the Constitution in 1920 was a result of
    A. the fact that many states had already extended suffrage to women before World War I
    B. the widespread belief that the time had come to stop classifying women with others most commonly denied the ballot: children, illiterates, the insane, and criminals
    C. the way women did "men's work" in war industries
    D. all of the above

1. During the post-World War I period, civil liberties were under attack. Which of the following is *not* an example of this experience?
   A. the conviction of Sacco and Vanzetti
   B. the Scopes trial in Dayton, Tennessee
   C. the revival of the Ku Klux Klan
   D. the novels of Sinclair Lewis

2. An experience of the majority of immigrants to the United States was that they
   A. Frequently met resentment
   B. settled in rural areas where cheap land was available
   C. were rapidly assimilated into the predominant lifestyle
   D. joined radical parties to bring about economic reform

3. President Calvin Coolidge once said, "The business of America is business." This slogan is most closely related to
   A. a laissez-faire attitude toward the economy
   B. government ownership of heavy industry
   C. the enactment of protective tariffs
   D. legislation benefiting organized labor

4. At various times throughout history, racial and religious prejudices have been exploited for the purpose of
   A. expanding cultural diversity
   B. reenforcing nationalistic sentiments
   C. expanding international trade
   D. furthering the growth of fine arts

5. All Native Americans achieved citizenship
   A. by the Dawes Act of 1887
   B. in 1968 as part of President Johnson's Great Society
   C. by an act of Congress in 1924
   D. by the Indian Reorganization Act of 1934

ESSAYS

1. During the period 1914–1929 (except for the years 1920–1921) the American economy made great advances, causing President Hoover to declare, "We are nearer today to the ideal of the abolition of poverty . . . than ever before in any land."
   a. Identify *three* factors that helped promote the growth of the economy during this period and discuss how each contributed to this growth.
   b. Using specific historical information, discuss one impact that industrialization had on the United States during the period 1914–1921.

2. Many aspects of United States society have been greatly affected by technological changes. Choose *three* of the aspects of United States society listed below. Explain how each one chosen has been affected by a specific technological development. [Use a different development for each aspect.]
   Aspects of United States Society
   Urbanization
   Agriculture
   Cultural homogeneity
   Rights of the individual
   Politics
   Environment

3. At various times, civil liberties have been seriously threatened in the United States. One such period was the decade following World War I. Give *three* examples of threats to civil liberties during this period.

   For *each* one mentioned, describe the threat and indicate briefly the outcome.

THEMATIC ESSAY

Directions: Write a well-organized essay that includes an introduction, several paragraphs addressing the task below, and a conclusion.

Theme: Changing Cultural Values

> The early decades of the 20th century proved to be a time of change in American cultural values.

Task:

> From your study of the early decades of the 20th century, identify *two* traditional cultural values that would be tested and subsequently experience considerable change.
>
> For each cultural value identified:
>
> - Identify the subject (women, minorities, children, educational values, music, etc.)
> - Discuss circumstances that led to the challenge of the traditional value.
> - Discuss one immediate or long-term effect of the challenge and change in the cultural value.

You may use any early 20th-century challenges and changes in American cultural values from your study of United States history. Some suggestions you may wish to consider are Prohibition (1920), women's suffrage (1919), Scopes Trial (1925), Child Labor Act (1919), developments in birth control and divorce, development of jazz, etc.

You are *not* limited to these suggestions.

DOCUMENT-BASED QUESTION ESSAY

The following questions (Part A and Part B) are based on the accompanying documents (1–6). Some of these documents have been edited for the purpose of this exercise. The question is designed to test your ability to work with historical documents and to demonstrate your knowledge of the subject matter being presented. As you analyze the documents, take into account both the source of the document and the author's point of view.

Historical Context: Although the "Golden 1920s" showed early signs of prosperity, a closer examination of the decade reveals that prosperity was not experienced by many.

Task: Using information from the documents and your knowledge of United States history, answer the questions that follow each document in Part A. Your answers to the questions will help you write the Part B essay, in which you will be asked:

Although the decade before the Great Depression was called the "Roaring 20s" or the "Golden 20s," a closer examination of the decade reveals that prosperity was not experienced by many. Identify the groups of Americans who were suffering economically and discuss how their conditions may have contributed to the collapse of the American economy in the 1930s.

Part A
Short Answer

The documents below relate to economic and social issues concerning the 1920s. Examine each document carefully and then answer the questions that follow.

DOCUMENT 1

By 1929, the richest 1 percent of the American population would own 40 percent of the nation's wealth. The bottom 93 percent would experience a 4 percent drop in real disposable per capita income between 1923 and 1929.

1. Identify one problem that may result when a large part of the population (in this case 93 percent) has less money to spend.

_____

_____

_____

_____

2. How much of the nation's wealth would the remaining 99 percent of the population own by 1929?

_____

_____

_____

_____

DOCUMENT 2

We worked to build this country, mister.
While you enjoyed a life of ease;
You've stolen all that we built, mister;
Now our children starve and freeze.

Think me dumb if you wish mister;
Call me green or blue or red;
This one thing I sure know mister;
My hungry babies must be fed.

I don't want your millions, mister,
I don't want your diamond ring.
All I want is the right to live mister;
Give me back my job again.

—Jim Garland, Coal Miner, Harlan County, Kentucky,
"I Don't Want Your Millions, Mister"

3. According to the author of the song, who was experiencing the benefits and profits of the working classes?

_____

_____

_____

_____

DOCUMENT 3

The present condition of American agriculture constitutes an emergency of the gravest character. The Department of Commerce report shows that during 1923 there was a steady and marked increase in dividends paid by the great industrial corporations. The same is true of the steam and electric railways and practically all other large corporations. On the other hand, the Secretary of Agriculture reports that in the fifteen principal wheat growing states more than 108,000 farmers since 1920 have lost their farms through foreclosure or bankruptcy....that more than 122,000 have surrendered their property without legal proceedings....

Almost unlimited prosperity for the great corporations and ruin and bankruptcy for agriculture is the direct and logical result of the policies and legislation which deflated the farmer while extending almost unlimited credit to the great corporations...

—Robert La Follette, Progressive Party Platform, 1924

4. According to candidate La Follette, how did American farmers compare with American corporations during the first four years of the 1920s?

_____

_____

_____

_____

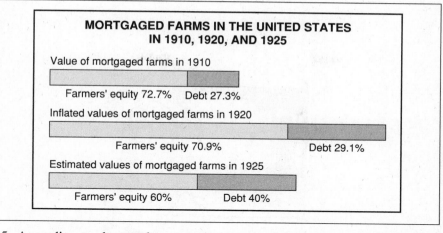

DOCUMENT 4

MORTGAGED FARMS IN THE UNITED STATES
IN 1910, 1920, AND 1925

Value of mortgaged farms in 1910

Farmers' equity 72.7%   Debt 27.3%

Inflated values of mortgaged farms in 1920

Farmers' equity 70.9%   Debt 29.1%

Estimated values of mortgaged farms in 1925

Farmers' equity 60%   Debt 40%

5. According to the graph concerning mortgaged farms (1910–1925), what was the trend regarding a farmer's amount of actual ownership of his farm?

_____

_____

_____

_____

DOCUMENT 5

The right of all to the opportunity for self-maintenance; a wider and fairer distribution of wealth; a living wage, as a minimum, and above this a just share for the worker in the product of industry and agriculture.

—*Social Creed of Protestant Churches*, Federal Council
of Churches, December, 1932

6. As the Depression hit following the 1920s, what issues did the Federal Council of Churches identify as in need of change?

_____

_____

_____

_____

DOCUMENT 6

—Two Chickens in Every Garage, 1932

7. How does the author of the political cartoon view President Hoover's promise to the American people of "A chicken in every pot and two cars in every garage?"

_____

_____

_____

_____

Part B
Essay

Your essay should be well organized with an introductory paragraph that states your position on the question. Develop your position in the next paragraphs and then write a conclusion. In your essay, include specific historical details and refer to the specific documents you analyzed in Part A. You may include additional information from your knowledge of social studies.

Historical Context: Although the "Golden 1920s" showed early signs of prosperity, a closer examination of the decade reveals that prosperity was not experienced by many.

Task:

Although the decade before the Great Depression was called the "Roaring 20s" or the "Golden 1920s," a closer examination of the decade reveals that prosperity was not experienced by many. Identify the groups of Americans who were suffering economically and discuss how their conditions may have contributed to the collapse of the American economy in the 1930s.

Guidelines:

In your essay, be sure to
• Develop all aspects of the task
• Incorporate information from at least *five* documents
• Incorporate relevant outside information
• Support the theme with many relevant facts, examples, and details
• Use a logical and clear plan of organization, including an introduction and a conclusion that are beyond a restatement of the theme

THE GREAT DEPRESSION AND THE NEW DEAL (1933–1940)

FAILURE OF THE OLD ORDER: HOOVER AND THE CRASH

> Our immediate and paramount task as a people is to rout the forces of economic disruption and pessimism that have swept upon us.
>
> Herbert Hoover, June 16, 1931

> A glance at the situation today only too clearly indicates that equality of opportunity as we have known it no longer exists . . . . Our task now is . . . distributing wealth and products more equitably, of adapting existing economic organizations to the service of the people.
>
> Franklin D. Roosevelt, September 23, 1932

Cracks in the Economic Foundation

Overproduction and Maldistribution of Purchasing Power

The short-lived prosperity of the late 1920s was built on a fragile economic base. Technological advances, coupled with overexpansion of credit, brought about a vast increase in industrial production. At the same time the maldistribution of wealth—the concentration of money among wealthy individuals and surpluses in business corporations—meant that farmers and laborers were not able to purchase the goods produced. For a time the gap was made up by installment buying and other forms of credit. But the day of reckoning had to come.

Overexpansion of Credit

Overexpansion of credit was encouraging reckless gambling in the stock market. An investor could purchase shares of stock "on margin," that is, by putting up as little as 10 percent of the cost with the rest of the money on credit. This enabled people to buy much more than they could afford. Stock prices became overinflated.

The Stock Market Crash

The Crash of 1929

Stock prices began to decline slowly in September 1929, and by October the decline gained momentum. The great crash came on **Black Tuesday**, October 29, 1929, when 16.5 million shares were traded in a precipitous decline that continued for the rest of the year. **U.S. Steel**, which sold for $262 a share in September, was quoted at $22 three months later.

Worldwide Economic Collapse

The economic crash and the resulting **depression** were worldwide. The banking systems of the world were interdependent. American banks had made large loans to their European affiliates. Banks on both sides of the Atlantic failed and caused others to fail. Between October 1, 1929, and August 31, 1932, 4,835 American banks failed. Their total deposits, representing

Many investors went bankrupt in the crash of 1929.

the lifetime savings of millions of Americans, amounted to $3.25 billion. To make matters worse, the **Hawley-Smoot Tariff** of 1930, with its high protectionist rates, served only to dry up the sickly streams of international trade.

Hoover and the Depression

President Hoover did make efforts to revive the economy but he was stopped from taking drastic action by his own economic philosophy. He believed that direct government aid to the needy would destroy "**rugged individualism**" and might even lead to socialism. Moreover, he believed that the depression would soon end and that "prosperity [was] just around the corner."

Moratorium on War Debts

In 1931 Hoover recommended a one-year moratorium (postponement) on the payment of war debts and on reparations owed by Germany to the Allies.

Trickle-down Economics—the Reconstruction Finance Corporation

Hoover also believed in "**trickle-down economics**," the idea that profits of big business would trickle down to average Americans. At Hoover's request, Congress established the **Reconstruction Finance Corporation** (1932). The RFC advanced some $2 billion in loans to state and local governments and to banks, railroads, farm mortgage associations, and large corporations in order to stimulate the economy. But the roots of the depression were too deep to be easily eradicated. Hoover's efforts to stem the tide proved to be inadequate, and the Republican party was swept out of office in the election of November 1932.

Misery and the Great Depression

Mass Unemployment and Its Effects

Mass unemployment was the hallmark of the Great Depression. Farms were abandoned, factories closed, and men and women stood on breadlines waiting for a handout. Youths rode the railroad lines in empty freight cars. Early in 1932, one fourth of the work force, some 10 million Americans, were unemployed. Some, like the fictional Joads in Steinbeck's *The Grapes of Wrath*, left their farms and drove West hoping for better times in California. In cities, men peddled apples on street corners. Women and children, helpless victims, perhaps suffered most, while minorities were hard hit by this unprecedented economic catastrophe.

Rundown shanty towns, their shacks put together with tin and paper collected in dumps, sprang up all over the country. They were named "Hoovervilles" in derision of an administration that was deemed inept, if not indeed lacking in compassion.

The Bonus Army in Washington

In the spring of 1932, about 15,000 veterans of World War I marched on Washington from all over the country to demand immediate payment of their bonus certificates, which were not due until 1945. They camped in shacks along the Anacostia River near the Capitol. When Congress failed to pass legislation to meet their demand, most of them departed. But some 2,000 remained, refusing the government's offer of funds to pay for their return home. Hoover ordered the Army to drive them out. Led by Chief-of-Staff General **Douglas MacArthur**, army infantry and cavalry units attacked the veterans in force, scattering them with tear-gas bombs, sabers, and tanks, and burned their shacks. MacArthur and Hoover were severely criticized for this tactic, which they claimed was "necessary under the circumstances."

1. From 1923 to early 1929 behavior of business cycles
   A. registered sharp fluctuations
   B. was indiscernible
   C. created the belief that a serious depression would never return
   D. created unrest and alarm

2. A criticism of President Hoover's policies in dealing with the Depression was
   A. he postponed action in the belief that prosperity was just around the corner
   B. he intervened excessively with businesses and corporations
   C. the policies of laissez-faire were violated by his administration
   D. he did less than earlier Presidents had done in similar crises

3. Which conditions are most characteristic of a depression?
   A. high production and high demand
   B. few jobs and little demand
   C. much money in circulation and high stock prices
   D. supply meeting demand and high unemployment

4. A condition that was for the most part unrelated to the causes of the Great Depression was
   A. the fact that large-scale construction of new highways was undertaken to accommodate the rapid introduction of the automobile
   B. that increased industrial production was not matched by a corresponding increase in the purchasing power of consumers
   C. that newly introduced laborsaving devices were causing technological unemployment
   D. that overextension of credit was encouraging debt as well as speculation in the stock market

FRANKLIN D. ROOSEVELT: RELIEF, RECOVERY, AND REFORM

> In broad terms I assert that modern society, acting through its government, owes the definite obligation to prevent the starvation or the dire want of any of its fellow men and women who try to maintain themselves but cannot.
>
> Franklin D. Roosevelt, speech in campaign
> for reelection as Governor of New York, 1930

New York Serves as a Prototype for the New Deal

The "Little New Deal"

Soon after his reelection as Governor of New York in 1930, **Franklin D. Roosevelt** called a special session of the legislature to face the problem of mounting economic distress. New York became the first state to appropriate public funds for unemployment relief. The **"New Deal"** was foreshadowed in Roosevelt's governorship. It was, in effect, a "Little New Deal." A State Power Authority was created to control public utilities and establish the principle that the water power of the state belonged to the people. An old-age Pension Law became a forerunner of **Social Security**. Legislation was introduced to end the 54-hour work week, and to require an **8-hour day** and **48-hour week** for women and children. **Minimum-wage legislation** for women was also proposed.

Mayor Fiorello LaGuardia

New York City had its own "Little New Deal," when it elected Fiorello LaGuardia (the "Little Flower") Mayor in 1933. Defeated in his bid for reelection to Congress in 1932, he formed the Fusion party and was elected Mayor of New York in 1933. He was reelected in 1937 and 1941. On first taking office he declared, "Our theory of municipal government is an experiment to try to show that a nonpartisan, nonpolitical local government is possible."

The LaGuardia administration found a sympathetic reception in Washington. During LaGuardia's first year in office, the federal government made significant commitments to New York City: $20 million for low-cost housing, $1.5 million toward completion of the Triborough Bridge, and $25 million to put 3,000 to work on subway construction. During LaGuardia's tenure, New York built 92 new schools and introduced the first inclusive health insurance plan in the nation for low-income city employees.

The New Deal in Washington

> I pledge you, I pledge myself, to a new deal for the American people.
> Franklin D. Roosevelt, accepting the Democratic
> nomination for the presidency, July 2, 1932

A Strong Cabinet

To help him tackle the problems facing the country and to bring relief, recovery, and reform to the beleaguered nation, Roosevelt surrounded himself with the best people he could find, regardless of their political affiliation. **Harold L. Ickes**, a former Republican, became Secretary of the Interior. **Henry Morgenthau, Jr.**, the President's close friend and Hyde Park neighbor, remained Secretary of the Treasury for twelve years. For Secretary of Labor, Roosevelt appointed **Frances Perkins**, the first woman to serve in a President's cabinet. Perkins, who had worked with Jane Addams at Hull House in Chicago, was to become a key figure in shaping New Deal labor legislation. **Henry A. Wallace**, a former Republican, who was to become Vice President during Roosevelt's third term, was Secretary of Agriculture and later Secretary of Commerce.

A "Brain Trust"

In addition to his Cabinet, Roosevelt brought to Washington a number of brilliant unofficial advisers who came to be known as the "brain trust." Chief among these was **Harry Hopkins**, a former social worker, who had the President's complete confidence and was entrusted with sensitive missions. Also in the "brain trust" were Rexford G. Tugwell, Adolphe A. Berle, Jr., and Raymond Moley, all members of the Columbia University faculty.

Relief of Human Suffering

> Let me assert my firm belief that the only thing we have to fear is fear itself.
> Franklin D. Roosevelt, First Inaugural Address,
> March 4, 1933

The first task set for the "New Deal" was relief of human suffering. Loss of people's life savings through bank failures had to be halted. The hungry had to be fed. The unemployed had to be put to work.

The Emergency Banking Relief Act

The day after his inauguration as President, Roosevelt summoned Congress into special session and proclaimed a national bank holiday, closing all the nation's banks for an indefinite period of time. Congress promptly passed the Emergency Banking Relief Act (March 9, 1933) granting extraordinary power to the President. Within a week the solvent banks reopened and deposits exceeded withdrawals. Swift action had restored public confidence in the banking system. Reform, to prevent future catastrophe, was to come later.

The Federal Emergency Relief Act

The Federal Emergency Relief Act (May 12, 1933) established a **Federal Emergency Relief Administration (FERA)** and authorized an appropriation of $500 million. The money was to be granted to states and municipalities for emergency relief. Harry L. Hopkins was appointed Administrator of the FERA. Ultimately, some $3 billion was spent under the act. A branch of the FERA was the **Civil Works Administration (CWA)**, established in November 1933 to provide temporary jobs during the winter emergency. The CWA came under criticism because many of the jobs, such as leaf-raking, hastily created during the emergency, were called "boondoggling," useless or wasteful activities.

Dealing with Unemployment

A **Public Works Administration (PWA)** was established in June 1933 under the **National Industrial Recovery Act (NIRA)**. It was directed by Secretary of the Interior Harold L. Ickes. The object of this legislation was called "pump priming," that is, the government pumps money into the economy to stimulate the economy. A full-scale attack on unemployment came in the spring of 1935 with the creation of the **Works Progress Administration (WPA)**. This act, administered by Harry Hopkins, provided 9 million useful jobs during the next eight years. Communities throughout the land were enriched by the construction of 6,000 school buildings, thousands of post-office and courthouse buildings, 128,000 miles of roads, and thousands of bridges. An effort was made to place people in jobs suitable to their education and experience. Unemployed architects designed buildings, engineers built dams, artists painted murals, authors, musicians, playwrights, and actors were enabled to work at their professions and contribute their talents as government employees during the Depression.

Aid to Youth

Agencies created specifically for the purpose of providing aid to needy youth were the **Civilian Conservation Corps (CCC)** and the **National Youth Administration (NYA)**. The CCC enrolled young men between the ages of 18 and 25 and assigned them to one of the 2,600 work camps throughout the country. There they cleared land for public parks, built dams for flood control, planted trees, and cleared swamps. The CCC ultimately enlisted 2.5 million young men. In addition to food, clothing, and shelter, they received money payments that went in part to their needy families. The **National Youth Administration (NYA)**, created in 1935, cooperated with schools and colleges in providing an income for needy students who performed tasks useful to their school or college. The NYA gave part-time employment to more than 600,000 college students and 1.5 million high school pupils. Aid was provided also to 2.6 million young Americans who were not in school. Some received vocational training; others were put to work renovating government buildings, repairing equipment, building playgrounds, and upgrading public parks.

Recovery for the American Economy

Besides trying to relieve human suffering caused by the Depression, the New Deal sought to restore the nation's economic health. The New Deal program for recovery set its sights on industry, agriculture, and housing.

Measures to Aid Industry

The **National Industrial Recovery Act (NIRA)**, which was signed into law June 16, 1933, created the **National Recovery Administration (NRA)** under General Hugh S. Johnson. Members of each industry were to establish "codes of fair competition" that, when approved by the President, were to be legally binding on the industry. The code of each industry was to prescribe wages, hours, and prices, provide for a minimum wage, and preserve labor's rights of collective bargaining. A blue eagle was adopted as a symbol that, when displayed, signified compliance with the code of that industry.

Helping Home Owners

The **Home Owners Loan Corporation (HOLC)** was established in June 1933 to help home owners save their homes. Every day 1,000 home owners were losing their homes to mortgage holders (banks) for failure to pay the mortgages. The HOLC loaned money at low interest to private home owners to pay off their old mortgages and new long-term mortgages were arranged at low interest rates. Within a year 300,000 loans amounting to almost $1 billion were made. During the three year period 1933–1936 the homes of more than a million families were saved by the HOLC. By insuring building loans made by banks, the **Federal Housing Authority (FHA)** created in 1934 encouraged banks to lend money for home repairs and for construction of homes and businesses.

Aid to Agriculture

To halt foreclosures on farms, a **Farm Credit Administration (FCA)** was established in June 1933. Farm mortgages were refinanced at low rates of interest for long terms, while farm debts were adjusted on favorable terms. In its first 18 months, the FCA refinanced the mortgages of nearly one fifth of America's family farms. To aid the poorest farmers—the tenant farmers and sharecroppers—a **Farm Security Administration (FSA)** was established in 1937. More than a billion dollars was extended in low-interest, long-term loans to enable tenants to buy farms.

- *The AAA (1933).* Major reform in agriculture was undertaken in two **Agricultural Adjustment Acts (AAA)**. The first AAA of May 1933 was designed to achieve "parity" between agriculture and industry by raising the prices of farm commodities, so that farm income would keep pace with nonfarm income. This was to be attained by curtailing production. Farmers signed agreements to reduce their planting by one fourth to one half, since lower production would help to raise the market price of farm commodities. In return, the government made "benefit payments" to farmers for their crop reduction. The AAA had an immediate effect on production and market prices of farm commodities. For example, with 10 million acres of cotton out of production, cotton prices rose from 5.5 to 9.5 cents per pound in the first year. The Supreme Court, by a 6 to 3 vote in January 1936, declared the AAA unconstitutional.

- *The SCDAA.* Congress then passed the **Soil Conservation and Domestic Allotment Act (SCDAA)** of 1936, which paid farmers for growing soil-conserving crops such as clover and soybeans and not growing soil-exhausting staples like cotton, corn, and tobacco.

- *Second AAA.* A second AAA in 1938 continued the soil conservation program of the 1936 act. With the approval of two thirds of the producers of a specific commodity, the government could decide the amount of corn, wheat, rice, cotton, or tobacco that could be marketed. Surpluses of each commodity were to be stored by the government and released when prices rose to the parity level. Despite all-out efforts at recovery, the level of unemployment and poverty remained above pre-Depression days well into Roosevelt's second term.

Reform Programs

> I see one-third of a nation ill-housed, ill-clad, ill-nourished.
> The test of our progress is not whether we add more to the abundance of those who have much; it is whether we provide enough for those who have too little.
> > Franklin D. Roosevelt, Second Inaugural Address,
> > January 20, 1937

The New Deal search for effective reform programs had a major impact on banking, stock market operations, social security and labor.

Banking Reform

The **Glass-Steagall Banking Act of 1933** was designed to protect depositors against bank failures. It separated commercial from investment banking and restricted the use of bank credit for financial speculation. Most significant was the provision creating a new agency, the **Federal Deposit Insurance Corporation (FDIC)**, which insured savings bank deposits up to $2,500. The guarantee was raised to $5,000 the following year and proved a boon to the banks as well as to their depositors. The amount insured—$100,000 in 1994—was steadily increased as the purchasing power of the dollar increased.

Stock Market Reforms

To provide basic protection to investors in the stock markets, the **Securities Act of May 1933** required every new stock offering to contain specific information to enable prospective investors to judge the value of a share and the financial circumstances of the corporation. The **Securities and Exchange Commission** was established the following year to enforce the act.

Social Security

A landmark achievement of the New Deal was the **Social Security Act** of August 14, 1935. The act provided for (1) a fund for **unemployment insurance** to be derived from taxes on payrolls of employers having 8 or more employees. Each state was to administer its own system in conjunction with the federal government; (2) a fund for old-age and survivors insurance to be derived from taxes levied on employers and their employees. This fund was to be administered by the federal government and was to make monthly pension payments to retirees when reaching the age of 65; (3) money grants to states for pensions provided by state law; and (4) grants to states for relief of blind, handicapped, and other destitute dependents.

The act was to be administered by a three-member **Social Security Board**. The act, which President Roosevelt described as "a cornerstone in a structure which is being built" had an immediate impact. Two years after the Social Security program was passed into law, 21 million workers were covered by unemployment insurance and 36 million were entitled to old-age pensions.

Labor Legislation

- *The Wagner Act.* Through patient and effective persuasion, Senator **Robert F. Wagner** of New York gained enough support from the business community to make possible the passage of landmark labor legislation. The **National Labor Relations Act** of July 5, 1935, known as the **Wagner Act**, was designed to reduce tension in labor relations and thus avoid strikes and labor disaffection. It provided for an independent **National Labor Rela-**

tions Board (**NLRB**) that would conduct plant elections for employees to choose their agents for contract negotiations and grievance resolution. The Board could also issue "cease and desist" orders against "unfair labor practices" such as interference with the union in collective bargaining, refusal to bargain collectively, and discrimination against union members.

• *The Fair Labor Standards Act.* The Fair Labor Standards Act (Wages and Hours Law) of 1938 set minimum wages (40 cents an hour initially) and maximum hours (40 hours per week) and forbade the employment of children under 16 in business establishments engaged in interstate commerce.

• *Formation of the CIO.* In 1935, **John L. Lewis**, president of the **United Mine Workers** and vice-president of the **American Federation of Labor** (**AFL**), took his union out of the AFL and started a new organization to be known as the **Congress of Industrial Organization** (**CIO**). Lewis charged that the AFL, whose membership consisted essentially of craft unions, showed little interest in organizing the low-skilled workers in the mass production industries. For the first time, unions organized on an industry basis (automotive, electrical, steel, etc.), were successful in bargaining for all their employees with such industrial giants as General Motors, United States Steel, and General Electric.

Exercise Set 4.5

1. In the early years of the New Deal, Roosevelt
   A. sought advice from very few others
   B. relied heavily on a "Brain Trust"
   C. consulted primarily business leaders
   D. sought advice only from politicians in his Cabinet

2. The policies of Franklin D. Roosevelt revealed
   A. a rejection of the capitalistic system
   B. a willingness to modify extensively American laissez-faire economic practices
   C. a Fascist philosophy of economic and political regimentation
   D. a timidity in dealing with the basic weaknesses of the free enterprise system

3. Franklin D. Roosevelt first gave his attention to what major problem?
   A. unemployment
   B. speculation in securities
   C. farm relief
   D. bank failures

4. A major difference between the New Deal and policies followed by earlier administrations was that the New Deal
   A. emphasized and encouraged rugged individualism
   B. advocated socialism as a solution to the problems of the times
   C. provided the government with a more active role in the economy
   D. was able to eliminate discrimination in employment

5. On the political spectrum Roosevelt's domestic program for relief, recovery, and reform was
   A. at the far left between socialism and communism
   B. at the far right between conservatism and fascism
   C. right of center between moderate and conservative
   D. left of center between moderate and liberal

CONSTITUTIONAL ISSUES AND THE NEW DEAL

When an act of Congress is appropriately challenged in the courts
. . . the judicial branch of government has only one duty—to lay the
article of the Constitution which is invoked beside the statute which
is challenged and to decide whether the latter squares with the former.

> Justice Owen J. Roberts, writing for the majority of six in
> *United States* v. *Butler* et al. (1936) invalidating
> the Agricultural Adjustment Act.

A tortured construction of the Constitution is not to be justified by
recourse to extreme examples . . . .

> Justice Harlan F. Stone, dissenting for the minority of three

The Supreme Court and New Deal Legislation

The Schechter Poultry Case

Foes of the New Deal were heartened by several key decisions of the
Supreme Court. A major piece of legislation, passed early in the New Deal,
was the **National Industrial Recovery Act** (June 1933), which established
a **National Recovery Administration** (**NRA**) designed to revitalize
industry while protecting labor and consumers. The act was declared unconstitutional by the Supreme Court in the case of *Schechter Poultry Corp.* v.
United States (1935). Chief Justice **Charles Evans Hughes**, writing for a
unanimous court, ruled that the excessive delegation of legislative power to
the executive was unconstitutional.

United States v. *Butler*—the AAA

The following year, the Court invalidated another major piece of New Deal
legislation, the **Agricultural Adjustment Act** of 1933. In a 6 to 3 decision,
the Court, in the case of *United States* v. *Butler,* declared the act unconstitutional on the ground that the processing tax was an abuse of the taxing
power in regulating agricultural output. The action of the Supreme Court
in declaring these and other acts of the New Deal unconstitutional brought
about a storm of resentment. The controversy raised one of the enduring
issues in American history: Is the judiciary the interpreter of the Constitution
or a shaper of public policy?

The Tennessee Valley Authority (TVA)

Purpose and Extent of the Project

One major agency of the New Deal, established by legislation in 1933, survived attacks in the courts. It was the **Tennessee Valley Authority (TVA)**, designed to revitalize one of the most economically depressed regions in the country. This region included parts of seven states—Virginia, North Carolina, Georgia, Alabama, Mississippi, Tennessee, and Kentucky. The TVA constructed 21 large dams on the Tennessee River to provide electric power for the region. Besides supplying cheap power, TVA served the region in many ways. It provided thousands of jobs to residents in the area. Additional benefits included flood control made possible by the newly built dams, prevention of soil erosion by the planting of millions of trees, establishment of public parks, schools, libraries, and hospitals, and improvement in river and road transportation.

The Election of 1936

In 1936, Roosevelt, running for reelection, was pitted against Governor Alfred M. Landon of Kansas. In a campaign speech at Madison Square Garden in New York City, Roosevelt declared:

> I should like to have it said of my first administration that in it the forces of selfishness and of lust for power met their match. I should like to have it said of my second administration that in it these forces met their master.

In 1936 Roosevelt's popular vote was 28 million against 17 million for Landon, but in the electoral college Roosevelt won every state but Maine and Vermont, giving him an electoral victory of 523 to 8. The New Dealers appropriately regarded this as a mandate, since they also won both houses of Congress and all but six governorships.

President Roosevelt and the Supreme Court

The "Court Packing" Proposal

Shortly after his reelection, Roosevelt asked Congress to give him authority to appoint one new Justice (not to exceed six) for every Supreme Court Justice who had reached the age of 70 and failed to retire. Since six of the nine Justices on the Court had reached the age of 70, this meant that, if Congress approved, Roosevelt could increase the Court to a membership of fifteen.

This proposal was described by its critics as a **"court packing"** scheme and was seen as a threat to the separation of powers.

Changes in the Court

After Roosevelt's attempt to reform the Court, the Court began to take a more liberal approach, giving rise to a popular saying: "a switch in time saves nine." Moreover, changes in the Court's membership came quickly. Within one term in office President Roosevelt had appointed a majority of the Court's members.

The Election of 1940

The election campaign of 1940 was waged during the dark days when Hitler's forces overran Western Europe and were poised to launch an all-out attack on Britain. The Republicans nominated the charismatic liberal corporation lawyer, **Wendell L. Willkie**, while the Democrats chose Franklin D. Roosevelt to run for a third term.

Third-Term Issue

If Roosevelt won the election, as seemed likely, it would upset the two-term tradition that George Washington had started. No President elected to two consecutive terms had ever sought a third. Despite public misgivings about violation of this tradition, Roosevelt won easily with 449 electoral votes to 82 for the Republicans. Opponents of aid to Britain had no real choice in 1940, for both major party candidates rejected isolationism in favor of opposition to the Nazi challenge. Roosevelt was to win a fourth term in 1944.

The Twenty-second Amendment

This reversal of the two-term tradition led to a reaction after the death of FDR. In 1951, the Twenty-second Amendment was added to the Constitution. It specifies: "No person shall be elected to the office of President more than twice . . . ."

Exercise Set 4.6

1. Which of the following New Deal acts or agencies was declared unconstitutional by the Supreme Court in *Schechter Poultry Corp.* v. *United States?*
   A. the AAA
   B. the NRA
   C. the TVA
   D. the WPA

2. Many Americans had misgivings about reelecting Roosevelt to a third term because
   A. it was a violation of precedent
   B. it was time to give someone else a chance since the problem of the Depression remained unsolved
   C. Roosevelt was an interventionist while his opponent was an isolationist
   D. Roosevelt was tampering with the Supreme Court

3. An argument advanced against the TVA by private power companies was that
   A. its lower rates would be subsidized by the taxpayers
   B. it would fail to provide cheap electric power for the people of the Tennessee Valley
   C. its activities would extend over too large an area
   D. it would eliminate jobs for residents of the area

4. Roosevelt's attempt to increase the number of Justices on the Supreme Court
   A. was acclaimed by most Americans as a brilliant solution to a Constitutional problem
   B. received solid support from the majority of both houses of Congress
   C. was narrowly defeated in the Senate Judiciary Committee
   D. was ridiculed in a popular book of the time entitled "Nine Old Men"

5. The election of 1936
   A. reflected grudging national support for the New Deal
   B. saw much debate over the Supreme Court issue
   C. may not be described as a landslide victory for the New Deal
   D. overwhelmingly endorsed the New Deal

6. FDR's attempt to reform the Supreme Court
   A. secured more decisions favorable to the New Deal
   B. was completely unsuccessful
   C. was the first attempt to change the number of members of the Supreme Court
   D. was endorsed by nearly all Democrats

THE HUMAN FACTOR

Franklin D. Roosevelt as Communicator

Franklin Delano Roosevelt had an extraordinary gift for communicating with the American people. From the very beginning of his first administration, he reached out to them in what he called "fireside chats." Within a week after his inauguration, as the banks reopened under the Emergency Banking Relief Act, he addressed his first nationwide radio audience of 35 million listeners, which included three out of four American families, and told them that it was now safer to keep their money in one of the reopened banks than "under the mattress." This was the first of what were to be some thirty "fireside chats," all calculated to communicate his message directly to the people.

Eleanor Roosevelt, the Eyes and Ears of the President

Eleanor Roosevelt, wife of Franklin D. Roosevelt, played a major, if unofficial, role in his presidential administration, as she had done when he was Governor of New York. By keeping informed of public sentiment on vital issues, Eleanor Roosevelt served as the keen and reliable eyes and ears of the President. From her extensive travels, she brought him extremely useful firsthand information. A humanitarian, she was deeply concerned with the plight of the underdog, victims of the Dust Bowl (the "Okies"), and especially African Americans, who were denied opportunities open to other Americans. On behalf of the underprivileged, Eleanor Roosevelt did not hesitate to speak out to the President.

Ravages of the Dust Bowl

When the plow destroyed the protective grasses of the semiarid plains east of the Rockies, the defenseless soil was ready for catastrophe. It came in the hot drought-ridden spring and summer of 1934. A great dust storm ravaged parts of Oklahoma, Arkansas, Colorado, Kansas, New Mexico, and Texas. Howling winds drove the dust a thousand miles east, covering homes and farms, blackening the sky, disrupting railroad schedules, and spreading despair. In *The Grapes of Wrath* (1939), novelist **John Steinbeck** tells the tragic story of the Joads, a family driven from its Oklahoma farm by the ravages of the Dust Bowl. A quarter of a million farmers, who saw their cattle suffocate, their crops destroyed, and their few possessions menaced by relentless mountains of dust, left their farms and drove west in quest of a better life.

Women During the New Deal Era

The appointment in 1933 of **Frances Perkins** as Secretary of Labor, the first woman to serve as a member of the Cabinet, heralded a new era in the status of women. Perkins remained in the Cabinet during the twelve years of Roosevelt's presidency and then served for seven years under President **Truman** as a member of the **Civil Service Commission**. Outstanding women authors of the period included Ellen Glasgow, literary historian of the South, who won the Pulitzer Prize in 1941 for *In This Our Life,* and **Willa Cather**, whose novels depicted the struggles of pioneer women in frontier Nebraska.

Minorities and the New Deal

African Americans

African Americans found new hope in the relief, recovery, and reform measures of the New Deal. Traditionally Lincoln Republicans—in opposition to the dominant whites who exercised control through the southern Democratic party—African Americans began switching to the Democratic party in 1934, and contributed significantly to the New Deal landslide of 1936, especially in the cities of the North.

Native Americans

The Native American minority, too, saw new hope as the **Indian Reorganization Act** of 1934 reversed the antitribal policy of the **Dawes Act** of 1887 and recognized tribal life as the normal and viable Native American mode.

Culture of the Depression

Like wars and other catastrophes, the Great Depression brought forth sympathetic responses in the arts. John Steinbeck's *The Grapes of Wrath* is the quintessential literary portrayal of this disaster, particularly as it affected the poor farmers of the Dust Bowl. **Langston Hughes** depicted the humiliation of African Americans in his semiautobiographical novel, *Not Without Laughter* (1930) and in his short story, *The Way of White Folks* (1934).

Escaping Reality—Movies and Comics

Hollywood and comic books provided an escape from the harsh reality of the Depression. A special Academy Award went to **Walt Disney** in 1932 for **Mickey Mouse**; to MGM in 1935 for *Mutiny on the Bounty*; and to Selznick International in 1939 for the box-office favorite *Gone With The*

Wind. Comic strips provided additional escape and became a regular feature of most newspapers. "Blondie" first appeared in 1930, "Dick Tracy" in 1931, "Li'l Abner" in 1934, and "Superman" in 1938. "Little Orphan Annie" dated back to 1924 and "Peanuts" had its debut in 1950.

The WPA and the Arts

The New Deal WPA provided funds for unemployed writers, actors, artists, and musicians. A series of WPA books on each of the states created an invaluable record of the period. Plays by Clifford Odets and music dramas like *Pins and Needles* entertained audiences that could not otherwise see a theater production, while it gave writers, actors, and directors a chance to practice their professions. In one WPA project, artists painted murals depicting historic scenes on the walls of public buildings, schools, libraries, and railroad centers.

Music

Music of the period evolved from **ragtime** developed by black orchestras in the South before World War I. A new form called **jazz** came into its own in the 1920s. Great performers and band leaders emerged, including the legendary cornetist **Bix Biederbeck** who died in 1931 at the age of 28, **Louis "Satchmo" Armstrong**, **Duke Ellington**, and the pianist and composer **"Fats" Waller**. **Swing** bands led by Paul Whiteman, Glen Gray, Tommy Dorsey, Glenn Miller, Benny Goodman, and Vincent Lopez played as couples danced to their music on large dance floors, and millions listened on the radio and bought their records. Musicals, too, came into their own with long-run performances of *Oklahoma, Show Boat, Porgy and Bess,* and the music of **Irving Berlin**, **Richard Rodgers**, **George Gershwin**, **Cole Porter**, and **Jerome Kern**.

Opposition to the New Deal

As might be expected, there were those who felt the New Deal had gone too far and others who believed it had not gone far enough to correct the system that had led to the Great Depression.

On the Left

At the far left were the **Communists**, who nominated Earl Browder for President in 1936. He garnered 80,000 votes out of a total of some 46 million cast in the election. The **Socialist party**, with Norman Thomas again the candidate, polled 187,000.

• *Communist and Socialist Doctrines Differ.* The Communists, influenced by the doctrines of **Karl Marx** and the Russian Bolshevik **Lenin**, believed that justice for the working class (proletariat) would come only through the violent overthrow of capitalism. The Socialists, led by **Eugene V. Debs** and Norman Thomas, believed that democratic methods supported by education and legal agitation would bring about the necessary radical changes in the economic system.

On the Right

Those who attacked the New Deal from the right presented a united front by nominating the former Republican Congressman William Lemke of North Dakota for President. The Union party was endorsed by most of the major rightist organizations. Lemke received 891,858 votes, about 2 percent of the total cast.

• *Fascists Inspired by Mussolini and Hitler.* At the far right of the political spectrum were the **Fascists**, who drew their inspiration from the systems imposed by force in Italy under Mussolini, in Germany under Hitler, and in Spain under Franco. In the United States, these found their counterparts in the pro-Nazi German-American **Bund** and Italian Fascist "Black Shirts."

Homegrown Demagogues

"Homegrown" demagogues gained a considerable number of converts by denouncing the New Deal and offering their own solutions.

• *Huey P. Long.* A serious challenge was mounted by Senator Huey P. ("Kingfish") Long of Louisiana, who launched a "Share Our Wealth" program with the promise to make "every man a king" and to distribute $5,000 to every family. Long, a skillful rabble-rouser, was planning to take his campaign to New York in a huge parade when he was assassinated in the Louisiana State capitol in 1935.

• *Father Charles F. Coughlin.* Father Coughlin was from Michigan and gained an army of followers through his weekly radio broadcast, which reached 40 million listeners. His call for "social justice" was accompanied by a steady stream of pro-Fascist, anti-Semitic messages that finally aroused his superiors in the church who in 1942 ordered him to discontinue his broadcasts.

Assessment of the New Deal

A brief assessment of the New Deal program suggests that it introduced at least one major new element in American life, the concept that the national government should assume responsibility for the welfare of the people. As Roosevelt expressed it: ". . . the government has the definite duty to use all its power and resources to meet new social problems with new social controls . . ." Roosevelt maintained that "it was this administration which saved the system of private profit and free enterprise after it had been dragged to the brink of ruin." The New Deal had saved the banking system, promoted the conservation of natural resources, and given new hope to the common people. Yet, on the eve of World War II, millions were still unemployed. It was World War II that finally revitalized the industrial machine and the national economy.

Exercise Set 4.7

1. Which of the following was *not* a factor in bringing about the landslide victory of the Democratic party in the 1936 election?
   A. the black vote
   B. "fireside chats"
   C. solution of the unemployment problem
   D. press conferences

2. Prominent women of the (Franklin) Roosevelt era include all of the following EXCEPT
   A. Susan B. Anthony
   B. Ellen Glasgow
   C. Frances Perkins
   D. Eleanor Roosevelt

3. Which of the following was a cause of the others?
   A. departure of thousands of poor farmers from Oklahoma and Arkansas
   B. publication of the novel *The Grapes of Wrath*
   C. the great dust storm of 1934
   D. creation of a "dust bowl" in parts of Texas, New Mexico, and Kansas

4. The plight of black Americans during the Depression is depicted in
   A. the novels of Willa Cather
   B. the works of Langston Hughes
   C. the photography of Walker Evans
   D. the movie *Gone With The Wind*

CHAPTER REVIEW QUESTIONS

1. The major difference between Herbert Hoover and Franklin Roosevelt was
   A. their political philosophy
   B. their wealth
   C. the difficulty of the problems they faced
   D. the cooperation each received from his own party

2. The election of 1940
   A. showed fundamental foreign policy differences between the two major parties
   B. was unique in that no minor parties participated
   C. caused the later adoption of the Twenty-second Amendment
   D. helped perpetuate the two-term tradition

3. Which is a valid conclusion based upon a study of the New Deal?
   A. labor, but not business, was affected
   B. it resulted in a government budget surplus
   C. it forced individuals to accept responsibility for their own economic welfare
   D. it continued to influence United States economic policy for many years

4. Although all segments of American society were affected by the Great Depression, those who suffered most severely were
   A. operators of small business
   B. the lower middle class
   C. senior citizens
   D. women and children

5. The Twenty-second Amendment to the United States Constitution
   A. eliminated the unproductive "lame duck" Congress
   B. changed the date of the President's inauguration
   C. limited Presidents to two terms
   D. specified that Congress would meet early in January of each year

6. Private business opposed the Tennessee Valley Authority (TVA) because
   A. it was thought the lakes would soon be filled with silt
   B. the project did not provide satisfactory protection against floods
   C. electricity was produced and distributed by a government agency
   D. it called for regimentation of the farmers of the district

7. FDR's attempt to reform the Supreme Court
   A. secured more decisions favorable to New Deal laws
   B. was completely unsuccessful
   C. was the first attempt to change the number of members of the Court
   D. was endorsed by nearly all Democrats

8. As President, Franklin D. Roosevelt did all of the following EXCEPT
   A. continue several of the policies he had put into practice as Governor of New York
   B. cease relying on his wife Eleanor as his eyes and ears
   C. demonstrate the same capacity for vote-getting as he had in New York
   D. bring to Washington a number of key political and personal associates from New York

ESSAYS

1. In attempting to measure how successful a person has been as President of the United States, the following qualities have been identified as important:

> Communication skills
> Ability to interpret the mood of the country
> Ability to project a positive public image
> Willingness to initiate bold programs
> Firmness, yet willingness to compromise

   a. Select *two* qualities from the list which you think are the most important qualities necessary for success as a President. For *each* one selected, show how this quality contributed to the success of a specific United States President during his presidency. [You may use the same or a different President for each quality discussed.]
   b. Explain how *one* of the qualities listed above was a significant factor in the 1940 presidential campaign. Include in your response references to a specific candidate.

2. Cultural expression has at times been used as a form of social criticism. At other times, cultural expression has been used to promote or glorify the values of a society. From the list below, select three forms of cultural expression. For *each* one chosen, identify a specific example of that form of cultural expression and show how that example was used either to criticize or to support the values of American society in the period between World War I and World War II.

> **Forms of Cultural Expression**
> Movies
> Literature
> Theater
> Music
> Painting or Sculpture

3. Periods of stress in American history have witnessed the emergence of antidemocratic forces either reacting to what they perceive as a reversal of traditional American values, or attempting to exploit stressful conditions in order to achieve their antidemocratic goals. Two such periods were the period immediately following World War I and the period of the Great Depression.

   For *each* period describe the conditions that caused stress. Explain how one antidemocratic group reacted to or attempted to exploit the stressful situation. Discuss the outcome of the antidemocratic activities.

THEMATIC ESSAY

Directions: Write a well-organized essay that includes an introduction, several paragraphs addressing the task below, and a conclusion.

Theme: Presidential Powers

> During times of crisis throughout our history, the executive branch has assumed, and many times been allowed, greater powers.

Task:

> From your study of the early decades of the 20th century, identify *two* presidential administrations that experienced crisis situations and have exercised extraordinary powers.
>
> For each administration:
>
> - Identify the crisis (war, economic, civil rights, etc.).
> - Describe the administration's response to the crisis.
> - Discuss how the powers of the presidency were expanded during the time of crisis.

You may use any presidential administration from your study of United States history. Some suggestions you may wish to consider are Thomas Jefferson (1801–1809), Abraham Lincoln (1861–1865), Franklin D. Roosevelt (1933–1945), or Lyndon Johnson (1963–1969).

You are *not* limited to these suggestions.

DOCUMENT-BASED QUESTION ESSAY

The following questions (Part A and Part B) are based on the accompanying documents (1–6). Some of these documents have been edited for the purpose of this exercise. The question is designed to test your ability to work with historical documents and to demonstrate your knowledge of the subject matter being presented. As you analyze the documents, take into account both the source of the document and the author's point of view.

Historical Context: The Great Depression of the 1930s resulted in dramatic adjustments to the American economic and political system. Some have claimed that the actions of President Franklin Delano Roosevelt and the programs of the New Deal were socialistic threats to capitalism, while others have held that the New Deal was designed to save capitalism.

Task: Using information from the documents and your knowledge of United States history, answer the questions that follow each document in Part A. Your answers to the questions will help you write the Part B essay, in which you will be asked:

Franklin Roosevelt's New Deal has been assessed in different ways. Some say it encouraged socialistic change to our form of government, while others say it helped maintain the capitalist system. Using the documents and your knowledge of United States history, answer the following question: Was the New Deal designed to preserve capitalism?

Part A
Short Answer

The documents below relate to the problems of the Great Depression and the tactics utilized by President Roosevelt and the New Deal. Examine each document carefully and then answer the questions that follow.

DOCUMENT 1

Long ago we stated the reason for labor organizations. We said that they were organized out of the necessities of the situation; that a single employee was helpless in dealing with an employer; that he was dependent ordinarily on his daily wage for the maintenance of himself and family; that, if the employer refused to pay him the wages that he thought fair, he was nevertheless unable to leave the employ and resist arbitrary and unfair treatment; that union was essential to give laborers opportunity to deal on an equality with their employer.

—National Labor Relations Board v. *Jones and Laughlin Steel Corp.* (1937)

1. The *NLRB* v. *Jones and Laughlin Steel Corp.* case upheld the Wagner Act of 1935, which recognized civil liberties of laborers. Why were many businesses against the Wagner Act and the holding of the Supreme Court?

_____

_____

_____

_____

DOCUMENT 2

UNITED STATES GOVERNMENT FINANCES, 1929–1941 (in billions of dollars)			
Fiscal Year	Expenditures	Surplus or Deficit (–)	Total Public Debt
1929	$3.127	$0.734	$16.9
1930	3.320	0.738	16.2
1931	3.577	–0.462	16.8
1932	4.659	–2.735	19.5
1933	4.598	–2.602	22.5
1934	6.645	–3.630	27.1
1935	6.497	–2.791	28.7
1936	8.422	–4.425	33.8
1937	7.733	–2.777	36.4
1938	6.765	–1.177	37.2
1939	8.841	–3.862	40.4
1940	9.589	–2.710	43.0
1941	13.980	–4.778	44.0

—U. S. Bureau of the Census

2. What is the argument against the increased spending (and therefore larger deficit) of the federal government between 1929 and 1941?

_____

_____

_____

_____

3. What is the argument for the increased spending (and therefore larger deficit) of the federal government between 1929 and 1941?

_____

_____

_____

_____

DOCUMENT 3

....Our greatest primary task is to put people to work. This is no unsolvable problem if we face it wisely and courageously. It can be accomplished in part by direct recruiting by the government itself, treating the problem as we would treat the emergency of war, but at the same time, through this employment, accomplishing greatly needed projects to stimulate and reorganize the use of our natural resources.

—Franklin D. Roosevelt, Inaugural Address, March 4, 1933

4. What is the government's role that President Roosevelt proposed in 1933 to help solve the problem of unemployment?

_____

_____

_____

_____

DOCUMENT 4

Out of the strains and stresses of these years we have come to see that the true conservative is the man who has a real concern for injustices and takes thought against the day of reckoning. The true conservative seeks to protect the system of private property and free enterprise by correcting such injustices and inequalities as arise from it. The most serious threat to our institutions comes from those who refuse to face the need for change.....

Wise and prudent men—intelligent conservatives—have long known that in a changing world worthy institutions can be conserved only by adjusting them to the changing time.

—President Franklin D. Roosevelt, Speech, Syracuse, New York, September 29, 1936

5. According to President Roosevelt in his Syracuse speech, what is the ultimate goal of the changes he and his administration have proposed?

_____

_____

_____

_____

6. Would you say that President Roosevelt's statements are evolutionary or revolutionary? Why?

_____

_____

_____

_____

DOCUMENT 5

No business whose existence depends on paying less than living wages to its workers has any right to continue in this country.

—President Franklin D. Roosevelt, Speech, 1933

7. What legislation resulted from the position put forth by President Roosevelt in the 1933 speech?

_____

_____

_____

_____

DOCUMENT 6

The following excerpts are from the 1935 Social Security Act. The Act brought the assumption of national responsibility for general social security and constituted a notable chapter in the history of federal centralization in the United States.

Sec. 1: ...for the purpose of enabling each state to furnish financial assistance...to aged, needy individuals.

Sec. 301:...for the purpose of assisting the states in the administration of their unemployment compensation.

Sec. 401:....for the purpose of enabling each state to furnish financial assistance to needy dependent children.

Sec. 801:....In addition to other taxes, there shall be levied, collected, and paid upon the income of every individual a (social security) tax....

—Social Security Act, August 14, 1935

8. How does the Social Security Act of 1935 change the federal government's role in caring for the welfare of the American people?

_____

_____

_____

_____

9. In your opinion, does this act encourage socialism or preserve capitalism?

_____

_____

_____

_____

Part B
Essay

Your essay should be well organized with an introductory paragraph that states your position on the question. Develop your position in the next paragraphs and then write a conclusion. In your essay, include specific historical details and refer to the specific documents you analyzed in Part A. You may include additional information from your knowledge of social studies.

Historical Context: The Great Depression of the 1930s resulted in dramatic adjustments to the American economic and political system. Some have claimed that the actions of President Franklin Delano Roosevelt and the programs of the New Deal were socialistic threats to capitalism, while others have held that the New Deal was designed to save capitalism.

Task:

Franklin Roosevelt's New Deal has been assessed in different ways. Some say it encouraged socialistic change to our form of government, while others say it helped maintain the capitalist system. Using the documents above, and your knowledge of United States history, answer the following question: Was the New Deal designed to preserve capitalism?

Guidelines:

In your essay, be sure to
- Develop all aspects of the task
- Incorporate information from at least *five* documents
- Incorporate relevant outside information
- Support the theme with many relevant facts, examples, and details
- Use a logical and clear plan of organization, including an introduction and a conclusion that are beyond a restatement of the theme

The United States in an Age of Global Crisis: Responsibility and Cooperation

KEY IDEAS Unit Five explores the American policy of isolation in the 1920s and 1930s and American involvement in World War II. It describes the effects of the war on the United States and America's role in the postwar world, with emphasis on the Cold War.

UNIT CONNECTIONS: By the end of the unit you should understand the following points.

- Isolationism in the 1930s
- United States involvement in World War II prior to congressional declaration in 1941
- The United States home front during World War II
- The role of the United States in World War II compared to World War I
- Wartime moral issues including rights of Japanese Americans, integration of African Americans, the Nazi Holocaust, and nuclear warfare
- War criminals and "crimes against humanity"
- Adjusting to a peacetime economy
- International involvement and the United Nations
- "McCarthyism," the Red Scare, and civil liberties
- The Cold War at home and abroad

CHAPTER 1

PEACE IN PERIL (1933–1950)

ISOLATION AND NEUTRALITY

Neutrality During the 18th and 19th Centuries

'Tis our true policy to steer clear of permanent alliances, with any portion of the foreign world.

George Washington's Farewell Address,
September 17, 1796

Washington's admonition against permanent alliances was still in the minds of America's leaders during the **Napoleonic Wars** of the early 19th century. There was pressure both on **Adams'** administration (1797–1801) and on that of his successor, **Jefferson** (1801–1809), to go to war against France as the Federalists urged, or against England as the Republicans demanded. But the sentiment for neutrality prevailed despite provocation by both warring nations. An undeclared naval war with France actually took place during two years of Adams' administration (1798–1800). Ultimately, the policy of noninvolvement failed and the United States became involved in the Napoleonic Wars in 1812. The **War of 1812** against Britain was fought to protect "neutral rights" on the high seas.

In the historic **Monroe Doctrine** (1823), President Monroe stated the policy of nonintervention in these words: ". . . our policy in regard to Europe . . . is not to interfere in the internal concerns of any of its powers." These sentiments prevailed and the United States avoided European conflicts for most of the rest of the 19th century, despite the efforts of the hawks during **Polk's** administration, who cried "Fifty-four forty or fight," calling for war with England unless our territory was extended to Russian Alaska (54° 40′ north latitude).

Efforts to Remain Neutral in World War I

When Europe was engaged in World War I, Wilson, echoing the sentiments of the American people, declared, "The United States must be neutral in fact as well as in name . . . We must be impartial in thought as well as in action." This was in 1914, but three years later he called for war, and American troops were sent to Europe. The postwar reaction was dramatic. Popular disillusionment following World War I contributed to the strong sentiment for isolationism that caused the U.S. Senate to reject membership in the League of Nations. It was this sentiment, still strong in the 1930s, that confronted the Roosevelt administration while Hitler moved step by step toward realization of the Nazi boast, "Today we rule Germany; tomorrow the world."

Of course, total isolationism by a great world power is impossible. In the 20th century the United States had territorial possessions in the Pacific Ocean, the Caribbean, and Central America. Moreover, American business interests were engaged in commerce and industry throughout the world, and American capital was a major source of support for worldwide industrial development. It was inevitable that defense of these commitments would make complete isolationism a practical impossibility.

The World Disarmament Conference

When the World Disarmament Conference convened in Geneva, Switzerland, in February 1932, President Hoover, whose Quaker background predisposed him to peace efforts, sent an American delegation. It was understood, however, that prevailing isolationist sentiment in the United States would make any American commitment for participation in international action unlikely. The Conference, sponsored by the League of Nations and attended by representatives of the Soviet Union as well as the United States, adjourned in March 1933 and reconvened in October. It adjourned again when Germany, now led by Hitler, withdrew from the Conference and later, from the League of Nations. Efforts at international disarmament had failed.

Isolationism and the Nye Committee Hearings

In 1934, the U.S. Senate created a special committee to prepare legislation on government control of the munitions industry. The committee, headed by a confirmed isolationist, Senator **Gerald P. Nye** of North Dakota, held widely publicized hearings for the next three years. The hearings disclosed that munitions manufacturers had made huge profits from World War I. They also charged that arms manufacturers had successfully exerted pressure for U.S. involvement in the war. Many who had supported America's participation in World War I now regarded it as a grave error. A spirit of pacifism, dominating college campuses, preached from pulpits, and bolstered on stage and in the cinema, reflected the prevailing national sentiment. The call for preparedness was answered with the phrase "never again."

United States Neutrality Legislation

It was in this atmosphere of isolationism that a series of neutrality laws were passed by Congress in the 1930s. In the summer of 1935, when Mussolini's troops were poised for the invasions of Ethiopia, Congress passed the **Neutrality Act of 1935**. The act required the President to place an **embargo** on arms to nations engaged in war and prohibited travel of U.S. citizens on belligerent vessels. It was designed to prevent any American armaments manufacturer, banker, or merchant from profiting from a foreign war or helping to embroil us in one. This meant that the United States had to remain neutral while Italy invaded and subjugated Ethiopia. Japan and Germany, of course, favored this American policy. Both had already embarked on programs leading to military conquest and expansion. In 1931 the Japanese invaded and occupied **Manchuria**, a large province of China, bordering on Korea, which Japan already controlled. The United States refused to recognize this conquest under the newly declared **Stimson Doctrine**. In 1936 Japan and Germany signed a military agreement called the Anti-Comintern Treaty. In the same year Germany and Italy formed an alliance called the **Rome-Berlin Axis**. With the addition of Japan in 1940, it became known as the **Rome-Berlin-Tokyo Axis**.

Civil War in Spain (1936–1939)

Events moved swiftly on the road to World War II. A "popular front" coalition of Liberals, Socialists, and Communists in Spain ousted the Conservative government in the 1936 national election. Five months later (July 1936) **Generalissimo Francisco Franco** led an uprising to overthrow the **Republican** government of Spain and replace it with a **Fascist** government. The **Spanish Civil War** that followed was a prelude to World War II. Germany and Italy openly aided Franco while England and France, following policies of nonintervention, looked on helplessly, and Russia, far from the scene, gave what help it could to the Spanish Republican government. The United States observed its own neutrality laws. Hitler's air force gained experience, valuable in the coming world war, by bombing Spanish cities and strafing their inhabitants. One such raid on Guernica, April 26, 1937, is depicted in a famous painting by the Spanish artist, Pablo Picasso. The war ended in March 1939 with the defeat of the Loyalists (those loyal to the Republic) and the establishment of a Fascist government under Franco.

American Isolationism and Axis Aggression

Meanwhile, in March 1936, Hitler's troops marched into the Rhineland in violation of the Treaty of Versailles. In 1937, Japan invaded China. In a speech in Chicago, President Roosevelt called on the democracies to "quarantine the aggressors," but his hands were tied by neutrality legislation and by the prevailing national sentiment of isolationism or, at least, nonintervention.

Neutrality Legislation of 1936 and 1937

The Neutrality Act of 1935 was due to expire at the end of February 1936. Congress replaced it with the Neutrality Act of 1936, which extended the legislation for another year and added a provision prohibiting loans by Americans to nations engaged in war. A third neutrality law, with no time limit, was passed by Congress in 1937. The legislation banned shipment of munitions to either side in the Spanish Civil War and was particularly disadvantageous to the Republicans, since Franco was receiving supplies from Italy and Germany. In his "quarantine" speech, Roosevelt urged that the United States join the other powers to "quarantine," or check, the aggressor nations. In an opinion poll taken shortly after the speech, only 31 percent of the public favored presidential action to check aggression, whereas the vast majority supported Congressional neutrality legislation.

1. In the years prior to 1939, an isolationist would be in most disagreement with which of the following?
   A. the speech of President Roosevelt urging a "quarantine" of the aggressors
   B. the hearings held in the U.S. Senate committee presided over by Senator Gerald P. Nye
   C. a tradition first expressed by President Washington in his Farewell Address
   D. the Neutrality Acts of 1935 and 1936

2. Neutrality legislation of the 1930s was designed to
   A. prevent aggression by the Rome-Berlin-Tokyo Axis
   B. give the United States time to prepare for the coming war
   C. protect American lives and property in Europe and Asia
   D. keep the United States out of war by avoiding the mistakes of pre-World War I

3. A major foreign relations problem of the Roosevelt administration after 1935 was to
   A. negotiate a military alliance with Great Britain and the USSR
   B. persuade the American people of the need to abandon the policy of isolationism
   C. persuade the Axis powers to rejoin the League of Nations
   D. persuade the Congress to disband the Nye Committee investigating corrupt practices in the munitions industry

4. Which of the following was the most important reason for the rise of dictatorships in Europe in the two decades following World War I?
   A. general illiteracy of the working class
   B. stresses caused by the constant threat of renewed warfare
   C. destruction of homes and factories during World War I
   D. widespread economic disorder

FAILURE OF PEACE: TRIUMPH OF AGGRESSION

The Road to World War II (1933–1939)

In retrospect, it is clear that the aggressions of the Axis powers during the 1930s culminated in a world war because the democracies were not willing to go to war to protect the freedom of the nations that the Axis powers invaded. Hitler began rearming Germany in violation of the Treaty of Versailles in 1933 and occupied the Rhineland in 1936. Despite promises to make each demand his last, he annexed **Austria** in 1938, dismembered **Czechoslovakia** in 1938, and demanded the **Polish Corridor** in 1939. Another Axis member, Japan, invaded **Manchuria** in 1931 and the rest of China in 1937. The third Axis member, Italy, invaded **Ethiopia** in 1935 and **Albania** in 1939. With the help of Germany and Italy, the democratic government of **Spain** was overthrown (1936–1939) and replaced with a dictatorship friendly to the Axis. To protect his eastern flank Hitler made a "nonaggression" pact with Stalin on August 23, 1939. On September 1, 1939, Hitler's armies invaded Poland. Two days later France and England declared war on Germany.

The Policy of Appeasement—the Munich Conference (1938)

The policy of appeasement, exemplified in the **Munich Conference** of September 1938, had disastrous consequences. This policy, adopted by British Prime Minister **Neville Chamberlain**, relied on Hitlers Germany's becoming a friendly member of the family of nations once Hitler's demands were met. When Hitler insisted that the Sudetenland of Czechoslovakia be turned over to Germany, there was grave concern among opponents of Fascism. Czechoslovakia was a strong democratic country. The Sudetenland was heavily fortified and the Czechs were prepared to resist. However, Chamberlain decided to appease Hitler and he called a conference of four powers—Britain, France, Italy, and Germany—to meet in Munich, Germany. In Munich it was quickly decided to yield to Hitler's demands to occupy the Sudetenland. Hitler promised in return to make no more territorial demands. Chamberlain flew back to England and was greeted with wild acclaim when he said he brought "peace in our time." Six months after the Munich conference Hitler sent his troops to occupy all of Czechoslovakia. **Winston Churchill**, a leading member of Parliament who was opposed to appeasement, called the Munich agreement an unmitigated disaster. Less than a year after the Munich Conference, Britain was at war with Germany.

Changing Public Opinion in the United States

In January 1939 President Roosevelt tried to persuade Congress to revise the neutrality legislation. He saw a war coming between Germany and the democracies of Western Europe—France and Britain. Under the then existing law the United States could not sell war supplies to the democracies. Congress, reflecting public sentiment, refused to change the law. However, after the war started in Europe, public opinion began to shift. On September 21, 1939, three weeks after the beginning of World War II, President Roosevelt addressed a joint session of Congress and urged a change in the neutrality law. He said, ". . . by the repeal of the embargo the United States will more probably remain at peace than if the law remains as it stands today." Congress responded by passing the **Neutrality Act of 1939**, which contained a "cash and carry" provision. Belligerents (that is, Britain or France) could purchase any supplies, including armaments, provided they paid cash and carried the supplies from the United States in their own ships. This would keep American ships out of the war zone and would prevent American banks from making loans that American troops might later have to redeem.

Agreement on Western Hemisphere Defense

One policy on which Americans were in agreement was the defense of the Western Hemisphere against foreign aggression. An Inter-American Conference at which the United States was a participant issued the **Declaration of Panama** (October 3, 1939) a month after the outbreak of war. It designated sea safety zones in the Western Hemisphere south of Canada and warned belligerent powers against naval action within these zones. On July 30, 1940, the 21 republics of the **Pan-American Union**, meeting in Havana, signed the **Act of Havana**. It provided that the American republics, individually or collectively, might take over any European possession in the Western Hemisphere endangered by aggression. The purpose of this act was to ensure against the occupation or transfer of any of these possessions to Germany. The achievement of unity in Latin America for support of U.S. foreign policy was attributable in part to the "**good neighbor policy**" that President Roosevelt had proclaimed in his first inaugural address and to which he adhered throughout his presidency.

Victories of the German Armies in Western Europe

The war in Europe took an ominous turn in the spring of 1940 as Germany quickly occupied neutral Norway and Denmark. German troops also overran Holland, Belgium, and Luxembourg. Operating from Belgium, the German army was able to bypass the powerful line of fortifications (**Maginot Line**) on which France relied for its security. German troops poured into France and defeated the British and French defenders. Britain was able to evacuate troops trapped in France at **Dunkirk** on the English Channel by a sea flotilla of civilian ships. Italy invaded southern France, prompting Roosevelt's statement in an address that day at the University of Virginia, "On this tenth day of June 1940 the hand that held the dagger has stuck it in the back of its neighbor."

Moving Toward War

Aid to Britain

Winston Churchill replaced Chamberlain as Prime Minister of Britain after the fall of France. He promised his people only "blood, toil, tears, and sweat." In an appeal to America he said, "Give us the tools and we will finish the job." As Commander-in-Chief of the Armed Forces, Roosevelt took the unprecedented step of making a swap with Britain by transferring to Britain 50 World War I destroyers in exchange for 99-year leases on a number of British air and naval bases in the Atlantic and West Indies. This transfer took place in September 1940.

Peacetime Conscription

Public opinion changed enough in the same month to secure the passage of a peacetime conscription bill of men between the ages of 21 and 35.

Franklin D. Roosevelt's Four Freedoms Message

Shocked by events in Europe, the United States began to see its own defense in a new light. Only the armed forces of Britain stood between the United States and the Nazi military machine. In a fireside chat on December 29, 1940, the month after defeating **Wendell Willkie**, his Republican opponent, for reelection to a third term, Roosevelt told the American people, "We must be the great arsenal of democracy." Public opinion was ready to accept this undertaking.

In his January 6, 1941, State of the Union message to Congress, the President proclaimed the "Four Freedoms":

> In the future days, which we seek to make secure, we look forward to a world founded upon four essential freedoms. The first is freedom of expression—everywhere in the world. The second is freedom of every person to worship God in his own way—everywhere in the world. The third is freedom from want . . . everywhere in the world. The fourth is freedom from fear . . . anywhere in the world.

Lend-Lease (February 1941)

The difficulty of serving as the **arsenal of democracy** was twofold. Britain could no longer pay cash for armaments, and the idea of extending credit raised the specter of old World War I debts that were never repaid. The solution was found in the **Lend-Lease Bill,** passed by Congress on March 11, 1941. Four days earlier, in his State of the Union message, the President had proposed to help Britain and other countries opposing Axis aggression by supplying "in ever-increasing numbers, ships, planes, tanks, guns." The lend-lease measure permitted the President to "sell, transfer, exchange, lease, or otherwise dispose of war equipment to any nation for use in the interests of the United States." The measure met fierce opposition from the **America First Committee** and its friends in Congress.

War Measures

With the passage of the Lend-Lease Act, the adoption of a draft, a vast increase in military appropriations, the repeal of the Neutrality Law of 1939, the use of American naval vessels to convoy supplies bound for Britain as far as Iceland, and the arming of American merchantmen to combat Nazi submarines, the United States was obviously moving toward war late in 1941.

The Atlantic Charter

The moral dimension of the war became the focus of world attention when Roosevelt and Churchill held a conference aboard a warship off the coast of Newfoundland in August 1941 and issued the Atlantic Charter. It declared (1) no territorial gains are sought by the United States or Britain; (2) territorial adjustments must conform to the wishes of the people involved; (3) people have a right to choose their own government; (4) trade barriers should be lowered; (5) there must be disarmament; (6) there must be freedom from fear and want; (7) there must be freedom of the seas; (8) there must be an association of nations.

The Attack on Pearl Harbor, December 7, 1941

At the very time that the Atlantic Charter was being prepared, the Japanese war department was making plans to attack the United States. A surprise attack was to be made on **Pearl Harbor**, the U.S. naval base in Hawaii. On Sunday morning December 7, 1941, at 7:55 A.M., a wave of 189 Japanese war planes—dive-bombers and torpedo planes—roared over Pearl Harbor meeting little opposition from the completely surprised base. A second wave of attack planes followed. One hundred and seventy American planes were destroyed on the ground. Eight battleships—the pride of the Navy—were sunk or severely damaged. Nineteen fighting ships, including cruisers and destroyers, were incapacitated. Some 2,400 officers and enlisted men were killed, and 1,300 wounded. Japanese losses totaled 29 planes and 6 submarines. It was the greatest disaster in the history of the U.S. armed forces. The next day, December 8, 1941, in his war message to Congress, President Roosevelt said, "Yesterday, December 7, 1941—a date which will live in infamy—the United States of America was suddenly and deliberately attacked by naval and air forces of the Empire of Japan."

With but one dissenting vote, Congress declared war against Japan. On December 11, Italy and Germany declared war on the United States. On the same day, Congress passed a declaration of war on Germany and Italy.

Exercise Set 5.2

1. Which of the following would have been most troubling to the isolation-istic views of the America First Committee?
   A. passage of the Lend-Lease Act
   B. assignment of African Americans to integrated army units
   C. passage of the 1939 Neutrality Law
   D. the Stimson Doctrine

2. The policy of appeasement, pursued by the British government under Prime Minister Neville Chamberlain
   A. achieved the goal of securing "peace in our time"
   B. was disapproved by public opinion in the democracies
   C. encouraged the Axis powers to engage in aggression
   D. gained the support of Winston Churchill in England

3. The first peacetime draft in American history, passed into law September 6, 1940,
   A. showed that the United States was now ready to go to war
   B. had a significant effect on the national election held two months later
   C. was approved by both houses of Congress with little dissent
   D. was reluctantly accepted by the American people as an essential defense measure

4. Which of the following would have been most clearly associated with the ideology of the Monroe Doctrine?
   A. the "lend-lease" law
   B. the exchange of destroyers for lease of bases
   C. the Declaration of Panama
   D. the Atlantic Charter

5. Hitler concluded a nonaggression pact with Stalin in August 1939 in order to
   A. protect his eastern flank while he made war on the west
   B. establish the supremacy of dictatorship over democracy
   C. carry out the understanding reached with England and France at Munich
   D. challenge the Atlantic Charter issued by Roosevelt and Churchill

HOME FRONT: THE HUMAN DIMENSIONS OF THE WAR

> We must be the great arsenal of democracy.
> Franklin Roosevelt, December 29, 1940

The United States, "Arsenal of Democracy"

With America's entry into the war, industry geared up rapidly to meet the challenge and soon performed incredible feats of productivity. By 1942 America's production of war materiel was equal to that of the three Axis powers combined. Two years later it had doubled. Before the war was over the United States had built 300,000 aircraft, 71,000 ships, and over 80,000 tanks. At war's end the fighting power of the Navy had been increased over that of 1941 by 6 more battleships, 21 more aircraft carriers, and 70 more destroyers, and America's merchant marine had become the largest in the world. Despite a decrease in farm labor brought about by military enlistments, agricultural production doubled during the war years. The Depression program of crop limitation gave way to an all-out war effort that produced bumper crops of cotton, corn, hogs, and other foods to supply our own needs as well as those of our allies.

Women, a Major Factor in the War Effort

America's capacity to produce was substantially increased by the addition of three million women—double the number previously employed—to the labor force. Women served in every industry, often performing tasks previously considered the exclusive province of men. More than 250,000 women served in the armed forces wearing uniforms of the Army WACS, Navy WAVES, and Coast Guard SPARS.

Mobilizing the Armed Forces

In 1940, fifteen months before the attack on Pearl Harbor, Congress passed a **conscription** law—the first peacetime draft in American history—designed to secure 1.2 million troops and 800,000 reserves for the armed forces. When the war came, there were 1.6 million in the army. Recruitment and training proceeded rapidly after Pearl Harbor. All men between 18 and 45 were made eligible for military service, though many were rejected for failure to meet standards of physical fitness and intelligence. Over 15 million men and women served in the armed forces during World War II.

Financing the War

Raising Funds for the War

For four years (1941–45) the United States was not only fighting a global war on land, sea, and in the air, but was serving as the "arsenal of democracy," supplying its allies with planes, tanks, guns, ships, and all the implements of warfare. It is not surprising, therefore, that the war cost $250 million a day. The national debt, which stood at $49 billion in 1941 (most of it incurred during World War I and the Depression of the '30s) zoomed to $258 billion in 1945.

Maintaining this giant enterprise required both taxing and borrowing, since it was impossible to operate on a "pay as you go" basis as President Roosevelt would have preferred. In seven massive **war bond drives**, the government borrowed $100 billion from its citizens.

Preventing Inflation

With full employment and high government expenditures, wages nearly doubled. It became necessary to take steps to prevent runaway inflation. An Office of Price Administration (OPA), headed by Leon Henderson, was established in August 1941. In April 1942 the OPA imposed a general **price freeze** including a freeze on rents. The OPA also distributed **ration booklets**, which limited civilian consumption of gasoline, meat, tires, and other commodities made scarce by the war.

Hollywood Goes to War

The movie industry gave its talents wholeheartedly to the war effort. War films depicted the bravery and skill of America's fighting forces, the cruelty and ineptness of the Axis forces, the sometimes exotic nature of war zones, and ultimately the goals for which we fought. Among outstanding war films were *Casablanca,* which portrayed the Free French in Africa standing firm against the Nazis; *Sahara,* which depicted soldiers of the allied nations gaining control of scarce water resources; *Air Force,* which pictured the exploits of a U.S. bomber "Flying Fortress"; and *A Walk in the Sun*, which presented U.S. Army units establishing a beachhead in Italy. Films that dealt with the war in Asia included *Bataan, Behind the Rising Sun,* and *Dragon Seed.* **Bob Hope**, one of Hollywood's best-known comedians, and many others went overseas to entertain the troops.

The War's Impact on Minorities

Impact on African Americans

World War II had a special impact on African Americans and on Japanese Americans. During the war, half a million African Americans moved from the deep South to seek employment in the defense industries in Northern cities. However, opportunities continued to be denied them despite the great need for labor in defense plants. Membership in the NAACP leaped from 100,000 to half a million in the first three years of the war.

When the **United States Employment Service**, a federal agency, continued to fill defense contracts from employers stipulating "whites only," A. Philip Randolph, president of the Brotherhood of Sleeping Car Porters, proceeded to organize 50,000 people for a protest march on Washington. President Roosevelt met with Randolph at the White House on June 18, 1941. Randolph refused to call off the march until a satisfactory employment directive was issued by the President.

On June 25, 1941, President Roosevelt issued Executive Order 8802, declaring it the policy of the United States "that there shall be no discrimination in the employment of workers in defense industries or government because of race, creed, color, or national origin." The President appointed a **Fair Employment Practices Committee** to "receive and investigate complaints of discrimination" and to take "appropriate steps to redress grievances." Partly as a result of this order the number of black employees in the federal government increased from 40,000 to 300,000.

Impact on Japanese Americans

On the West Coast there was considerable apprehension about the part that Japanese Americans might play in the war. There was also latent prejudice and animosity toward Japanese Americans. On February 19, 1942, two months after the attack on Pearl Harbor, President Roosevelt issued Executive Order 9066, transferring authority for security to the Army. The Army commander of the West Coast, Lt. General John DeWitt, ordered the removal of 127,000 Japanese Americans, more than two thirds of whom were American citizens, from their homes in the western parts of Washington, Oregon, and California, and from southern Arizona. Without any charges or trials, they were forcibly "**relocated**" to dismal camps in the Western deserts and the Arkansas swamplands.

A suit to void the order as unconstitutional came to the U.S. Supreme Court and was decided on December 18, 1944. In *Korematsu* v. *United States* the Court was confronted with one of the enduring constitutional issues in American history—the balance between government security and the civil liberties of the individual. By a vote of 6 to 3, the Court upheld the government's action. Writing for the majority, **Justice Hugo Black**, whose overall record marks him as a staunch defender of the Bill of Rights, wrote, "He [Korematsu] was excluded because we are at war with the Japanese Empire, because the properly constituted military authorities feared an invasion of the West Coast, and felt constrained to take proper security measures . . ." In dissent, **Justice Owen J. Roberts** said the facts exhibited "a clear violation of constitutional rights," and **Justice Frank Murphy** said the exclusion went over "the brink of constitutional power" and fell "into the ugly abyss of racism."

On August 10, 1988, the United States finally admitted that the **internment** of Japanese Americans was a "mistake," agreed to issue apologies to each of the surviving internees, and to pay to each $20,000 tax-free over a ten-year period.

Segregation in the Armed Forces

When the draft went into effect in 1940, African American enlistments, proportional to their population, exceeded white enlistments by 60 percent. Yet African Americans were not accepted into the Air Corps or Marine Corps; the Army assigned them to segregated units as laborers and servants, and the Navy placed them as officers' cooks and stewards. African American combat troops served under white officers.

Pressure on the President from the African American community finally resulted in the organization of a few African American combat units, the commissioning of a limited number of African American officers in the Air Force, and the promotion of Colonel Benjamin O. Davis to Brigadier General. The numbers gradually increased during the war and more than 80 African American Air Force officers won the Distinguished Flying Cross. *The Crisis,* journal of the NAACP, contended that "a Jim Crow army cannot fight for a free world," but African Americans fought with distinction in every theater of the war. Complete integration in America's fighting forces did not come until the Korean War in the 1950s.

The Holocaust (1933–1945)

Early in the war, Hitler declared the Nazi policy concerning all the Jews under his control in Germany and the occupied countries. He called it "**the final solution**." It consisted of the systematic murder of the entire Jewish people. The extermination of an ethnic group is called **genocide**. The Nazi "final solution," which resulted in the murder of six million Jews in Europe during the Third Reich (1933–1945), is known in history as the **Holocaust**. Major extermination centers were built at Auschwitz, Buchenwald, Treblinka, Bergen-Belsen, and Majdanek.

When American armed forces entered the death camps in April 1945, they were horrified at what they found—massive starvation, unchecked disease, thousands of unburied corpses. General Eisenhower called the findings "almost unbelievable." Slowly the truth was impressed on the incredulous public. As the cry, "Never again" was raised, Holocaust studies became part of the school curriculum in New York State and throughout the United States.

Failure of the United States to act on the reports of the Holocaust is attributable to a number of causes—disbelief, reluctance of the media to report what they knew, Roosevelt's preoccupation with other war matters and disinterest of the American public.

In the spring of 1944, President Roosevelt approved a request of the War Refugee Board to admit 1,000 refugees to Fort Ontario at Oswego, New

York. The refugees, at that time in southern Italy, were survivors of the death camps. They were to return to their homelands after the war. During the war, Sweden had welcomed 8,000 Jewish refugees from Denmark. But the admission of 1,000 to the United States under strict "security restrictions" met with bitter resistance from anti-Semites in the United States.

Exercise Set 5.3

1. During World War II the earnings of workers
   A. nearly doubled
   B. increased by 50 percent
   C. gained only slightly
   D. declined in terms of real wages

2. World War II was financed differently from World War I in that
   A. excess profits taxes were levied
   B. income taxes were levied
   C. more of the cost was raised by taxation
   D. the withholding tax was not used

3. Which statement best describes an important part of the experience of African Americans in the United States during the period between World War I and World War II?
   A. many African Americans moved back to the South in an attempt to recapture their roots
   B. interracial tensions increased because of the African American migration into Northern cities
   C. the influence of the Ku Klux Klan declined significantly
   D. the success of black soldiers in World War I led to equal treatment for African Americans

4. Which is a valid conclusion based on a study of the Holocaust?
   A. world opinion is effective in stopping genocide
   B. savage acts can be committed by an advanced society
   C. people should not become involved in partisan politics
   D. military commanders cannot be held responsible for acts committed during wartime

5. Agricultural policy during World War II
   A. favored the production of basic raw materials like cotton
   B. attempted to restrict production in order to enlist farm labor in the war production industries
   C. fostered bumper crops as a means of exchange for materials needed in defense industries
   D. was a reversal of New Deal agricultural policy

THE UNITED STATES IN WORLD WAR II

> More than any other war in history, this war has been an array of the forces of evil against those of righteousness . . . no matter what the cost, the war had to be won.
>
> Dwight D. Eisenhower, June 10, 1945

Allied Leadership and Strategy

Allied leadership and strategy were the key factors in attaining victory in World War II. The United States, under Commander-in-Chief **Franklin D. Roosevelt**, worked in close and harmonious cooperation with Britain, under the indomitable Prime Minister **Winston S. Churchill**. The military leaders of both nations, in a secret conference in March 1941, planned joint strategy. The primary effort was to be directed against Nazi Germany, because Germany, in control of the seacoast of western Europe, was using its **U-boats** to cut communications between Britain and the United States. Also, Germany had greater military power and resources than Japan, and there was great apprehension that Germany might develop the atom bomb or some other fearful weapon if given the time.

Marshall—the Architect of Victory

America's Chief of Staff **General George C. Marshall** was the leading architect of Allied strategy. Roosevelt turned down his request for a field command, asserting that Marshall's talents as an overall strategist were essential to victory.

Planning the Attack on "Fortress Europe"

Leadership of Eisenhower

General Dwight D. Eisenhower was **Supreme Commander of Allied Expeditionary Forces** in Western Europe. He commanded the successful Allied invasion of North Africa and was then assigned the task of the invasion of Europe as commander of all Allied forces in Europe with headquarters near London.

From North Africa to Italy

In November 1942 General Eisenhower, in cooperation with the British, made landings in Africa and took Casablanca, Oran, and Algiers. On February 14, 1943, Eisenhower took command of the Allied forces in North Africa. Aided by **General George S. Patton** and British **General Bernard Montgomery**, he forced the surrender on May 13th of 250,000 Axis troops and brought the African campaign to a close. In September 1943 **General Mark Clark** led an American invasion of Italy at Salerno, south of Naples.

D-Day—June 6, 1944

In June 1944 General Eisenhower was made Supreme Commander of the Allied Expeditionary Forces with Supreme Headquarters, Allied Expeditionary Forces (SHAEF) in London. After months of careful planning, the invasion of Europe, called by the code name "Operation Overlord," was launched on **"D-Day," June 6, 1944**. The first few hours of Operation Overlord included heavy air bombardment all along the French coast; 4,000 troop ships crossing the Channel with 176,000 troops; air cover by 11,000 planes; glider planes with parachute troops being dropped behind enemy lines; and about 600 fighting ships escorting the fighting forces and shelling enemy batteries.

V. E. Day—May 8, 1945

By July 1944 one million troops were in France; by September that number exceeded two million. In September 1944, American troops entered Germany. On **May 8, 1945 (V. E. Day)**, the German General Staff accepted the Allied terms of "unconditional surrender."

Turning Points in the War

At Sea—Midway

In the Pacific, the great air-naval battle of **Midway** (June 3–6, 1942) was a turning point in the war. Japan's attempt to take this strategic American base was repulsed with losses to the enemy of four carriers and about 275 planes.

In the Air—the Battle of Britain

A turning point in the air war in Europe came in the summer of 1940. Hitler's air force (**Luftwaffe**) bombed London and other British cities almost every night for three months. The **Royal Air Force** (**RAF**) downed 2,300 German planes during the **Battle of Britain**. Toward the end of August, the RAF gained control of the skies over Britain. They had won the battle and saved Britain. In the House of Commons on August 20, 1940, Churchill expressed Britain's tribute to the RAF in the classic statement: "Never in the field of human conflict was so much owed by so many to so few."

On Land—Stalingrad

The turning point in the land war between the Nazi army and the Soviet forces came at **Stalingrad** in the fall of 1942, when the Russians broke the back of the German offensive by destroying or capturing more than twenty divisions, containing some 300,000 of Germany's elite troops.

The Atomic Bomb

In 1939, scientists in the field of theoretical physics were aware that **nuclear fission** could be used to make a bomb of incredible destructive power. There was evidence that Germany was working on the **atomic bomb**. In July 1939, **Albert Einstein**, a refugee from Nazi Germany then working at Princeton University, signed a letter to President Roosevelt urging that the U.S. government sponsor a program to harness atomic energy and stating: "This new phenomenon would lead also to the construction of bombs." Roosevelt considered the idea carefully and decided that he must pursue a project that was recommended by Einstein and other leading physicists, including **Enrico Fermi**, a Nobel Prize winner refugee from Italy, and Niels Bohr, another Nobel Laureate refugee from Denmark.

The Manhattan Project

On the morning of July 16, 1945, the first atomic bomb was detonated in the desert south of Los Alamos, New Mexico. Three weeks later, on August 6, 1945, a U.S. Army plane dropped a single atomic bomb over Hiroshima, Japan. The bomb had a force equal to 20,000 tons of TNT (dynamite). A blinding flash was followed by a "mushroom cloud" of debris and atomic radiation that reached skyward and spread over the city and its environs. It killed 260,000 people. When the Japanese refused to surrender, a second bomb was dropped three days later on Nagasaki.

Reason for Truman's Decision to Use the A-Bomb

President Truman's decision to use the bomb was justified in his mind by the need to end the war quickly and save American lives. The war in the Pacific had been bitterly fought with heavy losses. Fighting in the Philippines, Coral Sea, Midway, Guadalcanal, Tarawa, the Marshall Islands, Saipan, and Guam in the Marianas, and the reconquest of the Philippines had contributed substantially to the million American casualties. Now the fighting was on Japanese soil as the main islands of Japan were being approached. Capturing the small island of Iwo Jima took the lives of 5,000 American marines. The conquest of Okinawa, 360 miles from the main islands of Japan, resulted in

11,000 Americans killed and 34,000 wounded. It was estimated that the successful allied invasion of Japan would result in a million casualties.

The Japanese Surrender

On **August 14, 1945 (V. J. Day)**, five days after the bomb was dropped on Nagasaki, Japan surrendered and World War II ended.

Formal Surrender Ceremonies

Formal ceremonies of surrender and signing of surrender documents took place aboard the battleship *Missouri* in Tokyo Bay, September 2, 1945. The surrender was accepted by General Douglas MacArthur on condition that **Emperor Hirohito** be allowed to remain on the throne as emperor-figurehead. In a brief statement MacArthur concluded: "If we do not devise some . . . more equitable system than war, Armageddon will be at our door."

Occupation of Japan

General MacArthur was virtually the ruler of Japan during most of the period of Allied occupation (1945–1951). The Japanese cooperated in carrying out the reforms he instituted in decrees establishing a democratic, nonmilitary government, redistributing land, restricting the power of the industrial monopolies, establishing labor unions, reforming education, and granting women suffrage. A beginning was made in rebuilding the Japanese economy.

1. Which of the following did *not* occur during the Allied occupation of Japan (1945–1951) after World War II?
   A. General MacArthur was not able to participate in the occupation because he was preoccupied with events in the Philippines
   B. The Japanese cooperated in carrying out the reforms requested by General MacArthur
   C. A new Japanese Constitution went into effect during the occupation
   D. The size of Japanese armed forces was substantially reduced

2. The first atomic bomb was developed in the United States with the help of a number of European scientists who were refugees from the Nazis. Which of the following was included in this group?
   A. Guglielmo Marconi
   B. Enrico Fermi
   C. Alessandro Volta
   D. Cyrus McCormick

3. The most accurate statement concerning U.S. foreign policy is that the United States has generally
   A. acted according to national self-interest
   B. reacted forcefully to imperialism around the world
   C. formed alliances with countries in need
   D. used military confrontation to solve disputes

4. President Truman's justification for using the atom bomb on Hiroshima and Nagasaki was
   A. to vindicate the expenditure of $2 billion on solving the problem of nuclear fission
   B. to avenge the Japanese use of suicide bombing against American ships
   C. to demonstrate to Stalin that the United States was the strongest military power on earth
   D. to save perhaps as many as a million American lives

5. Which group of U.S. residents was subjected to the greatest loss of constitutional rights during a period of U.S. military involvement?
   A. Hispanic Americans during the Spanish-American War
   B. German Americans during World War I
   C. Japanese Americans during World War II
   D. Chinese Americans during the Korean conflict

AFTERMATH OF WORLD WAR II

> The evidence relating to war crimes has been overwhelming in its volume and its detail . . . The truth remains that war crimes were committed on a vast scale, never before seen in the history of war.
> Report of the War Crimes Tribunal of the Nuremberg Trials, 1946

War Crimes Trials

The Nuremberg Trials

At the Nuremberg Trials (1945–1946) six German organizations and 24 top German civil, military, and naval leaders were charged with war crimes. The leaders included **Herman Wilhelm Goering**, the number two Nazi; Joachim von Ribbentrop, Nazi foreign minister; Julius Streicher, editor of *Der Sturmer*; **Rudolph Hess**, the number three Nazi; Generals Wilhelm Keitel and Alfred Jodl; and Admirals Eric Raedler and Karl Doenitz. (Hitler had committed suicide on April 30, 1945.) The charges included the killing of more than 10 million European civilians and captured war prisoners. Eleven of the defendants were sentenced to death by hanging, others to imprisonment for various terms.

War Crimes Trials in Japan

War crimes trials were also held in Japan at the direction of General MacArthur, who ordered the top Japanese war leaders to stand trial. General **Hideki Tojo**, the leading warmonger and former Premier, tried unsuccessfully to commit suicide. He and six of his colleagues were found guilty and hanged on December 23, 1948. The same fate overtook General Tomoyuki Yamashita, the Tiger of the Philippines. Sixteen others were given light sentences. Other trials were held throughout Japan before special courts; 4,200 were convicted, of whom 720 were executed.

The Pursuit of Nazi War Criminals

Many Nazi criminals involved in the slaughter of Jews during the Holocaust escaped from Germany to countries as far away as Argentina.

• *Adolf Eichmann.* A case that stirred worldwide interest was that of Adolf Eichmann, who had been assigned the task of deporting all the Jews from Europe to the extermination camps in Eastern Europe. On March 14, 1945, shortly before the surrender of the Nazis, Eichmann proclaimed, "I'll happily die with the certainty of having killed almost six million Jews." Instead, he fled in disguise to Argentina. Eichmann's capture in Buenos Aires in 1960 by Israeli commandos and his deportation to Israel for trial was made possible by the efforts of one man, Simon Wiesenthal, who spent

4½ years in Nazi concentration camps. In 1947 he founded the Vienna Documentation Center for tracing the whereabouts of war criminals. He helped bring 1,100 criminals, including Eichmann, to justice. He also established the Wiesenthal Center for Holocaust Studies in Los Angeles.

- *Klaus Barbie.* The French Fascist Klaus Barbie was captured in La Paz, Bolivia, in 1983. Barbie, who earned the title "Butcher of Lyons," worked with the Nazis during their occupation of France and was responsible for the murder of thousands of French Jews and resistance fighters.

Conversion to Peace

Demobilization

When the war ended, President Truman wished to demobilize the armed forces slowly in order to have a strong military presence in Europe and Asia in case of emergency. But there was tremendous pressure at home for immediate return of the troops. In less than a year the armed forces were reduced from 12 million to 3 million; the Air Force went from 85,000 to 9,000 planes, and the Navy withdrew hundreds of ships from active service.

End of Price Controls

There was also heavy pressure on the President to remove wartime price controls on consumer goods. When the Democrats lost control of both houses of Congress in the 1946 elections, Truman yielded and withdrew controls on everything but rent.

Postwar Inflation

As might have been expected, runaway inflation was unleashed. People had earned good wages during the war, but consumer goods such as automobiles, refrigerators, and home appliances were not available because industry was engaged in making ships, tanks, and guns. Savings mounted until nearly $50 billion was available for consumer purchases. By the spring of 1947, prices were one third higher than they had been less than two years before.

Labor Unrest

With this surge in prices came a demand by labor for wage increases. A wave of strikes swept across the country. Major industries, including automobiles, steel, and railroads, were hit. The federal courts intervened in a strike of bituminous coal miners, led by **John L. Lewis**, who defied a court injunction in 1946. The strike was broken when a federal district court imposed heavy fines on Lewis and the union.

The Taft-Hartley Act

The Republican-controlled Congress passed the 1947 Taft-Hartley labor law over Truman's veto. The law forbade the "closed shop" and outlawed the "check off," which required employers to deduct union dues from paychecks and turn the money over directly to the union. It authorized the President to seek a court injunction calling for a 60-day "cooling off" period for strikes and authorized an 80-day injunction against strikes affecting public health or safety. The new law was denounced by labor as a "slave labor" law. However, supporters in Congress and among the citizenry felt that it restrained the excessive power that organized labor had gained from the Wagner Act of 1935.

The law also forbade unions from making political contributions and required labor leaders, but not management, to take a non-Communist oath. In the face of a threatened strike of steel unions, President Truman ordered Charles Sawyer, his Secretary of Commerce, to take possession of the steel mills and run them by authority of the federal government. The procedure was declared unconstitutional by a 6 to 3 decision of the Supreme Court in *Youngstown Sheet & Tube Co.* v. *Sawyer* (1952).

Congress Opposes Truman's Reforms

In Social Legislation

Congress and the President were at odds. The President's efforts to expand public housing, Social Security, and federal aid to education were rejected.

In Civil Rights

African Americans continued to find it difficult to obtain a fair deal in housing, employment, and education. When President Truman attempted to put an end to racial injustice, he met even greater resistance. His call for anti-lynching and anti-poll tax laws, stronger civil rights laws, and a permanent Fair Employment Practices Committee was stalled when Southern senators prepared to filibuster against these measures. In December 1946 the President appointed a **Committee on Civil Rights** in response to racial murders in the South. Truman did, however, begin the desegregation of the armed forces. He also appointed African American judges to the federal courts and issued an executive order banning discrimination in federal employment.

The G.I. Bill of Rights

An important series of laws, called the "**G.I. Bill of Rights**," was passed by Congress in anticipation of the return of 10 million veterans to civilian life. One of the most far-reaching measures was the law providing subsidies for veterans who wished to continue their education. About 12 million veterans ultimately availed themselves of this opportunity for basic education as well as vocational education and the attainment of advanced professional diplomas and degrees. Other laws favorable to veterans provided reinstatement to their jobs with seniority rights, unemployment pay for up to one year, low-interest government loans for home building and for the purchase of farms or businesses, and provision for medical care.

The Election of 1948

As the election of 1948 approached, it seemed unlikely that President Truman would remain in office. There was even doubt that he would be nominated. The Democratic party split into three factions. Southern Democrats, called "**Dixiecrats**," alarmed by the President's civil rights agenda, organized a **States Rights** party and nominated Governor **J. Strom Thurmond** of South Carolina for President. Another wing of the Democratic party, led by former Vice-President **Henry A. Wallace**, opposed the President's "cold war" confrontation with the Soviet Union. Wallace was nominated for President by this faction under the name of the Progressive party.

Meanwhile the Republican party united behind Governor **Thomas E. Dewey** of New York. Dewey had lost to Roosevelt in 1944, when the war was still being fought. This time he was the strong favorite to win.

But the feisty President went around the country denouncing the "do-nothing, good-for-nothing" Republican-controlled Eightieth Congress. So certain were the Republicans of victory that the *Chicago Daily Tribune* published an early election edition with an eight-column front page headline: "Dewey Defeats Truman." Truman surprised the pollsters by winning 303 electoral votes to 189 for Dewey and 39 for Thurmond. The popular vote was 24.1 million to 21.9 million, with 1.17 million for Thurmond and 1.16 million for Wallace.

Truman's "Fair Deal" Program

In his State of the Union message (January 1949), Truman called for a "**Fair Deal**" for all Americans. The Democrats had gained majorities in both houses of Congress, and the President proposed to extend the social legislation of the New Deal. Most of his proposals met determined opposition by a conservative coalition of Republicans and Southern Democrats in Congress. But Truman did succeed with part of his "Fair Deal" program. Social Security benefits were extended to 10 million additional members; the minimum wage of the Fair Labor Standards Act of 1938 was raised from 40 cents to 75 cents an hour. The **National Housing Act** of 1949 provided for slum clearance and the construction of 810,000 housing units to be built during a six-year period for rental to low-income families. Proposals for strong civil rights measures, for repeal of sections of the Taft-Hartley Act, for a new farm subsidy program, for national health insurance, and for a comprehensive aid to public education program were rejected by Congress.

Exercise Set 5.5

1. An important outcome of the Nuremberg Trials held at the end of World War II was that they
   A. showed that many accounts of Nazi atrocities were exaggerated
   B. spread the blame for World War II among many nations
   C. held that moral and ethical considerations do not apply in wartime
   D. established that individuals are responsible for their actions

2. The term "open shop" refers to a plant or business where
   A. only unionized workers are hired
   B. either union or non-union workers are hired
   C. employees must join a union after six months
   D. only non-union workers are hired

3. The Taft-Hartley Act
   A. imposed unusual restrictions on employers
   B. gave labor greater power than ever
   C. was opposed by the Republicans
   D. sought to curb the power of unions

4. The success of President Truman in the 1948 election was due to
   A. his direct and forthright statement of his position on public issues
   B. his calls for civil rights legislation
   C. his conservative position during the period of postwar reaction
   D. the intellectual quality of his television appearances

5. The "G.I. Bill of Rights" refers to
   A. an amendment to the Constitution adopted shortly after the end of World War II
   B. rights of veterans affirmed by the Supreme Court in a series of post-war decisions
   C. legislation passed by Congress pertaining to education, unemployment compensation, loans for home building, and provisions for medical care of veterans
   D. guarantees for employment of veterans in federal government departments and agencies

1. Which statement best describes relations among the major powers during the period between World War I and World War II?
   A. major powers followed policies of international cooperation in order to insure peace
   B. major powers respected each other's territorial integrity
   C. the League of Nations was given the power to establish a strong multinational military force
   D. national interests took priority over international interests

2. Evidence that the United States generally followed a policy of isolationism during the period 1919–1939 is that the United States
   A. condemned Fascist aggression
   B. rejected the policy of appeasement
   C. refused to join the League of Nations
   D. participated in disarmament conferences

3. The neutrality legislation of 1935–1937 was based on the contention that one of the chief causes of American involvement in World War I was
   A. economic ties with the belligerents
   B. Wilson's failure to uphold American rights as a neutral
   C. creation by the press of hostile public opinion toward the Central Powers
   D. failure of the executive and legislative branches of the government to agree on foreign policy

4. The isolationist policies of the United States in the 1930s were broken down by the danger of
   A. a united Europe under the leadership of Soviet Russia
   B. a united Asia under the Chinese People's Republic
   C. a simultaneous two-ocean war against a united Europe and a united Asia
   D. the growth of British trade in Latin America and Canada

5. Roosevelt's decision to make the atom bomb was
   A. more difficult than Truman's decision to use it because there was greater opposition to it
   B. opposed by the leading scientists on both sides of the Atlantic
   C. based on reports that Germany was attempting to develop an atomic bomb or other decisive military invention
   D. not much of a risk since only a few million dollars were invested in the venture

ESSAYS

1. In the United States, the way of life is constantly changing. Listed below are some areas in which change has taken place in the 20th century.

      Areas of Change
      Global economic interdependence
      Role of government in everyday life
      Proportion of elderly in the population
      Population shifts
      Impact of technology on the work force

   Choose *three* of the areas listed. For *each* area chosen describe a change that took place during the 20th century and discuss how that change has affected life in the United States.

2. Discrimination has been a problem faced by many people throughout the world. Identify *two* specific groups that have experienced it.
   For *each* group identified:
   • Show how the group has experienced discrimination. Include a specific time period and a description of the historical setting.
   • Describe specific actions taken by the group to overcome the discrimination.
   • Discuss the extent to which the group's actions have been successful in overcoming the discrimination.

3. Some historians view the history of U.S. foreign policy as a sequence consisting of the stages listed below.

      1776–1823/Protecting national independence
      1824–1897/Fulfilling Manifest Destiny
      1898–1918/Entering the world scene
      1919–1940/Limiting international involvement
      1941–present/Accepting world leadership

   Choose *three* of the time periods listed above. For *each* one chosen, identify a U.S. foreign policy development. Explain how this development was consistent with the foreign policy stage of that time period and show how this development reflected a domestic need of the United States at the time.

THEMATIC ESSAY

Directions: Write a well-organized essay that includes an introduction, several paragraphs addressing the task below, and a conclusion.

Theme: Science and Technology

Science and technology have brought about great changes in many areas of American life.

Task:

From your study of the 20th century, choose *three* major scientific/technological developments.

For each administration:

- Identify the scientific/technological development.
- Describe the effects of the scientific/technological development on American life.
- Discuss the extent to which the development had a positive or a negative effect on American life.

You may use any major scientific/technological developments from your study of 20th-century United States history. Some suggestions you may wish to consider are mass production of the automobile (1900–1930), invention of the airplane and eventual trans-Atlantic flight (1903–1927), television (1945–present), nuclear weapons (1945–present), and home use of the personal computer (1980–present).

You are *not* limited to these suggestions.

DOCUMENT-BASED QUESTION ESSAY

The following questions (Part A and Part B) are based on the accompanying documents (1–6). Some of these documents have been edited for the purpose of this exercise. The question is designed to test your ability to work with historical documents and to demonstrate your knowledge of the subject matter being presented. As you analyze the documents, take into account both the source of the document and the author's point of view.

Historical Context: Although post-World War I isolationism ran deep in the United States during the 1930s and early 1940s, many believed that involvement in World War II was inevitable.

Task: Using information from the documents and your knowledge of United States history, answer the questions that follow each document in Part A. Your answers to the questions will help you write the Part B essay, in which you will be asked:

> Discuss the likelihood of U.S. involvement in World War II without the direct attack upon Pearl Harbor in December 1941.

Part A
Short Answer

The documents below relate to issues concerning United States foreign policy in the 1930s and early 1940s. Examine each document carefully and then answer the questions that follow.

DOCUMENT 1

> Sect. 1. (a) Whenever the President shall find that there exists a state of war between, or among, two or more foreign states, the President shall proclaim such fact, and it shall thereafter be unlawful to export, or attempt to export, or cause to be exported, arms, ammunition, or implements of war from any place in the United States to any belligerent state named in such proclamation, or to any neutral state for transshipment to, or for the use of, any belligerent state.

—The Neutrality Act of 1937 (May 1, 1937)

1. How did the Neutrality Act of 1937 distinguish, if at all, between the treatment of Great Britain and Germany?

_____

_____

_____

_____

2. How did the Neutrality Act of 1937 address the issue of shipping arms to neutral countries?

_____

_____

_____

_____

DOCUMENT 2

UNITED STATES IMPORTS and EXPORTS 1914–1945 (in millions of dollars)						
	Europe (total)		UK		Germany	
Year	Exports to	Imports from	Exports to	Imports from	Exports to	Imports from
1914	1,486	896	594	294	345	190
1915	1,971	614	912	256	29	91
1916	3,813	633	1,887	305	2	6
1917	4,062	551	2,009	280	—	—
1918	3,859	318	2,061	149	—	—
1919	5,188	751	2,279	309	93	11
1920	4,466	1,228	1,825	514	311	89
1921	2,364	765	942	239	372	80
1922	2,083	991	856	357	316	117
1923	2,093	1,157	882	404	317	161
1924	2,445	1,096	983	366	440	139
1925	2,604	1,239	1,034	413	470	164
1926	2,310	1,278	973	383	364	198
1927	2,314	1,265	840	358	482	201
1928	2,375	1,249	847	349	467	222
1929	2,341	1,334	848	330	410	255
1930	1,838	911	678	210	278	177
1931	1,187	641	456	135	166	127
1932	784	390	288	75	134	74
1933	850	463	312	111	140	78
1934	950	490	383	115	109	69
1935	1,029	599	433	155	92	78
1936	1,043	718	440	200	102	80
1937	1,360	843	536	203	126	92
1938	1,326	567	521	118	107	65
1939	1,290	617	505	149	46	52
1940	1,645	390	1,011	155	—	5
1941	1,847	281	1,637	136	—	3
1942	4,009	220	2,529	134	—	—
1943	7,633	240	4,505	105	—	—
1944	9,364	289	5,243	84	—	—
1945	5,515	409	2,193	90	2	1

—U. S. Bureau of the Census

3. How did import/export activity between the United States and Germany compare with import/export activity with Great Britain (UK) during the 1930–1940 period?

_____

_____

_____

_____

4. What argument could be made using the statistics in the table above for the eventual direction of United States foreign policy that favored protection of Great Britain against Germany?

_____

_____

_____

_____

DOCUMENT 3

It seems to be unfortunately true that the epidemic of world lawlessness is spreading. And mark this well! When an epidemic of physical disease starts to spread, the community approves and joins in a quarantine of the patients in order to protect the community against the spread of the disease.

—Franklin D. Roosevelt, "Quarantine Speech,"
October 5, 1937

5. What problems did the Neutrality Act of 1937 present to Roosevelt's position by October of 1937?

_____

_____

_____

_____

The Neutrality Act of 1937 made no distinction between aggressor nations (Germany, Japan) and victim nations (France, China). In September 1939 President Roosevelt addressed Congress and urged a repeal of the Act. The following response came from Michigan Senator Arthur Vandenberg.

In the midst of foreign war....we are asked to depart from the neutrality which the American Congress has twice told the world would be our role of conduct in such an event....We are asked to depart from international law itself, as we ourselves have officially declared it to exist. Consciously or otherwise, but mostly consciously, we are asked to depart from it on behalf of one belligerent whom our personal sympathies largely favor, and against another belligerent whom our personal feelings largely condemn. In my opinion, this is the road that may lead us to war, and I will not voluntarily take it.....

—Senator Arthur Vandenberg, Republican, Michigan,
October 4, 1939

6. Senator Vandenberg refers to two belligerents: one the United States favors and the other the United States condemns. Which country does the United States favor and which does the United States condemn?

_____

_____

_____

_____

7. Would Senator Vandenberg be labeled an isolationist or an interventionist? Why?

_____

_____

_____

_____

DOCUMENT 5

It is possible—I will put it that way—for the United States to take over British (war) orders, and, because they are essentially the same kind of munitions that we use ourselves, turn them into American orders..... That would be on the general theory that it may still prove true that the best defense of Great Britain is the best defense of the United States, and therefore that these materials would be more useful to the defense of the United States if they were used in Great Britain than if they were kept in storage here.

—President Franklin D. Roosevelt, Speech supporting
Lend-Lease Act, 1940

8. By 1940 it had become quite clear that United States foreign policy was designed to assist what major European warring nation?

_____

_____

_____

_____

DOCUMENT 6

I know I will be severely criticized by the interventionists in America when I say we should not enter a war unless we have a reasonable chance of winning...We have a one-ocean Navy. Our Army is still untrained and inadequately equipped for foreign war. Our air force is deplorably lacking in modern fighting planes because most of them have already been sent to Europe...

There is a policy open to this nation that will lead to success—a policy that leaves us free to follow our own way of life, and to develop our own civilization. It is not a new and untried idea. It was advocated by Washington. It was incorporated in the Monroe Doctrine....

—Charles A. Lindbergh, New York City, August 14, 1935

9. Explain Lindbergh's reference to Washington and Monroe and how the reference supports his argument.

_____

_____

_____

_____

DOCUMENT 7

Jan. 1, 1941

■ Allied Nations   ■ Axis Nations
▨ Allied Occupied Territory   ▨ Axis Occupied Territory

10. Nearly 11 months before the attack on Pearl Harbor, what concerns might the United States have had for the future of Western Europe?

_____

_____

_____

_____

Part B
Essay

Your essay should be well organized with an introductory paragraph that states your position on the question. Develop your position in the next paragraphs and then write a conclusion. In your essay, include specific historical details and refer to the specific documents you analyzed in Part A. You may include additional information from your knowledge of social studies.

Historical Context: Although post-World War I isolationism ran deep in the United States during the 1930s and early 1940s, many believed that involvement in World War II was inevitable.

Task:

> Do you feel that the involvement of the United States in World War II would have come without the direct attack on Pearl Harbor on December 7, 1941, or do you feel that the proponents of nonintervention would have been successful in keeping the United States out of war?

Guidelines:

In your essay, be sure to
• Develop all aspects of the task
• Incorporate information from at least *five* documents
• Incorporate relevant outside information
• Support the theme with many relevant facts, examples, and details
• Use a logical and clear plan of organization, including an introduction and a conclusion that are beyond a restatement of the theme

PEACE WITH PROBLEMS
(1945–1960)

INTERNATIONAL PEACE EFFORTS

> We must cultivate the science of human relationships—the ability of all peoples, of all kinds to live together and work together in the same world of peace
>
> Franklin D. Roosevelt's last written words, April 11, 1945

Organizing the United Nations

The San Francisco Conference (1945)

Allied leaders met in August 1944 at Dumbarton Oaks, in Washington, D.C.,where plans were laid for an international organization to be known as the **United Nations**. On April 25, 1945, 13 days after the death of President Roosevelt, delegates from 50 nations met in San Francisco to draft a charter (constitution) for the United Nations. The United States sent a 5-member delegation consisting of Secretary of State Edward Stettinius, two Republicans (Senator Vandenberg and Representative Eaton) and two Democrats (Senator Connally and Congressman Bloom).

The UN came into formal existence on October 24, 1945. The charter was ratified (approved) by the Senate on July 28, 1945, making the United States a charter member of the UN.

The United Nations Organization

The charter of the United Nations provides for six major organs and numerous specialized agencies. The **General Assembly** is the major legislative body, where each member has one vote. The **Security Council** is the peace-keeping authority. It consists of eleven members—five permanent and six others elected for two-year terms. The five permanent members—the United States, China, France, Russia, and Great Britain—each has the power to veto any decision of the Council. The **Secretariat**, headed by a Secretary General, is the administrative body of the UN. The other three major UN organs are the **Economic and Social Council**, the **Trusteeship Council** (to safeguard the interests of territories that were not self-governing), and the **International Court of Justice**. Headquarters of the United Nations are in New York City.

The Universal Declaration of Human Rights

Eleanor Roosevelt's Role

The first U.S. delegation to the UN, appointed by President Truman, consisted of five members, one of whom was Mrs. Eleanor Roosevelt. At first she hesitated to accept the appointment, saying she had no experience in foreign affairs. But President Truman insisted and she agreed to serve.

The delegation assigned her to the **Human Rights Commission**, where it was believed she would engage in trivial activities. She worked with careful attention to every aspect of the task. Delegates from other lands soon came to recognize her leadership qualities, and she was chosen to head the committee drafting the Human Rights Declaration.

Adoption and Contents of the Universal Declaration of Human Rights

It took three years before the Universal Declaration of Human Rights was adopted (December 10, 1948)—a tribute to Eleanor Roosevelt's patient and effective leadership. The vote in the UN General Assembly was 48 in favor and 8 members abstaining. These included six members of the Soviet bloc, Saudi Arabia, and South Africa. The Declaration consists of 30 articles, many with subsections. Included in the Declaration are the following:

Art. 1: All human beings are born free and equal in dignity and rights . . .

Art. 2: Everyone is entitled to all the rights and freedoms set forth in this Declaration without distinction of any kind, such as race, color, sex, language, religion, political or other opinion, national or social origin, property, birth or other status . . .

Art. 3: Everyone has the right to life, liberty, and security of person.

Art. 5: No one shall be subjected to torture or to cruel, inhuman, or degrading treatment or punishment.

Art. 9: No one shall be subjected to arbitrary arrest, detention or exile.

Art. 11: (I) Everyone charged with a penal offense has the right to be presumed innocent until proven guilty.

Art. 13: (II) Everyone has the right to leave any country, including his own, and to return to his country.

Art. 16: (II) Marriage shall be entered into only with the true and full consent of the intending spouses.

Art. 18: Everyone has the right to freedom of thought, conscience, and religion; the right includes freedom to change his religion or belief . . .

Art. 21: (I) Everyone has the right to take part in the government of his country . . .

Art. 22: Everyone, as a member of society, has the right to social security . . .

Art. 23: (I) Everyone has the right to work, to free choice of employment, to just and favorable conditions of work and to protection against unemployment.

Art. 23: (II) Everyone, without any discrimination, has the right to equal pay for equal work.

Art. 23: (IV) Everyone has the right to form and to join trade unions for the protection of his interests.

Art. 25: (II) Motherhood and childhood are entitled to special care and assistance. All children, whether born in or out of wedlock, shall enjoy the same social protection.

Attacks on United States Participation in the UN

John Foster Dulles, a prominent international lawyer in Washington, served as a U.S. delegate to the UN (1946–1950). When Eisenhower became President in 1953, he appointed Dulles Secretary of State. A period of reaction was setting in, and attacks were being mounted against U.S. participation in the UN. The cry was heard, "Take the United States out of the UN and the UN out of the United States." In the Senate, the Secretariat of the UN was portrayed by Senator **Joseph R. McCarthy**, Republican of Wisconsin, as a nesting place of Communist spies.

Displaced Persons and Refugees After WW II

The post-World War II problem of displaced persons and refugees was of great magnitude. There were approximately one million such refugees in displaced-person camps, most of them from Eastern Europe. Mrs. Roosevelt observed, "A new type of political refugee is appearing, people who have been against the present governments and if they stay at home or go home will probably be killed." The United Nations established a United Nations High Commission for Refugees (UNHCR) on January 1, 1951. They were to provide "legal protection and, when needed, material assistance to refugees, and to seek permanent solutions to refugee problems on a purely social, humanitarian and nonpolitical basis."

Exercise Set 5.6

1. The most representative legislative body of the United Nations is the
   A. Universal Declaration of Human Rights
   B. General Assembly in which each member nation has one vote
   C. Security Council in which each of the five permanent members has a veto power
   D. Trusteeship Council to safeguard the interests of territories that were not self-governing

2. The appointment of Eleanor Roosevelt as a member of the U.S. delegation to the United Nations
   A. was promptly accepted by Mrs. Roosevelt with great enthusiasm
   B. was considered by her colleagues as a good appointment from the very beginning
   C. was largely responsible for the creation of the Universal Declaration of Human Rights
   D. met with serious opposition in the U.S. Senate

3. The United Nations Universal Declaration of Human Rights was *not* approved by
   A. several African nations
   B. six member-states from Latin America
   C. China, Korea, and Indonesia
   D. Saudi Arabia, South Africa, and six members of the Soviet bloc

4. A factor that has strengthened the United Nations as compared with the League of Nations has been the U.S. policy of
   A. imperialism
   B. isolationism
   C. expansionism
   D. internationalism

5. Which foreign policy approach would advocates of the balance-of-power concept most likely support?
   A. creation of military alliances
   B. unilateral disarmament
   C. abolition of foreign trade
   D. reliance on world peace organizations

COMMUNIST EXPANSION AND CONTAINMENT IN EUROPE AND ASIA

> I believe that it must be the policy of the United States to support free peoples who are resisting attempted subjugation by armed minorities or by outside pressures.
>
> President Harry S. Truman, Message to Congress
> (The Truman Doctrine), March 12, 1947

Yalta Conference, February 1945

At Yalta, a Black Sea port in southern Russia, the big three—**Roosevelt**, **Churchill**, and **Stalin**—met in February 1945 to plan the final blows against the Axis and to make postwar arrangements. Agreement was reached about the new international organization (the United Nations) that was to be established soon after the end of the war. Stalin agreed to hold free elections in Poland, Bulgaria, and Romania, but these were never carried out. Roosevelt was anxious to have Russia enter the war against Japan, because it was expected there would be heavy casualties before Japan surrendered. Stalin agreed to enter the war against Japan within two or three months after the defeat of Germany. In return, Russia was to get the southern half of Sakhalin Island (which Russia had lost to Japan in the 1905 war) as well as the Kurile Islands. The Soviet Union was also to have special rights in parts of China—the railroads in Manchuria and the ports of Dairen and Port Arthur. Russia entered the war against Japan on August 8, 1945, exactly three months after V.E. Day.

Potsdam Conference, July–August 1945

A final summit conference was held at Potsdam, Germany, from July 17 to August 2, 1945, before the end of the war in Asia. President Truman met there with Churchill and Stalin. Later in the negotiations, **Clement Atlee**, the Labor Prime Minister who had defeated Churchill at the polls, represented Britain. The conference issued a declaration calling for the "unconditional surrender" of Japan. A democratic government was to be set up in Germany, and war criminals were to be tried by an international court. A council of foreign ministers of the victors was to draft treaties with Italy, Austria, Hungary, Bulgaria, Romania, and Finland. Zones of occupation in Germany were established, with East Germany assigned to the USSR, northwest Germany to Britain, southwest to the United States, and two small areas to France. Berlin, though located in the Russian zone, was to be divided into four zones, each to be occupied by one of the four powers.

Origins of the Cold War

The World War II alliance of Western democracies with the Soviet Union was really a "marriage of convenience or necessity." It broke up almost as soon as the war had been won. The hostility that developed, short of actual war, became known as the "**Cold War**." Instead of allowing free elections in neighboring countries, Stalin established Communist regimes in Poland, Romania, Bulgaria, and Albania. The Communists threatened the governments of Greece and Turkey in 1947. Soviet troops were used to install a Communist regime in Hungary (1956). In 1968, the Soviet Union sent 200,000 troops into Czechoslovakia to ensure Communist control of that country.

In a speech at Fulton, Missouri in March 1946, Winston Churchill declared, "From Stettin in the Baltic to Trieste in the Adriatic, an **iron curtain** has descended across the continent." President Truman, who was present during this address, was fully in accord with this statement. The U.S. response to Communist aggression was the policy of **containment**. It sought to "contain" or limit Soviet expansion and prevent the spread of Communism. The first step in this policy was the Truman Doctrine, which was applied to Greece and Turkey.

The Truman Doctrine (March 1947)

In a dramatic appearance before a joint session of Congress on March 12, 1947, President Truman announced a historic new turn in American foreign policy that became known as the Truman Doctrine. "One aspect of the present situation," said the President, ". . . concerns Greece and Turkey." President Truman was gravely concerned because, late in 1946, about 13,000 Communist-led guerrillas entered northern Greece from Albania, Yugoslavia, and Bulgaria. Britain, with a strained economy, was terminating its traditional support, leaving Greece alone to deal with this Communist insurgency.

By 1947, Greek Communists, supported by the Soviet Union, threatened to seize control of the government. In his message, President Truman told Congress: ". . . assistance is imperative if Greece is to survive as a free nation." As for Turkey, it too was under pressure from Russia to give up control of the strategic Dardanelles. Soviet control of Greece and the Dardanelles would enable it to dominate the eastern Mediterranean and the Suez Canal. President Truman told Congress, "As in the case of Greece, if Turkey is to have the assistance it needs, the United States must supply it." The heart of the message, the Truman Doctrine, was stated by President Truman in these words: "I believe it must be the policy of the United States to support free peoples who are resisting attempted subjugation by armed minorities or by outside pressures." Then the President made this request: "I therefore ask Congress to provide authority for assistance to Greece and Turkey in the amount of $400,000,000 for the period ending June 30, 1948." By 1950 the United States had invested nearly $1 billion to preserve the independence of Greece and Turkey.

The Marshall Plan (June 1947)

Europe lay in ruins and economic chaos following the war. The United States responded with a program of economic aid. The program for the rehabilitation of postwar Europe came to be known as the Marshall Plan. The plan was to give aid to 22 European countries including the Soviet Union, but the latter came to regard this plan as an anti-Soviet maneuver and refused to participate. In presenting his plan, Secretary of State **George Marshall** said, "The truth of the matter is that Europe's requirements, for the next 3 or 4 years, of foreign food and other essential products—principally from America—are so much greater than her present ability to pay that she must have substantial additional help, or face economic, social, and political deterioration of a very grave character. It is logical that the U.S. should do whatever it is able to do to assist in the return of normal economic health in the world, without which there can be no political stability and no assured peace." Sixteen European nations answered the call and formulated a four year "**European Recovery Plan**" calling for $16 to $24 billion in aid.

The plan met with mixed reactions in Congress. Opponents called the European Recovery Plan "operation rat-hole." However, after Russia overthrew the government of Czechoslovakia in March 1948 and established a Communist regime, Congress approved the Marshall Plan the following month.

Results of the Plan

Congress appropriated $6.8 billion for the European Recovery Plan for the first 15 months and prepared to extend further support. About $12 billion was spent during a four-year period. Britain, France, and West Germany made a remarkable economic recovery that may well have prevented serious political consequences.

The European Common Market

An outgrowth of the European Recovery Plan was the European Common Market (European Economic Community or EEC), organized in 1957 by France, West Germany, Italy, and the Benelux countries (Belgium, the Netherlands, and Luxembourg). Members reduced tariffs on each other's products and eased travel restrictions among members. Britain's efforts to join the Common Market during the 1960s were vetoed by France. In 1973

Britain, Ireland, and Denmark joined the Common Market. Greece was admitted in 1981. This economic union of 10 European nations stirred talk of political union. In the late 1980s a blueprint was drawn up for a European Parliament with a target date of 1992 for implementation. The nations of the Common Market have made significant progress towards economic cooperation, but political unity still seems far away.

The Berlin Crisis (1948–1949)

A major test of will in the cold war between East and West occurred over Berlin. Deep in the Soviet zone of occupation, Berlin itself had been divided into four zones of occupation among the United States, Britain, France, and the USSR. In the spring of 1948, the Western democracies proposed elections for a new German Federal Republic. In response, the Soviets determined to oust the West from Berlin. On June 24, 1948, they set up a blockade around the city so that no food, fuel, or other supplies could reach the 2 million inhabitants of the western zones of Berlin. Short of trying to break the blockade by force, the Allies had only one means of entry to the city—by air. The Allies undertook an "airlift" to circumvent the blockade and bring food, fuel, and supplies to the 2 million people of Berlin. For almost a year, planes delivered essential supplies to the city. They flew more than 100 million miles and brought more than 2 million tons of food and other necessities to the city. With the face-saving intervention of the United Nations, the crisis was solved and the blockade withdrawn in May 1949.

The North Atlantic Treaty Organization (NATO)

A "hot war" was narrowly averted over Berlin, but steps had to be taken to prepare for future crises. On May 19, 1948, the Senate approved a resolution pledging American support for collective security among the Western democracies. In line with this resolution, President Truman proposed the **North Atlantic Pact**, setting up the **North Atlantic Treaty Organization** (**NATO**), which was signed on April 4, 1949.

The original parties, in addition to the United States and Canada, were Belgium, Denmark, France, Iceland, Italy, Luxembourg, the Netherlands, Norway, Portugal, and the United Kingdom (Great Britain). Article V of the treaty reads: "The parties agree that an armed attack against one or more of them in Europe or North America shall be considered an attack against them all." The treaty, overwhelmingly approved by the public, was ratified in the Senate by a vote of 82 to 13.

Expansion of NATO

In 1951 General Eisenhower took command of all military forces of NATO. Greece and Turkey joined NATO in 1952 and West Germany became a member in 1955. It had become the largest peacetime military alliance in history.

The Warsaw Pact

The Soviet Union countered with a military alliance of its own in 1955 — the Warsaw Pact. This Pact united the Soviet Union with six allies in Eastern Europe: Poland, East Germany, Czechoslovakia, Hungary, Romania, and Bulgaria.

The USSR Explodes an A-Bomb (1949)

At the time NATO was organized (April 4, 1949), the Soviet Union did not yet have the atomic bomb, but Soviet scientists had been working frantically toward that end. On September 22, 1949, President Truman announced that the Soviet Union had successfully set off an atomic explosion. A huge buildup of armaments was in progress for NATO. The presence of American servicemen and women and U.S. armaments again became common throughout Western Europe. Before President Truman left office, $6 billion had been appropriated for NATO.

Truman's "Point Four" Program

In his inaugural address of January 1949, President Truman proposed a program of aid to the economically underdeveloped nations of the "Third World." This came to be known as the **Point Four Aid Program**. He spelled it out in detail in a special message to Congress on June 24, 1949:

> The grinding poverty and the lack of economic opportunity for many millions of people in the economically underdeveloped parts of Africa, the Near and Far East, and certain regions of Central and South America constitute one of the greatest challenges of the world today . . . I recommend the enactment of legislation to authorize an expanded program of technical assistance for such areas . . . To inaugurate such a program, I recommend a first-year appropriation not to exceed $45 million.

Congress approved the program and made an initial appropriation in 1950. This plan for underdeveloped nations was seen as both a means of defeating Communist encroachment in these areas and a spur to foreign trade by creating new markets for American industrial and agricultural products. During the period 1948–1960 the expenditures of the United States in foreign aid amounted to $72 billion.

Containment in Asia

Peace Treaty with Japan

On September 8, 1951, the United States signed a peace treaty with Japan bringing to an end the American occupation. No reparations were to be paid. Japan was to have the limited right to rearm. A security treaty, signed at the same time, gave the United States the right to maintain bases in Japan. In effect the United States was underwriting the security of Japan, a country now seen as an ally.

China Becomes Communist (1949)

China presented a different problem. For many years, the weakness of China was exploited by various powers. In 1927, **Chiang Kai-shek**, leader of the Chinese Nationalist government, sought to destroy the Chinese Communist forces under **Mao Zedong**. The latter fled deep into the interior of China. In 1931, Japanese forces invaded and overran Manchuria. In 1936, the Japanese invaded China. Faced with this crisis, the Chinese **Nationalists** and **Communists** fought the invader separately. But after the defeat of Japan in World War II, the fighting between the Chinese Communists and Nationalists resumed. The wily Mao had built a strong base of support among the Chinese peasants, while the arrogant Chiang became unpopular with the Chinese people. During 1948 and 1949 Mao's growing armies inflicted one defeat after another on the Nationalists. By December 1949 Chiang Kai-shek and his followers fled by air to the offshore island of Formosa, now called **Taiwan**, and established their government there. The Communist Chinese led by Mao Zedong now controlled all of mainland China.

The "Hot War" in Asia: Korea (1950–1953)

Korea Divided

Korea, formerly controlled by China, came under Japanese domination when Japan defeated China in 1894. At the end of World War II (as agreed at the Potsdam Conference), Russian forces entered Korea from the north, and American from the south. Two Koreas were formed with a dividing line drawn at 38° north latitude, between Communist-dominated North Korea and democratic South Korea. Attempts to reunite the country were unsuccessful. The Republic of (South) Korea was proclaimed in August 1948 and the People's Republic (North) in September. The USSR and the United States withdrew their military forces from Korea by 1949.

North Korea Attacks South Korea

On June 25, 1950, North Korean troops, alleging an attack from the South, suddenly crossed the line in force and launched a full-scale attack on South Korea. President Truman brought the matter at once to the Security Council of the UN, which voted 9 to 0 (the Soviets had been boycotting the UN) for a resolution ordering North Korea to withdraw.

UN and American troops were dispatched to Korea to drive back the invaders in what President Truman characterized as a "police action," since Congress never declared war. General Douglas MacArthur was placed in command of the combined forces, which included troops from 15 UN nations, South Koreans, and American land, naval, and air forces. At first, South Korean armies were driven back, but MacArthur conducted a successful offensive and then invaded North Korea. As MacArthur's troops approached the border with China at the Yalu River, they were caught in a trap by Chinese armies (so-called "volunteers") that had crossed into North Korea in force.

MacArthur Attempts to Make Policy

When UN forces again counterattacked, MacArthur proposed to drive north and invade China. This was contrary to the limited war policy laid down by President Truman. General **Omar Bradley**, chairman of the Joint Chiefs of Staff, testifying before a Senate committee on May 15, 1951, said that MacArthur's proposal would "involve us in the wrong war, at the wrong place, at the wrong time, and with the wrong enemy." The statement implied that a land war in China would leave the way open for Soviet expansion in Europe and the Middle East and could lead to World War III. MacArthur refused to accept Truman's policy decision and appealed to Congress over the President's authority. He continued to press for intensive military operations against the Chinese and proposed to assist Chiang Kai-shek's Nationalist troops to return to the mainland of China.

Truman Removes MacArthur

MacArthur's failure to implement the policy laid down by the President raised the constitutional question of the superiority of the civilian authority over the military. On April 11, 1951, President Truman informed General MacArthur that he was being relieved of his command in the Pacific and replaced by Lt. General Matthew B. Ridgway. President Truman explained his action by saying, "In the simplest terms, what we are doing in Korea is this: We are trying to prevent a third world war . . . By fighting a limited war in Korea we have prevented aggression from succeeding and bringing on a general war." Then he asked, "What would suit the ambitions of the Kremlin better than for our military forces to be committed to a full-scale war with

Red China?" Although there was a roar of outrage in Congress and loud public acclaim for MacArthur, the public supported the President.

Armistice in Korea

On July 10, 1951, General Ridgway began armistice negotiations with the North Koreans and Chinese. The negotiations continued at Panmunjom for two years. On July 27, 1953, North Korea and the UN reached an armistice agreement; an actual peace treaty was never signed. According to the armistice, the ceasefire line was established just north of the **38th parallel**, the previous boundary of the two Koreas. In 1954 the United States and Korea entered into a treaty whereby the United States agreed to come to the aid of South Korea if attacked again. Under the terms of the treaty, American troops have been stationed in Korea continually since 1954.

Exercise Set 5.7

1. The formation of the North Atlantic Treaty Organization (NATO) in 1949 is a significant event in U.S. diplomatic history because it
   A. committed the United States to a peacetime military alliance
   B. strengthened United States influence in oil-producing nations
   C. eased tensions with the Soviet Union and its satellites
   D. created new patterns of international trade

2. The term "iron curtain" used by Winston Churchill in a speech at Fulton, Missouri in 1946
   A. was a call for the use of the military to put an end to the Soviet dictatorship
   B. expressed a recognition of the existence of a "Cold War" between the USSR and the Western democracies
   C. suggested that trade agreements between the United States and Britain could restore the prewar dominance of the West in steel production
   D. was a first step in restoring diplomatic relations between the Soviet Union and the West

3. The attempt by the Soviet Union to force the Western Allies out of Berlin (1948–1949) failed because
   A. the United Nations intervened by sending relief supplies to the people of West Berlin
   B. the blockade did not prevent the British-American airlift from bringing food and fuel to the people of West Berlin
   C. the Berlin wall had not yet been built
   D. the people of West Berlin were able to manage on their own despite great hardships

4. The Truman Doctrine, announced in 1947,
   A. was a reversal of the Monroe Doctrine
   B. was the first step in the American policy of giving military aid to help nations resist communism
   C. called for the unification of the occupied zones of West Germany
   D. required the nations saved from German aggression to adopt democracy

5. The Marshall Plan and the Point Four Program were similar in that
   A. both were intended to resist Communist aggression in Europe
   B. both were designed to help economically distressed peoples to help themselves
   C. both were seen as measures that would help the United States become a creditor nation
   D. the United States would assume leadership in the United Nations if these plans were implemented

6. MacArthur was recalled by President Truman because
   A. MacArthur committed acts of insubordination
   B. MacArthur was a Republican
   C. American allies demanded his recall
   D. America was losing the Korean War

INTERNAL SECURITY AND CONSTITUTIONALISM

Truman and Government Loyalty Checks

The increasingly dangerous international situation and the tension of the Cold War had effects at home. Many Americans became concerned over internal security and Communist subversion within the United States.

Executive Order 9835 (1947)

On March 21, 1947, President Truman issued Executive Order 9835, also known as the Loyalty Order, designed to investigate the loyalty of government employees. Under this executive order some 3,000 persons were investigated, of whom 200 were dismissed. Though this was a small fraction of the 3 million government employees, the atmosphere in government service became poisoned. Many capable people who might otherwise have entered government service became reluctant to do so.

The National Security Act of 1947

In anticipation of the possible heating up of the Cold War, the National Security Act of July 26, 1947 was passed after two years of wrangling between the army and navy. A new **Department of Defense** was established, headed by a **Secretary of Defense** of Cabinet rank. A separate air force was created. Each service—army, navy, and air force—was to have its own secretary below Cabinet rank. To advise the President on security matters, a new agency, the **National Security Council**, was established, along with a new **National Security Adviser**. The Council was to include a new **Central Intelligence Agency** (**CIA**) to gather intelligence and conduct foreign activities associated with national security.

The McCarran Internal Security Act (1950)

The McCarran Internal Security Act required "Communist-front" organizations to register with the Attorney General. It authorized the government to arrest and detain anyone who might endanger the security of the United States by committing acts of espionage or sabotage. President Truman vetoed the act, calling it "a long step toward totalitarianism." But Congress passed it in 1950 over Truman's veto.

Earlier Attempts to Combat "Subversive Activities"

The Smith Act

In 1940, in the anxious days preceding the attack on Pearl Harbor, Congress had enacted the Alien Registration Act, commonly known as the Smith Act after its author, Senator Howard Smith of Virginia. The act made it illegal to advocate the overthrow of any government in the United States by force or violence or to become a member of any organization that adhered to this doctrine.

The House Committee to Investigate Un-American Activities (HUAC)

The House Committee to Investigate Un-American Activities (HUAC) was established in the House of Representatives in 1938, originally under the chairmanship of Congressman Martin Dies, Democrat of Texas. The committee held hearings, examined witnesses, issued reports and tarnished reputations over the years without ever defining "un-American" or disclosing anything not already known by the Justice Department.

The Supreme Court and Subversive Activities

Dennis v. United States (1951)

In 1949, under orders from President Truman, the Justice Department obtained the conviction of eleven high-ranking members of the U.S. Communist party for conspiring to advocate the violent overthrow of the U.S. government. The conviction (and imprisonment), based on the Smith Act of 1940, was appealed to the Supreme Court on the ground that the act was unconstitutional because it violated the freedom of speech provision of the First Amendment. The conviction was sustained by the Court in a 6 to 2 decision. Writing for the majority, **Chief Justice Frederick M. Vinson** declared that the defendants had conspired to teach and advocate the overthrow of the government of the United States and that this constituted a "clear and present danger" of an attempt to overthrow the government by force and violence.

Yates v. United States (1957)

In the *Yates* case, the Supreme Court again considered an appeal from members of the Communist party charged with violating the Smith Act. The Court, speaking through **Justice Harlan**, overruled the conviction of the defendants. In his concurring opinion, **Justice Black** said, "I believe that the First Amendment forbids Congress to punish people for talking about public affairs, whether or not such discussion incites to action legal or illegal.

Watkins v. United States (1957)

John Watkins, a labor union official, was questioned by the House Un-American Activities Committee. He refused to name former Communist party members, stating that this question was not relevant to the work of the Committee. The Court (with only one dissent) reversed his conviction of contempt of Congress, denying the Committee the authority to punish uncooperative witnesses at will. Each of these cases involved the enduring constitutional issue of civil liberties—the balance between government security and individual rights.

The Alger Hiss Case (1948)

This case stirred great public interest because Whitaker Chambers, a former Communist, charged that Alger Hiss, a former official in the State Department, had given him classified government documents. Hiss testified before the House Un-American Activities Committee, denied the charges, and brought a libel suit against Chambers, who then produced microfilm to prove his charges against Hiss. Consequently, Hiss was convicted of perjury (lying under oath) and served a five-year term in prison. His conviction for perjury helped set the stage for the most gruesome aspect of the "national security" drama.

McCarthyism

The Rise of Joseph R. McCarthy

In his quest for a popular cause, Senator McCarthy proposed alerting America to the Red Menace. In a Lincoln's Day address in February 1950 to the Women's Republican Club in Wheeling, West Virginia, McCarthy waved a sheet of paper and declared, "I have in my hand a list of 205 card-carrying members of the Communist party who hold important positions in the State Department." The speech won instant attention throughout the country. McCarthy had found his cause. Thorough investigation later disclosed not one case of a Communist in the State Department and McCarthy never produced the names. McCarthy then charged that General George C. Marshall was a "traitor" and that he and his protégé, General Eisenhower, were involved "in a conspiracy so immense and an infamy so black as to dwarf any previous such venture in the history of man."

By 1952, McCarthy had become the head of a Senate subcommittee on investigations. In this position, he investigated the State Department and other government agencies. Careers of many patriotic Americans in government, colleges, the arts, and the media were ruined by the "witch hunt" unleashed by McCarthy as he investigated and irresponsibly accused many individuals of having Communist affiliations.

The Army Hearings

Although some Americans were critical of McCarthy's unfair methods and accusations, many supported him. In 1954 he began to search for spies and Communists in the Army. Televised hearings were held April 22–June 17, 1954, investigating McCarthy's charges of subversion in the Army Signal Corps at Fort Monmouth, New Jersey.

Censure of McCarthy

After the hearings, Senator **Ralph Flanders**, Republican of Vermont, filed a resolution calling upon the Senate to censure Senator McCarthy. Among the charges were the Senator's contemptuous behavior in refusing to appear before a Senate committee. On December 2, 1954, by a vote of 67 to 22, the United States Senate voted to censure Senator McCarthy. Thereafter, McCarthy was shunned by his colleagues and his statements ceased to be reported in the press.

McCarthyism

McCarthy's tactics added the word "McCarthyism" to the English language. The historian Samuel Eliot Morison called McCarthy "one of the most colossal liars in our history." Eisenhower, in his memoirs, says, "McCarthyism took its toll on many individuals and on the nation." Reckless, unsupported charges of treason and conspiracy destroyed government officials, teachers, scientists, ministers and scholars. McCarthy's methods are summed up in the word **McCarthyism**.

Exercise Set 5.8

1. Which of the following internal security measures was adopted prior to World War II?
   A. the McCarran Internal Security Act
   B. President Truman's Executive Order for the investigation of government employees' loyalty
   C. the establishment of the House Un-American Activities Committee
   D. the investigation of Senator Joseph McCarthy's subcommittee

2. The Alger Hiss case stirred great public interest because
   A. Hiss, charged with passing classified information to the Communists, had held high public office
   B. Whitaker Chambers, who accused Hiss, denied having been a Communist
   C. Supreme Court Justice Felix Frankfurter testified against Hiss
   D. Hiss refused to appear before the House Un-American Activities Committee

3. Dr. J. Robert Oppenheimer was denied access to restricted government data and suspended from his position as consultant to the Atomic Energy Commission because he
   A. played a major role in the development of the atomic bomb
   B. had access to data which included vital government secrets
   C. was classified as a security risk by a 2 to 1 vote of a special Personnel Security Board
   D. was being considered for the position of Director of the Institute of Advanced Study at Princeton University

4. The term "McCarthyism" generally means
   A. efforts to restrict the spread of Communism
   B. effective use of the media to gain name recognition
   C. bringing false and reckless charges against people to secure publicity and political advantage for oneself
   D. the use of negative advertising during a political campaign

1. A major reason why a working system of international law has been difficult to achieve is that
    A. the many different languages in the world make communication difficult
    B. nations are unwilling to give up some of their sovereignty
    C. no precedent for international law exists
    D. many nations still lack even an internal system of law

2. Which was a major cause of tension in Europe during the decade following World War II?
    A. formation of Soviet-dominated Communist governments in many Eastern European nations
    B. failure of non-Communist nations to support the United Nations
    C. cutbacks in fuel supplies by oil-producing nations
    D. return of United States military forces to pre-World War II levels

3. Totalitarian societies in the 20th century could be most consistently identified by their
    A. unwillingness to allow free elections
    B. acceptance of a variety of political beliefs
    C. support for a state-controlled religion
    D. denial of public education to their citizens

4. "The parties agree that an attack against one or more of them shall be considered an attack against all."
    This statement most clearly illustrates which foreign policy concept?
    A. détente
    B. appeasement
    C. balance of power
    D. collective security

5. The relationship between the United States and Western European nations from 1945 to the present has most often been characterized by
    A. cooperation in efforts to gain political control of emerging nations
    B. division and resentment over competing economic systems
    C. continuance of military and economic interdependence
    D. economic conflict and military confrontation

6. The United States sells manufactured products to Third World nations and purchases raw materials from these nations. This fact illustrates
   A. economic protectionism
   B. global interdependence
   C. pooling of resources
   D. finance capitalism

7. Evidence that civil liberties in the United States were under attack in the period preceding the Cold War can be traced to
   A. the McCarthy speech at Wheeling, West Virginia
   B. the "iron curtain" speech of Winston Churchill
   C. the McCarran Internal Security Act
   D. the establishment of the House Un-American Activities Committee

ESSAYS

1. At various times, the United States has followed one or more of the foreign policies listed below.
   Foreign Policies
   Imperialism
   Isolationism
   Containment
   Nonrecognition
   Formation of military alliances
   Reliance upon international organizations

   Choose *three* of the policies listed above. For *each* one chosen, discuss a specific application of that policy by the United States. Include in your discussion one reason the United States applied that policy and one result of the application of that policy.

2. Below is a list of violations of human rights that have occurred throughout history.
   Violations of Human Rights
   Repression of dissidents
   Genocide
   Destruction of cultural heritage
   Denial of civil and legal rights
   Forced relocation

   a. Select *three* of the violations of human rights from the list above. For *each* one chosen, describe a specific historic example of that violation, including approximate time period and place. Use a different example for each violation chosen.
   b. Show how a specific group or organization, public or private, has promoted the cause of human rights.

THEMATIC ESSAY

Directions: Write a well-organized essay that includes an introduction, several paragraphs addressing the task below, and a conclusion.

Theme: Human Rights

> As a signatory to the Universal Declaration of Human Rights, the United States became responsible to its civil, political, economic, social, and cultural rights.

Task:

> From your study of U.S. history, choose *three* Articles from the Universal Declaration of Human Rights. (It will be necessary to obtain a copy of this document; see *www.hrusa.org*.)
>
> For each Article chosen:
>
> - Describe the human right provided in the specific Article.
> - Discuss the underlying reasons for the inclusion of the specific Article in the Universal Declaration of Human Rights.
> - Select a topic from U.S. history and discuss how the selected Article would apply to the topic chosen. (The question requires that you use three different Articles and three different topics from U.S. history.)

You may use any major topic from your study of U.S. history. Some suggestions you may wish to consider are: the drafting of the Bill of Rights, forced removal of the Cherokee Nation (1830s), the *Dred Scott* decision (1857), the Pullman Strike (1894), immigration restrictions and quotas, women's suffrage, Social Security Act (1935), Japanese relocation camps (1940s), McCarthy Hearings (1950s), student protests against the Vietnam War (1960s–1970s), and the death penalty.

You are *not* limited to these suggestions.

DOCUMENT-BASED QUESTION ESSAY

The following questions (Part A and Part B) are based on the accompanying documents (1–6). Some of these documents have been edited for the purpose of this exercise. The question is designed to test your ability to work with historical documents and to demonstrate your knowledge of the subject matter being presented. As you analyze the documents, take into account both the source of the document and the author's point of view.

Historical Context: Perhaps the most explosive constitutional issue arising out of the Cold War and the phenomenon of Communism was the tension between internal security requirements and civil liberties guarantees.

Task: Using information from the documents and your knowledge of United States history, answer the questions that follow each document in Part A. Your answers to the questions will help you write the Part B essay, in which you will be asked:

In the Cold War Era referred to in the documents (1945–1954) did the internal security measures taken by the federal government rise to the level of constitutional infringement of the civil liberties of Americans?

Part A
Short Answer

The documents below relate to issues concerning the perceived need for internal security measures and the conflicts with civil liberties, in particular, First Amendment rights. Examine each document carefully and then answer the questions that follow.

I feel that this committee could render a great service to the nation through its power of exposure in quickly spotlighting existing front organizations and those which will be created in the future.

The following are questions that Director Hoover proposed to be asked of organizations to determine if they were Communist:

A. Does the organization denounce American and British foreign policy while always lauding (praising) Soviet policy?
B. Does the organization utilize Communist "double-talk" by referring to Soviet-dominated countries as democracies, complaining that the United States is imperialistic and constantly denouncing monopoly-capital?
C. Have outstanding leaders in public life openly renounced affiliation with the organization?
D. Does the organization, if espousing (supporting) liberal progressive causes, attract well-known honest patriotic liberals or does it denounce well-known liberals?
E. Does the organization have a consistent record of supporting the American viewpoint over the years?

As Americans, our most effective defense is a workable democracy that guarantees and preserves our cherished freedoms.

—J. Edgar Hoover, Director of FBI, Testimony to House Committee on Un-American Activities, (March 26, 1947)

1. What First Amendment liberties may be in jeopardy if Director Hoover's "test questions" were to be put to use?

_____

_____

_____

_____

2. Identify the glaring contradiction in Director Hoover's testimony to the House Committee on Un-American Activities.

_____

_____

_____

_____

403

DOCUMENT 2

My definition of a free society is a society where it is safe to be unpopular.

—Adlai E. Stevenson, Democratic Presidential candidate, 1952

3. Compare and contrast Adlai Stevenson's thoughts on a free society with FBI Director Hoover's concerns with organizations suspected of being Communist (*see* Document 1).

_____

_____

_____

_____

DOCUMENT 3

I think it is high time for the United States Senate and its Members to do some real soul-searching and to weigh our consciences as to the manner in which we are performing our duty to the people of America, and the manner in which we are using or abusing our individual powers and privileges.

Those of us who shout the loudest about Americanism in making character assassinations are all too frequently those who, by our own words and acts, ignore some of the basic principles of Americanism—
The right to criticize.
The right to hold unpopular beliefs.
The right to protest.
The right of independent thought.
The American people are sick and tired of being afraid to speak their minds lest they be politically smeared as Communists or Fascists by their opponents. Freedom of speech is not what it used to be in America. It has been so abused by some that it is not exercised by others.

—Senator Margaret Chase Smith, Republican (Maine), responding to Senator Joseph McCarthy's allegations of Communist infiltration in government, June 1, 1950

4. In her criticism of Senator Joseph McCarthy's attacks, what does Senator Margaret Chase Smith cite as being contrary to the Constitution and un-American?

_____

_____

_____

_____

DOCUMENT 4

After Russia's explosion of an atomic bomb and China's transition to Communist control in 1949, President Truman directed the State Department and Department of Defense to reexamine American foreign policy and to establish national security objectives. National Security Council Document 68 (NSC 68) was the resulting report.

It is quite clear from Soviet theory and practice that the Kremlin seeks to bring the free world under its dominion by the methods of the Cold War....A comprehensive and decisive program to win peace and frustrate the Kremlin design should be so designed that it can be sustained for as long as necessary to achieve our national objectives. It would probably involve: a substantial increase in expenditures for military purposes....development of programs designed....to wage overt psychological warfare calculated to encourage mass defections from Soviet allegiance and to frustrate the Kremlin design in other ways....development of internal security and civilian defense programs.

—National Security Council Document 68, approved by President Truman, April 1950

5. How did NSC 68 influence the response of the United States to Communist North Korea's invasion of South Korea in June 1950?

_____

_____

_____

_____

DOCUMENT 5

The indictment of eleven high-ranking Communist leaders for allegedly conspiring to teach and advocate the violent overthrow of the government in violation of the Smith Act (1940) reached the Supreme Court of the United States and resulted in the 1951 decision. Below are segments from the majority decision by Chief Justice Vinson and the dissenting decision by Justice Douglas.

C.J. Vinson: …..We hold that Sec. 2 and Sec. 3 of the Smith Act (*advocating overthrow of government by force and violence and teaching such ideas*) do not…violate the First Amendment and other provisions of the Bill of Rights….Petitioners intend to overthrow the government of the United States as speedily as the circumstances would permit. Their conspiracy to organize the Communist party and to teach and advocate the overthrow of the government of the United States by force and violence created a "clear and present danger" …..They were properly and constitutionally convicted for violation of the Smith Act.

J. Douglas, dissenting:….Free speech has occupied an exalted position because of the high service it has given to our society. Its protection is essential to the very existence of a democracy. The airing of ideas releases pressures which otherwise might become destructive. When ideas compete in the market for acceptance, full and free discussion exposes the false and they gain few adherents…..

—*Dennis* v. *United States* (1951)

6. Which Justice is using a specific statute to support restrictions on the freedom of speech provided for by the First Amendment?

_____

_____

_____

_____

7. Does Justice Douglas support the ideas of the Communist party in his dissent? What does he say are the advantages of "airing ideas?"

_____

_____

_____

_____

—The Perils of McCarthyism (1954)

8. What does the author of the cartoon see as being sacrificed with the elimination of the "Communist Pest?"

_____

_____

_____

_____

Part B
Essay

Your essay should be well organized with an introductory paragraph that states your position on the question. Develop your position in the next paragraphs and then write a conclusion. In your essay, include specific historical details and refer to the specific documents you analyzed in Part A. You may include additional information from your knowledge of social studies.

Historical Context: Perhaps the most explosive constitutional issue arising out of the Cold War and the phenomenon of Communism was the tension between internal security requirements and civil liberties guarantees.

Task:

> In the Cold War Era referred to in the documents (1945–1954) did the internal security measures taken by the federal government rise to the level of constitutional infringement of the civil liberties of Americans?

Guidelines:

In your essay, be sure to
- Develop all aspects of the task
- Incorporate information from at least *five* documents
- Incorporate relevant outside information
- Support the theme with many relevant facts, examples, and details
- Use a logical and clear plan of organization, including an introduction and a conclusion that are beyond a restatement of the theme

A World in Uncertain Times

> **KEY IDEAS** Unit Six explores the global role of the United States in an increasingly interdependent world. It describes the social, political, and economic changes in American society in the period between the 1950s and 1990s as the United States entered the post-industrial era.

UNIT CONNECTIONS: By the end of the unit you should understand the following points.

- Post-World War II presidents; the Cold War; foreign policy of containment
- The continuing struggle for civil rights of African Americans
- Demographic changes in the 1950s and 1960s: the growth of the suburbs
- "New Frontier" policies of the Kennedy administration
- "Great Society" policies of the Johnson administration
- The 1960s and revolutionary change for African Americans, women, Hispanic-Americans, Native Americans
- The Warren Court and expansion of rights of the accused
- The Cold War and Southeast Asia: Vietnam War
- Richard Nixon and a departure from the "Great Society"
- The "Reagan Revolution" as a challenge to the New Deal and the "Great Society"
- Recent immigration patterns after 1975
- The Bush and Clinton administrations: Approaching the next century

TOWARD A POST-INDUSTRIAL WORLD: LIVING IN A GLOBAL AGE

> Why does this magnificent applied science which saves work and makes life easier bring us so little happiness? The simple answer runs: Because we have not yet learned to make sensible use of it.
>
> Albert Einstein, in an address at the
> California Institute of Technology, February 1931

UNITED STATES AND POST-INDUSTRIALISM

Changing Energy Sources: Toward Nuclear Power

In the years after World War II, nuclear energy created by fission, or the splitting of atoms, seemed to offer a cheap and unlimited source of power.

The Atomic Energy Commission (AEC)

In 1946, Congress established the Atomic Energy Commission (now called the **Nuclear Regulatory Commission**), a civilian agency with authority to make policy decisions about the use of nuclear power. A program was launched in 1954 whereby private power companies could construct nuclear power plants and operate them under license by the Atomic Energy Commission.

Problems of Nuclear Energy Plants

An accident in March 1979 at the **Three Mile Island** nuclear reactor near Harrisburg, Pennsylvania, caused grave concern about the danger of nuclear radiation escaping into the air and contaminating a wide area with cancer-causing by-products. On April 28, 1986, a major nuclear accident occurred at the Soviet Union's **Chernobyl** power station near the city of Kiev. The resultant cloud of radiation drifted over Europe as far north as Scandinavia. Then there was the March 2011 disaster at the Fukushima Daiichi plant following a devastating earthquake and tsunami that hit Japan. How many future deaths due to radiation exposure are yet to be known.

Changing Technology (Computers)

Advanced technology (hi-tech) is revolutionizing industry so rapidly that it is virtually impossible to keep abreast of developments. Extensive changes are occurring through the use of computers in business and industry, particularly in each of the following fields: missiles, spacecraft and aircraft, scientific instruments, drugs and medicines, electronics and telecommunications, and synthetic materials.

The computer is revolutionizing our lives in the fields of farming, manufacturing, management, business, education, banking, building and construction, entertainment, health, and other daily concerns and activities.

Changing Corporate Structures

The **multinational corporation**—an organization that carries on its business through branches in more than one country—is nothing new in world commerce. But the trend toward multinational corporations has gained momentum since the end of World War II. American corporations open factories, sales offices, mining branches, or other operating units in one or more foreign countries. A percentage of the capital may be raised in the foreign country, making it a joint venture with the percentage of ownership specifically stated. Many American multinationals operate in Africa, Asia, and Latin America, as well as in Europe. Their fields of interest include all types of business and industry, as indicated by names such as Exxon Mobil, General Motors, McDonalds, and Toyota. A major field for American multinationals is oil and petroleum products.

The Changing Nature of Employment

The total labor force in the United States has grown steadily, from 60 million at the end of World War II to 154 million by 2011. At the same time, there has been a dramatic change in the nature of employment.

Agriculture

The percentage of the labor force engaged in agriculture has declined rapidly since the 1930s. Of a total labor force of nearly 49 million in 1930, 10.5 million or 21.4 percent were engaged in farming. By 1970, the labor force had grown to 82 million, but the number of workers in agriculture had declined to 2.5 million or 3.1 percent of the labor force. A further decline continued during the 1970s and 1980s. By 1980, the percentage of workers employed in agriculture was 2.2 percent; in 1985 it was below 2 percent and in 2004, 1.8 percent.

Manufacturing and Service Industries

During the same period (1930–1970), the percentage of workers engaged in manufacturing increased steadily. Among their products were machinery, electrical equipment, textile products, processed foods, transportation equipment, printed materials, metal products, and many others. The percentage in the work force engaged in manufacturing rose from 20 percent in 1930 to 25 percent by 1970. However, the percentage of the work force engaged in manufacturing began to decline after 1970, with the astonishing growth of service occupations including retail sales, office workers, waiters/waitresses, medical services, advertising, and computer programming. By 1986, 75 percent of all employment was in service occupations.

Exercise Set 6.1

1. The potential of nuclear generators to supply America's needs for energy has not been realized because
   A. investors have not been willing to supply the necessary capital
   B. most of the required resources have been devoted to the production of nuclear weapons
   C. plans for the construction of new plants ordered after 1973 have been on the increase
   D. problems of safety, environmental degradation, and plant operation have caused delays in licensing

2. During the past half century there has been a marked shift in occupations from
   A. agriculture to industry to service occupations
   B. service to agriculture to industry
   C. business to industry to professions
   D. manual to electrical to mechanical

3. The domestic need for electricity in the United States supplied by nuclear reactors is approximately
   A. 5 percent
   B. 15 percent
   C. 25 percent
   D. 50 percent

THE WORLD AND POST-INDUSTRIALISM

> It is futile to expect a hungry and squalid population to be anything
> but violent and gross.
>
> Thomas Huxley, 1874

Developed and Developing Nations

Contrasts in a Divided World

The developed nations of the world—those with a strong industrial base—
are primarily located in North America and Europe, plus Japan in Asia. Most
of Africa, the Middle East, Asia, and Latin America are classified as third
world or developing nations. They differ from the developed nations— the
democratic nations of western Europe and North America, and the former
Soviet bloc—in their lower standard of living, lower educational standards,
and lower health standards. The division is sometimes seen as one of North/
South, with the former being developed and the latter developing. Another
point of reference uses the term East/West, with the latter being the area of
development and the former largely developing.

There was for many years an ongoing tension between the Soviet Union
and the Western democracies in an effort to gain influence over or, at least,
allegiance of the developing world. Areas of tension included Latin America
(notably in Central America), in the Middle East, the Persian Gulf, Africa,
and the third world generally. The developing nations, because they are poor
and relatively weak, became a political battleground between the super-
powers.

Third-World Debt

Efforts of third-world nations to make economic progress and raise the
standard of living of their people have led to extensive borrowing of capital
from banks in the developed world. But the money has not always been
properly used, and living standards have generally not risen. Meanwhile the
borrowers have gone deeper and deeper into debt, reaching a point where it
is obvious to both debtors and creditors that repayment cannot be made. By
1992, the debt owed to foreign bankers by less developed nations amounted
to more than one trillion (a thousand billion) dollars.

Low Income, Hunger, and Life Expectancy

There is a clear relationship between the per capita income of a nation and
its life expectancy. The developing nations with the lowest average national
income are also at or near the bottom of the scale in life expectancy.

Even developed industrial nations, including the United States, may have millions living below the poverty level, and many, especially children, suffering hunger and malnutrition. The poverty level is adjusted each year according to the cost of living. In 1986 in the United States, it was set at an income of $11,203 for a family of four. In that year 13.6 percent of Americans were below the poverty level. Children were the worst off, with 19.8 percent living below the poverty level.

Economic and Social Problems

Agriculture

The developing nations have two thirds of the world's population but produce only one third of the world's agricultural output. The greater output of the developed nations is due to the use of farm machinery, fertilizers and chemicals, irrigation, and other technology applied to production, harvesting, and methods of preservation of agricultural produce. The average American farmer cares for about 15 acres, while the average for a farm worker in the developing world is about 3 acres. The great farm belts of the United States and Canada produce more basic food crops (wheat, rye, barley, oats, and corn) than the entire output of the third world.

• *The Malthusian theory.* The theory propounded by the English economist Thomas Robert Malthus in the late 18th century stated that poverty, hunger, and starvation would soon be the lot of humankind, since the population increases by geometric ratio (2 to 4 to 8 to 16), while the food supply increases by arithmetic ratio (2 to 4 to 6 to 8).

• *The "Green Revolution."* The Malthusian theory, so far as food production is concerned, was challenged by the "Green Revolution," a term first used in the 1960s to describe efforts to produce greater yields from farm acreage. New varieties of rice, wheat, and other grains were developed. These new strains were resistant to plant disease, better able to withstand prolonged drought and cold, and had a greater yield per cultivated acre. Better methods of harvesting, soil conservation, and farm management were introduced. New fertilizers and pesticides were developed. Agricultural output in many parts of the world increased dramatically, causing the term "Green Revolution" to be applied.

World Population Growth

Prior to 1650, the world's population grew slowly. The graph shows the rapid increase in population growth since 1650. In the half-century from 1900 to 1950 the world's population increased by 50 percent. In the years after 1950 it increased by 100 percent. More than half the world's people live in Asia. The continent showing the most rapid population growth is Africa, where the popu-

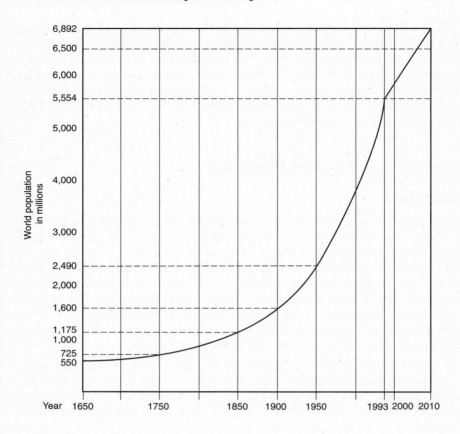

Figure 6.1 World Population (1650–2010)

lation catapulted from 199 million in 1950 to 677 million in 1993. Demographers (people who specialize in population studies) predict that the greatest population increase will be in developing countries. The combined population of Europe, North America (excluding Mexico), and Australia has remained relatively constant since the 1960s. While the population growth of the United States has not kept pace with that of world population, it has nevertheless been increasing steadily. The total population figures for the United States are:

Census Data	U.S. Population
1960	179,323,175
1970	203,302,031
1980	226,545,518
1990	248,709,873
2000	308,745,538

Figure 6.2 United States Population Increase

The astonishing momentum of world population growth is placing a heavy strain on the world's natural resources and contributing to grave environmental damage. The very survival of human life is in the balance.

Environmental Concerns

As crude a weapon as the cave man's club, a chemical barrage has been hurled against the fabric of life.

Rachel Carson, *Silent Spring*, 1962

Sooner or later, wittingly or unwittingly, we must pay for every intrusion on the natural environment.

Barry Commoner, *Science and Survival*, 1966

The Greenhouse Effect

The emissions into the atmosphere from the burning of fossil fuels (coal, oil, and natural gas) are causing a relentless global warming that has been named the **greenhouse effect**. The release of gases, especially carbon monoxide, into the atmosphere produces an artificial blanket that prevents heat from the sun from radiating back into space. This is thought to be the cause of a rise in the air temperature throughout the earth.

Air Pollution

The air on which our lives depend has become a receptacle for the discharges from motor vehicles, factories, airplanes, space exploration refuse, nuclear research, electric power plants, cooking and heating chimneys, forest fires, incinerators, and exhausts and dust from construction and demolition projects.

The **Clean Air Act of 1970** set national standards controlling six basic pollutants—notably carbon monoxide gas—but the act has not solved the air pollution problem.

Water Pollution

The first major Federal Clean Water Act was passed in 1965. The Federal Water Pollution Control Act of 1972 was passed over President Nixon's veto. The **Federal Clean Water Act of 1987** was passed by an angry Congress over President Reagan's veto. Despite these laws, our limited supply of clean water is at risk. Not only the nation's rivers and lakes, but also its subterranean groundwater (the sources of our drinking water) are threatened by contamination. There are 5,000 types of wastes that have been released into the nation's ground water from homes, farms, factories, and other sources.

The 20th-century phenomenon of water pollution is worldwide. On one of his exploratory voyages across the Atlantic Ocean, the scientist Thor Heyerdahl reported a 1,400-mile current of chemical contaminants.

Exercise Set 6.2

1. A characteristic of third-world nations is that they
   A. are all located in Asia or Africa
   B. have a weak industrial base
   C. are all lacking in natural resources
   D. have governments controlled by the military

2. Geographically, the developed nations are chiefly found in the continents of
   A. Europe, North America, and Australia
   B. Europe, Asia, and North America
   C. Africa, South America, and Australia
   D. North America, South America, and Europe

3. The "Green Revolution" refers to the
   A. fluctuation of the dollar in international finance
   B. terrorist activities of the Irish Republican Army
   C. the radical program of a West German political group
   D. the dramatic increase in agricultural output

4. The fact that the agricultural output per acre in developed nations is many times that of developing nations may be explained chiefly by
   A. the difference in soil quality, climate, and other natural advantages
   B. more advanced agricultural technology
   C. a higher education and health level
   D. government support through favorable tariff and tax legislation

5. World population growth
   A. declined between 1650 and 1850, then began a rapid advance
   B. grew relatively slowly but steadily between 1650 and 1950 and then picked up momentum rapidly
   C. shows signs of leveling off at the current figure of about 5 billion people
   D. is proceeding at approximately the same rate on each of the six major continents

6. The continent with the highest percentage of population growth is
   A. Africa
   B. Asia
   C. Europe
   D. South America

1. Since the establishment of the Atomic Energy Commission in 1946
   A. reliance on other sources of energy has gradually diminished
   B. the search for new sources of energy has been abandoned
   C. nuclear plants have become the major source of energy for home and industry
   D. the high expectations of the nuclear industry have failed to materialize

2. A drastic change in the categories of employment in the United States has come about primarily because of
   A. entrance of unprecedented numbers of women into the work force
   B. stringent state and federal regulation of employment of children
   C. technological developments in many fields of employment
   D. population shifts within the United States

3. The rapid increase in the employment of women after 1945 can be credited mainly to
   A. a decrease in the divorce rate
   B. the expansion of the service sector
   C. smaller families
   D. a sharp decrease in immigration

ESSAYS

1. Global interdependence has become an increasingly significant aspect of life in the second half of the 20th century. Listed below are several areas in which this development is clearly apparent.

   Areas of Global Interdependence
   Technological developments
   Environmental problems
   Rapid population growth
   Financial relationships
   Agricultural changes

   Choose *three* of the areas listed. For *each* area chosen, explain its impact on global interdependence indicating how the impact may be beneficial or detrimental.

2. An interrelationship has been shown to exist between certain socio-economic factors. Below are listed a number of these interrelated factors.

Socioeconomic Factors

Life expectancy—per capita income

Level of education—economic productivity

Agricultural output—technological development

Population explosion—financial dependency

Political stability—multinational economy

Choose *three* interrelated factors. For *each pair* chosen discuss the nature of the relationship and explain its effect on the nations involved.

CHAPTER 2

CONTAINMENT AND CONSENSUS
(1945–1960)

EISENHOWER POLICIES: FOREIGN AFFAIRS

> There is no nook or cranny in all the world into which Communist influence does not penetrate.
>
> John Foster Dulles, 1950

Threat of World Communism

Soviet Expansion In and After World War II

In 1940, while Germany was engaged in fighting France and Britain, the Soviets occupied and annexed the three Baltic States—Estonia, Latvia, and Lithuania. At the end of the war, Russia annexed eastern Poland and established a Communist government in the new Poland and in East Germany. Communist governments were also established in Czechoslovakia, Hungary, Romania, Bulgaria, Albania, and Yugoslavia.

Soviet efforts to overthrow the governments of Greece and Turkey were thwarted by American aid to these countries under the Truman Doctrine. In the Far East, the Soviets took from Japan the southern half of Sakhalin Island and the Kurile Islands. Communists dominated the northern half of Korea.

The Korean War

In 1950 North Korea attacked South Korea. In the ensuing Korean War, American and UN forces defeated Communist efforts to make all of Korea a Communist country. During the presidential campaign of 1952, Eisenhower promised to do all he could to bring the Korean War to an end. In a speech in October 1952, he said, "I shall go to Korea." After the election he kept his promise and in December 1952 went to Korea, where he conferred with American and UN leaders. Peace talks continued between negotiators for North and South Korea at Panmunjom, until finally an armistice agreement ending the war was signed on July 27, 1953. The boundary line between the two was set approximately where it had been before the war. A demilitarized zone was established between North and South Korea.

John Foster Dulles

> You have a row of dominoes set up, you knock over the first one, and
> what will happen to the last one is. . . that it will go over very quickly.
> Dwight D. Eisenhower, on the strategic importance of Indochina,
> in a press conference, April 7, 1954.

John Foster Dulles served as Secretary of State under Eisenhower from 1953 until Dulles died in 1959. During the Truman years, Dulles had contended that the Truman policy of **containment** of communism should be replaced by a policy of attempted liberation of Communist-controlled countries. As the architect of American foreign policy, Dulles adhered to the **domino theory** described in Eisenhower's statement, believing that if one nation in an area fell to communism, the rest, like a row of dominoes, would also fall to communism. This doctrine played an important role in the Vietnam War of the 1960s and 1970s.

Massive Retaliation

A Department of State bulletin issued by Secretary of State John Foster Dulles in January 1954 made two important changes in the nation's military policy. First, there was to be a cutback in the use of conventional military weapons. Second, there was to be greater reliance on atomic weapons. In 1952 the nation had successfully tested a new weapon, the **hydrogen** or **H-bomb**. This bomb had 500 times the destructive power of the A-bomb that had destroyed Hiroshima seven years before.

In the 1954 bulletin Dulles declared, "We want, for ourselves and the other free nations, a maximum deterrent at a bearable cost . . . Local defenses must be reinforced by the deterrent of massive retaliatory power." This came to be known as the policy of "**massive retaliation**" dependent on a preponderance of nuclear weaponry. Under this policy both the Soviet Union and the United States became involved in an arms race, each trying to build up a stockpile of nuclear weapons in order to show it could still destroy the other side, even if attacked first.

Brinkmanship

The Dulles conduct of relations with the Soviets came to be known as "brinkmanship." Dulles believed that the United States had to show the Communists it was willing to use force and to go to the brink of war in order to keep the peace. In an address in 1956, Dulles explained his policy in these words: "You have to take chances for peace just as you take chances in war . . . the ability to get to the verge without getting into the war is the necessary art. If you try to run away from it, if you are scared to go to the brink, you are lost."

The H-Bomb; Atoms for Peace

> The United States pledges... its determination to help solve the fearful atomic dilemma—to devote its entire heart and mind to find the way by which the miraculous inventiveness of man shall not be dedicated to his death, but consecrated to his life.
>
> Address by President Eisenhower
> to the United Nations General Assembly, December 8, 1953

The explosion of an H-bomb by the United States in 1952 was followed by the successful explosion of a similar bomb in 1953 by the Soviet Union. In his address, Eisenhower summarized the developments in atomic weaponry, predicted the spreading of these weapons of destruction to other nations, and urged that steps be taken to reverse the trend immediately. He offered to cooperate toward that end in implementing the UN resolution of November 1953. He proposed that ". . . this fissionable material would be used to serve the peaceful pursuits of mankind. Experts would be mobilized to apply atomic energy to the needs of agriculture, medicine, and other peaceful activities."

This atoms-for-peace proposal did not reverse the confrontational trend that was nourished by the cold-war atmosphere of suspicion and fear.

The Southeast Asia Treaty Organization (SEATO)

On September 8, 1954, a treaty negotiated by Secretary of State John Foster Dulles was signed in Manila. It had the same purpose and design for Southeast Asia as NATO did for the North Atlantic, namely, **collective security** measures against Communist aggression. The nations that signed the SEATO agreement were: Australia, France, New Zealand, Pakistan, the Republic of the Philippines, Great Britain, and the United States.

The SEATO agreement specified: "Each Party recognizes that aggression by means of armed attack against any of the Parties . . . would endanger its own peace and safety, and that it will in the event act to meet the common danger in accordance with its constitutional processes."

Aswan Dam and the Suez Canal

In 1956 a crisis developed over the Suez Canal. Egypt, led by **Gamal Abdel Nasser**, who had led a successful army coup against **King Farouk**, entered into an arms deal with the Soviets, who agreed to supply Egyptian armies for their military action against the new state of Israel on Egypt's eastern border. Afterwards, Nasser approached the United States for help in building a huge dam at **Aswan** on the Nile River for irrigation and flood control. The United States turned Nasser down because of Egypt's arms deal with the

Soviets. In response, Nasser seized the Suez Canal, which had been run by a joint Anglo-French company. He declared that the Canal was the property of Egypt and that revenues collected from its use would be applied to the building of the Aswan Dam. Great Britain and France were especially alarmed by Nasser's takeover of the canal, fearing it would interrupt the flow of oil from the Middle East to Europe.

On October 29, 1956, Israel attacked Egypt. Two days later, France and Britain joined Israel, and the three succeeded in gaining control of the Suez Canal. To avoid a military confrontation, both the United States and the Soviet Union supported Egypt and approved a UN resolution ordering a cease-fire and withdrawal from Egyptian territory. Troops of the three occupying powers were withdrawn and replaced by a United Nations peacekeeping force.

Polish and Hungarian Uprisings

In 1956, three years after Stalin's death, the new Soviet premier, **Nikita S. Khrushchev**, denounced Stalin as a tyrant who had committed grave crimes against his own people. This soon led to movements for more freedom in Poland and Hungary, two Communist-dominated Soviet satellite states. Polish workers rioted, demanding better working conditions. A new Polish Premier granted bargaining rights to labor. Khrushchev threatened to intervene but refrained when Poland continued its support of Soviet foreign policy.

In Hungary, the new premier, Imre Nagy, attempted to institute a democratic government and prepared to withdraw Hungary from the Warsaw Pact. An uprising in Hungary in 1956 was suppressed by Soviet troops. Hungary remained under Communist control.

The Eisenhower Doctrine—Intervention in Lebanon

Pressure from the United States resulted in the withdrawal of British, French, and Israeli troops from Egypt after the Suez Canal crisis. But the fear of Soviet infiltration and influence in the Middle East led President Eisenhower in 1957 to request authority from Congress to extend military and financial aid to any country in the Middle East threatened by Communist aggression. Congress responded in March 1957 with legislation that became known as the **Eisenhower Doctrine**. The doctrine applied specifically to "the general area of the Middle East" and authorized economic and military assistance, including the use of "armed force to assist any such nation or group of nations requesting assistance against armed aggression from any country controlled by international communism."

A crisis occurred in the spring of 1958 when Syria and Egypt attempted to overthrow the pro-Western government of Lebanon. When the President of Lebanon asked the United States for help, Eisenhower—in accordance with authority granted by Congress to implement the Eisenhower Doctrine—sent the Sixth Fleet into the Mediterranean and ordered 14,000 United States Marines to Lebanon. U.S. armed forces were withdrawn when Egypt and Syria agreed to refrain from intervention in Lebanon.

China Policy

When the **Nationalist** forces of **Chiang Kai-shek** fled from the mainland of China to the island of **Formosa** (**Taiwan**) in 1948, they also occupied the two offshore islands of Quemoy and Matsu. In the summer of 1958, the Chinese Communists began artillery fire against these islands, seemingly intending to occupy them by force. In a nationwide broadcast, Eisenhower warned that the United States would not "retreat in the face of armed aggression" and deployed the Seventh Fleet in the area as evidence of his determination. Meanwhile, Secretary Dulles flew to Formosa and prevailed on Chiang Kai-shek to give up his idea of invading mainland China. The shelling ceased, but in November the Chinese foreign minister issued this challenge: "The Americans must pull away their hand from the Taiwan Strait . . . We are determined to liberate Formosa and the offshore islands . . ." The issue remained unsettled, and in the 1960 election campaign, Kennedy and Nixon debated as to who would most effectively protect American interests in these islands off the coast of Communist China.

Summits and U-2s

In the fall of 1959, Premier **Nikita S. Khrushchev** of the Soviet Union toured the United States and had private talks with President Eisenhower at Camp David. Another summit meeting was planned to take place in Paris in May 1960. But on May 5, 1960, Khrushchev announced that the Russians had brought down an American **U-2 reconnaissance** (**spy**) **plane** four days earlier, 1,200 miles inside the Soviet Union. Two days later Khrushchev announced that the pilot, Francis Gary Powers, was alive and had confessed to spying. Powers was tried in the Soviet Union for espionage and was sentenced to ten years imprisonment but was released less than two years later.

A State Department bulletin of May 1960 stated that unarmed reconnaissance flights were common practice by many nations and admitted that the United States had been engaged in this activity over the Soviet Union for four years. The bulletin claimed that these flights would have been unnecessary if the Soviet Union had not rejected President Eisenhower's "open skies" proposal made in 1955.

In a subsequent statement, issued May 25, 1960, President Eisenhower declared that he had ordered that the U-2 reconnaissance flights be stopped. He refused Khrushchev's demand for a public apology, whereupon the Soviet leader canceled the summit conference scheduled for May.

Sputnik: The Space Missile Race

Experiments with rockets that could project missiles into outer space had been carried on long before World War II. In the last year of the war, the German army launched V-2 rockets, each carrying a ton of explosives, into cities in England, bringing death and destruction in their wake. There was no defense against this dreaded menace. After the war, Russia and the United States raced to perfect this new device, which would make it possible to send vehicles into orbit around the earth, reach out into space, and even land on the moon.

On October 4, 1957, the Russians launched the first successful earth satellite, which circled the earth and was called *Sputnik*, meaning "fellow traveler" (of the earth). A month later they launched *Sputnik II* with a dog on board to find out if an earth creature could live in space beyond the earth's atmosphere. It could!

The United States, stunned by the seeming superiority of Soviet science, quickly reacted to the challenge. The implications were ominous. Rocket-launched vehicles could soon carry the new H-bomb to pinpointed targets anywhere in the world. The first successful U.S. satellite, *Explorer I*, was launched in February 1958. Shortly thereafter, Congress passed the National Defense Education Act, appropriating $1 billion for science education. The defense budget for research, was increased by $4 billion, and the National Aeronautics and Space Administration (NASA) was established to carry out a program of space exploration and related defense applications.

Exercise Set 6.3

1. The Suez Crisis of 1956 was settled by
   A. the United States acting unilaterally
   B. Russia and the United States acting through the UN
   C. British and French voluntary withdrawal
   D. the defeat of Israeli military and naval forces

2. The belief in the 1950s and 1960s that the fall of one nation to communism would lead to the fall of neighboring nations was known as
   A. the domino theory
   B. massive retaliation
   C. brinkmanship
   D. economic nationalism

3. A scheduled 1959 summit meeting between Eisenhower and Khrushchev was canceled because of
   A. the Soviet testing of an H-bomb
   B. the U-2 incident
   C. U.S. intervention in suppressing uprisings in Poland and Hungary
   D. U.S. launching of *Explorer I*

4. The 1957 Eisenhower Doctrine empowered the president to extend economic and military aid to nations of
   A. Africa
   B. the Middle East
   C. Southeast Asia
   D. Central and Eastern Europe

5. The Dulles policy of "massive retaliation" was dependent on the use of
   A. nuclear weapons
   B. conventional forces
   C. joint action with our allies
   D. the overwhelming weight of public opinion

Exercise Set 6.4

1. In his farewell address, President Eisenhower warned against the growing power of the "military-industrial complex." He was referring to
   A. the arms race between the United States and the Soviet Union
   B. the confrontation between the members of NATO and the Warsaw Pact nations
   C. the alliance of the Pentagon and American arms manufacturers
   D. the growing power of the scientific community in American defense planning

2. Under President Eisenhower, social programs for health, education, and welfare were
   A. turned back from the federal government to state, local, and private control
   B. maintained but not expanded
   C. expanded by Congress at the request of the President
   D. passed by Congress over the President's veto

3. The Submerged Lands Act, advocated by President Eisenhower and signed into law by him in 1953, provided
   A. that control of the tideland (offshore) oil should pass to the states
   B. for joint exploitation of the tideland oil by state and federal agencies
   C. for sale of the offshore properties by the federal government to private interests
   D. that the potential oil resources be reserved to be available in case of national emergency

THE WARREN COURT AND CIVIL RIGHTS

It is the spirit and not the form of law that keeps justice alive.

Earl Warren, 1955

In 1953, President Eisenhower appointed **Earl Warren**, Republican three-term Governor of California, as Chief Justice of the United States. Warren held this high office until 1969. This 16-year period was to witness many changes, particularly in the area of civil rights.

Jackie Robinson

For a half century prior to World War II, professional baseball was completely segregated. No African American was signed by any major league club after 1884, though it was well known that there were many well-qualified players in the black leagues.

In 1947, the Brooklyn Dodgers took the first step by signing second baseman Jackie Robinson. It was not long before other African American players such as Roy Campanella, Willie Mays, Hank Aaron, Roberto Clemente from Puerto Rico, and many others were enriching the sport with their talents and underlining the all-American aspect of professional baseball.

Brown v. *Board of Education of Topeka* (1954)

In 1896, the Supreme Court, with only Justice **John Marshall Harlan** in dissent, ruled in the case of *Plessy* v. *Ferguson*, that segregation of the races was legal under the Fourteenth Amendment as long as the facilities provided the races were equal. This "separate but equal" doctrine was reversed by unanimous decision of the Warren Court in 1954 in the case of *Brown* v. *Board of Education of Topeka*. Writing for the Court, Chief Justice Warren said, "To separate them [African American children] from others of similar age and qualifications solely because of their race generates a feeling of inferiority as to their status in the community that may affect their hearts and minds in a way unlikely ever to be undone . . . . We conclude that in the field of public education the doctrine of 'separate but equal' has no place. Separate educational facilities are inherently unequal."

In a subsequent ruling on May 31, 1955 (*Brown* v. *Board of Education*), the Supreme Court instructed federal district courts to require local school authorities to move "with all deliberate speed" toward full compliance with this decision. But resistance to the Court's order was intense in the Southern states and in parts of the North as well. Delaware and the District of Columbia integrated their schools promptly. But a dozen years after the Brown decision thousands of public schools in the South still had 100 percent black student bodies.

Beginning of the Civil Rights Movement

Little Rock (1957): School Desegregation

An attempt was made at the beginning of the 1957 school year to integrate Little Rock's Central High School by enrolling nine African American students. Governor Orval Faubus, alleging that violence was about to erupt, sent units of the Arkansas National Guard to the school and ordered them to turn away the black students. When the guard was withdrawn on orders of a federal court, the black students entered the school through a back door, but a mob rushed the building and was barely restrained by the local police. Reporters and photographers on the scene were beaten.

   • *President Eisenhower Takes Action.* At this point, President Eisenhower decided to act. In an address to the nation on September 24, 1957, he declared; "In that city [Little Rock, Arkansas] under the leadership of demagogic extremists, disorderly mobs have deliberately prevented the carrying out of proper orders from a federal court. . . . the President's responsibility is inescapable. In accordance with that responsibility, I have today issued an Executive Order directing the use of troops under federal authority to aid in the execution of federal law at Little Rock, Arkansas."

Rosa Parks and the Montgomery Bus Boycott

On December 1, 1955, Rosa Parks, an African American seamstress in Montgomery, Alabama, boarded a crowded public bus on her way home from work. She sat down in a seat in the front part of the bus reserved for white passengers. The bus driver told her to give up her seat to a white passenger and move to the back of the bus. She refused to do so and was arrested for violating a Montgomery ordinance.

   At that time Dr. Martin Luther King, Jr., was a 26-year-old pastor in a Baptist church in Montgomery. The black community was outraged by the injustice of segregation and were ready to take violent action, but Dr. King urged **nonviolent resistance** and organized a **bus boycott**. Blacks refused to ride the buses of Montgomery until all riders were treated alike.

   The boycott went on for 381 days. Many walked long distances to and from work, while others organized car pools. A number of white people in Montgomery cooperated in the boycott, which attracted national attention. The Montgomery boycott achieved its purpose peaceably when the bus company gave up its practice of segregated seating.

Segregation in Interstate Transportation Unconstitutional

In *NAACP* v. *St. Louis-San Francisco Railway Company* (1955), the Interstate Commerce Commission ruled that segregation in interstate transportation was unconstitutional and ordered desegregation on all interstate transportation facilities.

Sit-ins, Civil Disobedience

The next step was to challenge local laws throughout the South requiring separate restaurants, lunch counters, or other public food and drink establishments for whites and blacks. This also included drinking fountains and restrooms, which were marked either "white" or "colored." The non-violent method used by blacks (aided by some whites) was the **sit-in**. A group entered a white restaurant or diner and sat down at the counter until they were served or forcibly removed. There were many arrests for violation of local ordinances. In May 1963 the Supreme Court ruled that the arrests were illegal because the segregation laws on which they were based were in violation of the Fourteenth Amendment's "privileges or immunities" clause.

First Civil Rights Legislation

In 1957, in a bipartisan effort supported by the Eisenhower administration, Congress passed the first **Civil Rights Act** since the Civil War. It addressed the key issue of **voting rights**, since blacks in the South were systematically disenfranchised by "literacy tests," poll taxes, and intimidation. The act created a Civil Rights Commission composed of members of both the Democratic and Republican parties and authorized the Justice Department to bring suits against persons interfering with anyone's right to vote.

When voting rights continued to be denied to blacks, a second and much stronger Civil Rights Act was passed in 1960. The act provided for the appointment of federal referees with power to issue voting certificates. It declared obstruction of voting rights by "threats or force" a federal crime. The number of black voters increased slowly but there was still a long way to go.

Exercise Set 6.5

1. In the landmark 1954 decision, *Brown* v. *Board of Education of Topeka*, the United States Supreme Court
   A. confirmed the earlier decision of *Plessy* v. *Ferguson*
   B. established the principle that "separate educational facilities are inherently unequal"
   C. ordered immediate integration of all public educational facilities
   D. divided 5 to 4 in favor of the plaintiffs

2. Implementation of the Supreme Court's school integration decision in Little Rock, Arkansas led to
   A. reluctant but prompt compliance by state authorities
   B. a subsequent reversal of the Court's decision
   C. an Executive Order by President Eisenhower directing the use of federal troops to enforce the Court's order
   D. disclosure of corruption in the local educational establishment

3. Throughout the year 1956, public attention in the nation was centered on Montgomery, Alabama, because
   A. the outcome of a nonviolent bus boycott could put an end to segregation on local public transportation facilities
   B. violence had erupted in connection with the bus boycott
   C. Rosa Parks had attempted to integrate the schools of Montgomery
   D. Dr. Martin Luther King, Jr., was a minister in Montgomery

4. The Warren Court is generally associated with
   A. a more liberal approach to the rights of minorities
   B. adherence to conservative principles of criminal justice
   C. split decisions representing divergent opinions of the justices on basic civil rights issues
   D. overwhelming public support of the Court's decisions

THE AFFLUENT SOCIETY

Postwar Consumption

Homes

The postwar economic boom, stimulated in part by the demand for housing, witnessed a vast building expansion, especially in the suburbs. The **Housing Act of 1955** provided for 45,000 new public housing units a year for four years. This obviously fell far short of the nation's needs.

By 1960, average real income in the United States had risen nearly 20 percent since the end of World War II, and 15 million new housing units had been constructed. By 1972, the Bureau of the Census reported that 45 million housing units (of a total of 70 million) were owned by their occupants.

Automobiles

The family car was a symbol of the affluent society. A few years after the end of World War II, when production of civilian goods had returned to high gear, 45 percent of American families owned an automobile. By 1970 it was 75 percent. The percentage increased to 80 in the next five years and, in addition, 30 percent of all American families now had at least two cars. Factory sales of passenger cars exceeded 8 million in 1985, with an additional 3.3 million trucks and buses. Over 255 million cars, trucks, and buses were registered in the United States in 2008.

Television

Television, with only a few thousand sets in use in the United States at the outbreak of World War II, became an important medium after the war. By 1960, nine of every ten American homes had television sets. A decade later TV had become the universal mass medium for communicating with the American public. People all over the world watched their TV screens in awe as the two American astronauts, Armstrong and Aldrin, walked on the moon in July 1969. As of 2010, the average American home had 2.93 TV sets per household.

Baby Boom

The post-World War II baby boom helped cause a marked increase in the population, which rose from 132 million in 1940 to 151 million in 1950. At the peak of the boom, the average number of children per family was 3.8. (It was below 2 in 1992.) The population boom continued in the 1950s with the total nearing 180 million by 1960. The number was swelled, in part, by the admission of 2.5 million refugees from war-torn regions. Although the boom slowed down during the 1960s and came to a halt in 1972, the population of the United States continues to increase. It was 226 million in 1980, 249 million in 1990, and 308,745,538 in 2010.

Year	Population	Year	Population	Year	Population
2010	308,746	1930	123,202	1860	31,443
1990	248,709	1920	106,021	1850	23,191
1980	226,545	1910	92,228	1840	17,069
1970	203,302	1900	76,212	1830	12,866
1960	179,323	1890	62,979	1820	9,638
1950	151,325	1880	50,198	1810	7,239
1940	132,164	1870	38,558	1800	5,308

Figure 6.3   U.S. Population (in thousands)

Migration and Immigration

Americans on the Move

About 3 percent of the population moves annually from one state to another. Special circumstances affect migration. For example, the figure was much higher during the Great Depression of the 1930s when people lost their jobs, their farms, and their savings, and many pulled up roots and went West looking for a new life.

The war years of the 1940s were another era of large-scale migration. This time the move tended to be from South to North and from rural to urban areas where there were better economic opportunities in the new war industries. An estimated 15 million people, or more than 10 percent of the population, were involved in this migration. Another 15 million or more in the military were moved from place to place before going overseas.

The momentum of westward migration was accelerated after World War II. The population of Arizona was half a million in 1940. By 1990 it was more than 7 times as great at 3.6 million. California grew from 7 million to 29 million in the same period. By 1964, California had surpassed New York as the most populous state in the nation, and in 2010 had 37,691,912 people. In the 1960s the previous migration trend (chiefly blacks) from South to North was sharply reversed by the new trend (chiefly whites) from North to South. The population of Houston, now the fourth largest city in the United States, leaped from half a million to 1.75 million since 1950. Dallas, the eighth largest city, more than doubled in population (434,000 to over 1 million) in the same period, and San Antonio went from 408,000 to 900,000. The "sunbelt" states of the South and Southwest became the fastest growing section of the country.

Suburbanization

A major postwar trend was the exodus of the middle class from the cities to the suburbs. Long Island, New York, long famous for its potato farms, was suddenly transformed into a strip of bedroom communities reaching eastward 100 miles from Manhattan.

The ingenious builder, William J. Levitt, secured large tracts of land, laid out plans approved by local authorities, and rapidly constructed thousands of reasonably priced homes on small plots of land. **Levittowns** sprang up within commuting distance of New York and Philadelphia. Other builders soon adopted this pattern to meet the almost insatiable appetite of migrants from the cities. When President Eisenhower delivered his farewell address in January 1961, the population of the suburbs already exceeded that of the cities.

New Immigration Patterns

The pattern of immigration (legal and illegal) has been changing. The new immigration stems from Mexico and other lands south of the border, from the Caribbean, and from Asia.

In an attempt to solve the problem of the vast number of immigrants who entered the United States illegally and had to remain "underground," the Immigration and Naturalization Service, as provided in the Immigration and Control Act of 1986, offered amnesty to those who could prove they had resided in the United States since January 1, 1982. By the deadline date of May 4, 1988, the Service had received applications for amnesty from 1.4 million illegal immigrants, 71 percent of whom had entered from Mexico and more than half of whom were living in California.

Immigration to the United States is limited to 270,000 annually, but additional provision is made under the **Refugee Act of 1980** for the admission of persons for humanitarian reasons who would be subjected to political persecution if they were returned to their country of last residence.

During the decade 1970–1980 a total of 1,588,200 immigrants were admitted from Asia, chiefly from the Philippines, Korea, and India. During the same period, nearly 2 million were admitted from countries south of the border—600,000 from Mexico, 271,000 from the West Indies, 265,000 from Cuba, and 170,000 from Colombia. In the 1980s the numbers increased.

Some 2 million were admitted from Asia by the end of 1990, and about 3.5 million from Latin America. The **Secure Fence Act** was passed in 2006 in an attempt to reduce illegal immigration across the Mexican border.

Exercise Set 6.6

1. During the decade following World War II, the United States experienced
   A. a recession similar to the one that followed World War I
   B. an economic boom stimulated in part by a vast building expansion
   C. a slow but steady rise in income keeping pace with inflation
   D. rapid fluctuations in stock and bond prices

2. In the post-World War II period, transportation trends were characterized by
   A. expansion in the use of canals, lakes, and rivers for moving heavy freight
   B. a rapid development of the railroads
   C. a leveling off of international air traffic
   D. the extensive use of the family car

3. In the affluent American society of the post-World War II period
   A. unemployment was virtually abolished
   B. television had become a standard source of entertainment and information in 90 percent of homes
   C. labor strife was a relatively rare occurrence
   D. the national budget showed a surplus in most years

4. Which has *not* been responsible for major migrations within the United States?
   A. loss of economic security brought on by the Great Depression
   B. dislocations resulting from World War II
   C. attraction of the wide open spaces of the Great Plains
   D. a movement to the so-called Sun Belt

5. A major cause of the movement to the suburbs in the decades following World War II was
   A. the growth of the middle class during the post-World War II period
   B. greater economic opportunities found in the suburbs
   C. the availability of comfortable and efficient railroad transportation from suburban to urban centers
   D. opportunities for minorities to find jobs and homes in the suburbs

1. In the case of *Brown* v. *Board of Education* (1954), the United States Supreme Court decided that
   A. busing children to overcome segregation is unconstitutional
   B. closing public schools to avoid integration is unconstitutional
   C. separate educational facilities are inherently unequal and unconstitutional
   D. the use of civil disobedience to achieve legal rights is constitutional

2. The development and operation of the Tennessee Valley Authority by the U.S. government is an example of
   A. a return to laissez-faire economics
   B. government's attempt to earn maximum profits in business
   C. experimentation with nuclear technology
   D. federal intervention to meet regional needs

3. An experience of the majority of immigrants to the United States was that they
   A. settled in rural areas where cheap land was available
   B. frequently met resentment
   C. joined radical political parties to bring about economic reform
   D. were rapidly assimilated into the predominant lifestyle

4. Which is a major difference between immigration to the United States during the period 1860–1920 and immigration since 1970?
   A. immigrants today are not likely to experience discrimination
   B. there is a greater need for unskilled labor today
   C. the primary areas of origin have changed dramatically
   D. today's immigrants tend to be members of the middle class

5. "A just society is one that treats fairly the most disadvantaged members of its society." Which government action would best illustrate this principle?
   A. creating "separate but equal" schools for minority groups
   B. shifting governmental funds from public schools to private schools
   C. establishing programs to train unskilled workers
   D. passing legislation making ownership of property a requirement for voting

ESSAYS

1. Many aspects of U.S. society have been greatly affected by technological changes. Choose *three* of the aspects of U.S. society listed below. Explain how *each* one chosen has been affected by a specific technological development. [Use a different development for each aspect.]

   Aspects of U.S. Society
   Urbanization
   Agriculture
   Cultural homogeneity
   Rights of the individual
   Politics
   Environment

2. American foreign policy has often been influenced by events or developments abroad. Following are terms used to describe foreign policies adopted by the United States:

   - the Truman doctrine
   - massive retaliation
   - the Eisenhower doctrine
   - collective security
   - joint action with the UN

   Choose *three* of the above policies adopted by the United States. For *each* policy chosen describe the events or developments that led to the policy and discuss the application of the policy in a specific international crisis.

THEMATIC ESSAY

Directions: Write a well-organized essay that includes an introduction, several paragraphs addressing the task below, and a conclusion.

Theme: Environment

> The second half of the 20th century has proven to be a time of growing environmental concerns.

Task:

> From your study of environmental concerns of the second half of the 20th century in the United States, identify *three* threats to the delicate environmental balance of the planet.
>
> For each environmental threat:
>
> - Identify the cause of the threat to the environment.
> - Discuss the dangers the problem poses to the environment.
> - Describe an action, either national or international, that has been taken to address the environmental problem.

You may use any dangers to the environment that have become an issue during the second half of the 20th century. Some suggestions you may wish to consider are depletion of the planet's ozone layer and resulting global warming (greenhouse effect), deforestation and increased release of carbon dioxide into the atmosphere, acid rain, water pollution, waste disposal (including nuclear), and air pollution.

You are *not* limited to these suggestions.

DOCUMENT-BASED QUESTION ESSAY

The following questions (Part A and Part B) are based on the accompanying documents (1–6). Some of these documents have been edited for the purpose of this exercise. The question is designed to test your ability to work with historical documents and to demonstrate your knowledge of the subject matter being presented. As you analyze the documents, take into account both the source of the document and the author's point of view.

Historical Context: The momentous school desegregation decision in 1954 started the Earl Warren Supreme Court (1953–1969) on a path that would undertake sweeping reforms in numerous areas. Many saw the Supreme Court's actions during the term of Chief Justice Earl Warren as encroachments on rights reserved to the States and to the People.

Task: Using information from the documents and your knowledge of United States history, answer the questions that follow each document in Part A. Your answers to the questions will help you write the Part B essay, in which you will be asked:

> The momentous school desegregation decision in 1954 by the Earl Warren Supreme Court (1953–1969) raised the debate concerning state versus federal powers. Was the Supreme Court's decision in *Brown* v. *Board of Education* (1954) an infringement upon state's rights, or was it the correct interpretation of the provisions of the Fourteenth Amendment?

Part A
Short Answer

The documents below refer to the era of the Warren Supreme Court. Examine each document carefully and then answer the questions that follow.

DOCUMENT 1

> We come then to the question presented: Does segregation of children in public schools solely on the basis of race, even though the physical facilities and other "tangible" factors may be equal, deprive the children of the minority group of equal educational opportunities? We believe that it does....
>
> Separate educational facilities are inherently unequal....

—Brown v. *Board of Education* (1954)

1. According to the Supreme Court in the *Brown* decision, what was making the education facilities (schools) not equal?

_____

_____

_____

_____

2. What type of educational facilities are being discussed in the decision?

_____

_____

_____

_____

DOCUMENT 2

Southern opposition to the Supreme Court's decision in the *Brown v. Board of Education* case was expressed in March, 1956 when 19 Southern Senators and 77 Southern Congressman expressed their concerns in a statement known as the "Southern Manifesto."

We regard the decision of the Supreme Court in the public school cases as a clear abuse of judicial power. It climaxes a trend of the Federal Judiciary undertaking to legislate, in derogation of the authority of Congress, and to encroach upon the reserved rights of the states.
    The original Constitution does not mention education. Neither does the 14th Amendment nor any other amendment....

—*Southern Manifesto* (March 1956)

3. What argument regarding the division of powers between the federal government and state governments (federalism) is being made in the "Southern Manifesto?"

_____

_____

_____

_____

DOCUMENT 3

> I have a dream that one day this nation will rise up and live out the true meaning of its creed: "We hold these truths to be self-evident; that all men are created equal."

—"I Have a Dream" speech, Dr. Martin Luther King, Jr.,
Washington, D.C. (1963)

4. What American document is Dr. King quoting in the segment of the "I Have a Dream" speech?

_____

_____

_____

DOCUMENT 4

> Then-Republican Presidential prospect Marion G. (Pat) Robertson was interviewed by the *Washington Post* on the subject of the Supreme Court and judicial review.
>
> A Supreme Court ruling is not the law of the land. The law of the United States is the Constitution, treaties made in accordance with the Constitution and laws duly enacted by the Congress and signed by the President....
> I am bound by the laws of the United States and all 50 states....I am not bound by any case or any court to which I myself am not a party....
> I am concerned, as I think millions of others are, when those justices (Supreme Court) say "the Constitution is what we say it is."

—Marion G. (Pat) Robertson, *The Washington Post* (June 27, 1986)

5. Having read candidate Robertson's response regarding the limited jurisdictional power of a Supreme Court decision, create a possible argument supporting the position that the holding in *Brown* v. *Board of Education* did not have to be applied to the individual states.

_____

_____

_____

DOCUMENT 5

In each of the cases, minors of the Negro race, through their legal representatives, seek the aid of the courts in obtaining admission to the public schools of their community on a nonsegregated basis. In each instance, they had been denied admission to schools attended by white children under laws requiring or permitting segregation according to race. This segregation was alleged to deprive the plaintiffs of the equal protection of the laws under the Fourteenth Amendment.

—Brown v. *Board of Education* (1954)

6. What specific provision of the Fourteenth Amendment was being quoted by the Supreme Court in the *Brown* decision in support of their decision that public schools segregated on the basis of race was unconstitutional?

_____

_____

_____

_____

DOCUMENT 6

The constitutional status of racial classification had been addressed in the case of *Plessy* v. *Ferguson* in 1896. The following is a segment of the Court's decision.

The statute of Louisiana, acts of 1890, c. 111, requiring railway companies carrying passengers in their coaches in that State, to provide equal, but separate, accommodations for the white and colored races.... .are not in conflict with the provisions either of the Thirteenth Amendment or of the Fourteenth Amendment to the Constitution of the United States.

—Plessy v. *Ferguson* (1896)

7. How did the Supreme Court's decision in the *Plessy* case in 1896 differ from the later decision in *Brown* v. *Board of Education* in 1954?

_____

_____

_____

_____

443

Part B
Essay

Your essay should be well organized with an introductory paragraph that states your position on the question. Develop your position in the next paragraphs and then write a conclusion. In your essay, include specific historical details and refer to the specific documents you analyzed in Part A. You may include additional information from your knowledge of social studies.

Historical Context: The momentous school desegregation decision in 1954 started the Earl Warren Supreme Court (1953–1969) on a path that would undertake sweeping reforms in numerous areas. Many saw the Supreme Court's actions during the term of Chief Justice Earl Warren as encroachments on rights reserved to the States and to the People.

Task:

> The momentous school desegregation decision in 1954 by the Earl Warren Supreme Court (1953–1969) raised the debate concerning state versus federal powers. Using the documents provided and your knowledge of United States history, answer the following question: Was the Supreme Court's decision in *Brown* v. *Board of Education* (1954) an infringement upon state's rights, or was it a correct interpretation of the provisions of the Fourteenth Amendment?

Guidelines:

In your essay, be sure to
• Develop all aspects of the task
• Incorporate information from at least *five* documents
• Incorporate relevant outside information
• Support the theme with many relevant facts, examples, and details
• Use a logical and clear plan of organization, including an introduction and a conclusion that are beyond a restatement of the theme

CHAPTER 3

DECADE OF CHANGE (THE 1960s)

THE KENNEDY YEARS: THE NEW FRONTIER

> We stand today on the edge of a New Frontier—the frontier of the
> 1960s—a frontier of unknown opportunities and perils—a frontier of
> unfulfilled hopes and threats.
>
> > John F. Kennedy accepting nomination for President
> > at Democratic National Convention, 1960

The 1960 Election

The election of 1960 pitted **John F. Kennedy**, Senator from Massachusetts, against **Richard M. Nixon**, Vice President. In this election, television
played a key role for the first time. The two candidates faced the nation in
four one-hour televised debates. An estimated 70 million Americans viewed
each debate. Kennedy, at 43, was the youngest candidate ever elected to the
presidency. In addition, he was a Roman Catholic, and no one of his religion
had ever been President. Kennedy faced the religious question head-on when
he said, "I believe in an America where the separation of church and state
is absolute . . ."

The 1960 election was one of the closest in American history. Of the total
votes cast—68.8 million—Kennedy's margin over Nixon was 119,450 votes
or 3/10ths of 1 percent. In the electoral college, Kennedy received 303 votes
to 219 for Nixon.

Domestic Policies and Programs

> Let the word go forth from this time and place, to friend and foe alike,
> that the torch has been passed to a new generation of Americans—
> born in this century, tempered by war, disciplined by a hard and bit-
> ter peace, proud of our ancient heritage, and unwilling to witness or
> permit the slow undoing of those human rights to which this Nation
> has always been committed . . .
>
> And so, my fellow Americans—ask not what your country can do for
> you—ask what you can do for your country.
>
> > John F. Kennedy, Inaugural Address, January 20, 1961

Domestic Gains

Kennedy did secure from Congress approval of a number of social programs—the minimum wage was raised, Social Security benefits were extended, unemployment compensation was increased, additional funds were appropriated for housing, mental health, and public works, and a Federal Water Pollution Control Act was approved. The President responded to an increase in steel prices by calling the steel magnates to his office and forcing them to rescind the price increases. He initiated a multi-billion-dollar program to put a man on the moon, which eventually bore fruit in July 1969.

Kennedy and Civil Rights

Appointments

Kennedy appointed members of the black community to key positions in the federal government. His appointment of **Thurgood Marshall** to the U.S. Circuit Court of Appeals later led to the elevation of Marshall to the Supreme Court by President Johnson in 1967. Marshall had been general counsel of the National Association for the Advancement of Colored People (NAACP) when he argued the case of *Brown* v. *Board of Education of Topeka* before the Supreme Court in 1954. Kennedy also appointed a number of African Americans to the federal bench as U.S. district court judges.

Attorney General Robert F. Kennedy

President Kennedy appointed his brother, Robert F. Kennedy, to the sensitive post of Attorney General in a time of turmoil over civil rights and other constitutional issues. "Bobby" Kennedy proved to be a firm advocate of civil rights. While he held office, the Justice Department brought over 50 suits to secure voting rights for African Americans in states where they were virtually disenfranchised. The suits were brought under the Civil Rights Act of 1960, which empowered the federal courts to appoint referees to investigate claims that citizens' voting rights had been violated by state voting regulations. The act authorized federal courts to levy heavy penalties on anyone who infringed on the civil rights of others.

James H. Meredith

In the fall of 1962 James H. Meredith, an African American Air Force veteran of the Korean War, attempted to enroll in the all-white University of Mississippi in his home state. The governor of the state took charge of the university and ordered that Meredith, who had met all necessary qualifications, be denied admission because he was black. When federal marshals escorted him to the university, a white mob touched off violence in which two people were killed and many were seriously injured. President Kennedy dispatched 5,000 federal troops to Mississippi and Meredith was registered in the university.

Medgar Evers

On June 11, 1963, President Kennedy, who was trying to get Congress to pass stronger civil rights legislation, delivered a stirring appeal to the nation on television. He asked his audience, "Are we to say . . . that this is a land of the free except for Negroes . . . that we have no class or caste system, no ghettos, no master race, except with respect to Negroes?"

That night, Medgar Evers, head of the NAACP of Mississippi, and a war veteran, was murdered outside his home by a white racist. Despite President Kennedy's efforts, stronger civil rights legislation had to wait until the administration of Lyndon Johnson.

Martin Luther King, Jr.

> I have a dream that one day on the red hills of Georgia the sons of former slaves and the sons of former slave owners will be able to sit down together at the table of brotherhood. . .
>
> I have a dream that my four little children will one day live in a nation where they will not be judged by the color of their skin but by the content of their character.

Martin Luther King, Jr.
at the Lincoln Memorial on the occasion of the Civil Rights March
in Washington, D.C., August 28, 1963.

Rise to Leadership

Martin Luther King, Jr., was born in Atlanta, Georgia, January 15, 1929, and died in Memphis, Tennessee, April 4, 1968, the victim of an assassin's bullet. Like his father and his maternal grandfather, he was a Baptist minister in Alabama.

King's rise to leadership in the civil rights movement began when he led the bus boycott in Montgomery, which began on December 1, 1955. Although he was arrested in January 1956 and his parsonage was bombed, his leadership succeeded in integrating Montgomery's buses. In February 1957, he became president of a new

Dr. Martin Luther King, Jr., (1929–1968) led the civil rights movement in the 1950s and 1960s.

antisegregation organization known as the **Southern Christian Leadership Conference** (**SCLC**). The organization sponsored nonviolent sit-ins at lunch counters and other nonviolent protests.

Birmingham Protest

Like Gandhi in India, King preached that racism and social injustice should be fought by disobedience but not by violence. King urged **civil disobedience** of Birmingham's segregation laws as a means of bringing injustice out where all could see it. He and his followers persisted despite violence against them instigated by Birmingham's police commissioner. King was arrested and put in solitary confinement in the jail, where he wrote his famous "Letter from a Birmingham Jail," giving the rationale for nonviolent disobedience to unjust laws.

March on Washington and Later Activities

In 1963 King led the famous march on Washington where, on August 28, he delivered the classic "I Have a Dream" speech. He continued to campaign for civil rights and for equal treatment of African Americans. In 1964 he was awarded the **Nobel Prize** for peace. In 1966 he led a campaign for slum clearance in Chicago. In 1968 he was in Memphis helping to coordinate a strike of sanitation workers. He was making plans to lead a Poor People's Crusade on Washington and had taken a public stand against the Vietnam War. King's life was cut short in Memphis on April 4, 1968, by a bullet that struck him in the head as he stood on the balcony of his hotel room. He received recognition as one of America's great leaders when his birthday was designated a national holiday by an act of Congress in 1983.

Exercise Set 6.7

1. Which would be most in accord with the ideals of Dr. Martin Luther King, Jr.?
   A. underpaid workers sabotage the machinery at their factory
   B. a minority worker assaults a bigot
   C. an 18-year-old pacifist accepts a jail term rather than register for military service
   D. radical leaders advocate black separatism if their group's demands are not met

2. "Under a government which imprisons any unjustly, the true place for a just man is also a prison."

   Henry David Thoreau

   Which idea does this quotation most strongly support?
   A. social control
   B. conformity
   C. suspension of civil liberties
   D. civil disobedience

3. President Kennedy's inability to secure passage of many of his legislative recommendations was due to
   A. a combination of Republicans and Conservative Democrats
   B. a lack of legislative experience on the part of the President
   C. distractions of foreign problems
   D. a Republican majority in one or both houses of Congress

4. President Kennedy made use of federal troops to force the racial integration of
   A. public schools in Little Rock, Arkansas
   B. the University of Mississippi
   C. the lunch counters of Greensboro, North Carolina
   D. the Montgomery, Alabama bus companies

ACTION IN FOREIGN POLICIES

Latin American Policies

Review of Earlier Policies

> The American continents are henceforth not to be considered as subjects for future colonization by any European Power. We should consider any attempt on their part to extend their system to any portion of this Hemisphere as dangerous to our peace and safety.
>
> President James Monroe, 1823

The principles established by the Monroe Doctrine became basic to American foreign policy and were followed throughout the 1800s. Concern in the United States over the ruthless conduct of the Spanish government against internal Cuban opposition came to a head in 1898 when the U.S. battleship *Maine* was blown up in Havana harbor and the United States declared war against Spain.

The years between the Spanish-American War and the New Deal era beginning in 1933 have been described as a period of "**dollar diplomacy**" in American foreign policy. American business invested heavily in economic exploitation of resources in Latin America. When the safety of these investments was threatened by local violence, the American response generally was to send in detachments of U.S. Marines "to restore order" and protect the investments. Under this policy during the 35-year period after the Spanish-American War, troops were deployed at various times in Cuba, Haiti, the Dominican Republic, Nicaragua, Honduras, and Panama.

In 1933 President Franklin D. Roosevelt changed American policy toward Latin America and declared, "I would dedicate this nation to the policy of the good neighbor." With the outbreak of World War II, the republics of the Western Hemisphere held an Inter-American Conference in 1939 and issued the Declaration of Panama, warning the combatants to keep armed vessels clear of a 300-mile zone surrounding the United States and Latin America.

The Bay of Pigs

Shortly after President Kennedy took office, he was informed that under the previous (Eisenhower) administration the **Central Intelligence Agency (CIA)** had been training, arming, and financing thousands of Cuban refugees in Florida and Guatemala for an attempt to overthrow the anti-American Castro dictatorship in Cuba. Kennedy met with his advisers and reluctantly agreed to let the plans go forward on condition that no U.S. military or naval forces be used in the invasion of Cuba. He was assured that the anti-Castro Cubans could accomplish the task on their own, with strong internal support.

On the morning of April 17, 1961, about 1,400 Cuban exiles who had embarked from Florida and Guatemala landed at the **Bay of Pigs** on the southern coast of Cuba. They were met by a force of some 14,000 well-armed defenders who, in three days of fighting, killed or captured almost all of the anti-Castro invaders. With the invasion a total failure, President Kennedy admitted that it was a mistake and accepted full responsibility for the outcome.

The Cuban Missile Crisis

Following the Bay of Pigs fiasco, **Fidel Castro** invited the Soviets to install intermediate-range ballistic missiles on Cuban soil. Installation of these missiles was under way when they were discovered by a **U-2 plane** taking photographs from high altitude on October 14, 1962. Careful analysis of the photographs revealed that launching pads were being installed and that nuclear warheads would soon be capable of striking as far north as Hudson Bay in Canada and as far south as Lima, Peru.

Kennedy convened top advisers from the Defense and State Departments, the CIA, the Cabinet, and his personal staff. They met daily and considered all possible responses for turning back this grave threat. Two possible courses emerged—a lightning air strike to destroy the installations, or a **blockade** to prevent offensive weapons from being delivered to Cuba. The latter course was agreed upon. The gravity of the crisis was clearly understood. "The worst course of all," said the President, "would be for us to do nothing." In a television address to the nation on Monday evening, October 22, he explained the threat contained in the installations and said, "A strict quarantine of all offensive military equipment under shipment to Cuba is being initiated . . . Let no one doubt that this is a difficult and dangerous effort on which we have set out."

Meanwhile, contact with the Soviets was maintained and every effort was made to enable Khrushchev to retreat gracefully without loss of face. Kennedy accepted Khrushchev's offer to remove the missiles in return for his public promise not to invade Cuba. Kennedy also agreed privately to withdraw American missiles from Turkey. Soviet ships bound for Cuba turned back and the tension was relieved. The missiles were subsequently removed and the launching pads dismantled under the eyes of UN observers. The Cuban missile crisis was resolved.

The Vienna Summit (Berlin Wall)

On January 6, 1961, two weeks before Kennedy's inauguration, Soviet Premier Nikita Khrushchev made a threatening speech about the city of Berlin. Located in East Germany, the city was divided into East Berlin, the Communist part, and West Berlin, the free part. Khrushchev threatened to end free access by the Western nations to West Berlin.

Khrushchev invited Kennedy to meet with him for a friendly talk in Vienna in June 1961. Khrushchev again threatened to close off West Berlin. Kennedy responded that our national security was involved in Berlin and that our abandoning it would mean abandoning our commitments not only to our allies but to all of Europe. Afterward, Kennedy made plans to defend Berlin, and he increased the military budget and the size of the armed forces.

In mid-August the Communists sealed off West Berlin by erecting the **Berlin Wall**, a wall of concrete and barbed wire between the two sectors. But access to Berlin from the West was not cut off and the crisis subsided.

In June 1963 Kennedy visited West Berlin and made the memorable statement: "All free men, wherever they may live, are citizens of Berlin, and therefore, as a free man, I take pride in the words 'Ich bin ein Berliner.' "

In November 1989 tremendous changes took place in East Germany as a result of demands and demonstrations by the people. The Berlin Wall was opened and East Germans were allowed to travel freely to West Berlin and all of West Germany for the first time in 28 years. In 1990 East and West Germany were reunited to form one nation.

The Peace Corps

In 1961, President Kennedy recommended to Congress the establishment of a permanent Peace Corps, which he had set in motion on an experimental basis by executive order. He described the Peace Corps as "an organization which will recruit and train American volunteers, sending them abroad to work with the people of other nations." Peace Corps members could help the people in the developing nations with their day-to-day problems. They could teach English in primary and secondary schools, help establish and operate public health and sanitation projects, aid in village development, and increase agricultural productivity by assisting local farmers to use modern implements and techniques.

The Peace Corps was approved by Congress on September 22, 1961 with an appropriation of $40 million. **Sargent Shriver**, who had proposed the idea, was appointed first director of the Peace Corps. At home, the Peace Corps was received with enthusiasm, and abroad, in the emerging nations of Asia, Africa and Latin America, it helped to replace the negative image of the "Ugly American" with one of American idealism and altruism.

452

The Race to the Moon

In April 1961 the Soviet astronaut **Yuri Gagarin** became the first human to orbit the earth. A month later, President Kennedy declared, "This nation should commit itself to achieving the goal, before this decade is out, of landing a man on the moon and returning him safely to earth." There was an immediate enthusiastic response from the nation and from Congress, and a $25 billion program was launched.

The Nuclear Test Ban Treaty

In August 1961, after the Berlin Wall was built, Khrushchev announced that the Soviet Union would again begin nuclear testing, in violation of a 1958 agreement between the United States, Great Britain, and the Soviet Union to suspend tests for three years. The Soviets began tests in the fall of 1961 and after they refused a test ban treaty, the United States agreed to set up a "hot line" telephone between Washington and Moscow, to be installed August 30, 1963. President Kennedy said the purpose of the line was "to avoid on each side the dangerous delays, misunderstandings, and misreadings of the other's actions which might occur at a time of crisis."

Finally, three-power talks between the United States, Great Britain, and the Soviet Union began in Moscow in July 1963. A treaty banning nuclear tests in the atmosphere, in outer space, and under water (but not under ground) was concluded on July 25. It was signed by the three powers in Moscow on August 5 and was ratified by the U.S. Senate on September 24. Two weeks later, President Kennedy approved the sale of $250 million of wheat to the Soviet Union. The nuclear test ban treaty was soon signed by more than 100 nations.

Assassination in Dallas

In November 1963 President Kennedy traveled to Texas to help heal a rift in the state Democratic party. On Friday, November 22, 1963, during the visit, President Kennedy was riding in an open car, sitting next to Governor **John B. Connally** of Texas, in a motorcade along the main street of Dallas, Texas. Suddenly he was hit in the head and neck by two rifle bullets. Governor Connally was wounded but recovered. The President died within an hour. The shots that killed the President were fired from a building adjoining the route of the motorcade. The suspected killer, **Lee Harvey Oswald**, was apprehended an hour and a half later.

Lyndon B. Johnson Sworn in as President

Vice President Lyndon B. Johnson, who was also riding in the motorcade, was unharmed. He was sworn in as President on a plane returning that day to Washington. Two days after the assassination, Oswald was being moved by police from the city jail to a more secure county jail when he was shot and killed by **Jack Ruby**, a Dallas night club operator.

The Warren Commission

President Johnson appointed a special commission to investigate the assassination of President Kennedy. The Commission was headed by **Earl Warren**, Chief Justice of the United States, and included leaders in the Senate and House of Representatives. The Commission conducted an exhaustive inquiry and presented its report on September 24, 1964. The report concluded that there was no conspiracy to assassinate the President and that "the shots which killed President Kennedy and wounded Governor Connally were fired by Lee Harvey Oswald." Warren asserted that "no one has produced any facts that are contrary to the commission's conclusion." But allegations continue to be made that the evidence is inconclusive and that there may have been a conspiracy to assassinate the President.

1. The most serious crisis in foreign affairs under Kennedy before the mid-term elections in 1962 was
   A. in Berlin
   B. in Cuba
   C. in Vietnam
   D. with Britain

2. In space exploration the idea of placing astronauts on the moon and bringing them back safely to earth was
   A. first undertaken by the Soviet Union
   B. at first rejected by the National Aeronautic and Space Administration
   C. considered too costly by Congress
   D. advocated by President Kennedy within a few months after his inauguration

3. Most consider which of the following to be a foreign policy failure of President Kennedy?
   A. the Bay of Pigs affair
   B. controversy over Berlin
   C. the Cuban missile crisis
   D. Peace Corps operations

4. The Warren Commission concluded that the assassination of President Kennedy
   A. had been planned for 1,000 days
   B. was planned and executed by conspirators
   C. was accomplished by Lee Harvey Oswald
   D. had no precedent in American history

5. The nuclear test ban treaty of 1963 was
   A. rejected by the U.S. Senate
   B. negotiated by representatives of more than 100 nations
   C. designed to prohibit testing of nuclear weapons in the atmosphere, in outer space, and under water, but not underground
   D. approved at a time when the United States and the Soviet Union were engaged in frantic testing of nuclear weapons

JOHNSON AND THE GREAT SOCIETY

> This nation, this generation, in this hour has man's first chance
> to build a Great Society, a place where the meaning of man's life
> matches the marvels of man's labors.
>
> Lyndon B. Johnson,
> Democratic National Convention, August 1964

Expanding the Kennedy Social Programs

Soon after he was sworn in as President on the day of Kennedy's assassination, November 22, 1963, **Lyndon B. Johnson** moved to implement and expand Kennedy's program of domestic civil rights and social legislation.

The War on Poverty

President Johnson prevailed on Congress to give him the key measure in his war on poverty, the billion-dollar Economic Opportunity Act (1964) creating the Office of Economic Opportunity (OEO). The act set up job- and work-training programs and provided for loans to college students and to small businesses for hiring the unemployed. The appropriation was doubled the following year with appropriations for rehabilitation in poverty-stricken Appalachia and for granting aid directly to needy elementary and secondary school students in public and nonpublic schools.

One agency in OEO was called Volunteers in Service to America (VISTA). It was organized in 1965 as the domestic counterpart to the Peace Corps. Volunteers receive training in working with children, the elderly, Native Americans, agricultural migrant workers, and the mentally ill. VISTA operated chiefly in pockets of poverty in rural areas.

Other programs of OEO included **Operation Head Start** for aid to preschoolers from underprivileged homes, a **Job Corps** for school dropouts, a **Neighborhood Youth Corps** for unemployed teenagers, and a Community Action Program whereby inner-city neighborhoods get financial aid for planning and executing programs of self-help.

Congress approved a rent-supplement program for poor families and established a **Department of Housing and Urban Development (HUD)** with Cabinet rank. The appointment of Robert C. Weaver as head of HUD made him the first Cabinet member from the African American Community.

Medicare and Medicaid

The Health Insurance Act for the Aged, passed in 1965 as an amendment to the Social Security Act, provided federally funded hospital insurance for people over 65. It also included limited nursing home care and home visits by nurses and health care workers other than physicians. Those covered by

Social Security could also secure medical care other than hospitalization by paying a small monthly fee. These fees were sharply increased during the 1980s. The plan called **Medicare** (for seniors) was accompanied by a plan called **Medicaid** for the needy of all ages. It required the states to administer financially aided programs of care for people below the poverty level as well as for needy families with dependent children, the blind, and the totally disabled.

Aid to Education

In a speech at the University of Michigan in May 1964, President Johnson declared, "The Great Society is a place where every child can find knowledge to enrich his mind and to enlarge his talents." This precept was advanced by the **Elementary and Secondary Education Act of 1965**. The act provided federal aid in the amount of $1.3 billion directly to pupils in school districts. To promote school integration as required by law the U.S. Office of Education now required proof as a condition of federal aid, that beginning with the 1966–1967 school year, desegregation had been undertaken in good faith.

The Moon Landing

Kennedy's prophetic vision to land a man on the moon was realized on July 20, 1969, when **Neil Armstrong** and Colonel **Edwin E. Aldrin, Jr.**, walked on the moon and returned safely to earth. Their spaceship, *Apollo 11*, carried a four-legged landing module, the *Eagle*, which placed them on the moon. When Armstrong descended from the *Eagle* and set foot on the moon he said, that's one small step for man, one giant leap for mankind." Colonel Aldrin joined him later while **Michael Collins**, the third astronaut on the mission, guided *Apollo 11's* command module, the *Columbia*, in orbit around the moon. The world watched this historic event on television.

A year later a Soviet spaceship left a robot on the moon to perform some of the same operations the astronauts had done.

The *Apollo 11* voyage was followed by six additional moon landings during which ten other American astronauts walked on the moon. The program was phased out after the last landing in December 1972.

The Struggle for Equal Rights

A Review: From Slavery to Equality Under the Law

A contingent of 20 blacks arrived in Jamestown, Virginia, in 1619, before the *Mayflower* landed at Plymouth Rock. These 20 Africans came as indentured servants, as did many thousands of whites prior to the American

Revolution. However, by the 1640s, blacks were enslaved to work in the sugar, rice, and tobacco fields on Southern plantations as well as to serve as domestics in the homes of their masters. With the invention of the cotton gin in 1793, cotton became the basis of the economy of the South and slavery spread. Since slaves were considered property, they had no legal rights and could be bought and sold according to the owner's whim.

Meanwhile the evils inherent in slavery caused thoughtful people in both the North and the South to seek its end. Jefferson, contemplating slavery in 1784, wrote: "I tremble for my country when I reflect that God is just." By the mid 1800s, many Northerners came to believe that slavery was morally wrong. In the North, **William Lloyd Garrison**, a leading abolitionist, began publishing *The Liberator* in 1831. Anti-slavery societies with nearly a quarter of a million members sprang up in the North and the "**underground railroad**" was established to help slaves escape to freedom.

At the outbreak of the Civil War, there were more than 4 million slaves in the United States. In the free states of the North there were close to half a million free blacks, many of them former slaves or descendants of slaves. With emancipation and the passage of the Fourteenth Amendment it was thought that equality for blacks would be secure. But this was not to be the case. Blacks were disenfranchised through the use of the poll tax, Grandfather clause, and intimidation. **Jim Crow laws** were passed in the South to separate the races. In *Plessy* v. *Ferguson* (1896) the Supreme Court's doctrine of "**separate but equal**" institutionalized the inferior status of the African Americans in American society. The reversal of this doctrine in *Brown* v. *Board of Education* (1954) opened the way for equality. But its complete attainment remained elusive.

Black Protest, Pride, and Power

With the passage of Jim Crow laws and disenfranchisement in the late 1800s, African Americans sought various means to gain equality. Over the years, they formed various organizations to struggle for their civil rights.

 • *The National Association for the Advancement of Colored People (NAACP).* This organization was founded in 1909 by a group of black and white leaders, including **W.E.B. Du Bois**, the black scholar and activist, **Jane Addams**, a white social reformer, and **John Dewey**, a white philosopher-educator. The NAACP provided leadership in the early 20th century in the struggle for civil rights and voting rights for African Americans. It was the NAACP chief counsel, **Thurgood Marshall**, who successfully argued for school integration in *Brown* v. *Board of Education* (1954). Under the leadership of Roy Wilkins, who joined the national staff of NAACP in 1931 and rose to the top position in 1955, the membership grew to over 400,000 by 1977. Its methods also became more militant, supplementing education, lobbying, and court action with demonstrations, sit-ins, and boycotts.

- *The National Urban League.* This organization was founded in 1910 and its efforts first concentrated on helping blacks who had migrated from the South to Northern cities find homes, jobs, and training programs in their new environment.

- *Congress of Racial Equality (CORE).* Another civil rights organization, the **Congress of Racial Equality**, founded in 1942, was committed to nonviolent, direct action to end racial discrimination. Many of its members were recruited on college campuses. Sit-ins and freedom rides were adopted as means to dramatize demands of equal treatment for blacks.

- *Southern Christian Leadership Conference (SCLC).* In 1957, **Dr. Martin Luther King, Jr.**, organized the Southern Christian Leadership Conference (SCLC). This organization provided the leadership for the 1963 **March on Washington**, where a quarter of a million people heard Dr. King deliver the memorable "I Have a Dream" speech at the Lincoln Memorial. The SCLC worked primarily in the South to attain "full citizenship rights, equality, and the integration of the Negro in all aspects of American life." "The Reverend **Ralph David Abernathy** became the leader of SCLC after the assassination of Dr. King in 1968.

- *Student Nonviolent Coordinating Committee (SNCC).* Founded in 1960 to eliminate segregation through nonviolent means, it was later led by **Stokely Carmichael** and other more militant leaders who favored "black power." SNCC had a substantial following on college campuses. One technique used by SNCC was to have buses with black and white "freedom riders" tour the South, stopping in various cities to demonstrate against discrimination. Another technique used by SNCC was the sit-in. College students sat at segregated lunch counters until they were served or evicted. In 1964 over 500 SNCC volunteers, blacks and whites, went to Mississippi to work on voter registration.

By 1967, under leader **H. Rap Brown**, SNCC began to resort to violence and discourage white membership. The term "black power" was first used in a march into Jackson, Mississippi, led by **James Meredith**, the first member of the black community to be admitted to the University of Mississippi.

- *Black Muslims.* Elijah Muhammad's **Nation of Islam** (sometimes called the **Black Muslims**) rejected integration and sought to establish a separate African American government in one or more of the United States. Its best known member was **Malcolm X**, who later broke with the Black Muslims and formed his own organization. His followers used "X" as a surname to designate their rejection of names acquired under slavery. A gifted speaker and writer, Malcolm X conveyed a message of hatred against white injustice, which he describes in his widely read *Autobiography*. He had begun to change and speak of alliances with white radicals before he was assassinated in 1965.

- *Civil Unrest.* In August 1965, **Watts**, the black ghetto district of Los Angeles, erupted in a week of terrible rioting. Shooting, burning, and looting resulted in 34 deaths and over 100 wounded. Violence during the "long hot summer" of 1965 was followed by more racial violence the following summer. The unrest reached its peak in the summer of 1967. In Detroit, 38 people died and property damage exceeded $200 million. Newark, New Jersey, and other cities also experienced racial violence. More than 100 riots raged in American cities in the 1960s. The racial violence, following on the heels of the Civil Rights Act of 1964 and the Voting Rights Act of 1965, caused disillusionment and even a backlash. President Johnson, a strong advocate of civil rights, understood the frustration of the African American people and said, "God knows how little we've really moved on this issue despite all the fanfare. As I see it, I've moved the Negro from D+ to C–. He's still nowhere and he knows it. That's why he's out in the streets."

Assassinations of the 1960s

President Kennedy once said, "Those who make peaceful revolution impossible will make violent revolution inevitable." He was assassinated in Dallas in 1963; Dr. Martin Luther King, Jr., was shot to death in Memphis, Tennessee in 1968; and Robert F. Kennedy, whose campaign for the presidency was gaining momentum, was fatally wounded by an assassin's bullet at the Ambassador Hotel in Los Angeles on the night of June 5, 1968.

Exercise Set 6.9

1. Which was *not* included in the Equal Opportunity Act sponsored by President Johnson?
   A. Volunteers in Service to America (VISTA)
   B. a new Department of Housing and Urban Development (HUD)
   C. loans to college students and to small business
   D. job- and work-training programs

2. Which was *not* part of President Johnson's program for aid to under-privileged inner-city residents?
   A. Operation Head Start
   B. Medicare and Medicaid
   C. a rent-supplement program
   D. the Alliance for Progress

3. In *Plessy* v. *Ferguson* (1896) the Supreme Court decided that
   A. the Dred Scott Decision was unconstitutional
   B. the "separate but equal" doctrine was not a violation of the Fourteenth Amendment
   C. blacks were full-fledged citizens of the United States and of the state wherein they resided
   D. the Court lacked jurisdiction in that case

4. The chief counsel of NAACP who argued *Brown* v. *Board of Education* before the Supreme Court was
   A. W.E.B. Du Bois
   B. Robert C. Weaver
   C. Thurgood Marshall
   D. Roy Wilkins

THE MOVEMENT FOR EQUAL RIGHTS

> The fight must go on. The cause of civil liberty must not be surrendered at the end of one or even one hundred defeats.
>
> Abraham Lincoln, November 19, 1858

> The core of the civil rights problem is the matter of achieving equal opportunity for Negroes in the labor market. For it stands to reason that all our other civil rights depend on that one for fulfillment. We cannot afford better education for our children, better housing or medical care unless we have jobs.
>
> Whitney M. Young, Director of the National Urban League, 1968

Truman and Civil Rights

In 1946, President Harry Truman appointed a **President's Committee on Civil Rights**. The Committee issued its report in 1947 in a document entitled "To Secure These Rights" and, based on this report, Truman called on Congress to pass a Fair Employment Practices law, to establish a Civil Rights Commission, to prohibit poll taxes, and to protect the right to vote. This blueprint for civil rights paved the way for a comprehensive civil rights program. Truman did all he could in the face of congressional resistance. He moved toward integration of the armed forces and issued an executive order prohibiting discrimination in employment in federal agencies.

The leading Supreme Court segregation case, *Brown* v. *Board of Education of Topeka* (1954), along with similar cases from South Carolina, Virginia and Delaware, moved through the lower federal courts during the Truman administration. The Supreme Court took jurisdiction and heard arguments in 1952, the last year that Truman was in office, and rendered its unanimous decision two years later.

Civil Rights Legislation

Beginning in the 1950s, laws were passed to ensure equal civil rights for all Americans.

Civil Rights Act of 1957

In 1957, Congress passed the first civil rights law in the 20th century. It established a bipartisan **Civil Rights Commission** with authority to investigate denial of voting rights and/or denial of equal protection as provided in the Fourteenth Amendment. It authorized federal courts to issue injunctions to prevent interference with voting rights.

Civil Rights Act of 1960

The act authorized federal courts to appoint referees with power to evaluate state voting qualifications. Suits could be brought against states, and heavy penalties could be imposed for violations of civil rights.

Civil Rights Act of 1964

This comprehensive civil rights legislation (1) prohibited discrimination in places of public accommodation (hotels and motels); (2) established an **Equal Opportunity Commission** to end job discrimination; (3) strengthened voting rights statutes; and (4) allowed federal funds to be withheld from school districts that violated integration orders.

Voting Rights Act of 1965

This landmark law was designed to end the denial of voting rights to blacks in the South. The act authorized the "appointment of federal examiners . . . to enforce the guarantees of the Fifteenth Amendment." It outlawed literacy tests and other voter-qualification tests in states or counties where fewer than half of those of voting age had registered or voted in 1964. It authorized the use of federal examiners to register voters in counties that practiced voter discrimination.

The act substantially increased the number of African American voters, particularly in the deep South. More than 150,000 black voters were registered in the three years following its passage. In Mississippi, where fewer than 7 percent of voting-age blacks were registered prior to the 1965 law, close to 60 percent were on the voting rolls in 1968.

Civil Rights Act of 1968

The last of the civil rights legislation passed during the Johnson administration contained a strong open-housing provision that prohibited discrimination in the sale or rental of housing. It also provided penalties for persons who intimidated or injured civil rights workers and for those who traveled from one state to another to "incite, organize, promote, encourage, participate in, or carry on a riot."

Twenty-fourth Amendment

The twenty-fourth Amendment to the Constitution, ratified in January 1964, abolished the poll tax in federal elections.

Court Decisions

Besides legislation to end discrimination and ensure equal civil rights, African Americans also received support for equal rights from the courts.

- *NAACP* v. *St. Louis-San Francisco Railway Company.* In this 1955 case the Interstate Commerce Commission ruled that segregation on interstate trains and buses was illegal.

- *Brown* v. *Board of Education of Topeka (1954).* This case struck down racial segregation in the public schools.

- *Baker* v. *Carr (1962).* This case involved the apportionment of legislative districts. Those who brought the case contended that failure by the state of Tennessee to redraw and reapportion districts for election to the state legislature for 60 years constituted a denial of "the equal protection of the laws accorded them by the Fourteenth Amendment by virtue of the debasement of their votes." The Court's ruling in this case, frequently referred to as "**one man, one vote**," was a major victory for equal representation in the state legislatures. This was particularly significant in crowded areas where blacks and poor people generally were underrepresented.

- *Heart of Atlanta Motel* v. *United States (1964).* In the area of civil rights the Court declared that Congress had the power under its authority to control interstate trade to forbid racial discrimination in motels and hotels serving interstate travelers.

The Drive for Equal Rights for Women

The colonial patriarchal tradition, derived from Europe, established the principle of the father's primary authority in the home, in the world of work, in politics, and in the church. Women in the 17th and 18th centuries had no political rights and were generally considered inferior.

- *The 19th Century.* During the period of reform between 1820 and the 1840s, the women's rights movement began. The first women's rights convention was held at **Seneca Falls**, New York, in 1848. The delegates adopted a Declaration of Sentiments that said, "All men and women are created equal" and listed demands for political, social, and economic equality with men. The earliest victories came in education as some schools were gradually opened to women, starting in the 1840s and 1850s.

Prominent 19th-century feminist leaders included **Susan B. Anthony**, a relentless advocate of women's suffrage; **Lucy Stone**, who was both a women's rights advocate and an abolitionist; **Elizabeth Cady Stanton**, the philosopher of the 19th century feminist movement; and **Lucretia Mott**, feminist, abolitionist, and a founder of Swarthmore College. **Harriet Tubman** and **Sojourner Truth**, better known for their efforts to free their people from slavery, were also ardent advocates of women's suffrage. **Carrie Chapman Catt**, in the early 20th century, carried forward the effort for women's suffrage.

The Modern Women's Movement

> We can no longer ignore that voice within women that says: "I want something more than my husband and my children and my home."
> Betty Friedan, in *The Feminine Mystique* (1963)

- *Kennedy Commission and the 1964 Civil Rights Act.* In 1963 President Kennedy appointed a Commission on the Status of Women headed by **Eleanor Roosevelt**. The Commission report disclosed that discrimination against women was rampant in virtually every aspect of American life. The following year, Congress passed the **Civil Rights Act** of 1964, designed to protect the civil rights of blacks. However, it also contained a provision pertaining to women's rights. The provision was introduced as an amendment to **Title VII** of the act banning discrimination on the basis of sex as well as race and made discrimination in employment on the basis of sex a violation of federal law.

- *NOW, 1966 to Present.* The **National Organization for Women** (**NOW**) was founded by **Betty Friedan** in 1966. NOW resorted to strikes, boycotts, and demonstrations to attain equality with men in all aspects of life in the 1960s and 1970s.

As the "**women's liberation**" movement gained momentum, women sought equal pay for equal work, equal opportunity for promotion, the right to maternity leave without loss of job or seniority, advancement to positions of responsibility and authority in government, industry, and in the professions, recognition of the value of work in the home, participation of men in the duties and responsibilities traditionally performed by women, recognition in textbooks of women's role in history, and a more positive image in the media than the traditional one of sex symbol.

NOW has continued to agitate for women's rights, particularly for the adoption of the **Equal Rights Amendment**. The organization includes both women and men in its membership. Its agenda comprises a broad spectrum of social reforms, including affordable child care, lesbian and gay rights, pay equity, keeping abortion and birth control legal, greater research on women's diseases such as breast cancer, and reducing military expenditures.

- *Shifting Roles and Images.* The roles and images of male and female in our society have undergone radical transformation in one generation. The idea of the wife as homemaker and the husband as breadwinner has given way to one of equal responsibility for home and work.

- *The Equal Rights Amendment (ERA).* The recognition that women often received the poorest paying jobs in the work force and that they were generally paid lower wages (sometimes as little as one-half those paid to men for the same work), led to a demand by the National Women's Party in 1923 for the adoption of an Equal Rights Amendment to the Constitution.

This would force states and cities to change laws and end practices that discriminated against women.

An Equal Rights Amendment was introduced in Congress in 1923 and every year thereafter until 1948, but failed to pass. During the ensuing years the measure was bottled up in the Judiciary Committee of the House of Representatives. It was finally forced out of Committee in 1970 and passed with an overwhelming vote in the House. Two years later it was approved by the necessary two-thirds vote in the Senate and sent to the states for ratification by the state legislatures. Approval by three fourths of the states, as required by Article V of the Constitution for ratification of amendments, proved difficult to attain.

The original time limit for ratification was set at March 22, 1979 (seven years after it was submitted by Congress to the states). Although the deadline was extended to June 30, 1982, it nevertheless failed to be ratified since by that date only 35 of the necessary 38 states (three fourths of the 50 states) had voted approval.

- *Roe v. Wade (1973).* In a 7 to 2 decision, written for the Court by Justice **Harry Blackmun**, the constitutional right of a woman to have an abortion was recognized. The Court held that this was part of the right to privacy implied by the **Bill of Rights**. The decision gave unqualified abortion rights to the pregnant woman during the first trimester (3 months), permitted the states to place limitations during the second trimester, and affirmed the right of the state to prohibit abortion during the final trimester except when the mother's life was in jeopardy.

With the appointment of three new justices by President Reagan and the elevation of Justice **William H. Rehnquist** to the position of Chief Justice, it was widely believed that the decision might be overturned. The Court agreed to hear challenges to the decision during its 1988–1989 term. On July 3, 1989, in *Webster* v. *Reproductive Health Services*, the Court upheld a restrictive Missouri abortion law, stopping just short of overturning *Roe* v. *Wade*. By a 5 to 4 vote, in an opinion written by Chief Justice William H. Rehnquist, the Court indicated that it no longer considered abortion to be a woman's fundamental right. The determination was left up to the individual states.

- *Equality in the Workplace.* During the 1970s and 1980s women entered the work force in ever-increasing numbers. Barriers fell as prestigious colleges became coeducational, women entered the professions on a par with men, and engaged in work such as mining, construction, heavy industry, transportation, police, and other arduous and dangerous jobs previously regarded as exclusively male occupations.

Admission of women to the service academies—West Point, Annapolis, and the Air Force Academy—began in 1976. By 1980 there were 19,000 women officers in the armed forces including a number of generals and admirals. In 2010 women made up 20 percent of the U.S. military forces. Women were governors of states, members of the Senate, and judges on both the federal and state benches. Thousands of women held legislative and judicial offices in the states. **Sandra Day O'Connor** became the first woman member of the Supreme Court in 1981 as the first Reagan appointee to the Court. Justice O'Connor has been followed by Ruth Bader Ginsburg (1993), Sonia Sotomayor (2009), and Elena Kagan (2010). In 1984 **Geraldine Ferraro** was the first woman vice-presidential candidate.

• *Affirmative Action.* In 1965 President Johnson signed an executive order requiring employers on federal contracts to take "affirmative action" to bring the number of women, African Americans, Hispanics, Native Americans, and Asians into better balance with the number of men and whites employed. The rationale was to correct past injustices done to these groups by giving preferences in employment, college admissions, and appointments to members of the disadvantaged categories who were equally qualified. The implementation of this directive aroused resentment and anger as some white men contended they were the victims of "reverse discrimination" based on past injustices to which they were not a party.

The Supreme Court faced this issue in two cases during the 1970s. In the case of *Regents of the University of California* v. *Bakke* (1978), the Court ruled 5 to 4 that the University of California at Davis, which was receiving federal funds, had acted unconstitutionally in setting up a 16 percent admission quota for minority students in its medical school, thus denying admission to **Allan Bakke**, a white applicant who was better qualified than some minority applicants admitted under their quota.

But in a 1979 case, *Kaiser Aluminum Co.* v. *Weber* (1979), Brian Weber sued the Kaiser Aluminum and Chemical Corporation when he was denied a place in a training program for advancement because less qualified black applicants were admitted under the 50 percent quota. The Court ruled 5 to 4 that this private company was within its constitutional right to adopt this quota system in an attempt to overcome past "patterns of social segregation and hierarchy."

Rising Consciousness of Hispanic Americans

Background

Spanish-speaking Americans (Hispanics or Latinos) have a cultural background reaching back to Columbus and before. Settlers from Spain have been in the Americas since 1492. Texas, New Mexico, Arizona, Utah, Nevada, California, and part of Colorado were part of Spanish-speaking Mexico until the middle of the 19th century. Puerto Ricans, whose culture is Hispanic, came under American rule about a century ago (1898), and became American citizens even more recently (1917). Cuba was part of the Spanish empire for four centuries before the Spanish-American War (1898).

Immigration

The term "**Chicanos**" designates Mexican-Americans, while the Mexicans refer to Americans as "Anglos." By the early 1990s there were more than 15 million Chicanos in the United States, though the actual number is certainly much larger because of illegal immigration. Many came during the Mexican Revolution, which caused turmoil in Mexico from 1910 until the end of World War I. Immigration was spurred by the demand for migrant labor to pick fruits and vegetables in California, Arizona, New Mexico, and Texas. Those who chose to remain, often without legal status, settled in the "barrios" (inner city neighborhoods — generally slums) of Los Angeles and other cities of the Southwest. As economic conditions worsened in Mexico, illegal immigration skyrocketed. These immigrants became the poorest-paid workers in the textile industry, in restaurants, as domestics, on farms, factories, ranches, and estates.

Migration from Puerto Rico to the United States on a permanent basis became legal after 1917, when Puerto Ricans became American citizens. By the early 1990s there were about 2 million Puerto Ricans living in the United States, chiefly in New York and other cities of the Northeast.

Immigration of Cubans to the United States dates from the overthrow of the **Batista** regime in Cuba in 1959 by revolutionary forces led by **Fidel Castro**. About 1 million Cubans fled to the United States, and most settled in the Miami, Florida, area.

After the attempt to overthrow the Castro regime failed at the Bay of Pigs (1961), the United States imposed an economic blockade. Despite the hardships suffered by the people of Cuba, Castro remained in power with considerable help from his communist ally, the Soviet Union. This aid vanished in 1989 with the demise of the Soviets. As economic conditions became intolerable, many Cubans attempted to escape to the United States. In 1994, the trickle became a deluge as Cubans began to arrive on rafts and by other hastily improvised means. Many were picked up at sea by the U.S. Coast Guard and taken to "temporary" quarters at the U.S. naval base at Guantanamo Bay in Cuba. By October 1994, there were over 15,000 Cubans at Guantanamo.

During the 1980s the Hispanic population of the United States grew four times as fast as the total population, reaching nearly 24 million or about 10 percent of the U.S. population. As of July 1, 2009, the estimated Hispanic population of the United States was 48.4 million; 16 percent of the U.S. population.

César Chavez

In 1963, César Chavez, a Chicano who had been a migrant farm worker, emerged as a leader of the exploited Mexican workers. He established the **United Farm Workers Organizing Committee** and led the union in a strike against the powerful grape growers of California. After a five-year struggle, during which he went on a 25-day fast to prevail upon his members to renounce violence, the union won contracts providing for an increase in pay and better working conditions.

Luis Muñoz Marin

Marin, a charismatic public figure, led Puerto Rico to "Commonwealth" status—partway between independence and statehood—within the United States. He was elected Governor of Puerto Rico in 1952. To raise the standard of living, he instituted a program called "Operation Bootstrap," whereby the resources of the Commonwealth—people, capital, and natural endowments—were marshaled to increase per capita income. The income level did rise, but it remained far below that of the United States, so, despite language problems, many Puerto Ricans chose to come to or remain in the United States. The people of Puerto Rico are divided about their political relationship with the United States. The majority prefer Commonwealth status, which gives them U.S. citizenship without requiring them to pay federal taxes on money earned in Puerto Rico. As a self-governing Commonwealth, they do not vote in U.S. national elections for President and Vice-President, nor do they elect members to the Senate or House of Representatives. They do have representation in Congress by a resident commissioner, who can speak but does not have a vote.

Hispanic Power

With growing numbers in the United States and a rising ethnic consciousness, Hispanics have become more aggressive in seeking recognition in economic, political, and cultural aspects of American life.

The time when the use of Spanish in the public schools was forbidden, as it was for a time in Texas, is long gone. Indeed in a number of states, English is now taught as a second language to Spanish-speaking immigrant children, who are instructed in Spanish in public schools until they become proficient in English. In many cities, election laws mandate the printing of ballots and other election instructions in both English and Spanish. Spanish has become the number one foreign language taught in the public schools of the United States. Fear that Spanish might force the United States to become a bilingual country, as French did in Canada, has caused a severe backlash and a strong movement for legislation to establish English legally as the sole official language of the United States.

Equality for Native Americans: American Indian Movement (AIM)

The relationship between the U.S. government and Native Americans is, for the most part, a shameful page in American history. In his book, *Custer Died for Your Sins*, **Vine Deloria, Jr.**, who is a Standing Rock Sioux and former Executive Director of the **National Congress of American Indians**, writes: "America has yet to keep one Indian treaty or agreement despite the fact that the United States government signed four hundred such treaties and agreements with Indian tribes."

When whites arrived in America, there were an estimated 850,000 Indians in what is now the lower 48 states. By 1890 that population had declined to 250,000. Since then, it has come back and surpassed the original number, but the economic status of Native Americans remains severely depressed. The 2010 census indicates that Native Americans comprise 0.9 percent of the U.S. population. An Indian is three times as likely to be unemployed as is a non-Indian living in the United States.

Alcatraz

In the 1960s Native Americans began to show a new militancy as they witnessed the developing counterculture of other disaffected Americans. In 1969, 78 Native Americans seized and held **Alcatraz Island**, a former federal prison, in San Francisco Bay. They were finally ousted by federal marshals, but not before nationwide publicity had brought their cause to the attention of the American public.

Wounded Knee (1973)

Indian Power manifested itself in surprising acts of defiance. In 1972, militant members of **AIM** (the **American Indian Movement**) occupied the Washington, D.C., offices of the Bureau of Indian Affairs, demanding that the Bureau be put in the hands of Indians and that treaty promises made to Indians be honored. They remained in control of the building for a week while talks were held with officials of the Department of the Interior.

A year later, about 200 armed members of AIM took control of the village of **Wounded Knee** on the Oglala Sioux Pine Ridge Reservation in South Dakota. They remained in the village for two months, during which violence broke out repeatedly in fighting with government agents. Major buildings were destroyed by the occupants and two Indians were killed in the fighting. The decision to occupy Wounded Knee was symbolic: it was near there that the last Indian resistance was broken when the U.S. 7th cavalry killed **Sitting Bull** and massacred 200 men, women, and children in 1890.

Example of Treaty Violation

The building of **Kinzua Dam** in western New York in the early 1960s inundated a large part of the Seneca reservation. Flooding the Indians out of their ancestral homeland was a violation of the **Pickering Treaty** of 1794, negotiated between the United States and the Seneca tribe of the Iroquois Nation and signed by George Washington as President of the United States.

Exercise Set 6.10

1. Of the five major civil rights acts passed during the period 1957–1968, the Voting Rights Act of 1965 is often regarded as the most far-reaching because
   A. prior to 1965 there was no legal guarantee of the right to vote for African Americans
   B. protection of the right to vote was regarded as a means whereby other basic rights could be secured
   C. voting rights would put an end to riots and racial violence
   D. Martin Luther King, Jr., was a strong advocate of the Voting Rights Act of 1965

2. The Supreme Court decision in *Baker* v. *Carr* (1962), involving reapportionment of state legislative districts, was a necessary complement to the 1965 Voting Rights Act because
   A. it protected voting rights in state elections
   B. the decision established the supremacy of federal over state voting regulations
   C. voting rights were reduced in practice by voting districts that were substantially unequal
   D. the appeal came from Tennessee, a state not directly involved in voting rights

3. The National Organization for Women (NOW)
   A. was founded in 1948 by Eleanor Roosevelt
   B. took the lead in support of the Civil Rights Act of 1964
   C. receives overt or tacit support from virtually all women
   D. includes in its membership both women and men

4. An Equal Rights Amendment to the Constitution
   A. was first proposed in 1970
   B. was declared unconstitutional by the Supreme Court
   C. failed to be approved by two thirds of each house of Congress
   D. failed to be ratified by the necessary three fourths of state legislatures

5. Women's organizations, for example—the National Organization of Women (NOW)—favored an Equal Rights Amendment (ERA) primarily because
   A. there is only one woman on the Supreme Court
   B. women in many jobs still receive lower pay than men for the same work
   C. educational opportunities for women are limited
   D. recent gains may be lost without a constitutional amendment

6. In the last decades of the 20th century, Native Americans
   A. ceased to be a recognizable ethnic group because of intermarriage
   B. steadily declined in population since the arrival of Europeans
   C. demanded a return of territory taken from them in violation of treaties with the American government
   D. no longer lived on reservations

CHAPTER REVIEW QUESTIONS

1. The Supreme Court decision that overturned a previous 19th-century civil rights case was
   A. *Pennsylvania Association for Retarded Children (PARC)* v. *Commonwealth of Pennsylvania*
   B. *Baker* v. *Carr*
   C. *Brown* v. *Board of Education*
   D. *Regents of the University of California* v. *Bakke*

2. African Americans realized they could not escape from the ghetto unless
   A. the right to vote was guaranteed
   B. open housing was assured
   C. children could be bused to integrated schools
   D. Black Power succeeded in establishing businesses owned and operated by blacks

3. The President responsible for beginning the program to land astronauts on the moon was
   A. Truman
   B. Eisenhower
   C. Kennedy
   D. Johnson

4. Which is a valid generalization about U.S. relationships with Latin America in the last 100 years?
   A. the success of democracy in Latin America is due largely to United States intervention
   B. Latin American resentment of the United States is due to Communist influence
   C. the United States has gradually realized that events in Latin America have little bearing on United States security
   D. economic interests have generally influenced United States policy toward Latin America

5. Which of the following describes the program of the Kennedy Administration?
   A. Great Society
   B. New Deal
   C. New Freedom
   D. New Frontier

6. The Kerner Commission reported: "Our nation is moving toward two societies, one black, one white—separate and unequal." The major reason for the failure to solve the race problem is
   A. failure of the black community to agree on a proper course of action
   B. preoccupation of administrations in Washington with foreign affairs
   C. lack of concern coupled with racism in the white society
   D. unfavorable Supreme Court decisions

ESSAYS

1. During the 19th and 20th centuries, women in the United States have worked to bring about change.

   a. Several women are listed according to the century in which they worked to bring about change. Select *one* woman from *each* list. For *each* woman chosen, identify an issue in which she was involved, describe her involvement in that issue, and discuss the impact of her involvement.

19th Century	*20th Century*
Harriet Tubman	Margaret Sanger
Elizabeth Cady Stanton	Eleanor Roosevelt
Susan B. Anthony	Gloria Steinem
	Geraldine Ferraro

   b. Many social issues of special concern to women are subjects of controversy today. Listed below are three such issues. Select *one* of these issues and discuss *two* conflicting viewpoints concerning that issue.

   Issues
   Government funding of day-care centers
   Guarantee of comparable worth
   Elimination of media exploitation of women
   Strengthening of affirmative action programs

2. Throughout U.S. history, the development of democracy has been affected by a variety of actions. Select *three* of the statements listed below. For *each* one chosen, discuss the extent to which the statement is accurate and use *two* specific examples from U.S. history to support your position. Use different specific examples for each statement.

   Statements
   Court decisions have been an important factor in the democratic process.
   Amendments to the U.S. Constitution have increased the rights of citizens.
   Citizen groups have had an impact on making government policies more democratic.
   Civil disobedience has been an effective way of achieving changes in society.
   Ethnic and racial groups have made gains in achieving political equality.

THEMATIC ESSAY

Directions: Write a well-organized essay that includes an introduction, several paragraphs addressing the task below, and a conclusion.

Theme: Civic Values and Citizenship

> Although the Reconstruction Period (1865–1870) saw the nationalization of civil rights with the addition of the Thirteenth, Fourteenth, and Fifteenth Amendments to the Constitution, it was not until nearly 100 years later that federal legislation and Supreme Court decisions started to enforce many of the rights granted in those amendments.

Task:

> From your study of the 1950s and 1960s, identify *three* actions by the federal government (legislation or Supreme Court decisions) that furthered the rights previously granted in the Thirteenth, Fourteenth, and Fifteenth Amendments.
>
> For each action:
>
> - Identify the action or Supreme Court decision.
> - Discuss the civil rights issue that necessitated the action.
> - Describe how the legislation or Supreme Court action helped address the civil rights issue.

You may use any examples of federal legislation or Supreme Court decisions that occurred in the 1950s and 1960s. Some suggestions you may wish to consider are *Brown* v. *Board of Education* (1954), *Baker* v. *Carr* (1962), Civil Rights Act of 1957, Civil Rights Act of 1960, Civil Rights Act of 1964, Voting Rights Act of 1965, and the Civil Rights Act of 1968.

You are *not* limited to these suggestions.

CHAPTER 4

THE LIMITS OF POWER: TURMOIL AT HOME AND ABROAD (1965–1972)

INVOLVEMENT IN ASIA

Prior to the 19th Century

United States involvement in Asia is not a recent development.

• *The China Trade.* In 1787 the Boston ship *Columbia*, loaded with ginseng, made a historic voyage from Boston to Oregon, where it picked up furs, and sailed across the Pacific Ocean to China, where it traded its cargo for tea and silk. The *Columbia* returned home in 1790, beginning a regular and profitable trade between the United States and China. From the late 1790s on, the China trade increased, and by 1850 the swift American clipper ships carried on most of the trade. After the **Opium War** with Britain (1839–1842), China opened more of its ports to trade. Prior to this, only Canton had been open to trade. In 1844, the American diplomat **Caleb Cushing** traveled to China with four warships and received generous trade arrangements for the United States. In the 1840s the first Chinese immigrants began to arrive in San Francisco. Chinese laborers were brought to California to help build the transcontinental railroads.

The 19th Century

The 19th century saw increased United States involvement in Asia.

• *Opening of Japan.* President **Millard Fillmore**, seeking trade with Japan, sent a special mission headed by **Commodore Matthew C. Perry**, that arrived in Tokyo Bay in 1853. He returned the following year with a fleet of seven warships and negotiated the Treaty of Kanagawa, a treaty of peace, friendship, and commerce. The Japanese, confronted with superior American power, agreed to open several ports to United States trade.

• *19th-Century Imperialism in Asia.* The United States became an imperial power in Asia toward the end of the 19th century by acquiring the Hawaiian Islands and Samoa in 1898 and the Philippine Islands from Spain at the conclusion of the Spanish-American War. Events in China at the close of the 19th century prompted Secretary of State **John Hay** to propose in 1899 the "**Open Door Policy**" for trade with China. This policy declared that China should be open to all nations on an equal basis. Hay announced (March 20, 1900) that the acceptance of the Open Door Policy by the major powers (Germany, Russia, Britain, France, Italy, and Japan) was "final and definitive." The United States returned to China part of the money awarded for damages resulting from the **Boxer Rebellion** of the same year.

The 20th Century

By the 20th century, the United States had become a major power, and its contacts with all areas of the world, including Asia, increased.

• *Theodore Roosevelt and the Russo-Japanese War.* In 1905, President Theodore Roosevelt helped bring to an end the war in Asia between Japan and Russia when he met with the envoys of the warring powers at Portsmouth, New Hampshire. He was awarded the Nobel Peace Prize for this act.

• *World War I (1914–1918).* While the war was fought primarily in Europe, there were repercussions in Asia. Japan joined the war against Germany in 1914. At the peace negotiations at Versailles, Japan acquired several islands in the Pacific previously held by Germany and was made a permanent member of the Council of the League of Nations.

• *World War II (1939–1945).* Asia was a major battleground of World War II. At the conclusion of the war, the United States had become the leading world power and a great power in Asia. The challenge was now perceived to be from the Soviet Union, itself a major power in Asia, the Middle East, and Europe.

• *The Korean War (1950–1953).* By prompt action, the United States and the UN prevented all of Korea from becoming a Communist outpost in Asia.

The French-Indochina War

The French in Indochina

Vietnam was part of a French colonial empire in Indochina that also included **Cambodia** and **Laos**. During World War II the Japanese took control of Indochina from the French and made it part of their "greater East Asia co-prosperity sphere." When the war ended, France attempted to reestablish its control over Vietnam. However, in 1946 the **Viet Minh**, a group of revolutionary nationalists and Communists led by **Ho Chi Minh**, began a war to drive out the French and their anti-Communist allies led by **Bao Dai**. In 1950, after it was found that Communist China was aiding the Viet Minh, President Truman sent military equipment and economic aid to the Vietnamese and French armies. Although President Eisenhower believed that a French defeat might lead to the Communist domination of Southeast Asia, he did not involve the United States in the war. He did continue to send military equipment, and the United States paid for much of the cost of the war. The civil war went on for eight years until a decisive battle at Dien

Bien Phu in May 1954 resulted in the defeat of the French. After the fall of Dien Bien Phu to the Communists, the French withdrew from Indochina and the Communist Viet Minh took over North Vietnam.

An international conference was held at Geneva, Switzerland, attended by representatives of both Vietnams, France, Great Britain, the Soviet Union, the People's Republic of China, and the United States. At the Geneva conference, the independence of Cambodia, Laos, and Vietnam was recognized. Vietnam was divided along the 17th parallel into North Vietnam and South Vietnam. North Vietnam became a Communist state under the leadership of Ho Chi Minh. South Vietnam became a republic and was led by Ngo Dinh Diem. Provision was made for elections to be held in 1956 to reunite Vietnam, but the elections were never held. Neither South Vietnam nor the United States signed these accords. When the time for the election to unify Vietnam arrived (July 1956), Ngo Dinh Diem, with approval of the United States, refused to participate in the election. He was convinced that he would lose to Communist North Vietnam, and American intelligence sources agreed with this conclusion.

The War in Vietnam

The Domino Theory

The American attempt to prevent a Communist victory in Vietnam was based primarily on the fear that such a victory would result in the spread of communism in Asia. According to President Eisenhower's domino theory, ". . . you knock over the first one [domino—in this case, Vietnam] and . . . the last one . . . will go over very quickly." Americans feared that the dominoes in Southeast Asia might include not only Indochina but also Thailand, Malaysia, Indonesia, the Philippines, and Burma, since each of these countries was also facing problems with Communist insurgencies.

Early American Involvement in Vietnam

• *Under Eisenhower.* President Eisenhower offered economic aid to South Vietnam soon after the Geneva Conference in 1954 and began sending **military advisors** there.

• *Under Kennedy and Johnson.* The war in South Vietnam carried on by the **Viet Cong**, Communist guerrilla forces aided by the North Vietnamese, was going badly for the South Vietnamese government. Consequently, President Kennedy, who also believed in the domino theory, increased the number of American military advisers.

In 1954 the United States had helped to install **Ngo Dinh Diem** in power in Saigon. In May 1963, Diem's troops killed nine Buddhists taking part in an anti-Diem demonstration in Hué. The demonstrators were protesting a government order barring the flying of flags and processions on Buddha's birthday. On June 11 the first of seven monks committed suicide by burning himself to death in Saigon to dramatize protest of government policies toward Buddhists. On November 1, 1963, a military coup deposed and assassinated Diem. The United States welcomed the coup but denied direct involvement.

When Lyndon Johnson became President (November 22, 1963) there were 15,000 American troops, including "Green Beret" special forces, in Vietnam. By January 1965, when Johnson began his full four-year term, there were 23,000 American troops in Vietnam.

Johnson and the Escalation of the War

In August 1964, two United States destroyers were reportedly fired upon by North Vietnamese patrol boats in the Gulf of Tonkin, off the coast of North Vietnam. At the time it was not known that these U.S. naval vessels, with President Johnson's approval, were cooperating with the South Vietnamese in raids on the North Vietnamese coastal areas. Johnson called these incidents "unprovoked attacks" and ordered retaliatory air raids on North Vietnam. He asked Congress for wider authority to take military action. On August 7, 1964, Congress overwhelmingly passed the **Gulf of Tonkin Resolution** authorizing the President to "take all necessary measures to repel any armed attack against the forces of the United States and to prevent further aggression."

The Gulf of Tonkin Resolution marked a turning point in the war and led to the beginning of large-scale American involvement. In February 1965 Johnson began the bombing of North Vietnam, which continued until 1968. More American troops were sent to Vietnam and committed to combat. Before this, Americans had served as military advisers. As American involvement increased, so too did North Vietnamese involvement. Supplies were sent from the north, and for the first time troops from North Vietnam went south to fight with the Viet Cong.

Prior to the November 1964 election Johnson said, "We will seek no wider war." He also told the voters, "We are not going to send American boys nine or ten thousand miles away from home to do what Asian boys ought to be doing for themselves." His Republican opponent, Barry Goldwater, called for more intensive bombing of North Vietnam. In the presidential election, the voters gave Johnson an overwhelming victory—more than 60 percent of the popular vote and a 486 to 52 triumph in the electoral college. It was clear that the people wanted no wider war in Asia, and Johnson was their "peace candidate." However, soon after the election Johnson proceeded to widen the war. In February 1965 after an attack on an American base in South Vietnam, Johnson ordered an escalation in the war. American planes began to bomb North Vietnam, and in June 1965 U.S. field commanders were authorized to send American troops into combat. By November 1966

479

the U.S. had 358,000 troops in Vietnam. By the middle of 1968, the number exceeded half a million.

Opposition to the Vietnam War

Early Opposition

From the very beginning, a few well-placed voices spoke out against the war. Some senators opposed the war because Americans were being drafted and sent into combat without a declaration of war by Congress. Heavy casualties were being incurred. The bombardment and the overwhelming fire power of the American forces were proving ineffective in the jungle against the hit-and-run guerrilla tactics of the Viet Cong.

Draft Resistance

At home the war was brought into people's living rooms on television screens. As they watched the horrors of war, Americans began to oppose the war, because there was no consensus as to what we were fighting for in Vietnam. Many young men sought to avoid the draft by failing to register or by seeking exemptions. Some fled to Canada, Sweden, and other foreign sanctuaries. Quotas were filled quickly in the National Guard and Coast Guard, two branches of the service not generally assigned to overseas duty.

Intensified Opposition

By 1967 many leading senators were openly demanding U.S. withdrawal from Vietnam. In an effort to answer the opposition, President Johnson addressed the nation on September 29, 1967, and once again used the domino theory to support the war.

But the nation did not accept the President's explanation. **Peace marches** and **protest meetings** throughout the United States showed the deep disaffection. Others were frustrated over the way the war was being fought, and many Americans believed that "hold back" tactics were being used. By March 1968, polls showed that only 36 percent of the people approved of Johnson's presidency.

Reports from the front fueled the discontent with the war. The nation learned of a massacre by American troops at **My Lai** village in March 1968. Frustrated American troops under the command of Lieutenant **William Calley** entered the village and murdered its inhabitants (old men, women, and infants). Many villages were destroyed in indiscriminate bombing. **Agent Orange**, a powerful chemical with long-lasting, serious health effects on people, was used extensively as a defoliant. Land mines took life and limb from countless civilians. In a war against guerrillas, it was impossible to distinguish combatants from noncombatants. Despite assurances from General **William Westmoreland**, Commander of American forces in Vietnam, that the war was being won, there was growing skepticism in Congress.

The Tet Offensive

In January 1968, during the Vietnamese New Year's holiday called "Tet," the Viet Cong and North Vietnamese launched a powerful offensive. Virtually all of South Vietnam, including the U.S. embassy in Saigon, was suddenly besieged. The attack was over in a few days and the North Vietnamese suffered tremendous losses. But the offensive demonstrated the Vietnamese will to continue to engage the U.S. military forces. Reports of the attack profoundly affected public opinion and the political situation in the United States. Opposition to the war intensified, and candidates in the Democratic party challenged President Johnson in the primaries for the November 1968 election.

On March 31, 1968, President Johnson delivered an address to the nation. He stated, "Tonight I renew the offer I made last August—to stop the bombardment of North Vietnam We ask that [peace] talks begin promptly . . ." He then startled the nation by declaring that he would not run for another term as President.

President Nixon and the Vietnam War

"Vietnamization" of the War

During the election campaign of 1968, **Richard Nixon** delared that he had a "secret plan" to end the war. Although President Johnson had tried to induce peace talks by halting bombing raids for short periods and offering economic aid, North Vietnam insisted that the United States leave Vietnam before talks could begin. In November 1969 Nixon unveiled his plan, which was later termed Vietnamization, of shifting the responsibility of fighting the war to South Vietnamese forces. He said, "We shall furnish military and economic assistance when requested in accordance with our treaty commitments. But we shall look to the nation directly threatened to assume the primary responsibility of providing the manpower for its defenses."

However, the fighting in Vietnam, including heavy bombing raids, continued. With the lack of success of peace negotiations being held in Paris, Nixon widened the war. In April 1970 he ordered American and South Vietnamese forces to invade **Cambodia**, a neutral nation neighboring Vietnam where the North Vietnamese and Viet Cong had bases. This action set off a chain of fierce protests, particularly on college campuses. To many, Nixon's credibility was minimal, and his assertion that the invasion was designed to facilitate the withdrawal of American troops from Vietnam was widely rejected. However, at the same time as the Cambodia invasion, Nixon began to withdraw American troops from the war. By the end of 1972, Nixon withdrew 500,000 American soldiers, leaving only about 24,000 in Vietnam Under the policy of Vietnamization, the United States armed and trained the South Vietnamese. Heavy bombing of Communist-controlled areas was undertaken.

Negotiations for a Cease-Fire

During this period the war continued while negotiations for a cease-fire, first begun under President Johnson in April 1968, were carried on in Paris by Nixon's foreign policy adviser (later Secretary of State) **Henry A. Kissinger**. On March 30, 1972, North Vietnamese forces launched a sustained offensive into South Vietnam. Heavy American bombing of North Vietnam was resumed, and on May 8, 1972, Nixon ordered the mining of North Vietnam's ports. Although United States participation in the ground war terminated in August 1972, aerial bombardment continued.

Shortly before the 1972 election, Kissinger announced from Paris that "peace is at hand." In November, Nixon was reelected in an overwhelming victory, defeating George McGovern, the Democratic anti-war candidate, by an electoral vote of 520 to 17. However, by December, no agreement had been reached and Nixon authorized the "carpet bombing" of North Vietnam declaring "I will show them no mercy." Hospitals, schools, and residences, were indiscriminately destroyed.

This attack caused peace talks to resume, and the long-awaited cease-fire agreement was finally reached on January 27, 1973, in the Paris negotiations between Henry Kissinger and Le Duc Tho, chief of the Vietnam mission. The United States agreed to respect the independence, unity, and territorial integrity of Vietnam and to withdraw all forces within 60 days. The Communist government of North Vietnam agreed to release all prisoners and to account for all soldiers missing in action. The final U.S. troops left Indochina on March 29, 1973. To achieve "peace with honor," the United States retained the right to recognize the government of **President Thieu** as the sole legitimate government of South Vietnam. But it was obvious to all that the Thieu government could not endure long against the forces of North Vietnam. The end came in April 1975, when North Vietnam mounted a major offensive and gained control of all of Vietnam. As Communist troops from the north besieged Saigon, President Thieu and his followers fled the country. Thousands of refugees fled to Thailand.

The Vietnam Veterans Memorial in Washington is engraved with the names of 58,156 Americans who died in Vietnam; 300,000 more were wounded. The monetary cost of the war was over $150 billion. The intangible costs are still being assessed and the lessons pondered. Nearly 5,000 American servicemen were missing in action (MIAs) at the end of the war.

The Pentagon Papers

Background

In June 1967 **Robert S. McNamara**, President Johnson's Secretary of Defense, authorized a comprehensive study to review the policy-making procedures whereby the United States became so deeply involved in Vietnam. After a year and a half of intensive study, a 47-volume report known as the **Pentagon Papers** was compiled. Only 15 copies were issued. They were classified as top secret and were given only to McNamara, former President Johnson, President Nixon, the State Department, and the Pentagon files. The *Papers* revealed new facts about the Tonkin Gulf incident of 1964, which President Johnson used to gain a free hand in Vietnam It appeared that the North Vietnamese attack on American destroyers in the Tonkin Gulf (if indeed, it ever *had* occurred) had been deliberately provoked by attacks on North Vietnamese territory carried out by South Vietnam and supported by U.S. destroyers in order to gain Congressional approval for the free hand sought by the President.

Publication of the Papers

One of the authors who compiled the *Pentagon Papers* was Daniel Ellsberg. Ellsberg had volunteered for service in Vietnam and spent two years in combat with the marines. He felt strongly that the American people should be informed of the contents of the *Pentagon Papers*. Considering it to be an act of the highest patriotism, he decided to release the report to the press. On June 13, 1971, *The New York Times* startled the nation with its front-page installment of the secret government report. The Justice Department indicted Ellsberg for theft, conspiracy, and espionage.

While Ellsberg awaited trial, the Nixon administration, via **John D. Ehrlichman**, assistant to the President for domestic affairs, sounded out the presiding judge on becoming the new director of the FBI. He also authorized a special secret contingent called "the plumbers" (leak stoppers) to break into the California office of Ellsberg's psychiatrist and steal whatever data they could find (they found none) about Ellsberg's personal affairs or problems. They also carried out other illegal activities, including wiretaps. When it was revealed that an illegal FBI wiretap had been in operation on Ellsberg's telephone from late 1969 to early 1970, the judge in the case dismissed the charges against Ellsberg, stating, "The conduct of the government has placed the case in such a posture that it precludes the fair, dispassionate resolution of these issues by a jury."

The New York Times Co. v. United States

When *The New York Times* began publication of the *Pentagon Papers*, the Justice Department obtained a court order enjoining the newspaper from further publication of any material contained in the confidential report. *The New York Times* sought an order from the Supreme Court vacating the injunction, on the grounds that prior restraint was a violation of the free press guarantee of the First Amendment. The government contended that disclosure of the contents would work "irreparable injury" to the "national security." The Court was asked to order prior censorship against a newspaper for the first time in American history.

The Court, in a 6 to 3 decision, rejected the government's request and vacated the injunction. Nine opinions, totaling over 11,000 words, were issued. The arguments against prior restraint were strongly stated by Justice Black with whom Justice Douglas joined in concurrence.

> Now for the first time in 182 years since the founding of the Republic, the federal courts are asked to hold that the First Amendment does not mean what it says . . .
>
> In revealing the workings of government that led to the Vietnam War, the newspapers nobly did that which the Founding Fathers hoped and trusted they would do . . .
>
> To find that the President has "inherent power" to halt the publication of news by resort to the courts would wipe out the First Amendment and destroy the fundamental liberty and security of the very people the government hopes to make "secure."

1. Which of the following did *not* involve U.S. relations with China prior to 1901?
   A. John Hay's "Open-Door Policy"
   B. building of the transcontinental railroads
   C. acquisition of the Philippine Islands
   D. the "Boxer Rebellion"

2. President Johnson's use of American troops to save the independence of South Vietnam was
   A. unpopular in Congress almost from the beginning
   B. a logical development of the policies pursued by Presidents Truman, Eisenhower, and Kennedy
   C. contrary to the advice of the Joint Chiefs of Staff of the Armed Forces
   D. tacitly approved by China, Japan, and Russia

3. The decision of the Supreme Court in *The New York Times Company* v. *United States* (1971) [the *Pentagon Papers* case] is important because
   A. it involved important officials in the U.S. government
   B. it was widely reported in newspapers throughout the country
   C. the government's attorneys lost the case in a 6 to 3 decision
   D. the Court ruled that the First Amendment prevented "prior restraint" of publication, even against a charge that such publication would jeopardize national security

4. U.S. actions in the Vietnam War demonstrated that
   A. the domino theory is an effective military tactic
   B. military policy in a democracy is affected by popular opinion
   C. advanced technology ensures victory
   D. limited use of tactical nuclear weapons can be successful

5. The executive branch of the U.S. government has traditionally gained power during periods when
   A. the presidency has been occupied by a high-ranking military officer
   B. the Republican party was in the majority in Congress and the President was a Democrat
   C. there has been a serious domestic or international problem facing the United States
   D. the Supreme Court and Congress have been in conflict over constitutional issues

PROTEST AND THE COUNTERCULTURE

Sources of Discontent

The decade of the 1960s was a period of rapid social change in American life. The traditional family underwent radical transformation. The authority of parents, teachers, churches, leaders in business, industry, the professions, and government was questioned, challenged, and attacked. By 1967 half of America's 200 million people had been born after the Great Depression and had no memory of the economic problems of that period.

Young people, impatient to correct injustice, found two areas for discontent: the unequal treatment of minorities and the war in Vietnam The Kerner Commission had found that the nation's two societies—one black and one white—were becoming increasingly "separate and unequal." Senator **Eugene McCarthy** of Minnesota described the war in Vietnam in his 1967 book *The Limits of Power*: "Vietnam is a military problem. Vietnam is a political problem; and as the war goes on it has become more clearly a moral problem."

Vexing social problems were associated with these sources of injustice— one was that a disproportionate share of fighting was being borne by young black Americans. For African Americans and other minorities and the poor, lack of opportunity, unequal education and health care, unemployment, hunger, and slum living produced a permanent underclass, alien to the tradition of the "American dream."

The Counterculture

The rejection of traditional American society, because of its many injustices, by many young Americans created a **counterculture**. Many young people rejected the norms and values of people "over 30."

The baby boom of the 1950s had produced a generation of 36 million Americans between the ages of 15 and 24 in 1970. In the 1960s many of these young people seriously questioned the injustice in American society and the unexplained war for which they were expected to risk their lives. They felt alienated from American society. The counterculture was one way of showing their rejection of their parents', teachers', and the older generation's values. Many wore long hair, beads, and bizarre clothing, and went barefoot. "Flower children" handed flowers to police officers. Many tried drugs, most commonly marijuana and LSD. Some followed Oriental gurus and went to live in communes. The "rock music" of groups such as the **Beatles** expressed their yearnings and feelings. In 1969, near **Woodstock**, New York, 400,000 gathered for an outdoor concert that became a symbol of the togetherness of this generation. Some young Americans rejected the

486

quest for economic advancement, turning to part-time occupations or crafts such as making furniture, pottery, or jewelry. They rejected ideas of personal achievement, material gain, and, above all, conformity. Rebellious youths referred to themselves as "**hippies**." (They were "hip" or wise to what was going on.)

The counterculture mood of rejection and rebellion was strongly reflected in the behavior of the military in Vietnam.

The Election of 1968

In 1968 a sharply divided Democratic party faced a united Republican party that chose **Richard Nixon** as its candidate. Nixon picked Governor **Spiro T. Agnew** of Maryland as his running mate.

The contest for the Democratic presidential nomination began in the New Hampshire primary on March 12, 1968. Senator **Eugene McCarthy** of Minnesota, virtually unknown outside his own state, ran as an "end the war" candidate and challenged President Johnson. To everyone's surprise, he received 42 percent of the vote and showed how vulnerable the President was in his own party. Four days later, Senator **Robert F. Kennedy** of New York announced his candidacy for the presidential nomination. And on March 31, in an address to the nation, President Johnson announced, "I shall not seek, and I will not accept the nomination of my party for a second term as your President." The way was now clear for Vice President **Hubert Humphrey** to seek the Democratic party nomination. The assassination of Robert F. Kennedy in Los Angeles on June 5 made the selection of Humphrey a virtual certainty, and it was confirmed at the Democratic convention in Chicago in August.

A third candidate, **George C. Wallace**, Democratic Governor of Alabama, ran as the Independent party candidate espousing segregation, hoping to garner enough electoral votes in the South to throw the election into the House of Representatives.

The Democratic convention was marred by a bitter battle over the party platform on Vietnam. The followers of Eugene McCarthy (and the Kennedy delegates) sought a quick withdrawal from Vietnam. However, the Humphrey delegates wrote a platform calling for stopping the bombing of Vietnam only when "it would not endanger the lives of our troops." But the greatest damage to the Humphrey candidacy was caused by what the voters saw on television. Outside the Chicago convention, fierce fighting broke out in the streets between antiwar demonstrators and the police, who were under orders from Chicago Mayor **Richard J. Daley** to preserve order, if necessary with their clubs. Among the demonstrators were the "**Yippies**" (**Youth International party**), who ridiculed the convention and nominated a pig named "Pigasus" for President.

During the campaign, which hinged on the issue of our involvement in the Vietnam War, Nixon said he had a secret plan to bring the war to a successful end. In the weeks before the November election, Humphrey gained steadily but failed to overcome the Republican lead. Nixon won in a close race by half a million votes of 73 million cast. Wallace received nearly 10 million votes. In the electoral college Nixon took 301 votes against 191 for Humphrey and 46 for Wallace.

Rallies, Protests, and Demonstrations

Students on the Offensive

Many young Americans, especially college students, expressed their resentment against the Vietnam War and other adult institutions and practices. Even before the war, students had begun to show a new militancy. At the University of California in Berkeley they had organized **a Free Speech Movement** and attempted to disrupt a San Francisco hearing conducted by the **House Un-American Activities Committee.** Some 800 members of Berkeley's Free Speech Movement staged a violent sit-in at the administration building and heard their spokesman, Mario Savio, claim, "There's a time when the operations of the machine become so odious . . . you've got to put your bodies on the gears . . . and make it stop."

At Greensboro, North Carolina, African American students from the nearby state university staged a sit-in in February 1960 at a segregated lunch counter in Woolworth's and started the process that brought integration to the nation's restaurants.

In colleges and universities around the country, indeed around the world, students were occupying and barricading buildings, holding vigils, and disrupting university procedures. During the first six months of 1968 there were major demonstrations in 101 American colleges and universities. In *Tinker* v. *Des Moines School District* (1969) the Court found high school antiwar protests, including the wearing of black armbands, to be protected speech, holding that students do not shed their freedom of expression "at the schoolhouse gate."

In Washington in November 1969, a quarter of a million people converged on the nation's capital to demand an end to the Vietnam War. The following May, the nation was shocked at President Nixon's announcement of the "incursion" of United States troops into Cambodia. A rally opposing this action was quickly organized, bringing 100,000 people to the capital.

Kent State and Jackson State

Meanwhile at colleges and universities, demonstrations against the widening of the war in Indochina were common occurrences. In April 1971 an "end the war" demonstration resulted in the arrest and imprisonment of some 10,000 protesters and spectators, who were held without trial in the Washington Redskins' stadium. Participating in the demonstration were the VVAW (Vietnam Veterans Against the War), who took the dramatic action of throwing their medals over a fence at the Capitol.

The extension of the war into Cambodia brought on a massive student demonstration at **Kent State University**. The Governor of Ohio sent 600 armed National Guard troops to the University to suppress the violence. The guardsmen fired a volley into the crowd, killing four of the demonstrators and wounding nine others. At **Jackson State College** in Mississippi, an institution with a predominantly black student body, protests against the invasion of Cambodia were broken up when the state highway patrol fired into a dormitory, killing two students.

Opposition to the War in Congress

After the invasion of Cambodia (April 29, 1970) a measure was introduced in the U.S. Senate by **Mark Hatfield** of Oregon and **George McGovern** of South Dakota, that would have required all U.S. troops to be recalled from Vietnam by the end of 1971. It was defeated 55 to 39. In June 1969 the Senate had approved by a vote of 76 to 10 a "sense of the Senate" resolution requiring the President to refrain from committing men or funds to any country without the express approval of Congress. And on June 24, 1970, the Senate voted 81 to 10 to repeal the Tonkin Gulf Resolution of 1964. On April 2, 1970, Massachusetts passed a law attempting to exempt its citizens from serving in combat overseas "unless such hostilities were initially authorized or subsequently ratified by a congressional declaration of war according to the constitutionally established procedures in Article I, Section 8, of the Constitution of the United States." The act underscored the fact that Congress had not declared war. The Supreme Court refused to hear arguments on the constitutionality of this Massachusetts act. But. the principle involved continued to surface.

The efforts of Congress to regain its constitutional war power, which was eroded during the Vietnam War era, culminated in November 1973 when Congress passed the **War Powers Act** over President Nixon's veto. The act provided that the President, within 48 hours of sending troops where they might be involved in combat in a foreign country, must fully explain his action to Congress. Unless Congress gave its approval, the troops were to be brought home within 60 days.

Exercise Set 6.12

1. The candidate running against Richard Nixon on the Democratic ticket in the election of 1968 was
   A. Robert Kennedy
   B. Adlai Stevenson
   C. Edmund Muskie
   D. Hubert Humphrey

2. The most important protest movements during President Nixon's first term were against
   A. war in Vietnam
   B. broken treaties with Native Americans
   C. discrimination against Native Americans
   D. pollution of the environment

3. Since World War II, African Americans in the United States have made the greatest gains in the area of
   A. equal economic opportunity
   B. major corporate leadership
   C. voting rights
   D. desegregation of social life

4. Which was *not* true of the election of 1968?
   A. The Democrats were badly divided
   B. Nixon won by a close vote in the electoral college
   C. Democrats retained control of both houses of Congress
   D. Humphrey lost overwhelmingly in the popular vote

5. U.S. participation in the undeclared war in Vietnam during the 1960s and 1970s raised a serious question in the United States about the
   A. loyalty of U.S. military commanders
   B. authority of the President to make war
   C. intervention of the Supreme Court in matters of national security
   D. ability of Congress to finance a war

6. The War Powers Act of 1973 was passed in order to
   A. strengthen the hand of President Nixon in pursuing the elusive victory on the battlefields of Vietnam
   B. modify the constitutional provisions pertaining to presidential power in wartime
   C. reassert the constitutional war-making power of Congress
   D. reassert the authority of the Supreme Court as an arbiter between the executive and legislative branches of government

CHAPTER REVIEW QUESTIONS

1. Which of the following is *not* true about support for the Vietnam War effort? It
   A. was maintained in Congress along partisan lines
   B. showed a steady buildup from the Eisenhower Administration well into the Johnson Administration
   C. was rejected by many of our traditional democratic allies abroad
   D. divided the American people into two groups generally described as "doves" and "hawks"

2. "We shall look to the nation directly threatened to assume the primary responsibility of providing the manpower for its defense." This statement represents
   A. President Johnson's strategy for successful prosecution of the war in Vietnam
   B. Senator Goldwater's position as candidate for President in 1964
   C. Senator McGovern's position as candidate for President in 1972
   D. Richard Nixon's "secret plan" to win the war as revealed after his election in 1968

3. Which of the following is not connected directly with the war in Vietnam?
   A. The Free Speech Movement at the University of California in Berkeley
   B. A rally in 1969 at which a quarter of a million people converged in Washington
   C. A demonstration which resulted in the arrest of some 10,000 people who were held without bail in the Washington Redskin's stadium
   D. The killing of two students at Jackson State College in Mississippi by members of the state highway patrol

4. The 1973 War Powers Act
   A. created an all-volunteer army
   B. required the president to report to Congress any commitment of American troops
   C. authorized the expansion of the war into Cambodia
   D. gave the president the power to declare war

ESSAYS

1. The period of the 1960s and 1970s was one of severe social and political upheaval in the United States.
   a. Choose *one* example of extreme social turmoil and *one* example of historic political upheaval. For *each* of these examples describe the unusual events that occurred and explain their significance.
   b. Choose *one* of the examples from "a" above and discuss its relationship to national developments of the period.

2. During the turbulent period of the Vietnam War, government policies and practices were greatly influenced by *nonelected* groups or individuals. Select *three* of the groups listed below and for *each* one chosen, show how that group or an individual within that group had an influence on the policies and practices of the United States government. Use specific historical examples to support your answer.

   Groups
   President's Cabinet
   The military
   Presidential advisers
   The mass media
   Interest/lobbying groups
   Public opinion consultants (pollsters)

Directions: Write a well-organized essay that includes an introduction, several paragraphs addressing the task below, and a conclusion.

Theme: Civic Values and Citizenship

Historical Context: The momentous school desegregation decision in 1954 started the Earl Warren Supreme Court (1953–1969) on a path that would undertake sweeping reforms in numerous areas of the electoral system, political representation, criminal justice within the states, race relations, freedom of speech, and the role of religion in public life.

> The Supreme Court during the term of Chief Justice Earl Warren (1953–1969) would hand down decisions resulting in sweeping reforms in the areas of the electoral system, political representation, criminal justice, race relations, and religion.

Task:

> From your study of the Warren Court years and decisions in the 1950s and 1960s, identify *three* issues that came to the Supreme Court.
>
> For each issue:
>
> - Name the Supreme Court case that addressed the issue.
> - Briefly describe the facts of the case.
> - Discuss the decision and its impact on American society.

You may use any appropriate decisions of the Warren Court (1953–1969). Some suggestions you may wish to consider are *Brown* v. *Board of Education* (1954), *Baker* v. *Carr* (1962), *Wesberry* v. *Sanders* (1964), *Mapp* v. *Ohio* (1961), *Gideon* v. *Wainwright* (1963), *Escobedo* v. *Illinois* (1964), *Miranda* v. *Arizona* (1966), *New York Times* v. *Sullivan* (1964), and *Engel* v. *Vitale* (1962).

You are *not* limited to these suggestions.

DOCUMENT-BASED QUESTION ESSAY

The following questions (Part A and Part B) are based on the accompanying documents (1–6). Some of these documents have been edited for the purpose of this exercise. The question is designed to test your ability to work with historical documents and to demonstrate your knowledge of the subject matter being presented. As you analyze the documents, take into account both the source of the document and the author's point of view.

Historical Context: At different times in the history of the United States, poignant protest against the policies of government and practices of society have been expressed through song. Bob Dylan's lyrics during the 1960s and 1970s addressed numerous issues including civil rights and war.

Task: Using information from the documents and your knowledge of United States history, answer the questions that follow each document in Part A. Your answers to the questions will help you write the Part B essay, in which you will be asked:

> From the documents, discuss some of the issues that were addressed and discuss how the popular music of protest was able to bring widespread attention to the issues mentioned.

Part A
Short Answer

The documents provided are excerpts from various songs by Bob Dylan (hereinafter referred to as "the author"). Examine each document carefully and then answer the questions which follow.

DOCUMENT 1

Come you masters of war
You that build all the guns
You that build the death planes
You that build the big bombs
You that hide behind walls
You that hide behind desks
I just want you to know
I can see through your masks

You fasten the triggers
For others to fire
Then you sit back and watch
When the death count gets higher
You hide in your mansion
As young people's blood
Flows out of their bodies
And is buried in the mud

And I hope that you die
And your death'll come soon
I will follow your casket
In the pale afternoon
And I'll watch while you're lowered
Down to your deathbed
And I'll stand o'er your grave
'Til I'm sure that you're dead

—Bob Dylan, "Masters of War" (1963)

1. Who are the "Masters of War" referred to in the selected lyrics from the song?

_____

_____

_____

_____

2. What is the relationship portrayed in the song between the "Masters of War" and those who actually fight the wars?

_____

_____

_____

_____

DOCUMENT 2

Medgar Evers, head of the National Association for the Advancement of Colored People (NAACP) and a war veteran was murdered outside his home on June 11, 1963, the very evening that President Kennedy made a passionate plea to the American people for the passage of stronger civil rights legislation. Dylan's "Only a Pawn in Their Game" was written shortly thereafter.

A bullet from the back of a bush took Medgar Evers' blood.....

A South politician preaches to the poor white man,
"You got more than the blacks, don't complain.
You're better than them, you been born with white skin," they explain.
And the Negro's name
Is used it is plain
For the politician's gain
As he rises to fame
And the poor white remains
On the caboose of the train
But it ain't him to blame
He's only a pawn in their game.

The deputy sheriffs, the soldiers, the governors get paid,
And the marshalls and cops get the same.
But the poor white man's used in the hands of them all like a tool.
He's taught in his school
From the start by the rule
That the laws are with him
To protect his white skin
To keep up his hate
So he never thinks straight
'Bout the shape that that he's in
But it ain't him to blame
He's only a pawn in their game.

—Bob Dylan, "Only a Pawn in Their Game" (1963)

3. How do the verses quoted above suggest that the politician is using the poor white population?

_____

_____

_____

_____

DOCUMENT 3

How many roads must a man walk down
Before you call him a man?
Yes, 'n how many seas must a white dove sail
Before she sleeps in the sand?
Yes 'n how many times must the cannon balls fly
Before they are forever banned?
The answer, my friend, is blowin' in the wind,
The answer is blowin' in the wind.

How many years can a mountain exist
Before it is washed to the sea?
Yes, 'n how many years can some people exist
Before they are allowed to be free?
Yes, 'n how many times can a man turn his head,
Pretending he just doesn't see?
The answer, my friend, is blowin' in the wind,
The answer is blowin' in the wind.

—Bob Dylan, "Blowin' in the Wind" (1962)

4. What two issues in particular does the author address in the two verses from "Blowin' in the Wind"?

_____

_____

_____

_____

DOCUMENT 4

Emmett Till was a 14-year-old black child from Chicago visiting a relative in Mississippi in 1955. After making a comment to a white woman in a local store, he was taken by a group of white men, beaten, tortured, murdered, and left in a nearby pond. Those charged with the murder were acquitted by an all-white Mississippi jury.

'Twas down in Mississippi not so long ago,
When a young boy from Chicago town stepped through a Southern door.
This boy's dreadful tragedy I can still remember well,
The color of his skin was black and his name was Emmett Till.

And then to stop the United States of yelling for a trial,
Two brothers they confessed that they had killed poor Emmett Till.
But on the jury there were men who helped the brothers commit this awful crime,
And so this trial was a mockery, but nobody seemed to mind.

I saw the morning papers but I could not bear to see
The smiling brothers walkin' down the courthouse stairs.
For the jury found them innocent and the brothers they went free,
While Emmett's body floats the foam of a Jim Crow southern sea.

—Bob Dylan, "The Death of Emmett Till" (1963)

5. How is the Mississippi trial presented in the lyrics by the author?

_____

_____

_____

_____

6. In your opinion, why has the reference to Jim Crow been made in the song "The Death of Emmett Till"?

_____

_____

_____

_____

...I've stumbled on the side of twelve misty mountains
I've walked and I've crawled on six crooked highways,
I've stepped in the middle of seven sad forests,
I've been out in front of a dozen dead oceans,
I've been ten thousand miles in the mouth of a graveyard,
And it's a hard, and it's a hard, it's a hard, and it's a hard,
And it's a hard rain's a-gonna fall.

.....I saw a black branch with blood that kept drippin',
I saw a room full of men with their hammers a-bleedin'...
I saw guns and sharp swords in the hands of young children...

I'll walk to the depths of the deepest black forest,
Where the people are many and there hands are all empty,
Where the pellets of poison are flooding their waters,
Where the home in the valley meets the damp dirty prison,
Where the executioner's face is always well hidden.....

—Bob Dylan, "A Hard Rain's A-Gonna Fall" (1963)

7. The author appears to be discussing a number of tragic issues in "A Hard Rain's A-Gonna Fall." Identify three of the issues mentioned in the lyrics above.

_____

_____

_____

_____

DOCUMENT 6

Bob Dylan wrote "Hurricane" in response to what he and many others felt was the wrongful conviction and imprisonment of middle-weight boxing contender Rubin Carter.

> Meanwhile, far away in another part of town
> Rubin Carter and a couple of friends are drivin' around.
> Number one contender for the middleweight crown
> Had no idea what kind shit was about to go down
> When a cop pulled him over to the side of the road
> Just like the time before and the time before that.
> In Paterson that's just the way things go.
> If you're black you might as well not show up on the street
> 'Less you wanna draw the heat.

—Bob Dylan, "Hurricane" (1975)

8. How does the author see the treatment of blacks in Paterson, New Jersey, compared to the treatment of others?

_____

_____

_____

_____

Part B
Essay

Your essay should be well organized with an introductory paragraph that states your position on the question. Develop your position in the next paragraphs and then write a conclusion. In your essay, include specific historical details and refer to the specific documents you analyzed in Part A. You may include additional information from your knowledge of social studies.

Historical Context: At different times in the history of the United States, poignant protest against the policies of government and practices of society have been expressed through song. Bob Dylan's lyrics during the 1960s and 1970s addressed numerous issues including civil rights and war.

Task:

> Using information from the documents and your knowledge of United States history, discuss some of the issues that were addressed and discuss how the popular music of protest was able to bring widespread attention to the issues mentioned.

Guidelines:

In your essay, be sure to
- Develop all aspects of the task
- Incorporate information from at least *five* documents
- Incorporate relevant outside information
- Support the theme with many relevant facts, examples, and details
- Use a logical and clear plan of organization, including an introduction and a conclusion that are beyond a restatement of the theme

CHAPTER 5

THE TREND TOWARD CONSERVATISM (1972–1992)

NIXON AND THE IMPERIAL PRESIDENCY (1969–1974)

> The truth is America's most potent weapon. We cannot enlarge upon the truth. But we can and must intensify our efforts to make the truth more shining.
>> Richard M. Nixon, *The Challenge We Face,* 1960

> Nixon is a shifty-eyed...liar... He's one of the few in the history of this country to run for high office talking out of both sides of his mouth at the same time and lying out of both sides.
>> Harry S. Truman, from Leo Rosten, *Infinite Riches* (1978)

In the election campaign of 1968, Richard Nixon ran against Hubert Humphrey. The three main issues in the campaign were the Vietnam War, violence and disorder at home, and racial strife. Nixon promised to end the war and to restore "law and order" in the United States. The election was very close, with Nixon winning by 260,000 votes. When he became President, the Vietnam War was the most pressing problem facing the nation. President Nixon began "**Vietnamization**" and increased bombing. American troops were withdrawn gradually and finally, in 1973, a cease-fire agreement was reached.

During the Nixon presidency some Americans realized that the President had grown increasingly powerful in the American political system. This power was largely the result of World War II and the Cold War, as the President took control of foreign affairs in a world situation of ever-increasing danger. Some Americans, alarmed by presidential power, began to speak of an "**imperial presidency**."

Foreign Affairs

President Nixon took charge of foreign affairs himself and used **Henry Kissinger** as his adviser. Kissinger served first as a member of the National Security Council and in 1973 became Secretary of State. Nixon's foreign policies, except for the Vietnam War, were widely approved by the American people. Especially popular was the policy of **détente**, or easing tensions, between the United States and the Communist nations.

Détente with the Soviet Union

Closer relations between the United States and the two Communist super-powers—the Soviet Union and the People's Republic of China—during the Nixon presidency could hardly have been foreseen from his adamant anti-Communist record at home. Shortly after he became President, Nixon began exploratory talks with the Soviets on a number of issues that concerned both powers, particularly the reduction or limitation of nuclear arms. In May 1972 Nixon arrived in Moscow for talks with the leaders of the Soviet Union. He was the first President to visit Moscow. Discussions proceeded over a wide range of subjects. Most important were the **Strategic Arms Limitation Talks** (**SALT**). Agreements were reached on arms limitation, particularly antiballistic missile systems (subject to ratification by the U.S. Senate) and a treaty was signed May 26, 1972. Under the treaty each party agreed "not to develop, test, or deploy ABM systems or components which are sea-based, air-based, space-based, or mobile land-based." Interpretation of this provision later caused controversy over President Reagan's proposal to develop the Strategic Defense Initiative (SDI), often called "**Star Wars**," in the 1980s. The treaty also provided that "ABM systems in excess of those prohibited by this treaty shall be destroyed or dismantled within the shortest possible agreed period of time."

Shortly after the signing of the ABM treaty, the United States sold $750 million worth of wheat, corn, and other cereals to the Soviet Union. The huge surplus of grains produced by American farms went to help relieve food shortages in the Soviet Union.

Détente with the People's Republic of China

When Nixon took office in 1969, the Communist government had ruled China for almost 20 years. Yet diplomatic relations between China and the United States had never been established because the United States still recognized the **Nationalist** (**Chiang Kai-shek**) government in Taiwan as the legitimate government of China.

In a television address to the nation, delivered July 15, 1971, President Nixon made a startling declaration: "The announcement I shall now read is being issued simultaneously in Peking and in the United States… Premier Chou En-lai and Dr. Henry Kissinger [President Nixon's Assistant for National Security Affairs] held talks in Peking from July 9 to 11, 1971… the government of the People's Republic of China has extended an invitation to President Nixon to visit China… President Nixon has accepted the invitation with pleasure."

On October 25, 1971, the People's Republic of China, with the acquiescence of the United States, was admitted to the United Nations. The UN General Assembly then recommended that the permanent seat on the Security Council held by the Nationalist government on Taiwan be turned over to the government of the People's Republic of China.

The historic visit of President Nixon and his wife to China took place in February 1972. Nixon met with Chairman Mao Zedong and Premier Zhou En-lai. The visit culminated in a joint communiqué issued at Shanghai February 27, 1972, stating: "…that Taiwan is a part of China. The U.S. government does not challenge that position… it affirms the ultimate objective of the withdrawal of all U.S. forces and military installations from Taiwan."

The Arab-Israeli War of October 1973

On the eve of Yom Kippur, the holiest day of the Jewish year, Israel was suddenly attacked by the armed forces of Egypt and Syria. At first the Israelis were driven back. The attackers had the initiative and were armed with Soviet military equipment. But, despite heavy losses, the Israelis, supplied with American equipment, drove the invaders back beyond their borders and occupied the Golan Heights previously held by Syria. Sporadic fighting continued until a cease-fire was urged on the Arabs and the Israelis by the United States and the Soviet Union and negotiated by May 31, 1974. But the uneasy peace was regarded on all sides as merely temporary.

The Arab nations were angered by the American support for Israel and several halted oil shipments to the United States. This **oil embargo** resulted in long lines at gas stations and calls for conservation measures.

Domestic Policies and Developments

Many pressing problems faced President Nixon when he took office. The Vietnam War divided American society as protests continued across the nation, while **inflation**, also largely a result of the war, caused problems at home.

Dismantling the Great Society

The Great Society of President Johnson was based on the idea that the federal government had a major responsibility to provide for the health, education, and welfare of the American people. Nixon rejected this idea and, instead, proceeded to shift the burden of responsibility to the states in what he called "**the new federalism**." Through **revenue sharing**, the federal government would aid the states in providing minimum levels of social benefits. The idea was that each state could decide its own needs and how to meet them. However, over the years, the diminishing share of federal funds left the states in a position of reducing these services or raising taxes. In 1969, with inflation mounting, 10 million Americans were on welfare. Unemployment among young people, especially African American teenagers, was at a post-World War II high. Also, as American troops left Vietnam, Americans in war industries were becoming unemployed. A **recession** was in progress and new economic measures had to be undertaken.

Economic Initiatives

Although he had previously rejected a Democratic proposal to freeze wages and prices in order to stem inflation, in August 1971, Nixon yielded and ordered a 90-day wage-price freeze (the first in peacetime). A special pay board and a price commission were authorized to grant or deny wage and price increases when the freeze expired.

To improve America's position in world trade, Nixon freed the dollar from its tie to gold, permitting the dollar to decline in relation to the currency of other nations. This gave American-made goods an advantage in foreign markets, because foreigners could pay for the goods with cheaper American dollars. Nixon also imposed a 10 percent surcharge on foreign imports. Improvements in the economy helped set the stage for Nixon's reelection in 1972.

Moon Landings

On Sunday, July 20, 1969, while Michael Collins guided the command module of *Apollo 11*, **Neil Armstrong** and **Edwin (Buzz) Aldrin, Jr.**, landed on the moon. As the world watched on TV, the two astronauts walked on the surface of the moon, set up scientific apparatus, collected rocks, and planted the American flag. The mission, planned eight years earlier by the Kennedy administration, was a 20th-century miracle.

In all, six Apollo missions landed twelve American astronauts on the moon, the last one in 1972.

The Environment

Congress took a strong stand on the environment by passing the **Water Quality Improvement Act of 1970**. The act created the **Office of Environmental Quality** and made oil companies responsible for cleaning up oil spills. It limited the use of pesticides and water pollutants and restricted thermal pollution of waters by discharges from power plants.

An oil spill that caused severe damage to the Santa Barbara coastline resulted in an order from Nixon's Secretary of the Interior Walter J. Hickel stopping undersea oil drilling in the area. Hickel also delayed the construction of an 800-mile oil pipeline in Alaska because of the potential damage to the flora, fauna, and other natural elements in the area. However, Nixon ordered work on the pipeline to be completed.

The Supreme Court

The Supreme Court under Chief Justice **Earl Warren** (1953–1969), former Republican Governor of California, who had been appointed by President Eisenhower, often came under attack during the 1950s and 1960s as being too "activist." Its liberal approach to civil rights, criminal procedures, church and state, and other social issues, was opposed by conservative Americans.

They were especially critical of the Court's decisions concerning criminal procedures. *Mapp* v. *Ohio* (1961) marked further incorporation of criminal procedure guarantees into the due process clause of the Fourteenth Amendment when the Court ruled that the federal exclusionary rule disallowing evidence wrongfully obtained would be applied to the states. In *Gideon* v. *Wainright* (1963) the Court set aside a state court verdict in a felony criminal case because the state had failed to furnish counsel for the defendant, an indigent person, at his request. In *Escobedo* v. *Illinois* (1964) and *Miranda* v. *Arizona* (1966) the Court set aside verdicts against the defendants because the police had failed to notify them of their right to remain silent and to be represented by counsel during questioning.

In 1962, in *Engle* v. *Vitale*, the Court ruled that a New York State decision permitting the reading of a "nonsectarian" prayer in the public schools was a violation of the First Amendment. The following year the Court prohibited Bible reading in public school assemblies or classrooms for the same reason.

In his 1968 campaign for election to the presidency, Nixon promised to reverse these trends by appointing "**strict constructionalist**" judges to the Supreme Court. Nixon's opportunity to reform the Court was not long in coming. In 1969 Chief Justice Earl Warren retired, and the President nominated **Warren E. Burger** of Minnesota to be Chief Justice. Burger, who was on the District of Columbia Federal Court of Appeals, was quickly confirmed by the Senate.

Twenty-Sixth Amendment

In 1971, during Nixon's first term as President, the Twenty-Sixth Amendment was added to the Constitution. Proposed by Congress in March 1971, it was ratified by the required 38 states by June 30, partly because it granted voting rights to many young Americans who served in Vietnam. The amendment provided: "The right of citizens of the United States, who are eighteen years of age or older, to vote shall not be denied or abridged by the United States or by any state on account of age."

The Election of 1972

Both parties held their national nominating conventions at the Miami Beach convention hall in Florida—the Democrats in July and the Republicans in August. The Republicans again nominated Nixon and Agnew. The chief contender for the Democratic nomination was Senator **George McGovern** of South Dakota, a liberal and an advocate of withdrawing American troops from Vietnam. Another contender was Governor **George Wallace** of Alabama, who had run as a third party candidate in 1968. His campaign was virtually ended when he was shot and paralyzed from the waist down while delivering a campaign speech at Laurel, Maryland. A third contender, **Edmund Muskie** of Maine, was the early Democratic front-runner.

During the election campaign, McGovern promised to end the war in Vietnam and to introduce basic economic and social reforms at home. Nixon was the "law and order" candidate and pointed to his impressive foreign affairs achievements in improving relations with the Soviet Union and the People's Republic of China. In October, shortly before the election, Nixon's campaign received a crucial boost when Henry Kissinger, who was then negotiating with the North Vietnamese, announced "peace is at hand."

The results of the 1972 election gave Nixon and Agnew an almost clean sweep in the electoral college. The vote was 521 to 17, with Nixon winning the entire country except for Massachusetts and the District of Columbia. The popular vote gave Nixon 46,631,189 votes to McGovern's 28,422,015.

The Resignation of Spiro Agnew

Vice President Agnew, a hard-line conservative, stood for "law and order." But after the 1972 election it was discovered that Agnew was himself a law-breaker. While serving as Governor of Maryland, he had taken bribes from contractors and was still receiving "kickbacks" while Vice President of the United States. He resigned as Vice President, was fined $10,000, and was placed on three years probation. He was also disbarred as a lawyer.

With the resignation of Vice President Agnew, the Twenty-Fifth Amendment to the Constitution, adopted in February 1967, came into effect. It provides: "Whenever there is a vacancy in the office of the Vice President, the President shall nominate a Vice President who shall take office upon confirmation by a majority vote of both houses of Congress." The choice in 1973 was of crucial importance because of the growing concern over the **Watergate** scandal. Nixon nominated **Gerald R. Ford** of Michigan, a twelve-term member and minority leader of the House of Representatives. Congress promptly confirmed the nomination, and Ford took the oath of office as Vice President on December 6, 1973.

Watergate: The Imperial Presidency in Trouble

> When the President does it, that means that it is not illegal.
> Richard M. Nixon, in a television interview, May 20, 1977

Nixon's second term was overshadowed by the Watergate affair, which included both the break-in at Democratic headquarters at Watergate and other political scandals in the Nixon administration, drawing up a list of enemies (those who opposed Nixon's policies) to be harassed by every means available to the administration, including the CIA, the FBI, and even the IRS. Many members of the press were on the enemies list, as were the leaders of the opposition to the Vietnam War. To discover who was "leaking" information to the press, Nixon also had illegal wiretaps placed on the telephones of suspects. He formed a special secret unit in the White House whose mission was to stop the leaks. The unit became known as "**the plumbers**," and they carried out a number of illegal activities.

The Break-in

On June 17, 1972, at the Watergate apartment complex in Washington, a burglary in progress was discovered in the Democratic National Headquarters. The burglars, who were rummaging through files, taking photographs, and installing bugging equipment, were arrested and pleaded guilty. It was discovered that some of them were connected to Nixon's "**Committee to Reelect the President**" (**CREEP**), including **James W. McCord, Jr.**, a former CIA wiretap expert; **G. Gordon Liddy**, a former FBI agent and White House consultant; and **E. Howard Hunt, Jr.**, a former CIA agent and a White House aide.

The Cover-up

Five days after the break-in, President Nixon said the matter was "under investigation...by the proper legal authorities" and that "the White House had no involvement whatever in this particular incident." At a news conference on August 29, 1972, the President said that, under his direction, his counsel **John Dean** had "conducted a complete investigation which disclosed that no one on the White House staff, no one in this administration, presently employed, was involved in this bizarre incident." Dean later testified under oath that he had had a series of meetings about Watergate with the President, that he had warned him that Watergate was "a cancer growing on the presidency" and that the President had taken part in the cover-up for eight months.

At first the President's cover-up statements were successful. The press seemingly lost interest in the case. However, two investigative reporters on the *Washington Post*—**Robert Woodward** and **Carl Bernstein**—pursued every lead and kept the story alive in the press. It was not until May 31, 2005, that it became known that Woodward and Bernstein's source for their information, known only as "Deep Throat" for more than thirty-three years, was William Mark Felt, Deputy Director of the FBI.

The Watergate Hearings

With pressure for a thorough investigation mounting, the U.S. Senate, in February 1973, adopted a resolution establishing the Senate Select Committee on Presidential Campaign Activities, headed by Senator Sam J. Ervin, Jr. The committee was directed to conduct an investigation into the extent to which illegal, improper, or unethical activities were involved in the 1972 presidential election. Televised hearings began in May 1973, and interrogation of witnesses continued for seventeen months.

Along with the establishment of the investigating committee, **Archibald Cox** of the Harvard Law School and former Solicitor General of the United

States, was appointed as special prosecutor (counsel) the day after the hearings began. He was to collect evidence that would eventually lead to the indictments, trial, and conviction of those who had committed crimes.

In April 1973, **H. R. Haldeman**, Nixon's Chief of Staff, and **John D. Ehrlichman**, his Chief Assistant for Domestic Affairs, resigned. Both were deeply involved in the matters under investigation. The same day, Nixon fired his counsel, John Dean, who had revealed damaging information in testimony before the Senate committee. On May 22, Nixon declared, "It is clear that unethical, as well as illegal surveillance activities took place in the course of the campaign. None of these took place with my specific approval or knowledge."

The Tapes

During testimony before the Senate committee, it was revealed that President Nixon had ordered the Secret Service to install listening devices in the White House Oval Office and other locations. Tapes of all conversations were made and stored "as a historical record."

When Nixon produced the tapes as ordered by the Federal District Court, it turned out that two of the key tapes were "missing" and that there was a "gap" of 18½ minutes in an important taped conversation that Nixon had with Haldeman, his Chief of Staff, three days after the Watergate break-in.

Special prosecutor Leon Jaworski demanded that the President release more of the relevant tapes. The Judiciary Committee of the House of Representatives also wanted the tapes to help them decide whether there were grounds for **impeachment**. In response, Nixon furnished edited tapes sprinkled with omissions and deletions. The President insisted that he had **"executive privilege"** to refuse Judge Sirica's subpoena to produce unedited tapes. Jaworski appealed to the Supreme Court, and in June 1974 the Supreme Court decided that the President was legally obligated to deliver the requested tapes to the Special Prosecutor. In *United States* v. *Nixon* (1974) the Court held that the importance of preserving confidentiality in White House conversations must be balanced against the need for evidence in a criminal trial. Nixon conceded that the tapes, which he was now required to release, were "at variance with my previous statements." In other words, he had lied in order to cover up illegal acts.

Impeachment Proceedings

Article I Section 2: The House of Representatives... shall have the Sole Power of Impeachment.

Article I Section 3: The Senate shall have the sole power to try all impeachments. When sitting for that purpose, they shall take an oath or affirmation. When the President of the United States is tried, the Chief Justice shall preside: and no person shall be convicted without the concurrence of two thirds of the members present.

> Judgment in cases of impeachment shall not extend further than the removal from office, and disqualification to hold and enjoy any office of honor, trust, or profit under the United States: but the party convicted shall nevertheless be liable and subject to indictment, trial, judgment, and punishment, according to law.

> Article II Section 4: The President, Vice-President and all civil officers of the United States shall be removed from office on impeachment for, and conviction of, treason, bribery, or other high crimes and misdemeanors.

The Judiciary Committee of the House of Representatives began conducting an inquiry and gathering data to prepare **Articles of Impeachment**. It had become clear that the President had engaged in "high crimes and misdemeanors" sufficient to warrant his impeachment.

On July 30, 1974, the Judiciary Committee of the House of Representatives voted for, and sent to the full House, three Articles of Impeachment: (1) the President was charged with obstruction of justice; (2) he was charged with abusing his authority and violating his oath of office; and (3) he was charged with subverting the Constitution by defying eight subpoenas for tapes in order to block impeachment. On August 5, the transcripts of Nixon and Haldeman's tape-recorded conversations from June 23, 1972, were made public. These tapes were considered a "smoking gun" because they showed that, contrary to Nixon's previous statements, he had attempted to cover up the Watergate burglary. There was little doubt that the House would vote to impeach him and the Senate would convict him. On August 8, 1974, President Nixon announced his resignation of the office of President of the United States to take effect the following day.

Indictments, Trials, and Convictions

Several important members of the Nixon administration were indicted for illegal activities. In March 1974, indictments were handed down against Mitchell, Haldeman, Ehrlichman, and four others connected with the Committee to Reelect the President, for crimes including obstruction of justice, conspiring to obstruct justice, and perjury. Mitchell, Haldeman, and Ehrlichman were convicted and sentenced to prison terms of from twenty months to five years.

Watergate was a blot on the American political record comparable to the scandals of the Harding and Grant administrations. On the positive side, it demonstrated the effectiveness of our democratic institutions. Freedom of the press and our two-party system worked in a crisis. The Constitution, with its carefully crafted procedures for checks and balances, provided the resilience necessary to meet the severe challenges presented by Watergate.

1. Which of the following is generally regarded as *the* major accomplishment of the Nixon administration?
   A. economic reforms
   B. environmental regulations
   C. détente with the Soviet Union and China
   D. Supreme Court appointments

2. The Watergate crimes were undertaken in order to
   A. assure success in the 1972 election
   B. secure approval for Nixon's domestic programs
   C. support continued prosecution of the war in Vietnam
   D. provide funds for "the plumbers"

3. Which of the following did *not* occur during Nixon's presidency?
   A. the Arab-Israeli War of 1973
   B. an attempt to cut back on the Great Society
   C. a 90-day freeze on wages and prices
   D. conviction of President Nixon of "high crimes and misdemeanors" by the Senate

4. In the United States, informing suspects in custody of their legal rights before they are questioned by a government official is required as a result of
   A. customs adopted from English common law
   B. state legislation
   C. decisions of the U.S. Supreme Court
   D. laws passed by Congress

5. Which description best characterizes the decisions of the U.S. Supreme Court of the 1950s and 1960s under Chief Justice Earl Warren?
   A. activist, with a liberal approach to interpreting the Constitution
   B. cautious, with a philosophy of strict construction
   C. traditional, with a stress on states' rights
   D. conservative, with a strong emphasis on "cracking down" on war criminals

6. Since World War II, a major goal of U.S. foreign policy in the Middle East has been to bring about
   A. permanent United Nations control of disputed territories
   B. a peaceful settlement of Arab-Israeli issues
   C. ownership of oil resources by Western nations
   D. an end to U.S. cooperation with Arab nations

THE FORD AND CARTER PRESIDENCIES (AUGUST 1974–JANUARY 1981)

I am a Ford, not a Lincoln.
Gerald R. Ford of Michigan upon being sworn in as Vice President,
Dec. 6, 1973

To me the presidency and the vice presidency were not prizes to be won but a duty to be done.
Gerald R. Ford in *A Time to Heal*, 1979

Gerald R. Ford served in the House of Representatives for 25 years (1949–1973), and was minority (Republican) leader from 1965 to 1973, when President Nixon appointed him Vice President to replace Spiro Agnew. Upon the resignation of Nixon, Ford became President on August 9, 1974. No other person has ever served in this high office without having been elected on a national ticket.

Domestic Developments Under President Ford

Vice President Rockefeller

To fill the vacancy in the vice presidency created by his elevation to the presidency, Ford followed the provisions of the Twenty-fifth Amendment to the Constitution. He nominated **Nelson A. Rockefeller**, Governor of New York from 1958 to 1973. Congress confirmed the nomination in December 1974. For the first time in history, the United States had an appointed President and Vice President, neither having been elected to office. Ford retained Henry A. Kissinger as Secretary of State along with most of the remaining members of the Nixon cabinet. The nation felt relieved at the transition from the Nixon administration to the frank, open, and amiable administration of the new President.

The Pardon

In September 1974, a month after taking office, Ford declared, "By virtue of the authority vested in me by the Constitution of the United States, I hereby grant to Richard M. Nixon a full, free and absolute pardon… for all offenses against the United States which he… has committed or may have committed or taken part in" during his presidency. The pardon was designed "to end the nightmare" and avoid the rancor of a public trial of the ex-President with its unpleasant consequences. Many Americans protested the pardon, claiming it was unfair to grant immunity to Nixon while those who had carried out his orders had served prison terms. It also raised the question of whether there had been a "deal" between Nixon and Ford.

The pardon was followed by a presidential announcement of **clemency** (but not amnesty) for draft evaders and deserters during the Vietnam War. Only about 25,000 of the 125,000 eligible accepted the offer. The others were later pardoned by President Carter.

Economic Difficulties

Within a year of Ford's assuming the presidency, the nation faced the worst **economic recession** since the 1930s. Unemployment reached an alarming level of nearly 10 percent in 1975, while annual inflation reached a high of 12 percent. The combination gave rise to a new term "**stagflation**," an economic anomaly. The economic situation improved slowly, but hard times continued throughout Ford's presidency and worked against his election in 1976.

Rising oil prices played a large part in the inflation of the 1970s. As the nation cut back on coal (an air pollutant) and nuclear energy (a safety hazard) and as the number of motor vehicles on the highways steadily increased, the use of oil (for gasoline) began to exceed the national production. The United States, traditionally an oil exporter, began to import oil in the early 1970s.

Led by **Venezuela**, oil producers in the Middle East, Asia, Africa, and Latin America formed a **cartel** (monopoly) named **Organization of Petroleum Exporting Countries** (**OPEC**). American motorists began paying five times what they had paid for gasoline only a few months earlier. Gas that sold for 16 cents a gallon in 1972 was now priced at $1.00, and oil companies made "windfall" profits.

Political Aspects

• *Freedom of Information Acts; Privacy Act.* The Freedom of Information Act of 1966 was strengthened by Congress in 1974 as a reaction to secret illegal dossiers compiled by the Nixon administration against his "enemies" and those who openly opposed his policies. Government agencies were required to open their files (except for national defense and foreign policy matters) and permit photocopying of contents by interested persons. The **Privacy Act of 1974** gave citizens the right to examine files compiled about them by government agencies.

• *Federal Election Campaign Finance Reform Act.* The act, passed in 1974 and revised in 1976, gave the President power to appoint a six-member Federal Election Commission. Candidates for President and Vice President in primary and national elections are required to file detailed accounts of sources of moneys received for their campaigns. Limitations are imposed on the amounts that **Political Action Committees** (**PACs**) of unions, corporations, or other organizations may contribute. Individuals who contribute over $100 must certify that the contribution was made without communicating with the candidate or the campaign committee. Violators are subject to severe civil and criminal penalties. The main source of presidential campaign funds was designed to be the $1.00 checkoff allotted to election campaigns from income tax return forms. This $100 million source plus small individual contributions takes the presidential election, to some extent, out of the control of large corporations, unions, and special interest political organizations. Efforts to impose similar restrictions on the election campaigns of members of Congress have proved unsuccessful.

• *Budget and Impoundment Act of 1974.* The act created a **Congressional Budget Office**, whereby Congress could maintain its own records of federal income and expenditures in order to monitor presidential compliance with the law.

• *Space Explorations. Viking 1*, launched in August 1975, landed on Mars in July 1976, and relayed back to earth detailed scientific research including photographs of the planet. It was designed for 90 days of operations but continued to function for almost 6½ years, until it ceased operating in November 1982. *Viking 2*, launched in September 1975, landed on Mars in September 1976, and continued to report its findings for 3½ years. Other launching and explorations (*Voyagers 1* and *2* of September 1977) explored the planets Jupiter, Saturn, and Uranus. *Voyager 2* passed Neptune in 1989 and sent back important new information on this planet. The Hubble Space Telescope was placed in orbit by the space shuttle *Discovery* in 1990. Problems with faulty equipment were repaired by astronauts in 1993.

• *Conrail (1976) and Amtrak (1971).* The **Consolidated Rail Corporation** (**Conrail**) was established in 1976 by combining seven freight lines in the Northeast. Conrail was granted a $2.1 million government loan to maintain the railroads, which were all in financial difficulties. The railroads would then be able to continue operating without a government takeover. Conrail handles about one fourth of the nation's freight and serves a population of 100 million.

Amtrak, a national passenger traffic combine, was organized in 1971 with federal subsidies to help maintain a viable system of national passenger transportation as an alternative to automobiles, buses, and airline transportation. Government subsidies were cut back during the Reagan administration. Yet Amtrak, despite its enforced elimination of many trains, has shown steady growth in the number of passengers served, particularly in the Northeast corridor (Boston–Washington), the Chicago area, and the West Coast. Because of motor vehicle highway gluts, air pollution, and accidents, it is expected that rail transportation will continue to increase in proportion to total passenger traffic.

Foreign Relations Under President Ford

Gerald Ford kept Henry Kissinger as Secretary of State and continued the policy of détente.

President Ford in the Soviet Union and Asia

In November 1974, three months after he took the oath of office as President, Ford met with Premier **Leonid Brezhnev** of the Soviet Union at a health resort near Vladivostok, the chief Soviet port on the Pacific Ocean. They agreed to place a ceiling on the number of **ICBMs** (intercontinental ballistic missiles) launched from submarines, of **MIRVs** (multiple independently targeted reentry vehicles), and bombers. The meeting, a signal that both sides sought détente, was a tacit recognition of the need to avoid a nuclear holocaust.

Angola

This former Portuguese colony in East Africa was one of the last colonies to gain its independence. A revolution in 1974 led Portugal to grant Angola its independence in 1975. American interest in Angola was based on the intervention by the Soviets, bolstered by Cuban troops. President Ford had Secretary of State Kissinger use his diplomatic skill to prevent a full-scale war or a Communist takeover. The problem was complicated by South Africa's control of **Namibia**, south of Angola. Namibia, the former German colony of Southwest Africa, became a trust territory of South Africa after World War I. Despite pressure from the UN, South Africa retained a dominant influence in Namibia, and was deeply involved in developments in Angola.

Capture of the *Mayaguez*

In May 1975, the United States merchant ship *Mayaguez*, with a crew of 39, was seized in the Gulf of Siam by Cambodian forces. After brief negotiations failed to free the crew, President Ford sent American forces to rescue the ship and crew. The Americans were freed, but 15 marines were killed in the battle, 23 died in a helicopter crash, 50 were wounded, and 3 missing.

South Vietnam

With the collapse of the Thieu government of South Vietnam in April 1975, Congress appropriated $405 million to aid refugees fleeing from the North Vietnamese Communists. President Ford admitted 140,000 South Vietnamese refugees to the United States after Congress rejected his appeal for military aid. Most of the refugees later became American citizens.

Helsinki Accords

In July 1975 President Ford attended a conference of representatives of 35 nations in Helsinki, Finland. Boundaries drawn in Eastern Europe at the end of World War II were officially legitimized. In return, the Soviet

Union and its satellites signed a "human rights" guarantee, which included a provision for the right to emigrate. The hopes raised by these agreements did not materialize when the Soviets failed to implement them.

President Jimmy Carter (1977–1981)

> As President I will not be able to provide everything that every one of you might like. I am sure to make many mistakes. But I can promise you that you will never have the feeling that your needs are being ignored, or that we have forgotten who put us in office.
>
> Jimmy Carter, in a televised address to the nation, February 1, 1977

The Election of 1976

In the 1976 election, the incumbent President Ford (Republican) ran against the little known challenger, **James Earl (Jimmy) Carter** (Democrat), former Governor of Georgia. To gain the nomination, each overcame strong competition from contenders in their respective parties. Ford was challenged by **Ronald Reagan**, the former Governor of California, who appealed to the conservative wing of the Republican party. Ford won the nomination on the first ballot by a close vote—1187 to 1070.

On the Democratic side there were a number of logical contenders for the nomination but no clear favorite. Among them were former Vice President **Hubert Humphrey**, Senator **Henry "Scoop" Jackson** of Washington, Congressman **Morris Udall** of Arizona, and Governor **George C. Wallace** of Alabama. However, it was Jimmy Carter who won the nomination by conducting a well-planned campaign. He entered his name in every primary and appealed to grassroots partisans willing to support an "outsider" who could bring a breath of fresh air to the stale politics-as-usual atmosphere.

In the November election, Carter and the Democratic party won a hard-fought victory. It was the first time since 1932 that an incumbent President was defeated in his bid for reelection. Only 53 percent of the eligible voters bothered to cast their ballots, The Democrats also retained control of the House and Senate and won nearly three fourths of the state governorships.

Domestic Policies of President Carter

Carter relied on his former Georgia associates when he took command in Washington. He and they had little experience with how the federal government worked. Moreover, Carter did not know many members of Congress, and he did not consult with them on his legislative program. As a result, Congress blocked many of Carter's programs.

President Carter did win the approval of Congress to add two new Cabinet-level departments to the executive branch—a **Department of Energy** in 1977 and a **Department of Education** in 1979.

516

Soon after he took office, Carter sought to end the Vietnam trauma. President Ford had offered clemency to draft evaders and deserters. Carter went further and pardoned some 100,000 Americans who were still subject to punishment.

• *The Economy.* Inflation plagued the Carter administration as it had Ford's. Led by rising oil prices, inflation reached 13 percent in 1979, while the economy remained in a slump. Mounting unemployment and skyrocketing interest rates (which reached more than 20 percent by 1980) added to the national economic malaise, while a budget deficit of $60 billion in 1980 called for new measures to turn the economy around. The proposal to raise taxes was rejected in favor of the alternative of reducing taxes in order to stimulate the economy. By 1980 the economy was suffering a recession. The same year, the Carter administration moved to bail out the **Chrysler Corporation**, which was facing bankruptcy, by supporting loan assurances of $1.5 billion.

The nation's economic problems were exacerbated by an energy crisis in 1979. Another oil shortage causing long gas lines was largely the result of a revolution in Iran, a major oil producer. The **Shah**, ruler of Iran, was forced to flee and was replaced by a fundamentalist Moslem religious regime headed by the **Ayatollah Ruhollah Khomeini**. As the Iranian oil supply temporarily stopped flowing into world markets, oil shortages developed and gasoline prices rose rapidly. Carter proposed a program to deal with the energy crisis. His proposals for making the nation independent of the OPEC oil included the development of synthetic fuels and other sources of energy such as solar, thermal, and nuclear, and a concerted national program of **energy conservation**.

• *The Environment.* President Carter secured Congressional approval of the Alaska National Interest Lands Conservation Act of 1980. This act set aside 103 million acres (an area larger than California) of unspoiled wilderness in Alaska. It was part of a compromise whereby other undeveloped areas in Alaska were opened for exploitation by oil, mining, and timber interests.

• *Judicial appointments.* President Carter made 265 appointments to the federal judiciary. His choice of a number of minority persons and women for the federal bench was widely hailed. No vacancies on the Supreme Court occurred during his term.

Foreign Affairs

Concern for human rights throughout the world was a key aspect of President Carter's foreign policy. He criticized the Soviet Union for failing to live up to the 1975 Helsinki Accords and denying dissidents and Jews the right to emigrate. His crusade for human rights was also directed against dictatorial regimes in Latin America and Africa. He denounced South Africa's practice of apartheid and castigated Cuba and Uganda for oppression. He cut off foreign aid to dictatorships in Argentina, Brazil, Ethiopia, and Uruguay. But he approved massive arms sales to Iran's dictatorial Shah because his government was serving as "a bastion against communism."

* *Panama Canal Treaties (1978).* By the Hay-Bunau-Varilla Treaty of 1903, a 99-year renewable lease to the Canal Zone in the newly established Republic of Panama was granted by Panama to the United States for the payment of an annual fee. In 1978 the lease still had 25 years to run, but discussions over the future of the Canal had been going on with Panama since the Eisenhower administration.

Two treaties were drawn up in 1977. One provided for the return of the Canal Zone and its operation to Panama by December 31, 1999. The other treaty provided that: "If operations [of the canal] are interfered with, the United States of America shall have the right to the use of force in the Republic of Panama."

* *Camp David Accord.* When Carter became President in 1977, three wars had already been fought between Israel and the neighboring Arab nations, which were determined to destroy the Jewish state. In 1977, President **Anwar el-Sadat** of Egypt surprised the world by accepting an invitation to visit Israel. He delivered a long, emotional plea for peace in an address to the Israeli Knesset (Parliament). President Carter promptly invited Sadat and Israeli Prime Minister **Menachem Begin** to join him at his Camp David retreat in the mountains of Maryland. In the ensuing dialogue, Carter acted to bring the positions of the two leaders closer together.

Finally, on September 17, 1978, a tentative agreement between Egypt and Israel was reached. President Carter went to Egypt and Israel in 1979 to facilitate peace negotiations and the peace treaty was signed in March 1979. Israel returned the **Sinai** peninsula to Egypt in return for guarantees of normal relations between the two countries. Exchange of ambassadors and the establishment of travel and trade relations raised hopes for an expanding good-neighbor relationship.

Shortly after this diplomatic success, President Carter took another significant move in foreign affairs by establishing full diplomatic relations with the People's Republic of China.

* *SALT.* The **Strategic Arms Limitation Treaty of 1972 (SALT I)**, between the United States and the Soviet Union, was scheduled to expire in December 1977. However, both sides continued to observe the terms of the treaty and a **SALT II** agreement was signed by President Carter and Soviet Premier Leonid Brezhnev in Vienna in June 1979. If ratified by the U.S. Senate, it would have extended arms limitations until December 1985. But it ran into strong opposition in the Senate and was tabled when Soviet troops invaded Afghanistan in December 1979.

- *Nicaragua.* Nicaragua, the largest country in Central America, was governed by the Somoza family from the 1920s until rebel forces known as **Sandinistas** succeeded in overthrowing the dictatorship of Anastasio Somoza in July 1979. The United States quickly recognized the new government, hoping to assist in the establishment of a democratic republic. But the Sandinistas proceeded to establish a Socialist regime modeled on Marxist economic principles.

- *Afghanistan.* In December 1979 the Soviet army launched a full-scale invasion of Afghanistan. This attempt to strengthen the faltering pro-Soviet government in Kabul met with unexpectedly strong resistance from guerrilla forces.

President Carter responded energetically to this challenge. He sent naval forces into the Persian Gulf, declaring that the area was "vital" to American interests. He ordered an embargo on the shipment of grain and high-technology machinery to the Soviet Union, called for a boycott of the 1980 Olympic Games in Moscow, and requested Congress to pass legislation requiring young men and women to register for a possible military draft.

Aid to Afghanistani rebel forces resisting the Soviet troops was stepped up throughout 1980 and reached a climax during the second term of the Reagan presidency. American military supplies flowed to the anti-Soviet forces. The Soviet air force was neutralized by sophisticated American Stinger missiles. The invasion turned out to be a disaster for the Soviets and in February 1986, the new Soviet leader, **Mikhail S. Gorbachev**, announced the withdrawal of Soviet forces "in the nearest future." Peace talks were held in Geneva under UN auspices, and accords providing for Soviet withdrawal were signed in April 1988. The last of 100,000 Soviet troops left Afghanistan in February 1989.

- *American Hostages in Iran.* The Shah of Iran was overthrown early in 1979 and replaced by a fanatical religious leader, the Ayatollah Ruhollah Khomeini. Fierce hatred of the United States by Muslim fanatics erupted in an unprecedented act of international terrorism. On November 4, 1979, a mob surrounded the American embassy in Teheran and seized its occupants, 52 members of the American diplomatic corps. Although President Carter worked to free the hostages, it wasn't until **Ronald Reagan** took the oath of office as 40th President of the United States that they were released—having served 444 days in captivity.

Exercise Set 6.14

1. Nelson Rockefeller became Vice President in the Ford administration as a result of
   A. his election to the office in 1974
   B. the decision of the Republican National Committee
   C. his nomination by President Ford and confirmation by both houses of Congress
   D. a decision by the U.S. Supreme Court

2. The Federal Election Campaign Finance Reform Act of 1974 as amended in 1976 provides for
   A. a limit on the amount that candidates for the Senate or House of Representatives may spend on their election campaigns
   B. a mandatory contribution to presidential campaigns by a $1.00 check-off on federal income tax returns
   C. the end of limitations on the amount that political action committees may contribute to candidates for national office
   D. candidates in primary elections and regular national elections must file detailed accounts with the Federal Election Commission specifying the amounts and sources of contributions to their campaigns

3. Least known among the early contenders for the presidential nomination in 1976 was
   A. George Wallace
   B. Edward Kennedy
   C. Henry Jackson
   D. Jimmy Carter

4. The largest contributor to the high rate of inflation during the Ford and Carter administrations was
   A. imports of oil
   B. high farm commodity prices
   C. high building costs
   D. budget deficits

THE REAGAN ERA (1981–1989)

The Election of 1980

> The Republican party is sharply different under Reagan from what it was under Gerald Ford and Presidents all the way back to Eisenhower.
>
> Jimmy Carter, Sept. 2, 1980

> In this present crisis, government is not the solution to our problems. . . . It is time to check and reverse the growth of government. . . .
>
> Ronald Reagan, first inaugural address, Jan. 20, 1981

As the 1980 election approached, the nation was plagued by unemployment, inflation, high interest rates, and frustration over the captivity of 52 American hostages in Iran. The apparent inability of the Carter administration to resolve these problems caused Senator **Edward M. (Ted) Kennedy** to challenge President Carter for the Democratic presidential nomination. Many members of the Democratic party feared that Carter would not be reelected. A public opinion poll in the summer of 1980 revealed that only 21 percent of the American people approved of President Carter's performance in office. This was an all-time low. Carter turned back Kennedy's challenge and won the nomination. He was opposed in the election by **Ronald Reagan**, who was nominated by the Republican party. Some voters turned to a third party, the Independent party, led by Representative John Anderson from Illinois, who won more than 5.7 million votes.

In the popular vote, Reagan received 51.6 percent against Carter's 41.7 percent, with 6.7 percent going to Anderson. But Reagan won an overwhelming majority of votes in the electoral college, 489 to 49.

In addition to winning the presidency, the Republicans gained control of the Senate for the first time in 28 years and picked up 33 seats in the House of Representatives.

Reagan Policies

Ronald Reagan had long been a leader of the conservative movement in the United States. He favored limited federal government, lower taxes, and reduced federal regulation of business. Although Reagan favored a more limited role for the federal government, in social issues he supported constitutional amendments to ban abortion and to permit prayer in public schools. He also favored a return to traditional values and family roles.

Attempt to Assassinate the President

On March 30, 1981, President Reagan was shot by **John W. Hinckley, Jr.**, a deranged young man. A bullet caused the collapse of the President's left lung, but after twelve days in the hospital, he returned to work. By April 28 he was able to deliver an address to Congress. His resiliency won public admiration.

Domestic Programs

President Reagan felt that he had a mandate from the electorate to carry out his programs for the nation. He immediately turned his attention to the nation's economic crisis.

Supply-side Economics

To bring down inflation, President Reagan adopted a policy known as **"supply-side" economics**, based on the belief that cuts in income taxes, especially on higher incomes, would result in business investment and act as a stimulus to business. Cuts in corporation taxes would promote business expansion, resulting in greater production of goods and bringing about full employment. Reagan prevailed on Congress to cut taxes on high incomes, corporations, and investors, and in July 1981, Congress passed the largest tax cut in the nation's history. American taxpayers received tax benefits of $750 billion over a five-year period.

The Federal Budget; Cuts and Priorities

To help him carry out his budgetary program, Reagan chose David Stockman as his director of the Office of Management and Budget. The goal of a balanced budget was to be attained through sharp cuts in federal expenditures. The one exception was the defense budget, which was expanded. Although the Reagan administration believed supply-side economics and cuts in the budget would painlessly decrease inflation, the economy did not respond as expected. Inflation came down, but within a year the nation was in a severe **recession**. In November 1982, unemployment reached 10.8 percent, with 11 million unemployed. By 1983, the economy began to recover and the twin demons — inflation and high interest rates — were brought under control. But the national budget remained unbalanced. By 1986, budget deficits, mounting annually, exceeded $200 billion. By 1989 the national debt was $3 trillion ($3 thousand billion). To remedy this, President Reagan called for an amendment to the Constitution requiring a balanced budget. In December 1985, Congress passed the **Gramm-Rudman-Hollings Act**, designed to achieve a balanced budget by 1991. The law set annual targets for reducing the deficit by across-the-board cuts in federal spending.

The first Reagan budget called for drastic cuts in social programs. The budget proposed a cut of $1.1 billion in aid to education with no provision for aid to handicapped or gifted students. Direct financial aid to college and university students (programs in existence since 1965) was phased out.

As for the poor, President Reagan spoke of a national "safety net," but this budget called for a reduction of $1.6 billion in school lunch programs for needy children, extinction of the Legal Services Corporation, reduction in Medicaid by nearly $1 billion, sharp cuts in federal aid to low-income housing, and a $2.3 billion cut in the food stamp program.

The "new federalism" of the Reagan administration offered grants to the states to help them assume responsibility for funding these programs.

Social Issues

The Reagan administration supported the position of conservatives on social issues, favoring organized prayer in the schools, support for nonpublic education, and less emphasis on civil rights. It opposed the Equal Rights Amendment, abortion, and sex education in the schools. Students' Fourth Amendment rights were redefined in *New Jersey* v. *T.L.O.* (1985) when the Supreme Court ruled that school officials needed only "reasonable suspicion" rather than "probable cause" to search students suspected of unlawful conduct. A later Supreme Court in 1995 would extend search rights over students to allow drug testing of student athletes in *Vernonia* v. *Acton* (1995).

Supreme Court Appointments

With the retirement of Justice Potter Stewart from the Supreme Court in 1981, President Reagan nominated **Sandra Day O'Connor** of the Arizona Supreme Court. She was confirmed by the Senate and sworn in September 25, 1981, the first woman to serve on the Supreme Court. Five years later additional openings came. Chief Justice **Warren E. Burger** retired in 1986 and President Reagan's nominee for the chief justiceship, Justice **William H. Rehnquist**, was confirmed by the Senate. The vacancy brought about by Justice Rehnquist's move to the chief justiceship was filled when the Reagan nominee, Judge **Antonin Scalia** of Virginia, was confirmed.

After the retirement of Justice Lewis F. Powell, Jr., in 1987, President Reagan nominated Judge Robert Bork of the United States Court of Appeals for the District of Columbia to fill the vacancy. Judge Bork, a former law professor at Yale Law School and Solicitor General in the Nixon administration, was a conservative whom Reagan described as "a powerful advocate of judicial restraint." He was opposed by many groups, and after hearings on the nomination the Senate Committee on the Judiciary recommended to the Senate that the nomination be rejected. Reagan's next nominee, Douglas Ginsberg, met with opposition because he admitted having once used marijuana. He asked to have his name withdrawn. Judge Anthony M. Kennedy of California was then nominated and promptly confirmed.

Meanwhile President Reagan nominated judges to fill vacancies on the lower federal courts—District Courts and Circuit Courts of Appeals—throughout the country. In selecting appointees, he was advised by his Attorney General, **Edwin Meese**, who sought candidates that satisfied the ideological criteria of conservative Republicans. During his eight years in office, Reagan appointed nearly 50 percent of all the judges on the federal bench.

The Environment

The assault on the environment caused by budget cuts for enforcement agencies such as the Environmental Protection Agency (EPA), the Food and Drug Administration (FDA), and the Occupational Safety and Health Administration (OSHA), was a source of concern for conservationists, environmentalists, and public health agencies.

In November 1986 President Reagan vetoed a clean water bill passed by Congress. The bill called for expenditure of $20 billion for facilities to treat sewage and water poisoned by toxic dumps. The bill was resubmitted and passed over the President's veto by the (new) 100th Congress in February 1987.

• *Depletion of Ozone.* In March 1989 the 12 European Community countries agreed to eliminate, by the end of the century, the production and use of chemicals that destroy the earth's protective ozone shield. The action was endorsed by William K. Reilly, head of the Environmental Protection Agency in the Bush administration. Ozone, the natural shield that gives protection from the sun's direct ultraviolet radiation, is declining steadily due to chemicals released into the air.

• *Greenhouse Effect.* The earth's temperature is slowly rising because of the "**greenhouse effect**." The global mean surface temperature has increased 0.5°F to 1.0°F since the late 19th century. Gases in the air, especially carbon dioxide released in automobile exhausts and industrial smoke stacks, prevent heat from the sun from radiating back into space. The rising temperature will have serious adverse effects on humans. Many scientists believe the glacial ice at the polar regions will melt, bringing about a disastrous rise in the ocean level.

The Election of 1984

As the election of 1984 approached, the nation was in an economic upswing. The recession of 1981–1982 was over, inflation and interest rates were down, and employment was up. In January 1984 President Reagan sounded his campaign theme, declaring "America is back, standing tall, looking to the '80s with courage, confidence and hope." Despite a doubling of the national debt during his first term, the President stood firm on his economic program of tax reduction. He was equally consistent on social issues: opposing abortion, the Equal Rights Amendment, affirmative action, and busing for school desegregation.

The front-runner for the Democratic nomination, former Vice President **Walter Mondale**, was strongly challenged by Senator **Gary Hart** of Colorado and Reverend **Jesse Jackson** of Chicago. However, Mondale secured enough delegates to clinch the nomination before the convention. For Vice President he chose Representative **Geraldine Ferraro** of New York, the first woman candidate for the vice-presidency nominated by a major party. Of the 92 million votes cast, 53,354,037 (59 percent) went for Reagan and 36,884,260 (41 percent) for Mondale. In the electoral college, the Republicans won 525 to 13.

Foreign Affairs

Cold War Resumed

During the 1980 election campaign, Ronald Reagan denounced SALT II, the Strategic Arms Limitation Treaty negotiated with the Soviets in 1979 by the Carter administration. The treaty, which was to run until 1985, was never acted on by the Senate because of the Soviet invasion of Afghanistan, but both sides observed its terms. In a press conference soon after his inauguration, President Reagan censured the Soviets, saying they were "prepared to commit any crime, to lie, to cheat" in order to achieve world conquest. Reagan's insistence on a hard-line approach toward the Soviet Union, as well as increased military spending and the placement of nuclear weapons in Europe, alarmed many. Fear of a global nuclear war increased throughout Europe and America. In New York's Central Park in June 1982, a peaceful demonstration against nuclear arms brought out more than 500,000 people. Antinuclear demonstrations took place in the major cities of our NATO allies. In 1985, a new leader, **Mikhail Gorbachev**, came to power in the Soviet Union. Reagan agreed to meet with him in Geneva in November.

Lebanon

On October 23, 1983, a truck carrying explosives drove into the marine barracks in Beirut, Lebanon, and blew up, killing 241 marines. The following year pro-Iranian terrorists took three American hostages in Beirut, including the CIA station chief, William Buckley, who died while being held captive.

Grenada

In October 1983 President Reagan made a surprise announcement of an invasion of the tiny eastern Caribbean nation on the island of Grenada by 6,000 U.S. marines and paratroopers. The leftist government of Grenada, supported by Cuba and the Soviet Union, was overthrown and replaced by a pro-American government. Protection of the 700 American medical students in Grenada was a factor in the invasion.

Nicaragua

In Central America, the Reagan administration found a more serious challenge. The **Somoza** dictatorship, which had governed Nicaragua since 1933, was overthrown in 1979 by the pro-Marxist revolutionists, called **Sandinistas**. Leftist guerrillas were also attempting to overthrow the government of neighboring **El Salvador**. The Reagan administration decided to support the opponents of the Sandinistas, called **Contras**, who operated from bases in Honduras. The United States financed and supplied the Contras with arms. Economic pressure was applied to Nicaragua. To prevent Soviet arms and supplies from entering Nicaragua, that country's harbors were mined by the CIA in violation of international law. Congress was divided, as were the American people, almost 50-50 as to whether this policy or a policy of seeking a political solution was preferable. The countries of Latin America, as well as some Americans, feared that force could lead to a wider war.

Reagan-Gorbachev Summit Meetings

In March 1985 Mikhail Gorbachev became the new General Secretary of the Soviet Communist party. His ideas began a new phase in both domestic and foreign policy in the Soviet Union. On the home front he called for "**glasnost**" (openness) and "**perestroika**" (restructuring). In foreign policy, he called for détente with the United States.

- *Geneva: November 1985.* President Reagan and Gorbachev held their first summit meeting in Geneva, where they met face-to-face for five hours. A stumbling block was Reagan's insistence on proceeding with the Strategic Defense Initiative (SDI), commonly called "Star Wars," which the Soviets regarded as destabilizing. Though no formal agreement was reached, the two leaders approved plans for arms control talks to make 50 percent reductions in strategic weapons their longterm goals. Provisions for cultural and educational exchanges were a concrete result of the talks.

- *Reykjavik.* The second meeting between Reagan and Gorbachev took place in October 1986 in Reykjavik, Iceland. On the American side, there was little planning for the hastily arranged meeting. The President made the astonishing proposal that all ballistic missiles—airborne, landbased, and seaborne—be eliminated by 1996. It fell apart when Reagan refused to agree to an interpretation of the 1972 ABM treaty that would restrict the Strategic Defense Initiative to laboratory research.

- *Washington—the INF (Intermediate Nuclear Forces) Treaty.* President Reagan and Soviet leader Gorbachev held their third summit meeting in Washington in December 1987. They signed a major arms limitation treaty providing for the dismantling of all short-range and intermediate-range (300–3,400 miles) missiles. This applied specifically to 1,752 American missiles in Europe, and 859 Soviet missiles in Europe facing them. The removal of these Soviet missiles was hailed by America's NATO allies as a long step toward ultimate security. After a four-month debate, the Senate, by a vote of 93 to 5, ratified the INF treaty for eliminating medium- and shorter-range land-based nuclear missiles. It was perhaps the most historic accomplishment of the Reagan presidency. In 1988, Reagan visited Moscow. Discussions were held regarding Soviet dissidents and the promotion of human rights.

Middle East

Constant turmoil in the Middle East marked the region as one of the danger areas requiring the constant attention of the United States.

- *Israel.* The Reagan administration's support for America's ally, Israel, was matched by Soviet support for Syria. In June 1981, Israeli war planes demolished an Iraqi atomic installation near Baghdad, charging that the plant was nearing completion for the production of atomic weapons. In June 1982 Israeli armed forces invaded southern Lebanon and advanced to Beirut. The area harbored **PLO** terrorist brigades that repeatedly attempted to infiltrate Israel. The immediate mission was accomplished, but the Israelis suffered losses and withdrew from Lebanon in 1985 without achieving any lasting results. An uprising ("**intifada**") of the Palestinians in areas occupied by Israel resulted in violence and was met by harsh repressive measures on the part of Israeli armed forces. In late 1988, **Yassir Arafat**, leader of the major PLO faction, seemed to renounce terrorism when he addressed the UN.

- *Libya.* A center of Middle East terrorism was Libya under the leadership of Colonel **Muammar Qaddafi**. Qaddafi, in power since 1969 and violently anti-American, trained and supplied international terrorists, using the profits of his oil-rich land to finance terrorist operations. In August 1981 Soviet-built Libyan fighter planes attacked American navy planes on maneuvers in the Mediterranean. In 1982 the United States placed restrictions on trade with Libya and in January 1986 all Libyan assets in the United States were frozen. In April 1986 American planes bombed Libyan military bases in retaliation for terrorist acts. In January 1989 two U.S. Navy F-14 fighter planes shot down two MIG-23 fighters off the coast of Libya.

- *The Persian Gulf.* A border dispute between Iraq and Iran, major oil-producing countries, precipitated a war in 1980. Oil tankers in the Persian Gulf came under attack from both Iraq and Iran. U.S. naval vessels were deployed in the Gulf to protect American shipping. Kuwait, a major oil-producing country on the Gulf, was supporting Iraq in the war. In March 1987 Kuwait asked the United States to protect its oil tankers in the Persian Gulf. In May 1987, an Iraqi aircraft, mistaking the *U.S.S. Stark* for an Iranian merchant vessel, fired two missiles killing 37 sailors and wounding 21 on the *Stark*. On the same day the United States agreed to replace the Kuwaiti flag with the American flag (called reflagging) on eleven Kuwaiti oil tankers and to provide naval escort for these ships in the Gulf. By the end of 1987, twelve major American warships were deployed in the Gulf to insure an uninterrupted flow of oil to America and its allies. In October 1987 one of the reflagged tankers was successfully attacked in Kuwaiti waters by Iranian Silkworm (Chinese-built) missiles. Other nations also sent ships to protect their countries' oil tankers and to keep the Gulf shipping lanes open. In April 1988 the Iranian navy attacked the United States fleet in the Persian Gulf. In less than one day the United States military destroyed one-fifth of Iran's navy while losing only one helicopter. In July 1988, an Iranian civilian airliner was destroyed over the Persian Gulf by gunfire from the *U.S.S. Vincennes*, which mistook the plane for a fighter jet. All 290 persons on the plane died in the attack. The destruction by a terrorist of a Pan Am flight bound from London to New York on December 21, 1988, was believed to be in retaliation for the *Vincennes* action. All 259 people on board the plane died, as well as 11 people on the ground, as the plane went down over Lockerbie, Scotland.

Reagan's Second Term

Income Tax Reform

The 1986 Income Tax Reform Act, which the President signed on October 22, completed a long overdue process. The tax code had become unwieldy, with patchwork changes and revisions introduced over the years. The 1986 act simplified the code, exempted millions of low-income families from federal income taxes, reduced the highest bracket to 28 percent, and closed numerous loopholes.

The Election of 1986

Attention focused on the Senate, where the Republicans had held a majority since the election of 1980. President Reagan toured the country to help elect Republicans to the Senate, but the voters gave the Democrats a resounding victory. They picked up eight seats, giving them a majority of 55 to 45.

Wall Street Crash

On Monday, October 19, 1987, the New York Stock Exchange registered its largest point decline in history when the Dow-Jones industrial average plummeted 508.32 points in a day of frenetic trading, as 604 million shares (by far the greatest number ever) changed hands. The Dow made a quick recovery and regained almost 300 points in the next two days.

The Balance of Trade

A worrisome aspect of the American economy was the persistent negative balance of trade which, during the Reagan years, had seen the United States change from a creditor to a debtor nation in international trade. The annual negative balance was running at $170 billion. The dollar, which was worth 360 yen during the first quarter century following World War II, was now trading at about 120 yen—one third its previous value. Americans were buying automobiles, cameras, computers, radio and television sets, even steel from Japan, while the Japanese were buying only unprocessed raw materials such as timber, oil, metals, grains, and fiber from the United States. The imbalance was causing the closing of factories and the displacement of labor in American industry.

The Iran-Contra Affair

On November 3, 1986, the Lebanese newspaper *Al-Shiraa* reported that the United States had sold arms to Iran after a secret visit by National Security Adviser Robert McFarlane. Less than 24 hours earlier, the U.S. hostage, David P. Jacobsen, who was kidnapped in May 1985, was released. Six hostages remained in Beirut. It was apparent that an "arms for hostages" deal had been made.

In an effort to win the release of the hostages, the Reagan administration secretly sold arms to Iran. The money paid by Iran for these arms was then used to fund the Contra rebels in Nicaragua. This secret and illegal diversion of funds was carried out by Lt. Colonel **Oliver North** with the knowledge of his superiors (Robert McFarlane and John Poindexter) on the National Security Council. It was an attempt by the Reagan administration to bypass Congress, which had passed the **Boland Amendment** outlawing aid to the Contras. Revelation of these activities caused a furor in the nation.

Investigation of the Iran-Contra Affair

Both the House and the Senate established select committees to investigate the Iran-Contra scandal. It was decided that the committees would meet jointly and conduct televised hearings. The hearings before the joint congressional committee opened in May 1987 and terminated three months later in August 1987. The committee's final report was submitted in November 1987. Criminal prosecution was assigned to an independent counsel, Lawrence E. Walsh.

Conclusion

Testimony at the hearing disclosed that high U.S. government officials provided the Contras with private and international sources of funds for conducting military operations against the Nicaraguan government.

In its final report, the majority concluded: "It was the President's policy—not an isolated decision by (Oliver) North or Poindexter—to sell arms secretly to Iran and to maintain the Contras, 'body and soul,' the Boland amendment notwithstanding . . ."

Independent counsel **Lawrence Walsh** secured indictment of **Oliver North** on twelve counts. North, a Lt. Colonel in the U.S. Marines, played a key role in the illegal Contra aid operations when he served as Assistant Director of the National Security Council from 1981 to 1986. He was tried in Federal District Court presided over by Judge Gerhard Gesell. The trial ended in a verdict of not guilty on nine counts and guilty on three counts: (1) aiding and abetting obstruction of Congress; (2) destroying government documents; and (3) receiving an illegal gratuity in the form of a security system for his home. North was fined $150,000 and given a three-year suspended sentence, but his conviction was later overturned on technical grounds. In 1994, North ran unsuccessfully for the U.S. Senate in Virginia.

Decline of President Reagan's Popularity

A "Special Review Board" was appointed by President Reagan on December 1, 1986 to investigate the Iran-Contra affair. John Tower was named chairman and the other two members were Edmund Muskie and Brent Scowcroft.

The Tower Commission report of February 26, 1987 stated "The President did not seem to be aware of the way in which the operation (arms for hostages) was implemented and the full consequences of U.S. participation . . . At no time did he insist on accountability."

In a nationally televised speech on March 4, 1987, President Reagan said, "I told the American people I did not trade arms for hostages. My heart and my best intentions still tell me that's true. But the facts and the evidence tell me it's not. . . . what began as a strategic opening to Iran deteriorated in its implementation into trading arms for hostages. It was a mistake." Disclosure of the arms deals had a dramatic impact on Reagan's standing in the polls. In *The New York Times*-CBS News poll reported December 1, 1986, his approval rating dropped from 67 percent a month earlier to 46 percent.

The decline in Reagan's popularity was reflected in his difficulty in gaining congressional support for his agenda. Congress overrode his veto of a transportation bill for spending $87.5 billion on highway and mass transit and allowing states to increase the speed limit to 65 m.p.h. The Senate rejected his nomination of Judge Robert H. Bork for the Supreme Court. In

February 1988, the House voted against military aid to the Contras and the Contra forces went into decline.

But Ronald Reagan was flexible enough to ride out the storm. Moreover, his success at the Moscow summit with the Soviet leader Mikhail Gorbachev that produced a nuclear arms agreement helped to restore his popularity. In Moscow the President and Gorbachev signed the historic **Intermediate Nuclear Forces (INF)** treaty.

Exercise Set 6.15

1. President Reagan's "supply-side" economic program was characterized by
   A. a budget brought into balance by income equal to expenditures
   B. a budget evenly balanced between spending for defense and spending for social programs
   C. an effort to maintain a favorable balance of trade
   D. a tax program designed to bring about an increase in the supply of consumer goods

2. Which of the following was *not* an aspect of the 1984 elections?
   A. Ronald Reagan scored a landslide victory
   B. television debates were held between the presidential and vice presidential candidates
   C. Democrats failed to gain control of the U.S. Senate
   D. there was a growing movement in favor of modifying the method of electing a President

3. Which of the following was *not* a foreign policy objective of the Reagan administration?
   A. cessation of violence and armed conflict between Arabs and Israelis in the Middle East
   B. immediate end of the apartheid policy of the South African government
   C. overthrow of the Marxist government of Nicaragua
   D. economic and diplomatic cooperation with the government and people of Japan

4. Which of the following was *not* a sign of President Reagan's declining influence during his second term?
   A. appointment of a congressional committee to investigate the Iran-Contra affair
   B. Democrats regain control of the Senate in the 1986 election
   C. Congress passes the 1986 Tax Reform Act
   D. Congress passes the Clean Water Act of 1987 over President Reagan's veto

5. Which of the following did *not* occur during President Reagan's second term?
   A. the trade deficits were brought back approximately into balance
   B. a severe crash occurred on the New York Stock Exchange
   C. Reagan and Gorbachev negotiated the Intermediate Nuclear Forces (INF) treaty
   D. Congress passed the Gramm-Rudman-Hollings Balanced Budget Act

PRESIDENT GEORGE BUSH (1989–1993)

The Election of 1988

The Primaries

Major contestants for the Republican nomination were Vice President George Bush, Senator Robert Dole of Kansas, minority leader of the Senate, television evangelist Pat Robertson, and Representative Jack Kemp of New York.

On the Democratic side there were more contestants. Former Senator Gary Hart was an early casualty of the media when he was caught in a liaison with a woman other than his wife. Others actively seeking the nomination were Governor Michael Dukakis of Massachusetts, the Reverend Jesse Jackson of Chicago, Senator Albert Gore of Tennessee, Representative Richard Gephardt of Missouri, Senator Paul Simon of Illinois, and Senator Joseph R. Biden, Jr., of Delaware.

In the first Republican primaries, Dole made a strong showing, but Bush fought back, gained the lead, and pulled ahead, clinching the nomination in April, four months before the Republican convention. The Democratic race narrowed down to a contest between Dukakis and Jackson, with the former steadily increasing his lead. Dukakis was nominated at the Democratic convention in July and chose Senator Lloyd Bentsen of Texas for Vice President.

In August, **Bush** won the nomination at the Republican convention. He made a controversial choice for a running mate, the young and relatively inexperienced Senator **Dan Quayle** of Indiana.

The Campaign and Election

Neither candidate evoked enthusiasm from the electorate, and the campaign seemed lackluster. It was fought chiefly on television and in the press. Bush was accused of using negative campaigning for calling Dukakis a "card-carrying liberal" and for running the controversial and racist "Willie Horton" TV ad campaign.

	Popular Vote	Percent	Electoral Vote
Bush	47,917,341	54	426
Dukakis	41,013,030	46	112

In Congress the Democrats gained strength in both houses while failing to win the presidency. The voters evidently determined to divide governmental power between the two parties. In the Senate, the Democrats gained one seat, giving them a majority of 55 to 45. In the House, they added 5 seats to give them a majority of 262 to 173.

The Bush Program and Promises

In a 20-minute inaugural address on January 20, 1989, President Bush singled out major problems that his administration would address. Referring to the national deficit he said, "We have more will than wallet; but will is what we need." He called the national epidemic of drug abuse a scourge and said, "Take my word for it: this scourge will stop." He called on the Democratic Congress, whom he referred to as his "friends" in the "loyal opposition," to join him in a bipartisan effort to solve the social problems of homelessness, poverty, and "the rough crime of the streets." Bush had earlier expressed the hope that he could lead "a kinder, gentler nation."

In a nationally televised address to Congress in February 1989, Bush outlined his budget proposals, encompassing broad outlines for the future. "We must make a very substantial cut in the federal budget deficit." In addition to the immediate goal of "meeting the targets set forth in the Gramm-Rudman-Hollings law," he asked for enactment of two-year budgets, a line-item veto provision, and the passing of a constitutional amendment requiring a balanced budget. He repeated his pledge of no new taxes.

Specific proposals included $2.2 billion for the National Science Foundation; a permanent tax credit law to promote basic research; a cut in the maximum tax rate on capital gains; and incentive awards for educational excellence. He said, "I'd like to be the Education President." President Bush asked for an increase of almost a billion dollars in budget outlays to escalate the war against drugs. Additional outlays were proposed for a new attack on organized crime; for education to prevent AIDS and research to find a cure; for upgrading and protecting the environment through a new Clean Air Act, and enforcement of laws against toxic wastes.

He called for a new child-care tax credit adjustment and guaranteed full funding of Social Security, including a full cost-of-living increase. He asserted his support for restoring the integrity of the failing savings and loan industry. He asked for a one-year freeze in the military budget, and overhauling of the defense procurement process.

On plans for world peace he would carefully assess the changes taking place in the Soviet Union and added, "I have personally assured General Secretary Gorbachev that . . . we will be ready to move forward."

Domestic Events

Savings and Loan Scandal

Savings and loan institutions (S&Ls or "thrifts") boomed following World War II, primarily by financing veterans' guaranteed home-mortgage loans at low interest rates. The S&Ls were legally restricted from matching the higher interest rates charged by other financial institutions, like commercial banks. In the early 1980s Congress and the Reagan administration **deregulated** the S&L industry, eliminated interest ceilings, and allowed the S&Ls to make commercial loans. Although the S&Ls were still regulated, and their deposits insured by the Federal Savings and Loan Insurance Corporation (FSLIC), a laissez-faire attitude prevailed, and following deregulation many of the S&Ls began to make high-risk loans and unsound investments, often in commercial real estate.

When the nation's economy faltered, many of the S&Ls' borrowers were unable to repay their loans, and the savings and loan institutions began to collapse. The FSLIC soon ran out of funds to back up the failing S&Ls, and the **Federal Deposit Insurance Corporation (FDIC)** had to assume the responsibility. The eventual cost to taxpayers over the next 40 years is estimated at $500 billion.

Census of 1990

Article I, Section 2, of the Constitution provides that a census be taken every ten years to determine the number of representatives a state shall have in Congress. According to the 1990 census, the nation's population in 1990 was approximately 249,500,000, an increase of about 23 million over the 1980 count. Adjustments in Congress, where the total number of Representatives remains at 435, included losses in New York (3 seats), Pennsylvania, Michigan, Ohio, and Illinois (2 seats each), and the loss of one seat in each of eight other states. Gains in congressional representation came in California (7 seats), Florida (4 seats), Texas (3 seats), and gains of one seat in each of five other states.

Americans with Disabilities Act (1990)

Passed by Congress July 13, 1990, the Americans with Disabilities Act (ADA) has been considered the most significant antidiscrimination legislation since the Civil Rights Acts of the 1960s. The law bans discrimination against people with physical or mental impairments in employment, transportation, public accommodations, and communications services.

Supreme Court Decisions

In *Cruzan* v. *Director, Missouri Department of Health* (1990), the Supreme Court addressed the issue of termination of life support. In a 6-3 decision, the Court found that a person did have a liberty interest under the due process clause of the Fourteenth Amendment to refuse medical treatment if there was clear and convincing evidence that they were competent when making the decision.

The issue of abortion was reviewed in *Planned Parenthood of Southeastern Pennsylvania* v. *Casey* (1992), when the Court reaffirmed a woman's right to have an abortion pursuant to *Roe* v. *Wade* (1973), but upheld waiting periods and parental notification by minors prior to obtaining an abortion.

Nomination and Confirmation of Clarence Thomas to the Supreme Court

President Bush selected Judge **Clarence Thomas** of the District of Columbia Circuit Court, a conservative Republican African American, to replace the retiring Justice **Thurgood Marshall**, an African American liberal and longtime proponent of civil rights. This nomination created some of the most heated Senate confirmation proceedings in the history of the nation. Major points of debate during the early hearings of the Senate Judiciary Committee were Thomas's opposition to **affirmative action** for minorities and women and questions about his stance on the *Roe* v. *Wade* decision on abortion rights.

In the course of the hearings, Democratic committee members raised allegations of sexual harassment, supported by testimony from law professor Anita Hill of the University of Oklahoma, who had worked for Judge Thomas at the Equal Employment Opportunity Commission during the Reagan administration. Judge Thomas reappeared before the committee to deny Professor Hill's charges and called the hearings a "high-tech lynching." After heated and partisan debate, the Senate confirmed his appointment on October 15, 1991, in a very close 52 to 48 vote, with 11 Democrats crossing party lines to vote with the Republicans.

Foreign Affairs

Invasion of Panama (December 20, 1989–January 3, 1990)

In April 1989 a report of the narcotics subcommittee of the Senate Foreign Relations Committee charged that the head of the Panamanian Defense Forces (PDF), **General Manuel Noriega**, "controlled all elements of the Panamanian government essential to the protection of drug trafficking and money laundering." Federal grand juries in Miami and Tampa, Florida, indicted Noriega on charges of drug trafficking. President Bush appealed for his overthrow, but Noriega survived economic sanctions and several coup attempts and annulled a May 1989 election in which he had been defeated.

On December 16, 1989, an off-duty American marine was shot to death by members of the PDF. With fairly wide approval, both in the United States and Panama, President Bush sent 10,000 American troops into Panama on December 20, 1989, to protect American lives and interests and to capture General Noriega and bring him to the United States to stand trial. Noriega surrendered on January 3, 1990, and was taken to Miami, where he was tried and found guilty of cocaine trafficking, racketeering, and money laundering; he was sentenced to a 40-year jail term. On December 11, 2011, Noriega was returned to Panama to serve a 20-year prison term. The invasion was condemned by the United Nations, but President Bush found legal support for the military action in a clause of the **1977 Panama Canal Treaty**, which allowed the United States to take action to protect the Panama Canal.

Operation Desert Storm

After unsuccessful talks about oil production and debt repayment between Iraq and its neighbor Kuwait, Iraqi president **Saddam Hussein** invaded and annexed Kuwait on August 2, 1990, declaring it to be a province of Iraq. Fearing that Iraq's next target might be Saudi Arabia, President Bush ordered 430,000 U.S. troops to Saudi Arabia to protect the world's largest oil reserves. "Operation Desert Shield," as this first phase was known, began on August 6, 1990, and its purpose was to "draw a line in the sand" (between Kuwait and Iraq) behind which Iraq's large army would have to retreat. On November 8, 1990, a United Nations Security Council resolution set a January 15, 1991, deadline for Iraq to withdraw from Kuwait.

The Iraqi withdrawal from Kuwait did not take place, and President Bush ordered a devastating air assault against military targets in Iraq and Kuwait. The phase of bombing and ground offensive by the allied powers was known as "Operation Desert Storm." The U.S. and allied forces carried out a massive bombing campaign for five weeks. On February 24, 1991, they began a ground campaign, directed by **General Norman Schwartzkopf**, that smashed through Hussein's armies, retaking Kuwait and occupying most of southern Iraq in only four days of combat. The retreating Iraqi forces set fire to over 500 of Kuwait's oil wells, causing a widespread environmental disaster. There were widespread fears that the Iraqis would resort to chemical and biological warfare, as they had previously done in their war with Iran and in campaigns against the Kurdish minorities. There has been no evidence that the Iraqis used any such weapons, although traces of nerve gas and mustard gas were detected, possibly from stockpiles destroyed by U.S. bombings.

On February 27, 1991, 100 hours after the land battle began, President Bush ordered a unilateral cease-fire, and on March 3, 1991, Iraq agreed to abide by the UN resolutions. An official cease-fire agreement was signed April 6, 1991.

South Africa

Although more than 75 percent of the people living in South Africa were black, throughout the 20th century the nation was ruled by its white minority, and blacks were not permitted to vote. In addition, the government had adopted **apartheid** a system of segregation that enforced a firm separation of different races and denied many basic civil rights to blacks. In 1986 Congress overrode a veto by President Reagan and passed legislation that implemented mandatory economic sanctions against South Africa, in an attempt to put pressure on its government to end apartheid.

In 1990 the South African government under President F. W. deKlerk, began to modify its policies. It recognized the African National Congress party and freed its leader, **Nelson Mandela** after 27 years' imprisonment. Later that year deKlerk began negotiations with Mandela regarding a new constitution which was adopted in 1993. In April 1994 the first multiracial elections were held in South Africa, which resulted in Mandela becoming president in May.

The End of the Cold War

The Soviet Union struggled under Gorbachev. Its economy had been weakened by years of mismanagement, poor achievement, and burden of supporting expensive military spending. Ecological disasters further strained the economy. Additionally, the war in Afghanistan, begun in 1979, proved unwinnable and unpopular, and caused unrest inside the Soviet Union and discredit outside. In February 1989 the last Soviet troops withdrew. Under Gorbachev the Soviet Union began rapidly loosening its grip on Eastern Europe and the various Soviet Republics. In August 1991 hard-line Communists with the Soviet government attempted to gain power through a coup. With the assistance of **Boris Yeltsin**, who later became the first elected President of Russia, the coup was defeated

Poland, Hungary, Romania, Bulgaria, Czechoslovakia, and East Germany, under Soviet control since the end of World War II, were permitted to become independent of Russian influence at the end of the 1980s and they began to change their Communist governments and adopt capitalism and democracy. In 1989 the **Berlin Wall**, the symbol of the Cold War, was torn down. Subsequently and peaceably, East Germany reunited with West Germany in 1990. The Warsaw Pact was disbanded.

The various republics that comprised the Soviet Union itself likewise became independent nations. In Europe, The Baltic republics of Estonia, Latvia, and Lithuania, and the more central republics of Belarus, the Ukraine, and Moldova become independent nations. In Asia, the transcaucasian republics of Georgia, Armenia, and Azerbaijan become independent nations, as did the central Asian republics of Kazakhastan, Uzbekistan, Turkmenistan, Kyrgyzstan, and Tajikistan. Finally, the vast majority of land and people comprising the former Soviet Union became the nation of Russia. In December 1991 the Soviet Union officially ceased to exist. President Bush stated that a "new world order" had begun, and in February 1992 he met with Russian President Yeltsin and they formally declared that the Cold War was over.

Exercise Set 6.16

1. In the United States, most new jobs created during the 1980s were jobs that
   A. were classified as managerial
   B. provided services rather than goods
   C. depended on heavy manufacturing
   D. were farm related

2. Both the Bay of Pigs invasion of Cuba (1961) and the invasion of Panama (1989) are examples of the U.S. attempt to
   A. eliminate unfriendly governments geographically close to the United States
   B. cultivate good relations with Latin American nations
   C. stop the drug trade
   D. end the Cold War

3. Under current federal laws, Americans with disabilities must be
   A. placed in federally funded institutions near their homes
   B. guaranteed access to public transportation and facilities
   C. educated and supported by their families without governmental help
   D. educated only until they complete the eighth grade

4. Which demographic trend has occurred in the United States during the past ten years?
   A. The average age of the population has decreased
   B. The birthrate has rapidly increased
   C. Life expectancy has decreased
   D. The proportion of the population over age 65 has grown

5. Which of the following was the result of a congressional declaration of war?
   A. The 1989 invasion of Panama
   B. Operation Desert Storm
   C. World War II
   D. Vietnam War

6. Presidential nominations of the Supreme Court Justices can lead to controversy because
   A. Congress consistently refuses to approve candidates who are not members of the majority parties
   B. Congress claims it has the sole right to nominate justices
   C. Presidents most often nominate their friends rather than persons with judicial experience
   D. The President and Congress sometimes have different views on the judicial philosophy that a proposed justice should hold

7. The results of the national census taken every ten years most directly affects which of the following?
   A. Number of justices on the Supreme Court
   B. Total electoral votes
   C. Composition of the House of Representatives
   D. President's Cabinet

CHAPTER REVIEW QUESTIONS

1. President Ronald Reagan's federal budget proposals came under sharp criticism because they
   A. lowered interest rates and decreased inflation
   B. increased social welfare spending
   C. included very large deficits
   D. advocated raising the income tax

2. In the United States in the 1980s, negotiations between labor and management frequently resulted in labor's acceptance of lower wages and greater automation in return for management's guarantees of job security for workers. This trend best indicates that
   A. labor and management are responding to the threats posed by foreign competition
   B. management is becoming more interested in strengthening labor unions
   C. legislation has required changes in labor contracts
   D. labor unions are becoming more powerful

Base your answer to question 3 on the cartoon below and on your knowledge of social studies.

3. The main idea of the cartoon is that
   A. regulation of the savings-and-loan industry is more important than campaign reform
   B. some problems cannot be solved by congressional action
   C. Congress cannot agree on spending priorities
   D. members of Congress sometimes avoid legislative actions that might limit their political careers

4. In the United States, large corporations would most likely support a congressional plan to
   A. require corporation-funded pension plans to workers
   B. grant capital investment tax credits
   C. mandate union shops in all corporations
   D. increase the minimum wage

5. In the 1980s, the reason that the federal government aided certain corporations that were on the verge of bankruptcy was that the government
   A. used the opportunity to break up monopolies
   B. pursued a trend toward public ownership of key industries
   C. sought to minimize the economic harm from collapse of these corporations
   D. wished to have more influence on the kinds of products made for sale to American consumers

6. A major reason for the ending of the Cold War Era was that
   A. the Soviet Union was seriously weakened by internal conflict and economic difficulties
   B. the United States and the Soviet Union were unable to destroy one another
   C. the Berlin Wall fell and Germany was reunited
   D. a recession forced the United States to cut military spending

ESSAYS

1. In the United States, situations frequently occur in which the interests of individuals have come into conflict with the perceived needs of society. Listed below are several issues that may lead to conflict.

Issues

Gun control
Affirmative action
Abortion
Death penalty
Prayer in public schools
Testing of individuals for drug use

   a. Choose *three* of the issues listed. For *each* one chosen, describe a perceived need of society related to the issue and show how the interests of individuals have come into conflict with this need.
   b. For *two* of the issues discussed in answer to "a," explain how a legislative or a judicial body has dealt with the conflict.

2. U.S. Presidents have used the power of their office to address a number of national and international issues. Each issue in the list below is paired with a specific President who addressed that issue.

Issues/Presidents

Reconstruction/Andrew Johnson
Environmental destruction/Theodore Roosevelt
Isolationism/Woodrow Wilson
Civil rights violations/Lyndon Johnson
Arab-Israeli tensions/Jimmy Carter
International aggression/George Bush

Choose *three* pairs from the list and for *each* one chosen:
- Describe conditions that let to the issue faced by the President
- Discuss how the President exercised a power of his office to deal with the issue
- Evaluate the success of the President's response in dealing with the issue

3. In the United States today, people hold different viewpoints concerning controversial issues. Some of these areas of controversy are listed below.

Areas of Controversy

Capital punishment
Right to die
Affirmative action
Censorship
Health care funding
Homelessness

Choose *three* of the areas of controversy listed and for *each* one chosen:
- State an issue involved in the controversy
- Discuss *two* different points of view concerning the issue
- Describe a specific action taken by government or a group to deal with the issue

THEMATIC ESSAY

Directions: Write a well-organized essay that includes an introduction, several paragraphs addressing the task below, and a conclusion.

Theme: Equality, Change, Equal Protection

> Throughout U.S. history, women have slowly gained equal status with men in the areas of voting, marriage rights, jury service, political office holding, and educational and professional opportunities, among others.

Task:

> From your study of the women's movement for equal rights throughout U.S. history, identify *three* occurrences (legislation, cases, organizations, etc.) that have furthered the equal status of women.
>
> For each occurrence selected:
> - Discuss the issue(s) addressed.
> - Describe the action(s) taken and results.
> - Explain how the legislation, case, organization, etc., has ultimately changed the position of women in U.S. society.

You may use governmental actions from any period in U.S. history. Some suggestions you might wish to consider are married women's property acts, Nineteenth Amendment (1920), Fair Labor Standards Act (1963), Civil Rights Act (1964), Title IX Equal Education Access (1971), *Roe* v. *Wade* (1973), National Organization of Women (1966–Present), and Affirmative Action.

You are *not* limited to these suggestions.

DOCUMENT-BASED QUESTION ESSAY

The following questions (Part A and Part B) are based on the accompanying documents (1–5). Some of these documents have been edited for the purpose of this exercise. The question is designed to test your ability to work with historical documents and to demonstrate your knowledge of the subject matter being presented. As you analyze the documents, take into account both the source of the document and the author's point of view.

Historical Context: From the Korean conflict (1950–1953) through Operation Desert Storm (1991) the question of the President of the United States being able to order U.S. troops to a warring area of the world without a declaration of war by Congress has been debated.

Task: Using information from the documents and your knowledge of United States history, answer the questions that follow each document in Part A. Your answers to the questions will help you write the Part B essay, in which you will be asked:

> Did the War Powers Resolution (1973) infringe upon the executive powers associated with the Commander in Chief's responsibilities enumerated in the Constitution?

Part A
Short Answer

The documents below refer to the era of the Warren Supreme Court. Examine each document carefully and then answer the questions that follow.

DOCUMENT 1

> Sec. 1. This joint resolution may be cited as the "War Powers Resolution."
>
> PURPOSE AND POLICY Sec. 2. (a) It is the purpose of this joint resolution to fulfill the intent of the framers of the Constitution of the United States and insure that the collective judgment of both the Congress and the President will apply to the introduction of the United States Armed Forces into hostilities, or into situations where imminent involvement in hostilities is clearly indicated by the circumstances, and to the continued use of such forces in hostilities or in such situations.

—War Powers Resolution (1973)

1. What two branches of the federal government are required by Sec. 2 (a) of the War Powers Act to participate in decisions involving deployment of United States Armed Forces into hostilities?

_____

_____

_____

_____

DOCUMENT 2

(b) Within sixty calendar days after a report is submitted or is required to be submitted pursuant to section 4(a)(1), whichever is earlier, the President shall terminate any use of the United States Armed Forces with respect to which such report was submitted (or required to be submitted), unless the Congress (1) has declared war or has enacted a specific authorization for such use of United States Armed Forces, (2) has extended by law such sixty-day period, or (3) is physically unable to meet as a result of an armed attack upon the United States. Such sixty-day period shall be extended for not more than an additional thirty days if the President determines and certifies to the Congress in writing that unavoidable military necessity respecting the safety of United States Armed Forces requires the continued use of such armed forces in the course of bringing about a prompt removal of such forces.

—War Powers Resolution (1973)

2. Under what three circumstances would Congress allow the continuation of the deployment of troops by the President?

_____

_____

_____

_____

In his veto message (October 24, 1973), President Richard Nixon argued that the War Powers Bill infringed upon his constitutional powers as Commander in Chief.

I hereby return without my approval House Joint Resolution 542—the War Powers Resolution......
I am particularly disturbed by the fact that certain of the President's constitutional powers as Commander in Chief of the Armed Forces would terminate automatically under this resolution sixty days after they were invoked.....

—President Richard Nixon, Veto of War Powers Bill (October 24, 1973)

3. What power (checks and balances) was President Nixon using in his message above?

_____

_____

_____

_____

4. What particular executive power did President Nixon see being jeopardized by the War Powers Bill?

_____

_____

_____

_____

DOCUMENT 4

On August 2–4, 1964, two United States destroyers in the Gulf of Tonkin were reportedly fired on by North Vietnamese torpedo boats. President Johnson used the incident to secure from Congress the following mandate for United States military intervention.

The Tonkin Gulf Resolution

Whereas naval units of the Communist regime in Vietnam, in violation of the principles of the Charter of the United Nations and of international law, have deliberately and repeatedly attacked United States naval vessels lawfully present in international waters, and have thereby created a serious threat to international peace;

.......Now, therefore, be it *Resolved by the Senate and House of Representatives of the United States of America in Congress assembled,* that the Congress approves and supports the determination of the President, as Commander in Chief, take all necessary measures to repel any armed attack against the forces of the United States and to prevent further aggression.

—Tonkin Gulf Resolution, House and Senate Joint Resolution
(August 7, 1964)

5. How does the Tonkin Gulf Resolution (1964) differ from the War Powers Resolution (1973) regarding presidential power to send United States troops into action?

_____

_____

_____

_____

DOCUMENT 5

Toward the end of the Vietnam War...Congress, seeking to limit the Presidential power that had been used so ruthlessly in Indochina, passed the War Powers Act....

Almost immediately, President Gerald Ford violated the act when he ordered the invasion of a Cambodian island and the bombing of a Cambodian town in retaliation for the temporary detention of American merchant seamen on the ship *Mayaguez*.....

In the fall of 1982, President Reagan sent American marines into a dangerous situation in Lebanon....again ignoring the requirements of the War Powers Act. The following year, over 200 of those marines were killed when a bomb was exploded in their barracks by terrorists.....

—Howard Zinn, *A People's History of the United States* (1995)

6. What specific incidents does Professor Zinn cite as violations of the 1973 War Powers Resolution?

_____

_____

_____

_____

Part B
Essay

Your essay should be well organized with an introductory paragraph that states your position on the question. Develop your position in the next paragraphs and then write a conclusion. In your essay, include specific historical details and refer to the specific documents you analyzed in Part A. You may include additional information from your knowledge of social studies.

Historical Context: From the Korean conflict (1950–1953) through Operation Desert Storm (1991) the question of the President of the United States being able to order U.S. troops to a warring area of the world without a declaration of war by Congress has been debated.

Task:

> Using the documents provided and your knowledge of United States history, answer the following question: Did the War Powers Resolution (1973) infringe upon the Executive powers associated with the Commander in Chief's responsibilities enumerated in the Constitution?

Guidelines:

In your essay, be sure to
- Develop all aspects of the task
- Incorporate information from at least *five* documents
- Incorporate relevant outside information
- Support the theme with many relevant facts, examples, and details
- Use a logical and clear plan of organization, including an introduction and a conclusion that are beyond a restatement of the theme

CHAPTER 6

THE CLINTON ADMINISTRATIONS

THE ELECTION OF 1992

> Political campaigns are designedly made into emotional orgies which
> endeavor to distract attention from the real issues involved.
> James Harvey Robinson, *The Human Comedy* (1937)

The national elections, besides ending 12 years of Republican control of the executive branch, had several interesting features.

The Primaries

Democrats

The major contestants for the Democratic presidential nomination were Governor Bill Clinton of Arkansas, former Governor Jerry Brown of California, former Senator Paul Tsongas of Massachusetts, Senator Robert Kerry of Nebraska, and Senator Thomas Harkin of Iowa. Tsongas, Kerry, and Harkin left the field early after poor showings in the early primaries and caucuses, and the Democratic race came down to Governor Clinton and former Governor Brown.

By June, Clinton had gained the support of enough delegates to assure him the nomination. At the Democratic National Convention in New York City in July the party's delegates selected Clinton to be the Democratic nominee for President. The delegates also approved Clinton's choice of Senator Albert Gore of Tennessee as the vice presidential candidate.

Republicans

The two main candidates for the Republican nomination were the incumbent President George Bush and conservative newspaper and television commentator Pat Buchanan. At the Republican National Convention in Houston in August, the party's delegates renominated George Bush for President and Dan Quayle for Vice President. The convention and the campaign were influenced, however, by conservative and religious elements within the Republican party who wanted stronger efforts to ban abortion and permit school prayer. Bush's efforts to accommodate the right-wing Republicans may have hindered his ability to appeal to more middle-of-the-road voters.

Independent

Ross Perot, a self-made Texas billionaire, entered the presidential race, withdrew, and then reentered. Perot's platform consisted mainly of a businessman's approach to economic reform. With the help of his "Volunteers," Perot succeeded in getting his name on the ballot in all 50 states, and in the November elections he polled 19 percent (19,236,411) of the popular vote, an unusually high showing for a third-party candidate.

The Campaign and the Election

Bush's popularity, based on his successes in foreign affairs (the Persian Gulf War, the end of Communism in the Soviet Union and Eastern Europe), appeared to assure him of an easy victory, but the realities of economic problems at home soon increased the electorate's demand for change. The recession of 1990 lingered on through 1992, and the unemployment rate remained at about 7.5 percent. Further reflecting a weak economy, the government reported that the poverty rate had risen again for the second consecutive year, to 14.2 percent of the population.

Governor Clinton's campaign concentrated on the economic issues, using the slogan "It's the economy, stupid." His platform included raising taxes on the wealthy and trimming tax breaks for corporations. President Bush criticized the Democratic platform as a "tax and spend" program and blamed the nation's economic troubles on the Democrat-controlled Congress.

Clinton Becomes the Nation's 42nd President

The total turnout of voters (101,129,210) for the presidential election represented about 55 percent of all those eligible to vote, an increase of about 5 percent over the 1988 election. Perot's showing in the election was the strongest for a third-party candidate since Theodore Roosevelt ran on the progressive Bull Moose ticket in 1912. Democrats maintained control of Congress, and four women were elected to the Senate (bringing the number of women Senators to six), including Carol Mosely Braun of Illinois, the first African American woman ever elected. The Senate also gained its first Native American member when Ben Nighthorse Campbell was elected as a Democrat from Colorado.

	Popular Vote	Percent	Electoral Vote
Clinton	43,727,625	43	370
Bush	38,165,180	38	168
Perot	19,236,411	19	0

PRESIDENT BILL CLINTON (1993–2001)

> All progress has resulted from people who took unpopular positions.
> Adlai E. Stevenson, Speech at Princeton University, New Jersey,
> March 22, 1954

Clinton Policies and Programs

President William Jefferson ("Bill") Clinton took the oath of office as the nation's 42nd President on January 20, 1993. Born in Hope, Arkansas, August 19, 1946, he was the first President born after World War II. In contrast to the laissez-faire policies of his immediate predecessors, Clinton immediately proposed a series of far-reaching domestic reforms. Focusing on the economy and health care, his agenda included a North American Free Trade Agreement (NAFTA), anticrime legislation—which he characterized by the phrase "three strikes and you're out"—welfare reform designed to put people to work, and a national service program whereby federal education loans could be repaid through community service.

Family Leave

One of President Clinton's first initiatives was the signing of a family leave bill, which had been vetoed by the previous Republican administrations. The law permits employees up to 12 weeks of unpaid leave without loss of seniority in order to respond to family needs, such as the birth of a child or the illness of a parent.

Economic Program

President Clinton had made economic recovery the centerpiece of his election campaign. He was not able to obtain passage of his economic stimulus package, designed to reduce unemployment, due to a Republican filibuster in the Senate. However, Clinton's main economic legislation was contained in his first federal budget bill, which included a sizable tax increase targeted to pay for new spending and to reduce the budget deficit. The bill squeaked through Congress by a vote of 218 to 216 in the House of Representatives and by Vice President Gore voting in favor to break a 50 to 50 tie in the Senate.

The U.S. economy rebounded very strongly under Clinton's presidency. Overall, more the 20 million new jobs were created between 1993 and 2000. Unemployment declined significantly, decreasing from 7.5 percent in 1992 to 4.3 percent in 1999. Inflation declined, generally being under 3 percent thorough Clinton's presidency, and concomitantly real wages rose 6 percent since 1993. The budget deficit declined, as the President and Congress presented balanced budgets. The stock market registered historic gains, with the Dow Jones average rising from the mid-3,000s in January 1993 to over 11,000 in 2000. One of the few remaining economic problems was the foreign trade deficit, which continued to grow, reaching a record $271.3 billion in 1999.

Anticrime Measures

Clinton made passage of the Brady Handgun Violence Prevention Act a priority. The bill was name for **James Brady**, President Reagan's press secretary, who was seriously wounded in the 1981 assassination attempt on Reagan. The bill, initially proposed seven years earlier, finally passed and was signed into law in 1993. The Brady Law took effect in February 1994 and mandated that anyone seeking to purchase a handgun had to wait five days while local law enforcement conducted a background check to ensure that no one forbidden from owning a gun was sold a handgun.

Crime Bill

In 1994 Clinton was able to secure passage of a major crime bill. One provision of the bill was designed to add 100,000 extra police officers to local police departments throughout the nation. The most controversial part of the bill banned semiautomatic assault weapons, guns that can fire up to six bullets a second and hold up to 50 rounds of ammunition. The National Rifle Association strongly opposed the measure as infringing on the Second Amendment. However, the provision was able to pass, and it forbade the manufacture of importation of semiautomatic assault weapons or guns holding more than ten bullets in a round.

Health Care

A prominent element of Clinton's agenda was health care reform. He supported the goal of trying to pass legislation to provide for universal health care for every American child and adult, which would have had the effect of extending health care to more than 37 million uninsured Americans. He appointed his wife, Hillary Rodham Clinton, to head a task force on health care reform. The comprehensive health care plan that the administration ultimately proposed was attacked by many for being too large and costly. Most Republican legislators opposed the plan as impinging too much on the private sector. Attempts to reach a compromise failed, resulting in a major setback for President Clinton. In 1996 Congress passed a much more limited measure, the Health Insurance Portability and Accountability Act, which limited health insurance exclusions for preexisting conditions and provided that persons who had insurance and switched jobs had a right to maintain their health insurance.

North American Free Trade Agreement (NAFTA)

The NAFTA pact was negotiated by the United States, Canada, and Mexico to stimulate trade among them by removing trade barriers, most notably tariffs. The international agreement was signed by President Bush in December 1992, and had strong Republican support. President Clinton worked diligently for its passage, arguing that in the increasing internationalized business world, such policies would assist American companies and consumers. It was opposed by labor groups, including the AFL-CIO, which feared that American workers would lose jobs to Mexico, where workers received lower wages and there were fewer government-mandated environmental and workplace protections. Former presidential candidate **Ross Perot** also opposed the agreement, stating the if NAFTA were adopted, there would be a large "sucking sound" of American jobs being siphoned off to Mexico. The final agreement included provisions for tighter enforcement of labor laws and environmental standards. A coalition of Republican and Democratic congressional votes enabled NAFTA to become law in November 1993.

1994 Midterm Elections

The Republicans won in a landslide in the 1994 midterm elections, gaining an additional 52 seats in the House of Representatives and 9 seats in the Senate, which enabled them to retake control of both the House and the Senate. It marked the largest midterm election gain since 1958, and was the first time since the 1952 election that the Republicans controlled Congress. Newt Gingrich became the first Republican Speaker of the House since 1952, and Robert Dole became Majority Leader of the Senate.

The Republican Agenda

The House Republicans sought to have a group of ten conservative programs, which they had labeled their "Contract with America," become law, achieving only mixed success. Initially, they successfully enacted into law measures that mandated that federal labor laws apply to Congress itself, and that prohibited Congress from passing "unfunded mandates," laws the federal government imposed upon the states, unless the states were also given funds for their enforcement. However, other measures ran into opposition from the Senate, the President, or even the House itself.

Term Limits, Line Item Veto, and Free Speech

The Twenty-second Amendment to the Constitution, adopted in 1951, prohibits the President from serving more than two terms. Since 1990, attempts were made to have term limits apply to the House and Senate. The House of Representatives voted on a number of bills, most of which would have limited members to 12 years in the House and 12 years in the Senate. No measure was able to pass with most Democrats and a significant number of Republicans voting in opposition.

In *Clinton* v. *City of New York*, the Supreme Court noted that the line item veto gave the President powers that "are not the product of the 'finely wrought' procedure that the Framers designed." The Court held that the procedures in the Line Item Veto Act violated Article I, Section 7 of the Constitution and the act was thus unconstitutional.

In *Reno* v. *A.C.L.U.* (June 1997), the Supreme Court held that the Communication Decency Act was too broad in its restrictions of Internet speech and therefore violated freedom of speech protected by the First Amendment.

The Government Shutdown

In the first year in which President Clinton faced budget negotiations with Republican-controlled Congress, there were significant disagreements over priorities. In November 1995 Clinton vetoed two temporary measures, including a continuing resolution bill (a stopgap measure designed to be in effect until a permanent bill was enacted). He claimed that these bills contained "extreme proposals" that would have endangered the environment and spending for education. The Republicans sought cuts in Medicare spending over 150 percent higher than those favored by the President. The Republican congressional leadership refused to compromise and allowed a government shutdown, in which all nonessential government employees, approximately 770,000 workers, were furloughed. The shutdown was temporarily ended on November 20, but another went into effect on December 16, before finally ending on January 6, 1996. Polls showed that there was significantly more support for the President than for Congress. A compromise was finally reached when Clinton agreed to submit a bill to balance the federal budget by 2002 and the Republicans modified their proposed Medicare decrease. In 1997 Clinton and the Republican-led Congress enacted a plan to balance the federal budget by 2002.

Welfare Reform

Clinton had supported a welfare reform plan in his campaign, but had not obtained one by 1994. The Republicans campaigned for their own plan in the midterm election. Clinton vetoed two earlier Republican welfare bills, but with additional modifications enacted he signed the welfare bill. The law imposed time limits that individuals would have before they were removed from welfare, and added more money for childcare spending so that individuals with children could return to work. It provided that block grants would be made to the states and that each state would be able to design its own welfare program.

Foreign Affairs—The Search for Peace and Stability in the Post-Cold War World

After the breakup of the Soviet Union, the United States became the sole superpower in the world. With the Cold War now over, there was no longer any need to engage in proxy wars such as in Korea and Vietnam, and the fear of a nuclear war was significantly decreased. However, new foreign problems, including how to combat the increased threat of terrorism and what circumstances justified the use of U.S. troops abroad, faced the United States.

NATO Expansion

When Germany unified in 1990, the former East Germany became part of NATO. In 1997 NATO signed an agreement with Russia to cooperate in furthering peace in Europe and engage in joint operations. In 1999 NATO expanded by admitting the Czech Republic, Hungary, and Poland.

Somalia

On December 9, 1992, a UN-sanctioned force entered Somalia, led by 1,800 American marines. The military was there on a humanitarian relief mission to ensure delivery of food supplies to a famine-plagued country where 250,000 people had died and central authority had broken down under the pressure from competing warlords. In October 1993 18 U.S. marines were killed in a street battle with heavily armed Somalian factions. In March 1994 the last American troops were withdrawn, and in March 1995 the final UN peacekeeping troops left. Throughout the mission significant relief work occurred; however, lawlessness and the absence of any central government persisted; 30 U.S. soldiers died in combat and more than 175 were wounded.

Bosnia-Herzegovina

Following the death of its longtime leader Tito and the demise of the Soviet Union, Yugoslavia began to break up as century-old ethnic and religious conflicts flared up in violence. In 1992 Serb forces began a campaign of territorial expansion against their Croatian and Muslim neighbors, forcing them from villages they had occupied for centuries in a campaign of **ethnic cleansing** that bore many aspects of genocide. President Clinton condemned the actions of the aggressors but resisted pressure for American military intervention that would run counter to the wishes of the majority of Americans. In August and October 1995, NATO planes bombed Serb military positions in retaliation for bombings of civilians. After engaging in U.S.-sponsored peace talks, in December 1995 the parties signed a peace treaty that divided Bosnia into two autonomous sections, a Moslem-Croat federation and a Serb republic. The agreement called for 60,000 NATO troops to be employed to maintain peace.

Kosovo

In early 1999 Serb military and police began a concerted effort to force the majority ethnic Albanian population to leave the Serb province of Kosovo. This new campaign of ethnic cleansing again included the use of force, rape, and murder. By March 24 approximately 250,000 ethnic Albanians had fled. With the killings in Bosnia fresh in world memory, Clinton stated that "ending this tragedy is a moral imperative," and after Serb President **Slobodan Milosevic** had rejected a compromise on this issue, on March 24 NATO forces, including those of the United States, began an air bombardment campaign against Serb forces in Kosovo and military and related targets in Serbia itself. This marked the first time NATO had ever conducted an offensive military campaign against a country. The heavy bombing led Serbia to agree to a peace accord with NATO on June 3, and seven days later the bombing campaign ended. On June 12 NATO peacekeepers began to enter Kosovo and the UN authorized a peacekeeping force of 50,000.

No American troops were killed during the bombing. However, faulty intelligence reports led a U.S. B-2 "stealth" plane to bomb the Chinese embassy in Belgrade, killing three Chinese and wounding another twenty, a major embarrassment to the United States. While the success of the campaign ended the Serb ethnic cleansing, doubts persisted as to whether the Serb and Albanian populations in Kosovo would ever be able to coexist without the presence of peacekeeping troops.

Other Troubled Areas

In several troubled areas of the world the United States provided no military assistance or peacekeeping forces, but nevertheless played an important role in encouraging the peaceful resolution of long-standing difficulties.

The Middle East

In 1993 a major breakthrough for peace in the Middle East occurred during secret talks held in Oslo, Norway, between Israel and the Palestine Liberation Organization (PLO). In September **Yasir Arafat**, the chairman of the PLO, publicly stated the PLO recognized Israel's right to exist, while **Yitzhak Rabin**, the Prime Minister of Israel, stated that Israel recognized the PLO as the representative of the Palestine people.

At the White House on September 13, 1993, before a large gathering of international dignitaries organized by President Clinton, Israel and the PLO signed an interim accord providing for Palestinian self-rule in the Gaza Strip and the West Bank town of Jericho. The accord was the initial step in the peaceful resolution of the long-standing Israeli-Palestinian confrontation.

Northern Ireland

Since 1922, when Great Britain granted the lower twenty-six Irish counties independence but retained the six northern Irish provinces, tensions have existed in Northern Ireland between the Protestant majority and the Catholic minority. This conflict intensified in recent decades, with the Catholic Irish Republican Army and various Protestant paramilitary groups carrying out terrorist acts against each other, the British police force, and the civilian population in Northern Ireland and England. In 1996 President Clinton appointed former Senate Majority leader George Mitchell as a special envoy to attempt to negotiate a resolution to this impasse. With the support of both British Prime Minister **Tony Blair** and Irish Prime Minister **Bertie Ahern**, the "Good Friday Agreement" was reached on April 10, 1998. The principal provisions of the compromise included decommissioning arms, establishing a regional government that included representation on a cross-community basis, and allowing the decision of whether to be aligned with Britain or Ireland to be decided by the majority vote of the people of Northern Ireland. The agreement was approved with a "Yes" vote of over 94 percent in Ireland and over 71 percent in Northern Ireland in May 1998. In December 1999 Britain officially relinquished power over Northern Ireland to a new provisional government, although difficulties remained in getting all parties to give up their weapons.

Haiti

After the election as President of Father Jean-Bertrand Aristide, a Catholic priest, in September 1991, Haitian military commanders took control of the government and forced him to flee. The new dictatorship caused more than 50,000 Haitians to seek refuge abroad, many losing their lives at sea in fragile boats that sank or capsized.

With some 3,500 Americans remaining in Haiti, there was considerable pressure on President Clinton to use American military forces to liberate Haiti and restore Father Aristide to power. The military junta in Haiti signed an agreement in 1992 promising to step down, but it did not carry it out. The United States then enforced an economic embargo sanctioned by the UN. In 1994, when the military still refused to cede power, President Clinton threatened military action. At that point an eleventh-hour compromise was reached. President Clinton then sent 20,000 U.S. troops to Haiti to oversee the transition to democracy.

Terrorist Attacks

World Trade Center Attack

On February 5, 1993, a large bomb exploded at the World Trade Center in New York City. The explosion blew a 100-foot crater in the bottom of the building, killed six people, and wounded more than 1,000 others. The bombing was planned and carried out by a number of Middle East Islamic terrorists, motivated by anti-America and anti-Israel hatred.

Oklahoma City Attack

On April 19, 1995, the Alfred P. Murrah Federal Building in Oklahoma City, Oklahoma, was destroyed by a powerful bomb, which killed 168 people and injured more than 500 others. The enormous wanton destruction and the location of the attack, in the country's heartland, brought home to all Americans the danger of domestic terrorist activity. Further troubling was the fact that this attack was not made by foreign terrorists, but was carried out by U.S. citizens, who possessed far-right antigovernment beliefs. Two Americans were convicted in separate trials.

United States Embassy Bombings in Kenya and Tanzania

On August 7, 1998, the United States embassies in the East African countries of Kenya and Tanzania were destroyed by powerful terrorist bombs that exploded within minutes of each other. The two bombs killed over 260 people, including 12 Americans, and wounded more than 5,000 others. Evidence indicated that the bombings were masterminded and funded by the Islamic fundamentalist terrorist **Osama bin Laden**, then living in Afghanistan. In retaliation for the attack, on August 20 President Clinton ordered the firing of 75 Tomahawk cruise missiles at suspected terrorist facilities in Sudan and Afghanistan. In 1999 the UN imposed economic sanctions on Afghanistan for refusing to turn over bin Laden.

Columbine High School Shooting

On April 20, 1999, two students at Columbine High School in Littleton, Colorado, assaulted the school with guns, including a semiautomatic handgun, and bombs. Their rampage lasted several hours, ending after they killed 13 people (12 students and a teacher), wounded more than 30 others, and then committed suicide. The Columbine attack was the deadliest school attack in U.S. history. The nation was stunned by the ferocity of the attack and disturbed because it marked the seventh time within two years that a student had committed a fatal shooting at a U.S. school.

THE ELECTION OF 1996

> Tonight we proclaim that the vital American center is alive and well.
> William Jefferson Clinton, November 5, 1996

The Primaries

Democrats

Throughout most of 1995 it appeared that President Clinton might face one or more primary opponents. However, by early 1996, with President Clinton stating that he was standing up to "extreme" Republican congressional poli-cies, and with the strong economy continuing, his popularity had rebounded sufficiently so that he was to gain renomination without a primary challenge. At the Democratic National Convention in August the party's delegates renominated Bill Clinton for President and Al Gore for Vice President. In his acceptance speech Clinton stressed his economic program and promised to seek enactment of pro-education and family measures "to build a bridge to the 21st century."

Republicans

The principal candidates for the Republican nomination were Senator **Robert J. Dole** of Kansas, the Senate majority leader, **Lamar Alexander,** former Governor of Tennessee, **Steve Forbes**, independently wealthy president of *Forbes Magazine*, and **Patrick Buchanan**, conservative press commentator.

At the Republican National Convention in August the party's delegates nominated Robert Dole for President and his choice, **Jack F. Kemp**, for Vice President. The convention stressed tax reduction, strengthening national defense, and reducing government.

Independent

Ross Perot again ran for President as the nominee of the independent Reform party. Although Perot stressed similar themes as in 1992, in this election he never showed sufficient strength to be a serious contender.

The Campaign and the Election

President Clinton was buoyed by a strong economy, which he made his central campaign issue, stressing the creation of 10 million jobs while maintaining low inflation and unemployment. President Clinton also stated that he was maintaining the center of the political spectrum, often acting as a bulwark against "extreme" Republican congressional proposals on such issues as Medicare and the environment. Senator Dole emphasized his long public service record, criticized Clinton's personal character, and stated that he would enact tax cuts to further stimulate the economy.

Clinton Easily Reelected; Republicans Maintain Congressional Control

The 1996 election essentially endorsed the status quo. President Clinton won, becoming the first Democrat to be reelected since Franklin Roosevelt, achieving just under 50 percent of the popular vote and a comfortable electoral vote majority. Meanwhile, the Republicans gained a few seats in the Senate and lost only a slightly larger number of seats in the House of Representatives, thus maintaining control of Congress. In 1996 only 49 percent of eligible voters actually voted, marking the first time that the majority of eligible voters did not vote in a presidential election. Perot, the Reform party candidate, garnered 8.5 percent, normally a strong third-party achievement but a significant decrease from the 19 percent he received in 1992.

	Popular Vote	Percent	Electoral Vote
Clinton	45,628,667	49.2	379
Dole	37,869,435	40.8	159
Perot	7,874,283	8.5	0

Clinton's Second Administration

Clinton's Team

President Clinton made several new key appointments following his reelection. He appointed **Madeleine K. Albright**, the U.S. ambassador to the UN, to be Secretary of State. Albright became the first woman to hold this position. President Clinton also appointed Senator William S. Cohen of Maine, a moderate Republican, to be Secretary of Defense.

The Paula Jones Lawsuit

In May 1994 Paula Jones filed a lawsuit in federal court against President Clinton. In the suit Ms. Jones alleged that in May 1999, when Mr. Clinton was Governor of Arkansas and she was a secretary working for the state, he sexually harassed her by asking her to have sex. She also claimed that he had defamed her character, a charge she later dropped. President Clinton denied these allegations, and his attorneys made legal claim that the lawsuit should not be permitted to proceed while Clinton was President because a civil lawsuit would distract a President from his official responsibilities and thus would undermine the institution of the presidency. The Supreme Court addressed this issue in 1997 in *Jones* v. *Clinton*, unanimously ruling that a civil lawsuit could proceed against an incumbent President.

Legal discovery in the lawsuit then continued. In April 1998 Judge Susan Webber Wright granted the defense motion to dismiss the lawsuit before trial, holding that "the plaintiff's allegations fall far short of the rigorous standards for establishing a claim of outrage under Arkansas law." Jones appealed this ruling, and in 1999, before the appeal was decided, she settled the case in return for a payment from President Clinton of $850,000.

After the lawsuit was settled, Judge Wright held President Clinton in civil contempt of court for giving "false, misleading and evasive answers that were designed to obstruct the judicial process." She imposed sanctions of just over $90,000 against Clinton to compensate opposing attorneys and the court for costs incurred by his untruthful testimony.

The Monica Lewinsky Scandal

In January 1998 Independent Counsel **Kenneth Starr** received permission to inquire whether President Clinton obstructed justice in the Jones lawsuit. Later that month it became public news that Starr's office was investigating President Clinton's relationship with **Monica Lewinsky**, whom President Clinton had first met in November 1995 when she was a 22-year-old intern at the White House. President Clinton publicly stated in January that he "did not have sex with that woman, Miss Lewinsky," and thereafter, although the news continued to be dominated by the scandal, he refused to discuss the matter publicly until August.

In August 1998 President Clinton testified before a federal grand jury. He admitted that he had "inappropriate intimate conduct" with Lewinsky, but denied that he had committed perjury in saying that he had not engaged in sexual relations, contending that his conduct had been outside the definition of sexual relations employed in the Jones case. Shortly thereafter, Clinton gave a televised speech in which he admitted to an "inappropriate relationship" with Lewinsky and asked for forgiveness. In September, Starr submitted a report to the House that provided intimate details of Clinton's physical relationship with Lewinsky, and listed 11 grounds for impeaching the President.

The Impeachment Proceedings

The Judiciary Committee of the House of Representatives held hearings on whether President Clinton should be impeached. Those in favor of impeaching the President claimed that he had committed perjury by denying he had engaged in sexual relations with Lewinsky in his civil testimony (and some contended in his grand jury testimony as well). They also claimed that Clinton had obstructed justice by attempting to cover up his relationship with Lewinsky. Some of those against impeachment stated that Clinton may not have technically committed perjury (as Clinton and his lawyers maintained), while more of those supporting the President claimed that even if he had committed perjury in denying a sexual relationship, this did not constitute a "high crime or misdemeanor" that should result in his being impeached.

After lengthy hearings, the Judiciary Committee voted in favor of four separate counts of impeachment. Although two of the counts were defeated, Clinton was impeached on two counts. The first count alleged that Clinton had committed perjury in denying under oath that he had a sexual relationship with Lewinsky. The second count alleged that Clinton obstructed justice in attempting to cover up his relationship with Lewinsky. This marked the first time a President had been impeached since Andrew Johnson in 1868. (President Nixon had resigned in 1974 after the Judiciary Committee had voted in favor of three impeachment counts against him, but before the House of Representatives as a whole had voted on impeachment.)

Pursuant to the Constitution, the Senate held a trial on the impeachment charges, at the end of which the President would be removed from office if two-thirds of the Senators voted to convict him on either count. The Senate decided to hear only brief additional testimony, relying principally on the evidence compiled in the House of Representatives. The same basic arguments made in the House supporting and opposing impeachment were repeated in the Senate. In February 1999 the Senate voted against removing President Clinton from office by a vote of 45 in favor, 55 opposed on the first count, and 50 in favor, 50 opposed on the second count. President Clinton was officially acquitted. He stated that he was "profoundly sorry" for his actions and called for "a time of reconciliation and renewal."

In the end the impeachment proceedings remained highly partisan—no Democratic Senator voted to impeach the President, while 50 of the 55 Republican Senators voted to impeach the President on at least one count. Although the country was divided on this issue, throughout the impeachment proceedings President Clinton's public approval ratings remained high and a majority of those polled were not in favor of removing him from office.

Comprehensive Test Ban Treaty Rejected

In September 1996 President Clinton was the first leader to sign the Comprehensive Test Ban Treaty, which was subsequently signed by 153 nations, including all nuclear-capable countries except India, Pakistan, and North Korea. The explosion of test nuclear bombs by both India and Pakistan in 1998, while they were in a state of undeclared war over Kashmir, emphasized the continued need for nuclear control. President Clinton pushed for a vote on the treaty the following year. Significant opposition among Senate Republicans revolved around concerns regarding whether treaty compliance could be adequately verified, as well as a dislike of the President. In October 1999 the treaty, which required a two-thirds affirmative vote to be ratified, did not even receive a majority, with 48 votes in favor to 51 votes against. This marked the first time since 1920 that a major arms control treaty had been defeated by the Senate.

THE ELECTION OF 2000

The Primaries

Democrats

From the time he was reelected Vice President, Al Gore was the odds-on favorite to secure the nomination. Former New Jersey Senator Bill Bradley was his only Democratic challenger. In the initial stages of the primary campaign, Vice President Gore obtained the endorsements of most elected party leaders and labor organizations. Senator Bradley ran as a reformist liberal, while Vice President Gore stressed that he would maintain and expand upon the policies of President Clinton. Although initially pressed, Vice President Gore won every primary, and Senator Bradley withdrew after losing all the "Super Tuesday" primaries in March.

Republicans

The principal candidates for the republican nomination were governor **George W. Bush** of Texas, son of the former President, Arizona Senator and war hero **John McCain**, and Steve Forbes, independently wealthy president of *Forbes Magazine*. Bush, who ran as a "compassionate Conservative" and McCain, who ran as a reformist Conservative alternated victories throughout the first month of primary contests. However, in the "Super Tuesday" primaries in March Governor Bush won most of the twelve states at stake, including the three with the most delegates, leading Senator McCain to concede the contest by "suspending" his campaign.

Nominations and Appointments During Clinton's Administrations

Supreme Court Justices

The retirement of Supreme Court Justice Byron H. White made Clinton the first Democratic President in 25 years to make a nomination for the Supreme Court. After two tentative choices, he nominated **Ruth Bader Ginsburg** of the U.S. Court of Appeals for the District of Columbia. The nomination was easily confirmed by the Senate, making Ginsburg the second woman on the high court, after **Sandra Day O'Connor** of Arizona, who was appointed in 1981 under President Reagan. In 1994 President Clinton nominated **Stephen G. Breyer**, Chief Judge of the U.S. Court of Appeals for the First Circuit in Boston, who was then confirmed by the Senate to sit on the Supreme Court.

The Presidential Election

The election of 2000 saw the nomination of Vice President Al Gore by the Democrats, Texas Governor George W. Bush by the Republicans, and a third party candidate, longtime consumer advocate, Ralph Nader, by the Green Party.

It was quickly realized as the popular vote returns were being tallied on November 7th that the election of 2000 would be one of the closest in U.S. history. (Al Gore: 50,158,094, George W. Bush: 49,820,518, Others: 3,835,594) The vote in Florida became crucial as the awarding of Florida's 25 electoral votes would give either Vice President Gore or Governor Bush the necessary 270 electoral vote majority. The popular vote in the State of Florida was so close (Governor Bush led by only a few hundred) that a recount was ordered pursuant to state law.

A separation of powers question arose between the Florida Supreme Court which supported the continuation of handcounts and the Florida Secretary of State who moved to end the recount and award the electoral vote to Governor George Bush. On December 9, 2000 the Supreme Court of the United States halted all recounts in the State of Florida and on December 12, 2000 the U.S. Supreme Court ruled in the case of *Bush* v. *Gore* that the recount ordered by the Florida Supreme Court had presented an "equal protection of the law" problem and ordered the recount to stop. This marked the first time that the Supreme Court of the United States had intervened in a presidential election.

On December 13, 2000 Vice President Al Gore conceded and Governor George W. Bush claimed victory.

1. The most successful example of the United States commitment to international trade under President Clinton was
   A. the World Trade Organization's 1999 meeting in Seattle
   B. the addition of Poland, Hungary, and the Czech Republic to NATO
   C. "fast track" approval of trade treaties
   D. NAFTA

2. Following President Clinton's signing of the Comprehensive Test Ban Treaty in September 1996, the treaty, which was eventually defeated, was submitted for ratification to which of the following governmental bodies?
   A. Supreme Court
   B. House of Representatives
   C. Cabinet
   D. Senate

3. The reason why President Clinton was acquitted after his trial on impeachment charges in the United States Senate is that
   A. the Senate did not have 12 more Republican members
   B. no Democratic Senator voted to convict him
   C. a majority of the Senate did not vote to convict him
   D. two-thirds of the Senate did not vote to convict him

4. Which of the following was the major trouble area for the United States economy under President Clinton?
   A. Lower unemployment
   B. Lower inflation
   C. Higher trade deficit
   D. Higher stock market prices

5. A major argument against granting the President the line item veto was that it
   A. violated the principle of checks and balances
   B. reduced "pork barrel" spending
   C. encouraged Congress to be wasteful
   D. prevented balanced budgets

6. One criticism of affirmative action programs is that these programs
   A. ignore the needs of women in business and education
   B. lead to discrimination against more qualified people
   C. have a negative effect on immigration
   D. have not eliminated segregated housing patterns

7. One way in which the Watergate scandal, the Iran-Contra affair, and the Paula Jones/Monica Lewinsky investigation are similar is that each led to
   A. the impeachment of a President
   B. the censorship of Congressional leaders
   C. the addition of new amendments to the Constitution
   D. a loss of respect for government leaders by the American people

8. Following the impeachment by the House of Representatives, President Clinton was tried and acquitted by the Senate in February 1999. Which individual presided at the Senate trial of President Clinton?
   A. Vice President Al Gore
   B. Independent Counsel Kenneth Starr
   C. Honorable Ryan K. Dugan
   D. Chief Justice William Rehnquist

9. Base your answer to question 9 on the cartoon below and on your knowledge of social studies.

   The main idea of this cartoon is that
   A. economic considerations dictate United States foreign policy
   B. a free-trade policy is largely responsible for the success of the American economy
   C. a President can benefit from a strong national economy
   D. the United States no longer has a trade deficit

UNIT SEVEN ————————————————————

The New Millennium

> **KEY IDEAS**   Unit Seven introduces the new millennium (2001) following the 2000 election. The new millennium is violated in its infancy, and the war on terror changes both foreign and domestic policies beyond what the most astute futurists would have ever predicted.

UNIT CONNECTIONS: By the end of the unit you should understand the following points.

- The complexities and oddities of our electoral process
- George W. Bush and the resurgence of neoconservatism
- The horror and significance of September 11, 2001
- International cooperation versus unilateral approach to foreign policy
- Fighting the global war on international terrorism
- The balancing of civil liberties and national security during times of war
- The interpretation of 20th-century international law in 21st-century conditions
- Constitutional issues of the 21st century
- The attempts to control nuclear proliferation as more countries possess nuclear capabilities
- Congressional elections and their reflection of administration policies
- The complexities of a volatile Middle East

CHAPTER 1

GEORGE W. BUSH
AND NEOCONSERVATISM

*I want everybody to hear loud and clear that I'm going to be the
president of everybody.*

George W. Bush, Washington, D.C.,
January 18, 2001

THE ELECTION OF 2000: AFTERMATH

Blue and Red States

The election of 2000 proved to be one of the closest elections in United
States history. Although **Governor Bush** won 271 electoral votes to **Vice
President Gore's** 266, the Vice President led the Governor in the national
popular vote 48.4 percent to 47.9 percent. In the case of ***Bush* v. *Gore* (Dec.
12, 2000)**, the Supreme Court reversed the Florida Supreme Court decision
ordering a manual recount of ballots, effectively ending the presidential
election in favor of George W. Bush. Consumer advocate and Green Party
candidate Ralph Nader polled 2.7 percent. Al Gore in 2000 joined Samuel
J. Tilden in 1876 and Grover Cleveland in 1888 in the group of presidential
candidates receiving the largest popular vote but failing to gain a majority in
the electoral college.

The media used the color blue to designate the states that Gore won and
red for the states Bush won. And soon commentators started to identify
America in terms of **"red"** and **"blue."** Gore carried the Northeast and the
West Coast; he also ran well in the Midwestern industrial heartland. Bush,
whose states were colored red, did very well in the South, the rest of the
Midwest, and the mountain states. George Bush took office in a climate of
extreme partisan bitterness. Although the percentage of eligible voters who
voted in 2000 increased from the presidential election of 1996, still, nearly
one half of the electorate did not vote.

571

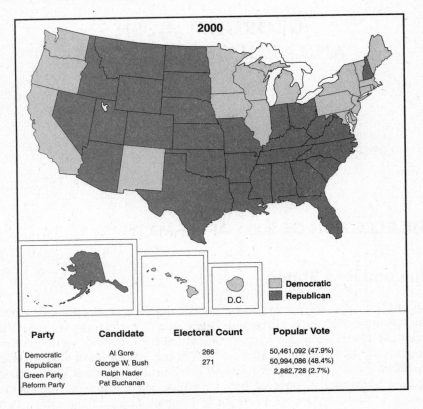

2000

Party	Candidate	Electoral Count	Popular Vote
Democratic	Al Gore	266	50,461,092 (47.9%)
Republican	George W. Bush	271	50,994,086 (48.4%)
Green Party	Ralph Nader		2,882,728 (2.7%)
Reform Party	Pat Buchanan		

Figure 7.1 Election 2000 results

The New Bush Administration

A **neoconservative** is one who is more inclined than other conservatives toward vigorous government in the service of the goals of traditional morality and pro-business policies. Neoconservatives tend to favor a very strong foreign policy. Although George W. Bush may not have been a neocon, his choice of **Richard Cheney** as a running mate, and Cheney's selection of personnel for the new administration, brought the neoconservative element to the presidency of George W. Bush. The choices of **Donald Rumsfeld** as Secretary of Defense, **Paul Wolfowitz** as Deputy Defense Secretary, **John Bolton** as Undersecretary of State, **Dr. Condoleezza Rice** as National Security Advisor, and **Elliot Abrams** as Deputy Assistant to the President set the stage for a very proactive, anti-**Saddam Hussein** foreign policy. Other appointments included Senator **John Ashcroft** from Missouri as Attorney General, **Colin Powell** as Secretary of State, Texan political consultant **Karl Rove** as Chief of Staff, and pro-Alaskan oil development Gale Norton as Secretary of the Interior.

The New Administration and Tax Cuts

The top item on Bush's domestic agenda, and a major campaign promise, a $1.6 trillion **tax cut**, was the subject of bitter debate in Congress. While Bush and his supporters claimed that the tax cuts would promote new investment and economic growth, the Democrats argued that the bill heavily favored the rich and would waste away the unprecedented budget surplus. The Senate eventually trimmed the tax cut to $1.35 trillion over 11 years, and Bush signed it into law on June 7. Almost 60 percent of the tax cuts were limited to the wealthiest 10 percent of Americans with the richest 1 percent of Americans receiving nearly 45 percent of the tax cuts.

In the final two years of the Clinton administration, there were budget **surpluses** of $122.7 billion (1999) and $230 billion (2000). As a result of the surpluses, the $5.7 trillion national debt had been reduced by $360 billion in the previous three years. One of the most controversial aspects of the Bush tax law was a plan to send checks to 95 million people. Those advanced payments were referred to as tax rebates. The rebates ranged from $300 to $600 depending on whether someone was single, married, or the head of a household. The total cost of the rebates was approximately $38 billion.

By the time Americans began receiving their tax rebate checks in August 2001, the country's budget surplus was beginning to disappear. The Congressional Budget Office attributed the change to a slowing economy and the Bush tax cut. By the fall, many believed that the country was heading toward a full-blown recession.

Bush–Cheney Energy Plan

Early in his administration, Bush and his advisors considered the oil supply essential to the health and profitability of leading U.S. industries. This concern prompted Bush to establish the National Energy Policy Development Group (NEPDG) and Vice President Richard Cheney was selected to lead the task force. Early on it appeared that the choice facing the policy planners was becoming ever more dependent on imported supplies or choosing the alternate route of reliance on renewable sources of energy and gradually reducing petroleum use.

The NEPDG wrestled with this dilemma and completed its report during the early months of 2001. At first glance, the Cheney report, as it is often called, appeared to reject the path of increased reliance on imported oil in favor of renewable energy. However, for all its rhetoric about conservation, the report did not propose a reduction in oil consumption. Instead, it proposed to boost production at home through the exploitation of untapped reserves in protected wilderness areas, including the Arctic National Wildlife Refuge (ANWR), an immense, untouched wilderness area in northeastern Alaska.

Exercise Set 7.1

1. When George W. Bush won the presidential election of 2000, he received
   A. a plurality
   B. a majority of the electoral votes
   C. a majority of the popular votes
   D. not a majority of the popular vote, but more popular votes than Vice President Gore

2. Which of the following would support the neoconservative foreign policies of the Bush presidency?
   A. Al Gore
   B. Donald Rumsfeld
   C. Ralph Nader
   D. Hillary Clinton

3. Which of the following would best describe a result of the economic policies of the Bush administration?
   A. deficit reduction
   B. accumulation of budget surplus
   C. growing national debt
   D. deflation

4. The economic policies of George W. Bush and his administration could be most closely associated with the policies of the
   A. Reagan administration
   B. Clinton administration
   C. Eisenhower administration
   D. Carter administration

5. One energy resource which was considered by the Bush–Cheney Energy Task Force and has caused considerable partisan disagreement in Congress, is
   A. the development of solar energy
   B. tapping oil resources in northeastern Alaska
   C. expansion of northwestern hydropower facilities
   D. development of coastal wind farms

CHAPTER 2

9/11 AND ITS AFTERMATH

All gave some, some gave all.

> Fire Department of the City of New York
> September, 2001

DOMESTIC AND WORLD EVENTS IN THE MONTHS BEFORE 9/11

Extraordinary incidents in history tend to make one forget those notable occurrences that immediately preceded the event. The following world and domestic events of the spring and summer of 2001 are certainly noteworthy.

Kyoto and Global Warming

The **United Nations Framework Convention on Climate Change** (Rio de Janeiro, 1992) is a treaty among 189 countries, including the United States, created to address global warming by reducing emissions from greenhouse gases. An amendment to this treaty became known as the Kyoto Protocol (Kyoto, Japan), which, for the first time, would require certain nations to cut the emissions of gases that contribute to global warming. Although the United States had originally signed on to the treaty (1998), President Clinton had never submitted it to the U.S. Senate for ratification; therefore, it was not binding on the United States. Actually, the Republican Senate had already passed a resolution on July 25, 1997 (95–0), stating that it would not ratify a climate treaty that would harm the U.S. economy or not require developing countries (such as China and India) to reduce emissions. After assuming office in January 2001, President George W. Bush announced that the United States would withdraw from the **Kyoto Treaty**, although it would continue to participate fully in the international meetings that developed the treaty. In July 2001, in Bonn, Germany, 165 countries (excluding the United States and Australia) ratified the Kyoto Treaty.

ATTACK ON AMERICA

9/11/01

The morning of September 11, 2001, a hijacked passenger jet, American Airlines Flight 11 out of Boston's Logan Airport, crashed into the north tower of the World Trade Center, tearing a gaping hole in the building and setting it afire. As people watched the burning tower in horror, a second hijacked airliner, United Airlines Flight 175 from Boston, crashed into the south tower of the World Trade Center at 9:03 A.M. and exploded. At approximately 9:43 A.M., American Airlines Flight 77 out of Washington exploded when it hit the Pentagon, killing all 64 aboard. At 10:05 A.M., the south tower fell, sending a huge cloud of dust and debris through the streets of lower Manhattan. At 10:10 A.M., United Airlines Flight 93 out of Newark and bound for San Francisco, also hijacked, crashed in Somerset County, Pennsylvania, southeast of Pittsburgh, killing 38 passengers, crew, and hijackers. At 10:28 A.M., the north tower of the World Trade Center collapsed. As it became apparent that terrorism was behind the attack, most realized that many things would no longer be the same. **September 11, 2001**, marked the largest single-day loss of life in U.S. history.

Osama bin Laden and al Qaeda

At some point between 10:00 and 11:00 on the morning of September 11, 2001, Secretary of State Colin Powell was quoted on the news saying that the U.S. government believed **Osama bin Laden** and the terrorist group **al Qaeda** were probably responsible. In 1993 the first World Trade Center bombing killed six people, and in 1998 the bombing of two United States embassies in Africa killed 224 people. Both were the work of al Qaeda and bin Laden, who in 1998 declared holy war on America, making him arguably the most wanted man in the world. As "9/11," as it would come to be known, became a reality in America, the name bin Laden and al Qaeda were already well known.

Shortly after the attacks of September 11, al Qaeda, under the leadership of Osama bin Laden, was suspected of being responsible. Bin Laden and the Muslim jihad had been supported by the United States in 1979 during the Soviet invasion of **Afghanistan**. Al Qaeda has its origins in the uprising against the 1979 Soviet occupation of Afghanistan. Bin Laden explained the origin of the term, in a videotaped interview with an **al Jazeera** (Arabic television channel) journalist in October 2001: "The name 'al Qaeda' was established a long time ago by mere chance. The late Abu Ebeida El-Banashiri established the training camps for our mujahedeen against Russia's terrorism. We used to call the training camp al Qaeda [meaning "the base" in English]. And the name stayed."

After the Soviets left Afghanistan, bin Laden returned to his native Saudi Arabia and then later set up bases in Sudan in northeast Africa. In 1994 Sudan expelled bin Laden, who moved his base of operations to Afghanistan. Bin Laden was welcomed by the **Taliban** ("Students of Islamic Knowledge Movement") who came to power during Afghanistan's long civil war and ruled Afghanistan from 1996 until 2001. The United States drove them from power in November 2001.

Among the claims of al Qaeda, which resulted in bin Laden's declaration of war against the United States, were America's participation in the first Gulf War, U.S. military involvements in Somalia and Yemen, and the U.S. military presence in Saudi Arabia. The attacks against the United States and its allies that have been credited to al Qaeda include:

- **February 1993.** Bombing of World Trade Center (WTC), New York City. The 1,500-lb nitrate-fuel oil device killed six and injured 1,042 people. It was intended to devastate the foundation of the north tower, causing it to collapse onto the south tower; six were killed. Those involved in the bombing received financing from al Qaeda member **Khaled Shaikh Mohammed**. Investigation of the WTC bombing reveals that it was only a small part of a massive attack plan that included hijacking a plane and crashing it into CIA headquarters.

- **October 1993.** Killing of U.S. soldiers in **Somalia**. Bin Laden confirmed that "Arabs affiliated with his group were involved in killing American troops in Somalia in 1993," a claim he had earlier made to an Arabic newspaper. The Battle of Mogadishu was the basis of the film *Black Hawk Down*.

- **August 1998.** Bombing of two U.S. embassies in Africa. On August 7, 1998, the U.S. embassies in Nairobi, Kenya, and Dar es Salaam, Tanzania, were bombed by terrorists, leaving 258 people dead and more than 5,000 injured. President Clinton's response was the launching of cruise missiles on August 20, 1998, striking a terrorism training complex in Afghanistan and destroying a pharmaceutical manufacturing facility in **Khartoum, Sudan**, that reportedly produced poison gases for military use, both believed to be financed by Osama bin Laden. Officials later said that there was no proof that the plant had been manufacturing or storing nerve gas, as initially suspected by the Americans, or had been linked to Osama bin Laden, who was a resident of Khartoum in the 1980s.

- **October 2000.** On October 12, 2000, 17 Americans died and 37 were wounded when suicide bombers attacked the U.S. Navy destroyer *Cole*, which was refueling in Aden, Yemen. It appeared that the small boat carrying the suicide bombers was carrying some form of highly explosive material powerful enough to rip a large hole, 40 feet by 60 feet, flooding the main engine spaces of the ship.

- **September 11, 2001.** Attacks on the **World Trade Center** and **Pentagon**. Four planes were hijacked and used as weapons resulting in the deaths of 19 hijackers, 246 passengers and crew, and 2,727 people who died at the World Trade Center and Pentagon. After the bombings bin Laden issued a videotape praising the hijackers and announcing that "America will not live in peace before peace reigns in Palestine, and before all the army of infidels depart the land of Muhammad."

- **June 2002.** On the morning of June 14, 2002, a truck with a fertilizer bomb driven by a suicide bomber was detonated outside the U.S. consulate in Karachi, Pakistan. Twelve people were killed and 51 injured, all Pakistanis.

- **June 2004.** Terrorists kidnap and execute (behead) Paul Johnson, Jr., an American helicopter engineer, in Riyadh, Saudi Arabia.

- **December 2004.** Militants, believed to be linked to al Qaeda, drove up to the U.S. consulate in Jiddah, Saudi Arabia, stormed the gates, and killed five consulate employees, none of whom were American. Saudi security forces subdued the attackers, killing four.

- **July 2005.** Four young Briton suicide bombers with possible ties to al Qaeda struck in central London on July 7, 2005, killing 52 people and injuring more than 770.

- **October 2010.** Two packages each containing a bomb were found on separate U.S. bound cargo planes.

America's Reaction

On September 20, 2001, President Bush addressed a joint session of Congress, members of the various branches of the national government, and the American people from the **House of Representatives**. He was quick to get to al Qaeda, bin Laden and the hosting government, the Taliban:

"And tonight, the United States of America makes the following demands on the Taliban: Deliver to United States authorities all the leaders of al Qaeda who hide in your land. (Applause.) Release all foreign nationals, including American citizens, you have unjustly imprisoned. Protect foreign journalists, diplomats and aid workers in your country. Close immediately and permanently every terrorist training camp in Afghanistan, and hand over every terrorist, and every person in their support structure, to appropriate authorities. (Applause.) Give the United States full access to terrorist training camps, so we can make sure they are no longer operating."

"These demands are not open to negotiation or discussion. (Applause.) The Taliban must act, and act immediately. They will hand over the terrorists, or they will share in their fate."

The Fall of the Taliban Government

On October 7, 2001, after the Taliban failed to respond to their demands, the United States, Great Britain, and coalition forces launched a bombing campaign on the **Taliban** government and al Qaeda terrorist camps in Afghanistan. Although the immediate goal was to destroy al Qaeda and capture bin Laden, the President stated that the "battle was broader." Perhaps the intentions of the administration were already on Iraq. Within two months the Taliban government had fallen. Although Osama bin Laden was not caught, the **al Qaeda** forces in Afghanistan were seriously weakened. After nearly a month and a half, the Taliban had lost their seat of government in **Kabul** and by December 9 they had been completely overpowered. On December 22, 2001, **Hamid Karzai**, who attended college in India, speaks fluent English, and enjoys strong support from the West was sworn in as interim chairman of the government. In January 2012, the Taliban influence and military strengths began to rise.

Balancing Civil Liberties and National Security

Forty-five days after the September 11 attacks, Congress, with little if any debate, passed the 342-page **USA PATRIOT ACT** (Uniting and Strengthening America by Providing Appropriate Tools Required to Intercept and Obstruct Terrorism Act). The vote in the House of Representatives was 357 to 66 and in the Senate 98 to 1 with **Senator Russ Feingold** of Wisconsin being the only Senator to vote against the Act. Included in the legislation were sections that provided:

• Domestic Terrorism definitions and greater authority to subject political organizations to surveillance.

• Greater powers to law authorities to conduct secret searches of phone, Internet, medical, banking, and student records with minimal judicial oversight.

• Greater powers to law authorities to investigate American citizens without probable cause if it's for "intelligence purposes."

• Incarceration of noncitizens for indefinite periods on mere suspicion with no right of counsel, **habeas corpus**, or opportunities to appear before public tribunals.

Since its passage, nearly 200 cities, towns, and three states have passed resolutions stating that the USA PATRIOT Act is not enforceable within their jurisdictions claiming that among other concerns, the **First, Fourth, Fifth, Sixth, Eighth,** and **Fourteenth Amendments** are being threatened. The PATRIOT Act has been sometimes compared to the **Sedition Act of 1918** (repealed 1921), which suppressed anti-government sentiments during

World War I. The USA PATRIOT Act has raised the tension that exists when a country is at "war" and national security is pitted against **civil liberties**. The difficult balance is the protection and security of society without sacrificing the very system that is being kept secure. Following successful constitutional challenges to some sections of the Act, the PATRIOT Act was renewed in March 2006 and then again in May 2011.

Exercise Set 7.2

1. The incident involving an April 1, 2001, U.S. Navy reconnaissance plane collision with a Chinese fighter plane piloted by Wang Wei can be most closely associated with which of the following?
   A. Gary Powers and the U-2 crisis of 1960
   B. The *Spirit of St. Louis* and the 1927 transatlantic flight
   C. The 1964 Gulf of Tonkin incident
   D. The Pan Am flight 103 crash at Lockerbie, Scotland

2. The execution of Timothy McVeigh on June 11, 2001, raised issues most closely associated with which of the following amendments?
   A. First
   B. Second
   C. Fourth
   D. Eighth

3. According to the Article II, Section 2 of the United States Constitution, which of the following bodies is responsible for ratifying treaties entered into by the United States?
   A. Cabinet
   B. Executive Branch
   C. Supreme Court
   D. Senate

4. The underlying issue being addressed by the Kyoto Protocol was
   A. proliferation of nuclear weapons
   B. military balance of power in the Far East
   C. global warming and reduction of greenhouse gases
   D. development of free trade agreements

5. The Islamic fundamentalist group al Qaeda had its origin in which of the following areas of the world?
   A. Kuwait during the Gulf War
   B. Afghanistan during the 1979 Soviet occupation
   C. United States following the 1993 World Trade Center bombing
   D. Iran following the overthrow of the Shah in 1979

6. Which of the following acts of terrorism against the United States was not credited to al Qaeda?
   A. 1993 bombing of the World Trade Center in New York City
   B. 1998 bombing of U.S. embassies in Kenya and Tanzania
   C. 2000 suicide bombing of the U.S. Navy destroyer *Cole* in Yemen
   D. 1995 Oklahoma City Federal Building bombing

7. On September 20, 2001, President Bush addressed America and sent a message to the government of Afghanistan whom he suspected of harboring Osama bin Laden. Which of the following was the governing body of Afghanistan in September 2001?
   A. Al Jazeera
   B. Taliban
   C. Hamas
   D. Fatah

8. The USA PATRIOT Act (October 2001) has caused much concern and intense debate primarily because it causes considerable tension between maintaining national security and preserving
   A. civil liberties
   B. adequate armed forces
   C. a federal form of government
   D. the safety of Americans overseas

9. Which of the following congressional acts does not belong with the other three?
   A. Sedition Act of 1918
   B. Voting Rights Act of 1965
   C. PATRIOT Act of 2001
   D. Alien and Sedition Acts of 1798

10. The branch of the federal government that determines the constitutionality of legislation like the USA PATRIOT Act is
    A. the executive branch
    B. the legislative branch
    C. the federal judiciary
    D. the Cabinet

11. According to the artist, the mastermind behind the September 11, 2001, attacks on America was
    A. Fidel Castro
    B. Vladamir Putin
    C. Yassir Arafat
    D. Osama bin Laden

CHAPTER 3

AMERICAN SOCIETY ENTERING THE 21ST CENTURY

I don't fear jail because I know I'm not guilty. I know I did nothing wrong. I did nothing criminal and I also believe my God will get me through this.

Kenneth Lay, convicted ex-CEO of Enron,
Born April 15, 1942, Died July 5, 2006

As the United States entered the 21st century, many issues were facing a maturing society that would present challenges, conflict, debate, and the need for solutions. These issues existed in their own right and shouldn't be overshadowed or ignored because of the dominance of the War on Terror.

Decisions of the Supreme Court 2000–2001

• *Bush* v. *Gore* (**December 12, 2000**). The Supreme Court reversed the Florida Supreme Court decision ordering a manual recount of ballots. In a 7–2 decision, the Court sent the case back to the Florida Supreme Court but, in a 5–4 split, which appeared to be along partisan lines, instructed that the deadline for the recount ended at midnight, effectively ending the presidential election in favor of George W. Bush.

• *United States* v. *Oakland Cannabis Buyers' Cooperative* (**May 14, 2001**). The issue of the medical use of marijuana was reviewed by the Court and in an 8–0 decision, the Court decided that federal law did not allow exception to use of the substance. Interestingly enough, the ruling did not overturn state laws giving patients access to the medicinal use of marijuana.

• *Kyllo* v. *United States* (**June 11, 2001**). In another search case, often conservative **Justice Scalia** wrote the decision that disallowed the use, without a warrant, of a thermal imaging device to determine whether a home is radiating abnormal heat (which might indicate the presence of high-intensity lamps used for growing marijuana indoors). The decision was 5–4.

Science in the New Millennium

The attempts to clone animals produced problems and defects and led to many scientific, moral, and religious debates about **cloning**. The National Academy of Sciences concluded that **global warming** was not simply a

583

cyclical stage of the earth's development and that human activity was also responsible. The Bush administration did little to curtail the emission of **carbon dioxide** pollution. Finally, the federal funding of embryonic stem cell research remains controversial. The **stem cells** come from a fertilized egg four days after conception. The debate pits pro-life advocates against many in the scientific community in favor of continuing research funding in hopes that the stem cells may also be able to replace damaged or sick cells in a patient with an injury or degenerative disease. The Bush administration's first veto was the veto of a stem cell research bill.

2002: Domestic

Enron, WorldCom, and Corporate Scandal

In December 2001, **Enron**, the largest energy corporation in the United States, filed for bankruptcy. Prior to this, Enron had been investigated for illegally driving up power prices during California's energy crisis. They did this by creating phantom congestion on electricity transmission lines and sending power outside the state and then reselling it back to California to avoid price limits for transactions within the state.

Enron had been under federal investigation for "cooking the books," in other words, falsifying higher earnings and hiding the company's debt. The illegal acts caused the loss of much of its employees' retirement funds. Within a year, Enron's stock prices fell from $80 to $.67 a share. Early in 2002 **Kenneth Lay**, the Chief Executive Officer and Chairman of Enron resigned. In 2002 **WorldCom**, a major telecommunications corporation went bankrupt after admitting to illegally altering its earnings and debt reports. Following Enron and WorldCom came Qwest, Global Crossing, Tyco, Adelphia as corporate America came under intense scrutiny for illegal activities, incredible greed, and criminal disregard for its employees.

The State of the Union

In his first **State of the Union** address to the nation, President Bush presented both his justification and plans for the war on terror and made it clear that the war against the terrorists was just beginning. The part of the speech quoted above has been since referred to as the "**axis of evil**" charge. The President charged North Korea, Iran, and Iraq as being dangers to the rest of the world and followed that the United States would wage war against countries developing weapons of mass destruction. There were parts of his address that were later found to be without any basis, i.e., "Our discoveries in Afghanistan confirmed our worst fears and showed us the true scope of the task ahead. We have found diagrams of American nuclear power plants." No such diagrams, or plants for that matter, were found.

Creation of Department of Homeland Security

On November 25, 2002, President Bush signed into law legislation creating a new **Cabinet**-level **Department of Homeland Security** and appointed **Tom Ridge**, ex-Governor of Pennsylvania, as its Secretary. The new Cabinet department would employ 170,000 people and combine all or part of 22 other agencies, including Immigration and Naturalization, the Coast Guard and Border Patrol to better protect the United States from terrorist attacks. The creation of the new department would bring the total number of departments to 15: Agriculture, Commerce, Defense, Education, Energy, Health and Human Services, Homeland Security, Housing and Urban Development, Interior, Labor, State, Transportation, Treasury, Veterans Affairs, and the Attorney General.

Nine States Sue the Environmental Protection Agency

New York, Connecticut, Maine, Maryland, Massachusetts, New Hampshire, New Jersey, Rhode Island, and Vermont brought a lawsuit against the Environmental Protection Agency in December 2002, challenging new regulations of the Bush administration that would remove some of the protections of the 1970 **Clean Air Act**. Of particular concern were the emissions of carbon dioxide and its contribution to **global warming**. The United States emits 25% of the world's carbon monoxide as the warming of the planet is unprecedented.

2002: Foreign

Anti-Ballistic Missile Treaty and the International Criminal Court

Since 1972 when U.S. President Richard Nixon and Soviet Union General Secretary Leonid Brezhnev signed the Anti-Ballistic Missile Treaty, there was a check on each other in their ability to launch multiple nuclear warheads upon the other. After the dissolution of the Soviet Union in 1991, the status of the treaty became somewhat unclear. On December 13, 2001, President Bush gave notice that the United States would be withdrawing from the Anti-Ballistic Missile Treaty marking the first time in recent history that the United States was withdrawing from a major international arms treaty. The United States withdrew on June 13, 2002.

The **International Criminal Court (ICC)** was established on July 17, 1998. Once 60 states (countries) had adopted the charter, the Court went into effect on July 1, 2002. Today, 104 countries have submitted to the jurisdiction of the ICC. The Court is based in **The Hague, Netherlands**, and hears cases involving international law including allegations of genocide, crimes against humanity, and war crimes, among others. To date, the United States has not ratified the ICC, arguing that prosecutions may be brought against U.S. nationals for political reasons.

The United Nations, Iraq, and Weapons of Mass Destruction

On May 14, 2002, the United Nations Security Council replaced sanctions on Iraq with "smart sanctions." "Smart sanctions" were meant to allow food, medical supplies, and goods into the country while restricting any trade that could be used for military purposes. These sanctions were designed to force Iraq to comply with United Nations resolutions about weapons of mass destruction. At the time, it was estimated by the United Nations that the sanctions had resulted in the deaths of over 1 million Iraqi civilians.

On November 8, 2002, the United Nations Security Council passed a unanimous resolution (Resolution # 1441) calling on Iraq to comply with earlier resolutions and disarm or face "serious consequences." The resolution called for United Nations arms inspectors to return to Iraq.

On December 7, 2002, Iraq handed over a 12,000-page, multi-CD-ROM voluminous weapons report to the United Nations stating that there were no prohibited weapons (chemical, biological, and nuclear) in Iraq.

Decisions of the Supreme Court 2002–2003

- *Ashcroft* v. *Free Speech Coalition* (**April 16, 2002**). In a 6–3 decision the Court struck down a 1996 child pornography law as unconstitutionally vague and therefore ruled that virtual child pornography was permitted.

- *Atkins* v. *Virginia* (**June 25, 2002**). The Supreme Court stopped the execution of mentally retarded individuals.

- *Ring* v. *Arizona* (**2002**). Juries rather than judges must decide who gets the death penalty.

- *Board of Education of Independent School District 92 of Pottawatomie County* v. *Lindsay Earls* (**June 27, 2002**). The *Pottawatomie* case involved the drug testing of students for any extracurricular activity in public schools. The issue presented to the Court was: "Does it violate the 4th Amendment's protection against unreasonable searches and seizures for a public school district to enforce a policy requiring students who wish to participate in extracurricular activities to submit to random, suspicionless urinalysis drug testing, if the policy is supported by no more than negligible evidence of drug abuse problems among students subject to the test?" The Court decided that the schools could drug test for all extracurricular activities.

- *Zelman, Superintendent of Public Instruction of Ohio, et al.* v. *Simmons-Harris et al.* (**June 27, 2002**). *Zelman* addressed the issue of whether students could have a choice of schools, paid for with public funds, and both religious and nonreligious schools in the district may participate, as may public schools in adjacent school districts. Tuition aid is distributed to parents according to financial need, and where the aid is spent depends solely upon where parents choose to enroll their children. The Court found the program (**voucher program**) did not offend the Establishment Clause.

• *Virginia* v. *Black* (**April 7, 2003**). Court, 6–3, rules that states can ban cross burning provided that the law as written places the burden on prosecutors to prove that the action was intended to intimidate and threaten, and not simply a form of expression. In an overlapping ruling, seven justices declare unconstitutional a part of a Virginia law that asserts any instance of cross burning is a form of intimidation.

• *Lawrence* v. *Texas* (**June 26, 2003**). Court, 6–3, overrules a Texas sodomy law and votes 5–4 to overturn 1986's *Bowers* v. *Hardwick* decision, which held that there's no constitutional right to have homosexual relations in private. "The state cannot demean their [gays'] existence or control their destiny by making their private sexual conduct a crime," wrote Justice Kennedy in the majority opinion. In his dissent to *Lawrence* v. *Texas*, Justice Scalia said the court has "largely signed on to the so-called homosexual agenda."

• *Grutter* v. *Bollinger* (**June 23, 2003**). In *Grutter* the justices, 5–4, upheld the University of Michigan Law School's consideration of race and ethnicity in admissions. In her majority opinion, Justice O'Connor said that the law school uses a "highly individualized, holistic review of each applicant's file." Race, she said, is not used in a "mechanical way." Therefore, the university's program is consistent with the requirement of "individualized consideration" set in 1978's *Bakke* case. "In order to cultivate a set of leaders with legitimacy in the eyes of the citizenry, it is necessary that the path to leadership be visibly open to talented and qualified individuals of every race and ethnicity," O'Connor said. However, the court, in *Gratz* v. *Bollinger*, 6–3, rules that the University of Michigan's undergraduate admissions system, which awards 20 points to black, Hispanic, and American-Indian applicants, is "nonindividualized, mechanical," and thus unconstitutional.

2003: Domestic

Space Shuttle *Columbia* Explodes upon Reentry

On February 1, 2003, the space shuttle **Columbia** exploded in the skies over central Texas as it was reentering the earth's atmosphere. The craft broke up about 200,000 feet above the ground minutes before its scheduled landing. All seven crew members, including Israel's first astronaut, Colonel Ilan Ramon, were killed in the tragedy. Terrorism was ruled out as a cause of the horrific catastrophe.

Bush Tax Cuts and Deficits

President Bush, very much in the economic spirit of **President Ronald Reagan**, formed his tax policies around "**trickle-down**" economics. By supporting significant long-lasting tax cuts, President Bush argued that it was better for the economy if individuals and businesses had more money to spend and invest. On May 28, 2003, Bush signed a ten-year $350 billion tax cut. Two-thirds of the tax cut would go to the top 10 percent of income earners in the country. Households making over $1 million per year would see an average tax cut of $93,500 in 2003 while households in the middle of the income spectrum would see an average reduction of $217 in 2003. The tax cuts also caused an increase in the deficit and necessitated spending cuts in **Medicaid**, student loans, veteran programs, school lunch programs, childcare, and many other programs.

Recall Used in California

Recall, a procedure that has its roots in the turn of the century age of **Progressivism,** was used in California in 2003. **Recall,** which provides for a special election and is either permitted or not permitted by state law, allows the voters to petition for a midterm election and may result in the removal of an incumbent politician before the end of their term. On October 7, 2003, such a vote was taken which removed Democrat **Governor Gray Davis** and replaced him with Republican **Arnold Schwarzenegger**. This was only the second governor recall in U.S. history.

2003: Foreign

North Korea Withdraws from the Nuclear Nonproliferation Treaty

On January 10, 2003, following U.S. accusations of nuclear weapons programs, North Korea announced that they were withdrawing from the Nuclear Nonproliferation Treaty. North Korea had ratified the treaty in 1985 and was the first country to ever withdraw from the treaty. In a roundtable discussion with the United States and China in Beijing on April 24, 2003, North Korean officials admitted for the first time that they possessed nuclear weapons. Furthermore, North Korean officials claimed to have reprocessed spent fuel rods and threatened to begin exporting nuclear materials unless the United States agreed to one-on-one talks with North Korea.

Libya Admits Guilt and Agrees to Pay for Lockerbie

On August 15, 2003, Libyan leader **Muammar Qaddafi** admitted guilt in Libya's role in the 1988 terrorist bombing of Pan American World Airways

Flight 103 over **Lockerbie**, Scotland, that took the lives of 270 people from 21 countries. Libya agreed to pay $2.7 billion to the families of the victims. In May 2006 President Bush took Libya off the United States list of terrorist countries and restored diplomatic relations for the first time in over a quarter of a century.

Exercise Set 7.3

1. Which of the following Supreme Court decisions primarily addressed the issue of federalism?
   A. *City of Indianapolis* v. *Edmond*
   B. *Kyllo* v. *United States*
   C. *Bush* v. *Gore*
   D. *Atkins* v. *Virginia*

2. The argument over the use of stem cells for medicinal purposes has raised the debate most closely associated with which of the following Supreme Court cases?
   A. *Roe* v. *Wade*
   B. *Miranda* v. *Arizona*
   C. *Brown* v. *Board of Education*
   D. *Dred Scott* v. *Sanford*

3. Interestingly enough, the "axis of evil" referred to by President Bush in his first State of the Union address did not include
   A. Iraq
   B. Venezuela
   C. Iran
   D. North Korea

4. Although the May 2001 switch of Senator Jim Jeffords from a Republican to an Independent gave the Democrats control of the Senate, following the midterm elections of 2002, Republicans had control of
   A. the Senate and the House of Representatives
   B. only the Senate
   C. only the House of Representatives
   D. neither the House of Representatives nor the Senate

5. The 1972 Anti-Ballistic Missile Treaty was originally an agreement between the United States and the Soviet Union and was signed by President Richard Nixon and
   A. General Secretary Leonid Brezhnev
   B. Soviet Premier Nikita S. Khrushchev
   C. Chairman Vadim Shvartsman
   D. President Mikhail S. Gorbachev

6. A "smart sanction" against a nation would most likely allow which of the following to be imported into the country?
   A. Medical supplies
   B. Munitions
   C. Plutonium
   D. Armored vehicle

7. United Nations Resolution #1441 (November 2002) was necessary because the United Nations Security Council believed that Iraq had not complied with demands following
   A. the removal of Saddam Hussein from power
   B. the Iraq-Iran War (1980–1988)
   C. the Soviet occupation of Afghanistan
   D. the Gulf War (1990–1991)

8. The issue at the heart of the *Grutter* v. *Bollinger* (2003) Supreme Court decision was
   A. affirmative action
   B. freedom of speech
   C. school vouchers
   D. capital punishment

9. "Trickle-down" economics, an economic policy favored by both the administrations of President Ronald Reagan and President George W. Bush, would favor tax cuts and economic inducements primarily for the
   A. lowest of economic classes
   B. lower-middle class industrial workers
   C. upper class and business interests
   D. unemployed and under employed

10. A supporter of the political process of recall would be one who supports
    A. less popular control of government
    B. greater popular control of government
    C. greater limits on direct democracy
    D. absolute term control by the incumbent

CHAPTER 4

OPERATION IRAQI FREEDOM

"As you know, you go to war with the Army you have. They're not the Army you might want or wish to have at a later time."

Secretary of Defense, Donald Rumsfeld, December 2004
in response to a soldier's question: "Why do we soldiers
have to dig through local landfills for pieces of scrap metal
and compromised ballistic glass to armor our vehicles?"

The United States call it Operation Iraqi Freedom, the name of the Operation for British troops is Operation Telic and for Australian troops involved, it is Operation Falconer. This concerted effort consisted of the largest special operations force since the Vietnam War. While the vast majority of special operations forces were American, the United Kingdom and the Australian militaries also provided significant forces.

Operation Iraqi Freedom

What was going to begin on March 19, 2003, at 9:34 P.M., Eastern Standard Time was known as **Operation Iraqi Freedom**. These military operations would be against the state of Iraq to rid Iraq of their weapons of mass destruction and remove **Saddam Hussein** and his government from power.

"The United States has no intention of determining the precise form of Iraq's new government. That choice belongs to the Iraqi people. Yet, we will ensure that one brutal dictator is not replaced by another. All Iraqis must have a voice in the new government, and all citizens must have their rights protected. Rebuilding Iraq will require a sustained commitment from many nations, including our own: we will remain in Iraq as long as necessary, and not a day more."

— President George W. Bush (February 26, 2003)

The 2002 State of the Union and the Axis of Evil

Article II, Section 3 of the United States Constitution requires that the President of the United States "from time to time give to the Congress Information on the State of the Union." "From time to time" has come to customarily mean annually and in that spirit, President Bush delivered, among other points, the following:

"States like these [North Korea, Iran and Iraq], and their terrorist allies, constitute an **axis of evil**, arming to threaten the peace of the world. By seeking weapons of mass destruction, these regimes pose a grave and growing danger. They could provide these arms to terrorists, giving them the means to match their hatred. They could attack our allies or attempt to blackmail the United States. In any of these cases, the price of indifference would be catastrophic."
— President George W. Bush (January 29, 2002)

A Call for Regime Change in Iraq

On September 12, 2002, President Bush addressed the United Nations and called for "regime change" in Iraq. Interestingly enough, the goal of regime change in Iraq was codified during the Clinton years with the passage of the Iraq Liberation Act in 1998 which stated that *"It should be the policy of the United States to support efforts to remove the regime headed by Saddam Hussein from power in Iraq and to promote the emergence of a democratic government to replace that regime."* Critics of the regime change policy claim that it was a violation of international law stating that regime change was not a permissible just cause of war. On October 11, 2002, Congress passed the **Joint Resolution to Authorize the Use of United States Armed Forces Against Iraq**. On November 8, 2002, the United Nations Security Council passed a unanimous resolution calling for tough new arms inspections and demanding that Iraq disarm or face serious consequences. This was followed by the return of United Nations weapons inspectors to Iraq for the first time in nearly four years. On December 7, 2002, Iraq submitted a statement on its chemical, biological, and nuclear capabilities, claiming it possessed no banned weapons.

UNITED NATIONS AND THE IRAQI WAR

As previously noted in this unit, United Nations Security Council had passed a unanimous resolution in November, 2002, calling on Iraq to disarm or face "serious consequences" (Resolution # 1441). United Nations arms inspectors were sent back to Iraq. On December 7, 2002, Iran submitted to the United Nations a lengthy declaration stating that it had no weapons that had been banned. In mid-January, United Nations inspectors discovered undeclared empty chemical warheads. During January, President Bush received a letter signed by 130 members of the House of Representatives, urging him to "let the inspectors work." By this time, nearly 200,000 U.S. troops were in the Middle East region. On January 28, 2003, the president delivered his State of the Union address and stated that Iraq was attempting to buy **uranium** from Africa, even though he already had the intelligence that Iraq had not done so. By February, United Nations weapons inspector Hans Blix indicated that there was some progress with Iraq's compliance, yet later that month the United States, Britain, and Spain submitted a proposed resolution to the UN Security Council stating that authorization for war was necessary. Germany, Russia, and France opposed the resolution.

World Wide Antiwar Protests

On February 15, 2003 "**The World Says No to War**," with massive peace demonstrations around the world, was the largest coordinated day of protest in world history, with more than 600 cities participating. In Rome alone nearly 3 million people protested, which is noted in the **Guinness Book of Records** as the largest antiwar rally in history. In New York City nearly 400,000 protestors had their **First Amendment** rights limited when they were not allowed to rally around the United Nations, but instead were "corralled" up First Avenue.

Secretary of State Colin Powell Addresses the United Nations Security Council

On February 5, 2003, Secretary of State Colin Powell attempted to convince skeptical members of the UN Security Council that Iraq was actively working to deceive UN weapons inspectors. Secretary Powell based his assertions upon satellite images, recorded conversations, drawings and diagrams illustrating Iraqi mobile biological labs, unaccounted-for nerve gas, assertions that Iraq was pursuing nuclear development, and assertions of ties to al Qaeda.

In later statements Powell said that his UN speech making the case for the U.S.-led war on Iraq was "a blot" on his record. Mr. Powell has also said that he had "never seen evidence to suggest" a connection between the September 11, 2001, terror attacks in the United States and the Saddam regime. The 9/11 Commission, an independent, bipartisan commission created by congressional legislation and the signature of President George W. Bush in late 2002 to prepare a full and complete account of the circumstances surrounding the September 11, 2001, terrorist attacks, later supported this conclusion. The 9/11 Commission concluded in its report that there was "no credible evidence that Iraq and al Qaeda cooperated on attacks against the United States." Secretary Powell was replaced by National Security Advisor Condoleezza Rice at the beginning of President Bush's second term.

"Shock and Awe"

By March 14, 2003, only 4 out of the necessary 9 votes on the UN Security Council supported military action. On March 19, 2003, President Bush declared war on Iraq and Operation Iraqi Freedom was commenced. On March 20, "**Shock and Awe**" started and, in the words of then-**Secretary of Defense Donald Rumsfeld,** "What will follow will not be a repeat of any other conflict. It will be of a force and a scope and a scale that has been beyond what we have seen before." However, Secretary Rumsfeld's prediction of a swift and efficient victory in Iraq failed to materialize, as the Iraq War would last longer than our involvement in World War II. The phrase "Shock and Awe" originated in a 1996 Pentagon publication entitled "Shock and Awe: Achieving Rapid Dominance," which supported a military strategy that would destroy the will to resist and cause one's enemy to accept our strategic aims and military objectives.

"Mission Accomplished"

On May 1, 2003, President Bush announced from the deck of the aircraft carrier *USS Abraham Lincoln* that major combat operations in Iraq were over. Behind him was a banner proclaiming "**Mission Accomplished**" and the President hailed a "job well done."

Saddam Hussein Captured

Shortly after the November 2003 statement by the Bush administration in which they agreed to transfer power to an interim Iraqi government in early 2004, **Saddam Hussein**, 66, was captured by American troops on December 13, 2003. He was found hiding in a dirt hole at a farmhouse about 10 miles south of his hometown, **Tikrit**. Saddam Hussein had not been seen since Baghdad fell to coalition forces in April 2003. On December 14, President

Bush addressed the nation and the people of Iraq and made the following statement: "And this afternoon, I have a message for the Iraqi people: You will not have to fear the rule of Saddam Hussein ever again."

The Continuation of Operation Iraqi Freedom

A major offensive by coalition troops took place in the city of **Fallujah** during April 2004. Following the March 31 murder and mutilation of four military contractors from the U.S. company **Blackwell USA**, a month-long offensive, including some of the most fierce fighting of the war, took place in the city. At the end of April, in an attempt to restore peace in Fallujah, U.S. Marines transferred security of the volatile city to a former Iraqi general.

The torture, physical and sexual abuse, and humiliation of Iraqi prisoners at **Abu Ghraib** prison near Baghdad was made public in April when photographs were released by the U.S. media. Abu Ghraib was a notorious prison and torture center during the rule of Saddam Hussein. The Pentagon-sponsored Schlesinger Report's investigation into the Abu Ghraib scandal called the prisoner abuse acts of "brutality and purposeless sadism" and also found that the acts were not simply the acts of lower level enlisted soldiers. Nicholas Berg, an American contractor, was beheaded by Iraqi militants, who claim the grisly murder was in retaliation for the treatment of Iraqi prisoners.

In early June, the UN Security Council unanimously passed a resolution endorsing the appointment of an interim government in Iraq. On June 28, 2004, the United States handed over power to the Iraqi interim government, and **Iyad Allawi** became Prime Minister.

Exercise Set 7.4

1. The last war in U.S. history that was declared by Congress in accordance with Article I, Section 8, was the
   A. Korean War
   B. World War II
   C. Operation Iraqi Freedom
   D. The Gulf War

2. An early statement by President Bush to the United Nations (September 2002) was that regime change was necessary in Iraq. Critics of President Bush claimed that invasion of a country solely for the purpose of regime change was a violation of
   A. Resolution #1441
   B. the Geneva Convention
   C. international law
   D. the Monroe Doctrine

3. In December 2002, for the first time in nearly four years, which of the following returned to Iraq?
   A. U.S. Ambassador
   B. UN weapons inspectors
   C. freedom of political dissent
   D. arms trade with the United States

4. Even though his administration already had information to the contrary, in his State of the Union address on January 28, 2003, President Bush told the American people that Iraq was attempting to do which of the following?
   A. Purchase nuclear warheads from Russia
   B. Stage a second invasion of Kuwait
   C. Surrender Kurdish northern Iraq to Turkey
   D. Purchase uranium from Africa

5. The author of the above political cartoon is suggesting that
   A. all Arabs should return to the Middle East
   B. the United States is a pluralistic society that includes Arab people
   C. there is a significant illegal Arab population in the United States
   D. all Americans are prejudiced against people from the Middle East

6. Colin Powell, the U.S. Secretary of State who presented arguments to the UN Security Council in support of military actions against Iraq was later replaced by
   A. Attorney General John Ashcroft
   B. Secretary of Defense Donald Rumsfeld
   C. Senator Bill Frist
   D. National Security Advisor Condoleezza Rice

7. In later statements, both Secretary of State Colin Powell and the 9/11 Commission concluded that there had never been any credible evidence that linked Iraq with
   A. Sunni Muslims
   B. al Qaeda's attack upon the United States
   C. chemical weapons used against their own people
   D. the 1990 invasion of Kuwait

8. The phrase that is not associated with the 2003 invasion of Iraq is
   A. Shock and Awe
   B. Operation Desert Storm
   C. Operation Iraqi Freedom
   D. Operation Telic

9. According to President Bush, following the events of December 13, 2003, near Tikrit, Iraq, the Iraqi people would no longer have to fear what?
   A. Taliban control
   B. Sunni and Shiite insurgents
   C. terrorists death squads
   D. the rule of Saddam Hussein

10. The primary reason given to the American people to justify the March 2003 war upon Iraq was that
   A. Saddam Hussein was in possession of weapons of mass destruction
   B. Osama bin Laden was being harbored by the Iraqi government
   C. the United States wanted to control the oil resources in Iraq
   D. Iraq had invaded and occupied Kuwait

CHAPTER 5

CONSERVATISM AND
ONE PARTY RULE

"Under democracy one party always devotes its chief energies to trying to prove that the other party is unfit to rule—and both commonly
succeed, and are right."

Journalist and social critic H.L. Mencken, 1956

America has had periods of single-party dominance before. It happened
under Franklin Roosevelt's New Deal, in the Republican 1920s, and in the
early 19th-century "**Era of Good Feeling**." In our system of republican
democracy, with the electoral process of selecting the President and Vice
President, the committee system in Congress, the enormous influence of lobbyists, the increasing use of gerrymandering to minimize the opposition, and
the appointment of federal judges, a nation in which a dominant party rules
for a prolonged period can jeopardize the democratic system.

2004 Elections

Although the 2004 elections were covered by the media with most attention being placed on the **Bush/Cheney** against **Kerry/Edwards** presidential
race, the congressional races were also highly contested and extremely
important to both parties in order to maintain control of the legislature.
Before the elections the Republicans held a 12-seat majority in the House of
Representatives, while in the Senate they held only a slim majority of 51–49.
As a result of the 2004 congressional elections, the Republicans increased
their control in the Senate to a 10-vote majority, and in the House of Representatives they added three more seats to their majority. Some of the gained
seats for the Republicans came as a result of redistricting (**gerrymandering**)
in Texas, led by Republican Representative, **Tom Delay**.

The Bush/Cheney campaign focused on national security, continuing the
war on terror that of course included the wars in Iraq and Afghanistan. The
Kerry/Cheney campaign supported more attention to domestic issues and
the claims that the war on terror, including Iraq and Afghanistan, had been
poorly executed.

 While the results of the election were contested, in the end it was a very tight victory for the incumbent administration of George Bush and Dick Cheney. A congressional study completed in January 2005 found that in Democratic pockets such as Columbus, Toledo, and Cincinnati, there were far too few voting machines, and voters were waiting in lines for as much as 10 hours. Many voters simply turned away and did not vote. The results were as follows: Bush/Cheney—popular votes 62,040,606, percentage 51%, electoral votes 286; Kerry/Edwards—popular votes 59,028,109, percentage 48%, electoral votes 252; Nader/Camejo—popular votes 411,304, percentage 1%, electoral votes 0. George Bush's victory in the presidential campaign came with the popular mandate that eluded him in the 2000 election and a stronger base in Congress that left him more powerful than ever before.

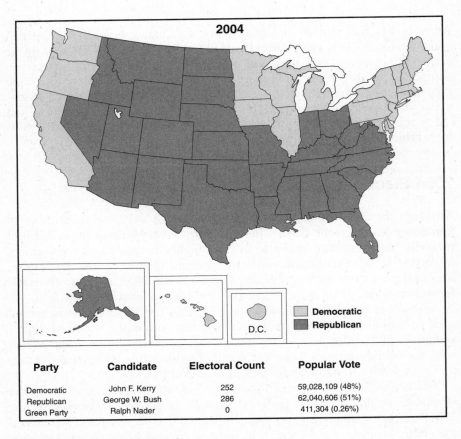

Figure 7.2 Election 2004 results

Decisions of the Supreme Court 2004–2005

- *Elk Grove* v. *Newdow* **(June 14, 2004).** In a unanimous 8–0 decision (**Justice Scalia** recused himself in the case), the court overturned a federal appeals court ruling that said the term "under God" in the Pledge of Allegiance was unconstitutional because it violates the separation of church and state. **Justices O'Connor** and **Thomas** and **Chief Justice Rehnquist** said the words "under God" were constitutional and were added in 1954 to set the U.S. apart from "godless Communism." The other five justices, however, said the plaintiff, Michael Newdow, did not have the legal standing to bring the case because he and the girl's mother, who opposed the suit, are in a custody battle.

- *Roper* v. *Simmons* **(March 1, 2005).** In *Roper* the Court decided, 5–4, that executing people who commit crimes before they turn 18 constitutes cruel and unusual punishment, a violation of the Eighth Amendment. Writing the majority opinion, Justice Kennedy points out that since the United States is the only country in the world that officially allows the execution of juveniles, it should be considered unusual punishment.

- *Gonzales* v. *Raich* **(June 6, 2005).** In a 6–3 decision the Court upheld the right of Congress to prohibit the use of medical marijuana and to prosecute those who violate the law even in the 11 states that have passed initiatives legalizing it for medical purposes.

- *Kelo* v. *City of New London*, **(June 23, 2005).** In one of the most controversial cases of the session, the Court ruled, 5–4, that a government can take possession of private property (**eminent domain**) against the owner's will and transfer it to private developers when the result will promote economic development. The Fifth Amendment allows the government to take private property for public use. In writing the majority opinion, **Justice John Paul Stevens** says "public use" also means "public purpose." "Promoting economic development is a traditional and long accepted function of government," he says. "Clearly, there is no basis for exempting economic development from our traditionally broad understanding of public purpose."

2004 and 2005: Domestic

Same-Sex Marriages Allowed in Massachusetts

On February 4, 2004, Massachusetts became the first state in the country to permit same-sex marriages on an equal basis with heterosexual marriages. The court's ruling gave the legislature six months to rewrite the law and rid the statute of language that banned same-sex marriage. The court rejected using "civil unions" as a remedy stating that it continued to place and relegate same-sex couples to a different status, a violation of the principles of equal protection of the law. President Bush's reaction was that he was "deeply troubled" stating that marriage is a "sacred institution between a man and a woman." As of January 1, 2012, six states and the District of Columbia allow same-sex marriage.

Final Report Concludes No Weapons of Mass Destruction Are in Iraq

Following a July 5, 2004, Senate Intelligence Committee report (Report of the U.S. Intelligence Community's Prewar Intelligence Assessments on Iraq), which stated that the intelligence on Iraq's weapons was inaccurate, overstated, and flawed, a final U.S. report on September 16 concluded that they had found no weapons of mass destruction (WMDs) in Iraq. The report also concluded that the intelligence that suggested the importation of nuclear materials and the capabilities for developing nuclear weapons was seriously flawed.

President Bush Sworn In for a Second Term and Addresses Social Security

On January 20, 2005, President Bush was sworn in for his second term. In his February 2, 2005, State of the Union address, President Bush announced his plan to reform Social Security. Among the reforms proposed was the establishment of personal accounts where Social Security deposits would go into bond and stock funds in the hopes of generating greater returns than the traditional Social Security deposits. This in turn would promote a "nest egg," in the President's words, that would be in addition to the worker's traditional Social Security check. Despite years of campaigning, his plan received only a lukewarm reception.

The Death of Terry Schiavo and the Right to Die

On March 31, 2005, Terry Schiavo, a 41-year-old brain-damaged woman, died in Florida nearly two weeks after doctors removed a feeding tube that had been keeping her alive for more than a decade. Terry Schiavo became the focal point of an ugly and, in many people's opinions, highly inappropriate and self-serving political battle over right to life and right to die. On March 21, three days after Schiavo's feeding tube was removed at the instruction of Terry's husband, Michael Schiavo, Congress passed a bill transferring jurisdiction of the case from Florida state court to a U.S. District Court, for a federal judge to review. President Bush signed it into law the next day. But federal courts refused to overturn the state courts' decision to allow her to die.

Hurricane Katrina

On August 25, 2005, Hurricane Katrina brought catastrophic damage on the Gulf coast resulting in more than 1,000 deaths and millions left homeless. Americans were shaken not simply by the magnitude of the disaster but also by how ill prepared all levels of government were in its aftermath. The **FEMA (Federal Emergency Management Agency)** chief testified that he informed White House officials on August 29 that the levees had breached and the city was flooding, but the Bush administration stated that they did not hear of the breach until August 30. In a radio interview, **Homeland Security Secretary Michael Chertoff** dismissed reports of the thousands at the convention center. Even when a Senate committee was requesting documents during an investigation of the government's response to the disaster, the White House refused claiming confidentiality.

Chief Justice William Rehnquist Dies

After having served on the Supreme Court for 33 years, 19 of those as chief justice and 14 as an associate justice (Nixon appointee), Chief Justice William Rehnquist died on September 3, 2005. The Rehnquist legacy has been that he turned back the liberal direction of the **Warren Court** and strengthened the legal position of the police, paved the way for swifter executions, defined constitutional limits on federal power, and permitted indirect government funding of religious schools. Chief Justice William Rehnquist was succeeded by **John Roberts** who became the 17th chief justice of the U.S. Supreme Court.

2004 and 2005: Foreign

NATO Admits Seven New Countries

On March 29, 2004, the North Atlantic Treaty Organization (NATO) admitted seven former communist eastern European countries: Bulgaria, Estonia, Latvia, Lithuania, Romania, Slovakia, and Slovenia. With the admission of the seven new countries, NATO now had 26 members.

Iyad Allawi Becomes Iraq's Prime Minister

On June 28, 2004, Iyad Allawi became the Prime Minister of Iraq. Allawi had been in exile since the early 1970s when he fell out of favor with Saddam Hussein. Allawi was appointed by the Iraq Interim Governing Council and became head of the Iraqi Interim Government. On April 21, 2006, **Nouri al-Maliki** was selected as the new Prime Minister and continues in that position.

Yasser Arafat Dies

On November 11, 2004, long-time leader of the **Palestine Liberation Organization** (PLO, formed 1964) and 1994 **Nobel Peace Prize** winner, **Yasser Arafat** died at Percy Military Hospital in Clamart, France, not far from Paris. Following the Oslo Accords of 1993, Palestinian elections took place in 1996, and Arafat was elected President of the Palestinian Authority. The exact cause of Arafat's death still remains somewhat of a mystery today.

Afghanistan Selects Its First President

Although he has been leading the post-Taliban Afghanistan government since December 2001, when the **Taliban** fell following the United States-led invasion, **Hamid Karzai** was elected President of the country after the first popular elections on October 9, 2004. The English-speaking leader enjoys strong support from the West and from many elements within Afghanistan. Born in Kandahar, Afghanistan, Karzai supported the **mujahideen** in their fight against the Soviet invasion in the 1980s. Following the Taliban take-over in 1996, Karzai opposed their radical reforms and in 2001 supported the American overthrow of their government. Since 2006 Karzai has been threatened with a resurgence of Taliban influence in Afghanistan.

Tsunami Kills More Than 220,000

On the day after Christmas 2004, an earthquake (9.3 on the **Richter** scale) under the Indian Ocean produced a number of **tsunami waves** that devastated coastal communities in Southeast Asia, including Indonesia, Thailand, India, and Sri Lanka. The death toll was estimated at over 220,000 people. An outpouring of worldwide aid totaling $7 billion to the area followed.

Terrorism in London

On July 7, 2005, London was hit by Islamic terrorist bombings that struck London's public transport system, killing 52 people and 4 suicide bombers and wounding about 700. It was Britain's worst attack since World War II.

G8 Meeting in London

In July 2005, the United Kingdom hosted the annual **G8 Summit** (Group of 8), a meeting of the world's eight leading industrialized nations (the G7, i.e., Britain, Canada, France, Germany, Italy, Japan, United States) plus Russia. The lead-up to the summit saw a lot of excitement from development and environmental groups. Public pressure seemed to have succeeded to get these most powerful nations to discuss various issues such as Africa (debt, unequal/unfair trade) and **climate change**. The countries agreed to double aid to Africa to $50 billion a year by 2010, cancel the debt of many poor countries, and open trade. Although some debt relief did result from the 2005 G8 Summit, open trade and climate control progress were disappointing.

Central American Free Trade Agreement

On August 2, 2005, President Bush signed the Central American Free Trade Agreement (CAFTA), which removed trade barriers between the United States and Costa Rica, the Dominican Republic, El Salvador, Guatemala, Honduras, and Nicaragua.

The Middle East in Turmoil

The War in Iraq

The war in Iraq continued through 2003 in spite of the "**Mission Accomplished**" claims of President Bush on May 1, 2003, on board the *USS Abraham Lincoln*. Following increased fighting, speculation about the administration's misuse of intelligence, and the realization that the war was going to last longer than originally hoped, good news came with the capture of Saddam Hussein. The announcement of **Ambassador Paul Bremer** on December 14, 2003, was "Ladies and gentlemen. We got him! Saddam Hussein had been captured hiding in a dirt cellar in the town of Abduar, about 15 kilometers from his hometown of Tikrit."

On January 17, 2004, the number of dead U.S. soldiers reached 500. Later that month **CIA** reports suggested that civil war was becoming a distinct possibility. This was further supported by a CIA intelligence report given to the Bush administration in September 2004. In September 2004 the death toll of U.S. soldiers reached 1,000. In October 2004, the British publication, *The Lancet*, estimated that 100,000 Iraqis had died as a result of the Iraq War.

On January 30, 2005, Iraq held elections to select a 275-seat National Assembly. The election results gave the Shiites a majority with the **Kurdish** community having a minority representation. The Sunni Arab community boycotted the election. On October 15, 2005, Iraqi voters ratified a new constitution. October also saw the beginning of the trial of Saddam Hussein and the number of U.S. soldier deaths reached 2,000. In December 2005 Iraq again held elections for the 275-seat National Assembly. In this election the Sunni community participated and the resulting Assembly is more representative of the different Iraqi factions. About 11 million Iraqis, 70% of the country's registered voters, participated in selecting their first permanent Parliament since the overthrow of Saddam Hussein. Once again, Shiites won a majority of the seats.

The threat of civil war increased as 2006 arrived with an increase in sectarian violence. Between January 4, 2006, and January 9, 2006, hundreds died at the hands of suicide bombers. In April the European Parliament announced that the CIA had conducted more than 1,000 secret flights over Europe, apparently transporting terrorism suspects to countries that would allow torture. Also in April **Jawad al-Maliki**, an advocate for Iraq's Shiite Muslims, was chosen to replace Ibrahim al-Jaafari as prime minister. On June 8, an attack by coalition forces north of Baghdad was successful in killing **Abu Musab al-Zarqawi**, the leader of al Qaeda in Iraq.

The month of July 2006 was the deadliest month of the war for Iraqi citizens with 3,438 civilian deaths. According to American military authorities, as reported in *The New York Times*, bomb strikes against American and Iraqi security forces numbered 1,666 bombs in the month of July. As of December 2011, American military casualties in Iraq reached 4,484.

Treatment of Detainees in War on Terror

Following continuing reports of the use of torture in the interrogation methods of the United States, on September 27, 2006, the House of Representatives voted 253–168 to support a bill drafted in part by **Senator John McCain,** which held the president to the guidelines of the **Geneva Convention**. The bill also banned the use of evidence gathered using cruel, unusual, and inhumane treatment. The Senate approved the bill by a vote of 65–34. When President Bush signed the bill into law, he did so with the use of a signing statement. A signing statement is used when a president is signing a bill into law and is a pronouncement of the president's interpretation of the law.

Saddam Hussein Is Found Guilty

On November 5, 2006, Saddam Hussein was found guilty by Iraq's High Tribunal and sentenced to death by hanging. Hussein was found guilty of crimes against humanity including the 1982 killings of 148 Shiites in the city of Dujail. Upon hearing the verdict, the former Iraqi leader shouted, "God is great."

Iran and Nuclear Development

The recent Iranian nuclear crisis can be traced back to 2002 when intelligence reports stated that Iran had built a large **uranium** plant without informing the United Nations. In December of 2002 satellite photographs confirmed that nuclear sites existed in Iran. After the United States accused Iran of developing weapons of mass destruction, Iran agreed to inspections by the International Atomic Energy Authority. In 2005 hardliner **Mahmoud Ahmadinejad** was installed as Iranian president, and Iran pledged an "irreversible" resumption of uranium enrichment. On January 3, 2006, Iran announced it would restart its nuclear energy program. The United States and several European nations condemned the move.

During April, President Mahmoud Ahmadinejad declared that Iran had successfully enriched uranium and would continue to produce nuclear fuel. The International Atomic Energy Authority (IAEA) announced that Iran had not cooperated with inspectors. On July 31, 2006, the UN Security Council resolution called on Iran to stop enriching uranium by August 31 or face the threat of sanctions. As of January 2012, the IAEA is still pursuing discussions of Iran's nuclear facilities to determine the countries nuclear intentions.

Exercise Set 7.5

1. The results of the 2004 national elections gave the
   A. Democrats control of the Congress, but not the White House
   B. Republicans control of the Congress, but not the White House
   C. Republicans control of the Congress and the White House
   D. Democrats control of the White House, but not the Congress

2. The issue of religion in the public schools reached the Supreme Court in 2004 in the *Newdow* case. At the heart of the case was
   A. "God" in the Pledge of Allegiance
   B. school prayer
   C. after-school religious clubs
   D. the display of a Christmas tree in the school

3. The power of the federal government to take private land for public use or "public purpose" is known as
   A. habeas corpus
   B. eminent domain
   C. gerrymandering
   D. log rolling

4. The *legal* issue which is at the core of the same-sex marriage debate is
   A. equal protection of the laws
   B. cruel and unusual punishment
   C. freedom of religion
   D. freedom of speech

5. The legacy of the Rehnquist Supreme Court would be consistent with
   A. judicial activism
   B. conservative jurisprudence
   C. liberal interpretation of the Constitution
   D. continuing the work of the Warren Court

6. Both NAFTA (North American Free Trade Agreement) and CAFTA (Central American Free Trade Agreement) support
   A. raising the levels of protective tariffs between trading countries
   B. isolationistic trade policies
   C. the reduction of trade barriers between member countries
   D. the greater use of trade sanctions between member countries

7. During December 2005, national elections in Iraq were held to select representatives to the National Assembly. Political/ethnic factions, which selected representatives to the National Assembly, did not include
   A. Kurds
   B. Sunnis
   C. Palestinians
   D. Shiites

8. The international agreement that addresses the use of torture upon enemy captives is known as
   A. Abu Ghraib
   B. NATO
   C. Resolution #1441
   D. Geneva Convention

9. The National Security Surveillance Act (2006), which allows wiretapping of electronic correspondence without a court's warrant, raises civil liberty issues protected by the
   A. First Amendment
   B. Fourth Amendment
   C. Sixth Amendment
   D. Eighth Amendment

10. In what appeared to be a vote against the way the war in Iraq was being conducted, in November 2006 the American people
    A. voted in a completely Democratic Congress
    B. voted to impeach President Bush
    C. recalled Secretary of State Donald Rumsfeld
    D. boycotted the midterm elections

CHAPTER 6

FINANCIAL CRISIS, BARACK OBAMA, AND AN UNEASY WORLD

The strongest democracies flourish from frequent and lively debate, but they endure when people of every background and belief find a way to set aside smaller differences in service of a greater purpose.

Barack Obama, press conference, Feb. 9, 2009

As the administration of George W. Bush approached its final year, the United States and much of Europe entered what may eventually prove to be the worst financial crisis since the Great Depression. Components of the crisis included increasing oil prices, the subprime mortgage crisis, collapse of the housing market, and the failures of major financial institutions, including **Lehman Brothers** in September, 2008. Both Presidents Bush and Obama and their administrations pushed into law unprecedented economic bailouts to economic institutions and the automobile industry. In October 2009, the unemployment rate peaked at 10.1%. In an attempt to prevent future economic disasters of this magnitude, Congress enacted the *Dodd–Frank Wall Street Reform and Consumer Protection Act*, which brought about changes in the financial regulatory system.

Populist Movements

Populist movements, both political and social, surfaced as the Obama administration entered its second year. On the domestic front the conservative **"Occupy"** movement addressed, among other things, the distribution of wealth in the United States, and the conservative **Tea Party** movement demanded reforms by Republicans and Democrats alike. The pro-democratic **Arab Spring** movement in the Middle East continues to battle oppressive regimes such as Syria and Bahrain and, of course, was successful in toppling the Gaddafi regime in Libya. With a democrat-controlled Congress, legislation of the Obama administration included the *Patient Protection and Affordable Care Act* (March 23, 2010) and the *Don't Ask, Don't Tell Repeal Act* (December 2010). Republicans regained control of the House of Representatives in the 2010 midterm elections, and the divided Congress debated debt ceilings and tax laws and saw their approval rating reach an all-time low of 11%. While United States involvement in Iraq approached an end, the debate continued regarding our involvement in Afghanistan.

Decisions of the Supreme Court 2006–2007

• *Rumsfeld* v. *Forum for Academic and Institutional Rights* **(March 6, 2006).** The Supreme Court, voting 8–0, upheld a federal law that provided that colleges and universities had to grant military recruiters the same access to students as other potential employers or else lose federal financing. A group of law schools had challenged the law, saying it violated their First Amendment right to free speech and association. The law schools objected to the military's presence on college campuses because of its policy of excluding openly gay men and women.

• *Georgia* v. *Randolph* **(March 22, 2006).** Justices ruled, 5–3, that if police do not have a warrant, they cannot search a home if one of the occupants objects, even if another occupant grants police permission. "A warrantless search of a shared dwelling for evidence over the express refusal of consent by a physically present resident cannot be justified as reasonable," Justice Souter wrote for the majority. John Roberts, Jr. issued his first dissent as chief justice.

• *Randall* v. *Sorrell* **(June 26, 2006).** Court voted 6–3 to prohibit Vermont's campaign finance statute, which limited the amount of money a candidate could spend on a campaign and how much individuals and political parties could contribute to a candidate. Justice Breyer, writing for the majority, said that such limits violate the First Amendment right of free speech of both candidates and political parties.

• *Hamdan* v. *Rumsfeld* **(June 29, 2006).** In a blow to the Bush administration, the Supreme Court ruled 5–3 that military commissions used to try suspected terrorists detained at the Guantánamo Bay prison camp in Cuba violate the Geneva Conventions and were established without Congress's authorization. The ruling forced the Bush administration to seek authorization from Congress.

• *Gonzales* v. *Carhart* **(April 18, 2007).** The Supreme Court upheld the **Partial-Birth Abortion Ban Act of 2003**. Under this law, "Any physician who, in or affecting interstate or foreign commerce, knowingly performs a partial-birth abortion and thereby kills a human fetus shall be fined under this title or imprisoned not more than 2 years, or both."

2006 and 2007: Domestic

• **Bush Addressed the Nation (January 31, 2006).** In his fifth State of the Union speech, the President denounced Iran, calling it a country "held hostage by a small clerical elite that is isolating and repressing its people." He also attacked Democrats for questioning the war in Iraq and urged Americans to end their "addiction" to oil, calling on the country to replace 75 percent of oil imports from the Middle East with **ethanol** and other energy sources.

- **Senate renewed the Patriot Act (March 2, 2006).** The Senate voted 89–10 to renew the controversial legislation. Bush signed the law, but included a **"signing statement"** that outlined his interpretation of the law, which stated he was not bound by its requirement to tell Congress how the law is being used.

- **Enron Executives Convicted (May 25, 2006).** Kenneth Lay and Jeffrey Skilling, former chief executives of **Enron**, were found guilty of fraud and conspiracy by a Houston jury.

- **Senate Defeated Ban on Same-Sex Marriage (June 7, 2006).** In a partisan vote of 49–48, the Senate rejected a proposed constitutional amendment to ban same-sex marriage.

- **Flag Amendment Defeated (June 28, 2006).** Sixty-six senators voted for a Constitutional amendment giving Congress the power to prohibit flag desecration, with 34 opposed; 67 votes had been needed.

- **Bush Vetoed Stem Cell Bill (July 19, 2006).** A day after the Senate voted 63–37 in favor of legislation that would expand the number of **stem cell** lines available for embryonic research using federal financing, the president used the veto for the first time.

- **Senate Extended Voting Rights Act (July 20, 2006).** A week after the House passed the bill, the Senate voted 98–0 to extend by 25 years the law that bans voter discrimination.

- **Senate Passed Abortion Restriction (July 25, 2006).** By a vote of 65–34 the Senate made it a federal crime to transport an underage girl across state lines to have an abortion and avoid the parental notification laws of certain states.

- **Congress Voted on Treatment of Terror Detainees (September 14, 2006).** Senate Armed Services Committee endorsed, 15–9, legislation introduced by Senator John McCain that expanded protections for foreign terror suspects. In approving the bill, the committee rejected legislation favored by the White House. The House of Representatives voted 253–168 for a compromise bill that stated the president cannot reinterpret what methods of interrogations are allowed under the **Geneva Conventions**.

- **U.S. Population Reached New Milestone (October 17, 2006).** The U.S. population officially reached 300 million.

- **Democrats Took Control of Congress in Midterm Elections (November 7, 2006):** Democrats gained 27 seats in the House of Representatives, giving them 230 seats to the Republicans' 205. In the Senate, Democrats gained six seats, enough for a 51–49 majority. Democrats selected **Nancy Pelosi** as speaker of the House and Steny Hoyer as House majority leader. Nancy Pelosi was the first woman to hold the position.

- **President Bush announced a surge** of an additional 20,000 troops would be deployed to Baghdad to try to stem sectarian fighting **(January 10, 2007)**.

- **Scientists Confirmed Global Warming (February 2, 2007).** A three-year study by the influential Intergovernmental Panel on Climate Change stated that global warming is very likely caused by human activity—specifically the emission and buildup of carbon dioxide in the atmosphere. The report also stated that the rise in temperatures and rising seas could be curtailed with quick action.

- **The minimum wage increased to $5.85 from $5.15 (July 24, 2007).** It was the first increase in 10 years. The wage would increase 70 cents each year through 2009, when it would be $7.25 an hour.

- **Median Household Income Increased, Number of Insured Down (August 28, 2007).** The Census Bureau reported that median household income increased to $48,201 due to longer work hours, but wages did not increase. The number of uninsured increased to 47 million in 2006, up from 44.8 million in 2005.

- **Federal Reserve Put Billions into Financial System (August 10, 2007).** Fed put $72 billion into the U.S. financial system over two days to steady the volatile markets that plummeted in response to losses in the American mortgage market.

- **Iraq Report to Congress (September 10, 2007).** In highly anticipated testimony, **Gen. David Petraeus** told members of the House Foreign Affairs and Armed Services committees that the U.S. military needed more time to meet its goals in Iraq. U.S. Ambassador to Iraq Ryan Crocker also testified, saying that while Iraqi leaders and the people are capable of—and desire to—bridge the sectarian divide, "I frankly do not expect that we will see rapid progress."

- **President Bush signed an energy bill (December 19, 2007).** The bill requires passenger vehicles sold in the U.S. to have fuel economy standards of 35 mpg by 2020.

2006 and 2007: Foreign

- **Iran's Defiant Nuclear Program (April 2006).** Iran announced that it had successfully enriched uranium. President **Mahmoud Ahmadinejad** refused to curb Iran's nuclear program, which he viewed as a source of national pride. After international negotiations and threats failed, a U.N. Security Council resolution was passed in July, demanding that Iran halt its nuclear activities by the end of August or face possible sanctions.

- **North Korea test fired missiles over the Sea of Japan (July 4, 2006)** and exploded a nuclear device in the North Korean mountains (October 9, 2006). The U.N. Security Council voted in favor of a resolution banning the sale of materials to North Korea that could be used to produce weapons (October 14, 2006). North Korea agreed to resume disarmament talks with China, Russia, the U.S., and South Korea (October 31, 2006).

- **The Taliban continued its resurgence in Afghanistan**, making 2006 the deadliest year of fighting since the 2001 war. Throughout the spring, Taliban militants infiltrated southern Afghanistan, terrorizing villagers and attacking Afghan and U.S. troops. In August 2006, NATO troops took over military operations in southern Afghanistan from the U.S.-led coalition. In September NATO launched the largest attack in its 57-year history. About 2,000—the vast majority Taliban fighters—were killed in military operations during the year.

- **Saddam Hussein** was convicted of crimes against humanity by an Iraqi court (November 5, 2006), and hanged in Baghdad.

- **The U.S. began its "surge" (February 7, 2007)** of some 30,000 troops to Iraq to stem increasingly deadly attacks by insurgents and militias.

- **India and U.S. reached an agreement (July 27, 2007)** on civilian nuclear power that allowed India, which had not signed the *Nuclear Non-proliferation Treaty,* to buy nuclear fuel from the U.S. to expand its civilian nuclear energy program and reprocess its spent fuel.

Supreme Court: 2008 and 2009

- *Baze* v. *Rees* **(April 14, 2008).** The court rejected a challenge to Kentucky's method of execution by lethal injection, ruling that there was insufficient evidence that the method posed an unconstitutional risk of pain and suffering.

- *Crawford* v. *Marion County Election Board* **(April 28, 2008).** By a vote of 6 to 3, the court upheld Indiana's voter identification law, which required would-be voters to present current state or federal photo identification to cast a ballot. The strictest of a half-dozen such laws, the Indiana statute was challenged as an unconstitutional burden on the right to vote. But Justice Stevens wrote in the lead opinion that no such burden had been demonstrated.

- *Boumediene* v. *Bush* **(June 12, 2008).** The Court ruled 5-to-4 that detainees at **Guantánamo Bay** have a constitutional right to go to federal court to challenge their continued detention. It was the court's third consecutive blow to the Bush administration in a Guantánamo-related case. Justice Kennedy, who had voted with the majority in the two earlier rounds, wrote the opinion in the case.

- ***District Attorney's Office v. Osborne* (June 18, 2009).** The Supreme Court ruled in a 5–4 decision that prisoners have no right to a **DNA** test to prove their innocence long after they are convicted of a crime. The Court claimed that most states already had laws in effect concerning DNA testing, so a federal law was unnecessary.

- ***Safford v. Redding* (June 25, 2009).** Can school officials legally strip-search students against their will for no specific reason? In an 8–1 ruling, the Court held that students have a Fourth Amendment right that precludes arbitrary strip searches.

- ***District of Columbia v. Heller* (June 26, 2008).** Striking down the District of Columbia's handgun ban, the court ruled that the Second Amendment protects an individual's right to own a gun for private use. Justice Scalia wrote for the court. Justices Stevens, Breyer, Souter, and Ginsburg dissented.

2008 and 2009: Domestic

- **Super Tuesday primary races (February 5, 2008).** Arizona Senator John McCain emerged as the clear front runner among Republicans in the Super Tuesday primary races and by March 4 had enough delegate votes to secure the Republican nomination. On the Democratic side, New York Senator Hillary Clinton won big states such as California and Massachusetts, but Illinois Senator Barack Obama took more states.

- **The federal government began to intervene in the U.S. financial system to avoid a crisis (March 11, 2008).** The Federal Reserve outlined a $200 billion loan program that let the country's biggest banks borrow Treasury securities at discounted rates. The Fed approved a $30 billion loan to JPMorgan Chase so it could take over Bear Stearns (global investment bank and securities trading and brokerage), which was on the verge of collapse.

- **Democratic Senator Barack Obama wins the presidential election (November 4, 2008).** Obama took 338 electoral votes to McCain's 161, and became the first African American to be elected president of the United States. Democrats increased their majority in the House and picked up five seats in the Senate.

- **President George W. Bush announced plans (December 19, 2008)** to lend General Motors and Chrysler $17.4 billion to survive the next three months.

- ***The American Recovery and Reinvestment Act of 2009***, commonly referred to as the Stimulus or The Recovery Act, was enacted by Congress and signed into law on February 17, 2009.

- **President Obama announced his intention to withdraw most American troops from Iraq by August 31, 2010 (February 27, 2009).** As many as 50,000 troops would remain there for smaller missions and to train Iraqi soldiers.

- **Unemployment in the U.S.** reached 8.1% in February 2009, the highest rate since 1983.

- **Insurance giant American International Group (AIG) reported a $61.7 billion loss for the fourth quarter of 2008 (March 2, 2009).** AIG lost $99.3 billion in 2008. The federal government, which had already provided the company with a $60 billion loan, would give AIG an additional $30 billion, making it the largest company loan the government provided during the bailout.

- **The Senate approved, 68 to 31, the nomination of Sonia Sotomayor (August 6, 2009)** to the Supreme Court. Sotomayor is the first Hispanic Supreme Court justice and the third woman to serve on the Court.

2008 and 2009: Foreign

- **Iraq's cabinet passed by a large margin an agreement (November 16, 2008)** that would govern the U.S. presence in Iraq through 2011. The pact called for the withdrawal of all U.S. combat troops by December 31, 2011.

- **Cease-fire between Israel and Hamas expired (December 28, 2008).** Hamas began launching rocket attacks into Israel, which retaliated with airstrikes that killed about 300 people.

- **Iraq held local elections to create provincial councils (January 31, 2009).** More than 14,000 people ran for just 440 seats. The elections are notable for their lack of violence and the noticeably diminished role the U.S. played in their implementation.

- **U.S. troops completed their withdrawal from Iraqi cities (June 30, 2009)** including Baghdad, and transferred the responsibility of securing the cities to Iraqi troops.

- **President Barack Obama announced that the U.S., China, India, Brazil, and South Africa (December 18, 2009)** reached an agreement to combat global warming. The agreement set up a system for monitoring pollution reduction, requiring richer nations to give billions of dollars to poorer nations more greatly affected by climate change.

Supreme Court: 2010 and 2011

- *Citizens United* **v.** *Federal Election Commission* **(January 21, 2010).** The Supreme Court ruled, 5–4, that the government cannot restrict the spending of corporations for political campaigns, maintaining that it's their First Amendment right to support candidates as they choose. This decision upset two previous precedents on the free-speech rights of corporations. President Obama expressed disapproval of the decision, calling it a "victory" for Wall Street and Big Business.

- *Berghuis* **v.** *Thompkins* **(June 1, 2010).** The Court considered the position of a suspect who understood his or her right to remain silent under *Miranda* v. *Arizona*, but did not explicitly invoke or waive the right. The Court held that unless and until the suspect actually stated that he was relying on that right, his subsequent voluntary statements could be used in court and police could continue to question him.

- *McDonald* **v.** *Chicago* **(June 28, 2010).** The Supreme Court ruled in a 5-to-4 decision that the Second Amendment's guarantee to bear arms applies to local and state gun control laws. Justice Samuel Alito, who spoke for the majority, said the right to self defense is fundamental to American civil liberties.

- *Brown* **v.** *Entertainment Merchants Association* **(June 27, 2011).** The Supreme Court struck down a California law enacted in 2005 that banned the sale of certain violent video games to children without parental supervision. In a 7–2 decision, the Court revoked the law, ruling that video games were protected speech under the First Amendment.

- *United States* **v.** *Jones* **(January 23, 2012).** The Court unanimously ruled that the police had violated the Constitution when they placed a Global Positioning System tracking device on a suspect's car and monitored its movements for 28 days. But the justices divided 5-to-4 on the rationale for the decision, with the majority saying that the problem was the placement of the device on private property. That ruling avoided many difficult questions, including how to treat information gathered from devices installed by the manufacturer and how to treat information held by third parties such as cellphone companies.

2010 and 2011: Domestic

- **"Don't Ask, Don't Tell,"** a policy that forbade openly gay men and women from serving in the military, was ended on September 20, 2011.

- *The Patient Protection and Affordable Care Act*, **which overhauled the health-care system was passed into law (March 23, 2010).**

Among other things, the bill allowed children to stay on their parents' health insurance plans until the age of 26, prevented insurance companies from denying coverage due to a patient's "pre-existing conditions," subsidized private insurance for low- and middle-income Americans, and required all Americans to have some sort of health insurance. The budget office estimated that the law would reduce federal budget deficits by $143 billion over the next 10 years. The government planned to earn money for the law with a tax on high-cost employer-sponsored health plans and a tax on investment income of the wealthiest Americans.

- **An explosion on a BP oil drilling rig off the coast of Louisiana killed 11 people and injured 17 (April 20, 2010).** After 86 days of gushing millions of gallons of crude oil into the Gulf of Mexico and several previous attempts to contain the flow, BP capped its leaking oil well.

- **Jan Brewer, governor of Arizona, signed into law the country's toughest immigration bill (April 23, 2010).** It is designed to identify and deport illegal immigrants. It allowed law enforcement officials to ask people suspected of being illegal immigrants for their proof of citizenship or visas. The United States Justice Department filed a lawsuit against the state of Arizona in protest of its new immigration law, and the Supreme Court decided to review the Arizona law (December 2011).

- **Congress approved a landmark financial regulation bill**, strongly supported by President Obama and the Democratic Party (July 15, 2010). The bill increased the number of companies that would be regulated by government oversight, a panel to watch for risks in the financial system, and a consumer protection agency. Republicans claim it gave the government too much power in the business sector.

- **The United States Senate voted 63 to 37 to confirm Elena Kagan** as the newest Supreme Court Justice (August 5, 2010). Kagan is only the fourth woman to ever hold this position.

- **Seven years after the war in Iraq began, President Obama announced the end of Operation Iraqi Freedom with a withdrawal of combat troops (August 31, 2010).** The U.S. would continue to be a presence in Iraq, mainly with civilian contractors but also with a smaller military contingent of approximately 50,000 troops.

- **President Obama announced that he would not approve an extension of the Bush-era law that gave a tax break for the wealthy (September 7, 2010)** or those families who earn over $250,000 per year and individuals who earn over $200,000 annually. President George W. Bush passed the tax cuts for those in the higher income bracket in 2001.

- **The percentage of Americans living below the poverty line** reached 14.3 percent, the greatest number since the Great Depression.

- **The Republican Party gained control of the House of Representatives (November 4, 2010)** in the midterm elections, but the Democratic party retained the majority in the Senate. Two members of the **Tea Party** won victories: Rand Paul of Kentucky and Marco Rubio of Florida.

- **Teachers and State Employees Protest in Wisconsin (February 15, 2011).** Wisconsin governor Scott Walker put forward a plan to cut the **collective bargaining** rights and benefits of public workers. Democratic senators flee Wisconsin in order to halt action in the state Senate.

- **President Obama Reserves Position on Defense of Marriage Act (February 23, 2011).** This 1996 law bars federal recognition of same-sex marriages. Two lawsuits challenging the 1996 law as unconstitutional forced President Obama and his legal team to revise their position, concluding that gay people qualify for the greater protection afforded to a handful of categories, like gender or race.

- **Osama bin Laden, founder of the militant Islamist organization Al-Qaeda, was shot and killed (May 2, 2011)** inside a private residential compound in Abbottabad, Pakistan, by U.S. Navy SEALs.

- **New York Legalized Same-Sex Marriage (June 24, 2011).** After making same-sex marriage one of his top priorities, Governor Andrew Cuomo emerged as a true champion of gay rights.

- **Standard & Poor's Lowered the U.S. Credit Rating (August 5, 2011).** In making the decision, Standard & Poor's wrote that the "gulf between the political parties" reduced confidence in the government's ability to manage its finances.

- **Occupy Wall Street Movement Continued to Grow (October 2011).** The group defines itself as a group of activists who stand against corporate greed, social inequality, and the disproportion between the rich and poor. It began in New York and has spread to Chicago, Los Angeles, and San Francisco.

- **Voters Reject Conservative Measures in General Election (November 8, 2011).** An anti-abortion measure in Mississippi, an anti-labor law in Ohio, and a measure to clamp down on voting rights in Maine were all rejected.

2010 and 2011: Foreign

- **United States and Russia Have Breakthrough in Arms Negotiations (March 24, 2010).** Both countries agreed to lower the limit on deployed strategic warheads and launchers.

- **Comprehensive Iran Sanctions, Accountability, and Divestment Act of 2010 (July 1, 2010)** was signed into law, extending economic sanctions on Iran.

- **Muammar Gaddafi**, deposed leader of Libya, was captured and shot to death (October 20, 2011).

- **U.S. troops** started to withdraw from Iraq under the terms of the U.S.–Iraq Status of Forces Agreement (December 18, 2011).

Exercise Set 7.6

1. In the last 20 years, the use of automation in U.S. industry has led to
   A. a shortage of consumer goods
   B. increased union membership
   C. the lowering of the legal minimum wage
   D. increased unemployment among unskilled workers

2. Some supporters of limits on Congressional terms favor limiting the number of years that members of Congress could serve to 12 years—six terms for House members and two terms for Senators. The major reason for increased support for this change discussed is the public's belief that
   A. most current members of Congress have taken bribes
   B. the President's political party should have a majority in Congress
   C. political disputes in Congress would be reduced
   D. the democratic process would be strengthened

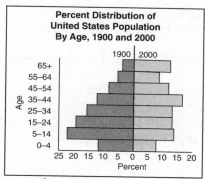

Source: United States Census Bureau (adapted)

3. The changes shown in the graph support the recent concerns of Americans about the
   A. future of Social Security and Medicare
   B. return to an agrarian society
   C. surplus of health care workers
   D. shortage of schools and colleges

4. During the next 30 years, what will be the most likely impact of the baby boom that followed World War II?
   A. More money will be spent on national defense.
   B. The cost of health care will decrease.
   C. Social Security will have to provide for increasing numbers of retired people.
   D. The elderly will be the smallest segment of the population.

Base your answers to questions 5 and 6 on the passage below and on your knowledge of social studies.

> . . . Keeping America competitive requires affordable energy. And here we have a serious problem: America is addicted to oil, which is often imported from unstable parts of the world. The best way to break this addiction is through technology. Since 2001, we have spent nearly $10 billion to develop cleaner, cheaper, and more reliable alternative energy sources. And we are on the threshold of incredible advances. . . .
>
> —President George W. Bush,
> State of the Union Address, January 31, 2006

5. In this passage, President George W. Bush suggests Americans can overcome oil "addiction" by focusing on
   A. conservation
   B. education
   C. scientific research
   D. discovery of new oil fields

6. Which goal related to United States energy needs is addressed in this speech?
   A. reduce dependence on the Middle East
   B. supply all energy needs from domestic sources
   C. decrease offshore drilling
   D. eliminate the use of all petroleum products

THEMATIC ESSAY

Directions: Write a well-organized essay that includes an introduction, several paragraphs addressing the task below, and a conclusion.

Theme: U.S. Immigration Policies

In the last 50 years United States immigration policies have reflected the prevailing needs and concerns of American society at a particular time.

Task:

From your study of immigration policies of the last 60 years, identify *three* legislative actions (legislation) by the federal government that have established immigration policies.

For each legislative action:

- Identify the particular law that was passed by Congress.
- Discuss the needs and/or concerns of American society that influenced the particular law.
- Evaluate the success of the law in addressing the needs and/or concerns.

You may use examples of federal legislation that occurred in the last 60 years. Some suggestions you may wish to consider are The Immigration and Nationality Act of 1952 (communism), Refugee Act of 1980 (post-Vietnam and Indochina conflicts), Immigration Reform and Control Act (IRCA) of 1986 (illegal immigration), Illegal Immigration Reform and Immigrant Responsibility Act (IIRAIRA) of 1996 (illegal immigration), REAL ID Act of 2005 (National Identification by 2008), and Secure Fence Act of 2006 (700-mile Mexican border fence).

You are *not* limited to these suggestions.

DOCUMENT-BASED QUESTION ESSAY

The following questions (Part A and Part B) are based on the accompanying documents (1–5). Some of the documents have been edited for the purpose of this exercise. The question is designed to test your ability to work with historical documents and to demonstrate your knowledge of the subject matter being presented. As you analyze the documents, take into account both the source of the document and the author's point of view.

Historical Context: Following the attacks on the United States on September 11, 2001, the question pitting national security against civil liberties created a debate regarding the Constitution and the powers it bestowed on the federal government and the function of the Constitution in protecting citizens from abusive governmental power.

Task: Using information from the documents and your knowledge of United States history, answer the questions that follow each document in Part A. Your answers to the questions will help you write the Part B essay in which you will be asked to:

Evaluate the following statement: "In creating greater domestic security from future attacks by terrorists, the United States government must not trample on American liberties in the name of preserving them."

Part A
Short Answer

The documents below relate to issues concerning the powers and function of the Constitution. Examine each document carefully and then answer the questions that follow.

DOCUMENT 1

During those first few hours after the attacks, I kept remembering a sentence from a case I had studied in law school. Not surprisingly, I didn't remember which case it was, who wrote the opinion, or what it was about, but I did remember these words: "While the Constitution protects against invasions of individual rights, it is not a **suicide** pact." I took these words as a challenge to my concerns about civil liberties at such a momentous time in our history; that we must be careful to not take civil liberties so literally that we allow ourselves to be destroyed.

— Senator Russ Feingold, Statement on the Anti-Terrorism Bill
(October 25, 2001)

1. Who, or what would be committing suicide?

_____

_____

_____

_____

2. What is the common name of the Anti-Terrorism Bill that Senator Feingold was speaking about on October 25, 2001?

_____

_____

_____

DOCUMENT 2

1. What is the main idea of the political cartoon?

_____

_____

_____

_____

2. The man leaving with the arm occupied what Cabinet position during the first George W. Bush administration?

_____

_____

_____

_____

DOCUMENT 3

"Those who would give up essential Liberty, to purchase a little temporary Safety, deserve neither Liberty nor Safety."

— Benjamin Franklin (1755)

1. Applying Benjamin Franklin's quote to the war on terror, give two examples of "Liberty" that some believe are being given up in order to protect the security of the United States.

_____

_____

_____

_____

DOCUMENT 4

USA PATRIOT ACT
SEC. 501. ACCESS TO CERTAIN BUSINESS RECORDS FOR FOREIGN INTELLIGENCE AND INTERNATIONAL TERRORISM INVESTIGATIONS.
(a)(1) The Director of the Federal Bureau of Investigation . . . may make an application for an order requiring the production of any tangible things (including books, records, papers, documents, and other items) for an investigation to protect against international terrorism or clandestine intelligence activities, provided that such investigation of a United States person is not conducted solely upon the basis of activities protected by the first amendment to the Constitution.

— Sec. 501 USA PATRIOT Act

1. The protections provided by which two amendments included in the Bill of Rights are applicable to this section of the USA PATRIOT Act?

_____

_____

_____

625

DOCUMENT 5

1. Who is the individual taking the oath and who is the individual giving the oath? Specific names are preferred, but titles are acceptable.

_____

_____

_____

2. What passages might not be protected and defended by the individual taking the oath? Give two examples.

_____

_____

_____

Part B
Essay

Your essay should be well organized with an introductory paragraph that states your position on the question. Develop your position in the next paragraphs and then write a conclusion. In your essay, include specific historical details and refer to specific documents you analyzed in Part A. You may include additional information from your knowledge of social studies.

Historical Context: Following the attacks on the United States on September 11, 2001, the question pitting national security against civil liberties created a debate regarding the Constitution and the powers it bestowed on the federal government and the function of the Constitution in protecting citizens from abusive governmental power.

Task:

> Evaluate the following statement: "In creating greater domestic security from future attacks by terrorists, the United States government must not trample on American liberties in the name of preserving them." Be sure to use the documents provided in structuring your response.

Guidelines:

In your essay, be sure to
• Develop all aspects of the task
• Incorporate information from at least *five* documents
• Incorporate relevant outside information
• Support the theme with many relevant facts, examples, and details
• Use a logical and clear plan of organization, including an introduction and a conclusion that are beyond a restatement of the theme

CHRONOLOGY OF MAJOR EVENTS IN AMERICAN HISTORY

1607	Founding of Jamestown in Virginia
1619	Virginia House of Burgesses formed. First Africans brought to Virginia.
1620	Mayflower Compact
1676	Bacon's Rebellion in Virginia
1688	Glorious Revolution in England
1754	Albany Congress proposes Plan of Union drafted by Benjamin Franklin for defense against Indians and French. Plan is rejected by the colonies.
1763	Treaty of Paris ending Seven Years War (French and Indian War) gives Canada to Great Britain and ends French threat to colonies.
1765	Stamp Act Congress (delegates from nine colonies) meets in New York to oppose Stamp Act and other British taxes.
1770	Boston Massacre
1773	Boston Tea Party
1774	Parliament passes Coercive Acts and Quebec Act. First Continental Congress meets in Philadelphia.
1775	Battles of Lexington and Concord (April 19). Second Continental Congress meets in Philadelphia.
1776	Thomas Paine publishes *Common Sense*. Congress adopts Declaration of Independence, July 4; begins drafting Articles of Confederation.
1778	Treaties with France bring important military supplies and naval support.
1781	Maryland is thirteenth and last state to ratify Articles of Confederation. British commander Cornwallis surrenders to Washington at Yorktown, Virginia, October 19, ending major fighting in the Revolutionary War.
1782	Preliminary peace treaty with Great Britain recognizes independent United States with borders of Great Lakes in the north, the Mississippi River on the west, and the 31st parallel to the south.
1783	British evacuate New York City November 25, but continue to hold forts in Northwest territories.
1786	Annapolis Convention discusses interstate cooperation and recommends a convention to revise the Articles of Confederation. Shays' Rebellion in Massachusetts suppressed.
1787	Constitutional Convention meets in Philadelphia, May–September Continental Congress adopts Northwest Ordinance. The Constitution submitted to Congress, September 20, and to the people in special state conventions, September 28.
1788	Eleven states (all but Rhode Island and North Carolina) ratify Constitution, putting new federal government into effect.
1789	New federal Congress convenes in New York City. George Washington receives all 69 electoral votes for President; nominates Thomas Jefferson as Secretary of State, Alexander Hamilton as Secretary of the Treasury, and John Jay as Chief Justice of the Supreme Court. Congress passes Judiciary Act creating federal court system. Proposed amendments to the Constitution approved by Congress and submitted to the states. North Carolina ratifies Constitution.

1790   Rhode Island ratifies Constitution. First American textile mill built in
        Pawtucket, R.I.

1791   Bank of the United States chartered. Vermont admitted to the Union.

1792   Washington reelected President, receiving all 132 electoral votes; vetoes
        first bill and veto is sustained by House. First ten amendments ("The Bill
        of Rights") officially ratified, March 1. Kentucky admitted to the Union.

1793   Supreme Court decision in *Chisolm* v. *Georgia* permits citizen of South
        Carolina to sue state of Georgia in federal court. Washington issues
        Proclamation of Neutrality in war between the new French Republic
        and Great Britain. Cotton gin invented by Eli Whitney.

1794   Whiskey Rebellion in Pennsylvania suppressed.

1795   Jay Treaty with England and Pinckney Treaty with Spain approved by
        Senate. Eleventh Amendment ratified, barring citizens of one state
        from suing another state in federal court.

1796   Washington refuses to furnish House of Representatives with documents
        about negotiation of Jay Treaty, establishing precedent for executive
        privilege; announces he will not seek a third term and publishes
        "Farewell Address." Oliver Ellsworth becomes Chief Justice.
        Tennessee admitted. John Adams elected President with 71 electoral
        votes to 68 for Thomas Jefferson, who is elected Vice President

1798   Congress passes Alien and Sedition Acts. Adams administration
        hampered by interference from Alexander Hamilton. Undeclared naval
        war with France; creation of Navy Department. Kentucky and Virginia
        Resolutions, passed by state legislatures, assert the Alien and Sedition
        Acts are unconstitutional and claim that states have the power to
        declare them void.

1800   Republican presidential and vice presidential candidates, Thomas
        Jefferson and Aaron Burr, receive 73 votes each in Electoral College
        (incumbent President John Adams receives 65), throwing election into
        House of Representatives. After 36 ballots over six days, Jefferson is
        elected President.

1801   Outgoing Secretary of State John Marshall becomes Chief Justice.
        Judiciary Act passed by lame-duck Congress. President Jefferson sends
        naval squadron to Mediterranean to protect American shipping from
        Barbary pirates in Tripoli.

1802   Congress repeals Judiciary Act of 1801.

1803   Louisiana Territory purchased from France for $15 million; treaty
        approved by Senate. Supreme Court decision in *Marbury* v. *Madison*
        declares the Judiciary Act of 1789 unconstitutional; decision establishes
        principle of judicial review of acts of Congress. Ohio admitted.

1804   Twelfth Amendment allows separate balloting for President and Vice
        President. Jefferson sends Meriwether Lewis and William Clark to
        explore and map Louisiana Territory. Vice President Aaron Burr kills
        Alexander Hamilton in a duel. Jefferson reelected President; George
        Clinton elected Vice President.

1807   Embargo Act prohibits exports to foreign nations.

1808   James Madison elected President. Importation of slaves prohibited.

1809   Non-Intercourse Act reopens trade with all nations except France and
        England.

1810   Supreme Court decision in *Fletcher* v. *Peck* establishes Court's power to declare state laws unconstitutional.

1811   Macon's Bill No. 2 allows trade with France and forbids trade with England.

1812   Madison reelected President. Louisiana admitted. War declared on Great Britain.

1814   British military expedition burns Washington, D.C. Hartford Convention of New England federalists declares states' right to oppose federal actions. Treaty of Ghent approved by Senate.

1816   Congress charters Second Bank of the United States; passes Tariff of 1816 and Bonus Bill for internal improvements (vetoed). Indiana admitted. Supreme Court decision in *Martin* v. *Hunters Lessee* sets appellate jurisdiction over state courts. James Monroe elected President.

1817   Mississippi admitted. Thomas Gallaudet founds first school for the deaf at Hartford, Ct.

1818   Illinois admitted.

1819   Supreme Court decision in *McCulloch* v. *Maryland* accepts broad implied powers of Congress, including power to create a bank, and asserts that states cannot tax federal agencies; in *Dartmouth College* v. *Woodward*, Court holds that states cannot interfere with contracts. Alabama admitted.

1820   Monroe reelected President. Maine admitted. Missouri Compromise bars slavery north of 36° 30' in Louisiana Purchase.

1821   Missouri admitted.

1823   James Monroe sets forth Monroe Doctrine to Congress, barring intervention by European powers in Western Hemisphere.

1824   Supreme Court decision in *Gibbons* v. *Ogden* asserts federal power to control interstate commerce. John Quincy Adams elected President in House of Representatives.

1825   Erie Canal completed; first American steam locomotive built in Hoboken, N.J.

1828   Tariff of Abominations. Andrew Jackson elected President.

1829   David Walker publishes *Appeal to the Colored Citizens of The United States* in Wilmington, N.C.

1830   Indian Removal Act

1831   Nat Turner's Rebellion in Virginia. William Lloyd Garrison begins to publish

Andrew Jackson (1767–1845), 7th President of the U.S., had the most popular and electoral votes for President in 1824, but was short of a majority. The House of Representatives decided the election in favor of John Quincy Adams.

The Liberator. Cyrus McCormick invents mechanical reaper. First regularly scheduled railroad service.

1832   Congress recharters Second Bank of the United States (vetoed). South Carolina nullifies Tariff of Abominations. Jackson reelected President.

1833   Congress passes Compromise Tariff. American Anti-Slavery Society founded.

1836   Roger B. Taney becomes Chief Justice. American settlers in Mexico revolt and declare Texas an independent nation. Martin Van Buren elected President.

1837   Michigan admitted. John Deere develops steel plow.

1838   Van Buren sends troops to force Cherokee removals to Oklahoma Territory, known as Trail of Tears. Frederick Douglass escapes from slavery in Maryland to Massachusetts.

1839   Vulcanized rubber developed by Charles Goodyear.

1840   William Henry Harrison ("Tippecanoe") elected President.

1841   Harrison dies; John Tyler becomes President.

1844   James K. Polk elected President. Telegraph developed by Samuel F.B. Morse.

1845   Florida and Texas admitted.

1846   Oregon Territory purchased from Great Britain. War declared on Mexico. Iowa admitted.

1848   Treaty ending Mexican War acquires territory from Texas to Pacific Ocean. Wisconsin admitted. Women's Rights Convention at Seneca Falls, N.Y., organized by Lucretia Mott and Elizabeth Cady Stanton. Zachary Taylor elected President.

1849   California Gold Rush

1850   Taylor dies; Millard Fillmore becomes President. Compromise of 1850, including Fugitive Slave Law, passed by Congress. First land grants for development of railroads. California admitted.

James K. Polk (1795–1849), 11th President of the U.S., used the Monroe Doctrine to justify annexing Texas and California.

1851   Indian Appropriations Act

1852   Harriet Beecher Stowe publishes *Uncle Tom's Cabin.* Franklin Pierce elected President.

1853   Gadsden Treaty purchases parts of Arizona and New Mexico from Mexico.

1854   Kansas-Nebraska Act.

1856   Mass production of steel developed by Henry Bessemer and William Kelly. John Brown and followers kill five proslavery settlers at

Pottawatomie Creek, Kansas. S.C. Representative Preston Brooks assaults Sen. Charles Sumner of Massachusetts with cane in Senate chamber. James Buchanan elected President.

1857   Supreme Court decision in *Dred Scott* v. *Sandford* denies slaves right to sue, declares Missouri Compromise unconstitutional, and opens territories to slavery.

1858   Minnesota admitted.

1859   Oregon admitted; John Brown leads attack on federal arsenal at Harper's Ferry, Va., hoping to begin popular insurrection.

1860   Abraham Lincoln elected President, winning 180 of 303 electoral votes in four-way race. South Carolina secedes.

1861   Virginia, North Carolina, Georgia, Florida, Alabama, Mississippi, Louisiana, Texas, Arkansas, and Tennessee secede. Lincoln attempts to resupply federal Fort Sumter in Charleston, S.C., harbor. Confederate forces attack fort April 12, and it surrenders April 15. Lincoln calls out 75,000 militia, orders blockade of Southern ports, and suspends habeas corpus in some areas. Kansas admitted.

1862   Lincoln abolishes slavery in District of Columbia. Congress passes Homestead Act, Morrill Land Grant Act, and Confiscation Act, granting freedom to slaves escaped from persons in rebellion. Lincoln issues Emancipation Proclamation September 22, to take effect January 1, 1863.

1863   Confederate invasion of North halted at Gettysburg July 3; Grant takes Vicksburg, Miss., July 4, securing federal control of Southwest. West Virginia, created from Virginia counties loyal to Union, admitted.

1864   Salmon P. Chase becomes Chief Justice. Nevada admitted. Lincoln reelected, with 212 of 233 electoral votes; Sherman marches from Chattanooga, Tenn., through Atlanta, Georgia, to the sea.

1865   Confederate army surrenders to Grant. Lincoln assassinated April 14 by actor John Wilkes Booth; Andrew Johnson, a Tennessee Democrat, becomes President. Thirteenth Amendment abolishes slavery. John D. Rockefeller buys oil-refining company.

1866   National Labor Union founded. Ku Klux Klan founded. Congress passes Civil Rights Act of 1866 and Freedman's Bureau Act.

1867   Congress passes Military Reconstruction Act and Tenure of Office Act. Senate ratifies treaty with Russia acquiring Alaska. Nebraska admitted. National Grange of the Patrons of Husbandry founded. Andrew Carnegie adopts Bessemer steel-making process.

1868   Johnson impeached but avoids removal by single vote. Fourteenth Amendment assures citizenship, equal rights, and due process to freed slaves, repeals "three-fifths clause," and repudiates debts of Confederate states. Ulysses Grant elected President.

1869   Knights of Labor founded. First transcontinental railroad completed. Wyoming Territory grants voting rights to women. First professional baseball team organized in Cincinnati. Black Friday financial panic on Wall Street, September 24.

1870   Fifteenth Amendment guarantees voting rights. Congress passes Force Act (federal supervision of elections). Department of Justice established. Standard Oil Co. founded by John D. Rockefeller.

1871	Congress passes Ku Klux Klan Act. Tweed Ring in New York City exposed.
1872	Amnesty Act restores suffrage to former Confederates. Yellowstone Park established. Grant reelected.
1874	Morrison R. Waite becomes Chief Justice. Women's Christian Temperance Union founded. Invention of barbed wire.
1875	Congress passes Specie Resumption Act, returning dollar to gold standard. Whiskey Ring in St. Louis exposed.
1876	Colorado admitted. Alexander Graham Bell patents telephone. Gen. George A. Custer's forces wiped out by Sioux and Cheyenne at Little Big Horn, Montana. Disputed returns in close presidential race between Rutherford B. Hayes and Samuel Tilden are decided by Congress in favor of Hayes, leading to his election by single electoral vote.

Rutherford B. Hayes (1822–93), 19th President of the U.S., a Republican, narrowly won the disputed election of 1876 and then ended Reconstruction in the South.

1877	Hayes withdraws last federal troops from South, ending Reconstruction. National railroad strike; Nez Perce Indian uprising.
1878	Thomas Edison forms Edison Electric Light Co.
1880	James Garfield elected President.
1881	Garfield assassinated; Chester Arthur becomes President. American Federation of Labor founded. Normal and Industrial Institute at Tuskegee, Alabama, founded by Booker T. Washington. Helen Hunt Jackson publishes *A Century of Dishonor*.
1882	Congress passes Chinese Exclusion Act.
1883	Congress passes Pendleton Act establishing Civil Service. Supreme Court decision invalidates Civil Rights Act of 1875 and allows segregation in public facilities.
1884	First skyscraper built in Chicago. Linotype machine patented. Grover Cleveland elected President.
1886	Haymarket Riot in Chicago. American Federation of Labor formed.
1887	Congress passes Interstate Commerce Act and Dawes Act.
1888	Melville Fuller becomes Chief Justice. Benjamin Harrison elected President.
1889	South Dakota, North Dakota, Montana, and Washington admitted. Andrew Carnegie publishes *The Gospel of Wealth*.
1890	Congress passes Sherman Antitrust Act. Army troops massacre 300 Sioux at Wounded Knee, S.D. Populist party founded. Wyoming and Idaho admitted.

1892   Homestead Strike against Carnegie Steel Co. Grover Cleveland elected President.

1894   Pullman Strike in Chicago. Congress repeals Force Acts of 1870–1875.

1895   J.P. Morgan Co. founded.

1896   Supreme Court decision in *Plessy v. Ferguson* sets "separate but equal" standard for segregation. Utah admitted. William McKinley elected President.

1898   Congress declares war on Spain, April 25. Senate approves treaty annexing Hawaii.

1899   Thorstein Veblen publishes *The Theory of the Leisure Class.* McKinley sends troops to Philippines to put down uprising. Open-Door Policy in China.

Grover Cleveland (1837–1908), 22nd & 24th President of the U.S., sent troops to Chicago to "protect the mails" during the 1894 Pullman strike.

1900   McKinley sends troops to China to help suppress Boxer Rebellion. Congress passes Gold Standard Act. McKinley reelected.

1901   Platt Amendment to Cuban constitution allows U.S. intervention. McKinley assassinated; Theodore Roosevelt becomes President. U.S. Steel Co. organized.

1902   Newlands Reclamation Act for Western irrigation.

1903   Elkins Anti-Rebate Act passed by Congress. Department of Labor and Commerce established. W.E.B. Du Bois publishes *The Souls of Black Folk.* First baseball World Series. Panama Revolt; Hay-Bunau-Varilla Treaty.

1904   Roosevelt reelected.

1905   Niagara Movement demands suffrage and civil rights for blacks. Industrial Workers of the World (IWW) founded.

1906   Upton Sinclair publishes *The Jungle.* Congress passes Pure Food and Drug Act, Meat Inspection Act, and Hepburn Act controlling railroads.

1907   Inland Waterways Act. Oklahoma admitted.

1908   William H. Taft elected President.

1909   International Ladies Garment Workers Union founded. National Association for the Advancement of Colored People (NAACP) founded. Congress passes Payne-Aldrich Tariff Act.

1910   Congress passes Mann-Elkins Act, extending control over telephone and telegraph systems. Edward White becomes Chief Justice. Ford Motor Co. begins production of Model T. National Urban League founded.

1911   Triangle Shirtwaist Factory fire in New York City kills 146 workers. U.S. troops sent to Nicaragua.

1912   New Mexico and Arizona admitted. Lawrence Textile strike by IWW. Woodrow Wilson elected President, defeating Republican William H. Taft and Bull Moose Theodore Roosevelt.

1913   Jewish Anti-Defamation League organized. Underwood Tariff Act and Federal Reserve Act passed by Congress. Sixteenth Amendment allows federal income tax; Seventeenth Amendment provides for direct election of senators.

1914   Congress passes Clayton Antitrust Act and Federal Trade Commission Act.

1915   Wilson sends U.S. marines to Haiti.

1916   Marcus Garvey founds Universal Negro Improvement Association. Wilson reelected. Congress passes Keating-Owen Act limiting child labor (ruled unconstitutional in 1918).

1917   Congress passes Selective Service Act, Espionage Act, and Jones Act (citizenship for Puerto Ricans). Wilson sends marines to Dominican Republic. War declared on Germany.

1918   Overman Act (presidential war powers) and Sedition Act passed by Congress. Wilson announces Fourteen Points.

1919   Eighteenth Amendment prohibits manufacture, sale, and transport of alcoholic beverages (Prohibition). Supreme Court decision in *Schenck* v. *United States* establishes "clear and present danger" standard for limiting free speech. Senate rejects Treaty of Versailles. Volstead Act (Prohibition enforcement) passed.

1920   Nineteenth Amendment extends voting rights to women. Republican Warren G. Harding elected President.

1921   Conviction of Sacco and Vanzetti in Massachusetts; Emergency Quota Immigration Act; William Howard Taft becomes Chief Justice.

1922   Dyer Anti-Lynching Bill defeated by Senate filibuster.

1923   President Harding dies; Calvin Coolidge becomes President.

1924   Congress passes Snyder Indian Citizenship Act and Immigration Act. Coolidge elected President.

1925   Trial of John Scopes in Tennessee. Supreme Court decision in *Gitlow* v. *New York* applies guarantees of Bill of Rights to the states.

1927   Congress passes Immigration Act of 1927. *The Jazz Singer* first talking movie. Charles Lindbergh first to fly across Atlantic.

1928   Herbert Hoover elected President.

1929   National Origins Act passed by Congress. Stock market crash on October 29 sets off Great Depression.

1930   Congress passes Hawley-Smoot Tariff Act. Charles Hughes becomes Chief Justice.

1932   Congress passes Norris-LaGuardia Act (labor). Drought turns much of Midwest into Dust Bowl. Hoover orders troops to disperse "Bonus Army" of WWI veterans in Washington. Franklin D. Roosevelt elected President defeating incumbent Hoover.

1933   Frances Perkins named Secretary of Labor, first woman to serve in Cabinet. Congress passes Emergency Banking Relief Act, Federal Emergency Relief Act, National Industrial Recovery Act, Glass-Steagall Banking Act, Tennessee Valley Authority, Civilian Conservation Corps, and First Agricultural Adjustment Act. Twentieth Amendment reduces "lame-duck" period by moving inauguration of President and beginning of Congressional term to January. Twenty-first Amendment repeals Prohibition.

1934   Congress establishes Federal Housing Authority, Home Owners Loan
        Corporation, and Securities and Exchange Commission, and passes
        Indian Reorganization Act.
1935   Supreme Court decision in *Schecter* v. *United States* declares National
        Recovery Act of 1933 unconstitutional. Congress passes National
        Labor Relations Act (Wagner Act), Neutrality Act, Social Security
        Act, and Works Progress Administration.
1936   Neutrality Act and Soil Conservation and Domestic Allotment Act passed
        by Congress. Roosevelt reelected President.
1937   Congress establishes Farm Security Administration.
1938   Congress passes Second Agricultural Adjustment Act, Fair Labor
        Standards Act, and Foreign Agents Registration Act.
1939   Congress passes Neutrality Act. John Steinbeck publishes *The Grapes of
        Wrath*.
1940   Smith Alien Registration Act passed. Harlan Stone becomes Chief Justice.
        Roosevelt reelected to third term.
1941   Congress on Racial Equality founded. Congress passes Lend-Lease Act
        and declares war on Japan and Germany following attack on Pearl
        Harbor, Hawaii, December 7.
1942   Naval battle at Midway, June 3–6, halts Japanese advance in Pacific.
        Military relocates 125,000 Japanese-Americans from West Coast to
        interior for security reasons.
1944   Supreme Court decision in *Korematsu* v. *United States* upholds
        internment of American citizens of Japanese descent. Allied forces
        invade Europe on D-Day, June 6. Roosevelt reelected to fourth term.
1945   Roosevelt meets with Stalin and Churchill in Yalta. Harry Truman
        becomes President when Roosevelt dies April 12. Germany surrenders
        on V-E Day, May 8. United Nations chartered. Truman at Potsdam
        Conference with Stalin and new British Prime Minister Clement Atlee.
        First atomic bomb exploded on Hiroshima, Japan. Japan surrenders on
        V-J Day, August 14.
1946   Congress passes Regulation of Lobbying Act and G.I. Bill of Rights.
        Frederick Vinson becomes Chief Justice.
1947   Truman announces Truman Doctrine and proposes Marshall Plan.
        Congress passes Taft-Hartley Act and National Security Act. Brooklyn
        Dodgers integrate Major League baseball by signing Jackie Robinson.
1948   Berlin airlift. Former State Department official Alger Hiss convicted
        of perjury before House Committee to Investigate Un-American
        Activities. Congress passes Displaced Persons Act. W.E.B. Du Bois
        dismissed from NAACP staff for criticising American foreign policy.
        Truman reelected, defeating Republican Thomas Dewey.
1949   Congress passes National Housing Act. North Atlantic Treaty
        Organization (NATO) formed.
1950   North Korean armies invade South Korea; United Nations and American
        troops committed. Congress passes McCarran Internal Security Act.
1951   Truman relieves Gen. MacArthur of command in Korea for attempting to
        broaden the war and invade China. Twenty-second Amendment sets
        two-term limit for President. Julius and Ethel Rosenberg convicted of

espionage for passing atomic secrets to Soviet Union (executed 1953). W.E.B. Du Bois arrested, tried, and acquitted of being a foreign agent.

1952   Congress passes McCarran-Walter Act, allowing deportation of subversives. Dwight D. Eisenhower elected President, defeating Adlai Stevenson.

1953   Secretary of State John Foster Dulles practices brinkmanship and declares policy of massive retaliation against Soviets. Earl Warren becomes Chief Justice. Submerged Lands Act gives oil drilling rights to states. Department of Health, Education and Welfare established.

1954   J. Robert Oppenheimer deprived of security clearance by Atomic Energy Commission. Sen. Joseph McCarthy censured by Senate. Supreme Court decision in *Brown* v. *Board of Education of Topeka* holds "separate but equal" standard to be unconstitutional, ends legal racial segregation of education.

1955   Bus boycott organized in Montgomery, Alabama.

1956   Eisenhower reelected, defeating Adlai Stevenson for second time.

1957   Eisenhower sends federal marshals and troops to enforce school integration in Little Rock, Ark. Congress passes Civil Rights Act of 1957. Southern Christian Leadership Conference organized by Dr. Martin Luther King, Jr.

1958   Eisenhower sends U.S. marines to Lebanon.

1959   Alaska and Hawaii admitted.

1960   Congress passes Civil Rights Act of 1960. Student Nonviolent Coordinating Committee (SNCC) founded. U-2 spy plane shot down over Soviet Union, leading to cancellation of Paris summit meetings. Democrat John F. Kennedy elected President, defeating Vice-President Richard M. Nixon.

1961   Freedom riders protest racial segregation in Southern bus systems. Kennedy permits invasion of Cuba by exile forces at Bay of Pigs. Twenty-third Amendment allows District of Columbia to vote in presidential elections.

1962   Supreme Court decision in *Engel* v. *Vitale* bans prayer in public schools; decision in *Baker* v. *Carr* establishes "one person, one vote" standard for apportionment. Kennedy orders blockade of Cuba to force removal of Soviet nuclear missiles.

1963   Supreme Court decision in *Gideon* v. *Wainwright* declares accused persons must be furnished an attorney. United Farm Workers organized by César Chavez. Poor Peoples' March on Washington. NAACP leader Medgar Evers assassinated in Mississippi. President Kennedy assassinated in Dallas by Lee Harvey Oswald; Lyndon B. Johnson becomes President.

1964   Congress passes Civil Rights Act of 1964, Gulf of Tonkin Resolution, Voting Rights Act, Federal Clean Water Act, Immigration Act of 1965, and Medicare Act. Twenty-fourth Amendment prohibits poll tax. Johnson reelected, defeating Republican Barry Goldwater.

1965   Malcolm X assassinated. Summer riots in Watts district of Los Angeles. Escalation of Vietnam War.

1966   Congress passes Freedom of Information Act. Supreme Court decision in *Miranda* v. *Arizona* requires persons arrested to be informed of their rights. National Organization of Women founded by Betty Friedan. Black Panthers founded in Oakland, Ca.

1967   Twenty-fifth Amendment allows for appointment of new Vice President to fill vacant office.

1968   Tet Offensive in Vietnam. Civil Rights Act of 1968 passed by Congress. Martin Luther King, Jr., assassinated in Memphis. American Indian Movement founded. Republican Richard M. Nixon elected President, defeating Vice President Hubert H. Humphrey.

1969   Warren Burger becomes Chief Justice. American astronauts Neil Armstrong and E. E. Aldrin walk on the moon. 250,000 march on Washington demanding end to Vietnam War.

1970   National Guard troops fire on students protesting invasion of Cambodia at Kent State University in Ohio, killing four. Congress passes Clean Air Act; Senate repeals Gulf of Tonkin Resolution. Earth Day celebrations held.

1971   Top-secret *Pentagon Papers* on Vietnam policy published in *The New York Times*, and right to publish them is upheld by Supreme Court. Amtrak, national passenger rail system, established with government subsidies. Twenty-sixth Amendment extends voting rights to citizens who have reached age 18.

1972   Federal Water Pollution Control Act passed by Congress. Burglary attempt at Democratic National Headquarters in Watergate Tower foiled; burglars appear to have links to Nixon reelection campaign. Nixon visits China. Nixon reelected, defeating Democrat George McGovern by 521 to 17 electoral votes.

1973   White House staff members H. R. Haldeman and John Ehrlichman resign, and John Dean is fired over involvement in Watergate coverup. Vice President Spiro Agnew resigns and pleads *nolo contendere* to charges of extortion and tax evasion, October 11. Nixon nominates Gerald Ford to be Vice President. Supreme Court decision in *Roe* v. *Wade* recognizes woman's right to an abortion. War Powers Act passed by Congress over Nixon's veto. U.S. troops leave Vietnam.

1974   Privacy Act and Federal Election Campaign Finance Reform Act passed by Congress. Nixon resigns August 8; Gerald R. Ford becomes President. Nelson Rockefeller appointed Vice President. Ford issues pardon to Nixon and offers amnesty to Vietnam draft evaders.

1975   Congress passes Education Act.

1976   Democrat Jimmy Carter elected President, defeating Gerald Ford.

1977   Carter pardons Vietnam deserters and draft resisters. Panama Canal Treaties negotiated. Department of Energy created.

1979   Strategic Arms Limitation Treaty (SALT II) signed in June, but not approved by Senate. Department of Education created. In November, Iranian extremists occupy American embassy in Teheran, holding 52 diplomats and others hostage. In December, Soviet troops occupy Afghanistan to support faltering Communist government.

1980   Congress passes Alaska National Interest Lands Conservation Act. Chrysler Corporation gets $1.5 billion in loan guarantees in government bailout. Republican Ronald Reagan elected President, defeating Carter by 489 to 49 electoral votes.

1981   Hostages in Iran freed the day Carter leaves office. President Reagan shot by John Hinckley, Jr., but recovers. Congress passes Economic Recovery Tax Act.

1983   U.S. forces invade Grenada to secure pro-American government. Forces committed to Beirut, Lebanon, to assist UN peacekeeping; 241 marines killed by terrorist bombing.

1984   Income Tax Reform Act passed by Congress. Reagan reelected President, defeating Democrat Walter Mondale, 525 to 13 electoral votes.

1985   Congress passes Gramm-Rudman-Hollings Act, requiring balanced budget by 1991. Summit meeting between Reagan and Soviet leader Mikhail Gorbachev in Geneva.

1986   Reagan attends summit with Gorbachev in Reykjavik. National Security Council staff Oliver North, John Poindexter, and Robert McFarland secretly and illegally sell anti-aircraft missiles and parts to Iran to gain the release of hostages held in Lebanon, and they divert money from the sales to the Contra rebels opposing the socialist Sandinista government in Nicaragua. Congress passes Federal Clean Water Act (vetoed) and Income Tax Reform Act. Justice William Rehnquist becomes Chief Justice.

1987   Federal Clean Water Act passed by Congress over Reagan's veto. Summit with Gorbachev in Washington. Intermediate Nuclear Forces Treaty signed. Wall Street crash on October 19.

1988   Reagan visits Moscow. Vice President George Bush elected President, defeating Democrat Michael Dukakis with slogan "Read my lips: no new taxes."

1989   Congress creates Resolution Trust Corporation to handle S&L bailout. Bush sends U.S. forces to invade Panama and capture Gen. Manuel Noriega, who is wanted on federal drug charges.

1990   Congress passes Americans with Disabilities Act.

1991   UN forces, including American troops, expel Iraqi army from Kuwait in Operation Desert Storm.

1992   Twenty-seventh Amendment bars Congressional pay raises from taking effect until after a new election. Democrat Bill Clinton elected President, defeating incumbent George Bush and independent Ross Perot.

1993   Congress passes Family and Medical Leave Act, Brady Bill on gun control, and economic package; ratifies North American Free Trade Agreement (NAFTA).

1994   Crime Bill passed by Congress. Military junta forced out of Haiti and elected president restored to power in a peaceful invasion by American troops. Republicans gain control of House and Senate in midterm elections.

1995   Domestic terrorists blow up federal building in Oklahoma City. Budget negotiation impasse leads Republican Congress to shut down federal government.

1996   Congress passes Welfare Reform Bill. Clinton reelected President, defeating Republican Robert Dole and Reform party candidate Ross Perot. Republicans retain Congressional control.

1997   Congress enacts plan to balance federal budget by 2002.

1998 Clinton presidency overshadowed by year-long Monica Lewinsky scandal concerning sex, perjury, and obstruction of justice. Independent Prosecutor Starr issues detailed report recommending impeachment, and House of Representatives impeaches Clinton on two counts. U.S. embassies in Tanzania and Kenya destroyed by terrorist bombs.

1999 Senate holds trial and acquits Clinton. Bombing campaign by NATO forces, spearheaded by U.S. armed forces, force Serb troops to withdraw from Kosovo. Senate rejects ratification of Comprehensive Test Ban Treaty.

2000 Democratic Vice President Albert Gore and Republican Governor of Texas George W. Bush obtain party nominations for President. Following one of the closest elections in United States history, by a 5–4 vote, Supreme Court justices overturn Florida bench and rule there can be no further counting of disputed Florida ballots in presidential election. Vice President Al Gore concedes election to George W. Bush, governor of Texas.

2001 President Bush signs new tax-cut law, the largest in 20 years. Oklahoma City bomber Timothy McVeigh executed. Terrorist hijackers ram jetliners into New York City's World Trade Center and the Pentagon. A fourth hijacked plane crashes 80 miles outside of Pittsburgh. Toll of dead and injured in thousands. Islamic militant Osama bin Laden and the al Qaeda terrorist network are identified as the parties behind the attacks.

2002 Kenneth L. Lay, chairman of bankrupt energy trader Enron, resigns; company under federal investigation for hiding debt and misrepresenting earnings. U.S. withdraws from International Court treaty. U.S. abandons 31-year-old Anti-Ballistic Missile Treaty. Bush addresses United Nations, calling for a "regime change" in Iraq. President Bush signs legislation creating Cabinet Department of Homeland Security.

2003 Space shuttle *Columbia* explodes, killing all seven astronauts. President Bush signs ten-year, $350-billion tax-cut package, the third-largest tax cut in U.S. history. Supreme Court upholds the right of affirmative action in higher education. California Governor Gray Davis ousted in recall vote; actor Arnold Schwarzenegger elected in his place. President Bush signs $87.5 billion emergency package for postwar Iraq reconstruction; this supplements $79 billion approved in April.

2004 John Kerry secures Democratic nomination. U.S. media release graphic photos of American soldiers abusing and sexually humiliating Iraqi prisoners at Abu Ghraib prison. Senate Intelligence Committee reports that intelligence on Iraq's weapons programs was "overstated" and flawed. September 11 commission harshly criticizes government's handling of terrorist attacks. George W. Bush is reelected president, defeating John Kerry.

2005 President Bush is officially sworn in for his second term as president. President Bush announces his plan to reform Social Security. The president signs the Central American Free Trade Agreement (CAFTA), which will remove trade barriers between the United States and Costa Rica, the Dominican Republic, El Salvador, Guatemala, Honduras, and Nicaragua. Hurricane Katrina wreaks catastrophic damage on the Gulf coast; more than 1,000 die, and millions are left homeless. Chief Justice William H. Rehnquist, who served on the U.S. Supreme Court for 33 years, dies and John Roberts becomes 17th chief justice.

2006   Surveillance debate over wiretapping of domestic phone calls and emails without obtaining legally required warrants. Republican lobbyist Jack Abramoff was convicted of fraud, tax evasion, and conspiracy to bribe public officials. The Iraq Study Group, led by former Secretary of State James Baker and former Democratic Congressman Lee Hamilton, concluded that "the situation in Iraq is grave and deteriorating" and "U.S. forces seem to be caught in a mission that has no foreseeable end." November midterm elections resulted in Democrats gaining control over the House of Representatives and the Senate for the first time in 12 years.

2007   President Gerald Ford, 38th president of the United States, dies. California Democrat Nancy Pelosi becomes first woman Speaker of the House of Representatives. Lewis "Scooter" Libby, former chief of staff to Vice President Dick Cheney, is found guilty of lying to FBI agents and to a grand jury in the investigation of who leaked to the press the name of a covert CIA agent. Attorney General Alberto Gonzales admits that the Justice Department made mistakes in firing eight federal prosecutors in late 2006.

2008   The federal government begins to intervene in the U.S. financial system to avoid a financial crisis. Democrat Senator Barack Obama wins the presidential election against Senator John McCain, taking 338 electoral votes to McCain's 161. President George W. Bush announces plans to lend General Motors and Chrysler $17.4 billion.

2009   The American Recovery and Reinvestment Act of 2009, commonly referred to as the Stimulus or The Recovery Act, is passed by Congress and signed by President Obama. President Obama announces his intention to withdraw most American troops from Iraq by August 31, 2010. The Senate approves the nomination of Sonia Sotomayor to the Supreme Court. Iraq's cabinet passes an agreement that will govern the U.S. presence in Iraq through 2011. The pact calls for the withdrawal of all U.S. combat troops by December 31, 2011.

2010   Supreme Court ruled that the government cannot restrict the spending of corporations for political campaigns, maintaining that it's their First Amendment right to support candidates as they choose. President Obama signed the health-care overhaul bill, called the *Patient Protection and Affordable Care Act*, into law. The governor of Arizona signed into law the country's toughest immigration bill. President Obama's most recent nominee to the U.S. Supreme Court, Elena Kagan, is confirmed by the Senate. The Republican Party gains control of the House of Representatives.

2011   "Don't Ask, Don't Tell" is repealed. Osama bin Laden is killed in Pakistan by U.S. troops. Standard & Poor's lowers the U.S. credit rating. Occupy Wall Street Movement continues to grow. Libyan civil war and death of Muammar Gaddafi. U.S. troops start to withdraw from Iraq.

NOTABLE AMERICANS

Adams, John (1735–1826) 2nd President, from 1797–1801; was first Vice President under George Washington; as member of the Continental Congress was instrumental in 1776 in getting the Declaration of Independence adopted; in 1783 was part of diplomatic team to conclude the Treaty of Paris recognizing American independence; was the last Federalist President.

Addams, Jane (1860–1935) social worker who founded Hull House in Chicago, one of the first settlement houses to serve as a community center to help the poor and work for social reform.

Anthony, Susan B. (1820–1906) leader of the women's suffrage movement; formed the National Woman Suffrage Association to agitate to gain the right to vote for women.

Astor, John Jacob (1763–1848) German-born immigrant who came to America in 1783 and made a fortune through fur-trading, the China trade, and New York real estate; the richest American of his time, he left an estate valued at $20 million.

Armstrong, Neil (1930–2012) astronaut who, as commander of NASA's *Apollo 11*, became the first man to set foot on the moon on July 20, 1969.

Barton, Clara (1821–1912) nurse, teacher, and organizer of medical relief for the Union army during the Civil War; organizer and first president of the American Red Cross.

Bell, Alexander Graham (1847–1922) invented the telephone in 1876; improved methods for teaching the deaf.

Brown, John (1800–1859) American abolitionist and fanatic; he led a massacre of proslavery settlers in Kansas in 1856 at Pottawatomie. Funded by extreme abolitionists, he led an armed band that seized the federal arsenal at Harpers Ferry, Virginia, on October 16, 1859, hoping to set off a general revolt of slaves. He was soon captured and convicted of treason and was hanged December 2, 1859.

Bryan, William Jennings (1860–1925) Democratic political leader and orator. Three-time unsuccessful candidate for President of the United States. His famous "cross of gold" speech advocated silver coinage (loose money) to help the interests of farmers and westerners. Resigned from Woodrow Wilson's cabinet, where he was Secretary of State, in 1916. Prosecuted the Scopes trial in Tennessee in 1925.

Bush, George (1924–) 41st President, from 1989–1993; was Vice President under Ronald Reagan, a member of the House of Representatives, United Nations ambassador, and director of the C.I.A.; organized the international coalition that invaded Iraq in 1991 to force it to withdraw from Kuwait in the Persian Gulf War.

Bush, George W. (1946–) 43rd and current President of the United States; elected Governor of Texas in 1994 and, after having served in that position for nearly six years, elected U.S. President in 2000, following one of the closest and most debated elections in U.S. history.

Calhoun, John C. (1782–1850) statesman and philosopher who served as Vice-President under John Quincy Adams and Andrew Jackson; defended the interests of the South by promoting the concept of states' rights to nullify federal legislation.

Carnegie, Andrew (1835–1913) immigrant from Scotland who rose from poverty to become a major industrialist producing steel and controlling mines and railroads; became a major philanthropist who used his wealth to fund 2800 libraries and establish the Carnegie Endowment for International Peace.

Carson, Rachel (1907–1964) biologist and author of many books on natural science; *Silent Spring* alerted the nation about the dangers to the environment from the use of pesticides in agriculture.

Carter, Jimmy (James Earl) (1924–) 39th President, from 1977–1981; signed treaties giving Panama eventual control of the Panama Canal; negotiated the Camp David Accords that brought peace between Israel and Egypt, and promoted an energy policy; after leaving office, became a leading advocate of human rights and programs to help the working poor.

Clay, Henry (1777–1852) leader in the House of Representatives and then of the Senate and frequent candidate for President; strong supporter of westward expansion of the United States; known as the Great Compromiser for his influence during times of national crisis.

Clinton, Bill (William) (1946–) 42nd President, elected in 1992 on a program of commitments to economic recovery and a national health care system; encouraged Arabs and Israelis to establish Palestinian self-rule. His second administration was tainted by scandal that resulted in the second impeachment of an American President.

Cooper, James Fenimore (1789–1851) first major novelist to write about frontier life; *The Deerslayer*, *The Last of the Mohicans*, and *The Pathfinder* created a glamorized myth of the frontier and showed the conflict between wilderness life and encroaching civilization.

Crockett, Davy (1786–1836) frontiersman and U.S. Congressman from Tennessee (1827–31 and 1833–35). He joined forces fighting for Texas independence from Mexico and died at the Alamo in 1836.

Davis, Jefferson (1808–1889) West Point graduate and officer in the Black Hawk and Mexican wars. Democratic congressman and senator from Mississippi; Secretary of War under Franklin Pierce. First and only President of the Confederate States of America (1861–65). Captured, charged with treason, and imprisoned; released on bail in 1867 and never tried.

Debs, Eugene V. (1855–1926) railroad union organizer and socialist; imprisoned for his part in Pullman strike of 1894. Five-time socialist candidate for President of the United States (1900, 1904, 1908, 1912, 1920). Opposed U.S. participation in World War I and was imprisoned under the Espionage Act. Pardoned and released in 1921 by President Harding.

Dix, Dorothea (1802–1887) social reformer who brought about improvement in the treatment of inmates in insane asylums.

Douglass, Frederick (1817–1895) leading 19th-century African American abolitionist and Republican party organizer. Escaped from slavery in Maryland and became speaker for abolition in the North and England. Founded and edited newspaper *The North Star* (1847) and assisted runaway slaves on the Underground Railroad. Helped enlist black regiments in the Civil War and served as federal marshal of the District of Columbia and as consul general to Haiti.

Du Bois, W.E.B. (1868–1963) African American civil rights leader and author who supported aggressive action to gain full civil, economic, and political equality for African Americans; cofounder of the National Association for the Advancement of Colored People (NAACP).

Edison, Thomas (1847–1931) productive genius in applying scientific principles to practical use; invented the light bulb, phonograph, and motion picture projector; developed a complete system for generating and distributing electricity in communities.

Edwards, Jonathan (1703–1758) the most influential American theologian and philosopher of the 18th century. A leader in the religious revival of the 1740s, known as the Great Awakening. Congregational minister in Northampton, Mass., and later president of the College of New Jersey (now Princeton University).

Einstein, Albert (1879–1955) born in Germany; emigrated to the United States in 1933 to escape the Nazis, and subsequently became a U.S. citizen. Formulated the theory of relativity, which produced the famous theorem $E = Mc^2$, awarded the Nobel Prize in Physics for his explanation of the photoelectric effect. His 1939 letter to President Roosevelt, advising of the possibility of atomic energy, helped lead to the creation of the Manhattan Project and the U.S. government's development of the atom bomb in 1945.

Eisenhower, Dwight D. (1890–1969) 34th President, from 1953 to 1961. A West Point graduate and career army officer, his talent for coordinating large troop maneuvers led to rapid promotion in World War II, and he oversaw successful troop landings in North Africa (1942), Italy (1943), and, as Supreme Allied Commander, the D-Day landing at Normandy, France (June 6, 1944). After the war he served as army chief of staff, president of Columbia University, and chief of NATO. As President of the United States he ended the war in Korea, and continued the Cold War opposition to the Soviet Union.

Emerson, Ralph Waldo (1803–1892) leading American writer, lecturer, essayist, and philosopher of the 19th century. One of the founders of transcendentalism, a philosophical and spiritual movement based on nature and inspiration.

Ford, Henry (1863–1947) industrialist who used assembly-line techniques to build the first inexpensive, mass-produced automobiles; the Model T and Model A Fords revolutionized communities and transportation by making automobiles affordable for the middle and working class.

Franklin, Benjamin (1706–1790) statesman, printer, scientist, inventor, and writer; experimented with electricity; was a delegate to the Albany Congress, a leader of the Continental Congress, and a member of the Committee that wrote the Declaration of Independence; served as ambassador to France during the Revolutionary War; was an influential member of the convention that drafted the Constitution in 1787.

Friedan, Betty (1921–2006) social reformer and feminist; author of *The Feminine Mystique*, a book that began the women's liberation movement; founder of The National Organization for Women (NOW).

Garrison, William Lloyd (1805–1879) leading New England abolitionist who advocated separation from the South. Founder and editor of *The Liberator* (1831) and a fiery and controversial speaker.

Garvey, Marcus (1887–1940) Jamaican organizer and business entrepreneur who brought his "Back to Africa" movement and United Negro Improvement Association to the United States in 1916. He was eventually convicted of mail fraud, pardoned by President Coolidge, and deported.

Gates, William (1955–) dropped out of Harvard University to devote attention to computer programming. Cofounder and chairman of Microsoft Corporation, which developed MS-DOS, the operating system used by most computers, and which assisted the growth of business and personal computer use.

George, Henry (1839–1897) American reformer famous for his book *Progress and Poverty* and his theory of the single tax.

Gompers, Samuel (1850–1924) founder and first president of the American Federation of Labor; supported efforts of organized labor to concentrate on improvement in wages and working conditions instead of political action; became a leading spokesman for the labor movement.

Grant, Ulysses S. (1822–1885) 18th President, from 1869 to 1877. West Point graduate and Mexican War veteran; subsequently worked in a variety of businesses prior to rejoining the army at the outbreak of the Civil War. In July 1863 he succeeded in taking Vicksburg, cutting the Confederacy in two. In November 1863 Lincoln appointed him to command the U.S. army, and he proceeded to doggedly use his superior manpower to wear down the Confederacy, resulting in Lee's surrender at Apppomattox, April 9, 1865. His presidential administration was rife with corruption.

Hamilton, Alexander (1755–1804) born on the island of Nevis, he attended Columbia College in New York, joined the Continental Army during the American Revolution, and served as an aide to Washington. After the war, he became a lawyer and politician, attended the Constitutional Convention in 1787, and coauthored *The Federalist* (with James Madison and John Jay) in 1788. He served as Secretary of the Treasury under Washington, organized the first Bank of the United States, and promoted the increase of central government power. A leading Federalist, after Washington's retirement he feuded with John Adams, paving the way for victory by the Jeffersonians in 1800. A dispute with Aaron Burr led to a duel in 1804 in which Hamilton was fatally wounded.

Hearst, William Randolph (1863–1951) wealthy newspaper and magazine publisher known for his many examples of "yellow journalism." Member of Congress from New York (1903–07).

Holmes, Oliver Wendell, Jr. (1841–1935) Harvard graduate and Civil War veteran, son of Dr. Oliver Wendell Holmes, the author. He taught at Harvard law school, served on the Massachusetts Supreme Court, and was appointed to the U.S. Supreme Court in 1902 by President Roosevelt. He wrote many famous court opinions, including that in *Schenck* v. *United States* setting forth the "clear and present danger" standard.

Houston, Sam (1793–1863) Congressman and Governor of Tennessee, he moved to Texas and commanded the army that secured independence from Mexico. Served as president of the Republic of Texas and as a Senator and its Governor after it was admitted to the United States. As Governor, he opposed secession in 1861, but was removed from office.

Jackson, Andrew (1767–1845) 7th President and first President from a state other than the original thirteen colonies; symbolized and supported the westward movement of the United States and growing democratization of politics; ended the eastern domination of politics.

Jackson, Helen Hunt (1830–1885) writer whose book, *A Century of Dishonor*, chronicled the government mistreatment of Native Americans and encouraged reform in federal Indian policy.

Jay, John (1745–1829) born in New York City, he represented New York in the First and Second Continental Congress, over which he presided; served as Secretary of Foreign Affairs and Chief Justice of the United States; negotiated the Jay Treaty with England in 1795, settling key financial and diplomatic issues.

Jefferson, Thomas (1743–1826) 3rd President, from 1801–1809, author of the Declaration of Independence and ambassador to France during the Constitutional Convention; as first Secretary of State under George Washington, opposed federalist policies of Alexander Hamilton; bought Louisiana Territory from France despite belief in strict construction of the Constitution.

Johnson, Lyndon (1908–1973) 36th President who, as Vice President, succeeded John F. Kennedy following the assassination; reelected in 1964 and supported civil rights legislation and an extensive "Great Society" program to help the poor; supported growing U.S. involvement in the war in Vietnam; declined to run again in 1968 following growing public opposition to the war.

Keller, Helen Adams (1880–1968) lost her sight and hearing before she was two as a result of a serious brain illness; grew up wild until the age of seven when a special education teacher, Anne Sullivan, taught her to read and communicate with her fingers; eventually graduated with honors from Radcliffe College and served as a model for the handicapped.

Kennedy, John F. (1917–1963) 35th President, elected in 1960 with a program of social and economic reforms, some of which were enacted after his assassination in 1963; supported the failed Bay of Pigs invasion to force Castro from power in Cuba, but succeeded in using the threat of force to convince the Soviet Union to remove missiles from Cuba.

Key, Francis Scott (1779–1843) a Washington, D.C. lawyer; wrote the words of *The Star-Spangled Banner* during the War of 1812; his inspiration for the anthem came as he witnessed the British bombardment of Fort McHenry in Baltimore Harbor.

King, Martin Luther, Jr. (1929–1968) African American minister and civil rights leader who encouraged civil disobedience to oppose segregation laws in the South; most widely known and respected leader in the struggle for political and economic equality for African Americans; awarded the Nobel Peace Prize in 1964; his birthday has become a national holiday.

Lee, Robert E. (1807–1870) West Point graduate, Mexican War veteran, and career army officer; declined Lincoln's offer to command U.S. Army in 1861 and accepted appointment to command Virginia forces and later the Confederate army; outnumbered and undersupplied, he surrendered to Grant at Appomattox, April 9, 1865, ending major fighting in the Civil War.

Lewis, John L. (1880–1969) labor leader who, as head of the mine workers union, sought to unionize unskilled industrial workers who were not eligible for membership in the trade-union-oriented American Federation of Labor; organized the Congress of Industrial Organization (C.I.O.) to greatly expand the membership and influence of organized labor.

Lewis, Sinclair (1885–1951) novelist who satirized the values and styles of middle-class American life in *Main Street* and *Babbit*; also satirized the medical profession in *Arrowsmith* and religious revivalism in *Elmer Gantry*.

Lincoln, Abraham (1809–1865) 16th President, whose election in 1860 triggered the secession of southern states; preserved the Union by using military force; issued the Emancipation Proclamation to include abolition of slavery as a goal of the Civil War; his speeches expressed the agony of war and sought to heal the wounds of the republic.

MacArthur, Douglas (1880–1964) American general who commanded the war in the Pacific against Japan during World War II, governed Japan after the war as it developed a representative form of government, and led allied forces during the Korean War until removed by President Truman for publicly opposing government policy.

Madison, James (1751–1836) 4th President; was a leader in the convention in 1787 to draft a new Constitution and supported ratification by writing many of the *Federalist Papers*; served as Secretary of State for Jefferson supporting embargo policies that later contributed to the War of 1812, which took place during his administration.

Mann, Horace (1796–1859) American educator and reformer who revolutionized public school organization and teaching.

Marshall, George Catlett (1880–1959) career soldier who was the head of the joint chiefs of staff and was the chief strategiest of the West in World War II; as postwar Secretary of State was architect of the Marshall Plan for the rehabilitation of Western Europe (1947).

Marshall, John (1755–1835) Chief Justice of the Supreme Court for 34 years and supporter of many important decisions that established judicial review and expanded federal influence by a loose interpretation of the Constitution.

Marshall, Thurgood (1908–1993) first African American member of the Supreme Court following a distinguished career as an attorney for the NAACP; successfully argued before the Supreme Court against school segregation in *Brown* v. *Board of Education of Topeka*.

McCarthy, Joseph (1908–1957) Senator who gained national attention in 1950 by accusations that the U.S. State Department was infiltrated by Communists; his name became associated with unverified and unjustified charges of subversion and an anti-communist national hysteria that led to the dismissal and resignation of government employees; his excesses ended when he was censured by the Senate.

McKinley, William (1843–1901) 25th President who supported industrialists, protective tariffs, and U.S. imperialism; supported the annexation of Hawaii and the Open-Door Policy; the Spanish-American War was fought during his administration.

Monroe, James (1758–1831) 5th President whose name is associated with the doctrine that became a cornerstone of American foreign policy for the Western Hemisphere; supported the Missouri Compromise, which resolved differences of slavery in the territories, and the purchase of Florida from Spain.

Morse, Samuel F.B. (1791–1872) successful portrait artist best known for inventing the telegraph that revolutionized communication.

Nader, Ralph (1934–) consumer advocate whose book, *Unsafe at Any Speed*, accused the automobile industry of emphasizing speed and style over safety and economy; instrumental in pressuring Congress to adopt automobile safety standards; formed other consumer groups attacking irresponsible actions of business and encouraging regulation to protect consumers; ran for President of the United States three times (1996, 2000, 2004).

Nixon, Richard (1913–1994) 37th President, elected in 1968 with a commitment to end the war in Vietnam; U.S. troops were withdrawn in 1973 after the war was first expanded into Cambodia and air attacks on North Vietnam increased; opened relations with communist China and improved relations with the Soviet Union; resigned in 1974 under the threat of impeachment due to the Watergate scandal.

O'Connor, Sandra Day (1930–) first woman to serve on the U.S. Supreme Court; appointed in 1981 by Ronald Reagan.

Owens, Jesse (1913–1980) African American athlete (sprinter, long jumper) who won four gold medals at the 1936 Munich Olympics, spoiling Hitler's claims of Aryan superiority.

Paine, Thomas (1737–1809) political theorist and writer of the widely read pamphlet *Common Sense*, which argued that the colonies should be independent of England; other writings encouraged the patriot cause during the Revolutionary War; he later went to France to support the French Revolution.

Parks, Rosa (1913–2005) African American whose refusal to give up her seat on a Montgomery, Alabama, bus to a white man in 1955 led to a bus boycott that was a seminal event in the civil rights movement.

Patton, George (1885–1945) American cavalry, tank, and army commander who led Allied forces in North Africa, Sicily, and France in World War II.

Pelosi, Nancy (1940–) first woman Speaker of the House; ranks second in the line of presidential succession; highest ranking woman in the history of the U.S. government; no woman has ever been closer in line to the U.S. presidency.

Reagan, Ronald (1911–2004) 40th President, elected in 1980 after a career in motion pictures and serving as Governor of California; advocated a balanced budget, but brought about a large increase in the budget deficit and national debt by supporting supply-side economics and making tax reductions while greatly increasing military spending; responded to changes in the Soviet Union by negotiating mutual reductions in nuclear missiles.

Robinson, Jackie (1925–1972) African American baseball player; in 1947 he played for the Brooklyn Dodgers, breaking the color barrier and integrating major league baseball.

Rockefeller, John D. (1839–1937) industrialist and philanthropist who became wealthy by organizing the Standard Oil Company, crushing competitors, and extracting rebates from railroads; funded foundations to sponsor research in medicine, education, and natural and social sciences.

Roosevelt, Eleanor (1884–1962) humanitarian and writer; as the wife of Franklin Roosevelt became active in promoting women's causes, civil rights for minorities, and help for the poor and unemployed; lectured throughout the nation and reported conditions and public opinion to her husband; following the President's death, she served as a delegate to the United Nations and supporter of the Declaration of Human Rights.

Roosevelt, Franklin D. (1882–1945) 32nd President, elected to four terms beginning in 1932 with a commitment called the New Deal to use the resources of government to fight the Great Depression; led the nation during World War II.

Roosevelt, Theodore (1858–1919) 26th President, who succeeded as Vice President following the assassination of McKinley in 1901; opposed business monopolies, supported consumer legislation, promoted conservation of natural resources, and expanded U.S. influence in the Caribbean; ran for President unsuccessfully in 1912 after a term out of office as the candidate of the Bull Moose party.

Sinclair, Upton (1878–1968) novelist best known for *The Jungle*, an exposé of the filthy and degrading conditions in the meatpacking industry that led to national legislation regulating food production; one of a number of muckrakers who attacked business practices.

Sitting Bull (1834–1890) Sioux leader at Little Big Horn, where Custer's forces were wiped out in 1876. Later retreated to Canada but returned and surrendered in 1881. Active in agitation for Indian rights, he was arrested and shot by guards in 1890.

Stanton, Elizabeth Cady (1815–1902) American crusader for abolition, temperance, education, and women's rights. With Lucretia Mott, she organized first women's rights convention in 1848. She worked closely with Susan B. Anthony and served as the first president of the National Woman Suffrage Association (1890–92).

Stowe, Harriet Beecher (1811–1896) novelist whose book, *Uncle Tom's Cabin*, was an immensely popular attack upon slavery that gained many supporters for the cause of abolition in the North and in Europe.

Tarbell, Ida (1857–1944) a muckraker whose book, *History of the Standard Oil Company*, chronicled the abuses of the company and led to a court case that caused the breakup of the monopoly.

Thoreau, Henry David (1817–1862) author and naturalist who influenced American thought by his individualism and opposition to conformity and materialism; *Walden*, his most famous book, described his solitary coexistence with nature; his support of civil disobedience to protest injustices of authority had influence within and beyond the United States.

Truman, Harry (1884–1972) 33rd President, who as Vice President succeeded upon the death of Franklin Roosevelt in 1945; led the United States during the postwar period and developed the policies opposing the Soviet Union during the Cold War; opposed North Korean aggression in the Korean War.

Tubman, Harriet (c.1820–1913) abolitionist and escaped slave who conducted hundreds of slaves to freedom though the "underground railroad" during the 1850s.

Twain, Mark (1835–1910) (Samuel Clemens) author, humorist, commentator on American life and values; portrayed 19th-century American life in *Adventures of Huckleberry Finn* and *The Adventures of Tom Sawyer*; other books of social criticism, fairy tales, and travel showed the breadth of his literary talents.

Warren, Earl (1891–1974) Chief Justice of the Supreme Court for 16 years beginning in 1953; led an activist court whose decisions showed regard for civil rights and civil liberties; wrote the unanimous decision declaring school segregation unconstitutional and supported decisions requiring legislative reapportionment and protecting defendants from police abuses.

Washington, Booker T. (1856–1915) born a slave, he gained an education and established the Tuskegee Institute in Alabama to provide technical education for African Americans; believed that African Americans should work to achieve economic improvement before striving for social and political equality.

Washington, George (1732–1799) First President, elected by unanimous vote of the electoral college after serving as commander of the Continental Army during the Revolutionary War and president of the Constitutional Convention; steered the new nation with a steady hand, asserted federal authority, mediated among his able cabinet members, established wise precedents, and avoided involvement in conflicts stemming from the French Revolution.

Webster, Daniel (1782–1852) Congressman from New Hampshire (1813–17) and Massachusetts (1823–27), Senator from Massachusetts (1827–41), and Secretary of State (1841–43 and 1850–52). One of the greatest orators of his day and a strong advocate of national union. He lost many former admirers when he supported the Compromise of 1850 and its Fugitive Slave Law, which he defended as necessary to preserve the Union.

Whitney, Eli (1765–1825) graduate of Yale College (1792); invented the cotton gin (engine) for cleaning picked cotton; this made slaves far more valuable and virtually ended the drive for emancipation in the South.

Wilson, Woodrow (1856–1924) 28th President who promoted progressive legislation curbing monopolies, supporting labor, and establishing the Federal Reserve System; led the nation during World War I and the peace negotiations after the war, but was disappointed by the Senate's failure to ratify the Treaty of Versailles and bring the United States into the League of Nations.

Wright, Orville (1871–1948) together with his brother Wilbur experimented with gliders and subsequently built the first powered airplane, *Flyer I*, which each successfully flew near Kitty Hawk, North Carolina, on December 17, 1903.

Wright, Wilbur (1867–1912) with his brother Orville experimented with gliders and subsequently built the first powered airplane, *Flyer I*, which each successfully flew near Kitty Hawk, North Carolina, on December 17, 1903.

QUOTATIONS

"No free man shall be detained or imprisoned, dispossessed, out-lawed, exiled, or destroyed in any way, except by the lawful judgment of his peers or by the law of the land."

Magna Carta, 1215

"God helps them that help themselves."

Benjamin Franklin, 1736

"Taxation without representation is tyranny."

James Otis, 1763

"By uniting we stand, by dividing we fall."

John Dickinson, *Liberty Song*, 1768

"There never was a good war or a bad peace."

Benjamin Franklin, 1773

"The God who gave us life, gave us liberty at the same time."

Thomas Jefferson, 1774

"A government of laws, and not of men."

John Adams, 1774

"I am not a Virginian, but an American."

Patrick Henry, Continental Congress, 1774

"Don't fire until you see the whites of their eyes."

Israel Putnam, 1775

"Is life so dear or peace so sweet as to be purchased at the price of chains and slavery? I know not what course others may take, but as for me, give me liberty or give me death."

Patrick Henry, Virginia House of Delegates, 1775

"Government, even in its best state, is but a necessary evil; in its worst state, an intolerable one."

Thomas Paine, *Common Sense*, 1776

"Yes, we must all hang together, or most assuredly we shall all hang separately."

Benjamin Franklin at the signing of the
Declaration of Independence, 1776

"I only regret that I have but one life to lose for my country."
Nathan Hale on the gallows, New York City, 1776

"These are the times that try men's souls."
Thomas Paine, *The Crisis*, 1776

"I have not yet begun to fight."
John Paul Jones aboard the *Bonhomme Richard*, 1779

"A national debt, if it is not excessive, will be to us a national blessing."
Alexander Hamilton, 1781

"There shall be neither slavery nor involuntary servitude in the said territory."
Northwest Ordinance, 1787

"The tree of liberty must be refreshed from time to time with the blood of patriots and tyrants. It is its natural manure."
Thomas Jefferson, 1787

"Every individual of the community at large has an equal right to the protection of government."
Alexander Hamilton,
Constitutional Convention, 1787

"To be prepared for war is one of the most effectual means of preserving peace."
George Washington, 1790

"The republican is the only form of government which is not eternally at open or secret war with the rights of mankind."
Thomas Jefferson, 1790

"'Tis our true policy to steer clear of permanent alliances with any portion of the foreign world."
George Washington, *Farewell Address*, 1796

"Millions for defense but not a cent for tribute."
Robert G. Harper, 1798

"A citizen, first in war, first in peace, and first in the hearts of his countrymen."
Henry ("Light-Horse Harry") Lee
on Washington, Congress, 1799

"We are all Republicans; we are all Federalists."

Thomas Jefferson, Inaugural Address, 1801

"It is emphatically the province and duty of the judicial department to say what the law is."

John Marshall, Opinion in *Marbury* v. *Madison*, 1803

"These lands are ours. No one has a right to remove us, because we were the first owners."

Tecumseh, 1810

"Protection and patriotism are reciprocal."

John C. Calhoun, House of Representatives, 1811

"We have met the enemy, and they are ours."

Oliver Hazard Perry, Battle of Lake Erie, 1813

"Oh, say, does that star-spangled banner yet wave
O'er the land of the free and the home of the brave?"

Then conquer we must, when our cause it is just,
And this be our motto, "In God is our trust."

Francis Scott Key, *The Star-Spangled Banner*,
September 14, 1814

"The power to tax involves the power to destroy."

John Marshall, Opinion in *McCulloch* v. *Maryland*, 1819

"The American continents are henceforth not to be considered as subjects for future colonization by any European powers."

James Monroe, Message to Congress, 1823

"Our sufferings will come to an end, in spite of all the Americans this side of eternity."

David Walker, *Appeal to the Colored
Citizens of the World*, 1829

"Our Federal Union! it must be preserved!"

Andrew Jackson, 1830

"Liberty and Union, now and forever, one and inseparable."

Daniel Webster, 1830

"Our country is the world—our countrymen are all mankind."

William Lloyd Garrison, *The Liberator*, 1831

"I have done nothing for which an Indian ought to be ashamed. I have fought for my countrymen against white men who came to take away our lands."

Black Hawk, 1832

"The politicians of New York see nothing wrong in the rule that to the victor belong the spoils of the enemy."

William Marcy, Senate, 1832

"We first crush people to the earth, and then claim the right of trampling on them forever, because they are prostrate."

Lydia Maria Child, *An Appeal on Behalf of That Class of Americans Called Africans*, 1833

Black Hawk (1767–1838), chief of the Sauk nation, led his people against the Americans in the Black Hawk War of 1832.

"The women of the South can overthrow this horrible system of oppression and cruelty, licentiousness and wrong. Slavery must be attacked with the whole power of truth and the sword of the spirit."

Angelina Grimké, *Appeal to the Christian Women of the South*, 1836

"Here once the embattled farmers stood,
And fired the shot heard round the world."

Ralph Waldo Emerson, *Concord Hymn*, 1837

"We have one country, one Constitution, one destiny."

Daniel Webster, 1837

"Our manifest destiny is to overspread the continent allotted by Providence for the free development of our yearly multiplying millions."

John L. O'Sullivan, *Democratic Review*, 1845

"If there is no struggle, there can be no progress."

Frederick Douglass, c. 1845

"I know no South, no North, no East, no West, to which I owe any allegiance. The Union, sir, is my country."

Henry Clay, 1848

"We hold these truths to be self-evident, that all men and women are created equal."

Elizabeth Cady Stanton, Women's Rights Convention, 1848

"Liberty is a spirit sent out from God, and like its great Author, is no respecter of persons. Slavery has prepared you for any emergency. Let it no longer be a debatable question, whether it is better to choose *Liberty* or *death*.

Henry Highland Garnet, *An Address to the Slaves of the United States of America*, 1848

"We are not a Nation, but a Union, a confederacy of equal and sovereign states."

John C. Calhoun, 1849

"It is not desirable to cultivate a respect for the law, so much as for the right."

Henry David Thoreau,
Civil Disobedience, 1849

"I would rather be right than President."

Henry Clay, 1850

"A democracy—that is a government of all the people, by all the people, for all the people."

Theodore Parker, 1850

"Eternal vigilance is the price of liberty."

Wendell Phillips, 1852

Newspaper publisher Horace Greeley (1811–1872) supported antislavery, but he later helped raise bail to get Jefferson Davis released from prison.

"Be not deceived. Revolutions do not go backward. The founder of the Democratic party declared that *all* men are created equal."

Abraham Lincoln, 1856

"For more than a century before the Declaration of Independence, the negroes had been regarded as beings of an inferior order who had no rights which a white man was bound to respect."

Roger B. Taney,
Opinion in *Dred Scott* v.
Sandford, 1857

"The principle laid down will enable the people of a slave state to introduce slavery into a free state; it protects the rights of the master and defies the sovereignty of the free state."

John McLean, Dissenting Opinion in
Dred Scott v. *Sandford*, 1857

Roger Brooke Taney (1777–1864), American jurist. Chief Justice Taney's decision in *Dred Scott* v. *Sandford* (1857) declared the Missouri Compromise of 1820 unconstitutional and opened up all U.S. territories to the expansion of slavery.

"The negro is my equal and the equal of Judge Douglas, and the equal of every living man."

Abraham Lincoln,
Debate with Stephen Douglas, 1858

"'A house divided against itself cannot stand,' I believe this government cannot endure permanently half slave and half free."

Abraham Lincoln, Illinois
Republican Convention, 1858

"You dare not make war on cotton. Cotton is king."

James H. Hammond, Senate, 1858

"I am now quite certain that the crimes of this guilty land will never be purged away but with blood."

John Brown, last statement, 1859

Abolitionist John Brown (1800–1859) resorted to violence and murder to oppose slavery in "Bloody Kansas"; he was hanged in 1859 for leading an attack on the federal armory at Harpers Ferry, Virginia.

"No terms except unconditional and immediate surrender can be accepted."

Ulysses S. Grant at Fort Donelson, 1862

"Damn the torpedoes—full speed ahead."

David Farragut, Battle of Mobile Bay, 1864

"I have been forty years a slave and forty years free, and would be here forty years more to have equal rights for all."

Sojourner Truth, 1867

"The Constitution, in all its provisions, looks to an indestructible Union composed of indestructible States."

Salmon P. Chase, Opinion in *Texas* v. *White*, 1868

"Let us have peace."

Ulysses S. Grant, accepting Republican
presidential nomination, 1868

"The true Republic: men, their rights, and nothing more; women, their rights, and nothing less."

Susan B. Anthony, *The Revolution*, 1868

"Join the union, girls, and together say *Equal Pay for Equal Work*."

Susan B. Anthony, *The Revolution*, 1869

"As long as I count the votes, what are you going to do about it?"

William Marcy ("Boss") Tweed, 1871

"The only question left to be settled now is: Are women persons?"

Susan B. Anthony, 1873

"We are an island of Indians in a lake of whites."

Sitting Bull, 1874

"My heart is sick and sad. From where the sun now stands I will fight no more forever."

Chief Joseph at the surrender of the Nez Percé, 1877

Sitting Bull (1837–1890), chief of the Hunkpapa Sioux, developed the tactics that led to Custer's annihilation at the Little Bighorn in 1876.

"He serves his party best who serves his country best."

Rutherford B. Hayes, Inaugural Address, 1877

"War is hell."

Gen. William Tecumseh Sherman, 1879

"The public be damned."

William H. Vanderbilt, 1882

"If nominated I will not run; if elected I will not serve."

Gen. William Tecumseh Sherman to the Republican National Convention, 1884

"Your every voter, as surely as your chief magistrate, exercises a public trust."

Grover Cleveland, Inaugural Address, March 4, 1885

"The growth of a large business is merely survival of the fittest."

John D. Rockefeller, c. 1890

"America! America! God shed His grace on thee And crown thy good with brotherhood from sea to shining sea.

America! America! God mend thine every flaw. Confirm thy soul in self-control, thy liberty in law."

Katherine Lee Bates, *America the Beautiful*, 1893

"All railway companies shall provide equal but separate accommodations for the white and colored races."

Louisiana statute of 1890, upheld by the Supreme Court in *Plessy* v. *Ferguson*, 1896

657

"Our Constitution is color-blind, and neither knows nor tolerates classes among citizens. In respect of civil rights, all citizens are equal before the law."

> John Marshall Harlan,
> Dissenting Opinion in
> *Plessy* v. *Ferguson*, 1896

"You shall not press down upon the brow of labor this crown of thorns. You shall not crucify mankind upon a cross of gold."
William Jennings Bryan, Democratic National Convention, 1896

Justice **John Marshall Harlan** (1833–1911) was the lone dissenting voice on the Supreme Court in the case of *Plessy* v. *Ferguson*, which legalized segregation.

"It could probably be shown by facts and figures that there is no distinctly native American criminal class except Congress."

> Mark Twain, 1897

"You furnish the pictures and I'll furnish the war."

> William Randolph Hearst, cable to
> Frederic Remington in Cuba, 1898

"The problem of the twentieth century is the problem of the color line."

> W.E.B. Du Bois, Pan-African Conference, London, 1900

"There is a homely adage which runs, 'Speak softly and carry a big stick; you will go far.' If the American nation will speak softly and yet build and keep a thoroughly efficient navy, the Monroe Doctrine will go far."

> Theodore Roosevelt, 1901

"A man who is good enough to shed his blood for his country is good enough to be given a square deal afterwards."

> Theodore Roosevelt, 1903

"Taxes are what we pay for civilized society."

> Oliver Wendell Holmes, Jr., 1904

"Wage workers have an entire right to organize."

> Theodore Roosevelt, Message to Congress, 1904

"America is God's crucible, the great melting pot where all races of Europe are melting and reforming."

> Israel Zangwill, *The Melting Pot*, 1908

"While there is a lower class, I am in it; while there is a criminal element, I am of it; while there is a soul in prison, I am not free."

Eugene Debs, 1913

"The United States must be neutral in fact as well as in name."

Woodrow Wilson, Message to the Senate, 1914

"America cannot be an ostrich with its head in the sand."

Woodrow Wilson, 1916

"The world must be made safe for democracy."

Woodrow Wilson, Address to Congress, 1917

"The most stringent protection of free speech would not protect a man in falsely shouting fire in a theater and causing a panic. The question is whether the words create a clear and present danger that they will bring about substantive evils that Congress has a right to prevent."

Oliver Wendell Holmes, Jr., Opinion in
Schenck v. *United States*, 1919

"Civilization and profits go hand in hand."

Calvin Coolidge, 1920

"The problem of birth control has arisen directly from the effort of the feminine spirit to free itself from bondage."

Margaret Sanger, 1920

"The business of America is business."

Calvin Coolidge, 1925

"They hired the money, didn't they?"

Calvin Coolidge, on the European war debts, 1925

"Panic is just like a war: you can talk your way into it, but you've got to fight your way out of it."

Will Rogers, 1929

"I pledge you, I pledge myself, to a new deal for the American people."

Franklin D. Roosevelt, Democratic National Convention, 1932

"The only thing we have to fear is fear itself."

Franklin D. Roosevelt, Inaugural Address, 1933

"In the field of world policy, I would dedicate this nation to the policy of a good neighbor."

Franklin D. Roosevelt, Inaugural Address, 1933

"No business whose existence depends on paying less than living wages to its workers has any right to continue in this country."

Franklin D. Roosevelt, 1933

"I see one-third of a nation ill-housed, ill-clad, and ill-nourished."

Franklin D. Roosevelt, Inaugural Address, 1937

"From the mountains to the prairies,
To the oceans white with foam,
God bless America, My home sweet home!"

Irving Berlin, *God Bless America*, 1938

"The 15th Amendment nullifies sophisticated as well as simple-minded modes of discrimination."

Felix Frankfurter, Opinion in *Lane* v. *Wilson*, 1939

"Yesterday, December 7, 1941—a date which will live in infamy—the United States was suddenly and deliberately attacked by naval and air forces of the Empire of Japan."

Franklin D. Roosevelt, Message to Congress, 1941

"Sixteen hours ago an American airplane dropped one bomb on Hiroshima."

Harry Truman, 1945

"From the Baltic to the Adriatic, an iron curtain has descended across the continent of Europe."

Winston Churchill, 1946

"Let us not deceive ourselves; we must elect world peace or world destruction."

Bernard Baruch to the United Nations
Atomic Energy Commission, 1946

"Our policy is directed not against any country or doctrine, but against hunger, poverty, desperation, and chaos."

George Marshall on the European Recovery Plan, 1947

"Let us not be deceived—we are today in the midst of a cold war."

Bernard Baruch, 1947

"We have grasped the mystery of the atom and rejected the Sermon on the Mount."

Omar Bradley, 1948

"I have here in my hand a list of 205 that were known to the secretary of state as being members of the Communist party and who nevertheless are still working and shaping the policy of the State Department."

Sen. Joseph McCarthy, 1950

"My definition of a free society is a society where it is safe to be unpopular."

Adlai E. Stevenson, 1952

"What's good for the country is good for General Motors, and vice versa."

Charles E. Wilson, Secretary of Defense, to the Senate Armed Services Committee, 1952

"Every gun that is made, every warship launched, every rocket fired, signifies a theft from those who hunger and are not fed, those who are cold and are not clothed."

Dwight D. Eisenhower, 1953

"Local defense must be reinforced by the deterrent of massive retaliatory power."

John Foster Dulles, 1954

"You have a row of dominoes. You knock over the first one, and what will happen to the last one is a certainty—it will go over very quickly."

Dwight D. Eisenhower, press conference, 1954

"We conclude that in the field of public education the doctrine of 'separate but equal' has no place. Separate educational facilities are inherently unequal."

Earl Warren, Opinion in *Brown* v.
Board of Education of Topeka, 1954

"In the councils of government, we must guard against unwarranted influence by the military-industrial complex."

Dwight D. Eisenhower, 1961

"And so, my fellow Americans, ask not what your country can do for you; ask what you can do for your country."

John F. Kennedy, Inaugural Address, 1961

"In a democratic society like ours, relief must come through an aroused popular conscience that sears the conscience of the people's representatives."

Supreme Court decision in *Baker* v. *Carr*, 1962

"No one has been barred on account of his race from fighting or dying for America—there are no 'white' or 'colored' signs on the foxholes or graveyards of battle."

John F. Kennedy, Message to Congress, 1963

"Injustice anywhere is a threat to justice everywhere."

Martin Luther King, Jr.,
Letter from the Birmingham Jail, 1963

"I have a dream that one day this nation will rise up and live out the true meaning of its creed: We hold these truths to be self-evident, that all men are created equal."

Martin Luther King, Jr., Speech at Washington, 1963

"We have talked long enough in this country about equal rights. It is time to write the next chapter—and to write it in the books of law."

Lyndon B. Johnson, Message to Congress, 1963

"This administration here and now declares unconditional war on poverty in America."

Lyndon B. Johnson, Address to Congress, 1964

"This nation, this generation, in this hour has man's first chance to build a Great Society, a place where the meaning of man's life matches the marvels of man's labor."

Lyndon B. Johnson, Democratic National Convention, 1964

"We are not fighting for integration, nor are we fighting for separation. We are fighting for recognition as human beings."

Malcolm X, 1964

"An unconditional right to say what one pleases about public affairs is what I consider to be the minimum guarantee of the First Amendment."

Hugo Black, Opinion in *New York Times
Company* v. *Sullivan*, 1964

"No Viet Cong ever called me 'nigger.'"

Muhammad Ali, 1966

"On public questions there should be 'uninhibited, robust, and wide-open' debate."

Supreme Court decision in *New York Times Company* v.
United States, 1971

662

"People have got to know whether or not their President is a crook. Well, I am not a crook."

Richard M. Nixon, press conference, 1973

"I believe that government is the problem, not the answer."

Ronald Reagan, 1976

"Human rights is the soul of our foreign policy, because human rights is the very soul of our sense of nationhood."

Jimmy Carter, 1978

"I think the government ought to stay out of the prayer business."

Jimmy Carter, 1979

"No government has the right to tell its citizens when or whom to love. The only queer people are those who don't love anybody."

Rita Mae Brown, Gay Olympics, San Francisco, 1982

"Read my lips: No new taxes."

George Bush, Republican National Convention, 1988

"I did have a relationship with Miss Lewinsky that was not appropriate."

Bill Clinton, August 17, 1998

"Conservation may be a sign of personal virtue but it is not a sufficient basis for a sound, comprehensive energy policy."

Vice President Dick Cheney, April 30, 2001

"Major combat operations in Iraq have ended. In the Battle of Iraq, the United States and our allies have prevailed. And now our coalition is engaged in securing and reconstructing that country."

George W. Bush, on board the
USS Abraham Lincoln, May 1, 2003

"My job is not to represent Washington to you, but to represent you to Washington."

Barack Obama, February 23, 2005

"Many of my comrades were subjected to very cruel, very inhumane and degrading treatment, a few of them even unto death. But every one of us—every single one of us—knew and took great strength from the belief that we were different from our enemies, that we were better than them, that we, if the roles were reversed, would not disgrace ourselves by committing or countenancing such mistreatment of them."

John McCain, Republican U.S. Senator, 2005

"The warnings about global warming have been extremely clear for a long time. We are facing a global climate crisis. It is deepening. We are entering a period of consequences."

Al Gore, 2005

"The ruling of *Citizens United* v. *Federal Election Commission* has the potential to be disastrous to our democracy."

Senator Charles E. Schumer, 2010

"As of September 20, service members will no longer be forced to hide who they are in order to serve our country."

President Barack Obama commenting
on repeal of "Don't Ask, Don't Tell," 2011

"Tonight, I can report to the American people and to the world that the United States has conducted an operation that killed Osama bin Laden, the leader of al-Qaeda, and a terrorist who's responsible for the murder of thousands of innocent men, women, and children."

President Barack Obama, 2011

ANSWER KEY

UNIT 1

Chapter 1

Exercise Set 1.1

1. D	4. B	7. C	10. C	13. A
2. B	5. A	8. B	11. A	14. C
3. A	6. B	9. C	12. B	15. D

Exercise Set 1.2

1. C	3. C	5. B	7. A	9. A
2. D	4. C	6. B	8. C	10. C

Exercise Set 1.3

1. D	3. B	5. C	7. C
2. C	4. B	6. A	8. B

Exercise Set 1.4

1. C	3. C	5. D	7. B	9. D
2. B	4. C	6. C	8. B	

Chapter Review Questions

1. D	5. B	9. A	13. B	17. C
2. B	6. C	10. D	14. B	18. B
3. C	7. A	11. C	15. B	19. D
4. C	8. C	12. B	16. A	20. A

Chapter 2

Exercise Set 1.5

1. C	3. A	5. C	7. D
2. C	4. D	6. C	

Exercise Set 1.6

1. C	3. B	5. A	7. C
2. B	4. D	6. D	

Chapter Review Questions

1. B	3. C	5. C	7. C	9. A
2. B	4. C	6. C	8. C	10. B

UNIT 2

Chapter 1

Exercise Set 2.1
1. D   3. A   5. D
2. B   4. C   6. B

Exercise Set 2.2
1. B   3. D   5. C
2. B   4. A

Exercise Set 2.3
1. D   3. C
2. C   4. D

Exercise Set 2.4
1. D   3. B
2. C   4. A

Chapter Review Questions
1. A   3. D   5. B
2. B   4. C   6. A

Chapter 2

Exercise Set 2.5
1. B   3. A   5. D
2. A   4. C

Exercise Set 2.6
1. A   3. D
2. B   4. D

Exercise Set 2.7
1. C
2. B
3. D

Exercise Set 2.8
1. A   3. B
2. C   4. A

Exercise Set 2.9

1. C	**3.** A
2. D	**4.** B

Chapter Review Questions

1. D	**3.** D	**5.** C	**7.** A	**9.** D
2. B	**4.** C	**6.** B	**8.** B	**10.** B

Chapter 3

Exercise Set 2.10

1. B	**3.** A
2. A	

Exercise Set 2.11

1. B	**3.** C	**5.** C
2. B	**4.** D	**6.** A

Exercise Set 2.12

1. D	**3.** B
2. B	**4.** C

Chapter Review Questions

1. C	**3.** A	**5.** A	**7.** D
2. B	**4.** B	**6.** D	**8.** A

UNIT 3

Chapter 1

Exercise Set 3.1

1. B	**3.** C	**5.** B
2. D	**4.** D	**6.** D

Exercise Set 3.2

1. D	**3.** B
2. D	**4.** A

Chapter Review Questions

1. C	**3.** A	**5.** B
2. C	**4.** B	**6.** C

Chapter 2

Exercise Set 3.3
1. D   3. A
2. C   4. A

Exercise Set 3.4
1. C   3. D   5. D
2. A   4. B   6. C

Exercise Set 3.5
1. C   3. A
2. D   4. B

Exercise Set 3.6
1. D   3. A
2. C   4. C

Exercise Set 3.7
1. C   3. B
2. C   4. B

Chapter Review Questions
1. A   3. D   5. C   7. B
2. B   4. B   6. A

UNIT 4

Chapter 1

Exercise Set 4.1
1. D   3. A   5. D   7. C   9. D
2. C   4. C   6. A   8. B

Exercise Set 4.2
1. A   3. C   5. B
2. A   4. C

Exercise Set 4.3
1. B   3. B   5. C   7. B   9. C
2. D   4. B   6. B   8. D   10. D

Chapter Review Questions

1. D	**3.** C	**5.** C
2. A	**4.** B	

Chapter 2

Exercise Set 4.4

1. C	**3.** B
2. A	**4.** A

Exercise Set 4.5

1. B	**3.** D	**5.** D
2. B	**4.** C	

Exercise Set 4.6

1. B	**3.** A	**5.** D
2. A	**4.** C	**6.** A

Exercise Set 4.7

1. C	**3.** C
2. A	**4.** B

Chapter Review Questions

1. A	**4.** D	**7.** A
2. C	**5.** C	**8.** B
3. D	**6.** C	

UNIT 5

Chapter 1

Exercise Set 5.1

1. A	**3.** B
2. D	**4.** D

Exercise Set 5.2

1. A	**3.** D	**5.** A
2. C	**4.** C	

Exercise Set 5.3

1. A	**3.** B	**5.** D
2. C	**4.** B	

Exercise Set 5.4

1. A	**3.** A	**5.** C
2. B	**4.** D	

Exercise Set 5.5

1. D	**3.** D	**5.** C
2. B	**4.** A	

Chapter Review Questions

1. D	**3.** A	**5.** C
2. C	**4.** C	

Chapter 2

Exercise Set 5.6

1. B	**3.** D	**5.** A
2. C	**4.** D	

Exercise Set 5.7

1. A	**3.** B	**5.** B
2. B	**4.** B	**6.** A

Exercise Set 5.8

1. C	**3.** C
2. A	**4.** C

Chapter Review Questions

1. B	**3.** A	**5.** C	**7.** D
2. A	**4.** D	**6.** B	

UNIT 6

Chapter 1

Exercise Set 6.1

1. D	**3.** B
2. A	

Exercise Set 6.2

1. B	**3.** D	**5.** B
2. A	**4.** B	**6.** A

Chapter Review Questions
1. D
2. C
3. B

Chapter 2

Exercise Set 6.3

1. B	3. B	5. A
2. A	4. B	

Exercise Set 6.4
1. C
2. C
3. A

Exercise Set 6.5

1. B	3. A
2. C	4. A

Exercise Set 6.6

1. B	3. B	5. A
2. D	4. C	

Chapter Review Questions

1. C	3. B	5. C
2. D	4. C	

Chapter 3

Exercise Set 6.7

1. C	3. A
2. D	4. B

Exercise Set 6.8

1. B	3. A	5. C
2. D	4. C	

Exercise Set 6.9

1. B	3. B
2. D	4. C

Exercise Set 6.10

1. B	**3.** D	**5.** B
2. C	**4.** D	**6.** C

Chapter Review Questions

1. C	**3.** C	**5.** D
2. B	**4.** D	**6.** C

Chapter 4

Exercise Set 6.12

1. C	**3.** D	**5.** C
2. B	**4.** B	

Exercise Set 6.13

1. D	**3.** C	**5.** B
2. A	**4.** D	**6.** C

Chapter Review Questions

1. A	**3.** A
2. D	**4.** B

Chapter 5

Exercise Set 6.14

1. C	**3.** D	**5.** A
2. A	**4.** C	**6.** B

Exercise Set 6.15

1. C	**3.** D
2. D	**4.** A

Exercise Set 6.16

1. D	**3.** B	**5.** A
2. D	**4.** C	

Exercise Set 6.17

1. B	**3.** B	**5.** C	**7.** C
2. A	**4.** D	**6.** D	

Exercise Set 6.18

1. D	**3.** D	**5.** A	**7.** C	**9.** C
2. D	**4.** C	**6.** B	**8.** D	

Chapter Review Questions

1. C	**3.** D	**5.** C
2. A	**4.** B	**6.** A

UNIT 7

Chapter 1

Exercise Set 7.1
1. B   3. C   5. B
2. B   4. A

Chapter 2

Exercise Set 7.2
1. A   3. D   5. B   7. B   9. B
2. D   4. C   6. D   8. A   10. C

Chapter 3

Exercise Set 7.3
1. C   3. B   5. A   7. D   9. C
2. A   4. A   6. A   8. A   10. B

Chapter 4

Exercise Set 7.4
1. B   3. B   5. B   7. B   9. D
2. C   4. D   6. D   8. B   10. A

Chapter 5

Exercise Set 7.5
1. C   3. B   5. B   7. C   9. B
2. A   4. A   6. C   8. D   10. A

Chapter 6

Exercise Set 7.6
1. D   3. A   5. C
2. D   4. C   6. A

GLOSSARY OF TERMS

Abolitionists   those who supported ending the institution of slavery.

Acid rain   rain, snow, or sleet containing nitric or sulphuric acid produced from the contamination of the atmosphere by smokestack and automobile emissions. It can damage plants and animals and erode stone and buildings.

Acculturation   the modification of a people's culture through adaptation or borrowing from other cultures; the merging of cultures.

Affirmative action   public policy of incorporating women and racial and ethnic minorities into economic, political, and social institutions; usually applied through legislation or court orders.

Albany Plan of Union   1754 plan of intercolonial defense by Benjamin Franklin that provided a federal plan of governing later used as a model for the United States Constitution.

Amendment   change or addition made in the Constitution; proposed by Congress or a national convention called by Congress and ratified by state legislatures or special state conventions.

American Federation of Labor   Early labor union (1881) of craft unions founded by Samuel Gompers. The AFL merged with the Congress of Industrial Organizations (CIO) in 1955.

Amnesty   a general pardon for political offenses.

Anarchist   one who believes in the abolition of government or is opposed to organized government.

Anarchy   the absence of government; a state of disorder or chaos.

Antifederalists   opponents of ratification of the Constitution in 1787 and 1788; opponents of the extension of federal power.

Antitrust   relating to the limitation or control of monopolies, trusts, or unfair business combinations.

Antitrust laws   legislation designed to prevent the abuses of large business organizations (i.e., monopolies).

Apartheid   racial segregation, specifically in South Africa.

Appalachia   vast region of the Appalachian Mountains characterized in many parts by poverty and economic underdevelopment.

Appeasement   attempts to conciliate an aggressor by making concessions. The policy of appeasement toward Hitler in the 1930s ultimately failed to avoid war.

Apportionment   allotment of voting districts as required by law.

Arab Spring   widespread wave of pro-democracy protests occurring in the Arab world that began at the end of 2010. The protests have resulted in despot rulers being removed in Tunisia, Egypt, Libya, and Yemen while uprisings continue in Bahrain and Syria.

Arbitration   process of settling a dispute by referring it to a third party; both sides usually agree beforehand to abide by the arbitrator's decision.

Armistice   a truce preliminary to a peace treaty.

Articles of Confederation   the charter of the first national government of the United States; in effect from 1781 until replaced by the Constitution in 1789.

Assembly   a gathering or body of representatives, usually of a state or locality.

Assembly line   manufacturing process in which parts are added to a product to create a finished product. Perfected by Henry Ford in 1913 in his automobile production factories.

Atlantic Charter   document issued in 1941 by President Franklin Roosevelt and Prime Minister Winston Churchill outlining the mutual wartime goals of the United States and England and their principles for assuring peace after the war.

674

Balance of power policy aimed at securing peace by maintaining approximate military equality among countries or blocs.

Balanced budget plan for government taxes and spending in which expenses do not exceed income.

Belligerent a participant in a war.

Berlin airlift in response to the 1948 blockade set up by the Soviets around Berlin, the United States, Great Britain, and France flew food and other necessities to the 2 million people there. The blockade was withdrawn in 1949.

Bicameral legislature lawmaking body made up of two houses or chambers.

Big stick policy willingness to use military power to influence foreign affairs. It derives from Theodore Roosevelt's saying, "Walk softly, but carry a big stick."

Bill of Rights first ten amendments to the Constitution, adopted in 1791.

Bipartisan involving the cooperation of two political parties.

Black codes a series of laws that sought to control and regulate the conduct of freed slaves during and after the Reconstruction period in the Southern states. Generally, they denied blacks their basic civil rights.

Bloc a group of countries or voters with similar political views.

Bolsheviks radical socialists and communists under the leadership of Lenin and Trotsky who came to power following the Russian Revolution in 1917.

Boston Massacre in 1770 five colonists were killed in Boston when British soldiers fired on a crowd throwing rocks and snowballs; the soldiers were tried and acquitted of murder.

Boston Tea Party incident in Boston, December 16, 1773, when colonists dressed as Indians forced their way aboard merchant ships in the harbor and threw overboard their cargoes of tea so that recently imposed British taxes on it could not be collected.

Bourgeoisie economic and social class between the aristocracy, or the very wealthy class, and the working class (the proletariat); the commercial or professional class; the middle class.

Boycott to join together in refusing to deal with or buy from a party in order to compel negotiation or concessions.

Brain trust experts without official positions who served as advisers to President Franklin Roosevelt.

Brinkmanship pushing a dangerous situation to the limit before stopping.

Budget deficit the amount by which expenses exceed revenue or income.

Bureaucracy administrative officials of government.

Cabinet the advisers to the President who also manage the principal executive departments of the U.S. government. The Cabinet is not mentioned in the Constitution, but has grown over time from custom and practice.

CAFTA (2003) United States–Central America Free Trade Agreement, which promotes lowering and doing away with tariffs between the United States and Costa Rica, El Salvador, Guatemala, Honduras, and Nicaragua. CAFTA is modeled after the North American Free Trade Agreement (1994).

Camp David Accords agreements reached in 1978 between President Sadat of Egypt and Prime Minister Begin of Israel, negotiated by President Carter at the presidential retreat in Camp David, MD. The accords evolved into a peace treaty between Israel and Egypt in 1979, providing for Egypt's official recognition of Israel and Israel's withdrawal from the Sinai Peninsula.

Capital 1) the seat or main location of a government; 2) money invested or used to return a profit.

Capitalism economic system in which the means of production and distribution are privately owned and operated for profit.

Capital punishment death sentence imposed by a court.

Capitol building in which state or federal legislature assembles.

Carpetbaggers Northerners who went to the South during the Reconstruction period to participate in and profit from its political reorganization.

Caucus a closed meeting of a political party.

Censorship preventing the publication of written material or the showing of a film, television program, or play because the government or a segment of society finds it objectionable.

Census a counting of the inhabitants of a region.

Central Powers In World War I, Germany, Austro-Hungary, and their allies.

Charter written document establishing the rules under which an organization will operate; an organization's constitution.

Checks and balances division of powers among the three branches of the federal government so that each branch may limit actions and power of the others. *See also* Separation of powers.

Chicanos Americans of Mexican origin or descent.

Citizen person entitled by birth or naturalization, to the rights and protection provided by the state or nation.

Civil disobedience refusal to obey a law in order to draw attention to its unfairness or undesirability.

Civil rights the liberties and privileges of citizens, especially those guaranteed in the Bill of Rights.

Civil Service system begun in 1880s for filling government jobs through impartial and nonpolitical means, such as standardized exams.

Civil war a war between factions or regions of one country (i.e., United States Civil War, Russian Revolution).

Clear and present danger standard established by the Supreme Court for determining when the right of free speech may be limited or denied—"when there is a clear and present danger that they will bring about the substantive evils that [the government] has a right to prevent."

Coalition temporary alliance of groups or factions.

Cold war a conflict between nations short of actual military conflict; the political, diplomatic, economic, and strategic competition between the United States and the Soviet Union from 1946 until 1991.

Collective bargaining method by which workers negotiate as a group with their employer through their union representatives.

Collective security agreement among a group of nations to help each other maintain their safety and territory; usually by agreeing that an attack by a foreign power upon one nation will be considered an attack upon all.

Colonialism national policy based on control over dependent areas or colonies.

Colony a territory ruled or administered by a distant nation, usually for the benefit of the ruling nation.

Commerce among the states business carried on across state lines, which Congress is given power to regulate by Article I, Section 8, of the Constitution.

Commodities common economic goods, such as agricultural products, that are bought and sold.

Common law body of law formed over time by accumulation of precedents and prior decisions, as opposed to laws enacted by legislative bodies.

Common Sense a pamphlet by Thomas Paine that helped rally public support for the Revolutionary War.

Commonwealth an organization of independent states; official designation (instead of state) of KY, MA, PA, and VA in the United States.

Communism political philosophy advocating collective ownership of property and the means of production and the abolition of the capitalist economic system.

Compact theory of union doctrine held by many states' rights supporters that the Union was a voluntary compact among the states and that states had the right to leave the Union in the same manner they had chosen to enter it.

Compromise of 1850 the results of debate and compromise by Henry Clay, Daniel Webster, Stephen Douglas, and John Calhoun; this set of laws temporarily resolved slavery/sectional balance questions raised by the Mexican War.

Confederate States the eleven Southern states that seceded or officially withdrew from the Union in 1860 and 1861 to form an independent nation called the Confederate States of America. They were defeated in the Civil War and reabsorbed into the Union.

Congress the legislative branch of the federal government; composed of the Senate and the House of Representatives.

Conscription compulsory enrollment into the armed forces; draft.

Consensus general agreement.

Conservative reluctant or resistant to change; favoring traditional views and values.

Constitution the basic charter of the U.S. government, effective since 1789; it was written by the Constitutional Convention in 1787, ratified by the states 1787–1788, and put into effect in 1789.

Constitutionalism belief that government is limited by legal and political restraints and accountable to the governed.

Constitutional Convention gathering of delegates from the thirteen states in 1787 in Philadelphia for the purpose of revising the Articles of Confederation; instead, they drafted an entirely new Constitution that was adopted in 1788 and put into effect in 1789.

Constitutional Republicanism elected government limited by legally defined guidelines.

Consumerism protection of the interests and rights of consumers against false advertising or faulty or dangerous products.

Containment policy adopted by the Western democracies after World War II to prevent the further expansion of communism and the Soviet Union.

Continental Congress 1) any of several assemblies of delegates from the American colonies before the Revolution to promote cooperation on various issues; 2) the national legislative body under the Articles of Confederation (1781–1788).

Cooperative a corporation owned collectively by members who share in the profits and benefits. Cooperatives were first developed by farmers in the late 19th century to avoid high prices charged by middlemen for grain storage, transportation, and farm supplies.

Corollary a proposition that follows a previous one, which it modifies or enlarges, such as the Roosevelt Corollary to the Monroe Doctrine.

Corporation an organization legally empowered to act as one person, including the ability to borrow and lend money, make contracts, own property, and engage in business.

Coup an overturning; a coup d'état is the overthrow of a government.

Court packing attempts by President Franklin Delano Roosevelt in 1937 to increase the number of justices on the Supreme Court in order to ensure passage of his New Deal legislation.

Craft union labor union made up of workers with the same skill or craft, such as carpenters or electricians.

Crédit Mobilier railroad construction company that cheated on government contracts and bribed Congressmen during the late 1860s.

677

Creditor nation a nation that exports more than it imports, so that it is owed money by other nations.

Cuban Missile Crisis October 1962 Cold War crisis that occurred when the Soviet Union placed nuclear missiles in Cuba. Resolved when the Soviets dismantled the missiles and the United States agreed to remove missiles from Turkey and end the Cuban blockade.

Cultural pluralism the acceptance of multiple ethnic, religious, and racial groups within one society; respect for ethnic diversity.

Darwinism 1) the theories of biologist Charles Darwin, who explained the evolution of species by natural selection; 2) social theories loosely based on Darwin's work and arguing that "the survival of the fittest" meant that government should not protect the weak from exploitation by the strong.

Debasement a reduction of value.

Debtor nation a nation that imports more than it exports and so owes money to other nations.

Declaration of Independence document passed and signed by the Continental Congress, effective July 4, 1776, declaring the United States an independent and sovereign nation.

Delegate a representative chosen to act for a group or another person.

Delegated power powers given to the national government by Article I, Section 8 of the United States Constitution.

Demilitarized zone area where no military equipment or personnel may be deployed.

Demobilize to discharge from military service.

Democratic party political party that evolved out of the Democratic Republicans around 1820.

Democratic Republicans political party formed around 1800 by Jefferson, Madison, and others opposed to the Federalists.

Demographic relating to the statistical study of human populations.

Desegregation the ending of segregation, which is the separation of whites and blacks.

Despot a sovereign or authority without legal restraints; an absolute monarch; tyrant.

Détente relaxation of strained relations or tensions.

Diplomacy the practice of conducting relations between countries by negotiations rather than force.

Direct election election in which votes are cast by the people themselves rather than by their representatives.

Directive order issued by a high authority calling for specific action.

Disarmament giving up or reducing armed forces.

Discrimination partiality, prejudice, or distinctions in treatment; the denial of rights and advantages to minority groups.

Disenfranchise to take away the right to vote.

Dissenting opinion written statement by a member of a court disagreeing with the court's decision.

Distribution of wealth statistical measure of how the property or wealth of a nation is divided among its population.

Dollar diplomacy use of American political and military power abroad (usually in Latin America) to promote or advance the interests of American businesses.

Domino theory belief in the 1950s and 1960s that the fall of one nation to communism would lead to the fall of neighboring nations.

"Don't Ask, Don't Tell" official policy of the United States from 1993–2011 regarding homosexual and bisexual members of the military. The policy prohibited discrimination as long as homosexual or bisexual military personnel did not demonstrate their sexual identity openly.

Due process of law doctrine that government's power cannot be used against an individual except as prescribed by established law. Applied to the state governments by the 14th Amendment.

Dust Bowl an ecological disaster for Plains farmers during the 1930s, which was created in part by bad weather and bad land management.

Eisenhower Doctrine statement made in 1957 by President Eisenhower that the United States would provide military and economic aid—and direct military intervention, if necessary—to nations of the Middle East if they were threatened by communist aggression.

Elastic clause part of the Constitution (Article I, Section 8) that gives the federal government the right to make laws "necessary and proper" to carry out its specific powers and functions; it has sometimes been used to expand the powers of the federal government; also known as the "necessary and proper clause."

Electoral college means of electing President and Vice-President established by the Constitution and subsequent amendments; voters in each state choose "electors" who later meet to elect the President and Vice-President. Electors were originally free to vote for any candidate they chose, but they are currently pledged to vote for specific candidates. The number of electors from each state is equal to the number of Representatives and Senators from that state.

Emancipation Proclamation issued by President Lincoln in 1863, it declared free the slaves in the Southern states in rebellion but did not affect slaves held in states loyal to the Union, such as Maryland, Kentucky, or Missouri.

Embargo prohibition of commerce with a nation or region, usually to apply pressure or force concessions.

Emigrate to leave one country or region to settle in another.

Encroachment step-by-step interference with the rights or possessions of others.

Enjoin to legally forbid or prohibit, usually by court order or injunction.

Enlightenment era during the 17th and 18th centuries when reason replaced religion as guide to politics, philosophy, and government.

Equal protection principle that all people or classes of persons be treated the same under the law.

Espionage the act or practice of spying.

Ethnic belonging to a particular group identified by nationality or national origin and culture or customs.

Ethnocentric believing that one's own ethnic group is superior to others.

Evolution change over time; an adjustment in the existing order.

Executive person or office having administrative and managerial functions; in government, the branch responsible for carrying out the laws and for the conduct of national affairs; it includes the President and Cabinet and the departments under their jurisdiction.

Executive privilege principle that an executive (such as the President) should not divulge certain sensitive or protected information.

Expansionism policy of adding to a country's territory, usually by seizing land from other nations.

Extraterritoriality right of a resident of a foreign country to be tried in the judicial system of his or her home country.

Fascism political philosophy advocating totalitarian government power, intense nationalism, and military expansionism. Mussolini's Fascist party governed Italy from the 1920s through World War II.

Far East the nations on the Pacific coast of Asia.

Favorable balance of trade exporting or selling more goods than are imported or bought.

Federal relating to the central national government created by the Constitution.

Federal Housing Administration federal agency established in 1934 to insure mortgages and set construction standards.

Federal Reserve Note Currency or paper money issued by the Federal Reserve System and representing a promissory obligation of the federal government.

Federal Reserve System federal agency created by Congress in 1913 to regulate the banking system. Federal Reserve banks in 12 districts supervise banking operations, lend money to banks, and issue currency; a Federal Reserve Commission sets and regulates interest rates.

Federalism system of government in which powers are divided between a central authority and local subdivisions.

Federalists advocates of adopting the Constitution in 1787–1788 and of more powerful central government during the period 1789–1820. Many Federalists later joined the Whig party.

Feminism movement advocating equal rights and privileges for women.

Filibuster use of delaying tactics, such as unlimited debate in one or both houses of Congress, to prevent action on a legislative proposal.

Fiscal having to do with government revenues, expenditures, and budgets.

Foreclosure the act of a lender's taking possession of mortgaged property from a borrower who is unable to make the required payments.

Foreign aid assistance in the form of money or goods supplied to a foreign country.

Foreign policy a nation's policy in dealing with other nations.

Fossil fuels buried combustible geologic deposits of organic materials, formed from decayed plants and animals. Fossil fuels include crude oil, coal, natural gas, etc.

Fourteen Points President Wilson's plan for international peace presented to Congress on January 22, 1918.

Franchise the right to vote; suffrage.

Free enterprise the freedom of private businesses to operate without undue government interference.

Free trade the freedom to exchange goods with other countries, especially without tariffs.

Freedman a freed slave, usually referring to a former slave freed by the Thirteenth Amendment.

Freedom of religion right of citizens to hold and practice religious beliefs without government interference.

Freedom of speech right of citizens to say or write their views without regulation or reprisal from government; restricted in some cases; *see* Clear and present danger.

Freedom of the press right of publishers to print material without prior approval by government; *see* Prior restraint.

Freedom riders civil rights advocates who traveled the South on buses to promote the desegregation of public facilities.

Free-Soil party political party before the Civil War opposed to the extension of slavery and the admission of slave states.

Frontier thesis the historical argument put forth by Professor Frederick Jackson Turner in 1893 that suggested that the spirit and success of the United States was directly tied to the country's westward expansion.

Fugitive Slave Law federal law passed in 1850 that required Northern states to return escaped slaves to their owners in the South. It was widely opposed by a variety of legal and extra-legal means.

Geneva Convention(s) four international treaties created and adopted in Geneva, Switzerland. The Geneva Conventions established much of the international law concerning humanitarian issues.

Genocide systematic annihilation of a particular group, usually racial, ethnic, or political in nature.

Gerrymandering drawing the boundaries of election districts to insure the victory of one party or faction by including or excluding neighborhoods of a particular ethnic or social class.

GI Bill of Rights (1944) congressional legislation granting monthly allowances to World War II veterans for education, loans to purchase farms, businesses, and homes.

Gilded Age in American history the "Gilded Age" refers to the post-Civil War and post-Reconstruction era, from 1865 to 1901, which saw economic, territorial, industrial, and population expansion.

Global warming warming of the planet Earth, which has been taking place throughout the last century. Scientists are more than 90 percent certain that most of it is caused by increasing concentrations of greenhouse gases produced by human activities such as deforestation and burning fossil fuels.

Good Neighbor Policy policy first announced by President Franklin Roosevelt to promote friendly relations with all Latin American nations.

Graduated income tax system of taxation that taxes those with a greater amount of disposable income, sometimes referred to as a progressive tax. Karl Marx argued for a progressive income tax in *The Communist Manifesto*.

Great Compromise agreement in the Constitutional Convention of 1787 to have two houses of Congress, one (the Senate) to represent the states equally and the other (the House of Representatives) to represent the people proportionately. Also known as the Connecticut Compromise.

Great Depression period from the stock market crash of 1929 until the start of World War II during which industrial production declined and unemployment rose to over one fourth of the labor force.

Great Society collective name for various social programs of President Lyndon Johnson, including the so-called War on Poverty and programs for job-training, subsidized housing, and free medical care for the poor and aged.

Greenhouse effect a global rise in temperature due to the accumulation of certain gases in the atmosphere (carbon dioxide, methane, among others) which traps the Earth's heat.

Green revolution the increase in agricultural crop yields brought about by the use of machinery, fertilizers, pesticides, and improved seeds.

Guerilla an active participant in a war who is not a member of the regular armed forces; a kind of warfare characterized by sabotage, harassment, and hit-and-run tactics.

Habeas corpus a writ or legal order directed to an official holding a person in custody, commanding the official to produce the person in court, show cause why the person has been confined, and prove that the person has not been deprived of liberty without due process.

Harlem Renaissance a movement among black writers, artists, and musicians centered in Harlem, New York City, during the 1920s.

Haymarket Riot 1886 gathering of labor activists and anarchists in Haymarket Square, Chicago, to protest a lockout of Knights of Labor union members by McCormick Harvester Company.

Head Start educational aid to preschool children from disadvantaged homes.

Hessians hired soldiers from the district of Hesse in Germany, employed by the British before and during the Revolutionary War.

Heterogeneous composed of unlike parts; a society made up of different races, nationalities, or ethnic groups.

Holocaust since World War II, it refers to the genocidal murders of six million European Jews by the Nazis.

681

Homestead Act passed by Congress in 1862, it gave 160 acres of Western land to any head of a family who agreed to cultivate it for five years; it encouraged the rapid settlement of the West by giving immigrants and Easterners free land.

Homogeneous made up of similar elements; a society consisting primarily of the same race, nationality, or ethnic group.

House of Burgesses (1619) first elected legislative body in the English Colonies (Virginia).

House of Representatives the half of Congress composed of representatives allotted among the states according to their population.

Immigration moving into a country where one is not a native to become a permanent resident.

Impeach to bring formal charges against a public official for misconduct. The House of Representatives has the power to impeach federal officials, and the trial is held by the Senate.

Imperialism the practice of forming and maintaining an empire; possession of foreign territories or colonies for the benefit of the home country; the policy of seeking to dominate economically, politically, or militarily weaker areas of the world.

Import quota a limit on the amount of a commodity that can be brought into the country.

Inauguration a ceremonial beginning, especially the installing of an official at the beginning of a term.

Incumbent person currently serving in political office.

Indians European term for the native inhabitants of the Americas.

Industrialization economic transformation of society by the development of large industries, machine production, factories, and an urban work force.

Industrial Revolution the transformation from an agricultural society to one based upon large-scale mechanized production and factory organization. It began in Europe (especially England) in the late 18th century and in America in the early 19th century.

Industrial Workers of the World Labor movement formed in 1905 under the leadership of Big Bill Haywood. Advocated militant agitation and damage to businesses if necessary to obtain demands. Also known as the Wobblies.

Infiltration gradual entrance or buildup with the intent of taking control.

Inflation general and continuing rise in the price of goods, often due to the relative increase of available money and credit.

Initiative process for the direct involvement of voters in the making of laws; by gathering enough signatures on a petition, a group can force a legislature to consider a proposal or require it to be placed on the ballot for public vote.

Injunction order issued by a court directing someone to do or refrain from doing some specific act.

Insurgency an uprising or revolt against an established authority, short of actual declared war.

Integration bringing together or making as one; unification; applied especially to blacks and whites.

Interdependent depending on one another, such as nations that rely on each other's trade.

Internal improvements roads, canals, and other means to assist transportation and commerce.

Internationalism policy of cooperation among nations.

Internment the detainment and isolation of ethnic groups for purposes of national security (such as Japanese Americans during World War II); this is now widely held to have been unconstitutional.

Interposition an argument that the states could legitimately object to acts of Congress if those acts exceeded Congress's legitimate authority. Interposition fell short of Nullification.

Interstate taking place across state lines; involving the citizens of more than one state.

Interstate Commerce Commission established by Congress in 1887 to regulate railroad rates and prevent abuses by railroads; it was later expanded to have jurisdiction over other forms of transportation.

Intervention interference in the affairs of another country, including the use of force.

Intolerable Acts series of acts of Parliament directed against the American colonies and intended to assert British authority and increase revenues from the colonies.

Invalidate to make null and void.

Iran-Contra Affair an illegal conspiracy by officials of the Reagan administration to provide funding for the anti-communist Contra rebels in Nicaragua by secretly selling missiles to Iran and diverting the money to the Nicaraguans.

Iron Curtain the series of fortified borders separating Western Europe from Soviet-dominated Eastern Europe; term made popular by Winston Churchill.

Isolationism policy of keeping a nation apart from alliances or other political relations with foreign nations.

Jacksonian Democracy the phrase "Jacksonian Democracy" has been the subject of much debate because, on one hand, it is the term that refers to the political platform of Andrew Jackson and his party, but the broader meaning, as described in Alexis de Tocqueville's classic *Democracy in America* (1835), suggests the blossoming of the democratic spirit in American life around the time of Jackson's presidency.

Jim Crow laws laws enforcing segregation or control of blacks in such a way as to make them unequal.

Joint resolution a legislative act that is the same in both houses of Congress.

Judicial activism developing social policy through court decisions instead of through legislative action, often in response to changing values and circumstances.

Judicial nationalism term used to describe the Supreme Court under the leadership of John Marshall, when its decisions consolidated the power of the federal government by centralizing responsibility for commerce, contracts, and finance.

Judicial restraint the preference of a court to avoid upsetting existing law or practice.

Judicial review power of the Supreme Court to void acts of Congress that are found to violate the Constitution.

Judiciary the branch of government that interprets the law and tries cases; the system of courts.

Jurisdiction authority of a court to interpret and apply the law; in general, the area of authority of a government.

Kansas-Nebraska Act (1854) Congressional legislation that provided for popular sovereignty to be applied to the Kansas Territory and the Nebraska Territory, assuming that Kansas would be slave and Nebraska would be free.

Kellogg-Briand Pact (1928) pact eventually signed by 62 nations "condemning recourse to war for the solution of international controversies."

Knights of Labor early labor union, formed in 1869.

Kremlin complex of government offices in Moscow; the center of government of Russia and the former Soviet Union.

Ku Klux Klan secret organization founded in 1866 to intimidate freed slaves and keep them in conditions of servitude through threats and acts of violence; it later developed into a nativist organization opposed to Jews, Catholics, and immigrants, as well as African Americans.

Laissez-faire doctrine opposing government regulation of economic matters beyond what is necessary to maintain property rights and enforce contracts. *Laissez-faire* is French for "let alone" or "let be."

Lame duck an official who has not been reelected and is serving out the remainder of a term.

League of Nations International organization of countries formed after World War I to promote world peace. It was supported by President Wilson, but the Senate refused to allow the United States to join. After World War II it was replaced by the United Nations.

Legislature a body of persons elected to make laws for a nation or state; a congress or parliament.

Lend-Lease Act (1941) congressional legislation that allowed the sale, transfer, exchange, or lease of war equipment to any nation for use in the interests of the United States.

Liberal advocating political or social views that emphasize civil rights, democratic reforms, and the use of government to promote social progress.

Line-item veto power of an executive to veto specific provisions of a bill without vetoing the entire bill that contains them. The President does not have line-item veto power.

Lobbying actions by private citizens or organizations seeking to influence (by legal means) the decisions of a legislature or executive department of government.

Loose construction, loose interpretation reading of the Constitution that allows broad use of the elastic clause and implied powers.

Louisiana Purchase the purchase from France by the United States in 1803 for $15 million of the Louisiana Territory, stretching from New Orleans west to the Rocky Mountains, more than doubling the size of the United States.

Loyalists American colonists who remained loyal to England during the American Revolution; also known as Tories.

Magna Carta agreement signed by King John I of England in 1215, granting certain rights (including trial by jury and habeas corpus) to the barons who had taken him prisoner.

Manifest Destiny belief, held by many Americans in the 19th century, that the United States was destined to control the continent between the Atlantic and Pacific Oceans.

March on Washington (1963) civil rights massive demonstration in Washington, D.C. Site of Martin Luther King's "I Have a Dream" speech. The march was attended by some 250,000 people; it was the largest demonstration ever seen in the nation's capital and one of the first to have extensive television coverage.

Market economy an economic system in which decisions about production and pricing are based on the actions of buyers and sellers in the marketplace; usually associated with capitalism.

Marshall Plan the program of U.S. aid to Europe following World War II to help those nations recover from the extensive damage to their cities, industries, and transportation.

Mayflower Compact an agreement made by Pilgrims and others aboard the Mayflower (1620) which established a civil government for "the general Good of the Plymouth Colony."

McCarthyism term that had its origin in the investigative methods of Senator Joseph McCarthy (1950s) and came to mean the practice of making accusations of disloyalty, especially of pro-Communist activity, in many instances unsupported by proof.

Mediator person who solves differences between two parties. Both sides do not usually agree beforehand to accept the decisions of the mediator, as they usually do with an arbitrator.

Mercantilism the economic policies of European nations from the 15th century until the Industrial Revolution, based on mercantile (commercial, trading) activities and characterized by the acquisition of colonies and the establishment of a favorable balance of trade. The American colonies were established under the mercantile system.

Mexican War military conflict fought between the United States and Mexico from 1846 to 1848 resulting in the U.S. gain of the Mexican Cession.

Middle class the members of a society having a socio-economic position between the very wealthy and the poor.

Militaristic characterized by military discipline and aggressiveness.

Military-industrial complex the combined power of the Defense Department and the industries that supply it with equipment. The phrase was popularized by Eisenhower, who claimed that it worked for unnecessary increases in armaments.

Militia part-time soldiers who do not belong to the regular armed forces.

Minimum wage federally established minimum hourly wage that can be paid to most workers. Adopted in the United States at the federal level in 1938. Currently $7.25/hour (July 2009). Many states have raised their own considerably higher than the federal government's rate.

Missouri Compromise an agreement in 1820 between Congressional advocates and opponents of the extension of slavery that preserved sectional balance. It included the simultaneous admission of the slave state Missouri and the free state Maine and the prohibition of slavery in the northern parts of the Louisiana Purchase.

Monopoly the exclusive control or ownership of an industry by a single person or company.

Monroe Doctrine policy announced in 1823, during the presidency of James Monroe, that the United States would oppose European attempts to extend their control of the Western Hemisphere. It became and remains a basic principle of American foreign policy.

Montgomery bus boycott (1954) in response to the arrest of Rosa Parks for violating city Jim Crow ordinances, a 381 day refusal by many in Montgomery, Alabama, to use public transportation. Led by Martin Luther King, Jr. The city and the bus companies removed the segregationist policies.

Moratorium agreement to postpone payment of a debt or other obligation.

Muckraker journalists in the late 19th and early 20th centuries who reported on political or commercial corruption.

Munitions armaments and ammunition used in warfare.

NAACP National Association for the Advancement of Colored People formed in 1909 by, among others, Jane Addams, W. E. B. DuBois, and John Dewey.

NAFTA North American Free Trade Agreement (1994). Agreement between the United States, Canada, and Mexico to encourage the reduction of trade duties and tariffs.

Nationalism 1) sense of pride in one's country; 2) extreme devotion to national interests.

National Labor Relations Board federal agency established in 1935 to enforce laws against unfair labor practices.

National Origins Act laws passed in 1921, 1924, and 1929 that limited immigration into the United States and established quotas for nations based on the number of persons from those nations living in the United States according to an earlier census. It was regarded as discriminatory because it favored immigrants from Western Europe.

Native one who is connected with a place by birth; an original inhabitant as distinguished from immigrants or visitors.

Native Americans descendants of the original inhabitants of the Americas.

Nativism in the United States, the policy of favoring native-born Americans and opposing immigrants.

Naturalization the process of conferring citizenship upon an immigrant.

Natural rights rights or liberties to which one is entitled as a human being, as distinguished from those that are created by laws or governments.

Necessary and proper clause portion of the Constitution granting Congress power to "make all Laws which shall be necessary and proper for carrying into Execution" its other powers.

Neutrality policy of not helping either side in a war.

Neutrality Acts laws passed in 1935 and 1937 to avoid U.S. involvement in a war in Europe; they placed an embargo on arms sales to any nation engaged in war.

New Deal name adopted by President Franklin Roosevelt for the reforms and social programs instituted by his administration, beginning in 1933.

New Freedom program of President Wilson to regulate banking and currency to influence the direction of the economy and to support stronger anti-trust legislation.

New Nationalism program of President Theodore Roosevelt during his unsuccessful campaign for the presidency in 1912. It promised greater government supervision of the economy to balance the power of big business.

Nineteenth Amendment granted suffrage (the right to vote) to women; enacted in 1920.

Nonintervention policy of not becoming involved in the affairs of other nations.

Nonpartisan not based on party interests or bias.

Nonsectarian not affiliated with any religious group.

Normalcy the state of being normal; the term was applied to the era of the 1920s, following the disruptions of World War I.

North Atlantic Treaty Organization (NATO) collective security military alliance formed in 1949 by the United States, Canada, and nations of Western Europe to oppose the threat posed by the Soviet Union and Warsaw Pact nations to Europe.

Northwest Territory federal administrative district west of the Allegheny Mountains, north of the Ohio River, south of the Great Lakes, and east of the Mississippi River, including the present states of Ohio, Indiana, Michigan, Illinois, and Wisconsin, and part of Minnesota. The Territory was organized by the Continental Congress in 1787 from lands claimed by several eastern states.

Nullification argument or doctrine claiming that states could refuse to abide by acts of Congress if the states felt Congress had exceeded its enumerated powers. Used by states' rights advocates; championed by John C. Calhoun of South Carolina.

Nuremberg Tribunal international military court held in Nuremberg, Germany, in 1945–46; top Nazi leaders were tried and convicted of crimes against humanity and violations of international law.

Occupy Movement among the prime concerns of the movement begun in the summer, 2011, is the claim that big corporations and the global financial system control the world in an unstable way that benefits only few and is undermining democracy.

Open-Door policy an attempt by the United States in 1899 to preserve trade interests in China by asking European nations to respect the territorial integrity of China and to permit free access to ports they held in Asia.

Ordinance a law or regulation, usually of a local municipality.

Organized labor workers represented by labor unions.

Original jurisdiction the first court with authority to consider and decide a case, as opposed to appellate jurisdiction.

Parity government support of prices for agricultural products to insure that farm income keeps pace with income in other economic sectors.

Parliament the legislative body of Great Britain, consisting of the House of Commons and the House of Lords.

Partition division of a country into two or more separate parts.

Patriot Act this anti-terrorism legislation was passed during the administration of George Bush in response to the attacks of September 11, 2001.

Peace Corps U.S. government agency formed by President Kennedy in 1961; it sought to assist developing countries by sending American volunteers to teach and provide technical assistance.

Pentagon headquarters of the U.S. armed forces, near Washington, D.C.

Persian Gulf War (1990–1991) war following Iraq's invasion of Kuwait. Mandated by United Nations and led by United States forces with a coalition of approximately 30 nations.

Plea bargaining pleading guilty to a lesser charge in order to avoid standing trial for a more serious one.

Pluralistic type of society in which diverse ethnic, racial, and national groups coexist while maintaining their own cultural heritage.

Plurality a number of votes greater than any other candidate but less than a majority of all the votes cast.

Pocket veto an automatic veto that occurs if the President does not sign a bill passed by Congress during the last ten days of its session.

Pogrom organized, officially encouraged persecution or massacre of a group.

Political machine combination of party and political officials who maintain themselves in office, sometimes through corrupt means.

Poll tax 1) a tax paid to register or vote in elections (prohibited under the Twenty-Fourth Amendment). 2) a per-person or per-capita tax, not based on income or employment.

Pools business agreements designed to fix prices and divide profits.

Popular sovereignty 1) doctrine in democratic forms of government that power ultimately derives from the people and that the consent of the governed is exercised through the vote; 2) in the years before the Civil War, a political position advocating that the legality of slavery in the western territories be decided by popular vote of the inhabitants; it was ridiculed by its opponents as "squatter sovereignty."

Populism movement that began in agricultural areas in the late 19th century seeking government regulation to curb excesses and exploitation by big business.

Power of the purse the power to authorize revenues and spending; in the federal government, Congress holds the power of the purse.

Pragmatism belief in a practical (rather than an ethical or theoretical) approach to problems and affairs.

Preamble introductory part, especially the opening of the Constitution, which begins "We the people...."

Precedence the right to be first or have more authority.

Precedent rule or decision that serves as a guide for future actions or decisions.

President the chief executive officer of the federal government.

Price supports government measures to maintain the price of a commodity at an artificially set level.

Prior restraint the prohibition of publication of an article, book, or story by a court order before the material is disclosed to the public. Permissible only in cases of obscenity or of "clear and present danger."

Primary election   election in which members of a political party choose their candidates for the upcoming election.

Progressive Era   the period roughly from 1900 to 1920, marked by political, economic, and social reform movements.

Progressive tax   a tax that is higher for the wealthy than for the poor, such as income tax.

Progressivism   a broad reform movement during the late 19th and early 20th centuries that sought to remedy the worst effects of industrialism and urbanization by imposing governmental controls on big business, improving social justice, and increasing direct democratic participation in politics.

Prohibition   period from the enactment of the 18th Amendment in 1919 until its repeal by the 21st Amendment in 1933, during which the manufacture, sale, import, export, and transportation of alcoholic beverages was illegal.

Proletariat   the industrial working class, who sell their labor and do not own the means of production.

Protective tariff   tax on imported goods intended to protect the interests of internal or domestic industries by raising the price of imports.

Protectorate   an area under the control and protection of a country that does not have full sovereignty over it.

Proviso   clause in a document or statute making some condition or provision.

Pullman strike   (1894) strike by Pullman Car Company workers under the leadership of American Railway Union president Eugene V. Debs. President Cleveland sent federal troops to end strike in the interest of "protecting the delivery of the mails."

Pure Food and Drug Act   (1906) congressional legislation during the progressive administration of President Theodore Roosevelt requiring the contents of food and drug preparations be described on the labels of the product.

Quartering   forcibly housing soldiers in private residences.

Quota   a maximum limit; a share or portion assigned to a group.

Racism   belief that some races are inherently superior to others.

Radical, Radicalism   favoring extreme and fundamental changes.

Ratification   formal legal approval and adoption.

Rearmament   rebuilding of a nation's armed forces, often with new and better weapons.

Recall   political reform procedure for removing a public official from office before the end of a term by popular vote; it is usually initiated by a petition.

Reconstruction   period from 1865 through 1876, when Southern states were occupied by federal troops and under the control of the national government.

Red Scare   fears about the danger of communist subversion or invasion; after World War II, "Red Scare" tactics were used by Senator Joseph McCarthy and others for political purposes.

Referendum   a proposal submitted to a popular vote before putting it into effect.

Reform   to improve or change, especially a social institution.

Regulatory   enforcing the rules or laws.

Reparations   payments imposed on nations defeated in war to help the victors recover the costs of war.

Representative   1) a delegate or agent of another person or group of people; 2) a federal legislator; 3) a type of government by persons chosen from among the governed, usually by election.

Republican party   political party formed in the 1840s, opposed to the extension of slavery; Lincoln was the first Republican elected President (in 1860).

Reserved powers powers not specifically granted to Congress or the federal government under the Constitution, and so held to be reserved to the states.

Restraint of trade language used in the Sherman Antitrust Act (1890) to describe combinations and activities of groups (businesses, labor unions) that were prohibited under the Act.

Return to normalcy Republican campaign slogan of Warren G. Harding in 1920 following World War I.

Revenue the income of governments from taxation, tariffs, and other fees.

Reverse discrimination prejudice or bias against a class or person for the purpose of correcting discrimination against another class or person.

Right to counsel entitlement of an accused person to have an attorney present during questioning or trial.

Rights individual liberties protected by the state or federal constitutions.

Rights of Englishmen an expression of the American colonists during their struggle with England; they claimed to want only the same liberties and privileges enjoyed by British subjects in England, as established by Magna Carta, common law, and the English Bill of Rights, including habeas corpus, trial by jury, and representation in Parliament.

Rights of the accused include the 5th Amendment guarantee against self-incrimination and the right to counsel; also known as "Miranda rights," after the Supreme Court decision in the case of *Miranda* v. *Arizona* (1966).

Roaring Twenties the decade between the end of World War I and the beginning of the Great Depression.

Robber barons business owners of the latter part of the 19th century who often used unscrupulous methods to make their fortunes.

Roosevelt Corollary supplement to the Monroe Doctrine asserted by President Theodore Roosevelt, who claimed the right of the United States to exercise international police power in the Western Hemisphere and to intervene in the affairs of Latin American nations.

Rosie the Riveter World War II icon demonstrating the domestic contributions of women in the war effort.

"Rule of Reason" term used by the Supreme Court in its decision in the case of *Standard Oil Co.* v. *United States* (1911), which held that only "bad" trusts were illegal.

Salutary neglect phrase describing the belief that the American colonies benefited from lack of interest in their affairs by the British government during the period before 1763.

Satellite state a nation controlled by a more powerful nation.

Scopes trial the trial of John T. Scopes in Dayton, Tennessee, in 1925 for violating a state law prohibiting the teaching of Darwinian evolution. William Jennings Bryan was the prosecutor and Clarence Darrow represented Scopes, who was found guilty and fined $100.

Search and seizure police power to look for and hold evidence in the investigation and prosecution of a crime; evidence from unreasonable searches or searches without probable cause may be excluded from a trial.

Secession withdrawal of a member from a political group; withdrawal of a state from the Union.

Sectarian a member of a sect, which is a group of people forming a distinct unit within a larger group. Sectarians can be partisan and sometimes narrow-minded.

Sectionalism development of internal divisions based on geographic and economic alliances; rivalry between different areas of the country.

Securities and Exchange Commission federal agency established in 1934 to regulate the stock market and to prevent the abuses practiced during the 1920s that led to the stock market crash of 1929.

Sedition the act of stirring up rebellion against a government.

Segregation the isolation or separation of one group from another, usually applied to keeping whites and blacks apart.

Senate the part of the federal legislature made up of two members from each state.

Seneca Falls Convention convention held in Seneca Falls, New York, on July 19–20, 1848. It was the first women's rights convention held in the United States.

Separate but equal legal doctrine established by the Supreme Court in the case of *Plessy* v. *Ferguson* (1896) that separate accommodations for blacks and whites did not violate the Fourteenth Amendment if the accommodations were of equal quality. Overruled by the later Supreme Court decision in *Brown* v. *Board of Education* (1954).

Separation of church and state doctrine that government may not restrict the free exercise of religious beliefs nor support any religious group or principle.

Separation of powers doctrine that liberty of the people is best assured by the division of government into separate branches. *See also* Checks and balances.

Sexual harassment policy or practice of compelling female employees to submit to the sexual advances of male superiors or to endure verbal or physical harassment, in violation of the Civil Rights Act of 1964.

Sharecroppers tenant farmers who leased and cultivated pieces of land in exchange for a percentage of the crop.

Shays' Rebellion armed insurrection in western Massachusetts in the fall of 1786 led by Captain Daniel Shays and others in protest against economic policies and foreclosures of farms for fail-

ure to pay taxes. It was suppressed by the state militia, but it had a significant effect on the framing of the Constitution the following summer.

Sherman Antitrust Act passed in 1890 declaring combinations in restraint of trade to be illegal; it was passed to maintain competition in private industry and to correct abuses of companies that had gained monopoly power.

Sit-in action of protesters in occupying a public place to force concessions; especially by civil rights advocates seeking desegregation of public facilities.

Social contract the implied agreement among individuals in a community or between the people and their rulers.

Socialism political philosophy advocating ownership and operation of the means of production (such as land, mines, factories) by society as a collective whole, with all members sharing in the work and benefits. Socialist economic systems usually include government ownership and operation of industries.

Social mobility movement up or down the class scale within a society.

Social Security Act passed in 1935 to provide an income for persons who are disabled or aged and for families without a wage earner; it has become the basic means of support for retired persons who lack private pensions from employers.

Social welfare organized services for helping disadvantaged people.

Sovereign holding supreme authority.

Sovereignty the ultimate power and authority to make laws, either directly or through representatives; in a democracy, sovereignty lies in the people.

Special interest group or industry that seeks to influence government for its own benefit.

Spoils system system wherein government positions and offices are awarded to political supporters on the basis of party loyalty or service rather than qualification or merit; based on the saying "To the victor go the spoils"; the system was replaced to some extent by the Civil Service in the 1880s.

Stamp Act   enacted by Parliament in 1765, it required a tax stamp on all printed and legal documents. It was soon repealed after American resistance.

Star-Spangled Banner   the name by which the flag of the United States is known.

States' rights   group of doctrines holding that the states retained the power to overrule, oppose, or withdraw from the federal government if they chose.

Stock market crash   a rapid fall in the price of stocks. The great crash of 1929 was caused by overspeculation that increased stock prices far above their true value; prices started to fall when knowledgeable investors began to sell their shares; that forced speculators, who had invested with borrowed money, to sell as well, and the combined rush to sell caused a panic, which drove prices even lower.

Strict construction   doctrine that the Constitution limits governmental powers to those explicitly stated; contrast with Loose construction.

Subjugation   the act of bringing under control.

Subpoena   official written order commanding a person to appear in court or to produce specific items.

Subsidiary   in business, a company that is controlled by another company.

Subversion   the undermining, overthrowing, or destroying of an established institution, such as government.

Suffrage   the right to vote.

Supremacy clause   portion of the Constitution declaring it "the supreme law of the land" and overriding any state or local laws in conflict with it.

Supreme Court   the highest court in the federal judicial branch.

Taliban   Islamist militant and political group that ruled large parts of Afghanistan and its capital, Kabul, from September 1996 until October 2001. It gained diplomatic recognition from only three states: Pakistan, Saudi Arabia, and the United Arab Emirates. The main leader of the Taliban movement is Mullah Mohammed Omar. Today the Taliban continue to operate in Afghanistan and northwest Pakistan.

Tariff   taxes on imports into a country to collect revenues or to protect domestic industries.

Tea Party   an American populist political movement that is generally recognized as conservative and libertarian. The movement has supported political candidates since 2009.

Teapot Dome   federal oil reserve in Wyoming that was secretly and illegally leased to a financial backer of President Harding.

Temperance   moderation in the consumption of alcoholic beverages; a movement supporting governmental measures to curb alcohol consumption.

Tennessee Valley Authority   federal public works project established in 1933 that constructed dams and reengineered waterways to control flooding and generate electricity in seven Southern states.

Tenure   the act or right of holding an office.

Terrorism   the use of violence as unconventional warfare to intimidate a population. Terrorists usually do not belong to any recognized national armed force.

Third parties   political parties existing at various times in the United States other than the two predominant political parties.

Third World   the group of nations, especially in Asia and Africa, that were not aligned with either the Communist bloc or the Western democracies.

Three-fifths clause   clause in the Constitution saying that three fifths of the number of persons held as slaves be included in calculating representation in Congress, even though those persons were not citizens and were not entitled to vote. Superceded by the Fourteenth Amendment.

"Too Big to Fail" term that implies certain financial institutions are so large and so interconnected that their failure will be disastrous to an economy, and therefore a government has a responsibility to support them when they face difficulty.

Tories supporters of British rule during the Revolutionary War; also known as Loyalists.

Totalitarian characterized by the government's having total control over the lives of citizens.

Town meeting meeting of the citizens of a town as a legislative body.

Trade deficit the amount by which imports exceed exports; how much is owed to other nations.

Trade gap difference in amount between imports and exports.

Trail of Tears the forced relocation in 1838 of, among others, the Cherokee Native American tribe to the Western United States, which resulted in the deaths of an estimated 4,000 Cherokees. The Cherokees were not the only Native Americans forced to emigrate as a result of the Indian Removal efforts of the United States.

Treason acts that intentionally endanger the security or sovereignty of one's own nation; waging war against one's country or giving aid to its enemies.

Triangular trade pattern of commerce pursued in the late 18th and early 19th centuries by New England merchants who carried sugar and molasses from the West Indies to New England, rum and manufactured goods from New England to Africa, and slaves from Africa to the West Indies.

Truman Doctrine policy announced by President Truman in 1947, stating that the United States would provide military and economic aid to nations threatened by subversion or invasion; it was established specifically to assist Greece and Turkey, which were threatened with communist takeover.

Trust a combination of companies or industries established to reduce competition and increase profits.

Tweed Ring 1860s and 1870s corrupt, political boss of New York City's Democratic Party (Tammany Hall). Exposed by cartoonist Thomas Nast.

Tyranny absolute and arbitrary power without legal restraints.

Uncle Tom's Cabin inflammatory 1851 anti-slavery literary work by Harriet Beecher Stowe. Sold 300,000 copies in one year.

Unconditional surrender total surrender without exceptions or conditions; the phrase was made popular by Ulysses S. Grant.

Unconstitutional prohibited by or in opposition to the principles of the Constitution.

Underclass class of the permanently poor.

Underground railroad extensive system of escape routes for slaves coming to the north and many on to Canada. Harriet Tubman; underground railroad conductor.

Unicameral of a legislature, having only one house or chamber.

Union 1) the political combination of the states; 2) the northern and border states that opposed secession during the Civil War; 3) an organization of workers seeking collective bargaining with their employer.

United Nations an organization of over 150 nations formed in 1945 to deal with international disputes and threats to world peace.

Universal suffrage the right of all citizens to vote, regardless of sex, race, or economic status.

Unwritten Constitution governmental practices and institutions not specifically set down in the Constitution but based upon custom and practice.

Utopian advocating impossibly idealistic or impractical forms of government or society.

Versailles Treaty peace treaty signed in 1919 between Germany and the Allies; it required Germany to give up its colonies, pay substantial reparations, and surrender territory to France, Poland, and Czechoslovakia.

Veto action by an executive official preventing the enactment of a legislative act. A veto by the President can be overridden by a two-thirds majority of Congress. *See also* Pocket veto.

VISTA Volunteers in Service to America, a program of President Johnson's 1964 Economic Opportunity Act.

Wagner Act (1935) New Deal legislation that established the National Labor Relations Board to solve labor/management disputes and avoid strikes and job actions.

War on Poverty President Johnson's domestic programs for social renovation, including the VISTA, Job Corps, and Head Start programs and the establishing of the Department of Housing and Urban Development.

War Powers Act law passed in 1973 to limit the power of the President to use armed forces in combat without the authorization of Congress; it was adopted in response to the Vietnam War, in which millions of armed forces were sent to Vietnam without a declaration of war.

Warsaw Pact organization of Soviet-led countries in response to the 1949 creation of the North Atlantic Treaty Organization.

Watergate hotel in Washington, D.C., where the national Democratic party headquarters were burglarized in 1972 by operatives of the Republican Committee to Reelect the President (Nixon). Attempts by the White House staff to cover up links to the burglars led to a widespread scandal and the resignation of President Nixon.

Weapons of mass destruction (WMD) arms that have the ability to kill massive numbers of people. Usually refers to nuclear, chemical, biological, and radiological weapons.

Whigs in the United States from around 1800 until the Civil War, a political party opposed to the Jeffersonian Republicans and Jacksonian Democrats. Many of its supporters later joined the Republican party.

Whiskey Rebellion armed insurrection in 1792 by settlers in western Pennsylvania and Virginia protesting federal excise tax on distilled spirits (whiskey). Suppressed by federal troops under Washington, who pardoned most of the participants.

Yalta Agreements agreements reached between Roosevelt, Churchill, and Stalin at Yalta in February 1945, regarding the organization of postwar Europe in anticipation of the defeat of Germany. The agreements divided Germany and Berlin into temporary zones of occupation and established the basis for the United Nations.

Yellow journalism irresponsible, sensational, or misleading reporting of news.

Zimmermann note (1917) publication of German correspondence with Mexico in which Germany promised Mexico recovery of the Mexican Cession if Mexico would assist Germany in the world war. It inflamed anti-Germany feelings.

Examination June 2014

United States History and Government

PART I: MULTIPLE CHOICE

Directions (1–50): For each statement or question, write in the space provided the *number* of the word or expression that, of those given, best completes the statement or answers the question.

Base your answers to questions 1 and 2 on the time line below and on your knowledge of social studies.

1 Which conclusion is best supported by the information on the time line?

1 Britain eventually granted the colonies representation in Parliament.
2 Only elected British officials had the right to levy taxes.
3 Britain's efforts to increase control over the colonies were not successful.
4 Creation of the First Continental Congress was an immediate reaction to the passage of the Stamp Act.

1 _____

2 Which of these events would be placed on the time line before 1763?

1 Boston Massacre
2 French and Indian War
3 Battle of Saratoga
4 passage of Northwest Ordinance

2 _____

3 From the 1600s through the 1800s, the major reason for the westward movement of settlers was to

1 escape urban unrest in coastal cities
2 avoid high taxes in the East
3 find manufacturing jobs in the Midwest
4 acquire new areas of fertile soil for agriculture

3 _____

4 Colonial-era New England town meetings and the Virginia House of Burgesses were both

1 early social reform movements
2 attempts to build a strong national government
3 steps in the growth of representative democracy
4 efforts to regulate trade with Native American Indians

4 _____

5 The years between the end of the American Revolution and the ratification of the Constitution are sometimes called the "critical period" because

1 the western territories were left ungoverned
2 the United States fought a war with France
3 Spain refused to sell Florida to the United States
4 the central government failed to solve many economic problems

5 _____

Base your answers to questions 6 and 7 on the speakers' statements below and on your knowledge of social studies.

Speaker A: Our national government should be strong. State governments should have only limited powers.

Speaker B: A bicameral legislature would protect the power of both the large states and the small states.

Speaker C: The expansion of the national government will lead to tyranny.

Speaker D: The executive branch should have significant power.

6 Which speaker is expressing an idea that was included in the Great Compromise during the drafting of the Constitution in 1787?

1 *A*   3 *C*
2 *B*   4 *D*

6 _____

7 During the debate over ratification of the Constitution, people who agreed with the statements of *Speakers A* and *D* became known as

1 Loyalists
2 Federalists
3 Antifederalists
4 Democratic Republicans   7____

---

8 Which protection guaranteed by the first amendment to the United States Constitution was influenced by the trial of John Peter Zenger (1735)?

1 freedom of the press
2 freedom of religion
3 right to assemble
4 right to petition   8____

9 The term *judicial review* is best defined as the

1 right of a defendant to appeal the verdict of a jury
2 ability of Congress to create new federal courts
3 authority of the Senate to confirm Supreme Court justices
4 power of the Supreme Court to determine the constitutionality of laws   9____

10 According to the United States Constitution, the federal census is used to determine the

1 size of the United States Supreme Court
2 maximum number of cabinet members
3 apportionment of members in the House of Representatives
4 number of senators allotted to each state   10____

11 During George Washington's presidency, the authority of the federal government was strengthened by the

1 elimination of political parties
2 suppression of the Whiskey Rebellion
3 formation of a military alliance with England
4 establishment of a national language   11 _____

12 Under the leadership of Chief Justice John Marshall (1801–1835), the Supreme Court expanded the influence of the national government by

1 forcing states to grant relief from personal debt
2 authorizing the president to use troops without congressional approval
3 ending the importation of enslaved Africans
4 strengthening federal powers over interstate commerce and banking   12 _____

Base your answer to question 13 on the map below and on your knowledge of social studies.

The Louisiana Purchase

Source: *American Military History*, Center of Military History, United States Army, 1989 (adapted)

13 The map shows the exploration routes of Lewis and Clark and of Zebulon Pike. A valid conclusion based on this map is that these expeditions

1 faced few barriers from natural features
2 avoided land claimed by other countries
3 used river systems to help them on their journeys
4 took the most direct routes to reach the Pacific Ocean

13 _____

14 Between 1800 and 1830, the National Road and the Erie Canal were built to connect which regions?

1 Atlantic Coast and Midwest
2 South and New England
3 Pacific Coast and Gulf Coast
4 Great Plains and Rocky Mountains   14____

15 During the 1840s, supporters of Manifest Destiny favored

1 closing the frontier to settlement
2 ending the American System
3 acquiring Texas and California
4 ceding the Oregon territory to Russia   15____

16 Which constitutional principle was the main focus of the North–South conflicts that led to the Civil War?

1 States rights
2 due process of law
3 separation of powers
4 presidential veto power   16____

17 Slavery throughout the United States was permanently abolished by the

1 ratification of the Constitution of the United States
2 approval of the Republican Party platform of 1860
3 issuance of the Emancipation Proclamation
4 adoption of the 13th amendment to the Constitution   17____

18 "Since the Southern states never legally left the Union, they should be restored to the Union as soon as possible."

The position expressed in this statement is most closely associated with the beliefs of

1 Robert E. Lee   3 Jefferson Davis
2 Thaddeus Stevens   4 Abraham Lincoln   18 _____

Base your answer to question 19 on the poem excerpt below and on your knowledge of social studies.

"Keep ancient lands, your storied pomp!" cries she
With silent lips. "Give me your tired, your poor,
Your huddled masses yearning to breathe free,
The wretched refuse of your teeming shore.
Send these, the homeless, tempest-tost to me,
I lift my lamp beside the golden door!"
     — Emma Lazarus, "The New Colossus," 1883

19 Which attitude about immigration is reflected in this poem, which is inscribed on the Statue of Liberty?

1 People from all nations should be welcomed.
2 Educated professionals should be given preference.
3 Quotas should be adopted to limit certain ethnic groups.
4 The influx of unskilled people should be restricted.   19 _____

20 A major result of the Spanish-American War (1898) was that the United States

1 adopted a policy of isolationism
2 assumed a more prominent role in world affairs
3 gave up control of territories outside the Western Hemisphere
4 increased foreign aid to European allies   20 _____

21 During the Progressive Era, support for a graduated income tax was based primarily on the

1 desire of corporations to reduce their taxes
2 need to raise income from the lower classes
3 belief that all people should be taxed the same
4 resentment over the unequal distribution of wealth   21 _____

22 President Theodore Roosevelt strengthened the Monroe Doctrine by establishing the policy that the United States would

1 require Latin American nations to end trade with Europe
2 reduce Asian influence in Latin America
3 intervene in Latin America to prevent European interference
4 develop military alliances with Pacific naval powers   22 _____

Base your answers to questions 23 and 24 on the cartoon below and on your knowledge of social studies.

The Protectors of Our Industries.

Source: Bernhard Gillam, *Puck*, 1883 (adapted)

23 Which statement most accurately expresses the main idea of this 1883 cartoon?

1 Most workers in the United States can become business owners.

2 Business owners have achieved wealth through their own hard work.

3 Social classes arise from the natural differences in the abilities of individuals.

4 The wealthy are benefiting from the efforts of the working class.

23 _____

24 The problem shown in the cartoon was addressed during the late 1800s primarily by the

1 organization of labor unions
2 implementation of the Populist Party platform
3 elimination of child labor
4 increase in immigrant workers

24 _____

Base your answers to questions 25 and 26 on the cartoon below and on your knowledge of social studies.

A NAUSEATING JOB, BUT IT MUST BE DONE

Source: *Utica Saturday Globe*, 1906 (adapted)

25 Which book was responsible for prompting the investigation illustrated in this cartoon?

1 *The Octopus* by Frank Norris
2 *The Jungle* by Upton Sinclair
3 *The Shame of the Cities* by Lincoln Steffens
4 *How the Other Half Lives* by Jacob Riis

25 _____

26 In 1906, the federal government responded to the situation shown in the cartoon by

  1 taking control of meatpacking facilities
  2 sending federal troops to end a strike by meat-packers
  3 banning imported meat products
  4 authorizing government inspection of meat processing plants

26 _____

Base your answer to question 27 on the passage below and on your knowledge of social studies.

We intend to begin on the first of February unrestricted submarine warfare. We shall endeavor in spite of this to keep the United States of America neutral. In the event of this not succeeding, we make Mexico a proposal or alliance on the following basis: make war together, make peace together, generous financial support and an understanding on our part that Mexico is to reconquer the lost territory in Texas, New Mexico, and Arizona....

— Zimmerman telegram, 1917

27 The disclosure of this document contributed to

  1 a declaration of war against Mexico
  2 the entry of the United States into World War I
  3 the passage of the Treaty of Versailles
  4 a restriction on immigration from Latin America

27 _____

28 **"Harding Rejects Wilson's Foreign Policy—Wants Return to 'Normalcy'"**

"Coolidge Declares: 'The Chief Business of the American People Is Business'"

"Hoover Calls for 'Rugged Individualism'; Rejects Paternalism and Socialism"

Which policy of Republican presidents in the 1920s is most consistent with the positions stated in these headlines?

1 The United States should assist unions and provide old-age insurance.
2 The United States should acquire and protect an empire.
3 The federal government should support the poor and raise farm prices.
4 The federal government should assist business and limit foreign commitments.

28 _____

29 During the 1920s, which economic trend helped cause the Great Depression?

1 buying goods on credit
2 saving rather than spending
3 continuing shortages of consumer goods
4 imposing low tariffs on imported products

29 _____

30 What was a major result of President Herbert Hoover's use of the military to drive the Bonus Army out of the nation's capital?

1 Army veterans widely approved President Hoover's decision.
2 President Hoover's reelection campaign was damaged.
3 Habeas corpus was suspended across the country.
4 The Supreme Court declared the action unconstitutional.

30 _____

31 The primary purpose of the National Labor Relations Act of 1935 (Wagner Act) was to

1 allow factory owners to use court injunctions against workers
2 guarantee collective bargaining rights
3 establish the Social Security system
4 ban the use of strikes by unions

31 _____

32 What was one economic consequence of President Franklin D. Roosevelt's New Deal?

1 Bank deregulation encouraged investment.
2 Major industries were nationalized.
3 Balanced budgets became the model for economic stability.
4 The role of the federal government in the economy expanded.

32 _____

Base your answer to question 33 on the passage below and on your knowledge of social studies.

...We must be the great arsenal of democracy. For us this is an emergency as serious as war itself. We must apply ourselves to our task with the same resolution, the same sense of urgency, the same spirit of patriotism and sacrifice as we would show were we at war....

— President Franklin D. Roosevelt, December 29, 1940

33 In urging the United States to become the "arsenal of democracy," President Franklin D. Roosevelt meant the nation should

1 make its neutrality laws more restrictive
2 create a military draft
3 provide war materials to Allied nations
4 send troops to Europe to fight in the war

33 _____

Base your answer to question 34 on the poster below and on your knowledge of social studies.

"No loyal citizen of the United States should be denied the democratic right to exercise the responsibilities of his citizenship, regardless of his ancestry.

"The principle on which this country was founded and by which it has always been governed is that Americanism is a matter of the mind and heart.

"Americanism is not, and never was, a matter of race or ancestry.

"Every loyal American citizen should be given the opportunity to serve this country wherever his skills will make the greatest contribution—whether it be in the ranks of our armed forces, war production, agriculture, government service, or other work essential to the war effort."

THE PRESIDENT OF THE UNITED STATES, FEBRUARY 3, 1943

Source: Office of War Information, 1943 (adapted)

34 What was one purpose of this World War II poster?

1 discouraging discrimination in employment
2 supporting the internment of Japanese Americans
3 requiring all citizens to take a loyalty oath
4 promoting a more diversified economy

34 _____

35 During World War II, the federal government urged Americans to support the war effort by

1 manufacturing more consumer goods
2 increasing spending to stimulate the economy
3 reducing consumption of resources needed for the military
4 investing their savings in the stock market

35 _____

36 The United States created the Marshall Plan (1947) as a program to

1 develop an atomic bomb
2 increase civil defense during the Cold War
3 provide economic aid to war-damaged Europe
4 deliver weapons to Nationalist China

36 _____

Base your answer to question 37 on the cartoon below and on your knowledge of social studies.

"Be Sure To Give Mine Special Attention"

Source: Herblock, *Washington Post*, November 23, 1955 (adapted)

37 The cartoon suggests that during the 1950s leaders in government and education

  1 were challenged by the baby boom that followed World War II

  2 provided greater resources for rural schools than for urban schools

  3 placed excessive burdens on schools through federal legislation

  4 supported separate classrooms for students based on gender   37 _____

---

38 In 1948, the United States responded to the Soviet blockade of West Berlin by

  1 tearing down the wall between East Berlin and West Berlin

  2 supporting United Nations peacekeeping efforts in West Germany

  3 shutting down transportation to East Berlin

  4 organizing an airlift of supplies to West Berlin   38 _____

39 What was a major effect of the creation of the interstate highway system on the United States?

  1 the loss of population in the Sun Belt

  2 a decline in federal funding for urban renewal projects

  3 an increase in suburbanization

  4 an increase in congressional representation from New England   39 _____

Base your answer to question 40 on the newspaper headlines below and on your knowledge of social studies.

SOVIET FIRES EARTH SATELLITE INTO SPACE;
IT IS CIRCLING THE GLOBE AT 18,000 M. P. H.;
SPHERE TRACKED IN 4 CROSSINGS OVER U. S.

Source: *New York Times*, October 5, 1957

MEN WALK ON MOON
ASTRONAUTS LAND ON PLAIN;
COLLECT ROCKS, PLANT FLAG

Source: *New York Times*, July 21, 1969

40 Which statement most accurately explains the relationship between the events described in these newspaper headlines?

1 The launch of *Sputnik* prompted the United States to expand its space program.
2 Space exploration ended competition between the United States and the Soviet Union.
3 Congress reduced military spending to fund space exploration.
4 The United States and the Soviet Union began sharing space technology.

40 _____

41 In the 1960s, a common goal of President John F. Kennedy's Alliance for Progress and Peace Corps was to

1 improve Arab-Israeli relations
2 fight the spread of the AIDS epidemic
3 end colonialism in Latin America and Asia
4 support developing nations while containing communism

41 _____

711

42 Both the Nuclear Test Ban Treaty of 1963 and the Strategic Arms Limitation Treaty (SALT) of 1972 were attempts to

1 settle boundary disputes in Europe
2 promote the peaceful use of atomic energy
3 ease Cold War tensions
4 share military technologies with developing nations   42 _____

Base your answer to question 43 on the passage below and on your knowledge of social studies.

...In this present crisis, government is not the solution to our problem; government is the problem. From time to time we've been tempted to believe that society has become too complex to be managed by self-rule, that government by an elite group is superior to government for, by, and of the people. Well, if no one among us is capable of governing himself, then who among us has the capacity to govern someone else? All of us together, in and out of government, must bear the burden. The solutions we seek must be equitable, with no one group singled out to pay a higher price....

— President Ronald Reagan, Inaugural Address,
January 20, 1981

43 The Reagan administration tried to deal with the situation described in this statement by

1 limiting the role of the federal government
2 reducing military defense expenditures
3 increasing regulations on business
4 expanding the power of federal employee unions   43 _____

Base your answer to question 44 on the statement below and on your knowledge of social studies.

My fellow citizens, events in Iraq have now reached the final days of decision. For more than a decade, the United States and other nations have pursued patient and honorable efforts to disarm the Iraqi regime without war. That regime pledged to reveal and destroy all its weapons of mass destruction as a condition for ending the Persian Gulf war in 1991....

— President George W. Bush, March 17, 2003

44 Which action did President George W. Bush take following this statement?

1 withdrawing from the Persian Gulf War
2 ordering American forces to invade Iraq
3 removing economic sanctions on Iraq
4 threatening Iraq with nuclear weapons

44 _____

Base your answer to question 45 on the cartoon below and on your knowledge of social studies.

GOING DARK

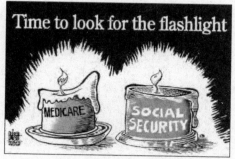

Source: Randy Bish, *Pittsburgh Tribune-Review*, May 15, 2009 (adapted)

45 Which statement most accurately expresses the main idea of this cartoon?

  1 Medicare and Social Security are not helping Americans.
  2 The financial future of Medicare and Social Security is in jeopardy.
  3 Social Security will run out of money before Medicare.
  4 Medicare and Social Security have been abolished.

45 _____

46 The migrations of African Americans from the South to the North during World War I and World War II are most directly related to

  1 the availability of factory jobs
  2 a widespread farming crisis
  3 plans to pursue military careers
  4 access to free land

46 _____

47 President Lyndon B. Johnson's Great Society programs built on ideas set forth in President Franklin D. Roosevelt's New Deal by

  1 supporting the expansion of social welfare programs
  2 reinstating government loyalty lists
  3 opposing new immigration reform measures
  4 relying on balancing the federal budget

47 _____

48 Which action illustrates the concept of checks and balances?

1 President Harry Truman issuing an executive order to desegregate the military
2 Congress overriding President Richard Nixon's veto of the War Powers Act
3 the House of Representatives Ethics Committee reviewing members' financial records
4 President Jimmy Carter selecting Walter Mondale as his vice presidential running mate

48 _____

49 Which action did the federal government take in response to Cold War tensions after World War II and again in response to the September 11, 2001, terrorist attacks?

1 expanding civil rights protections
2 monitoring persons suspected of endangering national security
3 withdrawing from international organizations
4 restricting trade with allies

49 _____

50 Both President Franklin D. Roosevelt and President Barack Obama undertook banking and financial reforms during their administrations to

1 give states a greater role in the regulatory process
2 end foreign influence in the banking systems
3 restore stability to the national economy
4 reduce government involvement in the economy

50 _____

In developing your answer to Part II, be sure to keep these general definitions in mind:

    (a) <u>describe</u> means "to illustrate something in words or tell about it"

    (b) <u>explain</u> means "to make plain or understandable; to give reasons for or causes of; to show the logical development or relationships of"

    (c) <u>discuss</u> means "to make observations about something using facts, reasoning, and argument; to present in some detail"

PART II: THEMATIC ESSAY

Directions: Write a well-organized essay that includes an introduction, several paragraphs addressing the task below, and a conclusion.

Theme: Change—The Supreme Court

> Throughout United States history, the Supreme Court has dealt with many controversial issues. The Court's decisions in these cases have had a significant impact on the United States and/or on American society.

Task:

> Select *two* United States Supreme Court decisions that have had a significant impact on American society and for *each*
> * Describe the historical circumstances surrounding the case
> * Explain the Court's decision in the case
> * Discuss the impact of the decision on the United States and/or on American society

You may use any Supreme Court decision from your study of United States history. Some suggestions you might wish to consider include *Worcester* v. *Georgia* (1832), *Dred Scott* v. *Sanford* (1857), *Plessy* v. *Ferguson* (1896), *Schenck* v. *United States* (1919), *Korematsu* v. *United States* (1944), *Engel* v. *Vitale* (1962), *Miranda* v. *Arizona* (1966), *New York Times* v. *United States* (1971), *Roe* v. *Wade* (1973), and *United States* v. *Nixon* (1974).

You are *not* limited to these suggestions.

Do not use Brown v. Board of Education of Topeka as one of your Supreme Court decisions.*

Guidelines:

In your essay, be sure to:
- Develop all aspects of the task
- Support the theme with relevant facts, examples, and details
- Use a logical and clear plan of organization, including an introduction and a conclusion that are beyond a restatement of the theme

---

*Students were instructed not to use *Brown* v. *Board* because information in the Document-Based Question on this exam would have helped them write their thematic essay. However, students could have used their knowledge of *Brown* in their discussion of Dr. Martin Luther King Jr.'s "Letter from Birmingham Jail" in their DBQ essay.

In developing your answers to Part III, be sure to keep these general definitions in mind:

(a) <u>describe</u> means "to illustrate something in words or tell about it"

(b) <u>discuss</u> means "to make observations about something using facts, reasoning, and argument; to present in some detail"

PART III: DOCUMENT-BASED ESSAY

This question is based on the accompanying documents. The question is designed to test your ability to work with historical documents. Some of these documents have been edited for the purposes of this question. As you analyze the documents, take into account the source of each document and any point of view that may be presented in the document. Keep in mind that the language used in a document may reflect the historical context of the time in which it was written.

Historical Context:

During the 1960s, writers frequently reflected social conditions that influenced United States history. These writers increased public awareness of critical issues facing the nation and had an important impact on the United States and on American society. Three such writers were **Dr. Martin Luther King Jr.** (**"Letter from Birmingham Jail"**), **Rachel Carson** (*Silent Spring*), and **Betty Friedan** (*The Feminine Mystique*).

Task:

Using the information from the documents and your knowledge of United States history, answer the questions that follow each document in Part A. Your answers to the questions will help you write the Part B essay in which you will be asked to

Choose *two* writers from the 1960s mentioned in the historical context and for *each*
- Describe the historical circumstances surrounding an issue addressed by the writer
- Discuss how the writer influenced the United States and/or American society

718

Part A: Short-Answer Questions

Directions: Analyze the documents and answer the short-answer questions that follow each document in the space provided.

Document 1a

> ...In any nonviolent campaign there are four basic steps: (1) collection of the facts to determine whether injustices are alive; (2) negotiation; (3) self-purification; and (4) direct action. We have gone through all of these steps in Birmingham. There can be no gainsaying [denying] of the fact that racial injustice engulfs this community. Birmingham is probably the most thoroughly segregated city in the United States. Its ugly record of police brutality is known in every section of this country. Its unjust treatment of Negroes [African Americans] in the courts is a notorious reality. There have been more unsolved bombings of Negro homes and churches in Birmingham than any city in this nation. These are the hard, brutal, and unbelievable facts. On the basis of these conditions Negro leaders sought to negotiate with the city fathers. But the political leaders consistently refused to engage in good faith negotiation....

Source: Dr. Martin Luther King Jr.,
"Letter from Birmingham Jail," April 16, 1963

Document 1b

During civil rights protests in Birmingham, Alabama, Public Safety Commissioner Eugene "Bull" Connor was in charge of the police and fire departments. Acting on his orders, firefighters turned their hoses on demonstrators.

Source: AP/World Wide Photos, May 1963

1 Based on these documents, what were **two** examples of racial injustice addressed by Dr. Martin Luther King Jr.? [2]

(1)_____

_____

(2)_____

_____

Document 2

Two years after writing "Letter from Birmingham Jail," Dr. Martin Luther King Jr. was asked by an interviewer if the events that followed its publication justified the sentiments expressed in that letter.

> ...I would say yes. Two or three important and constructive things have happened which can be at least partially attributed to that letter. By now, nearly a million copies of the letter have been widely circulated in churches of most of the major denominations. It helped to focus greater international attention upon what was happening in Birmingham. And I am sure that without Birmingham, the march on Washington wouldn't have been called— which in my mind was one of the most creative steps the Negro [African American] struggle has taken. The march on Washington spurred and galvanized [strengthened] the consciences of millions. It gave the American Negro a new national and international stature. The press of the world recorded the story as nearly a quarter of a million Americans, white and black, assembled in grandeur as a testimonial to the Negro's determination to achieve freedom in this generation....

Source: James M. Washington, ed., *A Testament of Hope: The Essential Writings and Speeches of Martin Luther King, Jr.*, HarperCollins

2 According to Dr. Martin Luther King Jr., what were *two* effects of his "Letter from Birmingham Jail"?   [2]

(1)_____

_____

(2)_____

_____

Document 3

...Today we are committed to a worldwide struggle to promote and protect the rights of all who wish to be free. And when Americans are sent to Viet-Nam or West Berlin, we do not ask for whites only. It ought to be possible, therefore, for American students of any color to attend any public institution they select without having to be backed up by troops....

Now the time has come for this Nation to fulfill its promise. The events in Birmingham and elsewhere have so increased the cries for equality that no city or State or legislative body can prudently choose to ignore them.

The fires of frustration and discord are burning in every city, North and South, where legal remedies are not at hand. Redress is sought in the streets, in demonstrations, parades, and protests which create tensions and threaten violence and threaten lives....

I am, therefore, asking the Congress to enact legislation giving all Americans the right to be served in facilities which are open to the public—hotels, restaurants, theaters, retail stores, and similar establishments....

Source: President John F. Kennedy, Radio and Television Report to the American People on Civil Rights, June 11, 1963

3 According to President John F. Kennedy, why should Congress pass civil rights legislation? [1]

_____

_____

Document 4

Rachel Carson, a friend of Olga Owens Huckins, was sent a copy of this letter in 1958.

To the Editor of The [Boston] Herald:

Mr. R. C. Codman, who wrote that he "is actively associated" with the Commonwealth of Mass. aerial spraying programs for alleged mosquito control, also says that state tests have proved that the mixture used—fuel oil with DDT [chemical insecticide]—last summer over Plymouth and Barnstable Counties was entirely harmless....

Dr. Robert Cushman Murphy, distinguished scientist, observed after New York State sprayed Long Island in the same way, that no fish in still waters survived. All bees in a large section of the state were killed. Indeed, evidence of the havoc wrought by all air spraying of DDT is accumulating so rapidly that Mr. Codman's placid [calm] assurance becomes absurd.

The mosquito control plane flew over our small town last summer. Since we live close to the marshes, we were treated to several lethal doses as the pilot crisscrossed our place. And we consider the spraying of active poison over private land to be a serious aerial intrusion....

The remedy of this situation [killing the mosquitoes] is not to double the strength of the spray and come again. It is to STOP THE SPRAYING OF POISONS FROM THE AIR everywhere until all the evidence, biological and scientific, immediate and long run, of the effects upon wild life and human beings are known....

Olga Owens Huckins
Duxbury, 1958

Source: Adler and Adler, eds., *Letters of the Century: America 1900–1999*, Dial Press

4 According to this letter, what is **one** reason Olga Huckins is concerned about spraying DDT?   [1]

_____

_____

Document 5a

In *Silent Spring*, Rachel Carson warned about what might happen if the use of dangerous pesticides such as DDT continued.

...There was a strange stillness. The birds, for example—where had they gone? Many people spoke of them, puzzled and disturbed. The feeding stations in the backyards were deserted. The few birds seen anywhere were moribund [dying]; they trembled violently and could not fly. It was a spring without voices. On the mornings that had once throbbed with the dawn chorus of robins, catbirds, doves, jays, wrens, and scores of other bird voices there was now no sound; only silence lay over the fields and woods and marsh....

The roadsides, once so attractive, were now lined with browned and withered vegetation as though swept by fire. These, too, were silent, deserted by all living things. Even the streams were now lifeless. Anglers [fishermen] no longer visited them, for all the fish had died.

In the gutters under the eaves and between the shingles of the roofs, a white granular powder [DDT] still showed a few patches; some weeks before it had fallen like snow upon the roofs and the lawns, the fields and streams....

Source: Rachel Carson, *Silent Spring*,
Houghton Mifflin, 1962 (adapted)

Document 5b

Source: L.D. Warren, *Cincinnati Enquirer*,1972,
in Jerry Robinson, ed., *The 1970s: Best Political
Cartoons of the Decade*, McGraw-Hill

5 Based on these documents, what is **one** possible effect of DDT on the environment? [1]

_____

_____

Document 6a

According to a 1970 Gallup poll, 53 percent of the American public saw controlling air and water pollution as a critical issue, up from only 17 percent five years earlier. This made the environment an important political concern for many elected officials, including President Richard Nixon.

> ...The great question of the seventies is, shall we surrender to our surroundings, or shall we make our peace with nature and begin to make reparations [compensation] for the damage we have done to our air, to our land, and to our water?...
>
> We still think of air as free. But clean air is not free, and neither is clean water. The price tag on pollution control is high. Through our years of past carelessness we incurred a debt to nature, and now that debt is being called....
>
> I shall propose to this Congress a $10 billion nationwide clean waters program to put modern municipal waste treatment plants in every place in America where they are needed to make our waters clean again, and do it now. We have the industrial capacity, if we begin now, to build them all within 5 years. This program will get them built within 5 years....
>
> The automobile is our worst polluter of the air. Adequate control requires further advances in engine design and fuel composition. We shall intensify our research, set increasingly strict standards, and strengthen enforcement procedures—and we shall do it now....

Source: President Richard M. Nixon,
State of the Union Address, January 22, 1970

6a According to the 1970 State of the Union address, what is **one** proposal made by President Richard M. Nixon to address the concerns of environmentalists such as Rachel Carson? [1]

_____

_____

Document 6b

> ...*Silent Spring* planted the seeds of a new activism that has grown into one of the great popular forces of all time. When Rachel Carson died, in the spring of 1964, it was becoming clear that her voice would never be silenced. She had awakened not only our nation but the world. The publication of *Silent Spring* can properly be seen as the beginning of the modern environmental movement....

Source: Vice President Al Gore, introduction
to 1994 edition of *Silent Spring*

6*b* According to Vice President Al Gore, what was one effect of the publication of *Silent Spring*? [1]

_____

_____

Document 7

...It also is time to stop giving lip service to the idea that there are no battles left to be fought for women in America, that women's rights have already been won. It is ridiculous to tell girls to keep quiet when they enter a new field, or an old one, so the men will not notice they are there. In almost every professional field, in business and in the arts and sciences, women are still treated as second-class citizens. It would be a great service to tell girls who plan to work in society to expect this subtle, uncomfortable discrimination—tell them not to be quiet, and hope it will go away, but fight it. A girl should not expect special privileges because of her sex, but neither should she "adjust" to prejudice and discrimination....

Source: Betty Friedan, *The Feminine Mystique*,
W.W. Norton, 1963

7 According to Betty Friedan, what is *one* form of discrimination experienced by women in the early 1960s? [1]

_____

_____

Document 8

...With its impassioned yet clear-eyed analysis of the issues that affected women's lives in the decades after World War II—including enforced domesticity, limited career prospects and, as chronicled in later editions, the campaign for legalized abortion—"The Feminine Mystique" is widely regarded as one of the most influential nonfiction books of the 20th century. Published by W. W. Norton & Company, the book had sold more than three million copies by the year 2000 and has been translated into many languages.

"The Feminine Mystique" made Ms. Friedan world famous. It also made her one of the chief architects of the women's liberation movement of the late 1960's and afterward, a sweeping social upheaval that harked back to [recalled] the suffrage campaigns of the turn of the century and would be called feminism's second wave....

Source: Margalit Fox, *New York Times*, February 5, 2006

8 According to Margalit Fox, what is **one** issue addressed in *The Feminine Mystique* that concerned American women after World War II?   [1]

_____

_____

Document 9a

> DON'T iron while the strike is hot," advised the slogan of the Women's Strike for Equality. No one knows how many shirts lay wrinkling in laundry baskets last week as thousands of women across the country turned out for the first big demonstration of the Women's Liberation movement. The strike, on the 50th anniversary of the proclamation of the women's suffrage amendment, drew small crowds by antiwar or civil rights standards, yet was easily the largest women's rights rally since the suffrage protests....
>
> Betty Friedan, whose 1963 book *The Feminine Mystique* is credited with reviving the feminist movement, originally called the strike at the conference of the National Organization for Women in March. As head of the hastily assembled National Women's Strike Coalition, she had predicted an impressive turnout and was not dismayed by the figures. "It exceeded my wildest dreams," Friedan said. "It's now a political movement; the message is clear. The politicians are taking heed already."...

Source: *Time*, September 7, 1970

9a Based on this document, what was **one** way *The Feminine Mystique* influenced the women's movement of the 1960s and early 1970s?   [1]

_____

_____

Document 9b

...Many factors have contributed to that record of [women's] achievement. The reform efforts of suffragists in the nineteenth and early twentieth centuries were important, as were those of the feminists of the 1960s. American women owe a great deal to those who fought for the passage of civil rights legislation in the 1960s, particularly the Equal Pay Act of 1963 and the Civil Rights Act of 1964. Demographic and economic trends also shaped women's experiences.

The personal choices women have made are perhaps the most important and least appreciated factor in women's economic progress over the years. Decisions to enter previously male-dominated fields of education and employment, to marry and bear children later in life, to join the work force, and to leave the work force to raise children have all had an enormous effect on whether women can achieve total parity with men. Some of those choices, such as leaving the work force for a time to raise children or working part-time, have a negative effect on women's earnings. Others, such as entering previously all-male fields, have led to remarkable gains for women in the work force....

Source: Furchtgott-Roth and Stolba, *Women's Figures: An Illustrated Guide to the Economic Progress of Women in America*, The AEI Press and Independent Women's Forum, 1999

9b According to Furchtgott-Roth and Stolba, what is **one** factor that contributed to the economic progress of women? [1]

_____

_____

Part B: Essay

Directions: Write a well-organized essay that includes an introduction, several paragraphs, and a conclusion. Use evidence from *at least four* documents in your essay. Support your response with relevant facts, examples, and details. Include additional outside information.

Historical Context:

During the 1960s, writers frequently reflected social conditions that influenced United States history. These writers increased public awareness of critical issues facing the nation and had an important impact on the United States and on American society. Three such writers were **Dr. Martin Luther King Jr.** (**"Letter from Birmingham Jail"**), **Rachel Carson** (*Silent Spring*), and **Betty Friedan** (*The Feminine Mystique*).

Task:

Using the information from the documents and your knowledge of United States history, write an essay in which you

Choose *two* writers from the 1960s mentioned in the historical context and for *each*
- Describe the historical circumstances surrounding an issue addressed by the writer
- Discuss how the writer influenced the United States and/or American society

Guidelines:

In your essay, be sure to:
- Develop all aspects of the task
- Incorporate information from *at least four* documents
- Incorporate relevant outside information
- Support the theme with relevant facts, examples, and details
- Use a logical and clear plan of organization, including an introduction and a conclusion that are beyond a restatement of the theme

Answers
June 2014
United States History and Government

Answer Key

PART I

1. 3	14. 1	27. 2	40. 1
2. 2	15. 3	28. 4	41. 4
3. 4	16. 1	29. 1	42. 3
4. 3	17. 4	30. 2	43. 1
5. 4	18. 4	31. 2	44. 2
6. 2	19. 1	32. 4	45. 2
7. 2	20. 2	33. 3	46. 1
8. 1	21. 4	34. 1	47. 1
9. 4	22. 3	35. 3	48. 2
10. 3	23. 4	36. 3	49. 2
11. 2	24. 1	37. 1	50. 3
12. 4	25. 2	38. 4	
13. 3	26. 4	39. 3	

INDEX

734